Media & Entertainment Law

Media & Entertainment Law presents a contemporary analysis of the law relating to the media and entertainment industries both in terms of its practical application and its theoretical framework, providing a broad and comprehensive coverage of these fast changing branches of the law.

Fully restructured to complement how media law is taught today in the digital age, this third
edition explores recent updates in the law including the outcomes of the *Google Spain* case and the
'right to be forgotten', the use of drones in breach of privacy laws, internet libel and the boundaries of media freedom and press regulation following the Leveson inquiry. *Media & Entertainment Law*
uses the most up-to-date authorities to explore privacy and confidentiality subjects, such as the
Prince Charles 'black spider' letters, the *Maximilian Schrems* and the celebrity superinjunction *PJS v Newsgroup
Newspapers cases*. The book also covers defamation, contempt of court and freedom of information,
plus Scots law. New to this edition:

- A brand new chapter is dedicated to exploring technology and the media, including contemporary issues such as the dark web, the surveillance state, internet censorship and the
  law and social media, including bloggers, vloggers and tweeters.
- The chapters on regulatory authorities have been expanded to provide greater clarification
  and explanation of broadcasting, press and advertising regulation, including the protection
  of journalistic sources and comparisons with EU Law.
- The chapter on intellectual property and entertainment law has been streamlined to match
  media law courses more effectively.

This text provides students with detailed coverage of the key principles, cases and legislation as well
as a critical analysis of this vibrant subject.

Ursula Smartt lectures in law at New College of the Humanities, London where she is subject
leader of Public Law and English Legal Systems. She is a Researcher and Visiting Lecturer in Media
and Entertainment Law at the University of Surrey, Guildford.

Ursula Smartt

Media &
Entertainment Law

THIRD EDITION

Ursula Smartt

With a Foreword by Sir Keir Starmer QC, MP

Routledge
Taylor & Francis Group

LONDON AND NEW YORK

Third edition published 2017
by Routledge
2 Park Square, Milton Park, Abingdon, Oxon, OX14 4RN

and by Routledge
711 Third Avenue, New York, NY 10017

Routledge is an imprint of the Taylor & Francis Group, an informa business

Second edition published by Routledge 2014

British Library Cataloguing-in-Publication Data
A catalogue record for this book is available from the British Library

Library of Congress Cataloging-in-Publication Data
Names: Smartt, Ursula, author.
Title: Media and entertainment law / Ursula Smartt.
Description: Third edition. | New York : Routledge, 2017. | Includes
    bibliographical references and index.
Identifiers: LCCN 2016035810 | ISBN 9781138961876 (hardback) |
    ISBN 9781138961883 (pbk.) | ISBN 9781315659626 (e-book)
Subjects: LCSH: Mass media—Law and legislation—Great Britain. | Performing
    arts—Law and legislation—Great Britain. | Copyright—Great Britain.
Classification: LCC KD2870 .S63 2017 | DDC 343.41/07830223—dc23
LC record available at https://lccn.loc.gov/2016035810

ISBN: 978-1-138-96187-6 (hbk)
ISBN: 978-1-138-96188-3 (pbk)
ISBN: 978-1-315-65962-6 (ebk)

Typeset in Joanna
by Apex CoVantage, LLC

Contents

Foreword

The way we communicate has changed profoundly in the last decade. Old established frameworks which distinguished journalists from others are largely redundant; social media provides a new world-wide platform for everyone; the Leveson Inquiry shone a bright torch on murky practices; and, as the recent EU Referendum campaigns showed, the capacity for whipping up division, hatred and hostility is formidable. We live in rapidly changing times. The ability of the law to keep up is a real challenge.

This book acts as a trusted guide in these uncertain times. The title *Media and Entertainment Law* does not do justice to the contribution that Ursula Smartt makes. Of course, on one level, this is a book for students of law. But it is much more than that; it puts law into its historical, political and social context. The breadth of coverage is wide, taking in privacy, freedom of expression, technology, regulation, defamation, intellectual property and much more. The depth of coverage is striking. For example, before getting to an analysis of Article 10 of the European Convention on Human Rights, Smartt takes us through not only the historical development of free speech and press freedom, but also the theoretical foundations of media freedom. Real issues are brought to life by real examples: thus the privacy arguments are illustrated by reference to the way Gwyneth Paltrow announced her 'conscious uncoupling' from Chris Martin on her Goop website, and the way Olympic diver, Tom Daley, came out in a YouTube posting in December 2013.

Nor is Smartt unafraid to reach strong conclusions. Take this example in Chapter 3, which covers technology and the media: 'one thing is clear: online communication is no longer constrained by legal boundaries . . .'. What follows is an analysis of questions, such as, 'is trolling a criminal offence?' As well as the strict legal answer, Smartt gives us context, which leads her to conclude that 'there is a clear anomaly in the law and the way in which internet abuse is treated and investigated by the police depending on whether the victim is in the public eye or an ordinary member of the public . . .'. Internet service providers are also subjected to withering analysis.

This book acts as a beacon. It helps readers to understand not only what the law is, but also why the law is what it is. In a fast-changing world, that is an invaluable contribution.

Keir Starmer QC, MP
4 July 2016

Preface

Much has changed since the first and second editions of this book and the fall-out of Brexit is being felt in all areas of law. The forewords to the first, second and latest editions of this book summarize many of the areas of change in the field of media, internet and intellectual property law. Legal commentator, Joshua Rozenberg (2011), wrote in his foreword to the first edition about the fast-moving news channels (e.g. BBC News Online) and the 'biggest challenges' to court reporting and contempt legislation being social networks. Prominent lawyer, Michael Mansfield QC (2014), in the foreword to the second edition, worried about the surveillance state in the post-Snowden world and that the boundaries of privacy had become blurred to non-existent. Sir Keir Starmer QC, in his foreword to this edition, draws on his experience as former Director of Public Prosecutions, well aware of the power and dangers of social media.

Drone cameras have replaced some long lens paparazzi practices (featuring on the cover of the second edition) and digital technology and the internet have transformed not only our lives but also the law. The courts have been kept busy with more privacy claims – such as the controversial injunction of *PJS v News Group Newspapers Ltd*, where the celebrity couple and one partner's extramarital affair were mentioned in print in the Scottish newspapers, but not in England and Wales (**see Chapter 1.6**).

The important concepts of confidentiality and privacy are at the heart of this book and permeate each chapter. Leading authorities prior to the Human Rights Act 1998 (HRA) will be discussed as well as the notion of an evolving tort of privacy, based on Strasbourg jurisprudence as well as leading UK authorities. Most cases will feature challenges of Articles 8 ECHR ('privacy') and 10 ECHR ('freedom of expression') in the form of (super)injunctions and the courts' treatment of celebrities' misdemeanours and the media's reporting on these. It is clear that this area of human rights law is not changing, until and unless the UK government decides to repeal the Human Rights Act 1998 (**see Chapters 1 and 2**).

'Internet law' is covered to a much greater extent in this edition, with a stronger focus on 'regulators' of the media, communications and advertising industries.

Due to the fast-changing developments in media (internet) law this third edition has been completely revised. Extensive feedback was sought from students and teachers of law and journalism in relation to the contents and layout of chapters and topics, which shaped the didactic structure of this edition. As with linguistic changes in the area of 'new' media and entertainment (IP) law, new subject areas have been included such as bloggers and tweeters, the increasing use of social media, Instagram imaging, vlogging and viral advertising.

With ever-increasing user-generated content (UGC) media lawyers are kept busy with privacy, harassment and possible defamation claims (**see Chapters 3, 6** and **7**). Relevant media content has been included in the form of internet sources, traditional law reports and judgments (provided in the footnotes). Non-traditional platforms such as Vice News and Buzzfeed have also been consulted, in addition to traditional accredited news organizations, such as BBC News Online and Reuters. Due to the demise of the 'red top' *News of the World* (NoW) and the aftermath of the *Leveson Report*, the case load of scandalous cases has (regrettably) been reduced (**see Chapter 6**).

A landmark ruling by the Court of Justice of the European Union (CJEU) introduced 'the right to be forgotten' against Google Inc. Mr Mario Costeja González had requested that a Spanish newspaper and the Google Spain search engine remove his personal data. *Google Spain* (2014), paved the way for claims to be made for damages for distress caused by data breaches which in turn led to the strengthening of the EU General Data Protection Regulation. The law now empowers EU citizens to ask ISPs and operators of websites to correct inaccurate data or stop their personal information (including photos) being misused (**see Chapter 3**).

While those – like myself – who wished to see the UK remain within the EU, are understandably disappointed, the vote to leave on 23 June 2016 ('Brexit') might well provide an opportunity for the UK to introduce new more flexible data protection laws and become a 'data haven'. Once outside the EU there could be more opportunity to reach bilateral trade agreements with major, high growth countries which have been unable to agree deals with the EU, such as India, China and Turkey. The Information Commissioner's Office (ICO) has made clear that there already exists adequate data protection status in the form of the Data Protection Act 1998 (DPA) and that Britain operates in a jurisdiction that fosters innovation (**see Chapter 4.10**).

Since its inception the Freedom of Information Act 2000 (FOIA) has been a resounding success. Not only did FOIA requests (mainly by the media) lead to the revelation of the Prince of Wales's 'spider letters' and memos to government department and ministers – thanks to the tireless requests and ten-year long legal quest by *Guardian* journalist Rob Evans, but we finally saw the publication of the Chilcot Report on 6 July 2016, following the Iraq Inquiry and answers as to whether the 'War on Iraq' was legal (**see Chapter 4**).

Changes in defamation laws following the Defamation Act 2013 saw the end of libel juries in England and Wales and generally a reduction in libel actions due to the high threshold of the 'serious harm' test. Whilst Scotland and Northern Ireland continue using common law defamation practices it could be argued that libel tourism has shifted from London to the Edinburgh and Belfast High Courts. Any potential libel claims now largely involve online and social media publications with potential harm to celebrities as well as innocent victims (**see Chapter 7**).

In the chapter on regulators, the book deals with the 'fallout' of the Leveson Inquiry and its effect on media practices. We examine the new print press regulator IPSO as well as the regulation of advertising, film and related EU media and IP legislation (**see Chapter 6**).

The reporting of court proceedings forms a large part of this book with contempt of court being a British peculiarity in law which all journalists must adhere to during 'active' court proceedings. The prosecution by the Attorney General of some 'tweeting' jurors is highlighted as they disobey judges' orders not to use the internet for research on cases they are hearing. The debate whether suspects of historical child sexual abuse should be named in the media (prior to charge) is being considered, following the Jimmy Savile atrocities. Important (and at times rather confusing) reporting restrictions for juveniles and anonymity orders in criminal and non-criminal court proceedings are explained with plenty of case examples (**see Chapter 8**).

The final chapter features developments in intellectual property law, largely dominated by EU law. It is this area of law which could be particularly affected by the Brexit result as present legislation impacts on the music and publishing industries. We will look at the legality of peer-to-peer file-sharing, music streaming services and artists' royalty collection agencies. The chapter features the extended sound recording rights for music performances to 70 years, championed by Sir Cliff Richard before the EU Commission and resulting in the EU Copyright Term Directive (2011/77/EU) – affectionately known as 'Sir Cliff's Law'. Recent changes in patent and design laws highlight the complexities in IP law, such as the Supreme Court's *Trunki* judgment (2016) (**see Chapter 9**).

One thing is sure in the post-Brexit world: students and teachers of law, readers of this book and lawyers in the area of EU law will be extremely busy during the next decade, considering the implications of a post-EU world for the United Kingdom. Crucial areas are intellectual property, competition and personal data protection laws.

Though this edition of *Media and Entertainment Law* falls within the post-Brexit era, it is up to date in the fast-moving fields of internet, media and IP law, taking into account the frequency with which the Strasbourg (ECtHR) and Court of Justice of the European Union (CJEU) cases arise in litigation in these particular fields.

I hope readers enjoy the book as much as I enjoyed writing and researching it.

Ursula Smartt
Guildford, Surrey.
February 2017

Acknowledgements

For the third edition of this book, there have been a large number of individuals and professionals who have given their support, time and advice to shape the contents of the book. I want to thank them all.

First to my husband **Mike Smartt OBE**, for his continued love, support and patience. I value Mike's knowledge as an award-winning BBC journalist and former editor in chief and originator of the BBC news online website. It is his professional advice which has shaped the journalistic detail of this book and makes some of the legal jargon and cases more readable.

I am indebted to **Sir Keir Starmer MP** who gave up his time to write the foreword and thereby endorse the book. Ever since I read his book, *Miscarriages of Justice* (1999), I have been an admirer of his (and his co-author Clive Walker). As Director of Public Prosecutions (2008–2013) he was greatly admired by those in the criminal justice system, and I personally welcomed his guidelines on assisted dying which shaped the euthanasia debate in Parliament. Keir has been a Member of Parliament (Holborn and St Pancras, Labour) since 2015 and his tireless work has made it difficult for us to meet, since he was appointed first as Shadow Home Office Minister, then as Shadow Brexit Secretary after Jeremy Corbyn's victory in the Labour leadership election in September 2015. As one of the most eminent QCs and human rights lawyers in the UK, Keir Starmer has represented many individuals in cases against the police and the security and intelligence services.

It was with great sadness that during the writing of this edition I learnt of the death of my good friend, **Lord Avebury** (Eric Lubbock of Orpington by-election-fame in 1962) on Valentines Day 2016. Though he had been suffering a long-term illness he was still working on legislation – such as the Investigatory Powers Act 2016 – almost to the very end of his life. He was a defender of civil and human rights and his continued advice shaped the constitutional and human rights content of this book.

Fiona Clark of 8 New Square Chambers is a leading barrister in all aspects of intellectual property law. I am proud to say she is a former student of mine. She helped shape the final chapter of this book, with her detailed knowledge of IP law, particularly in trade marks and designs.

Dr Heike Gading, Secretary to the Scottish Law Commission, for keeping me up to date with developments in Scottish defamation laws.

Cheryl Grant – my dear friend – has advised on all editions of this book with her vast experience of the music publishing and entertainment industry. Cheryl founded her own record label, White Label Productions, and is at the forefront of important strategic developments in the UK's entertainment industry with regard to copyright and branding.

Rosalind McInnes, Principal Solicitor for BBC Scotland, is author and editor of *Scots Law for Journalists*. She provided great insight into the current state of Scottish libel laws and has been lobbying the Scottish Parliament to adopt the Defamation Act 2013 into Scots law.

John McLlellan, Chief Executive of the Scottish Newspaper Society and former editor of *The Scotsman*, was of particular help with his practical 'take' on the post-Leveson 'fall-out' in respect of current press regulation and arbitration under IPSO.

David McKie, Solicitor and media lawyer with Levy & McRae, St Vincent Street, Glasgow, is chief adviser to the Scottish media and newspaper industry and advised on the Scots law sections in this book.

Richard Walker, at the time of my meeting in Glasgow in August 2015, was editor of the *Sunday Herald*. He helped shape the practical parts of the privacy and superinjunction sections of this book and shared his story of how he exposed the Ryan Giggs superinjunction. Richard provided a lively insight into the Scottish print press.

Fiona Briden, my Senior Commissioning Editor, who sadly left Routledge as this book went into production, has championed all three editions of this text and has become a good friend. I hope she will be as successful at Edward Elgar Publishing as she has been with this publishing house.

Emily Wells, Editorial Assistant, saw the editorial process through for the first half of the book, followed by the meticulous diligence of **Jade Lovitt**, who saw the book through to its production stage and made sure the right cover photograph and colour were chosen for this edition to attract the readers' attention.

My gratitude goes to the anonymous reviewers, whom I only know as A, B and C. Their tremendous contributions in the form of scrupulous and painstaking reviews of each chapter made the book what it is. I value their fresh ideas and their tremendous attention to detail.

Legal references in this book are accurate to the best of my knowledge as at 1 January 2017. Views and legal opinions and interpretations expressed in the text are mine. I have also consulted a large number of legal journals and scholarly opinion specifically related to the field of media, internet and IP law. No liability can be accepted by me or the publishers Routledge (Taylor & Francis Books) for anything done in reliance on the matters referred to in this book.

Ursula Smartt
Guildford
January 2017

Glossary of acronyms and legal terms

A

A & R (Artists and Repertoire)	The division of a record label that is responsible for talent-scouting and the artistic development of a recording artist. A & R acts as liaison between artist and record label.
ABC	Audit Bureau of Circulations. The industry body for media measurement.
Acquis (communautaire)	EU law: this is a French term meaning, essentially, 'the EU as it is', i.e. the rights and obligations that EU countries share. The acquis includes all EU law, such as treaties, Directives, Regulations, declarations and resolutions, international agreements on EU affairs and the judgments given by the Court of Justice. Accepting the acquis means taking the EU as you find it. Candidate countries have to accept the acquis before they can join the EU, and make EU law part of their own national legislation.
Acte clair	EU law: the idea that there is no need to refer a point of law, which is reasonably clear and free from doubt, to the European Court of Justice (ECJ), e.g. this court found the matter acte clair and declined to refer the interpretation of Article 5 to the ECJ.
Actio injuriarum (or: iniuriarum)	Scots private law 'injuries to honour'; action covers affront-based delicts such as defamation, wrongful arrest, personal molestation and harassment, breaches of confidentiality and privacy.
Acts of Adjournal	Scots law: regulations as to court procedure made by the High Court of Justiciary in criminal law.
Acts of Sederunt	Scots law: Acts passed by the Lords of Council and Session relating to civil procedure.
Adduce	Introduce.
Admissible evidence	Evidence allowed in proceedings.
Advocate	Scots law: a member of the Scottish Bar.
Advocate, Lord	Scots law: Senior Scottish Law Officer responsible for the prosecution of crime and investigation of deaths in Scotland, and the principal legal adviser to the Scottish government.
Advocate Depute	Scots law: an advocate appointed by the Lord Advocate to prosecute under his/her directions, and paid by salary.

Advocate General (ECtHR)	The Court of Justice is composed of 27 judges and eight Advocates General. Advocates General are appointed by governments of Member States for a term of six years (renewable) (see also: Court of Justice).
Advocate General (Scotland)	UK government Minister and the UK government's chief legal adviser on Scots law.
Affidavit	A written, sworn statement of evidence.
AG	Attorney General. The AG is the government's principal legal adviser. Usually a Member of Parliament, they provide advice on a range of legal matters. As well as carrying out various civil law functions, the AG has final responsibility for the criminal law. Their deputy is the Solicitor General.
Alternative dispute resolution (ADR)	Collective description of methods of resolving disputes otherwise than through the normal trial process.
Anton Piller order	An *ex parte* court injunction that requires a defendant to allow the claimant to (a) enter the defendant's premises, (b) search for and take away any material evidence, and (c) force the defendant to answer questions (usually in copyright infringement actions). Its primary objective is to prevent destruction or removal of evidence. *Anton Piller* is not a search warrant. The defendant is in contempt of court if he refuses to comply. Named after the case of *Anton Piller KG v Manufacturing* (1976).
Arraign	To put charges to the defendant in open court in the Crown Court.
Arraignment	The formal process of putting charges to the defendant in the Crown Court which consists of three parts: (1) calling him to the bar by name; (2) putting the charges to him by reading from the indictment; and (3) asking him whether he pleads guilty or not guilty.
ASA	Advertising Standards Authority.
Assignment	The transfer of property or rights from one party to another (copyright).
Authorities	Judicial decisions or opinions of authors of repute used as grounds of statements of law.
AVMS	Audio Visual Media Services Directive.

B

BBFC	British Board of Film Classification.
Bill of indictment	A written accusation of a crime against one or more persons – a criminal trial in the Crown Court cannot start without a valid indictment.
Bitcoin	A type of digital currency in which encryption techniques are used to regulate the generation of units of currency

	and verify the transfer of funds, operating independently of a central bank.
BitTorrent	BitTorrent tracker is a server that assists in the communication between peers using the BitTorrent protocol for peer-to-peer (P2P) file-sharing. These sites are typically used to upload music files.
BPI	British Phonographic Industry (originally 'The British Recorded Music Industry').
BSI	British Standards Institution.
BTOP	Broadband Technology Opportunities Programme – a US government project.

C

CAA	Civil Aviation Authority
Case stated	An appeal to the High Court against the decision of a magistrates' court on the basis that the decision was wrong in law or in excess of the magistrates' jurisdiction.
CDPA	Copyright, Designs and Patents Act 1988.
CFA	Conditional fee agreement (also known as 'no win, no fee' agreement) whereby fees and expenses only become payable in certain circumstances (most commonly used in personal injury claims but also in defamation cases). Until 1 April 2013, lawyers entered into CFAs at their own risk, and as a result of this a 'success fee' was usually charged in addition to the lawyer's standard fees if the case was won. If a success fee was also payable it was expressed as a percentage of the standard fee, although it could not be more than 100 per cent of those fees. Part 2 of the Legal Aid Sentencing and Punishment of Offenders Act 2012 (and associated Regulations and changes to the Civil Procedure Rules) abolished the recovery of success fees under CFAs and also abolished the recovery of ATE (after the event) insurance premiums from the losing side, with the exception of clinical negligence cases where some of the ATE premium was likely to be recoverable. From 1 April 2013, claimants are still able to use CFAs but will now have to pay their lawyer's success fee and any ATE insurance.
Champertous	A vexatious claim by a stranger in return for a share of the proceeds.
CJEU	Court of Justice of the European Union (formerly: European Court of Justice – ECJ) based in Luxembourg. The CJEU ensures compliance with EU law and rules on the interpretation and application of the treaties establishing the European Union.

Community (EU)	In the 1950s, six European countries formed three organizations: the European Coal and Steel Community (ECSC), the European Atomic Energy Community (Euratom) and the European Economic Community (EEC). These three communities – collectively known as the 'European Communities' – formed the basis of what is now the European Union (EU). With the Lisbon Treaty in 2009 the word 'community' disappeared, replaced by the 'European Union'. Many texts still use the word 'community'; it means more or less the same as 'EU'.
Complainant	A person who makes a formal complaint. In relation to an offence of rape or other sexual offences the complainant is the person against whom the offence is alleged to have been committed.
Contempt of Court	Disobedience or wilful disregard of the judicial process (Contempt of Court Act 1981). 'Contempt' can also relate to any attempt to interfere with proceedings or to obstruct or threaten Members of Parliament in the performance of their parliamentary duties.
Contra mundum injunction	Order 'binding on the whole world'. Injunctions are usually made against named individuals (*in personam*). When made *contra mundum*, they are made against the entire world (i.e. no media organization is allowed to publish details of the case or person/s).
Convention	This term has various meanings, including (in the EU context) a group of people representing the EU institutions, the national governments and parliaments, who come together to draw up an important document. Conventions of this sort have met to draw up the Charter of Fundamental Rights of the European Union or new EU treaties; the European Convention on Human Rights and Fundamental Freedoms is also meant by this term (see: Convention right).
Convention right	A right under the European Convention on Human Rights (see: ECHR).
Counsel	Barrister. In Scotland a member of the Faculty of Advocates practising at the Bar.
Counterclaim	A claim brought by a defendant in response to the claimant's claim, which is included in the same proceedings as the claimant's claim.
Court of Session	Scots Law. Scotland's supreme civil court that sits in Parliament House in Edinburgh as a court of first instance and a court of appeal. The court is divided into the **Outer House** and the **Inner House**. The Outer House consists of 22 Lords Ordinary sitting alone or, in certain cases, with a civil jury. They hear cases at first instance on a wide range of civil matters, including cases based on delict (tort) and contract, commercial cases and judicial review. All appeals go to the UK Supreme Court.

CPD	Criminal Practice Direction.
CPR	Civil Procedure Rules or Criminal Procedure Rules.
Cross-examination	Questioning of a witness by a party other than the party who called the witness.
Cy-près	Scots law: approximation; as near as possible.

D

DAB	Digital Audio Broadcasting.
Damages	A sum of money awarded by the court as compensation to the claimant.
De facto	According to the fact; in point of fact.
De jure	According to law, or in point of law.
De minimis	'Of minimum importance' or 'trifling'; *de minimis* doctrine means the law has no interest in trivial matters.
Declaration of incompatibility	A declaration by a court that a piece of UK legislation is incompatible with the provisions of the European Convention on Human Rights (see: ECHR).
Defender	Scots law: defendant. A person who disputes the claim of the pursuer and lodges defences (see also: pursuer).
Deposition	Written record of a witness's written evidence.
Derivative work	A work that is based on (derived from) another work (copyright), e.g. a painting of a photograph. As the adaption of copyright work is a restricted act, unless covered under fair dealing rules, the artist will normally require the permission of the copyright owner before making a derivative work.
Devolution	The decentralization of governmental power such as the Scottish Parliament, the National Assembly for Wales and the Northern Ireland Assembly.
Dictum (pl. *dicta*)	'Remark'; refers to a judge's comment in a ruling or decision which is not required to reach the decision, but may state the judge's interpretation of a related legal principle.
Diplock courts	Juryless courts in Northern Ireland from 1973 to 2007.
DMB	A Digital Multimedia Broadcasting – Audio.
DNS	Domain Name System.
DOCSIS	Data Over Cable Service Interface Specification – a technology for next generation broadband services over the cable network.
DPA	Data Protection Act 1998
DPI	Digital Phone Interphase Technology.
Draft Bill	A bill that has not yet been formally introduced into Parliament and enables consultation and pre-legislative

	scrutiny before a bill is issued formally. This process is known as pre-legislative scrutiny.
DRM	Digital Rights Management.
DS	Developers' System.

E

ECHR	European Convention on Human Rights and Fundamental Freedoms ('The Convention').
ECJ	European Court of Justice (now: 'The Court of Justice of the European Union').
ECtHR	European Court of Human Rights: an international court set up in 1959 in Strasbourg; it rules on individual or state applications alleging the violations of civil, political or human rights set out in the European Convention on Human Rights (ECHR) (also known as 'the Strasbourg Court') (see also: Grand Chamber) (see also: HUDOC).
Estoppel	Equitable doctrine that may be used to prevent a person from relying upon certain rights or facts, e.g. words said or actions performed, which differ from an earlier set of facts.
Estreatment (of recognizance)	Forfeiture.
European Arrest Warrant (EAW)	The UK adopted the EAW in 2002, following the terrorism atrocities of 9/11. The EAW is widely used to secure the arrest and surrender of suspected criminals across the European Union.
Evidence-in-chief	The evidence given by a witness for the party who called him.
Ex parte	A hearing where only one party is allowed to attend and make submissions, mainly in judicial review; now cited as, for example, *R (on the application of Animal Defenders International) v Secretary of State for Culture, Media and Sport* [2008] 1 AC 1312. Proceedings are *ex parte* when the party against whom they are brought is not heard.
Exemplary damages	Or: punitive damages. Awarded by a court when the defendant's wilful acts were malicious, violent, oppressive, fraudulent, wanton, or grossly reckless. They reward the claimant for his/ her suffering, for example, damage to his/ her reputation (defamation) or harassment. These damages go beyond compensating for actual loss and are awarded to show the court's disapproval of the defendant's behaviour.

F

Fair dealing (or 'fair use')	Acts which are allowable in relation to copyright works under statutory legislation. What constitutes 'fair use'

	may differ from country to country, but normally includes educational and private study and news reporting.
Fatal accident inquiry	Scotland. An inquiry before a sheriff into the circumstances of a death of a person. Such an inquiry must be held where the person died at work or in legal custody.
FOIA or FOI	Freedom of Information Act 2000.
FOISA	Freedom of Information (Scotland) Act 2002.
Footprints	Deliberate mistakes or hidden elements that are only known to the author or creator of a work (copyright), e.g. the software designer who includes redundant subroutines that identify the author in some way.
Forfeiture	A broad term used to describe any loss of property without compensation. In contract law, one party may be required to forfeit specified property if the party fails to fulfil its contractual obligations. In criminal procedures, it is the loss of a defendant's right to his property which has been confiscated by the police when used during the commission of a crime. For example, the seizure by police of a car which was used during a bank robbery; or the forfeiture of illegal narcotics (possession of class A drugs).
Forum conveniens	A discretionary power in common law where a foreign court will accept jurisdiction over matters where there is a more appropriate forum available to the parties.
Forum non conveniens	As applied to a court which, although having jurisdiction, is not the appropriate court for the matter in issue. This doctrine is employed when the court chosen by the plaintiff is inconvenient for witnesses or poses an undue hardship on the defendants, who must petition the court for an order transferring the case to a more convenient court, e.g. a lawsuit arising from an accident involving a foreign resident who files the complaint in his home country when the witnesses and doctors who treated the plaintiff are in the country where the accident occurred, which makes the latter country the most convenient location for trial.
FTT	First Tier Tribunal (formerly: Information Tribunal). Appeals to the First Tier Tribunal are against the decisions from government departments and other public bodies (see also: FOIA) (see also: Upper Tribunal – UT).

G

GDPR	General Data Protection Regulation 2016
General Court	Formerly Court of First Instance as part of the European Court of Justice.
Grand Chamber	(of the European Court of Human Rights – ECtHR) The Grand Chamber is made up of 17 judges: the Court's President and Vice-Presidents, the Section Presidents and the national judge, together with other judges

selected by drawing of lots. The initiation of proceedings before the Grand Chamber takes two different forms: referral and relinquishment (see also: ECtHR).

Green Paper
A consultation document produced by the government. The aim of this document is to allow people both inside and outside Parliament to debate the subject and give the department feedback on its suggestions.

H

Hansard
The official report of the proceedings of Parliament, published daily on everything that is said and done in both Houses of Parliament. In the House of Commons the Hansard reporters sit in a gallery above the Speaker and take down every word that is said in the Chamber. In the Westminster Hall Chamber they sit next to the Chairman. The Hansard reporters in the House of Lords sit below the Bar of the House, facing the Lord Speaker. The name Hansard was officially adopted in 1943 after Luke Hansard (1752–1828), who was the printer of the *House of Commons Journal* from 1774. The first detailed official reports were published in 1803 in *William Cobbett's Political Register* by the political journalist of the same name.

Harmonization
This may mean bringing national laws into line with one another; in EU Law this means removing national barriers that obstruct the free movement of workers, goods, services and capital. Harmonization can also mean co-ordinating national technical rules so that products and services can be traded freely throughout the EU (e.g. in copyright and IP law).

Her Majesty's Advocate
Scotland. The senior Law Officer responsible for the prosecution of crime and investigation of deaths and the principal legal adviser to the Scottish government. Referred to as 'Her Majesty's Advocate' in criminal matters and the 'Lord Advocate' in civil matters.

High Court of Justiciary
Scotland. Usually referred to as 'the High Court' in Edinburgh. Consists of two appellate courts (the Court of Criminal Appeal and the Justiciary Appeal Court) and a court of first instance (i.e. a court trying persons on indictment with a jury). The judges of the High Court are formally called Lords Commissioners of Justiciary. The judges of the court are also the judges of the Court of Session.

HRA
Human Rights Act 1998.

HUDOC
A database which provides access to the case law of the European Court of Human Rights (Grand Chamber, Chamber and Committee judgments, decisions, communicated cases, advisory opinions and legal summaries from the Case Law Information Note), the

European Commission of Human Rights (decisions and reports) and the Committee of Ministers (resolutions) (see also: ECtHR).

I

IAB	Internet Advertising Bureau.
IC	Information Commissioner (see also: FOIA).
ICANN	The Internet Corporation for Assigned Names and Numbers is a non-profit organization that is responsible for the coordination of maintenance and methodology of several databases of unique identifiers related to the namespaces of the internet and ensuring the network's stable and secure operation. ICANN performs the actual technical maintenance work of the central internet address pools and Domain Name System (DNS) registries pursuant to the Internet Assigned Numbers Authority (IANA) function contract. ICANN's main aim is to help preserve the operational stability of the global internet community.
ICT	Information and Communication Technology.
IFPI	International Federation of the Phonographic Industry; represents the recording industry worldwide. IFPI safeguards the rights of record producers and expands the commercial uses of recorded music (see: BPI).
In camera	Court proceedings in private where the public is not allowed access, though the media may be permitted access by special permission from the legal adviser or judge.
Indemnity	A right of someone to recover from a third party the whole amount which he himself is liable to pay.
Indictment	The document containing the formal charges against a defendant; a trial in the Crown Court cannot start without this.
Informant	Someone who lays information.
Infringement (copyright)	The act of copying, distributing or adapting a work without permission.
Injunction	An injunction is a court order which orders a person to stop (called a 'prohibitory injunction') or to do (a 'mandatory injunction') a particular act or thing. A breach of an injunction is generally punishable as a contempt of court and in some circumstances can lead to imprisonment. Interim injunctions are either obtained 'on notice' or 'without notice'. With an 'on notice' application, the other side is told that the application for an injunction is being made and when

	and where it will be heard (see also: *contra mundum* and 'interim injunction').
Inner House	Scots law: the two appellate divisions of the Court of Session, so called originally on the simple topographical ground that their courts lay further from the entrance to the courthouse than did the Outer House (see also: Outer House).
Intellectual property (IP)	A product of the intellect, including copyright works, trademarks and patents.
Inter alia	Among other things.
Inter partes	A hearing where both parties attend and can make submissions (see: *ex parte*).
Interdict	Scots law: a judicial prohibition or court order preventing someone from doing something. It is comparable to the English (interim) injunction. This judicial prohibition is issued by the Court of Session or Sheriff Court. In an emergency, interim interdict can be obtained in the absence of the person against whom the order is sought (i.e. *ex parte*).
Interested party	A person or organization who is not the prosecutor or defendant, but who has some other legal interest in a case.
Interim injunction	The applicant applies for 'interim relief' from the court for the purposes of preserving evidence or assets (in intellectual property law) at the very outset of the proceedings. Interim injunctions are applied for at the commencement of legal proceedings, without a full examination by the court of the facts said to justify a final injunction.
International Court of Justice (ICTJ)	Judicial organ of the United Nations, based in The Hague. Those who commit crimes on a large or systematic scale such as genocide are tried here. The Court has roots in international legal obligations dating back to the Nuremberg trials, the most recent trials being the International Criminal Tribunals for the former Yugoslavia (ICTY) and Rwanda (ICTR).
IP	Intellectual Property (or Internet Protocol).
IPO	Intellectual Property Office
IPSO	Independent Press Standards Organisation. Regulator for the newspaper and magazine industry (incl. online editions).
IPTV	Internet Protocol Television – television services delivered over the internet.
ISB	Independent Spectrum Broker.
ISDN	Integrated Services Digital Network – a data transfer technology using the copper phone network.

ISP	An internet service provider (ISP) is an organization that provides services for accessing, using, or participating in the internet. Internet services typically provided by ISPs include internet access, internet transit, domain name registration or web hosting. Top ISPs in the UK are: BT, Sky Broadband, Virgin Media, EE, Talk Talk, Kingston Communications.

J

Jigsaw identification	The ability to identify someone by using two or more different pieces of information from two or more sources. The media refers to the 'jigsaw effect' in *sub judice* proceedings, where a person's identity is to be kept anonymous for legal reasons (e.g. children and young persons under 18).
Judge Rapporteur	EU law: the Judge Rapporteur draws up the preliminary report of the general meeting of the judges and the Advocates General before the Court of Justice known as 'measures of inquiry' (see also: European Court of Justice).
Judicial review	A remedy used by the Administrative Court (or the Court of Session in Scotland). If a public body (or authority) has made a decision in breach of any public law principle then that decision may be challenged by an individual or group action. Court proceedings can be by judge-alone hearings where the lawfulness of a decision or action made by a public body is reviewed. For example, where the challenge is based on an allegation that the public body has taken a decision unlawfully (*ultra vires*) and usually where there is no adequate alternative remedy.

L

Laches	Equity: A defence to an equitable action that bars recovery by the plaintiff because of the plaintiff's undue delay in seeking relief.
Law Lords	Highly qualified, full-time judges, the Law Lords carried out the judicial work of the House of Lords until 30 July 2009. From 1 October 2009, the UK Supreme Court assumed jurisdiction on points of law for all civil law cases in the UK and all criminal cases in England and Wales and Northern Ireland. The existing 12 Lords of Appeal in Ordinary (Law Lords) were appointed as Justices of the Supreme Court and were thereafter disqualified from sitting or voting in the House of Lords. When they retire from the Supreme Court they can return to the House of Lords as full members, but newly appointed Justices of the Supreme Court will not

	have seats in the House of Lords (see also: Supreme Court).
Leave to appeal	Permission granted to appeal the decision of a court.
Licence (Copyright)	An agreement in copyright that allows use of a work subject to conditions imposed by the copyright owner.
Limited right	Right by virtue of the HRA 1998 (see: HRA) – so that, within the scope of the limitation, the infringement of a guaranteed right may not contravene the Convention.
Lisbon Treaty	EU law: the treaty was signed on 13 December 2007 in Lisbon and entered into force on 1 December 2009. Technically, the Lisbon Treaty consists of several specific changes of articles compared to the previous treaties.
Litigation	Process by which a person or company begins a civil lawsuit. Full legal action tends to be avoided and dispute resolution is often used (e.g. libel actions). Most top law firms have specialist litigation and dispute resolution departments, whilst smaller or specialist firms concentrate all their resources on litigation.
Lord Chief Justice (LCJ)	The name given to the judge who presides over the Queen's Bench Division of the High Court (QBD). Since the passing of the Constitutional Reform Act 2005 the LCJ is now Head of the Judiciary of England and Wales, a role previously performed by the Lord Chancellor. In addition, he is President of the Courts of England and Wales and responsible for representing the views of the judiciary to Parliament and the government.
Lucas Box meaning	Defamation: A defendant in a libel action must set out in his/her statement of case the defamatory meaning he/she seeks to prove to be essentially or substantially true ('justification').

M

Mandatory order (formerly: mandamus)	Order from the divisional court of the Queen's Bench Division mandamus or 'writ of mandate') ordering a body (such as a magistrates' court) to do something (such as rehear a case). The writ can order a public agency or governmental body to perform an act required by law when it has neglected or refused to do so. Example: after petitions were filed with sufficient valid signatures to qualify a proposition for a ballot, a town council has refused to call an election, claiming it has a legal opinion that the proposal is unconstitutional.
Mareva order	*Mareva* injunctions (also known as 'asset-freezing orders') are court orders that negate the banker's duty to pay or transfer funds as per the instructions of the customer. A *Mareva* order is an interlocutory order (injunction), granted ancillary to a substantive claim involving money,

	that seeks to prevent a defendant from rendering a decree against him worthless by removing his assets from the jurisdiction of the court.
Master	Procedural judge for the majority of the civil business in the Chancery (Ch) and Queen's Bench Divisions (QBD). A Master at first instance deals with all aspects of an action, from its issue until it is ready for trial by a trial judge – usually a High Court judge. After the trial the Master resumes responsibility for the case.
Master of the Rolls (MR)	Ranks immediately below the Lord Chief Justice. He presides over the Court of Appeal and is responsible for the records or 'rolls' of the Chancery Court (see also: Lord Chief Justice).
MCPS	The Mechanical Copyright Protection Society (now part of the PRS). Collects royalties whenever a piece of music is reproduced for broadcast or online.
Moral rights	Are concerned in copyright with the protection of the reputation of the author, in particular the right to be attributed with the creation of a work, and the right to object to defamatory treatment.

N

NDPB	Non-departmental public body which has a role in the process of national government but is not a government department, or part of one and therefore operates to a greater or lesser extent at arm's length from ministers (see also: Quango).
Nobile officium	Scots law: 'the noble office or duty of the Court of Session' is an equitable jurisdiction in the High Court of Justiciary or the Inner House of the Court of Session which can provide a remedy where none other would be available, or to soften the effect of the law in a particular circumstance.
Nolle prosequi	'Will not prosecute'; formal entry in the records of the case in the court by the prosecutor in a criminal case that they are not willing to go any further in the case. This means that the CPS withdraws the charge(s) against the defendant(s).
Norwich Pharmacal Order (NPO)	A *Norwich Pharmacal* Order requires a respondent to disclose certain documents or information to the applicant. The respondent must be involved in a wrongdoing (whether innocently or not) and is unlikely to be a party to the potential proceedings. An NPO will only be granted where 'necessary' in the interests of justice. Orders are commonly used to identify the proper defendant to an action or to obtain information to plead a claim. An NPO can be obtained pre-action, during the course of an action, and post-judgment. An NPO can be

made in one jurisdiction to identify a defendant for the purpose of proceedings in another jurisdiction. For a third party to be liable to present the information requested by the claimant, they must have been involved, innocently or not, in the wrongdoing against the claimant. It must also be clear that justice will be served by the revelation of this information.

Notice of transfer	Procedure used in cases of serious and complex fraud, and in certain cases involving child witnesses, whereby the prosecution can, without seeking judicial approval, have the case sent direct to the Crown Court without the need to have the accused committed for trial.

O

Obiter dictum (*'obiter'*)	Judge's opinion given incidentally, not legally binding.
OECD	Organisation for Economic Co-operation and Development.
Ofcom	Office for Communications. Independent regulator and competition authority for the UK communications industries.
Offence triable either way	A statutory criminal offence (or 'either-way-offence'), which may be tried either in the magistrates' or Crown Court.
Offence triable only on indictment	An offence which can be tried only in the Crown Court.
Offence triable only summarily	An offence which can be tried only in a magistrates' court.
OFT	Office of Fair Trading. The organization promotes and protects consumer interests in the UK.
Ombudsman	Now 'Parliamentary and Health Service Ombudsman', which combines the two statutory roles of Parliamentary Commissioner for Administration (the Parliamentary Ombudsman) and Health Service Commissioner for England (Health Service Ombudsman). Investigates complaints from members of the public about government departments; has wide powers to obtain evidence; makes recommendations about cases s/he hears.
Open court	In a courtroom which is open to the public (see also: open justice principle; *in camera*).
Open justice principle	The public (and media) has the statutory right to attend most court proceedings – unless held *in camera* (see: *in camera*; see: open court).
Operators of websites	s 5 Defamation Act 2013 provides website operators with a defence to defamation provided they follow the procedure set out in the Defamation (Operators of Websites) Regulations 2013.
Ordinary, Lords	Scots law: the judges who try cases at first instance in the Court of Session.

P

PACT	Producers Alliance of Cinema and Television.
Parliament Acts	The Parliament Act of 1911 was introduced to reform Parliament, and the House of Lords (HL) in particular. It deprived the HL of any power over money bills and gave the Speaker the power to decide what was a Money Bill. It allowed bills that had been passed by the Commons in three successive sessions, but rejected by the Lords in all three, to become law. The Parliament Act 1949 reduced the powers that the HL had to delay a bill from becoming law if the House of Commons approved it. Since the Parliament Act 1911 the HL had been able to delay legislation for two years. The 1949 Act reduced this to one year.
Passing off (Copyright)	Using the work or name of an organization or individual without consent to promote a competing product or service.
Patent	A grant made by a government that confers upon the creator of an invention the sole right to make, use and sell that invention for a set period of time.
PCC	Press Complaints Commission.
Per incuriam	Through negligence, mistake or error.
Perjury	Offence committed by a witness in court proceedings involving the affirmation of a deliberate falsehood on oath or on an affirmation equivalent to an oath.
Petition	A document by which court proceedings are initiated, like a summons but used for specific types of case. Can have various meanings. An indictment is originally called a petition until the Crown is in a position to indict the accused on the charges. In civil business the term also relates to certain types of applications to the court.
Phonogram (Copyright)	The symbol 'P' in a circle is a distinct right applied to an individual sound recording, which will operate separately from rights existing in the underlying musical composition.
PII	Public Interest Immunity certificate, where the prosecution contends that it is not in the public interest to disclose any sensitive material (secret courts) (see also 'in camera').
PLR	Public Lending Right.
PPL	Phonographic Performance Ltd licenses sound recordings and music videos for use in broadcast, public performance and new media.
Practice direction	Direction relating to the practice and procedure of the courts.
Precedent	The decision of a court regarded as a source of law or authority in the decision of a later case.

Preliminary ruling	EU law: to ensure effective and uniform application of EU law, national courts can refer to the Court of Justice (or ECJ) and ask it to clarify a point in EU law; reference for a preliminary ruling can also seek the review of the validity of an act of EU law (Treaty provision).
President, Lord	Scots law: the highest civil judge in Scotland, who presides over the First Division of the Court of Session.
Prima facie case	A prosecution case which is strong enough to require the defendant to answer it.
Primary legislation	Acts of Parliament.
Privilege	The right of a party to refuse to disclose a document or produce a document or to refuse to answer questions on the ground of some special interest recognized by law.
Privy Council	Privy Counsellors are members of the Queen's own Council: the 'Privy Council'. There are about 500 members who have reached high public office. Membership includes all members of the Cabinet, past and present, the Speaker, the leaders of all major political parties, archbishops and various senior judges as well as other senior public figures. Their role is to advise the Queen in carrying out her duties as monarch. Privy Counsellors are referred to as 'The Right Honourable Member'. The Judicial Committee of the Privy Council, situated in the Supreme Court building, is the court of final appeal for the UK overseas territories and Crown dependencies, and for those Commonwealth countries that have retained the appeal to Her Majesty in Council or, in the case of Republics, to the Judicial Committee.
Procurator Fiscal	Scots law: literally, the procurator for the fiscal or treasury; now the style of the public prosecutor in the sheriff court.
PRP	Press Recognition Panel. An independent body set up by Royal Charter to ensure that regulators of the UK press are independent, properly funded and able to protect the public.
PRS	The Performing Right Society. Body which represents music publishers (see also: MCPS).
PSB	Public Service Broadcasting.
PSN	Public Sector Network.
Pursuer	Scots law: the party initiating a law suit (English law: plaintiff or claimant).

Q

Qualified right	Right by virtue of the HRA 1998 so that, in certain circumstances and under certain conditions, it can be interfered with (see: HRA).

Quango	Quasi-autonomous non-governmental organization; also known as Non-Departmental Public Bodies (NDPBs). Quangos are organizations funded by taxpayers, but not controlled directly by central government. For example, ACAS (Advisory, Conciliation and Arbitration Service); the Big Lottery Fund; the Boundary Commission for Wales; UK Anti-Doping (see: NDPB).

R

Remand	A criminal court sends a person away when a case is adjourned until another date; the person may be remanded on bail (when he can leave, subject to conditions) or in custody.
Reporter	Scots law: a person appointed to hold a public inquiry or to whom the court may remit some aspect of a case for investigation or advice (such as the Children's Hearings in Scotland).
Representation order	An order authorizing payment of legal aid for a defendant.
Resident Sheriff	Scots law: the Sheriff who holds the commission to sit at a particular court (as opposed to a Sheriff sitting part time) (see also: Sheriff).
Respondent	The party in a civil action defending on appeal.
Restraining Order	Criminal law: a restraining order can be a significant part in managing the risks to a victim in preventing further harassment or harm. Conditions on the perpetrator can include: no contact with the victim; not to go near the victim's address, etc. (under section 12 Domestic Violence, Crime and Victims Act 2004; or section 2 Protection from Harassment Act 1997).
Restraint order – Civil Restraint Order (CRO)	Civil law: a CRO is an order issued against people who have had more than one court claim or application dismissed or struck out for being totally without merit. The order prevents that person from issuing further claims or making applications in some or all of the county courts in England and Wales and also in the High Court, without first getting the permission of the judge named in the order.
RIPA	Regulation of Investigatory Powers Act 2000.
Royal Assent	The monarch's agreement to make a bill into an Act of Parliament.
Royal Commission	A selected group of people appointed by the government to investigate a matter of important public concern and to make recommendations on any actions to be taken.
Royalties	A share paid to an author or a composer out of the proceeds resulting from the sale or performance of his or her work (copyright).
RPAS	Remotely Piloted Air Systems ('drones').

S

Safe harbour	Privacy agreement of 2000 ('pact') between the EU and USA regarding online privacy. The pact allows firms to transfer data from the EU to the USA if they provide safeguards equivalent to those required by the EU data-protection directive ('safe-harbour') (see: *Max Schrems* case).
Secretary of State	The title held by some of the more important government ministers, for example the Secretary of State for Foreign Affairs. Usually a member of the Cabinet (the executive).
Security money	Deposited to ensure that the defendant attends court (also known as 'surety').
Sending for trial	Procedure whereby indictable offences are transferred to the Crown Court (or 'sent') without the need for a committal hearing in the magistrates' court.
Set aside	Cancelling a judgment or order or a step taken by a party in the proceedings.
Sheriff	Scots law: legally qualified person who sits in judgment at the sheriff court.
SI	Statutory Instrument. SIs are a form of legislation which allow the provisions of an Act of Parliament to be subsequently brought into force or altered without Parliament having to pass a new Act. They are also referred to as secondary, delegated or subordinate legislation.
Sine qua non	Latin for '[a condition] without which it could not be' or 'but for . . .' or 'without which [there is] nothing that can be effectively done'. The term refers to an indispensable and essential action, condition, or ingredient; a necessary condition without which something is not possible.
Skeleton argument	A document prepared by a party or their legal representative setting out the basis of the party's argument, including any arguments based on law; the court may require such documents to be served on the court and on the other party prior to a trial.
Slander	Defamation: spoken words which have a damaging effect on a person's reputation.
SOCA	Serious Organised Crime Agency. SOCA tackles serious organized crime that affects UK citizens.
Solatium	Scots law: extra damages allowed in certain delict cases in addition to actual loss – for 'injury to feelings' or 'wounded feelings' (see also: *actio injuriarum*).
Special measures	Measures which can be put in place to provide protection and/or anonymity to a witness (e.g. a screen separating witness from the accused; or hearing child witnesses on a live link).

SSI	Scots law: Scottish Statutory Instrument. The form in which Scottish orders, rules and instruments, regulations or other subordinate legislation are made.
Stay	A stay imposes a halt on court proceedings, e.g. in contempt of court actions. Proceedings can be continued if a stay is lifted.
Strict liability	Not all offences require proof of *mens rea*. By a crime of strict liability is meant an offence of which a person may be convicted without proof of intention (*mens rea*), recklessness or even negligence. The prosecution is only obliged to prove the commission of the *actus reus* and the absence of any recognized defence (see *R v Adomako* (1994)).
Strike out	Striking out means the court ordering written material to be deleted so that it may no longer be relied upon, e.g. a police interview transcript.
SUA	Small Unmanned Aircraft.
Sub judice	A rule that prevents any journalist or Member of Parliament from referring to a current or impending court case (see: contempt of court).
Subpoena	A summons issued to a person directing their attendance in court to give evidence (see: summons).
Summons	A document signed by a magistrate after information is laid before him/her which sets out the basis of the accusation against the accused and the time and place at which they must appear.
Supreme Court	The Supreme Court of Justice is the final court of appeal in the UK for civil cases. It hears appeals in criminal cases from England, Wales and Northern Ireland.
Surety	A person who guarantees that a defendant will attend court, usually linked to a bail hearing.

T

Territorial Authority	A national authority which has power to do certain things in connection with co-operation with other countries and international organizations in relation to the collection of the hearing of evidence.
TFEU	Treaty on the Functioning of the European Union (consolidated version, also known as the Lisbon Treaty).
Time-shifting	A person is allowed to make a copy of a broadcast for private and domestic use to watch or listen to at a more convenient time, or for educational purposes, using methods such as video recording or the BBC iPlayer©.
Trademark (™ or ®)	A name, symbol or other device identifying a product or company. Trademarks are registered via national trademark or patent offices and legally restrict the

	use of the device to the owner; it is illegal to use the ® symbol or state that the trademark is registered until the trademark has in fact been registered.
Tribunal	There are tribunals in England, Wales, Scotland and Northern Ireland covering a wide range of areas affecting day-to-day life. HM Courts & Tribunals administers many of them although some are the responsibility of the devolved governments in Scotland, Wales and Northern Ireland, for example, employment tribunals or immigration and asylum tribunals. Tribunal judges are legally qualified; they usually sit with two tribunal members who are specialist non-legal members of the panel and include doctors, chartered surveyors, ex-service personnel or accountants.
Troll(s)	Internet slang: a 'troll' is someone who posts inflammatory or off-topic messages in an online social networking community, such as a forum, chat room, or blog, with the primary intent of provoking readers into an emotional response.
TSI	Trading Standards Institute.

U

UAS	Unmanned Aerial Systems.
UAVs	Unmanned Aerial Vehicles ('drones').
Universal Declaration of Human Rights	Text adopted by the United Nations in 1948 in order to strengthen human rights protection at international level.
Upper Tribunal (UT)	The Upper Tribunal hears appeals from the First Tier Tribunal (FTT) on points of law, i.e. an appeal made over the interpretation of a legal principle or statute. Further appeals may be made, with permission, to the Court of Appeal (see also: FTT).

V

VCS	Video Standards Council – regulator of the video industry.
Venire de novo	A Queen's Bench Division (QBD) order requiring a new trial following a verdict given in an inferior court. In criminal matters the court of trial may, before verdict, discharge the jury and direct a fresh jury to be summoned; and even after verdict, if the findings are so imperfect as to amount to no verdict at all.
Vlogging	Video blog or Video Blogger; a form of blog for which the medium is video. Vlog entries often combine embedded video (or a video link) with supporting text, advertisements, images and other metadata.

W

Warrant of distress	Court order to arrest a person (Distress warrant).
Wash-up period	Refers to the last few days of a Parliament, after a General Election has been announced but before dissolution. All the unfinished business of the session must be dealt with swiftly and the government seeks the co-operation of the Opposition in passing legislation that is still in progress. Some bills might be lost completely; others might be progressed quickly but in a much-shortened form (e.g. Digital Economy Act 2010).
Wasted costs order	An order that a barrister or solicitor is not to be paid fees that they would normally be paid by the Legal Services Commission.
White Paper	A document produced by the government setting out details of future policy on a particular subject. A White Paper will often be the basis for a bill to be put before Parliament. The White Paper allows the government an opportunity to gather feedback before it formally presents the policies as a bill.
WIPO	World Intellectual Property Organization.
Without prejudice	Negotiations with a view to a settlement are usually conducted 'without prejudice', which means that the circumstances in which the content of those negotiations may be revealed to the court are very restricted.

Table of cases

Table of legislation

Table of international instruments and treaties

Chapter 1

Confidentiality and privacy

Chapter contents

Key points

This chapter will cover the following questions:

○ What is the difference between confidentiality and privacy in common law?
○ How does privacy law differ before and after the Human Rights Act 1998?
○ Does a child have its own right to privacy – independent of that of his parents?
○ What is the meaning of the 'public interest test'?
○ Is there one privacy law for the rich and famous and another for the 'commoner'?
○ Has judge-made law created a tort of privacy since the HRA?

1.1 Overview

Max Mosley, Naomi Campbell, Michael Douglas and his wife Catherine Zeta-Jones, Princess Caroline of Monaco, Elton John's husband David Furnish, Jeremy Clarkson and Andrew Marr, and footballers Ryan Giggs, Rio Ferdinand and John Terry are just some of the celebrities who have asked the courts, with varying degrees of success, to protect their privacy by way of (super)injunctions. Whilst France and Germany have strict privacy laws, the UK stands out as not providing an actionable right to privacy – that is, the ability to sue someone who has seriously invaded the secrets of your private life.[1]

To this day, there is no UK statute which covers expressly an individual's right to privacy, as the court in *Kaye v Robertson* (1991)[2] famously and uncompromisingly pointed out: there is no tort of privacy known to English law. This can often be to the detriment of the claimant as they have to fit their privacy claim into existing tortious actions. Some newspaper editors, such as Paul Dacre of the *Daily Mail*, would argue that common law judge-made development has created a privacy law 'via the back door', a view he gave in a lecture to the Society of Editors in November 2008, referring *inter alia* to Eady J's ruling in the *Max Mosley* case.[3]

This chapter deals with the concepts of confidentiality and privacy at common law and how the notion of privacy was further developed by the courts since the coming into force of the Human Rights Act 1998 (i.e. 1 October 2000 and in Scotland in 1998[4]). Chapter 2 then looks at concepts of free speech (dating back to the Bill of Rights 1689) and freedom of expression (Article 10 ECHR). The aim of this chapter is to clarify and distinguish the terms 'confidentiality' and 'privacy' in English common law and European Court of Human Rights (ECtHR) jurisprudence.

The concept of 'privacy' was first mentioned during the late 1880s by two American lawyers and partners in a Boston law firm, Samuel D. Warren (1852–1910) and Louis D. Brandeis

---

1   See: Markesinis, B. S. and Unberath, H. (2002).
2   (1991) FSR 62.
3   See: 'Society of Editors: Paul Dacre's speech in full', *Press Gazette*, 9 November 2008: www.pressgazette.co.uk/story.asp?storycode=42394.
4   The Human Rights Act 1998 and the Scotland Act 1998 were enacted at the same time in Scotland. The primary function of the Scotland Act 1998 was to set up a system of devolved government for Scotland, but it also included important provisions relating to the protection of the rights guaranteed by the Convention ('Convention rights'). It is necessary to read both Acts in order to understand the status of Convention rights in Scots law.

(1856–1941) in their seminal 1890 article, 'The Right to Privacy' in the *Harvard Law Review*.[5] Their privacy theory was based on natural rights, responding to privacy threats from new sources such as the telephone and paparazzi photography and sensationalist journalism, the 'yellow press'[6] (see: *Midler (Bette) v Ford Motor Co. and Young & Rubicam* (1988)[7]).

Raymond picks up Warren and Brandeis' argument almost 100 years later, when he argued that the emergence of newspapers and the mass media brought freedom of expression into the public domain but to the detriment of a person's privacy.[8]

The concept of 'private and public spheres' was further developed during the 1960s by German philosopher Jürgen Habermas.[9] His definition of the 'public sphere' later had a great impact on privacy applications by German celebrities, such as Caroline von Hannover (see: *von Hannover v Germany* (No 1) (2005)[10]).

Once the concepts of confidentiality and privacy have been explained this chapter focuses on superinjunctions and how the courts have made use of these 'double gagging' orders to restrain publication in the media in order to grant certain celebrities anonymity with a view to keeping confidential information, such as an illicit affair, from the public eye via the media.

1.2 Confidentiality: legal conventions and common law remedies

As English common law developed, before the Human Rights Act 1998 (HRA) came into force, the law concerned itself mainly with constitutional convention rights (such as collective cabinet confidentiality) and the obligation of confidence to control confidential information. Whereas a privacy right serves to protect a personal and private state of affairs, preventing information that the individual has chosen not to convey from being disclosed. This explanation was first given by John Stuart Mill in his writings *On Liberty*, where he argued that privacy allows people to engage in 'experiments in living'.[11]

1.2.1 Conventions and breach of confidence

One of the first legal cases involving a breach of confidential information and the Royal Household was that of *Prince Albert v Strange* (1849).[12] His Royal Highness, the Prince Consort, Prince Albert, had to ask the courts for an order to restrain the printer William Strange and his publishers Jasper Tomsett Judge and Son from reproducing private royal family drawings and etchings for 'mass' publication and to exhibit these 'sketches' in public.

Her Majesty Queen Victoria and her husband Prince Albert had occasionally, for their amusement, made drawings and etchings principally of subjects of the Royal Household at Windsor and Osborne House on the Isle of Wight. These were not meant for publication but limited copies had been made by a private press (Strange) and the plates were kept by Her Majesty under lock and key at her private apartments at Windsor. The defendants Strange, Judge, and J. A. F. Judge had in

---

5 See: Warren, S. D. and Brandeis, L. D. (1890) at pp. 193–220.
6 'Yellow Press' or 'yellow journalism' is an American term, akin to 'tabloid' journalism in the UK, meaning 'exaggeration', 'scandalmongering' and 'sensationalism'. See: Campbell, W. J. (2001).
7 [1988] 849 F 2d 460 Case No: 87-6168) United States Court of Appeal (for the Ninth Circuit) on 22 June 1988. The case centred on the protectability of the voice of the celebrated chanteuse from commercial exploitation without her consent (2005) 40 EHRR 1.
8 See: Raymond, J. (1998), pp. 109–136.
9 See: Habermas, J. (1962, translation 1989).
10 (2005) 40 EHRR 1.
11 See: Mill, J. S. (1859).
12 *Albert (Prince) v Strange* [1849] 1 Macnaghten & Gordon 25, (1849) 41 ER 1171.

some manner obtained some of these impressions, which had been surreptitiously taken from some of such plates. Copies of these etchings had then been exhibited in the form of a gallery collection which were then intended for a public exhibition without the permission of Her Majesty and Prince Albert and against their will. The defendants had also compiled and printed a catalogue entitled,

'A Descriptive Catalogue of the Royal Victoria and Albert Gallery of Etchings [then followed a quotation from Shakespeare]. London. Price Sixpence.'[13]

The catalogue comprised a list of 63 etchings. On 8 February 1849 the Lord Chancellor (Cottenham) granted a permanent injunction restraining the defendants from publishing any 'work being or pretending to be a catalogue of the etchings'. The defendants were also asked to 'deliver up' all the etchings and prints which had been made for the catalogue and large costs were awarded against the defendants which subsequently bankrupted the publishers.

The *Prince Albert* case set the precedent for confidentiality in relation to private material, kept under lock and key, for His Majesty's private use or pleasure and that such information should be kept from public knowledge.

Some 157 years later HRH Prince Charles found himself in the same predicament as his royal ancestor when his private travel journals had fallen into the wrong hands, namely the *Mail on Sunday*, and some extracts of his journals were published. In *HRH Prince of Wales v Associated Newspapers*,[14] Prince Charles asked the courts to restrain 'mass' publication of his private thoughts in his diaries which had fallen into the hands of a journalist. The Prince of Wales successfully gained a court order (by way of an injunction), restraining any further publications of the other seven journals, citing breach of confidence and copyright as well as his right to privacy under Article 8 ECHR. The *Mail* had used the 'public interest test' defence which later became prominent in the 'Prince Charles spider letter' case (see: *R (on the application of Evans) v Attorney General* (2015)[15].

See Chapter 4.6

One thing is clear in both the *Prince Albert* and *Prince Charles* cases: the courts will interfere by way of an injunction with any party who avails themselves of unauthorized material in violation of any right or breach of confidence which is of contractual nature (see: *Ashdown v Telegraph Group Ltd* (2001)[16]).

1.2.2 Official secrets and collective cabinet confidentiality

There have been three famous cases in UK legal history which have tested the notion of state secrecy and the doctrine of cabinet confidentiality; two were decided prior to the Human Rights Act 1998, namely the *Crossman Diaries*[17] and *Spycatcher*[18] cases, with the *David Shayler*[19] case decided post the Convention's incorporation into UK law involving, *inter alia*, criminal action. In *Crossman Diaries* and *Spycatcher*, prior restraint orders to stop publication were applied for by the Attorney General on behalf of the respective governments at the time, citing breach of confidence.

The *Crossman Diaries* case presented the first court action that tested the Convention of Collective Cabinet Confidentiality, a paradigm of restraining government ministers from any publication of Cabinet 'secrets'. In this case, the government had applied via the Attorney General to injunct the publication of Cabinet Minister Richard Crossman's posthumous diaries covering the period of

13 Ibid., at 1173.
14 [2006] EWHC 522 (Ch).
15 [2015] UKSC 21.
16 [2001] Ch 685 (Ch D).
17 *AG v Jonathan Cape Ltd; AG v Times Newspapers Ltd* [1976] QB 752 (*Crossman Diaries* case).
18 *AG v Guardian Newspapers Ltd (No 2)* [1990] 1 AC 109, at 283–284 (Lord Goff of Chieveley) (*Spycatcher* case).
19 *R v Shayler* [2003] 1 AC 247.

Harold Wilson's government between 1964 and 1970. Following Crossman's death in April 1974, volume one of the book, *Diaries of a Cabinet Minister*, which covered the years 1964–1966, had been sent to the Secretary of the Cabinet for his approval but was rejected on the ground that publication was against the public interest in that the doctrine of Collective Cabinet Responsibility would be harmed by the disclosure of details of Cabinet discussions. In July 1974 Crossman's literary executors gave an undertaking not to publish the book without giving prior notice to the Treasury Solicitor but, in January 1975, the first extracts from the book were published in the *Sunday Times* without the consent of the Cabinet Secretary.

On 18 June 1975, the Attorney-General issued a writ against the first defendants, the publishers Jonathan Cape Ltd and Hamish Hamilton Ltd and against the second group of defendants, Crossman's literary estate, namely his wife Anne Patricia Crossman, writer Graham Greene and Labour Party leader Michael Foot, seeking an injunction to restrain the defendants from printing, publishing, distributing, selling or otherwise disclosing in any manner, or causing to be printed, published, distributed, sold or otherwise disclosed, the contents of the book *Diaries of a Cabinet Minister* or any extracts from it. The Attorney-General also applied for an injunction against the *Sunday Times* to restrain publication of any extracts of the three volumes of the book.

The Court of Appeal dismissed the actions and lifted all injunctions on the grounds of public interest. The court ruled that volume one of the *Diaries* could be published immediately since it was dealing with events ten years previously and that Cabinet discussions should no longer remain confidential.[20] Lord Widgery CJ made it abundantly clear that the convention of Joint Cabinet Responsibility was in the public interest:

> it is unacceptable in our democratic society that there should be a restraint on the publication of information relating to Government when the only vice of that information is that it enables the public to discuss, review and criticise Government action. Accordingly, the court will determine the Government's claim to confidentiality by reference to the public interest. Unless disclosure is likely to injure the public interest, it will not be protected.[21]

The British secret services, particularly MI5, have always been the object of conspiracy theories, according to Cambridge professor Christopher Andrew, author of the first official history of MI5.[22] Layers of official secrecy were exposed by Peter Wright's sensational publication of *Spycatcher: the Candid Autobiography of a Senior Intelligence Officer* which had come into the Australian market. The former MI5 officer – by now retired in Tasmania – described in detail how 'we bugged and burgled our way across London at the State's behest, while pompous, bowler-hatted civil servants in Whitehall pretended to look the other way'.[23]

See Chapter
4.2

The *Spycatcher* (No 1)[24] and (No 2)[25] actions are best known for their numerous injunctions. The Attorney General, on behalf of the British government, attempted to restrain prior publication of Wright's memoirs in order to preserve the confidentiality of government and secret service material. Wright had, of course, signed the Official Secrets Act 1911 and was bound by this beyond his employment.[26] The question arose whether the UK High Court and the Crown could injunct a publication outside the United Kingdom?[27] The short answer was 'no'. And the book was published outside the UK and serialized in the *Sunday Times*. The restraining order was directed at the *Guardian*

---

20 [1976] QB 752 at pp. 765D–E, 769H–770A, 770B–D, 770G–771H, 772A–C.
21 Ibid., at 735 (Lord Widgery).
22 See: Andrew, C. (2009).
23 See: Wright, P. (1987), pp. 104–106.
24 *Attorney-General v Guardian Newspapers Ltd and Ors (No 1)* [1987] 1 WLR 1248 (*Spycatcher*).
25 *Attorney-General v Guardian Newspapers Ltd (No 2)* [1990] 1 AC 109.
26 For further discussion see: Barendt, E.(1989), p. 204; also: Bindman, G. (1989), p. 94.
27 See: Lee, S. (1987), p. 506; see also: Leigh, I. (1992), p. 200.

and the *Sunday Times* (and thereby *contra mundum*) and *Sunday Times* editor at the time, Andrew Neil, was severely criticized by Lord Keith of Kinkel, referred in his judgment in *Spycatcher No 2* to Mr Neil's blatantly ignoring the interim injunction as employing 'peculiarly sneaky methods'.[28]

Had Peter Wright returned to the UK he would, no doubt, have been arrested and charged with offences contrary to the Official Secrets Act 1911. Such was the case involving another MI5 whistleblower, David Shayler.[29] He too had disclosed official secrets to the press, the *Mail on Sunday*. The paper ran a front-page story on 24 August 1997, headlined 'MI5 Bugged Mandelson', with the claim that Tony Blair's favourite Cabinet Minister at the time had his phone tapped for three years during the late 1970s. Among his claims were that the intelligence service was paranoid about 'reds under the bed' and that it had investigated other Labour ministers such as Jack Straw and Harriet Harman. On 19 July 1998 Mr Shayler published further revelations on his own website www.shayler. com, such as an MI5 plot to kill the Libyan leader, Colonel Gaddafi.

Shayler was arrested in a Paris hotel by French police and extradited to the UK where he was convicted for unlawfully disclosing official documents to the media, thereby breaching the Official Secrets Act 1989.[30] He unsuccessfully used freedom of expression as a defence. Shayler was sentenced to six months in prison.

1.2.3 What is a breach of confidence?

See above
1.2.1

The common law or, more precisely, the courts of equity, have long afforded protection to the wrongful use of private information by means of the cause of action which became known as breach of confidence. A breach of confidence has been defined in equity as a form of unconscionable conduct, akin to a breach of trust. A breach of confidence goes back to the time when the cause of action was based on improper use of information disclosed by one person to another in confidence. To attract protection the information had to be of a confidential nature. The cause of action in confidence then is that information of this nature has been disclosed by one person to another in circumstances 'importing an obligation of confidence'.

The *Coco* case[31] is important here, concerned with the protection of trade secrets (namely the 'Coco Moped' with an Italian designed two-stroke engine). Mr Coco sought a court order by way of an interlocutory injunction to stop Mr Clark of the UK firm A. N. Clark (Engineers) Ltd manufacturing a copy, named the 'Scamp Moped'. The defendant engineering company had given an oral undertaking to pay a royalty of five shillings per engine. But since there was no written contract, Mr Coco could only rely on the duty of confidentiality, which he argued had arisen between himself and Mr Clark. Unfortunately, Mr Coco had already imparted his knowledge and trade secrets to the British company arguing at the first hearing that such information had to be kept 'strictly confidential'.

See Chapter
9.9

In the end the trial never took place since British intellectual property laws were weak at the time. The 'Coco engine' was subsequently discontinued after a short production run estimated at 3,000 and A. N. Clark (Engineers) Ltd went into administration.[32]

This meant that inventions and trade secrets could easily be stolen or copied and the inventor would not have any redress.

The 'Coco Engineers' case is important however because it established fundamental principles of law in the area of breach of confidence. Megarry J in the High Court Chancery Division had to decide what amounted to a breach of confidence and secondly whether the case was one where an injunction could be granted. He noted that the equitable jurisdiction in cases of breach of confidence was 'ancient' (referring to *Prince Albert v Strange*). Megarry J said that there was no breach

---

28 See: *AG v Guardian Newspapers (No 2)* [1990] 1 AC 109 at 261 (Lord Keith of Kinkel).
29 See: *R v Shayler* [2003] 1 AC 247.
30 For further discussion see: Hollingsworth, M. and Fielding, N. (1999).
31 See: *Coco v A. N. Clark (Engineers) Ltd* [1969] RPC 41 at 47 (Megarry J).
32 For further discussion see: Richardson, M. and Thomas, J. (2012).

of contract in the *Coco* case for no contract had ever come into existence. Accordingly he could only consider the pure equitable doctrine of confidence in the realms of commerce (referring to *Saltman Engineering Co. Ltd v Campbell Engineering Co. Ltd* (1948)[33]).[34]

Megarry J named three elements which set the precedent for a breach of confidence action to succeed:

1. the information itself must have the necessary quality of confidence about it;
2. the claimant must have disclosed the information to the defendant in circumstances which created an obligation of confidence; and
3. the information must have been used to the detriment of the claimant without authorization.[35]

The ruling in *Coco* is still valid in common law today: the definition of a 'breach of confidence' needs to be made up of all three essential elements

1.2.4 Remedies for breach of confidence before the Human Rights Act 1998

Once a breach of confidence has been established, an equitable remedy for such a breach comes into existence, including:

1. injunctions;[36]
2. compensatory damages;
3. exemplary damages;
4. account of profits;
5. delivery-up;
6. proportion of costs.

How then are damages awarded by the courts for breach of confidence? Ten years after the leading judgment in *Coco*, Sir Robert Megarry VC commented in *Malone* on the unsatisfactory state of the law of equity in that:

> the right of confidentiality is an equitable right which is still in the course of development, and is usually protected by the grant of an injunction to prevent disclosure of the confidence. . . . In such a case, where there is no breach of contract or other orthodox foundation for damages at common law, it seems doubtful whether there is any right to damages, as distinct from an account of profits.[37]

With no relationship between confider and confidant, the obligation of confidence is not established and a claimant will not succeed in a confidentiality action.

1.2.5 'Kiss and tell' tales: breach of confidence in the domestic setting

From the 1960s onwards, we can observe two branches of 'confidentiality' developing in common law, one in relation to trade and business secrets (i.e. *Coco* or *Campbell Engineering*-type cases) and the second in relation to misuse of private information in the form of 'kiss and tell' stories involving celebrities.

---

33 (1948) 65 RPC 203.
34 For further discussion see: Carty, H. (2008) at pp. 416–455.
35 *Coco* [1969] RPC 41 at 47 (Megarry J).
36 See: Practice Direction CPR 25A 'Interim Injunctions'.
37 See: *Malone v Metropolitan Police Commissioner* [1979] 1 Ch 344 (Sir Robert Megarry VC).

When people kiss and later one of them tells, the person who does so is almost certainly breaking a confidential arrangement. Though this book advances the 'open justice' principle it is worth noting that private communication between couples should be free from distribution to the press (and this includes modern practices such as text messaging, emails, etc.). This point was developed in the sensational divorce proceedings concerning the *Duchess and Duke of Argyll*[38] (for confidentiality see also: *Stephens v Avery* (1988)[39]). However, in another famous divorce case, *Scott v Scott* (1913),[40] the courts gave a carte blanche approach to the disclosure of confidential information.

See Chapter 8.2

The *Argyll v Argyll* (1967)[41] case was the scandal that rocked the nation at the time. Central to the Duke and Duchess of Argyll's divorce proceedings were the discourse of sexually explicit photos taken with a Polaroid camera in which the Duchess sought to invoke 'confidentiality'. The photos shown in court were 'headless' in a sexually very explicit pose with the Duchess. We learnt of the subjects' identities some 41 years later when, on 10 August 2000, a Channel 4 TV documentary named the two men (after their deaths): the actor Douglas Fairbanks Jr and Cabinet minister Duncan Sandys.

A few individuals have been able to rely on the *Argyll* judgment in their confidentiality actions against former partners or lovers, but many have been unsuccessful. John Lennon of the Beatles (1940–1980) could not rely on *Argyll*.[42] His divorced wife, Cynthia Lennon (1939–2015) had written her memoirs[43] after her bitter divorce from John and had sold the story to the *News of the World*. John Lennon was unsuccessful in seeking to injunct the publications. The court ruled that he could not rely on *Argyll* for breaches of marital confidences on the grounds that:

1.   he himself had publicized the most intimate details of their marriage; and
2.   there was nothing left which was confidential; all the information was already in the public domain.

Confidentiality injunctions were difficult to obtain where the couple was not married, particularly involving same-sex couples (this changed with the Civil Partnership Act 2004). The ruling in *Barrymore*[44] is therefore particularly significant.

On 17 March 1997 (just a year before the HRA 1998), *The Sun* outed TV personality Michael Barrymore as gay. He sought an *ex parte* injunction (not naming his lover Paul Wincott), claiming breach of confidence at common law in relation to 'A Trust and Confidence Agreement' made between him and his lover in 1995. The agreement – made by deed – included the obligation not to disclose or make use of any confidential business or personal information. The High Court granted the injunction to restrain any further publications, citing Lord Wheatley's judgment in *Argyll*, and extending the principle of confidentiality in correspondence between married couples to that of 'close relationships'. Jacob J said:

> The fact is that when people kiss and later one of them tells, that second person is almost certainly breaking a confidential arrangement.[45]

---

38   See: *Argyll v Argyll and Others* [1967] Ch 301.
39   [1988] 1 Ch 449.
40   [1913] AC 417.
41   [1967] Ch 301.
42   *Lennon v News Group Newspapers* [1978] FSR 573.
43   See: Lennon, C. (2005).
44   See: *Barrymore v Newsgroup Newspapers Ltd and Another* [1997] FSR 600 (Ch D)
45   Ibid., at 602 (Jacobs J).

However, it became near impossible for Michael Barrymore to sue the newspaper for compensatory and exemplary damages.

In *Stephens v Avery*[46] the court granted an equitable injunction restraining publication concerning a lesbian relationship. Sir Nicholas Browne-Wilkinson VC made clear that the law of confidence is capable of protecting relationships outside that of husband and wife, though possibly only where the confidence was 'express'. Though the court stressed that gross sexual immorality might not be protected from disclosure, information about sexual activities could be protected under a legally enforceable duty of confidence, where it would be unconscionable for someone who had received information on an expressly confidential basis to disclose it.

The media will always oppose injunctions since the publication of a juicy 'kiss and tell' story will increase revenue. In the *Jamie Theakston* case,[47] the popular broadcaster tried unsuccessfully to 'injunct' a story which had been leaked by a prostitute to the *Sunday People* and *News of the World*. Theakston (now presenting on Heart FM) was best known at the time as a presenter on BBC Radio 1 and hosted the BBC's *Top of the Pops* and *Live and Kicking* – i.e. he was seen as a youngsters' role model. The headlined articles showed Theakston coming out of a Mayfair brothel. Ouseley J granted an interim injunction in January 2002, banning the newspapers from using any photographs of the young presenter taken inside the brothel because the prostitute had used threatening text messages, demanding 'ransom' money from Theakston.[48]

The order was subsequently discharged because the story was seen as having a 'public interest' element which the law of confidence should not protect. The fact that the popular presenter had behaved in the manner he did was in the public interest, given his public role as perceived by young people as a role model and respectable figure. However, the photos were permanently injuncted because they had been taken by the prostitute without Theakston's consent. Ouseley J granted Article 8 ECHR ('privacy') rights in the photos. Phillipson argues that Ouseley J appreciated the need for proportionality in his decision in that the photographs taken of the claimant at the brothel had a lower level of public interest than the disclosure of the actual brothel visit.[49]

This leaves the concept of breach of confidentiality rather open-ended and perhaps too flexible. In 'privacy' cases before the HRA 1998 came into force those individuals seeking injunctions had to exhaust the UK courts' hierarchy first before they could seek redress at the Strasbourg Human Rights Court (ECtHR). This made for a rather uneasy relationship as demonstrated in the *Earl Spencer* case.[50] In his privacy action before the Strasbourg Court, the ninth Earl Spencer, brother of the late Diana, Princess of Wales, submitted that the UK had failed to comply with its obligations to protect his and his wife's right to respect for their private life under Article 8 ECHR.

The Earl claimed that the state had failed to prohibit the publication and dissemination of information relating to Countess Spencer's private affairs and therein failed to provide a legal remedy. He argued that the UK ought to have prevented the release of private and confidential information concerning the Spencers' private affairs by restraining the newspaper from publishing their stories and photographs, and that the UK courts ought to have provided damages for his wife's distress and the family's harassment by the media. Reasons for the media frenzy were that both Earl Spencer's wife Victoria[51] and his sister, Diana, had been suffering from an eating disorder.

---

46 [1988] 1 Ch 449.
47 See: *Theakston (Jamie) v MGN and Ors* [2002] EWHC 137 (QB).
48 Ibid., at 69 (Ouseley J).
49 Phillipson, G. (2003) at pp. 54–72.
50 *Earl Spencer and Countess Spencer v UK* (1998) 25 EHRR CD 105 (App Nos 28851/95, 28852/95) of 16 January 1998.
51 Victoria Lockwood had married Earl Spencer in 1989, with Prince Harry as a pageboy.

KEY CASE   *Earl Spencer and Countess Spencer v United Kingdom* (1998) 25 EHRR CD 105 (ECtHR)

Precedent

* There are adequate remedies available in the UK courts for breach of confidence.
* Before an application can be made to the European Court of Human Rights (ECtHR) in Strasbourg the applicant has to exhaust the domestic courts' remedies to the full; otherwise he will not be heard.

Facts

The *News of the World* (*NoW*) published an article on 2 April 1995, entitled 'Di's sister-in-law in booze and bulimia clinic'. This detailed some of the personal problems of Countess Spencer and included a photograph taken with a telephoto lens while she walked in the grounds of a private clinic. Earl Spencer complained to the Press Complaints Commission, which concluded there was a clear breach of Code 3 ('privacy') vis-à-vis his wife. The second publication was an article in the *People* on the same day, referring to the Countess's admission to a private clinic for an eating disorder. The third article was published in the *Sunday Mirror*, on the same day, alleging that the Countess had a drink problem.

Instead of suing the newspapers, the Earl and Countess applied to the European Commission on Human Rights (and therein to the Strasbourg Court), complaining that English law had failed to provide adequate respect for their privacy and so violated Article 8. Apart from arguing the breach of confidence action, the Spencers complained that the UK had no effective remedy in common law for the invasion of their privacy by the media.

Decision

The ECtHR declared inadmissible an application by Earl and Lady Spencer on the basis that they had not exhausted their domestic remedies, rejecting the Spencers' complaints under Article 8 on the basis that the couple had not completely exhausted the domestic remedies available to them for breach of confidence as outlined in *Spycatcher No 2* and *Barrymore*. The Commission also found their complaint under Article 13 ill-founded within the meaning of Article 27(2) of the Convention.

Analysis

The Strasbourg Court found in the *Earl Spencer* case that the UK's common law provisions in the law of confidence were adequate and reasonable to remedy the Spencers' complaint. However, since the Spencers had chosen not to avail themselves of any domestic court action in 'privacy' (not following the hierarchy of the courts) they were not entitled to seek redress in the Human Rights Court.

But the watershed was yet to come with case law building up following the introduction of the Human Rights Act 1998 in the United Kingdom.

FOR THOUGHT

Discuss the remedies available in the UK courts for breach of confidence for an unauthorized disclosure of personal information, accompanied by unsolicited photographs of a famous claimant.

1.3 Privacy: developments since the Human Rights Act 1998

The protection of someone's privacy is frequently seen as a way of drawing the line as to how far society can intrude into an individual's private affairs. To define 'privacy' is perhaps most difficult, as the notion of privacy differs from country to country and from culture to culture. Individual states have defined their constitutional laws and substantive case law as the notion of privacy has developed.[52] But privacy is not just about celebrities as the Leveson Inquiry showed. The inquiry into phone hacking by newspapers and unethical media standards and practices was told in May 2012 for example how the teenager Milly Dowler's mobile phone was hacked into by *News of the World* reporters, and how the police knew about it. Thirteen-year-old Milly disappeared in March 2002 and Levi Bellfield was convicted of her murder in June 2011, and sentenced to a whole life tariff.

See Chapter 6.3

Article 8(1) of the European Convention on Human Rights and Fundamental Freedoms (ECHR – or 'the Convention') makes it clear that the concept of privacy is not limited to isolated individuals, but includes the general 'zone' of the family, the home, correspondence with others, telephone conversations and a person's well-being. Article 8(1), 'Right to respect for private and family life', reads:

> Everyone has the right to respect for his private and family life, his home and his correspondence.

However, Article 8 is not an absolute right and may be 'qualified' which means a Member State to the Convention may derogate under Article 8(2) ECHR:

> There shall be no interference by a public authority with the exercise of this right *except* such as is in accordance with the law and is necessary in a democratic society in the interests of national security, public safety or the economic well-being of the country, for the prevention of disorder or crime, for the protection of health or morals, or for the protection of the rights and freedoms of others.

1.3.1 What is 'privacy'?

Before we examine definitions in common law let us consider how some scholars have defined 'privacy' before we look at leading authorities. Barber argues that privacy prevents others from learning everything about our activities.[53] American Sociologist Barrington Moore defines 'privacy' within the following categories:

- Information privacy involves the establishment of rules governing the collection and handling of personal data such as credit information and medical records.

---

52 See: Hixson, R. (1987).
53 See: Barber, N. W. (2003).

- Bodily privacy concerns the protection of people's physical selves against invasive procedures such as drug testing.
- Privacy of communications covers the security and privacy of mail, telephones, email and other forms of communication.
- Territorial privacy concerns the setting of limits on intrusion into the domestic environment such as the workplace or public sphere; to control the channels through which one's image is distributed.[54]

Rachels contends that privacy is valuable in that it allows us to limit the information that others know about us: that there are different sorts of social relationships that bring different levels of intimacy. Some information remains confidential to us.[55]

The by now famous dictum by Glidewell LJ in *Kaye v Robertson*[56] stated expressly that there is no right to privacy in English law:

> it is well known that in English law there is no right to privacy, and accordingly there is no right of action for breach of a person's privacy.[57]

In this case the editor and publishers of the *Sunday Sport* had published 'lurid and sensational style' photographs accompanied by an interview with the well-known actor Gorden Kaye, who was lying in hospital on life support. The actor, best known for his role as René in the popular TV series *'Allo'Allo!* had sustained severe head injuries on 25 January 1990 when, as he was driving in London during a gale, a piece of wood from an advertisement hoarding smashed through his windscreen and struck him on the head.

See below
1.7

This case established that 'hospital beds' are out of bounds for the media. It is worth noting that subsequent authorities demonstrate that Lord Glidewell's *dicta* in *Kaye v Robertson* have been superseded, although courts continue to use and perhaps distort the action for breach of confidence instead of recognizing they have created a tort of 'misuse of private information'.

As Glidewell LJ opined, privacy legislation was urgently needed in the UK:

> We do not need a First Amendment to preserve the freedom of the press, but the abuse of that freedom can be ensured only by the enforcement of a right to privacy. This right has so long been disregarded here that it can be recognised now only by the legislature.

So far Parliament has not found it necessary to enact any privacy laws relying mainly on Article 8 ECHR which has not changed substantive law in this respect. As the law of confidence developed by way of common law jurisprudence in the UK courts, the notion of 'privacy' developed alongside, arguably changing from the law of confidence to privacy with the inception of the Human Rights Act 1998 (HRA).

1.3.2 Public interest defence and privacy claims

See below
1.4.2

As common law developed post-HRA 1998 we can observe that the public interest defence advanced by newspapers and media organizations can be successful. The case which specifically examined the distinction between the public interest and what the public is interested in, was undoubtedly that of *Max Mosley*.[58]

---

54 Source: Moore, B. (1984), p. 5.
55 See: Rachels, J. (1975), p. 323.
56 (1991) FSR 62.
57 Ibid., at 66 (Glidewell LJ).
58 See: *Mosley (Max) v Newsgroup Newspapers Ltd* [2008] EWHC 1777 (QB).

See below
1.4.4

Case law informs us that the public interest defence now tends to be limited to matters of genuine political, legal, constitutional, social or economic relevance and importance, and whether the publication is capable of contributing to a debate in a democratic society. The Strasbourg Human Rights Court held in *von Hannover* (No 1)[59] that the individual claiming privacy and confidentiality (e.g. in photographs) must carry out public functions.

The public interest defence was advanced by the publishers of the *Daily Mail*, Associated Newspapers, in the *Carina Trimingham* case[60] (see below). The journalist and former press officer to and lover of Chris Huhne MP, applied for a privacy injunction under Article 8 ECHR in August 2010 against the *Daily Mail* and *Mail on Sunday* in respect of a series of articles and photographs published about her having an affair with the MP.[61] At the time of the affair Mr Huhne was married to Vicky Pryce for almost 25 years; the couple had five children, three together, and two from Ms Pryce's first marriage.[62] Until 20 June 2010, Ms Trimingham was living with her civil partner. The comments in the newspapers focused on her appearance, referring to her as 'bisexual' and a 'lesbian' and that she had previously lived in a civil partnership with another woman. Whilst Ms Trimingham did not action in defamation (because the allegations were substantially true) her legal complaint focused on repeated 'pejorative' references to her sexuality and appearance in eight articles. She actioned in harassment, privacy and breach of copyright in respect of the photographs.

❖ KEY CASE — *Trimingham v Associated Newspapers Ltd* [2012] EWHC 1296 (QB)

Precedent

❖ Claimants cannot rely on their Article 8 ECHR privacy rights if they are not a private individual; in the case of a public figure performing a public function the expectation of privacy is limited.

❖ The public interest defence (for the media) exists where the conduct and behaviour of the claimant in his or her personal life is likely to affect the business of government.

❖ A reasonable person with the same characteristics as the claimant would not think it unreasonable to disclose matters of genuine public interest (here Ms T was a press officer and journalist and had the knowledge of media practices).

❖ It would be a serious interference with freedom of expression (Article 10 ECHR) to silence the views of the press by subjective claims of harassment.

❖ There is no 'privacy' in photos if the claimant publishes personal photos on social media (e.g. Facebook).

Facts

Carina Trimingham (T) had worked as a press officer in three political campaigns and had been the campaign director for the Electoral Reform Society. She began to have an affair with married MP, Chris Huhne (Lib Dem) (H), in 2010, then a leading figure in the Coalition government and for whom Ms T had worked as a press officer. At the time Ms T was in a civil partnership with another woman and both she and Mr H's wife were unaware

---

59 See: *von Hannover v Germany* (No 1) (2005) 40 EHRR 1.

60 See: *Trimingham v Associated Newspapers Ltd* [2012] EWHC 1296.

61 Mr Christopher Huhne MP had been re-elected as the Member of Parliament for Eastleigh in Hampshire at the General Election held in May 2010. He became Secretary of State for Energy in the Coalition government. He was one of the leading figures in the government and in the Liberal Democrat Party.

62 Mr Huhne and his by now ex-wife Vicky Pryce, a prominent economist, were convicted of perverting the course of justice after she took speeding points for him following an incident on the M11 in 2003. Pryce had claimed the defence of marital coercion. Both were found guilty at Southwark Crown Court in March 2013 and given an eight months' prison sentence each.

of the affair. Numerous articles appeared in the *Mail Online* and the print editions of the *Daily Mail* and the *Mail on Sunday*, calling T 'bisexual' and 'lesbian' and making comments about her appearance, for example:

> 'Chris Huhne's bisexual lover: Life and very different loves of the PR girl in Doc Martens' by Barbara Davies, *Daily Mail* 21 June 2010.

> 'First picture of Chris Huhne's lover and the lesbian civil partner she has left broken-hearted' by Barbara Davies, *Daily Mail* 22 June 2010.

> 'It's Chris Huhne's hypocrisy and lies that matter, not his sex life' by Richard Littlejohn, *Daily Mail* 22 June 2010.

Photographs which had been taken by a professional photographer and personal friend of T at her home prior to her going to her civil partnership ceremony and at the ceremony were published in the *Daily Mail* and the *Mail on Sunday* (eight articles in August 2011 and other newspapers such as *The People*). T submitted that the *Mail* had:

(1) pursued a course of conduct amounting to harassment under section 1(3)(c) Protection from Harassment Act 1997;
(2) misused private information under Article 8 ECHR and breach of confidentiality; and
(3) breached copyright contrary to section 85 Copyright, Designs and Patents Act 1988 (CDPA) by publishing the photographs.

Ms T sought aggravated damages and a privacy injunction at trial.

Decision
The claim was dismissed with an order for costs against Ms Trimingham. Tugendhat J gave the following reasons:

1. The harassment claim
The judge considered that repeated publication in the media of offensive or insulting words about a person's appearance, sexuality, or any other characteristic *did not* amount to harassment.[63] Reasons advanced were:

(a) Ms T was *not* a private figure and in her private capacity she had conducted a sexual relationship with H which she knew would be likely to lead to a political scandal.[64] The scope of her protected private life was therefore limited (see: *Saaristo v Finland* (2010)).[65]
(b) T claimed that the defendant newspaper *ought* to have known that their conduct by publication amounted to harassment. Tugendhat J applied the 'reasonable person' test and pointed out: 'she was tough, a woman of strong character, not likely to be upset by comments or offensive language, a woman who was known to give as good as she got'[66] (applying *Banks v Ablex Ltd* (2005)[67]). The judge found that the newspaper's hostility was directed towards her conduct, not her appearance. The words 'bisexual'

---

63 *Trimingham* [2012] EWHC 1296 at para. 70 (Tugendhat J).
64 Ibid., at para. 249.
65 [2010] ECHR 1497
66 *Trimingham* [2012] EWHC 1296 at para. 252.
67 [2005] EWCA Civ 173.

and 'lesbian' were not normally understood to be pejorative and no reasonable reader of the words complained of would understand them in a pejorative sense[68] (applying *Jeynes v News Magazines Ltd* (2007)[69]).

(c) The reasonableness of the course of conduct. The judge found that it is not unreasonable for a newspaper to refer to these facts and if a journalist is criticizing a person for deceitful, unprofessional or immoral behaviour in a sexual and public context, it is not unreasonable to refer to that person as 'lesbian' or 'homosexual' given the newsworthiness of events.[70]

2. The Article 8 privacy and breach of confidentiality claims

Tugendhat J said these were rather limited since Ms T was not a purely private figure. She had openly and publicly declared her sexuality and previous sexual relationships[71] (applying: *Murray v Express Newspapers plc* (2007)[72]). The judge said it would be a serious interference with freedom of expression (Article 10 ECHR) if members of the media, wishing to express their own views, could be silenced by, or threatened with, claims for harassment based on subjective claims by individuals that they felt offended or insulted.

3. The breach of copyright claim

Section 85 CDPA affords rights to a person who 'commissions' the taking of a photograph. The photographs published in the newspapers had been commissioned by Ms T for her civil partnership ceremony; and Ms T had given these pictures to the *Evening Standard* in 2008 and posted them on her Facebook page. She only removed them from the site after the 'Huhne' story had broken. Tugendhat J held that the publication of the 'wedding' photographs disclosed no significant information and that T had no reasonable expectation of privacy in respect of these photos[73] (applying: *Ultraframe (UK) Ltd v Fielding* (2005)[74]).

Analysis

This **Carina Trimingham** case touches on several areas of law: protection from harassment, copyright, privacy under Article 8 ECHR and confidentiality. Like *Max Mosley*, Ms Trimingham decided not to sue in defamation. She chose the Protection from Harassment Act 1997 which obliges the state to prevent interference with an individual's right to privacy and the protection of their private lives under Article 8 ECHR. Was Ms T a public or private figure? The judge determined that T was *not* a private individual because of her association with a politician. She also had a high-profile career as PA to Mr Huhne. She could not claim privacy in the photographs because she had herself disclosed photos and matters about her private life on Facebook.

The case is a good example where the courts are balancing 'privacy' and 'freedom of expression' – Tugendhat J decided in favour of the latter. He also dismissed Ms T's harassment claim (s 1(3)(c) PHA 1997) because the conduct of the newspaper was held to be not so unreasonable in the particular circumstances and there was a 'pressing social need' to publish the story. This means that the privacy rights of the individual came second to the right of press freedom.

---

68 Trimingham [2012] EWHC 1296 at para. 255.
69 [2007] EWCA Civ 1270
70 Trimingham [2012] EWHC 1296 at para. 261.
71 Ibid., at para. 263.
72 [2007] EWHC 1908 (Ch).
73 Trimingham [2012] EWHC 1296 at paras 328, 337, 338.
74 [2005] EWHC 679 (Ch).

1.4 The public interest test and the 'red carpet' rule

British tabloid journalism is well known for its intrusion into the private lives of celebrities. Photographs are a record of a frozen moment in time and therefore have a permanence and presentational power which the human eye and words alone cannot capture. Paparazzi photographs taken on a public beach will not normally be considered private, while those taken in a private location will. Celebrities whose behaviour is seen as 'discreditable' and those who mislead the media about the truth are unlikely to have their secrets preserved.

Witzleb expresses concern that the lack of a substantive privacy law has led to insufficient legal remedies for invasions of privacy in the UK.[75] Though Bennett maintains that this may have been negated somewhat by the courts' flexibility in interpreting the equitable action for breach of confidence and in how they assess breaches of privacy, and the fact that it is considered on a case-by-case basis.[76] However, the flexible nature of privacy in English common law has meant that a person's privacy right does not sit comfortably with press freedom, particularly when the opposing rights of confidential information and freedom of expression coincide (see: *Spencer v UK* (1998)[77]).

If not in statute, how can the term 'public interest' be defined? The Independent Press Standards Organisation (IPSO)[78] definition probably comes closest to defining 'public interest' as:

1. The public interest includes, but is not confined to:
   (i) Detecting or exposing crime or serious impropriety.
   (ii) Protecting public health and safety.
   (iii) Preventing the public from being misled by an action or statement of an individual or organization.
2. There is a public interest in freedom of expression itself.
3. Whenever the public interest is invoked, the regulator will require editors to demonstrate fully that they reasonably believed that publication, or journalistic activity undertaken with a view to publication, would be in the public interest and how, and with whom, that was established at the time.
4. The regulator will consider the extent to which material is already in the public domain, or will become so.
5. In cases involving children under 16, editors must demonstrate an exceptional public interest to override the normally paramount interest of the child.[79]

See Chapter 6.4

The definition is deliberately loose, in order to allow the IPSO adjudicator to judge each complaint fully on its merits.

1.4.1 Privacy in public and private places

The first 'red carpet' case which tested the notion of privacy under Article 8 ECHR in the English courts was that of *Douglas v Hello! Ltd.*[80] What mattered in this case was the question whether the celebrity couple Catherine Zeta-Jones and Michael Douglas ('the Douglases') had a reasonable

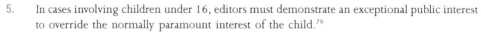

---

75 See: Witzleb, N. (2009).
76 See: Bennett, T. D.C. (2010).
77 (1998) (28851/95, 28852/95) 25 EHRR CD 105.
78 IPSO is the UK regulator charged with enforcing the Editors' Code of Practice, enshrined in the contractual agreement between IPSO and newspaper, magazine and electronic news publishers.
79 Source: IPSO – The Editors' Code of Practice, 1 January 2016.
80 [2001] EMLR 563 (QB).

expectation of privacy at their wedding at the Plaza Hotel in New York in November 2000? And would this notion of privacy include the exclusivity of their wedding photographs which they had sold for £1 million to OK magazine? Whilst the couple later recovered damages against Hello! magazine in the Chancery Division of the High Court,[81] the main issue in the 2001 privacy action was their claim under Article 8 ECHR. On 8 January 2000, Sedley LJ stated:

> We have reached a point at which it can be said with confidence that the law recognises and will appropriately protect a right of personal privacy.[82]

The judge gave two reasons for his comment. First, that equity and the common law had to respond to an increasingly invasive social environment. Secondly, that such recognition was now required by the HRA and in particular Article 8 ECHR (the HRA 1998 had only just come into force in October 2000). Sedley LJ went on to say that since *Kaye v Robertson* had been decided, 'the legal landscape has altered' and that the right of privacy was grounded in the equitable doctrine of breach of confidence. Sedley LJ's observations in the *Douglas* case in respect of balancing the Douglases' right to privacy and the media's freedom of expression are highly relevant when he said:

> the Convention right, when one turns to it, is qualified in favour of the reputation and rights of others and the protection of information received in confidence. In other words you cannot have particular regard to Article 10 without having equally particular regard at the very least to Article 8.[83]

A day after their wedding at the Plaza Hotel in New York, on Monday 20 November, the Douglases obtained an *ex parte* injunction restraining publication of Hello! issue 639. This was discharged by the Court of Appeal on Thursday 23 November. Edition 639 of Hello! containing the six unauthorized photographs went on sale on the following day, Friday 24 November, on the same day as issue 241 of OK which included OK's 'exclusive' coverage of the wedding. OK had hurriedly brought forward this publication. Hello's sales figures for issue 639, about 523,000, were some 150,000 above average. The High Court ruled that a wedding has to be essentially a public affair and the Douglases' private life was already in the public domain and they had sold their photographs for financial gain. Their Article 8 right had not been breached and the court ruled in favour of freedom of expression.

Photographs can have a special intrusive effect, as was held in the *Beckham*[84] case conveying visual information which words alone could not achieve. Compared with the *Douglas* case, where the claimants had set out to make a profit from their wedding, the claimants in *Beckham* did not have that commercial backdrop in that the photographs had been taken inside the Beckham's private home.

In this case, Eady J reversed the decision of the duty judge that the Beckhams had given a cross-undertaking not to publish photographs of their house, holding that this would have prejudiced their basic rights of privacy and freedom of contract. Eady J then upheld the interim injunction in favour of the Beckhams, preventing the *Sunday People* from publishing photographs of their matrimonial home and protecting the claimants from unwarranted intrusions into their privacy under Article 8, 'with regard to material which the law recognizes as being confidential'.[85] Although David and Victoria were themselves considering selling the rights to allow publication of certain

---

81 See: OBG Ltd and others v Allan and others, Douglas and another and others v Hello! Ltd and others, Mainstream Properties Ltd v Young and others and another [2007] UKHL 21 (on appeal from: [2005] EWCA Civ 106, [2005] EWCA Civ 595, [2005] EWCA Civ 861 (sub nom Douglas v Hello! No 7) – judgment of 2 May 2007 (HL)).
82 Douglas v Hello! Ltd [2001] EMLR 563 at 236, para. 115 (Sedley LJ).
83 Ibid., at 236, para. 138.
84 See: Beckham v Mirror Group Newspapers Ltd (28 June 2001, unreported).
85 Ibid., at 9, line C (Eady J).

photographs of their house, they were particularly concerned that the unauthorized photographs might reveal and thereby jeopardize some of the security measures taken to protect them and their home.

In determining whether photographs taken in a public place are capable of protection the courts have taken account of the context in which the photographs were taken and published, and whether the person photographed had a reasonable expectation of privacy in relation to their subject matter, and whether the photographs were taken surreptitiously. Additionally, the information conveyed by photographs has to be judged by reference to the captions and surrounding text.

The next case which touched on a similar privacy claim as the Douglases' was Naomi Campbell's common law claim on the basis of breach of confidence in 2001.[86] Her action was initially presented to the courts exclusively on the wrongful publication by the *Daily Mirror* of private information (in conjunction with an action in defamation).

In the first Naomi Campbell action *Campbell v MGN* (2002) a cause of action arose in February 2001 upon the publication of surreptitiously taken photos when the *Daily Mirror* published an image of and extensive articles on the famous supermodel receiving drug rehabilitation treatment at a Narcotics Anonymous clinic in 2001. Miss Campbell sued the newspaper for damages for breach of confidentiality. The *Mirror* carried a number of stories at the time on the supermodel, with headlines such as 'Naomi: I am a drug addict' and 'Pathetic – No hiding Naomi'. The articles in question contained the information that Campbell was a drug addict, and that she was receiving treatment at the Narcotics Anonymous rehabilitation clinic, as well as details of that treatment. The stories were supported by pictures of Miss Campbell leaving a drug therapy clinic. During the first proceedings Miss Campbell claimed damages for breach of confidence and compensation under the Data Protection Act 1998. Morland J did not grant Miss Campbell the right to privacy though he upheld a data protection claim, awarding her £2,500 plus £1,000 aggravated damages.[87]

The newspaper appealed and the CA, allowing the appeal, discharged the injunction. Miss Campbell appealed to the House of Lords on 23 February 2003. Their Lordships Lord Nicholls of Birkenhead, Lord Hoffmann, Lord Hope of Craighead, Baroness Hale of Richmond and Lord Carswell held that the law of confidence does not protect the trivial.[88] Their Lordships stated that Miss Campbell could not complain of the exposure of her drug-taking, especially since she had previously denied that she was a drug addict, but the HL felt that the Court of Appeal had erred in holding that the details of the claimant's treatment and attendance at the clinic plus the photographs were not private and confidential and that the article could not credibly have been written without the inclusion of that material.

Allowing the appeal (Lord Nicholls of Birkenhead and Lord Hoffmann dissenting), the House of Lords set the threshold test as to whether information was private: whether a reasonable person of ordinary sensibilities, placed in the same situation as the subject of the disclosure (rather than its recipient), would find the disclosure offensive. Miss Campbell's details of her drug therapy should have been afforded privacy related to her physical and mental health. The treatment she was receiving amounted to confidential information contained in her medical records and the publication clearly breached that confidentiality and her right to privacy. Their Lordships found the disclosure of the photographs highly offensive, stating that this had caused the claimant a setback in her recovery. The publication of that information went beyond disclosure which was necessary to add credibility to the legitimate story that the claimant had deceived the public and went beyond the journalistic margin of appreciation allowed to a free press. Though the photographs of Miss Campbell were taken in a public place, the context in which they were used and linked to the articles added to the overall intrusion into the claimant's private life.

---

86 *Campbell v Mirror Group Newspapers Ltd* [2002] EWHC 499 (QB).
87 Ibid., at 502 (Morland J) (CA).
88 *Campbell v MGN* [2004] 2 AC 457 (HL).

In summary, when a public figure chooses to make untrue statements about their private life, as was the case with Naomi Campbell denying her drug addiction, is it not the press who should be entitled to set the record straight? Should disclosure not be justified when it serves to prevent members of the public from being misled? The *Daily Mirror* argued that the photos and details about Miss Campbell's drug treatment exposed her lies, demonstrating that the newspaper had done an excellent piece of investigative journalism. The House of Lords argued that it depends how the information was obtained and by what means, such as by covert or surreptitious long-lens photography by paparazzi or phone-hacking, without the subject's consent or in a private place (see also: *Wainwright v Home Office* (2004);[89] *Fressoz and Roire v France* (1999);[90] *Jersild v Denmark* (1994);[91] *Peck v UK* (2003)[92]).

Their Lordships in *Campbell* took the Mirror's publication as a whole and examined all the circumstances including her going through drug rehabilitative treatment. They ruled that Ms Campbell's Article 8 right to privacy outweighed the newspaper's right to freedom of expression. Accordingly, the publication of the articles and the accompanying photos in the Mirror constituted an unjustified infringement of Miss Campbell's right to privacy whilst undergoing treatment; therefore she was entitled to damages.

Patten J argued in the *J. K. Rowling (David Murray)* case[93] that there is a clear difference between celebrities' and private individuals' private lives:

> If a simple walk down the street qualifies for protection then it is difficult to see what would not. For most people who are not public figures in the sense of being politicians or the like, there will be virtually no aspect of their life which cannot be characterized as private. Similarly, even celebrities would be able to confine unauthorized photography to the occasions on which they were at a concert, film premiere or some similar occasion. . . . Even after *von Hannover [No 1]* there remains, I believe, an area of routine activity which when conducted in a public place carries no guarantee of privacy.[94]

In July 2012, the mother of actor Hugh Grant's baby, Ms Ting Lang Hong, received a High Court 'permanent undertaking' from the picture agency *Splash News* not to pursue, doorstep or harass her or her child.[95] The order was made under section 1(1)(a) of the Protection from Harassment Act 1997, a ruling by Tugendhat J which has been used by celebrities in subsequent actions, providing enhanced measures of protection against paparazzi and media intrusion. Ms Hong claimed that on several occasions as many as ten journalists had camped outside her house, staying all night even in the rain, in the hope of getting a picture. An illustrated article appeared in the *News of the World*, dated 8 April 2011, headlined 'Hugh's Secret Girl'. At the time of the publication Ms Hong had no idea that she was being followed and photographed.[96]

1.4.2 Social utility and the protection of private information: the *Max Mosley* case

As the line between public and private blurs on the internet, can the courts truly protect what they regard as 'private' and 'confidential' in an attempt to protect a person's reputation, including personal image and photographs? In recent years, English law has adapted the action for breach of

---

89 [2004] 2 AC 406.
90 (1999) 31 EHRR 28.
91 (1994) 19 EHRR 1.
92 (2003) 36 EHRR 719.
93 *Murray v Big Pictures* [2008] EWCA Civ 446 (Patten J).
94 Ibid. at 65–66.
95 *Ting Lang Hong and Child KLM v XYZ and Others* [2011] EWHC 2995 (QB).
96 Ibid., at para. 5.

confidence to provide a remedy for the unauthorized disclosure of personal information such as in the *Naomi Campbell* case. This development has been mediated by the analogy of the right to privacy conferred by Article 8 ECHR and has required a balancing of that right against the right to freedom of expression conferred by Article 10 of the Convention. More recently, the Strasbourg Court confirmed in the *Axel Springer* case[97] that Articles 8 and 10 ECHR are of equal value, as long as the 'balancing exercise' is genuinely conducted by domestic courts, following the margin of appreciation.

Their Lordships said in *Campbell* (2004) that the law of confidence does not protect useless information or trivia. In *Mosley*,[98] Eady J extended the confidentiality notion to what amounts to personal conduct and what would be regarded as 'socially harmful'. He then applied the terms 'social utility' and 'pressing social need',[99] first coined in *Francome*[100] by Sir John Donaldson MR, where he explained that:

> the 'media', to use a term which comprises not only the newspapers, but also television and radio, are an essential foundation of any democracy. In exposing crime, anti-social behaviour and hypocrisy and in campaigning for reform and propagating the view of minorities, they perform an invaluable function.[101]

Max Mosley sued the *News of the World* (News Group Newspapers Ltd), complaining about a number of articles.[102] *News of the World* (NoW) journalist, Neville Thurlbeck, headlined the 'exclusive' on 30 March 2008: 'F1 Boss Has Sick Nazi Orgy With 5 Hookers', with the subheading: 'Son of Hitler-loving fascist in sex shame'. Of 'public interest' – the newspaper argued – was that Mr Mosley, the youngest son of the right-wing fascist leader Sir Oswald Mosley[103] and Diana Mitford, had engaged not only in an orgy with call girls, but in a 'Nazi orgy'. Mr Mosley knew nothing of the article before publication nor of the clandestine video footage which had been taken by an undercover reporter posing as a prostitute. The first he knew of the scoop was on the very same Sunday that millions of people were reading the article and watching the accompanying footage on the NoW website.

Mosley's cause of action centred on both a breach of confidence (i.e. the unauthorized disclosure of personal information) and an infringement of Mr Mosley's privacy under Article 8 ECHR. Eady J referred to the principle of 'pressing social need, where revealing someone's identity in court and therefore in the media was useful to society and 'of social utility', for the purpose of revealing criminal misconduct and antisocial behaviour (see: *X v Persons Unknown* (2006)[104]). Clearly, it was not alleged that the Formula 1 boss had engaged in unlawful sexual activity. The sensational newspaper reports centred on his sexual activities between consenting adults in private. Eady J stressed that Mr Mosley's conduct was in private and not socially harmful. He drew the analogy between the law on consumption of alcohol with that on other intoxicating substances: was such conduct in private and by consenting adults in the public interest and of social utility?

Eady J ruled that that the photographs of and articles on the Formula 1 chief's sadomasochistic activities with hired call girls were of *no social utility* at all. They rather amounted to 'old-fashioned breach of confidence' by way of conduct inconsistent with a pre-existing relationship, rather than simply of the 'purloining of private information'. The judge stressed that the content of the

97 *Axel Springer v Germany* (2012) (Application No 3995/08) Strasbourg judgment of 7 February 2012 (ECtHR).
98 *Mosley v NGN* [2008] EWHC 1777 (QB).
99 Ibid., at 173.
100 *Francome v MGN* [1984] 1 WLR 892.
101 Ibid., at 989 (Sir John Donaldson MR).
102 Mr Mosley was at the time President of the Fédération Internationale de l'Automobile (FIA) – Formula One's governing body (1993–2009).
103 Sir Oswald Ernald Mosley, 6th Baronet (1896–1980) was an English politician, known principally as the founder of the British Union of Fascists (BUF) in 1932.
104 [2006] EWHC 2783 (QB).

published material was inherently private in nature, consisting of S & M sexual practices. Moreover, there had been a pre-existing relationship of confidentiality between the participants, who had all known each other for some time and took part in such activities on the understanding that they would be private and that none of them would reveal what had taken place. Clearly 'Woman E' had breached that trust by recording her fellow participants.[105]

Max Mosley had chosen not to sue the newspaper in defamation. Though he was successful in the privacy claim it still meant that the offending articles and video footage of the 'Nazi Orgy' available on the *NoW* website were already in the public domain and the damage to Mr Mosley's reputation had been done.

On 29 September 2008, Max Mosley filed an application before the European Court of Human Rights (ECtHR) heard on 11 January 2011 in Strasbourg. Mr Mosley had asked the court to rule in favour of 'prior notification', which would compel the British (and EU) press to notify the subject of a story before publication.[106] He lost his claim. The ECtHR ruled against any pre-notification regimes concerning the media which would require powerful civil or criminal sanctions. The ruling stated that such a measure would have an adverse impact on media freedom beyond the limits of 'entertainment journalism' and the trade in the private lives of celebrities. The Strasbourg Court concluded:

> The limited scope under Article 10 for restrictions on the freedom of the press to publish material which contributes to debate on matters of general public interest must be borne in mind. Thus, having regard to the chilling effect to which a pre-notification requirement risks giving rise, to the significant doubts as to the effectiveness of any pre-notification requirement and to the wide margin of appreciation in this area, the Court is of the view that Article 8 does not require a legally binding pre-notification requirement.[107]

See Chapter 3.6

During his testimony at the Leveson Inquiry on 24 November 2011, Max Mosley disclosed that he was suing the Google search engine in France and Germany in a libel action, in an attempt to force the internet company to monitor and censor search results about his alleged sadomasochistic orgy and the *NoW* video.[108] His action was superseded by the *Google Spain* case (C-131/12)[109] action in the CJEU, resulting in the 'right to be forgotten' ruling.

We have seen in *Mosley* (2008) that the courts protect the individual when the intrusion into a claimant's life has been 'highly offensive' and when the objective 'sober and reasonable man' would agree that intrusion has been unacceptable.

 FOR THOUGHT

Compare the rulings in *Theakston* [2002], *Campbell* [2004] and *Mosley* [2008]. In what circumstances will the courts grant privacy protection in the absence of 'Max Mosley-style' pre-notification regulations to editors?

---

105 *Mosley v NGN* [2008] EWHC 1777 QB at 2–6 (Eady J).
106 *Mosley v UK* (Application No 48009/08) Judgment by the Strasbourg European Court of Human Rights of 10 May 2011 (ECtHR).
107 Ibid., at 132.
108 Source: Witness statement by Max Rufus Mosley to the Leveson Inquiry at MOD100023418 and MOD100023425 signed and dated 31 October 2011: www.levesoninquiry.org.uk/wp-content/uploads/2011/11/Witness-Statement-of-Max-Mosley.pdf.
109 *Google Spain SL, Google Inc. v Agencia Española de Protección de Datos, Mario Costeja González* ('right to be forgotten' Case C-131/12) Court of Justice of the European Union, Luxembourg, 13 May 2014.

1.4.3 Balancing the public interest with the individual's right to privacy

A factor which often dictates whether or not an individual's privacy is protected is the consideration of 'public interest'. Before the Human Rights Act 1998 came into force in October 2000, common law recognized that the public interest could justify the publication of information that was known to have been disclosed in breach of confidence. This was initially limited under the 'iniquity rule', whereby confidentiality could not be relied upon to conceal wrongdoing, upheld in *Lion Laboratories v Evans* (1985).[110] The public interest consideration is the argument that intrusion into people's private lives should be permitted where it is in the public's interest for them to be made aware of the private information. This may be considered a defence to a breach of privacy (or confidence), now supported by Article 10 ECHR when the courts balance freedom of expression with that of the right to privacy (see: *Francome v Mirror Group Newspapers Ltd*[111]).

In *Jameel*,[112] Lord Bingham made the following observations within the context of confidentiality and the public interest:

> the necessary precondition of reliance on qualified privilege in this context is that the matter published should be one of public interest. In the present case the subject matter of the article complained of was of undoubted public interest. But that is not always, perhaps not usually, so. It has been repeatedly and rightly said that what engages the interest of the public may not be material which engages the public interest.[113]

At a trial for a claim for misuse of private and confidential information, a claimant must first establish that he has a reasonable expectation of privacy in relation to the confidential information of which disclosure is threatened, as established in *Murray v Express Newspapers* (2008):[114]

> whether a reasonable person of ordinary sensibilities would feel if he or she was placed in the same position as the claimant and faced the same publicity.[115]

See below

1.5

That case concerned photographs of a young child (David, son of J. K. Rowling) in a public place taken covertly and published without the parents' permission.

The *Max Mosley*[116] privacy ruling made it clear that matters concerning the 'extramarital bed', 'death bed' or 'hospital bed' are out of bounds as far as freedom of expression and media reporting are concerned. In *AMP*[117] a British university student used her mobile phone to take explicit naked photos of herself at her home; the mobile phone was subsequently stolen while she was on a tram in Nottingham in 2008. After the phone was found, her photos were uploaded to the BitTorrent network and circulated under the name 'Sexy Rich Chick Mobile Phone Found By IRC Nerdz'. Her application for an interim (super)injunction to prevent transmission, storage and indexing of any part or parts of these photographic images was granted by Ramsey J in December 2011 to protect the claimant's rights to privacy under Article 8 ECHR and to prevent harassment under section 3 Protection from Harassment Act 1997.

110 [1985] QB 526.
111 [1984] 1 WLR 892.
112 *Jameel (Mohammed) v Wall Street Journal* [2007] 1 AC 359.
113 Ibid., at 31–33 (Lord Bingham).
114 [2008] EWCA Civ 446.
115 Ibid., at 24.
116 *Mosley v NGN* [2008] EWHC 1777 (QB).
117 *AMP v Persons Unknown* [2012] All ER (D) 178.

Until *von Hannover (No 1)*[118] there existed some confusion as to the meaning of 'public' and 'private' domain' as to what would be regarded in the 'public interest' in relation to an individual's right to privacy. This was perhaps better defined in *Spycatcher (No 2)*,[119] where the ECtHR ruled that the public interest test does not always amount to a justification for publication of confidential information. Since *Spycatcher (No 2)* the law imposes a 'duty of confidence' in common law whenever a person receives information which he knows or ought to know is fairly and reasonably to be regarded as confidential. Nevertheless, the law remains awkward and bewildering, caused partly by confusing case law relating to trade secrets with misuse of private personal information, which may require different parameters and treatment. This has given rise to ever greater legal actions. As common law has developed, 'public interest' is now the most common justification for publishing information which is either confidential or which has been challenged in the tort of defamation.

See Chapter 7

1.4.4 Genuine public interest or mere 'tittle-tattle'? The *von Hannover Nos 1–3* and *Axel Springer* actions

The German weekly 'gossip' magazines such as *Bunte* or *7 Tage* have always been interested in the private lives of European royalty, focusing particularly on Princess Caroline of Monaco[120] during her various marriages, the last being to Ernst August von Hannover. The applicant, Princess Caroline von Hannover, is a Monegasque national who was born in 1957 and lives in Monaco. The German media interest has always been focused on the royal family in Monaco, starting with the marriage of Prince Rainier III (1923–2005) to the Hollywood and Oscar-winning actress Grace Kelly (1929–1982) in 1956 and their children Princess Caroline, Prince Albert II and Princess Stephanie.

Princess Caroline has made repeated attempts to prevent the publication of photographs portraying her private life, often by taking legal action in the German courts. Two series of photographs, published in 1993 and 1997, were the subject of three sets of proceedings. Those proceedings were the subject of the judgment of 24 June 2004 in *von Hannover v Germany (No 1)*[121] in which the European Court of Human Rights (ECtHR) held that the court decisions in question had infringed the applicant's right to respect for her private life under Article 8 ECHR.

In a joint action, Caroline and her husband, Ernst August von Hannover,[122] subsequently brought several sets of proceedings seeking injunctions against the publication of further photographs published in German glossy and gossip magazines between 2002 and 2004. The German Federal Court of Justice dismissed their claims in part and the Federal Constitutional Court rejected a constitutional complaint by the applicants. Those proceedings were the subject of the Grand Chamber judgment of 7 February 2012 in the case of *von Hannover v Germany (No 2)*,[123] in which the Court held that the court decisions at issue had *not* infringed the right of Princess Caroline von Hannover and her husband to respect for their private life.

Noteworthy in *von Hannover (No 1)* was the judgment by presiding Judge Zupani who made the distinctions between the different levels of 'privacy' which were rather confusing in German copyright law and constitutional jurisprudence (*Begriffsjurisprudenz*). The ECJ criticized Germany's Constitutional Court for allowing publication of the pictures four and a half years previously and

---

118 *von Hannover v Germany (No 1)* [2004] EMLR 21.
119 *AG v Guardian Newspapers Ltd (No 2)* [1990] 1 AC 109 (*Spycatcher*).
120 Her official title is: Princess Caroline Louise Marguerite, Prinzessin von Hannover, Herzogin zu Braunschweig und Lüneburg. She married Ernst August Prinz von Hannover on 23 January 1999, her second marriage, after Caroline of Monaco had married Philippe Junot on 28 June 1978; their marriage was annulled on 9 October 1980.
121 *von Hannover (No 1)* (2005) 40 EHRR 1.
122 Born 1954 and of particular interest since he is a member of the royal House of Hannover as: Ernst August, Prince of Hanover, Duke of Brunswick and Lüneburg (Ernst August Albert Paul Otto Rupprecht Oskar Berthold Friedrich-Ferdinand Christian-Ludwig Prinz von Hannover Herzog zu Braunschweig und Lüneburg Königlicher Prinz von Großbritannien und Irland).
123 *von Hannover v Germany (No 2)* (2012) (Application Nos – 40660/08, 60641/08) (unreported) Judgment of 7 February 2012.

said there had been no 'legitimate interest' in Princess Caroline's private life and that the general public did not have a legitimate interest in knowing her whereabouts or how she behaved generally in her private life. The ECtHR raised the standard of protection of private life to a level higher than in Germany similar to the privacy laws of France. Zupani's ruling set the precedent for the 'balancing test' in human rights legislation between the public's right to know and freedom of the media to report under Article 10 ECHR and the celebrity's right to privacy:

> he who willingly steps upon the public stage cannot claim to be a private person entitled to anonymity. Royalty, actors, academics, politicians etc. perform whatever they perform publicly. They may not seek publicity, yet, by definition, their image is to some extent public property.[124]

The ruling in *von Hannover* (No 1) significantly impacted on media practices throughout Europe at the time. Paparazzi had to make sure when taking a celebrity photo: was it taken in a clandestine and secret long-lens way by peeping over a fence into a private garden or was the celebrity individual undertaking an official duty in public? *Von Hannover* (No 1) set the scene for the 'public' or 'private sphere'. And if the picture was of public interest it could safely be published, irrespective of consent.

The ruling in *von Hannover* (No 2) was different. The ECtHR did not really reverse the ruling in the No 1 action but did not grant the Article 8 'privacy' right to Princess Caroline von Hannover for different reasons. The action concerned the publication of photographs in the 'gossip' magazine *Frau im Spiegel* in 2002, showing the Princess and her husband, Prince Ernst August von Hannover (joint applicants), on a skiing holiday in St Moritz. The accompanying article reported on the deteriorating health of the Princess's father, Prince Rainier III of Monaco and that the Princess should have been at his bedside as he was dying. The ECtHR ruled that the publication of the said photo and the accompanying article did not breach the applicants' privacy rights because the subject matter (the poor health of the reigning Prince of Monaco) was of general public interest. The Strasbourg Court also confirmed that the link between the photographs and the subject matter of the accompanying article was sufficiently close so as to render their publication justifiable. The case was jointly heard with the *Axel Springer* case (see below).

❖ KEY CASE

Axel Springer v Germany (2012) (joint application No 3995/08 with *von Hannover No 2*) Strasbourg judgment of 7 February 2012 (ECtHR)

Precedents (in both actions: *Axel Springer* and *von Hannover No 2*)

- ❖ The domestic courts must strike a balance between Articles 8 and 10 ECHR, depending on the facts and circumstances.
- ❖ **Contribution to a debate of general interest** – this covers not only political issues or crimes but sporting issues or performing artists.[125]
- ❖ **How well known the person was and the subject of the report** – a distinction has to be made between private individuals and persons acting in a public context, as political or public figures.[126]
- ❖ **Prior conduct of the person concerned: the conduct of the person prior to the publication is a relevant factor** – although the mere fact of having co-operated with the press cannot be an argument for depriving a person of all protection.[127]
- ❖ **Method of obtaining the information and its veracity** – these are important factors – the protection of Article 10 is subject to the proviso that journalists are acting in

---

124 *von Hannover* (No 1) (2005) 40 EHRR 1 at 32 (Judge Zupani).
125 *Axel Springer v Germany* (2012) at para. 90.
126 Ibid., at para. 91.
127 Ibid., at para. 92.

good faith, on an accurate factual basis, providing reliable and precise information in accordance with the ethics of journalism.[128]

❖ **Content, form and consequences of the publication** – the way in which the photo or report is obtained and the way in which the individual is represented are factors to take into account.[129]

❖ **Severity of the sanction imposed.**[130]

❖ **Courts have to balance Articles 8 and 10 ECHR equally.**

❖ **Article 8 does not create an 'image right', nor does it create a 'right to reputation'.**

❖ **Individuals who seek the public limelight have their Article 8 right to privacy severely curtailed.**

Facts

The applicant, Axel Springer-Verlag, is the publisher of the daily German tabloid *Bild-Zeitung* ('*Bild*'), registered in Hamburg since 1952, with a circulation of about 2.6 million per day (in 2004). *Bild* is famous for its salacious gossip and sensational journalistic headlines.

The case concerned two articles about X, a well-known TV actor.[131] X had been the subject of two stories and photos in *Bild* in 2004 and 2005, after he was arrested in a beer tent at the Munich Oktoberfest for possessing cocaine. The story made the headlines: 'Cocaine! Superintendent caught at Munich Beer Festival', with a photo of X. The second article was published some ten months later and reported details of X pleading guilty to the drug possession offence and how he was sentenced to a €18,000 fine. Axel Springer claimed that prior to publication the journalist had confirmed the arrest with the police sergeant present at the scene; the public prosecutor had also verified the charges.

Whilst the Hamburg regional court had granted X an injunction, restraining *Bild* (and other publications) from publishing the story, *Bild* went ahead and published the story and photos. The Hamburg court found Axel Springer guilty of contempt by disobeying the existing court order. The applicant publishers petitioned the ECtHR relying on their Article 10 right.

Decision: *Axel Springer*

The Grand Chamber (of the ECtHR) disagreed with the German courts' reasoning for granting the injunction to the actor. Judges of the Grand Chamber opined that X's arrest and conviction were of general public interest, particularly since the public prosecutor had confirmed the criminal charges of possession of class A drugs. It was also in the public interest and therefore of importance to uphold the law, since X had been a role model for young people, playing the character of a police superintendent (*der Kommissar*) whose job it was to combat crime. The Court noted that X had regularly contacted the press himself or via his PR company and that he had previously revealed detailed information about his private life in a number of media interviews. The Court reasoned that X's 'legitimate expectation' of protection for his private life was reduced by virtue of the fact that he had 'actively sought the limelight'. Because 'TV cop' X was a well-known actor, known particularly as a law enforcement officer on screen, the ECtHR held:

---

128 Ibid., at para. 93.
129 Ibid., at para. 94.
130 Ibid., at para. 95.
131 The German left-wing daily newspaper *TAZ* (*Tageszeitung*) disclosed X's identity, that of Bruno Eyron, well known for playing a RTL-TV cop, 'Kommissar Balko'. Source: 'Caroline von Monaco zu Recht geknipst. Ein europäisches Gericht stärkt die deutsche Pressefreiheit: Ein Foto von Caroline von Monaco durfte gedruckt werden. Ebenso das Bild eines koksenden Schauspielers', by Christian Rath, *TAZ*, 7 February 2012.

he was sufficiently well known to qualify as a public figure. That consideration . . . reinforces the public's interest in being informed of X's arrest and of the criminal proceedings against him.[132]

The Grand Chamber found by 12 votes to five that the German courts had violated the publishers' Article 10 rights by their overzealous injunctive sanctions imposed on the tabloid newspaper. The restraining order had been too severe and accordingly there had been a violation of the publishers' Article 10 right. The newspaper publishers were awarded damages and costs in the domestic proceedings and in the Strasbourg action.

Analysis of *Axel Springer* and *von Hannover (No 2)*

The difficulty with both the conjoined cases was compounded by a series of appeals and cross-appeals by the applicants and various publishers, including complaints in respect of publications and photographs elsewhere. Nevertheless, the ECtHR's decision in both cases is an important win for the media, particularly as media practices were severely criticized at the Leveson Inquiry in London's High Court of Justice. The *Axel Springer* and *von Hannover (No 2)* judgments remind us of the important role played by a free and uncensored press in a pluralistic democracy where the Human Rights Court undertook a careful balancing exercise between freedom of expression and the individuals' privacy rights. In both cases the Grand Chamber of the ECtHR explained the criteria, based on existing human rights law, which are to be applied when balancing the competing Article 8 and 10 rights in the public interest. Both the ECtHR decisions in *Axel Springer* and *von Hannover (No 2)* can be seen as important victories for the media and for press freedom in general. With the Leveson Inquiry into media ethics and phone-hacking dominating the headlines at the same time as the Grand Chamber judgment in 2012, the judgment provides suitable encouragement and support for the media across Europe in relation to the publication of stories and photographs about the private lives of celebrities.[133]

The *von Hannover* (No 3) (2013)[134] action concerned a complaint lodged by Princess Caroline von Hannover relating to the refusal of the German courts to grant an injunction prohibiting any further publication of a photograph of her and her husband Ernst August taken without their knowledge while on holiday in their villa on an island off the Kenyan coast. In its judgments in *Axel Springer AG* and *von Hannover* (No 2) (see above) the ECtHR had set out the relevant criteria for balancing the right to respect for private life against the right to freedom of expression. These were: contribution to a debate of general interest, how well known the person concerned was, the subject of the report, the prior conduct of the person concerned, the content, form and consequences of the publication and, in the case of photographs, the circumstances in which they were taken.

In *von Hannover* (No 3), the Strasbourg Court noted that the German Federal Constitutional Court had taken the view that, while the photograph in question had not contributed to a debate of general interest, the same was not true of the article accompanying it, which reported on the current trend among celebrities towards letting out their holiday homes. The Federal Constitutional Court and, subsequently, the Federal Court of Justice had observed that the article was designed to report on that trend and that this conduct was apt to contribute to a debate of general interest. The Court also noted that the article itself did not contain information concerning the private life of the applicant or her husband, but focused on practical aspects relating to the villa and its letting. It could not therefore be asserted that the article had merely been a pretext for publishing the photograph in question or that the connection between the article and the photograph had been purely contrived. The characterization of the subject

---

132 Ibid., at para. 99.
133 See also: Pillans, B. (2012).
134 *von Hannover v Germany* (No 3) (2013) (Application No 8772/10) ECHR 264.

of the article as an event of general interest, first by the Federal Constitutional Court and then by the Federal Court of Justice, could not be considered unreasonable. The Human Rights Court could therefore accept that the photograph in question had made a contribution to a debate of general interest.

The Strasbourg Court reiterated that on several occasions the applicant and her husband were to be regarded as public figures who could not claim protection of their private lives in the same way as individuals unknown to the public. Noting that the German courts had taken into consideration the essential criteria and Strasbourg jurisprudence in balancing the various interests at stake, the court concluded that they had not failed to comply with their positive obligations and that there had been no violation of Article 8 of the Convention.

The Strasbourg Human Rights Court messages sent out in *von Hannover* (No 2) and *Axel Springer* (2012) and *von Hannover* (No 3) are helpful, making a distinction between what is of genuine public interest and what is not. In *von Hannover* (No 2), the article did not centre on Princess Caroline. Instead, its main focus was her father, Prince Rainier of Monaco, and his deteriorating health, which was a matter of public interest given his official role as reigning head of state. In *von Hannover* (No 1) the photographs at issue depicted Princess Caroline's personal relationships and day-to-day life and activities, such as horse riding, skiing and playing tennis, which the ECtHR decided were purely private. What is clear from the three *von Hannover* judgments is that where an article and accompanying photo can be shown to contribute to a debate of genuine public interest, it can be justified and be published. Let us call this the 'red carpet' rule, where the ECtHR defined what is meant by 'public' and 'private sphere' more clearly in relation to celebrities and public figures.

Nicol J did not grant the claimant David Axon 'a reasonable expectation of privacy' because of his 'very public position' as the Commanding Officer of a Royal Navy frigate, *HMS Somerset*. Complaints that Axon had bulled junior officers on the ship had been published in *The Sun* in December 2004. The judge concluded that the fact of Axon's removal from command was a public fact and his role was that of a 'very public position'.[135]

 FOR THOUGHT

Should the UK Parliament legislate for a right of privacy, building on existing common law of breach of confidence? Discuss with reference to leading authorities.

1.5 A child's right to privacy

A child's welfare is of paramount importance, a principle enshrined in the United Nations Convention on the Rights of the Child 1989 which provides in Article 3:

1. In all actions concerning children, whether undertaken by public or private social welfare institutions, courts of law, administrative authorities or legislative bodies, the best interests of the child shall be a primary consideration.

And Article 16:

1. No child shall be subjected to arbitrary or unlawful interference with his or her privacy, family, home or correspondence, nor to unlawful attacks on his or her honour or reputation.

2. The child has the right to the protection of the law against such interference or attacks.

---

135 See *Axon v Ministry of Defence* [2016] EWHC 883; [2016] 3 Costs L.O. 401 (QBD) 19 April 2016.

Article 24 of the Charter of Fundamental Rights of the European Union 2000 provides:

> (2)   In all actions relating to children, whether taken by public authorities or private institutions, the child's best interests must be a primary consideration.

See Chapter
8.3

In English law the Children and Young Persons Act 1933[136] and the Children Act 1989 protect the upbringing and – if necessary – anonymity of a child going through care and court proceedings until the age of 18. The Victims and Witnesses (Scotland) Act 2014 introduced the same reporting restrictions as England and Wales in September 2015.[137] These principles ensure that all decisions made in respect of children must be in their best interest and must be respected by all persons, including a child's parents or guardian and all private and public bodies. Any interference with a child's right to privacy will ultimately be decided by the courts who have the welfare of the child in mind.

There have been decisions made by the courts which conflict with the parents' interest and that of the child. Where there exists such conflict with the parents' interests, the courts tend to rule in the child's best interest and welfare though relief will not always be granted under Article 8 ECHR according to the ruling in the *AAA*[138] case (see below). Increasingly we see children participate in reality TV shows where parents have clearly waived the child's privacy right – some for financial gain. While reality shows featuring children may cause television ratings to go up, children participating in these shows face immense pressure.

The court ruling in the *David Murray* case (see below) made it clear that a child's right to privacy is not entirely separate from that of his parents. Rather the court posed the question as to whether the child's right to privacy is engaged should not be determined by reference to the parents' own interest and actions. The court made reference to parental conduct and motive when assessing whether an interference with the child's privacy is justifiable. The court recognized that parents can, in limited circumstances, waive a child's right to privacy – which many celebrities have done, such as the Beckhams with their children – but for financial gain.

1.5.1 A child's right to privacy is distinct from that of each of its parents

The leading case in this respect is the *David Murray* action[139] concerning the then 19-month-old son David Murray whose mother is the famous Harry Potter author. The child was photographed covertly with a long lens by paparazzi from the Big Pictures agency in a buggy as the author was strolling in a public street in Edinburgh in November 2004. Big Pictures is a well-known celebrity photo agency which licenses its photos in the UK and internationally. The child's photograph was published in April 2005 (without the parents' permission) in the *Sunday Express* magazine, accompanying an article on Joanne Rowling's attitude to motherhood. Rowling and her husband Dr Murray sought an injunction to stop publication on behalf of their son David.

The question before the Court of Appeal was whether a small child being pushed in a buggy down the high street was 'private'? The CA found that it depends on the circumstances in which the

---

136 The Criminal Justice and Courts Act 2015 inserted s 39A into the 1933 Act including 'Prohibition on publication of certain matters: providers of information society services' extending publication beyond the realm of 'newspapers'.

137 Section 15 Victims and Witnesses (Scotland) Act 2014 ('Reporting of proceedings involving children') amended restrictions on reporting proceedings involving children in s 47 Children (Scotland) Act 1995 so that they apply to a person under 18, rather than under 16. Section 47 of the 1995 Act puts certain restrictions on newspapers to prevent them revealing the identity of persons under 16 who are involved in criminal proceedings (as the person against or in respect of whom the proceedings are taken, or as a witness). However, the court has discretion to dispense with these requirements if it is satisfied that it is in the public interest to do so. The provisions also apply to sound and television programmes.

138 *AAA (by her litigation friend BBB) v Associated Newspapers* [2013] EWCA Civ 554; [2012] EWHC 2103 (QB).

139 *Murray (David) v Express Newspapers and Others* [2008] EWCA Civ 446 (CA) (also known as: *Murray v Big Pictures*).

photograph was taken which would determine if Article 8 ECHR can be engaged. The David Murray photograph was taken in a clandestine way and the photo was subsequently published for the purpose of sale and publication which was sufficient to establish an interference with the child's privacy. Furthermore the court ruled that a child's right to privacy is distinct from that of each of its parents owing to its vulnerability and youth.[140]

The CA stated that the circumstances in which a child has a legitimate expectation of privacy are wider than those in which an adult has such expectations: adults can expect a greater degree of intrusion as part of their daily lives whilst a young child may be unaware of media hype. Citing the 'legitimate expectation' test in *Campbell*, Lord Hope asked:

> what a reasonable person of ordinary sensibilities would feel if she was placed in the same position as the claimant and faced with the same publicity?[141]

At the same time the CA pointed out that children, unlike adults, are very unlikely to derive any benefit from publication of information. This does not mean that children should never be photographed in public, as long as it is not detrimental to the child at the time of publication or in the future. In any case this should be in line with normal parental responsibility and the statutory duty to protect the child's well-being.

In *Re Z*[142] the CA granted an injunction to prevent publicity and identification of a child who attended a special school. The mother had consented to a TV company filming the child's particular treatment and the TV programme was to show the results of the child's institutional care as well as the child's treatment in which the child and mother would play active roles. The CA held that the parent's right to waive a child's privacy rights is strictly limited, reiterating Lord Oliver's judgment in *Re KD (A Minor) (Ward: Termination of Access)*.[143]

Since the *J. K. Rowling (David Murray)* case there has been a tendency by celebrities to include their children in lifestyle magazines or reality programmes which enhance their celebrity status as 'yummy mummy' or 'superdad'.[144] When we see the Beckhams' children Brooklyn, Romeo, Cruz and Harper Seven or Kim Kardashian and Kanye West's daughter North or Tamara Ecclestone breast feeding baby Sophia in glamour magazines, we can be sure that the celebrities will have allowed publication of the images for financial gain. Otherwise we would see celebrity children's photographs pixelated.

Between 2010 and 2011 the *Daily Mail* published eight articles about the then Conservative Mayor of London Boris Johnson and his 'philandering' past. The 'siege' by newspaper journalists and paparazzi had taken place during a 12-day period in the summer of 2010. According to the claimant baby AAA, the journalists and photographers had laid siege to her family home in London, eventually forcing the claimant to stay at her grandparents' house in Kent. The newspaper (and its online edition) had openly reported on the married Mayor's affair with Helen Macintyre who subsequently gave birth to her daughter Stephanie. The paper ran eight stories, speculating over the paternity of Stephanie, showing a photo of the one-year-old child born in November 2009 with a wild mop of flaxen hair and instantly recognizable features similar to those of Mr Johnson. As soon as the scandal broke, the child – only known as AAA at the time – sought damages against Associated Newspapers and a 'superinjunction' for lifelong anonymity because the mother had chosen not to reveal the identity of the father and had not named the father on the child's birth certificate.

AAA v Associated Newspapers (2012)[145] was a six-day private hearing in London where High Court judge Nicola Davies J ruled that AAA's (the claimant baby) mother had compromised the child's

140 For further discussion see: Carter-Silk, A. and Cartwright-Hignett, C. (2009) pp. 212–217.
141 See: *Campbell v MGN Ltd* [2004] 2 AC 457 (HL).
142 *Re Z (A Minor) (Identification: Restrictions on Publication)* [1996] 2 FCR 164 CA.
143 *Re KD (A Minor) (Ward: Termination of Access)* [1988] FCR 657 (HL).
144 *Murray (David) v Express Newspapers and Others* [2008] EWCA Civ 446 (CA) (also known as: *Murray v Big Pictures*).
145 [2012] EWHC 2103 (QB).

right to privacy by hinting at the identity of the father at a party. The claimant served proceedings on the defendant in June 2011. Solicitors acting for the claimant alleged breaches of the baby's privacy rights under Article 8 ECHR and under the Protection from Harassment Act 1997. Associated Newspapers disputed the claim, but promised to remove the photograph from the *Daily Mail's* website and to adhere to the PCC Code. But more articles followed and the baby's photograph was republished despite the assurance given. At the end of the trial the judge ordered the *Mail's* publishers, Associated Newspapers, to pay £15,000 in privacy damages for publishing photographs of Stephanie but ordered the legal representatives of the baby to pay 80 per cent of the *Mail's* legal costs, an estimated £200,000.

Miss Macintyre (the child's mother) appealed against the decision not to award her damages for details about the affair and resulting child being published, and the refusal to grant an injunction preventing the *Mail* from reprinting the information. But the Court of Appeal rejected her application.[146] Master of the Rolls Dyson LJ said: 'It is not in dispute that the legitimate public interest in the father's character is an important factor to be weighed in the balance against the child's expectation of privacy.' The court also rejected any further privacy injunction since much information had already been put in the public domain by the child's mother so that an injunction to prevent any further publication upon this topic would have served no real purpose. The court had evidence of the claimant's mother's numerous conversations with friends and that she had told a senior magazine executive at a party that Boris Johnson was the father of Stephanie (AAA). These facts had clearly compromised the claimant child's reasonable expectation of privacy.

Davies J in the High Court action referred to *Murray* in assessing AAA's reasonable expectation of her private life, her welfare and upbringing. But different to the *David Murray* (the infant child of J. K. Rowling) case, the court found that the conduct of AAA's mother as identified in the above paragraph demonstrated ambivalence towards, and an inconsistent approach, with her stated aim in these proceedings. The court further ruled that the matter was in the public interest which the electorate was entitled to know when considering his fitness for high public office. The core information was that AAA's father (Boris Johnson) had an adulterous affair with the mother (Miss Macintyre), deceiving both his wife and the mother's partner, and that the child, born about nine months later, was likely to be the father's child.

The photograph of the claimant AAA had been taken in a public place, when she was less than one year old and her mother was unaware of it being taken. Davies J said that there was no suggestion that the taking of the photograph caused distress to the claimant. The same photograph accompanied the first, second and eighth articles published by the defendant's newspaper (though no consent had been obtained from the claimant's mother). The *Daily Mail* argued that the publication of the photo was necessary in order to permit readers to see whether or not there was any family resemblance as between the baby and her supposed father.[147] The judge found that the claimant's mother and nanny were not reliable witnesses, pointing out discrepancies and inaccuracies in their evidence. Davies J further pointed out that much of the information was already in the public domain, citing the CA in *Douglas v Hello* (2006):

> Once intimate personal information about a celebrity's private life has been widely published it may serve no useful purpose to prohibit further publication.[148]

Davies J also noted that the claimant in *Murray v Express Newspapers* had sued the photographic agency (Big Pictures) as well as the newspaper's publisher. This course of action had been open to

---

146 *AAA v Associated Newspapers* [2013] EWCA Civ 554.
147 [2012] EWHC 2103 (QB) at 121–122 (Davies J).
148 [2006] QB 125 at 105

the claimant in the *AAA* case, but had not been taken: at most, the photographic agency would have known that the defendant may have been interested in obtaining the photograph.

The claimant child had relied on the privacy aspect in *Reklos and Davourlis v Greece* (2009).[149] But Davies J pointed out that in this case the Strasbourg Human Rights Court (ECtHR) had stated that neither the child's lack of awareness of the taking or the existence of photographs, nor the fact that they revealed no private information (other than what the baby looked like), nor anything potentially embarrassing, had prevented there being an infringement of the child's Article 8 right of privacy.

At the appeal hearing the CA balanced the defendant newspaper's Article 10 rights with the claimant's Article 8 rights and justified publication as a high one of 'exceptional public interest', due to the baby's father's professional and private life as a high profile politician, married man, father of four children and his notoriety for extramarital adulterous liaisons.[150] The claimant baby AAA was alleged to be the second such child conceived as a result of an extramarital affair of the supposed father. The CA said that such information went to the issue of recklessness on the part of the supposed father, relevant both to his private and professional character, in particular his fitness for public office.[151] For these reasons the CA held that the claimant's reasonable expectation of privacy under Article 8 was to be given less weight than would have been the position had the claimant's mother said or done nothing (as was the case with *David Murray* and his mother J. K. Rowling).

In balancing the claimant's expectation of privacy against the public interest in AAA's supposed father and in particular the recklessness, relevant to his character and fitness for public office, the CA found that the publication of the fact of the claimant's birth in the circumstances alleged was justified.[152] So much of AAA's birth and supposed paternity had already been in public domain, that an injunction to prevent any further publication upon the topic would have served no real purpose. As Davies J had concluded: 'This was a story which was going to be published. If the defendant had not done it, another newspaper would.'[153]

1.5.2 Protecting the right to life: anonymity orders for child killers

The HRA and European Convention have enabled the law of confidence to develop to protect a citizen's right to life (under Article 2 ECHR) and right not to be subjected to torture or to inhuman or degrading treatment or punishment (under Article 3 ECHR).

The issue of lifelong anonymity orders in respect of children who kill was first raised in the case of *Mary Bell* when, in 1968, ten-year-old Mary was convicted at Newcastle Crown Court of the murder of two little boys, aged three and four, by strangulation. After conviction Mary Bell spent 12 years at Red Bank Approved School near Newton-le-Willows in Lancashire and was released on licence in 1980 with a new identity. There followed a number of applications to the courts for the anonymity order to continue beyond her coming of age. The first application on 25 May 1984 concerned an injunction to conceal the identity of her baby daughter (Y) and the baby's father after the *News of the World* had tracked down Mary Bell and her child (*Re X* (1985)[154]). Balcombe J granted a restraining order lasting until Y's 18th birthday, preventing identification of Mary's daughter as well as the child's father, and continuing the order on Mary (X) indefinitely. In 1988 the identities

149 (2009) (Application No 1234/05) (ECtHR).
150 [2013] EWCA Civ 554 (CA) at 39 (Master of the Rolls, Tomlinson LJ).
151 Ibid., at 118–119.
152 For full coverage of the story see: 'Boris's secret lovechild and a victory for the public's right to know: Judge rejects lover's attempts to keep daughter's birth quiet', by Michael Seamark, *Daily Mail*, 20 May 2013 at: www.dailymail.co.uk/news/article-2328067/Boris-Johnsons-secret-lovechild-daughter-Stephanie-victory-publics-right-know.html.
153 [2012] EWHC 2103 (QB) at 129 (Davies J).
154 *Re X (a woman formerly known as Mary Bell) and CC v A* [1985] 1 All ER 53.

of X and Y (then aged four) had been revealed to the press by villagers where the mother and daughter lived at the time.

The third period was in 1998 after the publication of Gitta Sereny's book on the story of Mary Bell, *Cries Unheard*, whereby Sereny had paid Mary a 'substantial sum of money' to co-author the book.[155] Home Secretary Jack Straw did not succeed in injuncting the publication of the book and condemned the payment to Bell in an open letter to the *Sun*, stating that, by collaboration on the book, Mary Bell should forfeit her right to anonymity. Prime Minister Tony Blair criticized the payments to the former child killer as 'inherently repugnant'.

The fourth period began in December 2002 when Mary's acquitted co-accused 'Norma' demanded in the *Sunday Sun* on 15 December that it was 'time to unmask Mary Bell'. The *Newcastle Evening Chronicle* published a lead article on 11 April 2003, 'Still Haunted', in which family members of the two killed boys demanded that Mary Bell's identity be disclosed.[156]

The waiver of a child's privacy may not be permanent, though the (family) court can reimpose privacy at any time even if it has previously been waived. One of the most notorious cases involved two ten-year-old child murderers, Jon(athan) Venables and Robert Thompson, who killed 18-month-old James (Jamie) Bulger in February 1993. In *Venables and Thompson v News Group Newspapers Ltd*[157] the 18-year-old claimants applied for injunctions preventing disclosure of their new identities, current physical appearance and their time spent in secure units since their conviction at the adult Preston Crown Court in November 1993. The murder of little James Bulger had shocked the nation and Venables and Thompson continued to be the object of death threats. They were given new identities to assist in their reintegration into the community.

Butler-Sloss P held that, as the court was a public authority under section 6(3) of the HRA, she had to act compatibly with the Convention rights and have regard to Strasbourg jurisprudence. She recognized that any restriction on freedom of the press had to fall within one of the exceptions in Article 10(2), which should be construed narrowly and the onus of proof of which was on the claimants.[158] Dame Elizabeth Butler-Sloss, when granting a lifelong anonymity order *contra mundum* on the – by now – 18-year-old Venables and Thompson, cited Article 2 ECHR, 'right to life' as a reason for granting the order.

She referred to the fact that the evolution of the common law, and in particular the law of confidence, had been given considerable impetus by the HRA. Taking into account Articles 2, 3 and 8 ECHR, and the real possibility that the claimants may be the objects of revenge attacks, she stated that:

> the court does have the jurisdiction, in exceptional cases, to extend the protection of confidentiality of information, even to impose restrictions on the press, where not to do so would be likely to lead to serious physical injury, and there is no other way to protect the applicants.[159]

Butler-Sloss P granted the injunctions as they satisfied the requirements of Article 10(2), namely:[160]

1. they were in accordance with the law, namely the law of confidence;
2. they would be imposed to prevent the disclosure of information received in confidence;
3. there was a very strong possibility, if not probability, that on the release of the claimants there would be serious efforts to find them and if that information became public they would be

155 See: Sereny, G. (1998).
156 *Re X: A Woman Formerly Known as 'Mary Bell' and another v O'Brien and Others* [2003] EWHC 1101 (QB).
157 *Venables and Thompson v News Group Newspapers Ltd* [2001] Fam 430.
158 Ibid., at 268, para. 25.
159 Ibid., at 288, para. 82 (Butler-Sloss P).
160 Ibid., at 286–290, paras 77–87.

pursued by those intent on revenge. Their rights under Articles 2 and 3 gave a strong and pressing social need in a democratic society for their confidentiality to be protected; and

4. the injunctions were proportionate to the legitimate aim pursued, namely protecting the claimants from the real and serious risk of death or physical harm.

The defendant newspapers had argued that the young killers' rehabilitation process and education whilst in youth custody were matters of genuine public interest and for that reason Venables and Thompson's identities should be revealed, citing – *inter alia* – freedom of expression. Butler-Sloss P granted the permanent injunctions against the whole world (*contra mundum*), stating that:

> in the light of the implementation of the Human Rights Act, we are entering a new era, and the requirement that the courts act in a way compatible with the Convention, and have regard to European jurisprudence, adds a new dimension to those principles.[161]

For these reasons the court had a duty of care to grant lifelong anonymity orders on the young men (see also: *Davies v Taylor* (1974);[162] *Re H (Minors) (Sexual Abuse: Standard of Proof)* (1996)[163]).

In March 2010, the by now 27-year-old Jon Venables – now on life licence – disclosed his identity to prison and probation staff. On 8 March the *Daily Mirror* broke the news that the 'Jamie Bulger killer' was back in prison on suspicion of a 'serious sexual offence'. Justice Minister Jack Straw released a press statement which confirmed the identity of the 'Bulger-killer' in preventive custody, though stating that Venables had not been charged with any sexual offence. This angered the press and the blogosphere was wild with speculation about Venables' identity and the alleged crime. The *Daily Mirror* and the *Sun* demanded that the lifelong anonymity order on Venables and his accomplice Thompson be lifted. On 9 March 2010, Baroness Butler-Sloss addressed the House of Lords, giving reasons why the *contra mundum* anonymity order must never be lifted, repeating her reasons at the time based on Article 2 ECHR and the state's duty to protect the Bulger killers' individual lives in spite of the heinous crime they committed in 1993. She opined that the risk of harm to Jon Venables in the present case would be too great and the court had a duty of care to protect even the most dangerous offenders (see also: *Osman v UK* (1998)[164]).

See Chapter 8.3

 FOR THOUGHT

> Is it right for media companies to rely on parental consent where it is clear that publication is not in the interest of the child's welfare? Discuss with reference to legal rights of a child.

1.6 Superinjunctions

There has been a steady rise in superinjunctions to stop reporting of potentially embarrassing revelations of celebrities and the royals since 2009. Superinjunctions that were sought – but not granted or subsequently lifted – involved, for instance, the then Chelsea football captain John Terry, England striker Wayne Rooney and Manchester United and Wales footballer Ryan Giggs, all of

161 Ibid., at 295, para. 101.
162 [1974] AC 207.
163 [1996] AC 563.
164 (1998) 29 EHRR 245.

whom had had extramarital affairs and had the financial means to use expensive lawyers to exercise legal rights denied to ordinary members of the public. Some TV personalities such as former *Top Gear* presenter Jeremy Clarkson or TV personality Andrew Marr, would argue that superinjunctions are a waste of time and money, spoilt largely by the 'Twitterati'. Andrew Marr – like Jeremy Clarkson – also decided to speak out about his own superinjunction, thereby technically breaking his own injunction and being in contempt of court. Mr Marr told the *Daily Mail* in April 2011: 'I did not come into journalism to go around gagging journalists. Am I embarrassed by it? Yes. Am I uneasy about it? Yes.'[165]

Greater protection is usually extended to privacy rights than to rights in relation to confidential material (see: *OBG Ltd v Allan* (2007);[166] *K v News Group Newspapers Ltd* (2011)[167]). A claim for misuse of private information may well survive when information is already in the public domain, depending on how widely known the facts are, but it is diminished because many readers already know what the defendant newspaper has already published. The claimant may still have a damages claim, but the injunction is clearly weakened. Looking at recent case law it has become clear that the claimant's Article 8 rights to privacy weigh less when the courts have carried out the balancing exercise (of Articles 8 and 10 ECHR) when the facts are already generally known about the celebrity's indiscretions.

In January 2016, a celebrity only named as PJS applied to the London High Court for an interim injunction to prevent the *Sun on Sunday* publishing a story on a 'celebrity threesome', and further preventing *The Sun* (and other newspapers) from printing details of PJS's extramarital affairs. Interestingly, this was not a superinjunction (since the newspaper was known). This resulted in the fact that – by March 2016 – every British editor knew the true identity of PSJ and YMA, and everyone who really wanted to find out about the marital commitment of the two men and their two small children could either find their names via social media or *Scottish Mail on Sunday* which released the names and photos of the 'celebrity couple' on 10 April 2016 in their print edition (on the front page and page 6). Lawyers for PJS later regretted not taking out a 'double gagging' order;[168] nor had they sought an interdict in the Scottish courts. American and Canadian newspapers (and their online editions) also reported about the 'celebrity couple' and that the 'betrayal by a cheating husband' would result in a '\$450m Divorce'.

The Sun and *Guardian* newspapers appealed the injunction, arguing that such a 'gagging order' had become meaningless in the internet and social media age. The Court of Appeal duly dismissed the interim injunction with the proviso that PJS had a couple of days in which to appeal to the Supreme Court.[169] This meant that the 'well-known' celebrity who reportedly had a 'three-way sexual encounter' between 2009–2011 and his husband were still to be kept anonymized.

A new ground for the application of an interim injunction had been sought, namely, 'in the interest of children'. Lord Jackson stressed, however, that children should not be used 'as a trump card'. He also said that the two children would, in due course, learn about these matters from their mates in the playground and via social media. Clearly reasons for privacy injunctions had shifted: there were no longer claims of blackmail or threats to PJS' other family members, as had been the reason given in the *John Terry*[170] or *Jeremy Clarkson*[171] superinjunctions.

The UK Supreme Court gave one if its speediest rulings in legal history (within one month) in May 2016 in PJS,[172] upholding the interim injunction by a majority in the light of extensive media

165 'Gagging orders are out of control, says Andrew Marr as he abandons High Court injunction over his extra-marital affair', by Sam Greenhill, *Daily Mail*, 26 April 2011.
166 [2007] UKHL 21.
167 [2011] EWCA Civ 439.
168 Referred to as 'superinjunctions'.
169 See: *PJS v News Group Newspapers Ltd* [2016] EWCA Civ 100 (Jackson and King LJJ).
170 See: *John Terry (LNS) v Persons Unknown* [2010] EWHC 119 (QB).
171 See: *AMM v HXW* [2010] EWHC 2457 (Jeremy Clarkson superinjunction)
172 *PJS* [2016] UKSC 26 (Lord Mance, Lord Neuberger, Lady Hale and Lord Reed; Lord Toulson dissenting).

interest. The judgment was streamed on live TV and is available via YouTube. The grounds cited by the Supreme Court justices centred on the privacy interests of the appellant (PJS), his partner (YMA) and their two young children (pending a trial). Their Lordships commented that the forthcoming trial against the newspapers was likely to involve further tortious invasion of privacy of the appellant and his partner as well as of their children, who had of course no conceivable involvement in the conduct in question.

The court observed that those interested in a prurient story could, if they so wished, easily read about the identities of those involved in the Scottish and American media and find in great detail all the unpleasant details about PJS' conduct with another couple.

The UKSC found no evidence of 'public interest' in any legal sense in the story involving PJS, though the respondent newspapers (mainly The Sun) hoped during the interim injunction that further evidence would emerge at trial. The court ruled that the media storm which would ensue had their Lordships discharged the injunction would have unleashed more enduring media and social networking attention with an even more damaging and ever-lasting invasion of privacy particularly of the children.[173]

The celebrity couple eventually settled out of court and the injunction regarding PJS' and YMA's identities and those of their children were permanently protected by a final injunction granted at the Queen's Bench Division on 4 November 2016. Other ciphers for three persons – AB, CD and EF – with whom PJS had had a relationship and/or sexual encounter were also permanently protected by the order and Art 8 ECHR[174]

Louise Berg and Michael Skrein of the media law firm Reed Smith commented on the company's website that PJS 'will have fought tooth and nail to preserve the injunction' and that 'maybe he just didn't like to lose'.[175] The lawyers accused the UKSC however of failing to acknowledge the realities of a connected and globalized media landscape, echoing the dissenting judge, Lord Toulson, who warned, 'the court must live in the world as it is and not as it would like it to be'.[176]

1.6.1 What are superinjunctions?

A superinjunction (referred to by the media as a 'double gagging order') is a term commonly given to an order restraining disclosure and publication of the claimant's identity and the fact the claim has been brought. These are usually interim court orders which prevent news organizations from revealing the identities of those involved in legal disputes, or even reporting the existence of the injunction at all. They were originally used exclusively in the family courts as a result of privacy and in camera proceedings, mostly concerning the protection of juveniles and children in care, adoption or divorce proceedings. In their simplest form, superinjunctions prevent the media from reporting what happens in court, usually on the basis that doing so could prejudice a trial or someone's right to privacy. Superinjunctions in their strictest form mean derogation from the open justice principle in that they seek:

1.   a private hearing (in camera);
2.   anonymity for the applicant (and other persons involved in the 'relationship');
3.   that the entire court file should be sealed;[177] and
4.   that the court order should prohibit publication of the existence of the proceedings, usually until after the conclusion of any trial.[178]

---

173 Ibid., at paras 44–45.
174 PJS v News Group Newspapers Ltd [2016] EWHC 2770 (QB); [2016] All ER (D) 29, 4 November 2016.
175 Source: 'Privacy in a Connected World: The Celebrity Threesome Injunction', by Louise Berg and Michael Skrein, 20 May 2016 at: www.reedsmith.com/Privacy-in-a-Connected-World-The-Celebrity-Threesome-Injunction-05–20–2016.
176 Ibid., at para. 86 (Lord Toulson dissenting).
177 Criminal Procedure Rules (CPR) 5.4C(7).
178 For a detailed discussion how to conduct any privacy action see: Tugendhat and Christie (Warby, M., Mareham, N. and Christie. I., eds) (2011) pp. 706–719.

See Chapter
2.4

If such an order is disclosed, say by a newspaper, this can amount to contempt of court – but only if the publication is in breach of an express prohibition: for example, where the court order expressly prohibits the publication of certain information relating to the hearing or the proceedings, to third parties with knowledge of such an order.

1.6.2 Superinjunctions and children

Lady Hale's judgment in PJS is worth noting regarding the interests of the two children whom PJS has with YMA. She said:

> It is simply not good enough to dismiss the interests of any children who are likely to be affected by the publication of private information about their parents with the bland state-ment that 'these cannot be a trump card'. Of course they cannot always rule the day. But they deserve closer attention than they have so far received in this case, for two main reasons. . . . Not only are the children's interests likely to be affected by a breach of the privacy interests of their parents, but the children have independent privacy interests of their own. They also have a right to respect for their family life with their parents.[179]

See Chapter
6.4

She cited the IPSO Code (which came into force in January 2016) which provides that:

> Editors must demonstrate an exceptional public interest to over-ride the normally paramount interests of [children under 16].

This means that courts will have to consider carefully the nature and extent of the likely harm to children's interests, which will result in the short, medium and longer terms from the publication of this kind of information about their parents. Lady Hale hoped that superinjunctions would make it possible that children could be protected from any such risk, by a combination of the efforts of their parents, teachers and others who look after them and some voluntary restraint on the part of the media.

An earlier precedent that the rights of children not to have 'distressing experiences in the playground' was set in the case of ETK v News Group Newspapers (also known as 'K')[180] in 2011, when the News of the World (NoW) was prevented from reporting that a woman had been sacked from her job after the colleague she had previously had an affair with told his bosses 'he would prefer in an ideal world not to have to see her at all and that one or other should leave', because the court ruled that his children might find it upsetting if they found out.

ETK, a married man working in the entertainment industry, had begun a sexual relationship with another woman 'X', also married. The source of the NoW's information suggested that this relationship became obvious to those with whom ETK and X were working. Towards the end of April 2010 the appellant's wife confronted him with her belief that he was having an affair. He admitted it. This was deeply distressing for the wife but she and her husband determined, not least for the sake of their two teenage children, to rebuild her trust and their marriage. To that end the appellant accepted that he would end his sexual relationship with X and he so informed her.

Balancing Articles 8 and 10 ECHR, the CA held that that K's right to privacy, that of his family and children, wholly outweighed the newspaper's right to freedom of expression, since the harm that would be done to his family life would be detrimental. Ward LJ held that K and X's sexual relationship was essentially a private matter and the knowledge of their work colleagues did not put the information into the public domain (citing Browne v Associated Newspapers Ltd (2007)[181] and X v

179 Ibid., at para. 72 (Lady Hale).
180 ETK v News Group Newspapers Ltd [2011] EWCA Civ 439 (also known as: K v News Group Newspapers Ltd).
181 [2007] EWCA Civ 295.

Persons Unknown (2006)[182]). Weight had to be given not only to K's Article 8 rights but also to those of his wife, children and X.

The case of ETK (*Re K*) has been widely used by celebrities and public figures, most notably by Andy Coulson and Rebekah Brooks (themselves former editors of *NoW*) in their attempts to prevent their own extramarital affair from being reported during the phone hacking trial.

ETK was also cited in *Edward Rocknroll v News Group Newspapers Ltd* (2013),[183] where actress Kate Winslet's new husband had asked the High Court for an interim injunction prohibiting *The Sun* from printing semi-naked photographs of 'Ed' taken in 2010. Briggs J granted the (interim) superinjunction under Article 8 ECHR, establishing that his right to respect for his family life – and that of Kate Winslet's children – should prevail over the newspaper's Article 10 right to freedom of expression.

In the leading case of *Re S (A Child) (Identification: Restrictions on Publication)* (2005),[184] very careful consideration was given, first in the Court of Appeal and then in the House of Lords, to balancing the public interest in publishing the name of a woman accused of murdering her child against the welfare interests of her surviving child who was living with his father. The public interest, in the legal sense, in publication was very strong. There was expert evidence of the welfare interests of the surviving child. This case was very different from that of PJS, as Lord Mance demonstrated in his leading judgment, when he said that there was no public interest in the legal sense in the publication of any information relating to PJS and his partner.[185]

See Chapter 6.3

1.6.3 Restraining publication: section 12 HRA

A claimant who applies for an interim restraining order (or superinjunction) against publishers (of newspapers or online editions for example) is obliged to give advance notice of the application under section 12 HRA, especially where the publisher or media organization relies on their Article 10 ECHR right to 'freedom of expression'. In Scotland such an order would be called an interdict and would have to be applied for separately at the High Court in Edinburgh.

The order is then binding on the party against whom injunctive relief is sought by application of the *Spycatcher* principle, *unless*:

1. the claimant has no reason to believe that the non-party has or may have an existing specific interest in the outcome of the application; or
2. the claimant is unable to notify the non-party having taken all practicable steps to do so; or
3. there are compelling reasons why the non-party should not be notified.

Section 12 HRA will only apply at any trial or at the application of a superinjunction or possible life-long anonymity order when the freedom of expression under Article 10 ECHR is challenged. Section 12 HRA reads:

1. This section applies if a court is considering whether to grant any relief which, if granted, might affect the exercise of the Convention right to freedom of expression.
2. If the person against whom the application for relief is made ('the respondent') is neither present nor represented, no such relief is to be granted unless the court is satisfied:

    (a) that the applicant has taken all practicable steps to notify the respondent; or
    (b) that there are compelling reasons why the respondent should not be notified.

---

182 [2006] EWHC 2783 (QB).
183 [2013] EWHC 24 (Ch).
184 [2005] 1 AC 593.
185 *PJS v News Group Newspapers Ltd* [2016] UKSC 26 at paras 1–45 (Lord Mance).

3.   No such relief is to be granted so as to restrain publication before trial unless the court is satisfied that the applicant is likely to establish that publication should not be allowed.

4.   The court must have particular regard to the importance of the Convention right to freedom of expression and, where the proceedings relate to material which the respondent claims, or which appears to the court, to be journalistic, literary or artistic material (or to conduct connected with such material), to:

(a)   the extent to which (i) the material has, or is about to, become available to the public; or (ii) it is, or would be, in the public interest for the material to be published;

(b)   any relevant privacy code.[186]

See below
1.6.6

The problem in the *John Terry* superinjunction[187] was that the famous Chelsea footballer claimed not to know the name of the newspaper that had a specific interest in his story. In Terry's case Tugendhat J did not accept that explanation since it had become quite clear that the *News of the World* intended to publish on Sunday 24 January 2010 the story about Terry's affair with the lingerie model, Vanessa Perroncel, then girlfriend of Terry's best friend and fellow England defender Wayne Bridge. The public interest lay in the fact that Terry was England football captain at the time and had portrayed himself as a 'clean-living' family man.

The effect of section 12(3) HRA is that a court is not to make an interim restraint order unless satisfied that the applicant's prospects of success at trial are sufficiently favourable to justify such an order being made in the particular circumstances of the case and taking into account the relevant jurisprudence under Article 10 ECHR. Looking at the judgment by Tugendhat J in *LNS*, it appears that the general approach by the courts in the granting (or continuation) of superinjunctions tends to be 'exceedingly slow', by making an interim restraint order where the applicant has not satisfied the court that he would probably succeed at trial.[188] However, where the potential adverse consequences of disclosure are particularly grave – say, in family cases, or where a short-lived injunction is needed to enable the court to hear and give proper consideration to an application for interim relief pending trial or any relevant appeal – the courts have granted such restraining orders under section 12 HRA with great expediency (see: *X (a woman formerly known as Mary Bell) and another v O'Brien and others* (2003)[189]).

See also
Chapter 8.4

The Supreme Court in *PJS* specifically considered section 12(4) HRA and the effect of the social media and internet disclosures already in the public domain (Scotland and USA) and how these would – in future – impact on the children of the celebrity couple.[190] The court said that there had been too much focus on those disclosures, and not enough emphasis on the 'qualitative difference in intrusiveness and distress' that was likely to be involved if there was unrestricted publication by the English media in hard copy, as well as on their own internet sites.[191] Lord Mance said:

> There is little doubt that there would be a media storm. It would involve not merely disclosure of names and generalised description of the nature of the sexual activities involved, but the most intimate details. This would be likely to add greatly and on a potentially enduring basis to the intrusiveness and distress felt by the appellant, his partner and, by way of increased media attention now and/or in the future, their children.[192]

---

186 For example the IPSO Editors' Code of Practice Clause 3 'Privacy'.
187 *John Terry (LNS)* [2010] EWHC 119 (QB).
188 Ibid., at 120 (Tugendhat J).
189 [2003] EWHC 1101 (QB).
190 *PJS* [2016] UKSC 26 at paras 33–34.
191 Ibid., at para. 35.
192 Ibid., at para. 35 (Lord Mance).

The interpretation of 'public interest' then became an issue where the Supreme Court disagreed with the CA which had argued that there was only a 'limited public interest' in publishing the details of someone's extramarital sexual relations (e.g. 'Gag couple alleged to have had a threesome'[193]).

Courts then have to balance Articles 8 and 10 ECHR, whereby section 12(4) HRA provides particular regard and importance to the right of freedom of expression. Where the court proceedings relate to journalistic material (or conduct connected to such material) the courts must also have particular regard under section 12(4)(a) to two specific factors which point potentially in different directions:

(i)   the extent to which the material has, or is about to, become available to the public and
(ii) the extent to which it is, or would be, in the public interest for the material to be published.

Under section 12(4)(b), the courts must also have particular regard to any relevant privacy code (such as IPSO).

Section 12(4)(a)(ii) provides guidance on how the evidence available to the court must be approached and whether there is effectively (no) public interest in a legal sense in further disclosure or publication. As to the factor in section 12(4)(a)(i), the requirement is to have particular regard to the extent to which journalistic material (or conduct connected with such material) 'has, or is about to, become available to the public'. And the question whether material has, or is about to, become available to the public will then be considered by the court with reference to, *inter alia*, the medium and form in relation to which injunctive relief is sought.

The effect of section 12(3) HRA is that a court is not to make an interim restraint order unless satisfied that the applicant's prospects of success at trial are sufficiently favourable to justify such an order being made in the particular circumstances of the case and taking into account the relevant jurisprudence under Article 10 ECHR. Looking at the judgment by Tugendhat J in LNS ('John Terry Superinjunction') it appears that the general approach by the courts in the granting (or continuation) of superinjunctions tends to be 'exceedingly slow', by making an interim restraint order where the applicant has not satisfied the court that he would probably succeed at trial.[194]

If there is any public interest, Article 10 will triumph over the individuals' right to privacy.

1.6.4 Do superinjunctions interfere with the right to freedom of expression?

The media's defence of 'public interest' in privacy actions will be considered by the courts in respect of a 'pressing social need'. This test is based on the ruling in *Max Mosley*.[195] Where a litigant intends to serve a prohibitory injunction upon a publication, the courts rely on the *Spycatcher* principle, in that the individual author, journalist or publisher should be given a realistic opportunity to be heard on the appropriateness of granting the injunction and the scope of its terms, mirrored closely by the provisions contained in section 12 HRA 1998.

As the Strasbourg Court observed in *von Hannover* (No 1):

> the court considers that a fundamental distinction needs to be made between reporting facts – even controversial ones – capable of contributing to a debate in a democratic society relating to politicians in the exercise of their functions, for example, and reporting details of the private life of an individual who, moreover, as in this case, does not exercise official functions. While in the former case the press exercises its vital role of 'watchdog' in a democracy by contributing to 'impart[ing] information and ideas on matters of public interest' it does not do so in the latter case.[196]

---

193 PJS [2016] EWCA Civ 393 at para. 47(ii) (CA).
194 John Terry [2010] EWHC 119 (QB) at 120 (Tugendhat J).
195 Mosley v NGN [2008] EMLR 679.
196 von Hannover v Germany (No 1) [2005] 40 EHRR 1 at 63.

What should be borne in mind is that if an individual is properly entitled to a privacy injunction, the whole purpose of that injunction may in some situations be undermined by disclosure of the fact that an injunction has been obtained by that individual. In such circumstances the alternative to justice being done behind closed doors is that justice will not be done at all.

Where the potential adverse consequences of disclosure are particularly grave – say, in family cases – the courts have granted restraining orders under section 12 HRA with great expediency.

A media organization may well be in contempt if they disclose the information that the court has ordered not to be disclosed. In *Re H (A Healthcare Worker)* (2002)[197] the claimant was seeking to prevent the disclosure by N, a health authority, of confidential information that he was HIV positive. Kennedy LJ held that the court could properly make an order in the proceedings, restraining the publication of information made available in the course of the proceedings which, if disclosed, would pre-empt the decision of the court on the issues before it.

See Chapter 8.5

The UK courts increasingly regard personal information as 'private' and 'confidential' when a reasonable person of ordinary sensibilities who finds themselves in the same position as the claimant would have had a reasonable expectation of privacy in all the given circumstances. Such was the case in *AMP*,[198] where the judge granted a superinjunction against 'Persons Unknown' to prevent the transmission of sensitive, personal photos belonging to the claimant who had lost her mobile phone. When some of her naked photos were uploaded on to Facebook, the court order not only protected her and the images (which were subsequently removed) but also stopped the threats which not only endangered her reputation but also that of her father's business; her father had allegedly been blackmailed over some of his daughter's images.

There is now a basic framework within Articles 8 and 10 in Strasbourg jurisprudence that provides for a social equilibrium between individuals, the media and society. It is argued that superinjunctions have curtailed the extent to which a newspaper or media organization can report on individuals in the public interest (see also: *Fressoz and Roire v France* (1999)[199]).

1.6.5 The *Trafigura* superinjunction

The United Nations 'Minton Report',[200] commissioned in September 2006, based on 'limited' information, had exposed that a toxic waste-dumping incident had taken place at locations around Abidjan in Ivory Coast in August 2006, involving the multinational Dutch oil company Trafigura.[201] The Minton Report revealed that truck- and shiploads of chemical toxic waste from a Trafigura cargo ship, the *Probo Koala*, had been illegally fly-tipped. The Ivorian authorities claimed that tens of thousands of people in Abidjan had been affected by fumes, reporting serious breathing problems, sickness and diarrhoea, and that 15 people had died.

On 12 October 2009, Labour MP Paul Farrelly tabled a question in the House of Commons (HC) for the then Justice Secretary, Jack Straw, to answer questions in relation to Trafigura's alleged dumping of toxic oil and the UN Minton Report. The second part of Mr Farrelly's question was of greater interest to freedom of speech in Parliament, as it concerned the superinjunction obtained by solicitors Carter-Ruck, acting on behalf of Trafigura at the time. Strictly speaking the 'Trafigura' *contra mundum* superinjunction of 11 September 2009 had prevented the *Guardian* (and therefore all other UK media outlets) from identifying the MP, what the question in Parliament was, which

197 *H (A Healthcare Worker) v Associated Newspapers Ltd* [2002] EMLR 425.
198 See: *AMP v Persons Unknown* [2012] All ER (D) 178.
199 [1999] 31 EHRR 28.
200 The United Nations 'Minton Report' (September 2009) had exposed a toxic waste-dumping incident in August 2006 in Ivory Coast, involving the multinational Dutch oil company Trafigura.
201 The author of this initial draft study, John Minton, of consultants Minton, Treharne and Davies, said dumping the waste would have been illegal in Europe and the proper method of disposal should have been a specialist chemical treatment called wet air oxidation. Source: 'Minton Report: Carter-Ruck give up bid to keep Trafigura study secret', by David Leigh, *Guardian*, 17 October 2009.

minister might answer it and where the question was to be found. All that could be reported was that the case involved the London libel lawyers Carter-Ruck.[202]

The *Guardian* had requested disclosure of the Minton Report under 'freedom of information' legislation (i.e. FOIA) in December 2009, but all matters concerning the report and the spilling of toxic waste off Ivory Coast had been 'gagged' under a superinjunction against the newspaper. The Twitterati revealed that Trafigura lawyers Carter-Ruck had attempted to prevent the issue being raised in Parliament, relying on the *sub judice* rule. Nevertheless, Mr Farrelly still referred to the 'Trafigura' superinjunction in Parliament, thereby breaching the *sub judice* rule of the injunction, relying on his defence of parliamentary privilege.

See Chapter 4.3

Thousands of tweets called into question the privilege which guarantees free speech in Parliament. The High Court privacy 'Trafigura' superinjunction was then lifted and senior managers at Trafigura and their lawyers admitted that their approach may have been a little 'heavy-handed', insisting it had not been their intention to try to silence Parliament. Trafigura agreed to pay out more than £30 million to some 30,000 Abidjan inhabitants who had been affected by the toxic waste. But all was not over.

Trafigura subsequently sued the BBC's *Newsnight* for libel after the company was criticized on the programme on 13 May 2009.[203] Trafigura's lawyers claimed that the oil traders had been wrongly accused of causing deaths and not just sickness in Ivory Coast. The BBC's defence was that it had merely focused on the gasoline waste dumped by Trafigura in Abidjan in August 2006, with *Newsnight* reporting that Trafigura's actions had caused deaths, miscarriages, serious injuries and sickness with long-term chronic effects. After lengthy negotiations with Trafigura's director, Eric de Turckheim, the BBC eventually agreed to settle on 17 December 2009, by apologizing for the investigatory programme and paying £25,000 to a charity. As part of the 'offer of amends' the public broadcaster had to withdraw any allegation that Trafigura's toxic waste dumped in West Africa had caused deaths. The BBC still issued a separate combative statement, pointing out that the dumping of Trafigura's hazardous waste had led to the British-based oil trader being forced to pay out £30 million in compensation to victims. The BBC's decision to settle caused dismay in journalistic circles because the public broadcaster was penalized for trying to report what had been factually raised in Parliament and by the United Nations.

See Chapter 7

1.6.6 Celebrity superinjunctions: John Terry, Ryan Giggs, Jeremy Clarkson and others

Since the disclosure of the *Trafigura* oil scandal in 2009 by way of parliamentary privilege, MPs have repeatedly broken several superinjunctions by naming public figures such as Ryan Giggs or former Royal Bank of Scotland (RBS) chief, (the then Sir) Fred Goodwin[204] in Parliament. All individuals, named initially in the law reports only by computer-generated acronyms (such as LNS or CTB), had used the courts and costly media lawyers to suppress information about their personal lives. The Ryan Giggs 'gagging order'[205] made sensational headlines in the Glasgow-based *Sunday Herald* featuring a picture of the England footballer with just a thin black band across his eyes and the word 'censored' in capital letters. The Scottish newspaper named the footballer in spite of the (English) court order.

Let's take the individual superinjunctions (or 'gagging orders' as the media call them) which followed each other in fairly rapid succession and ask the question: have such privacy injunctions actually

---

202 Source: 'Guardian gagged from reporting Parliament', *Guardian*, 12 October 2009
203 See: *Trafigura Limited v British Broadcasting Corporation* (2009) QBD 15 May 2009. Claim No: HQ09X02050. Unreported.
204 See: *Goodwin (Sir Fred) v News Group Newspapers* [2011] EWHC 1309 (QB). May 19. The Liberal Democrat Peer Lord Stoneham revealed during a debate in the House of Lords that Sir Fred Goodwin had obtained an injunction to stop reports that he had a sexual relationship with a colleague.
205 See: *CTB v News Group Newspapers* [2011] EWHC 1326 (QB) ('Ryan Giggs superinjunction').

worked and whether they have become meaningless in the digital age? Because of the limited reporting of such cases, frequently known only by acronyms and randomly selected letters of the alphabet, it is difficult to find such cases via Westlaw or Lexis, for example (see: *G and G v Wikimedia Foundation Inc.* (2009)[206]).

On 22 January 2010, lawyers acting for the then England football captain, John Terry, asked the High Court for a prohibition in the form of an interim superinjunction on publishing details of a 'specific personal relationship' between their client and another person. This became known later as the 'John Terry Superinjunction' (*LNS v Persons Unknown* (2010)[207]). Terry's lawyers argued that the intended publication in the *News of the World* (*NoW*) would amount to a breach of confidence and misuse of private information in that £1 million had been promised to an informant to keep the story quiet. The newspaper was about to publish their scoop on the footballer's adulterous affair with French underwear model Vanessa Perroncel, who happened to be the former girlfriend of Terry's friend and team-mate Wayne Bridge. The story was to be the front-page headline on Sunday 24 January 2010.

The *John Terry* (*LNS*) 'double gagging order' (where neither the individual nor the newspaper are named) sought complete privacy, stating that any publication of any information, including photographs, evidencing the extramarital relationship could lead to harming the private family life of the applicant. Opposing the injunction at the hearing on 29 January 2010, News Group Newspapers (NGN), made a strong submission before Tugendhat J, supporting freedom of expression under Article 10 and the public's 'right to know' in this case, i.e. that John Terry as England football captain was a role model to many young people and prided himself on being a family man. Tugendhat J considered Articles 6, 8 and 10 of the Convention in turn, giving additional consideration to the open justice principle. Balancing one right against the other, he considered the right to speak freely, the right to private life and reputation and the right to a fair hearing.

In the *John Terry* application Tugendhat J noted that there was no evidence before the court and no personal representation from the applicant of proof to convince him to apply the right to privacy under Article 8, nor was there proof that any confidentiality had been breached: no photographs were produced, nor was there any confidential or private information disclosed. For this reason the judge lifted the interim order granted initially a few days earlier, stating that privacy law was not there to protect someone's reputation, which in this case also included the footballer's commercial interests (e.g. sponsorship by Daddies Sauce, Umbro, Samsung and Nationwide).

After *John Terry* the press – particularly in Scotland – became increasingly daring and aggressive in their revelations about other infidelities and indiscretions of celebrities, often completely ignoring any superinjunctions which might have been in place at the time. One of these was the *Ryan Giggs superinjunction*.[208] Despite the court anonymity order, the extramarital affair of the married Manchester United and Wales football star – referred to only as 'CTB' in the restraining order – with lingerie model Imogen Thomas was widely exposed on Twitter and other social networking sites in May 2011 and the Lord Chief Justice, Lord Judge, warned that 'modern technology was totally out of control', granting search orders in the form of *Norwich Pharmacal* orders against the US-based microblogging site on Friday 20 May 2011 in an attempt to compel Twitter to identify those responsible for naming the footballer. Mr Giggs' lawyers hoped that the High Court orders would force Twitter to hand over the names, email and IP addresses of those persons behind the Twitter accounts of UK individuals who had disclosed Giggs' identity and that they would be prosecuted for breaches of a court order (i.e. contempt of court).

See Chapter 8.5

Richard Walker, editor of Glasgow's *Sunday Herald*, then took the daring and unprecedented decision to name Ryan Giggs on the front page on Sunday 22 May 2011. The newspaper's front-page 'splash' featured the footballer with a thin black band across his eyes and the word 'censored' in capital letters. The player was easily recognizable and the caption below the photograph read:

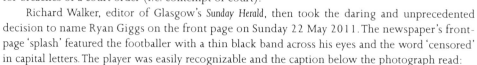

206 [2009] EWHC 3148 (QB).
207 [2010] EWHC 119 ('John Terry Superinjunction').
208 *CTB (Ryan Giggs)* [2011] EWHC 1326 (QB).

Everyone knows that this is the footballer accused of using the courts to keep allegations of a sexual affair secret. But we weren't supposed to tell you that . . .[209]

In an accompanying editorial Richard Walker commented that he had taken the decision to identify the footballer just hours before the paper went to press (on Saturday), following legal advice from Paul McBride QC[210] and media lawyer David McKie[211] that the privacy injunction did not apply in Scotland because an interdict ought to have been applied for by Giggs' London lawyers at the High Court in Edinburgh at the same time as the superinjunction application in the English High Court.[212] Or at the very least, the footballer's lawyers (Schillings) should have informed all editors of the Scottish and Northern Irish press that an (English) injunction was in place. They had done no such thing. In an interview with the author, Richard Walker said:

Our piece, naming Ryan Giggs, was not so much about his sexual infidelities but about the principle of privacy and superinjunctions taken out by famous celebrities having been exposed on Twitter and that the internet was now exposing stories about Strauss-Kahn's alleged past sexual behaviour and that of others, such as (Sir) Fred Goodwin and his superinjunction trying to suppress an affair with a senior colleague at Royal Bank of Scotland. Initially we were looking to portray Ryan Giggs as a pixelated front page photo but then it occurred to me that the injunction would not be in force in Scotland so I took legal advice and the advice was that that was indeed the case.[213]

Worthy of note in this case was the difference between Scots and English law. The reason why the *Sunday Herald* was able to publish the full disclosure of the Ryan Giggs superinjunction was that:

(a)   There was no interdict from the Scottish High Court in Edinburgh which imposed a 'gagging' order on the Scottish media.
(b)   The newspaper was not sold or distributed 'south of the border' (in England and Wales).
(c)   There was no internet or online publication of the Ryan Giggs article.

Two days after the Ryan Giggs front-page 'splash' in the *Sunday Herald* the footballer was identified by the Liberal Democrat MP John Hemming in the House of Commons, using parliamentary privilege. By the time the High Court revisited the anonymized 'Ryan Giggs' injunction a year later in March 2012, it appeared to have blown up in Mr Giggs' lawyers' faces. Ultimately, the injunction was compromised between Mr Giggs and Ms Thomas. Because on 15 December 2011, supermodel Imogen Thomas had issued a public statement categorically denying that she was the source of the *Sun* article and that she had not blackmailed Giggs (as he had alleged when applying for the injunction on 14 April 2011).

Eventually Tugendhat J struck out the injunction (*Giggs No 2*), a full six months *after* the world had learnt of Mr Giggs' identity. As Tugendhat J noted in his March 2012 judgment:

There can be few people in England and Wales who have not heard of this litigation. The initials CTB have been chanted at football matches when Mr Giggs has been playing for Manchester United. And Mr Giggs has been named in Parliament, raising questions as to the proper relationship between Parliament and the judiciary.[214]

209 See: *Sunday Herald*, front page, 22 May 2011.
210 Paul McBride (1964–2012) was a leading Scottish criminal lawyer. He died suddenly on a trip to Pakistan aged 47.
211 David McKie is a partner in the Glasgow law firm Levy & McRae. In an interview with the author on 2 July 2015, Mr McKie recounted the complex legal background to the Ryan Giggs' publication in the *Sunday Herald*.
212 Source: 'Sex, lies and private laws'. Analysis by Richard Walker. *Sunday Herald*, 22 May 2011, pp. 12–16.
213 Source: Richard Walker in an interview with the author on 2 July 2015 at the *Glasgow Herald* headquarters.
214 *Ryan Giggs* (No 2) [2012] EWHC 431 (QB) at para. 1 (Tugendhat J).

Clearly the *Ryan Giggs No 1* and *No 2* privacy orders did not achieve their purpose. Had Mr Giggs known in April 2011, at the time the principal injunction was sought, that Imogen Thomas was not the source of the *Sun* article it may well be that the footballer would not have sought an order against News Group Newspapers (NGN) to gag the press. But Mr Giggs' lawyers thought otherwise. In *Giggs No 2* (March 2012) his lawyers asked for aggravated damages seemingly only directed against Imogen Thomas. Tugendhat J dismissed the application for damages, adding that there was 'no purpose' in allowing the superinjunction to continue.

On 26 April 2011 BBC journalist Andrew Marr revealed his own superinjunction – taken out in 2008 – which was intended to gag the press about his extramarital affair, followed by Prime Minister David Cameron expressing his concern about the prolific use of these 'gagging orders', commenting that Parliament should determine privacy law and not judges.

In October 2011, former BBC *Top Gear* presenter Jeremy Clarkson 'outed' his own superinjunction by stating that these 'gagging orders' are 'pointless'. Clarkson told the *Daily Mail*: 'Super-injunctions don't work. You take out an injunction against somebody or some organization and immediately news of that injunction and the people involved and the story behind the injunction is in a legalfree world on Twitter and the internet.'[215]

In the aptly named *AMM* ('Aston Martin Man') v *HXW* ('His ex-wife'),[216] Mr Clarkson had applied for a 'gagging' order in September 2010 to restrain his former wife, Alex Hall, from publishing a book about their extramarital affair, *after* the couple had divorced and Clarkson had remarried. Edwards-Stuart J granted the injunction after hearing that Ms Hall (HXW) had blackmailed Mr Clarkson by threatening to expose their relationship to the media unless he paid a 'very substantial sum' of hush money. As soon as the order was served on the *Daily Mail* (Associated Newspapers Ltd) on 30 September 2010, the 'Jeremy Clarkson superinjunction' story reached the 'Twittersphere', with the 'red tops' freely reporting on it.[217]

In May 2011 the Neuberger Report[218] established the framework in which future applications for superinjunctions ('anonymized injunction') should be made. Master of the Rolls, Lord Neuberger's Committee had been formed in April 2010 following a report of the Culture, Media and Sport House of Commons Select Committee, and in the light of growing public concerns about the use and effect of superinjunctions and the impact they were having on open justice. The Report stresses the fundamental principles of open justice and freedom of speech. And that 'secrecy orders' should only be made if they are 'strictly necessary' in the interests of justice; a fair balance should be struck by the courts in making such orders between the principles of freedom of expression and an individual's right to privacy.

As common law and ECtHR jurisprudence have developed the courts have stressed that the 'necessity' for any restriction on freedom of expression must be convincingly established as a matter of general principle. Mindell argues that there are two forms of privacy that are protected in English law: the torts of trespass (to the person and to land) and protection under the Human Rights Act 1998.[219] The author further argues that there exist 'secondary forms of privacy', the first being 'the informational realm' and the other 'territorial information', depicted in *Peck v UK*[220] (personal information).

---

215 Source: 'Jeremy Clarkson lifts the gag on his ex-wife: She claims she had an affair with Top Gear star after he remarried', by Michael Seamark, *Daily Mail*, 27 October 2011.

216 [2010] EWHC 2457 (QB); [2010] All ER (D) 48 (Oct) ('Jeremy Clarkson superinjunction').

217 See: Smartt, U. (2011), pp. 135–140.

218 See: Master of the Rolls (2011) Report of the Committee on Super-Injunctions: Super-Injunctions, Anonymised Injunctions and Open Justice ('the Neuberger Report'): www.judiciary.gov.uk/Resources/JCO/Documents/Reports/super-injunction-report–20052011.pdf.

219 Mindell, R. (2012), pp. 52–58.

220 (2003) 36 EHRR 719.

 **FOR THOUGHT**

With social media's widespread dissemination of protected information about celebrities' private lives would you agree that the main objective of a superinjunction is now largely unachievable? Discuss.

1.7 A tort of privacy

The question which has arisen over the past decade or so with ever-developing case law is whether a tort (or *delict*) of privacy exists such as in France or Germany? We know there is as yet no UK law that protects an individual's privacy. One could argue that a 'tort' of privacy was created by Parliament when it introduced the HRA by way of Article 8 ECHR ('right to privacy'). An 'informal' tort was first expressed by the House of Lords in the *Naomi Campbell* case (2004), that 'protects the right to control the dissemination of information about one's private life'.[221] In the same year, Lord Hoffmann was unequivocal in *Wainwright v Home Office* (2004) when he said that English law recognizes *no* common law tort of invasion or breach of privacy:

> I would reject the invitation to declare that since at the latest 1950 there has been a previously unknown tort of invasion of privacy.[222]

As far back as 1973, the Younger Committee advised against enactment of any general tort of invasion of privacy, recommending that the then regulator the Press Council should deal with the continued regulation of the print press and that any breaches of privacy be dealt with on a case-by-case basis.[223] In 1990, the Calcutt Committee[224] recommended that a tort of infringement of privacy should not be introduced. This meant that the courts continued to iron out deficiencies in existing law with piecemeal common law jurisdiction. The facts of the *Gorden Kaye*[225] and many subsequent cases suggested in this chapter remain a graphic illustration of the desirability of Parliament considering whether and in what circumstances statutory provision can be made to protect the privacy of individuals in English law.

See Chapter 6.4

As common law continued to develop post the HRA 1998, we saw an increase in truth-telling 'kiss and tell' stories and an increase in media applications for free speech and the defence of the public interest test, advanced when newspapers had reported on a celebrity's indiscretions. Following the ECtHR's judgments in *von Hannover* (No 1)[226] and *von Hannover* (No 2),[227] one could possibly begin to define 'breach of confidence' as the tort that protects private information. Though it is important to note that in *von Hannover* (No 1)[228] the Human Rights Court ruled that a celebrity has a 'public' and a 'private sphere', the latter being strictly protected by privacy with no invasion by the paparazzi or the press. In the *Beckham* case[229] the ruling was similar, in that famous couples like Victoria and David Beckham and their children have a right to privacy in the comfort and circumference of their own home.

---

221 *Campbell v MGN Ltd* [2004] 2 AC 457 at 51.
222 Ibid., at 34.
223 Source: House of Commons (1973) 'Privacy: Younger Committee's Report'. HC Debate, 6 June 1973.
224 House of Commons (1990) 'The Calcutt Report'. HC Debate, 21 June 1990.
225 (1991) FSR 62.
226 *von Hannover v Germany* (No 1) (2005) 40 EHRR 1.
227 *von Hannover v Germany* (No 2) (2012) (Application Nos – 40660/08, 60641/08) Strasbourg Judgment of 7 February 2012.
228 *von Hannover v Germany* (No 1) (2005) 40 EHRR 1.
229 *Beckham v MGN Ltd* (28 June 2001; unreported).

There now exists a wide interpretation by the UK courts of the concept of privacy and what amounts to 'confidential information'. The argument advanced in *Spycatcher* was that the second *Coco* requirement, the need for a confidential relationship, would justify equity's interference with freedom of speech, as it served as the link between the recipient's conscience in not revealing the confidential information and the doctrine itself. This meant that the maintenance of confidential relationships was thereby sidelined. This standpoint was challenged by the press in the *Rio Ferdinand*[230] superinjunction case, and subsequently clarified by the Strasbourg Court in Princess Caroline's second privacy action, i.e. *von Hannover* (No 2).[231] Neither Rio Ferdinand nor Princess Caroline von Hannover in her second action were awarded Article 8 rights to privacy in their actions, because the court held that the matters in question were in the public interest. More recent jurisprudence has given greater weight to the public interest test, by allowing the media their Article 10 right.

Legal uncertainly continued to exist, creating ambiguity for both the claimant in the level of 'tortious' protection in their privacy rights and for the media on the other hand, whose editors have to make decisions on such common law considerations. Some answers were however provided by the seminal case of *Vidal-Hall v Google Inc.* (2015).[232] Master of the Rolls McFarlane LJ ruled in the Court of Appeal that misuse of private information is distinct from breach of confidence and should now be recognized as a tort. In this case, three claimants (respondents to this appeal) pursued Google for claims that Google (the 'data controller'), through its use of internet 'cookies', had misused their private information and breached their confidence; that Google had infringed section 13(2) of the Data Protection Act 1998 (DPA). All three individuals had used Apple computers and Safari browsers, between summer 2011 and 17 February 2012, to access the internet during that time. They sued Google (situated in California, USA) in the London High Court.

The issues before the Court of Appeal were:

(1)   whether the cause of action for misuse of private information is a tort, and
(2)   whether there can be a claim for compensation without pecuniary loss within the meaning of damage in section 13(2) of the Data Protection Act 1998?

The CA ruled that:

(1)   the misuse of private information constitutes a tort for the purposes of the rules providing for service of proceedings out of the jurisdiction; and
(2)   the claimants could recover damages for non-material loss;[233]
(3)   that section 13(2) DPA should be disapplied on the grounds that it conflicts with the rights guaranteed by Articles 7 ('right to private and family life') and 8 ('right to protection of personal data') of the EU Charter of Fundamental Rights.

Google then applied for permission to appeal to the Supreme Court which granted permission to appeal in part. The Court ordered that permission to appeal be refused on ground 1 (the issue whether the claim is in tort) because this ground does not raise an arguable point of law. The Court ordered that permission to appeal be granted on all other grounds.

---

230 *Ferdinand (Rio) v Mirror Group Newspapers Ltd* [2011] EWHC 2454 (QB).
231 *von Hannover v Germany* (No 2) (2012) (Application Nos – 40660/08, 60641/08) Judgment of 7 February 2012.
232 See: *Judith Vidal-Hall, Robert Hann and Marc Bradshaw and the Information Commissioner v Google Inc.* [2015] EWCA Civ 311 (CA).
233 The issue of compensation for a contravention by a data controller is dealt with in Article 23 of the Directive (95/46/EC). The CA found it was not possible to interpret s 13(2) DPA in a way that was compatible with Article 23.

Vidal-Hall v Google Inc is a landmark decision, not only for the confirmation that misuse of private information is a tort, but for the disapplication of primary domestic legislation on the basis of incompatibility with an EU Directive and provisions of the Articles 7, 8 and 47 of the EU Charter of Fundamental Rights (see also: *Benkharbouche v Embassy of the Republic of Sudan* (2015)[234]). This means that claims for compensation for breach of the Data Protection Act can be made for damages for distress even though one has not suffered any pecuniary loss; moreover this case was not related to purposes of journalism, the arts or literature.

See Chapter 4.7

If we then accept that there now exists a tort of privacy ('misuse of private information') it follows that we can safely assume that this law now affords protection to information in respect of which there is a reasonable expectation of privacy, even in circumstances where there is no pre-existing relationship. This in itself will then give rise to an enforceable duty of confidence. The law now seems to be concerned with the prevention of the violation of a person's autonomy, dignity and self-esteem taking into account Convention rights as well as common law development since the coming into force of the HRA 1998 and the *Douglas* case in 2001.

Is it not about time that Parliament addresses a statutory tort of privacy, particularly in the digital age of online blogs and social networking? Mindell argues that 'proper' privacy legislation could acknowledge breaches of privacy 'in both primary and secondary forms and understanding the remedial possibilities of each' so that the law could ultimately protect private information because it is 'private' and undisclosed, rather than because it is 'confidential information'.[235]

Eady J observed in his speech on 'privacy' to intellectual property lawyers in 2009 that the statutory tort could be less restrictive of the media than the law of privacy as it subsequently developed. For example, it would have excluded anything touching on the conduct of a business, trade or profession, and it would have been directed purely at the protection of personal life. It would also have excluded anything occurring in a public place.[236]

Clearly there are misunderstandings and social differences in what some deem 'private' and some regard or even misuse as 'confidential' information. The law in this area could then provide objective criteria for the courts to apply when misuse of another's private information has taken place.

 FOR THOUGHT

> Former Liberal Democrat MP, John Hemming, who named footballer Ryan Giggs as the subject of a superinjunction by using parliamentary privilege in 2011, said such privacy orders were unfair as they were only available to the rich and famous, who could 'gag' the media with the application of 'large sums of money'. He said, 'I just don't think that it is a reasonable use of state power.' Would you agree that once a superinjunction has been breached in Scotland or abroad and leaked via social networking sites they just become 'a complete nonsense'? Discuss with reference to leading authorities.

---

234 [2015] EWCA Civ 33.
235 Mindell, R. (2012) at pp. 52–58.
236 Source: Sir David Eady's Speech on Privacy to TIPLO (The Intellectual Property Lawyers' Organisation), House of Lords, 18 February 2009: www.publications.Parliament.uk/pa/cm200809/cmselect/cmcumeds/memo/press/uc7502.htm.

1.8 Further reading

Bingham, T. (1996) 'Should there be a law to protect rights of personal privacy?', European Human Rights Law Review, 5, 455–462.
Lord (Tom) Bingham discusses the protection of breach of confidence and whether there should be law to protect personal privacy following the *Gorden Kaye* case (where he was one of the judges). Bingham argues that the expansion and distortion of any confidence action cannot serve as an adequate substitute for a full privacy action and a 'proper' privacy law, unless, by either judicial sleight of hand or the bold grasping of the privacy nettle, a free-standing tort of privacy emerges fully from any from confidence action.

Carter-Silk, A. and Cartwright-Hignett, C. (2009) 'A child's right to privacy: "out of a parent's hands"', Entertainment Law Review, 20(6), 212–217.
This article discusses whether children have a fundamental right to privacy separate from that of their parents and what happens if the parents 'waive' their children's rights in order to gain financially. The authors argue that some celebrities use their children to obtain privacy via the back door. The authors ask whether any purported waiver of that privacy right is void unless it is in the child's best interest?

Foster, S. (2015) 'Reclaiming the public interest defence in the conflict between privacy rights and free speech', Coventry Law Journal, 19(2), 1–23.
Steve Foster discusses some of the leading authorities regarding privacy applications and the press defence of 'public interest'. Foster argues that the distinction between what is in the public interest and what is mere 'tittle-tattle' has become blurred when dealing with revelations about the private lives of public figures.

Mindell, R. (2012) 'Rewriting privacy: the impact of online social networks', Entertainment Law Review, 23(3), 52–58.
This article discusses the meaning of 'privacy' in English common law in relation to technological innovations, such as Twitter and Facebook, which have put privacy at risk. He argues that the force of social media remains uncontrolled.

Phillipson, G. (2003) 'Breach of confidence, celebrities, freedom of expression, legal reasoning, newspapers, privacy, public interest, right to respect for private and family life', European Human Rights Law Review (Special Issue on 'Privacy'), 54–72.
The article criticizes the legal reasoning applied by the Court of Appeal in *A v B plc* in respect of two key issues: (1) the horizontal application of Article 8 ECHR in cases concerning media intrusion, and (2) the circumstances in which there is a public interest justification for publication. The author questions the meaning of public interest in relation to 'public figures'.

Pillans, B. (2012) 'Private lives in St Moritz: von Hannover v Germany (No 2)', Communications Law, 17(2), 63–67.
Brian Pillans discusses the judgments in *Axel Springer* and *von Hannover (No 2)*. He looks at the nature of the individuals involved and the publications and examines the ECtHR's balancing test in respect of the right to freedom of expression and the individual's right to privacy.

Smartt, U. (2011) 'Twitter undermines superinjunctions', Communications Law, 16(4), 135–140.
The article discusses common law in respect of personal privacy, grounded in the equitable doctrine of breach of confidence and relevant case law with specific discussion of *Douglas v Hello! Ltd* (2001) and the development of superinjunctions (*CTB v NGN* (2011) and *DFT v TFD* (2010)). Smartt examines the remedies available in an action for breach of confidence and asks whether superinjunctions have become meaningless in the age of social media.

Warren, S. D. and Brandeis, L. D. (1890) 'The right to privacy', Harvard Law Review, 4(5) (15 December 1890), 193–220.
This classic publication by Warren and Brandeis developed the concept of an individual's right to privacy at the time when this was absent in (US) law and is often cited in scholarly research.

Chapter 2

Media freedom and freedom of expression

Chapter contents

Key points

This chapter will cover the following questions:

- How has press freedom developed over time?
- Who were the historical freedom of speech fighters?
- Can there be a fundamental right to receive freedom of information? The *Sugar v BBC* case.
- Can there be total press freedom after the Prophet Mohammed controversies in Denmark and Charlie Hebdo in France?
- What constitutes 'obscene publication' in UK legislation today?
- What are the boundaries of media freedom in relation to an individual's right to privacy?

2.1 Overview

The digital growth of many national newspapers has shown great potential for global coverage online (in spite of some paywalls, such as *The Times*, *Sunday Times*, *Financial Times* and the *Daily Telegraph*). *MailOnline* is the most visited global English-language newspaper website, averaging 11.5m page views a day in 2016.[1]

With the demise of the print press (e.g. *The Independent*), there is no doubt that popular journalism has become more aggressive in order to sell what remains of daily newspapers.

This chapter looks at the history of the development of freedom of expression and the struggle of individual writers who fought for press freedom and freedom of speech in their societies.

We then examine examples of political cartoons which have led to acts of terrorism, such as the Prophet Mohammed cartoons in Danish newspaper *Jyllands-Posten* in 2005 and the *Charlie Hebdo* killings in Paris in 2015.

2.2 Historical development of free speech and press freedom

Freedom of speech arguably dates back to the Greek philosopher Socrates (470 BCE – c.399 BCE). Socrates argued that democracy established in Athens was designed to be impartial and create better citizens; one of the main principles of a democratic society was freedom of speech.[2]

Magna Carta of 1215 ('Great Charter of Freedoms'), signed into law by King John I of England, remains one of the most important statutes that limited the power of the monarch. Though Magna Carta did not guarantee freedom of speech it began a tradition of civil rights in Britain that laid the foundation for the first Bill of Rights some 400 years later which granted freedom of speech as a legal right granted by Parliament in 1688.

---

1   Source: *Mailonline* by numbers, at: www.dailymail.co.uk/home/stats/index.html.
2   Isocrates (Norton, G.) (1980).

2.2.1 Censorship of free speech and the press in Britain

One of the key issues of the English Civil War (1642–1649) was freedom of speech and one of the first great proponents of free speech was Cromwell's secretary, John Milton, who in his *Areopagitica* (1644), vehemently opposed literary censorship, after Parliament had issued the 'Licensing Order of 16 June 1643' which was designed to bring publishing (and therein copyright) under Crown control by creating a number of official censors.[3] *Areopagitica* remains the most influential and eloquent philosophical work, defending the principle of the right to freedom of speech and embodies the cornerstone of press freedom. Crown licensing eventually ended in 1695 when the House of Commons refused to renew the licensing legislation.

See Chapter 9.3

The Bill of Rights 1688/1689 significantly established freedom of speech in Parliament relating to debates and proceedings in that they ought not to be questioned in any a court of law. This in essence established parliamentary privilege as a means of stopping a monarch from interfering with the workings of Parliament. To this day, parliamentary privilege means that all parliamentarians have the right to say whatever they like in Parliament without fear of being sued for libel or slander (such as mentioning a superinjunction). There were still a large number of constraints on freedom of the press which remained in place until recent times, such as the offences of criminal and seditious libel, which remained punishable at common law. These rather outdated offences were abolished under section 73 of the Coroners and Justice Act 2009, thus sweeping away the old common law offences of sedition, seditious libel, obscene libel and defamatory libel.

See Chapter 1.6

During the Second World War, the British government (re)implemented the Defence of the Realm Act (DORA) by way of secondary legislation by way of regulation 2D. The main purpose of the regulation was to stop subversive newspaper propaganda which would impede the war effort.[4] Relying on regulation 2D, the government closed down two communist papers and warned the *Daily Mirror* and the *Sunday Pictorial* that the papers must cease publishing anti-government war propaganda.[5] Following mass rallies in response, the ban was lifted.

2.2.2 Freedom of speech fighters

The fight for freedom of speech continues around the world and there are numerous examples of writers and journalists who either had to go into exile or died for their courage. Here are just a few.

No doubt the drive towards freedom of speech was inspired by some of the philosophers of the European educated middle classes such as Immanuel Kant, Voltaire, Jean-Jacques Rousseau and John Locke, who spread the ideas and values of the Age of Enlightenment through the late seventeenth and early eighteenth centuries, when the concepts of equality and freedom of the individual had become paramount to their thinking and writing.

When Edmund Burke, an intellectual Protestant and Whig in the English Parliament, published his criticism of the French Revolution in his *Reflections* (1790), he repudiated the belief in divinely appointed monarchic authority and the idea that the people had no right to depose an oppressive government. Burke advocated that citizens should have a stake in their nation's social order which would aid constitutional reform (rather than by revolution, as in France). Burke advocated specific individual rights such as freedom of speech including writing and printing – a form of freedom of expression against oppression by government. Burke famously detested injustice and abuse of power.

---

3   See: Milton, J. (1644) at p. 41.
4   See: Memorandum by the Home Secretary 8 October 1940 on 'subversive newspaper propaganda'. Secret Copy No W.P. (40) 402. 8th October 1940. The National Archives at: http://ukwarcabinet.s3.amazonaws.com/documents/cab-66–12–32–0001.pdf.
5   Ibid.

In America the First Amendment of the Bill of Rights 1791 reflected some of these ideas and guaranteed freedoms of religion, speech, the press and the right to free assembly.[6]

English philosopher John Stuart Mill fought for freedom of speech in Parliament and in his writings. In his essay *On Liberty* (1859) he argued in favour of tolerance, individuality and freedom of expression.[7] Mill also fought for 'liberty of the press' as the paramount safeguard against 'corrupt or tyrannical government'.[8]

In Europe, after the twentieth-century dictatorships of Adolf Hitler[9] in Germany, Benito Mussolini[10] in Italy and General Franco in Spain,[11] freedom of speech was formally identified as an absolute human right under Article 19 of the Universal Declaration of Human Rights of 1948.[12]

The Russian dissident, Aleksandr Solzhenitsyn, experienced a Siberian labour camp ('the Gulag') during the Stalinist era in Russia, for publishing his famous autobiographical account *One Day in the Life of Ivan Denisovich* some 50 years ago.[13] Solzhenitsyn was imprisoned for eight years after 1945 for writing derogatory comments about Joseph Stalin, when serving in the Red Army during the Second World War.

On 14 February 1989, British Indian author Salman Rushdie was telephoned by a BBC journalist and told that he had been 'sentenced to death' by the Ayatollah Khomeini. For the first time he heard the word *fatwa*. His crime? To have written a novel called *The Satanic Verses* (1988)[14] which was accused of being 'against Islam, the Prophet and the Qur'an'. Sir Salman Rushdie became another dissident who had to live in exile for his writings. In his memoirs, *Joseph Anton* (2012),[15] Rushdie describes the extraordinary story of his life in exile, forced underground, living with the constant presence of an armed police protection team. He was asked to choose an alias that the police could call him by. He thought of writers he loved and combinations of their names; then it came to him: Conrad and Chekhov – Joseph Anton. His story is of one of the crucial battles for freedom of speech. In April 1989 two bookshops, Dillons and the left-wing Collets, were firebombed for stocking the Rushdie novel. There followed explosions in High Wycombe and London's King's Road and a bomb in Liberty's department store, which had a Penguin bookshop – because Penguin had published *Satanic Verses*. Rushdie lived in secretly guarded exile for ten years until 1998 when the *fatwa* was withdrawn.

In November 2002, Nigerian journalist Isioma Daniel incensed Muslims in her country by writing about the Prophet Muhammad in a newspaper article. In her fashion column for a Lagos newspaper she commented about the Miss World pageant which was about to be held in Nigeria:

> the Muslims thought it was immoral to bring 92 women to Nigeria and ask them to revel in vanity. What would Mohammed think? In all honesty, he would probably have chosen a wife from one of them.[16]

---

6 The first ten amendments to the US Constitution are collectively known as the 'Bill of Rights'; there are five freedoms guaranteed by the First Amendment, the fifth being the right 'to petition the government for a redress of grievances'.

7 Mill, J. S. (1859), Introduction, p. 26.

8 For further discussion see: Wragg, P. (2013b).

9 Chancellor of Nazi Germany 1933–1945.

10 Italian Fascist dictator and founder of the Organizzazione per la Vigilanza e la Repressione dell'Antifascismo (OVRA) (Organization for Vigilance and Repression of Anti-Fascism), 1927–1945.

11 General Francisco Franco, the military head of Spain from 1936 to 1975.

12 The Universal Declaration of Human Rights (UDHR) was drafted by representatives with different legal and cultural backgrounds from all regions of the world. The Declaration was proclaimed by the United Nations General Assembly in Paris on 10 December 1948 (Resolution 217 A III).

13 Aleksandr Solzhenitsyn, *One Day in the Life of Ivan Denisovich* (first published in the Soviet literary magazine Noviy Mir (*New World*) in November 1962).

14 The title refers to a group of Qur'anic verses that allow for prayers of intercession to be made to three pagan goddesses in Mecca. See: Rushdie, S. (1989; new edition 1998).

15 See: Rushdie, S. (2012).

16 Source: *Thisday* press office release, Kaduna, 27 November 2002.

A *fatwa* was issued on Isioma Daniel by the deputy governor of Zamfara state because her article had incited major religious riots for being held a 'blasphemous' publication. Information Minister Umar Dangaladima reiterated Zamfara state policy by his public announcement:

> it's a fact that Islam prescribes the death penalty on anybody, no matter his faith, who insults the Prophet.[17]

In August 2012 Russian judge Marina Syrova sentenced three members of the punk band Pussy Riot to two years in a prison labour camp for staging a 40-second punk feminist 'flash mob' inside Moscow's official church as they performed a 'punk prayer'. One Pussy Riot member, Yekaterina Samutsevich, was set free by a Moscow appeal court in October 2012, leaving Maria Alyokhina and Nadezhda Tolokonnikova – found guilty of hooliganism and blasphemous religious rioting – to serve two years in a Russian labour colony. No doubt the punk band members had offended many Russian Orthodox believers by screaming lyrics such as 'Shit, shit, the Lord's shit' inside the Cathedral of Christ the Saviour, but the trial itself became an old-fashioned Soviet show trial, one of the first criminal crackdowns of President Vladimir Putin's campaign against political activists.

The anti-corruption and anti-Putin blogger, lawyer and political activist, Alexei Navalny (born 1976), was imprisoned in 2015 for his prominent opposition (via social media) during the controversial presidential elections in Russia in December 2011. Navalny blogged about allegations of malpractice and corruption on his blog, 'rospil.info'.[18] In November 2016 the Russian Supreme Court overturned Navalny's conviction for embezzlement.

2.2.3 Towards human rights and constitutional freedom of speech

Most democratic societies now enshrine freedom of speech in their constitutions such as the German Constitution (*Grundgesetz*). Since the United Kingdom which does not have a written constitution it has to reply on the European Convention Article 10 for 'freedom of expression', now enshrined in the HRA 1998.[19]

In 1948, the Universal Declaration of Human Rights was adopted by the UN General Assembly. Its main aim was to promote human, civil, economic and social rights, including freedom of expression and religion, among all its subscribing nations. There followed the European Convention on Human Rights and Fundamental Freedoms (ECHR), adopted in 1950. The subsequent International Covenant on Civil and Political Rights 1966 (ICCPR) recognized the right to freedom of speech as 'the right to hold opinions without interference'.[20]

Worth noting is that Article 10(1) ECHR is a protection for individual rather than corporate freedom of expression and does not expressly refer to media or journalistic (press) freedom. *Centro Europa* (2012)[21] first recognized the importance of pluralism in the media, noting that 'there can be no democracy without pluralism. Democracy thrives on freedom of expression.'[22]

---

17 Source: 'Fatwa is issued against Nigerian journalist', by James Astill and Owen Bowcott, *Guardian*, 27 November 2002.

18 Boris Yefimovich Nemtsov (1959–2015) was a Russian physicist, statesman and liberal politician. Nemtsov was one of the most important figures in the introduction of capitalism into the Russian post-Soviet economy.

19 For further discussion see: Stein, E. (2000), p. 347.

20 International Covenant on Civil and Political Rights (ICCPR), United Nations Treaty, New York, 16 December 1966. UN Treaty Series, vol. 999, p. 171 and vol. 1057, p. 407 (procès-verbal of rectification of the authentic Spanish text); depositary notification C.N.782.2001.

21 *Centro Europa 7 S.R.L. and Di Stefano v Italy* (Application No 38433/09), [2012] ECHR 974 (ECtHR). Grand Chamber judgment of 7 June 2012.

22 The applicants were Centro Europa 7 S.R.L., an Italian company based in Rome, and Francescantonio Di Stefano, its statutory representative.

The case concerned an Italian TV company's inability to broadcast, despite having a broadcasting licence, due to lack of television frequencies allocated to it. The Italian broadcasting authorities had granted the company a licence for national TV broadcasting via Hertzian waves in 1999, but the national frequency allocation plan of 1998 was never implemented. Due to a series of interim legislative schemes, existing TV channels were allowed to extend their use of frequencies that they should in principle have given up. As a result, Centro Europa had no frequency attributed to it and it was unable to broadcast. The applicants complained that this amounted to an unjustified breach of their right to impart information, relying on Article 10 ECHR (freedom of expression and information), and that they had suffered discrimination, relying on Article 14 (prohibition of discrimination) of the Convention.

The ECtHR held by 16 votes to one that there had been a violation of Article 10 ECHR and ruled that the respondent state (Italy) was to pay the applicant company €10 million within three months (plus any tax in respect of pecuniary and non-pecuniary damages). The court held unanimously that Italy was to pay the applicant company a further €100,000, plus any tax that may be chargeable to the applicant company, in respect of costs and expenses within three months.[23]

2.3 Theoretical foundations of media freedom

Media freedom can be defined as the ability and opportunity for journalists to say and write what they want without restriction or interference from the state and elsewhere. Though the UK prides itself on having a free press, journalistic activities today are restricted by numerous pieces of legislation, the majority of which form the subject matter of this book. As common law has developed, particularly in the area of human rights, it will be demonstrated that the courts have attempted to strike a fine balance between the freedoms and responsibilities of the press, while safeguarding an individual's right to privacy.

The idea that citizens can receive free and objective information and engage in free debate and critical reflection was adopted in the twentieth century by the German philosopher Jürgen Habermas, who traced the rise of free speech back to the Age of Enlightenment, made possible by a free press. Habermas believed that the emancipation of the informed citizen could be brought about only by 'critical communication and analysis of modern institutions'. The only way such informed criticism could take shape is through a free and uncensored press, which he included in his 'three normative models of democracy'.[24]

For daily practical journalistic and investigative purposes we need to place our trust in the media and broadcasting institutions – it is hoped that post-Leveson, this will be done well. Today press freedom accepts certain restrictions on providing information, such as war reporting,[25] contempt, blasphemy, the protection of minors, racial discrimination and national security. Frost argues that it can be rather confusing that many people in Britain and other Western European countries appear to support freedom of speech and a free press on the one hand, while supporting censorship on specific matters on the other, such as the coverage of terrorism or sexually explicit material.[26] Ultimately, there are ethical and moral issues that govern war reporting or news-gathering. These are usually left to broadcasting organizations' policy, such as the BBC's editorial code.

---

23 *Centro Europa* [2012] ECHR 974 at para. 227 (Françoise Tulkens, President, Grand Chamber, ECtHR).
24 See: Habermas, J. (1994).
25 For further discussion see: Burchill, R., White N. D. and Morris, J. (2005).
26 Frost, C. (2011).

2.3.1 Media coverage of terrorism activities and the law

Large numbers of people across the world now access online news and information services such as Reuters. International news organizations have to report international conflicts, including wars, acts and planned acts of terror, sieges and emergencies. It is important that war correspondents give impartial analyses by offering a wide range of views and opinions. Because of the dangerous conflicts that now exist in parts of the world (e.g. Ukraine, Syria, Iraq), reliable information is often hard to come by, and journalists need to be scrupulous in applying principles of accuracy and impartiality. This increasingly puts journalists and camera teams at risk. Additionally, there are laws which may curtail free and open reporting.

The Prevention of Terrorism (Temporary Provisions) Acts of 1974 and 1989 were a series of Acts that conferred emergency powers upon police forces, particularly aimed at the 'Troubles' in Northern Ireland with suspected terrorism from the IRA (Irish Republican Army). It had been Prime Minister Margaret Thatcher's unrelenting aim to stop violence in Northern Ireland. The policies her government actually did implement from 1979 included a decree whereby members of the republican political party Sinn Féin and several other paramilitary organizations were banned from speaking about the conflict in media broadcasts. Thatcher claimed this would deny terrorists 'the oxygen of publicity'.

A complete ban began on 19 October 1988 and affected 11 loyalist and republican organizations but Sinn Féin, the political wing of the IRA, was the main target. It meant that instead of hearing Gerry Adams or Martin McGuinness, BBC viewers and listeners would hear an actor's voice reading a transcript of the individuals' words. This proved not to be a straightforward task and Danny Morrison, former director of publicity for Sinn Fein, commented that there was 'total confusion'.

Sanders highlights journalistic coverage of terrorism as being particularly difficult in terms of free speech and ethics.[27] She specifically examined broadcast reporting during the Troubles from 1989 to the Belfast (Northern Ireland) Agreement in 1998, looking particularly at interviews with IRA and INLA (Irish National Liberation Army) members, concluding that these were difficult times for press freedom.

A BBC documentary by Paul Hamann featuring an extensive interview with Martin McGuinness of Sinn Féin was banned by the government, and McGuinness's voice was replaced by an actor until the start of the peace talks in 1994. Media restrictions in Northern Ireland were gradually lifted and both Terrorism Acts 1974 and 1989 were repealed. Hamann's documentary – *Real Lives: At the Edge of the Union* – could finally be shown in 1994. There is no doubt that the documentary and subject matter caused immense controversy between the Thatcher Conservative government and the BBC in the mid-1980s.

Since the atrocities of 9/11 (2001) in New York and the London bombings in July 2005, the UK Parliament has passed a number of 'terrorism' statutes. On 29 August 2014, the independent Joint Terrorism Analysis Centre (JTAC) raised the UK national terrorist threat level from 'substantial' to 'severe'. This meant that a terrorist attack was 'highly likely'. By the end of 2014, some 600 people from the UK were known to the security services who had travelled to Syria in order to join ISIS.[28] In the context of this heightened threat to the UK's national security, Parliament passed the Counter-Terrorism and Security Act 2015. The aim was to strengthen the legal powers and capabilities of law enforcement and intelligence agencies to disrupt terrorism and prevent individuals from being radicalized in the first instance.

---

27 Sanders, K. (2003), p. 71.
28 Islamic State of Iraq and the Levant (abbreviated ISIL or ISIS).

Journalists covering news from highly dangerous areas such as Syria and Iraq have been made aware by the UK government to focus on four main areas of their work:

1.   the pursuit of the investigation and disruption of terrorist attacks;
2.   the prevention of people becoming terrorists or supporting terrorism and extremism;
3.   the protection of UK citizens by the security services to stop a terrorist attack; and
4.   ongoing work by the security and law enforcement agencies to minimize the impact of an attack and to recover from it as quickly as possible.

See Chapter
6.6

Alongside normal ethical considerations terrorism legislation places legal obligations on journalists to disclose certain information to the police as soon as reasonably practicable. Reporters need to be aware that their broadcasts need to be sensitive when reporting from war zones because matters reported will involve loss of life, as well as human suffering or distress with some listeners or viewers having relatives and friends directly involved.

2.3.2 The BBC and freedom to broadcast

The background to the *Sugar* case involved a BBC inquiry into news coverage of the Israeli–Palestinian conflict, resulting in the 'Balen Report', compiled by senior BBC journalist Malcolm Balen in 2004. The inquiry had been commissioned by the BBC's former director of news, Richard Sambrook, following allegations of anti-Israeli bias during the BBC's coverage of the Israeli–Palestinian conflict in 2003–2004.[29] Hundreds of viewers and listeners had complained to the Corporation in 2003–2004, when the Middle East correspondent Barbara Plett revealed that she had cried at the death of Yasser Arafat. There were also allegations of pro-Jewish bias. The Balen Report was then presented to the BBC's Journalism Board for consideration in 2004.

Following the Hutton Report[30] in January 2004 there had been several changes in the top management of the BBC. The BBC governors had sacked Director General Greg Dyke within 24 hours of the report's publication and Gavyn Davies, the BBC's chairman, had resigned. Mark Byford became Deputy Director-General of the BBC, and in August 2004, Richard Sambrook became Director of Global News and Helen Boaden took over Mr Sambrook's place as Director of News. Mark Thompson, the new Director-General, set up three new boards, including a Journalism Board of which Mr Byford was the chair and Mr Sambrook, Ms Boaden and other senior managers were members. The Board was to be responsible for setting the strategy which would direct, and for defining the values which would inform, journalism across all areas of the BBC's output. The Balen Inquiry then became of an equally sensitive nature as the Hutton Report, alleging the BBC's systematic and anti-Semitic bias against Israel.

On 8 January 2005, a commercial lawyer, Steven Sugar, asked to see the Balen Report and made a request to the BBC under the Freedom of Information Act 2000 (FOIA). The BBC governors refused, reasoning that the Balen Report was an internal document aimed at checking its own standards of journalism. This meant that information held by the BBC for the purposes of journalism was effectively exempt from production under the FOIA, even if it was held for

29 Mr Balen had at one time been editor of the BBC's *Nine O'Clock News* but, by 2003, he had ceased to be employed by the BBC and was working as Head of News for a commercial television channel. Richard Sambrook asked Mr Balen to re-join the BBC under a one-year contract, which took effect on 1 November 2003.
30 'Report of the Inquiry into the Circumstances Surrounding the Death of Dr David Kelly CMG' (the Hutton Report'), HC 247.

other, possibly more important, purposes.[31] Mr Sugar complained to the Information Commissioner (IC), stating that the BBC – as a public body – was under a duty to disclose the requested information under FOIA. On 24 October 2005, the IC ruled in favour of the BBC. Mr Sugar subsequently appealed to the Information Tribunal, which ruled in favour of Mr Sugar on 29 August 2006. This meant the BBC should disclose the report and could not derogate under FOIA.[32]

The BBC appealed against the tribunal's decision. The grounds of appeal before the High Court were as follows: that the tribunal did not have jurisdiction to hear an appeal from the IC; and, even if it did, the IC's decision had been flawed as a matter of law. On 27 April 2007, High Court judge Davies J backed the IC's decision and held that the Balen Report was 'for the purpose of journalism'. Additionally, the judge imposed restrictions on potential appeals to the Information Tribunal in the future, stating, *inter alia*, that the tribunal lacked jurisdiction.[33] The Court of Appeal[34] rejected Mr Sugar's appeal, ruling that the Balen Report was to be prohibited and exempt under section 44 FOIA.[35]

See Chapter 4.5.2

Eventually the case reached the UK Supreme Court with a judgment in February 2012.[36] Sadly the appellant, Mr Steven Sugar, died during the proceedings in January 2011 and the court appointed his wife Fiona Paveley to represent his estate in the appeal.

The Supreme Court justices held that the CA had been correct in stating that once it is established that the information sought from the BBC is held 'for the purposes of journalism', it is effectively *exempt* from production under the FOIA. Their Lordships ruled that the BBC, as a public service broadcaster, should be free to gather, edit and publish news and comment on current affairs without the inhibition of an obligation to make public disclosure of or about their work under FOIA.[37] Lord Brown held that the Balen Report was held *predominantly* for purposes of journalism and accordingly fell within the exemption of the Act.[38] Their Lordships also commented that Article 10 of the Convention created no general right to receive freedom of information.[39]

The Supreme Court's decision in *Sugar* disappointed the Jewish community, which wanted to know whether the Balen inquiry found any evidence of anti-Israeli bias in news programming and reporting at the BBC. It had taken seven years from Steven Sugar's first submission of his request to the BBC under the FOIA in January 2005 to the final decision by the UK Supreme Court in 2012, with Mr Sugar dying in the meantime and his wife Fiona Paveley continuing the legal battle on his behalf. We will therefore never know whether the BBC's coverage of the Middle East conflict was biased either way. The Balen Report was never published. This case will also be discussed in Chapter 4 (Freedom of information).

---

31 'For the purposes of journalism, art or literature' within the meaning of Sch. 1, Part VI FOIA.
32 *Sugar v BBC* [2007] EWHC 905.
33 [2009] EWHC 2348 (Admin).
34 [2008] EWCA Civ 191.
35 For further discussion see: Johnson, H. (2008a), pp. 174–176.
36 *BBC and Another v Sugar (deceased) (No 2)* [2012] UKSC 4.
37 Ibid., at para. 61 (as per Lord Walker with Lord Phillips, Lord Brown, Lord Mance agreeing).
38 Ibid., at paras 57, 60 (as per Lord Brown).
39 Ibid., at paras 94 and 98.

 **FOR THOUGHT**

In *Sugar v BBC (No 2)* (2012), Mr Steven Sugar argued that he had the right to disclosure of the BBC's *Balen Report* under Article 10(1) ECHR and the FOIA. Discuss Lord Brown's judgment (at paras 84–103) and Strasbourg case law in this respect (e.g. the trilogy of *Matky v Czech Republic, Tarsasag v Hungary* and *Kenedi v Hungary*).[40]

2.4 Cartoons and the boundaries of press freedom

Cartoonists and caricaturists can often say a great deal more than a journalist can through their visual medium.

In many Islamic countries blasphemy laws remain stringent and are strictly enforced, often with severe penalties; even potentially death. This demonstrates that the extent and scope of national laws protecting religious beliefs remain very culture-specific.

2.4.1 Abuses of freedom of expression: the provocative power of cartoons

In Britain, caricatures and satires are generally dealt with by the tort law of defamation.[41] In *Charleston v News Group Newspapers Ltd* (1995),[42] the House of Lords considered the digitally enhanced photomontage that showed the faces of two famous Australian actors, Anne Charleston ('Madge') and Ian Smith ('Harold'), of the popular TV series *Neighbours*, superimposed on the nearly naked bodies of others in pornographic poses and agreed with Blofeld J's order to strike out the libel action against the publishers of the *News of the World*. Their Lordships, applying the 'bane and antidote' defence, declined to find defamation in *Charleston*. They further commented if the readers who did not take 'the trouble to discover what the article was all about, carried away the impression that two well-known actors in legitimate television were also involved in making pornographic films, they could hardly be described as ordinary, reasonable, fair-minded readers'.[43]

See Chapter 7

When the Danish newspaper *Jyllands-Posten* published 12 editorial cartoons of the Prophet Muhammad in September 2005 it caused outrage in the Muslim world, with violent protests erupting across the Middle East. Newspapers and magazines around the world reprinted the cartoons, leading to a global wave of protests and riots by Muslims who claimed that the caricatures were just another expression of Western colonialism. Hundreds of Iranians attacked the Danish embassy in Tehran and Saudi Arabia recalled its ambassador to Denmark, while Libya closed its embassy in Copenhagen and Lebanese demonstrators set the Danish embassy in Beirut on fire. By 2009, 11 Danish newspapers had been contacted by the Saudi lawyer Faisal Yamani, representing eight Muslim organizations claiming to represent in turn 94,923 descendants of Muhammad, demanding that *Jyllands-Posten* and the other newspapers remove the cartoons from their websites and print apologies. On 26 February 2010, Danish newspaper *Politiken* published an apology for reprinting the cartoons. Though this was welcomed by the Danish Prime Minister, he equally stressed the

40 See: *Matky v Czech Republic* (Application No 19101/03) 10 July 2006 (Matky), *Tarsasag A Szabadsagjogokert v Hungary* (2009) 53 EHRR 130 (14 April 2009) (Tarsasag), and *Kenedi v Hungary* (Application No 31475/05) (unreported) 26 August 2009.
41 See: Rogers, W. V. H. and Parkes, R. (2010) *Gatley on Libel and Slander, first supplement to the eleventh edition*, para. 3.4. For further detail see *Gatley on Libel and Slander* (2013).
42 [1995] 2 AC 65 (HL).
43 Ibid., at 76 (Lord Bridge of Harwich).

importance of press freedom. The editor of *Jyllands-Posten* said that its sister paper had failed in the fight for freedom of speech and called it a 'sad day' for the Danish press.

On 7 January 2015, gunmen shot dead 12 people at the Paris office of French satirical newspaper *Charlie Hebdo* in an apparent militant Islamist attack with the gunmen shouting 'We have avenged the Prophet Muhammad' and 'God is the Greatest' in Arabic ('*Allahu Akbar*'). The attack took place during the magazine's daily editorial meeting. Cartoonist Philippe Honoré ('Honoré') (73) was amongst those killed. He had drawn the last cartoon for the magazine, showing the leader of ISIS, Abu Bakr al-Baghdadi, presenting his New Year message, saying 'and especially good health!' Nine months later, French opinion was deeply divided about the controversial Mohammed cartoons in *Charlie Hebdo*. Its senior cartoonist, Luz – the man who designed the famous green cover of the first edition after the attacks[44] – announced his resignation in October 2015; columnist Patrick Pelloux announced the same.

A month later, on Friday 13 November 2015, gunmen and suicide bombers hit the Bataclan Concert Hall, the Stade de France and restaurants and bars, almost simultaneously in Paris, leaving 130 people dead and hundreds wounded. The attacks were described by President François Hollande as an 'act of war', organized by the Islamic State (IS) militant group. The man suspected of killing a policewoman in a shooting in Montrouge, was a member of the same jihadist group as the two suspects in the attack on *Charlie Hebdo*.

 FOR THOUGHT

Opinions about the appropriateness of publishing the Mohammed cartoons in the French magazine *Charlie Hebdo* and the Danish cartoons in *Jyllands-Posten* vary considerably. Discuss whether religious attacks are likely to increase if an editor of a magazine, newspaper or online edition chooses to publish such cartoons, believing strongly in his or her freedom of expression under Article 10(1) ECHR and editorial freedom.

2.5 Obscenity laws and freedom of expression

The Obscene Publications Act of 1959 put an end to aspects of 'obscene' or 'seditious' libel in English common law and therein ended these criminal offences. The offences of blasphemy and blasphemous libel were abolished by section 79 of the Criminal Justice and Immigration Act of 2008. 'Blasphemy' consisted of words that tended to vilify Christianity or the Bible.

The definition of 'obscene' still exists in English law and consists of words and statements that would be likely to deprave and corrupt those people who would be likely to read them. This legislation is used when judging films, publications or works of art in the UK.

2.5.1 Obscenity in English law

The Obscene Publications Act of 1959 has been used in the past in cases involving works of art, literature, drama or photography, which were said to adversely affect the morality and sensibilities of the ordinary 'decent' citizen. Such prominent cases are (still) heard before criminal juries. Here are some examples.

---

44 The edition of 14 January 2015 of *Charlie Hebdo* had a print-run of 1 million copies and contained cartoons of Prophet Mohammed, along with jibes against world religions.

There were the 'saucy seaside postcards' painted by Donald McGill (1875–1962) that fell foul of Britain's obscenity laws (Obscene Publications Act 1857 and Obscene Publications Act 1959). McGill had produced about 12,000 postcard designs between 1904 and 1962 and local 'policing' groups and 'friendship societies' took it upon themselves to remove these 'obscene' postcards from shops. On 15 July 1954 a jury at Lincoln Crown Court found Donald McGill guilty of obscene publications under the 1857 Act. He was fined £50 plus £25 court costs and all existing postcards and their templates were ordered to be destroyed. McGill went bankrupt.

As soon as the Obscene Publications Act 1959 came into force, the publishers of *Lady Chatterley's Lover* were charged under section 1(1) of the 1959 Act for the 'unacceptable' erotic portrayals in D. H. Lawrence's novel.[45] The indictment was based on the premise that the novel put promiscuity on a pedestal, and that the majority of the book was merely 'padding' between graphic scenes of sexual intercourse and filthy language.

Lawyers for the defence at the notorious 'Lady C's trial' called upon a string of expert witnesses to defend the book's literary merit, including several members of the clergy, one of whom remarked that the work 'was a novel and novels deal with life as it is'. On 10 November 1960, the jury acquitted Penguin of all charges.[46]

As soon as the verdict was pronounced, London's largest bookstore, W&G Foyle Ltd, reported a run on their bookshop with 300 copies sold in just 15 minutes and orders for 3,000 more copies. The case marked a famous turning point, with a victory for more liberal publishing houses, making literary prosecutions more difficult and increasingly rare.

Ten years after the 'Lady C' trial, the *Trial of Oz* in 1971 became the longest obscenity trial in English legal history, held at the Old Bailey under the auspices of Judge Michael Argyle QC.[47] Issue 28 of May 1970, *Schoolkids Oz*, led to the convictions of editors Richard Neville, Felix Dennis and Jim Anderson (all later overturned on appeal). Central to the obscenity allegations was the notoriously explicit cartoon by Robert Crumb, depicting Rupert Bear in a sexual position ravishing a gypsy granny. What made it worse was that the editors had invited young readers, aged between 15 and 18, to edit Issue 28. The 'Schoolkids' issue, with its French erotic cover design ('Desseins Erotiques'), contained 48 pages of content on homosexuality, lesbianism and sadism.

John Mortimer QC (late author of the famous *Rumpole of the Bailey* short stories and TV series) acted for the defence. Amongst the defence witnesses was DJ John Peel, musician George Melly (who at one point explained a Latin sexual term in detail to the jury) and comedy writer Marty Feldman, who called the judge a 'boring old fart'. At one point in the trial the defendants turned up at court dressed as schoolgirls, an obvious hint at the *Hicklin* 'innocent schoolgirl' test.[48]

The Old Bailey jury found the three young editor defendants guilty of publishing an obscene magazine under the 1959 Act in 1971. The sentences were severe: Judge Argyle set out a prison term of 15 months for the editor, Richard Neville, and 12 months and nine months respectively for his associates. The Court of Appeal subsequently revoked the sentences with a judgment by Lord Widgery LCJ, where the court recognized 14 errors of law. The ruling was appealed and the House of Lords dismissed the (counter) appeal, stating that the offence could be committed by encouraging 'obscene' conduct which although not itself illegal might be calculated to corrupt public morals (applying *Shaw v DPP* (1962)[49]). *Oz* ceased publication not long after the trial.

---

45   See: *R v Penguin Books Ltd* [1961] Crim LR 176.
46   See: Palmer, T. (1971), which contains court transcripts of the actual trial.
47   The controversial underground magazine *Oz* was first published in Sydney, Australia in 1963.
48   See: *R v Hicklin* (1868) LR 3 QB 360 established the 'innocent schoolgirl' test in common law as 'obscene' or 'immoral'. The test was whether the publication had a tendency to deprave and corrupt 'upright' members of society, particularly 'innocent schoolgirls', should the publication fall into their hands.
49   [1962] AC 220.

⊙ FOR THOUGHT

The law on obscenity in the UK centres on the notion that a publication – a book, magazine, or photograph – has to have a tendency to 'deprave and corrupt' those who are likely to view it. The Obscene Publications Act 1959 provides a defence if it can be shown that the publication is in the public interest – for example, because of an article's literary value. Discuss whether the statute should be repealed.

2.5.2 Strasbourg jurisprudence in relation to obscenity and blasphemy laws in Europe

Various obscenity and blasphemy laws in Europe prohibit film, video and video games releases. Strasbourg jurisprudence remains vague and non-committal in this area and generally applies only to anything which might encourage criminal activity by those watching the movies, especially if it encourages violence or sexual violence. When examining human rights law it could be argued that the ECtHR has – in general – not interfered with a country's freedom of religion under Article 9 ECHR in favour of Article 10 ('freedom of expression') (see: *Murphy v Ireland* (2000)[50]).

The controversial case of *Otto-Preminger*[51]-*Institut v Austria* (1994)[52] concerned the forfeiture of the film *Council of Love* (*Das Liebeskonzil*), based on a nineteenth-century play in which the Eucharist is ridiculed and God the Father is presented as a senile, impotent idiot, the Virgin Mary as a wanton woman who displays erotic interest in the devil and Jesus Christ as a low-grade mental defective given to fondling his mother's breasts.

Das Liebeskonzil was to be screened at a private film club before an informed adult audience in the Tyrol in 1987, but the Innsbruck court injuncted the film because of its blasphemous content which, the court reasoned, would shock the predominantly Roman Catholic audience in the Tyrol.[53] Preminger opposed the injunction citing Article 10(1) ECHR as 'freedom of [artistic] expression'. On appeal the Austrian Constitutional Court in Vienna held the film to be blasphemous because it contained provocative and offensive portrayals of the objects of veneration of the Roman Catholic religion. The Austrian court cited Article 10(2) of the Convention as a reason for derogating against 'freedom of expression' and confirmed the injunction as permanent: the court ruled that the Innsbruck court had not overstepped the 'margin of appreciation'.[54]

One of the leading cases in human rights law is *Jersild v Denmark* (1994)[55] (see below), where the Strasbourg Court recognized journalistic freedom of expression under Article 10 ECHR. The Danish government had classed the TV documentary as racist and obscene – and the ECtHR noted the repressive measures in Danish criminal law applied to the media at the time.[56]

---

50 (2000) 38 EHRR 13 (ECtHR).
51 Otto Ludwig Preminger (1905–1986) was a famous Austro-Hungarian film director. Living mostly in the USA, he directed over 35 Hollywood movies which tended to be of the film noir genre. Topics were intentionally blasphemous and provocative e.g. *Fallen Angel* (1945), *The Moon is Blue* (1953), *The Man with the Golden Arm* (1955), the *Anatomy of a Murder* (1959) and *Advise and Consent* (1962).
52 (1995) 19 EHRR 34, [1994] ECtHR 26 (Case No 13470/87) 20 September 1994 (ECtHR).
53 Contrary to s 188 of the Austrian Penal Code.
54 Judgment by the ECtHR of 20 September 1994 with the result of the immediate withdrawal of the movie by the Austrian Constitutional Court (Urteil vom 20. September 1994, A/295-A EGMR Einziehung des Films Das 'Liebeskonzil', verstößt nicht gegen Art 10 EMRK).
55 (1994) 19 EHRR 1.
56 Namely the Danish Penal Code Article 266(b) and the 1991 Media Liability Act (Denmark).

KEY CASE   *Jersild v Denmark* (1994) 19 EHRR 1

Precedent

❖ A journalist's publication and remarks are not racist if the aim of the publication is to protect the rights and reputation of others.

❖ A publication or broadcast is justified under Article 10(1) ECHR if (given the margin of appreciation) the article (or broadcast) contributes discussions of matters of public interest.

❖ The publication should not be banned under Article 10(2) ECHR.

Facts

On 31 May 1985 the Danish *Sunday News Magazine* (*Søndagsavisen*) published an article describing the racist attitudes of members of a group of young people, calling themselves 'The Greenjackets' (*grønjakkerne*), at Østerbro in Copenhagen. In the light of this article, the editors of the *Sunday News Magazine* decided to produce a documentary on the Greenjackets. The applicant, Mr Jens Olaf Jersild, a Danish journalist, contacted representatives of the group, inviting three of them, together with Mr Per Axholt, a social worker, to take part in a TV interview. During the interview, the three Greenjackets made abusive and derogatory remarks about immigrants and ethnic groups in Denmark. The edited film – lasting only a few minutes – was broadcast by Danmarks Radio on 21 July 1985 as part of the Sunday news magazine programme. The documentary feature included avowed racist views.

In their statements the youths described black people as belonging to an inferior subhuman race ['. . . the niggers . . . are not human beings . . . Just take a picture of a gorilla . . . and then look at a nigger, it's the same body structure. . . . A nigger is not a human being, it's an animal, that goes for all the other foreign workers as well, Turks, Yugoslavs and whatever they are called'].

Following the programme, no complaints were made to the Radio Council or to Danmarks Radio, but the Bishop of Ålborg complained to the Minister of Justice. Subsequently, the three youths were convicted for making racist statements and Mr Jersild for aiding and abetting them in making racist comments in a public place.[57] Mr Jersild, but not the three Greenjackets, appealed against the City Court's judgment to the High Court of Eastern Denmark (*Østre Landsret*), but his appeal was rejected and his conviction was upheld by the Danish Supreme Court.

Decision

The ECtHR jointly dissented with the opinion and judgment of the Danish Supreme Court. Judges Gölcüklü, Russo and Valticos stated, 'We cannot share the opinion of the majority of the Court in the Jersild case.' The ECtHR held that Mr Jersild's Article 10 right to freedom of expression had been violated and that he was not a racist. He had a valid defence in the making the programme. The reasons given by the Danish court in support of Jersild's conviction and sentence (and derogation under Article 10(2) ECHR) were not sufficient to justify interference with a journalist's right of free expression in a democratic society.

---

57   Under Article 266 (b) of the Danish Penal Code.

Analysis

It is interesting that the Strasbourg Court in *Jersild* did not show any concern or sensibility towards vulnerable groups in the face of racial abuse compared with its judgment in the *Otto Preminger* case, where the Catholic population of the tiny Tyrol region was very much taken into consideration over the offending film. Were the religious sensibilities so fundamentally different in character in the satirical film by Otto Preminger to the 'nigger' quote in the Danish documentary by Jersild? Why did the ECtHR not apply the 'margin of appreciation' in the *Jersild* case?[58] The Strasbourg Court found it particularly important in *Jersild* to send a message to combat racial discrimination. This, in fact, had been Mr Jersild's intention when making the Danish TV documentary. The ECtHR stressed that freedom of expression at times constitutes publications (or broadcasts) which may shock or offend, but that this is one of the essential underpinnings of a democracy and the media plays an important role in the duty to inform.

The ECtHR ruling in *Jersild* provides journalists and media outlets the protection needed to disseminate controversial opinions; however, it does caution against the dissemination of unbalanced and overly obscene or blasphemous communication.[59]

2.6 Freedom of expression under Article 10 ECHR

The right to freedom of expression is crucial in a democracy, helps to inform political debate and is essential to the media to report on government transparency and the checks and balances imposed by Parliament on the executive.

Article 10(1) ECHR gives everyone the right to freedom of expression, which includes the freedom to hold opinions and to receive and impart information and ideas without state interference. The type of expression protected includes:

- political expression (including comment on matters of general public interest);
- artistic expression; and
- commercial expression, particularly when it also raises matters of legitimate public debate and concern.

To ensure that free expression and debate are possible, there must be protection for elements of a free press, including protection of journalistic sources. Interferences with press freedom usually involve restrictions on publication (injunctions or superinjunctions).

See Chapter 6.6

Article 10 is a qualified right and as such the right to freedom of expression may be limited under Article 10(2) ECHR which provides that freedom of expression 'carries with it duties and responsibilities' and may be limited as long as the limitation:

- is prescribed by law;
- is necessary and proportionate; and
- pursues a legitimate aim.

---

58 For a detailed discussion see: Mahoney, P. (1997), pp. 364–379.

59 For further reading see: Council of Europe (2010) 'Blasphemy, insult and hatred: Finding answers in a democratic society', *Science and Technique of Democracy* 47. Brussels: Council of Europe Publication.

Such 'legitimate aim' might include the interests of national security, territorial integrity or public safety, but can also include the prevention of disorder or crime, the protection of health or morals, the protection of a person's reputation or preventing the disclosure of information received in confidence (confidentiality).

Freedom of speech must at times yield to other cogent social interests, such as national security, recognized in the *Spycatcher*[60] action well before the European Convention entered UK domestic law. In *Derbyshire County Council v Times Newspapers Ltd*[61] Lord Keith of Kinkel, speaking for a unanimous House, observed about Article 10:

> As regards the words 'necessary in a democratic society' in connection with the restrictions on the right to freedom of expression which may properly be prescribed by law, the jurisprudence of the European Court of Human Rights has established that 'necessary' requires the existence of a pressing social need, and that the restrictions should be no more than is proportionate.

 FOR THOUGHT

> Should an editor of a newspaper (and its online edition) apologize for a cartoon or a satirical poem which has offended a religious community or a leader of state? Or does this attack the artist's freedom of expression? Discuss with reference to leading examples.

2.6.1 What is the link between Article 10 ECHR and section 12 HRA 1998?

See Chapter 1.4

Whenever an application for a (super)injunction concerning a celebrity, royal or public figure is made, the media will invoke their Article 10 ECHR right to freedom of expression, and the courts will weigh up the applicant's privacy right (Article 8 ECHR) – as well as consider the 'public interest' test – against the media's Article 10 right. At the same time the application is made (by the media for discharging an injunction) section 12 HRA is invoked. The courts are then asked to have particular regard to the importance of the right to freedom of expression and to not impose any orders without the other party being first notified (usually representatives of the media) unless there is strong justification for doing so.

According to section 12(3) of the HRA, an injunction before trial is not granted unless the court is satisfied that the applicants are likely to establish that publication should not be allowed. And in coming to its finding on that question, the court is obliged to and does have regard to the public interest and to the other matters set out in section 12(4) HRA, which reads:

> (4)   The court must have particular regard to the importance of the Convention right to freedom of expression and, where the proceedings relate to material which the respondent claims, or which appears to the court, to be journalistic, literary or artistic material (or to conduct connected with such material), to –
>
> (a)   the extent to which – (i) the material has, or is about to, become available to the public; or (ii) it is, or would be, in the public interest for the material to be published;
>
> (b)   any relevant privacy code.[62]

---

60   See: *AG v Guardian Newspapers Ltd (No 1); AG v Observer Ltd; AG v Times Newspapers Ltd* [1987] 1 WLR 1248 (Spycatcher case); see also: *AG v Guardian Newspapers Ltd (No 2)* [1990] 1 AC 109 (Spycatcher No 2).
61   *Derbyshire County Council v Times Newspapers Ltd and Others* [1993] AC 534, [1993] 2 WLR 449 (HL).
62   This reference used to mean section 3 of the PCC Code; now the IPSO Editor's section 2 'Privacy'.

Section 12(3) HRA requires that an interim injunction be refused unless the court is satisfied that the claimant is likely to establish at trial that the publication should not be allowed. The court in balancing all Convention rights has to have particular regard to the importance of the media's Article 10 right, and under section 12(4)(a)(i) HRA it has to consider the extent to which the material has, or is about to, become available to the public. That now involves a fact-sensitive assessment as to what has occurred, what would occur prior to the trial, and what the result would be at trial.

In the *Fred Goodwin* case (2011)[63] (formerly known as MNB[64]), the *News of the World* were content in keeping the name of the lady with whom 'Sir Fred' was having an affair a secret as part of the original injunction; however their application to the court was to be able to publish information which would identify him.[65] On 19 May 2011 Lord Stoneham on behalf of Lord Oakeshott identified Sir Fred Goodwin's superinjunction in Parliament, applying parliamentary privilege. The injunction was swiftly discharged in its entirety.

Recent authorities have shown that section 12 HRA does not provide any defence to the tort of misusing private information, but it enhanced the weight which Article 10 rights carry in the balancing exercise, and it has raised the hurdle which the claimant has to overcome to obtain an interim (super)injunction.

2.7 Balancing freedom of expression and the right to privacy: analysis and discussion

Strasbourg jurisprudence encourages domestic courts to apply the balancing test between Articles 8 ('privacy') and 10 ECHR ('freedom of expression'). This has led to a more nuanced approach to freedom of expression in Europe compared with the more absolutist approach in the USA, where freedom of expression is a rather dominant right compared with privacy and other rights.

2.7.1 How have the courts balanced the right to privacy and freedom of expression?

We have seen in Chapter 1 that the ECtHR pronounced very different judgments in the three *von Hannover* actions. The first action granted Princess Caroline of Monaco privacy.[66] In the conjoined judgments of *von Hannover* (No 2)[67] and *Axel Springer*,[68] the Grand Chamber carefully balanced Articles 8 and 10 ECHR and ruled in favour of 'freedom of expression', thereby granting the publications the right to contribute to a debate of general and genuine public interest. *Von Hannover* (No 3)[69] repeated that message.

See Chapter 1.4

It is only when a fine balance has been struck by the courts between the competing privacy rights of the individual and the right to free speech that the issue of whether a matter is in the public interest can be decided. Publication at all costs, merely designed to satisfy the public's curiosity and to increase newspaper sales, should be avoided. The ECtHR has stressed, however, that Article 8 should not extend to the protection of someone's reputation or commercial interest (*Karakó v Hungary* (2009)).[70]

---

63 See: *Goodwin (Sir Fred) v News Group Newspapers* [2011] EWHC 1309 (QB).

64 See: *MNB v News Group Newspapers Ltd* [2011] EWHC 528 (QB) (Sharp J).

65 Former CEO of the Royal Bank of Scotland (RBS), Fred Goodwin oversaw the multi-billion-pound deal to buy Dutch rival ABN Amro at the height of the financial crisis in 2007, which led to RBS having to be bailed out to the tune of £45 billion by taxpayers. He was stripped of his knighthood in 2012.

66 See: *von Hannover v Germany* (No 1) (2005) 40 EHRR 1 (Application No 59320/00) (ECtHR).

67 *von Hannover v Germany* (No 2) (2012) (Application Nos – 40660/08, 60641/08) Strasbourg judgment of 7 February 2012 (ECtHR).

68 *Axel Springer v Germany* (2012) (Application No 39954/08) Strasbourg judgment of 7 February 2012 (ECtHR).

69 *von Hannover v Germany* (No 3) (2013) (Application No 8772/10) ECHR 264 (ECtHR).

70 (2009) (Application No 39311/05) Strasbourg, 28 April 2009 (ECtHR).

❖ KEY CASE   *Karakó v Hungary* (2009) (Application No 39311/05)
Strasbourg, 28 April 2009 (ECtHR)

Precedent
❖   Article 8 ECHR does not extend to 'reputation'.
❖   Member states to the Convention have their own legislation to deal with a person's
    reputation (e.g. defamation laws).

Facts
During the Hungarian parliamentary elections of 2002, Mr László Karakó (K), Member of
Parliament for the Fidesz Party ('the Civic Union') and a candidate in one of the electoral dis-
tricts of Szabolcs-Szatmár-Bereg County, complained that the respondent state (Hungary)
had breached his Article 8 rights. K had pressed criminal charges and brought a private
prosecution for libel against 'LH', chairman of the county regional assembly (Szabolcs-
Szatmár-Bereg). LH had accused K of regularly voting against the interests of the county.
The prosecuting authorities decided not to pursue K's libel charges, also dismissing his
private prosecution. K argued before the Strasbourg Court that the Hungarian authorities
had failed to assist him to pursue his libel actions against his political opponent, claiming
that this had violated his right to reputation which he argued breached his Article 8 right.

Decision
As K claimed a violation of Article 8 by way of 'injury to his reputation', the Strasbourg
Court had to determine whether Article 8 included 'reputation' as part of the privacy
right. The Court found that the impugned statement was a value judgement, dismissing
K's complaint on the grounds that the 'right to privacy' under Article 8 did not imply a
right to reputation. The judgment referred to the principle established in *von Hannover
(No 1)*,[71] where the ECtHR had extended the protection of private life to the protection of
personal integrity which did not extend to 'reputation'.

This meant that the complainant's allegation that his reputation as a politician had been
harmed by an allegedly libellous statement was not a sustainable claim regarding the
protection of his right to respect for personal integrity under Article 8 ECHR.

Analysis
In *Karakó* the ECtHR held that there was sufficient legislation in several Member States to
the Convention (such as the UK), whereby reputation had traditionally been protected by
the law of defamation.[72] A limitation on freedom of expression for the sake of Karakó's (K's)
reputation would have been disproportionate under Article 10. Consequently, there had
been *no* violation of K's Article 8 right.

The Strasbourg Court decision in *Karakó* is an important one and impacts on many other
cases thereafter (such as *LNS – John Terry*). In this case K had not shown that the publication constituted such a serious interference with his private life as to undermine his personal integrity. Accordingly, it was K's reputation alone which was at stake in the context of
an expression made to his alleged detriment.[73]

---

71   *von Hannover v Germany* [2004] EMLR 21.
72   See paras 21–29 of the judgment.
73   For further discussion see: Milo, D. (2008), pp. 15–43.

In summary, the ECtHR decision in *Karakó* conformed with Convention rights and standards in carefully balancing Articles 8 and 10 ECHR. The Court concluded that national laws of Member States were adequate enough to deal with claims of defamation[74] or other causes of action, such as 'harassment' (see: Protection from Harassment Act 1997).

Unfortunately the Strasbourg Court has not always sent out the same message and can conflict in its own jurisprudence. In *Lindon v France* (2007)[75] the ECtHR determined that the right to reputation should always be considered as safeguarded by Article 8. This case arose from a novel published in France entitled *Jean-Marie Le Pen on Trial* (*Le Procès de Jean-Marie Le Pen*) in respect of which Monsieur Le Pen and his rightwing National Front party brought defamation proceedings in France against the writer and publisher of the book.[76]

The serious and murderous allegations against Monsieur Le Pen and the National Front were found to be factually incorrect, defamatory and unproven and the Paris court upheld the defamation claims. The three applicants (Lindon, Otchakovsky-Laurens and July – respectively, the author, the chairman of the board of directors of the publishing company P.O.L. and the publication director of the newspaper *Libération*) were found guilty of defamation.

The three applicants claimed that their Article 10 right had been breached, that any exceptions to freedom of expression should be 'construed strictly' and that politicians ought to 'display a great degree of tolerance'. The ECtHR ruled that the French appeal court had made a reasonable assessment of the facts in finding that to liken Monsieur Le Pen to a 'chief of a gang of killers' overstepped the permissible limits of freedom of expression. The *Lindon* case was in stark contrast to the UK *Reynolds*[77] jurisprudence, whereby Judge Loucaides in the ECtHR particularly emphasized both the importance of truth and of media organizations being accountable to those against whom they make false or defamatory allegations.

See Chapter 7

2.7.2 Analysis and discussion

How impartial should the media be? What is the difference between comment, conjecture and fact and what are the boundaries of a free press? One of the few certainties in the world of journalism and editorial policy is that the age-old tension between freedom of expression and the right to robust and occasionally rude debate will, from time to time, come into conflict with the sensibilities of those who feel insulted or abused and minorities who can feel oppressed by the slights, real or imagined, of the majority.

Freedom of expression and freedom of the press do not always go hand in hand: there can be abuses by powerful media moguls which threaten media pluralism, as the Leveson Inquiry has shown. There are increasing challenges facing the use of new technologies and there is an urgent need for more stringent compliance with international legislation that protects both freedom of expression and an individual's right to privacy. Certainly, there needs to be clarification as to how human rights are to be protected if there is to be freedom of expression in electronic media. This will be discussed in the next chapter.

---

74 See: *Gatley on Libel and Slander* 11th edn, §27.17 and the cases there cited.
75 *Lindon, Otchakovsky-Laurens and July v France* (2007) (Applications Nos 21279/02 and 36448/02) judgment of 22 October 2007 (ECtHR).
76 See: Lindon, M. (1998).
77 See: *Reynolds v Times Newspapers Ltd* [2001] 2 AC 127.

2.8 Further reading

Frost, C. (2015) *Journalism, Ethics and Regulation* **(4th edn). Harlow: Longman.**
Though this book is principally aimed at working journalists and editors, it is a comprehensive volume addressing ethical considerations, dilemmas and challenges that practising journalists face. The text looks at practical challenges in the digital age, such as news-gathering in line with ethical and regulatory frameworks. The text illustrates the conflicts between the law, ethics and the public's right to be informed from a journalistic perspective.

Jordan, B. (2010b) 'Reputation and Article 8: *Karako v Hungary.* **Case Comment',** *Entertainment Law Review,* **21(3), 109–111.**
The article discusses the *Karakó* Human Rights Court case and the complainant's allegation that his reputation as a politician had been harmed by an allegedly libellous statement and that this should be protected under Article 8 ECHR.

McInnes, R. (2016) *Scots Law for Journalists* **(9th edn). Edinburgh: W Green/Sweet & Maxwell.**
The book is the authority on Scots law in this field, written primarily for practising journalists and editors. It provides good comparative coverage of English and Scots law on topics such as 'freedom of information' and human rights legislation, as well as case law in the area of privacy.

Rawls, J. (orig. 1971; 1999) *A Theory of Justice* **(reprinted and updated edn). Oxford: Oxford University Press.**
This is a twentieth-century classic, discussing John Rawls's highly regarded and compelling theory of social justice. For example, Rawls's political liberalism does not endorse welfare state capitalism.

Sanders, K. (2003) *Ethics and Journalism.* **London: Sage.**
This book provides readers with a summary of philosophical perspectives relevant to the topic in relation to the print press and broadcast journalism. There are also relevant references to film and literature.

Spencer, J. R. (1989) *Jackson's Machinery of Justice* **(8th edn of the original publication by Professor R. M. Jackson in 1903). Cambridge: Cambridge University Press.**
This is a classic text. First published in 1940, R. M. Jackson's *Machinery of Justice* has long been an established text on the subject of 'justice' in England and Wales. For this edition, J. R. Spencer has undertaken a full-scale revision, incorporating major topical issues such as PACE (Police and Criminal Evidence Act of 1984) and the Prosecution of Offences Act 1985.

Wragg, P. (2013b) 'Mill's dead dogma: the value of truth to free speech jurisprudence', *Public Law,* **April, 363–385.**
The purpose of this article is not so much to articulate fresh insights into John Stuart Mill and his famous work *On Liberty* but to scrutinize the role of Mill's argument in the UK in relation to Article 10 ECHR jurisprudence. Paul Wragg argues that Mill's theory is sometimes misrepresented in the academic literature as chiefly concerned with 'the truth' about uninhibited discussion. The author looks at the complexity of Mill's argument on free speech which, Wragg argues, has at times been oversimplified. The author argues that, given certain societal conditions, absolute freedom of thought and 'almost' absolute freedom of expression represent the optimal conditions by which 'truth' may be discovered.

Chapter 3

Technology and the media

Chapter contents

Key points

This chapter will cover the following questions:

○ How – if at all – can social media be regulated in cyber space?

○ How far can freedom of expression be permitted on the internet?

○ What are the human rights issues regulating the boundaries of social media freedom?

○ What is the 'right to be forgotten'? The *Google Spain* (*González*) case.

○ Is there a fundamental human right to receive information (via the internet)?

○ What are the implications of drone photography and the recording of images in terms of data protection and privacy laws?

3.1 Overview

There are now millions of amateurs who blog or tweet and share photos via Instagram, Snapchat or upload some of their most intimate detail on YouTube. Most of these individuals will be ignorant of the law in this area, such as defamation, mental abuse and harassment. In the absence of any privacy laws in the UK one could even argue that there exists no restraint or protection for an individual other than resorting to court restraining orders against an Internet Service Provider (ISP) or operator of a website – most of these are located in the USA or outside the European Union. Asking an operator of a website to take down offending statements or photos visible to the world at large can be near impossible for some (see: *Godfrey v Demon Internet*[1]).

See Chapter 7

One of the questions asked in this chapter: what is the responsibility of ISPs and operators of websites? Can they be held liable, for instance, for unlawful user-generated hate speech posted on their websites? The rise in defamation cases linked to the internet has been inevitable, where blogs or tweets have failed to put in place the same kind of pre-publication controls that traditional media use. As a result, there exists an ongoing battle between individuals trying to protect their privacy and the media trying to publish ostensibly private material. This will be further discussed in the 'defamation' chapter.

Hate speech and trolling via social media have increased enormously embracing nationality, race or religion – aimed to shock, offend or disturb, often hiding behind 'freedom of expression'. The United Nation's International Covenant on Civil and Political Rights (ICCPR)[2] not only permits states to prohibit hate speech but actually requires them to do so. Article 2(1) ICCPR reads:

> Each State Party to the present Covenant undertakes to respect and to ensure to all individuals within its territory and subject to its jurisdiction the rights recognized in the present Covenant, without distinction of any kind, such as race, colour, sex, language, religion, political or other opinion, national or social origin, property, birth or other status.

---

1 [2001] QB 201.

2 Adopted and opened for signature, ratification and accession by General Assembly resolution 2200A (XXI) of 16 December 1966, entry into force 23 March 1976, in accordance with Article 49.

In addition, one particular form of hate speech – incitement to genocide – is one of only a few types of acts recognized as a crime under international law, akin to war crimes and crimes against humanity. Article 20(2) ICCPR reads:

> Any advocacy of national, racial or religious hatred that constitutes incitement to discrimination, hostility or violence shall be prohibited by law.

This chapter will also look at the scale and scope of drone camera use which has taken law enforcement agencies by surprise. Because drones are relatively cheap, they are now widely used for commercial aerial photography not only by geographers and TV companies, but also by paparazzi to track the movements of celebrities and the royals, such as pictures of Prince George or Princess Charlotte when the Duke and Duchess of Cambridge travel abroad (e.g. Australia). Kensington Palace issued an unprecedented warning to paparazzi in August 2015, accusing photographers of harassing the Duke and Duchess of Cambridge and their children by using increasingly dangerous tactics to obtain drone images of the children. The aggressive tactics by unscrupulous paparazzi drones have been compared with the harassment experienced by Prince Harry's late mother, Diana, Princess of Wales. We will question the role of drones in relation to privacy.

How – if at all – can legislation manage the privacy of online users? If people voluntarily post their most intimate details and thoughts on social media sites, what protection is there for them? Legal boundaries are blurred between countries, making privacy invasion online less actionable in international law. And if information which a site visitor thinks is secure can be harvested by illegal – and sometimes legal – means, what can be done about it, especially if the information-thief or snooper is in a country many thousands of miles away? Pippa Middleton, sister of the Duchess of Cambridge, successfully sought an injunction when her iCloud account was hacked in September 2016.[3]

3.2 Internet privacy

We live in an era where people routinely share extremely personal information online or via social media. When Mark Zuckerberg, founder of *Facebook*, discovered that his wife was expecting a baby in August 2015, he chose to announce the news on Facebook. His message was viewed by 33 million people. Gwyneth Paltrow also shared her announcement of her separation from Chris Martin on her website 'Goop' with the headline 'conscious uncoupling'. Olympic diver Tom Daley came out as gay on a YouTube posting in December 2013.

Can the internet be controlled by privacy laws or would this interfere with the right to receive information and amount to internet censorship? This was the point made by former CIA agent Edward Snowden (then 29) in 2013 when he revealed himself to be the whistleblower behind the exposure of secret US National Security Agency (NSA) surveillance programmes. Snowden left the USA in May 2013 after leaking to the media details of extensive internet and phone surveillance by American intelligence. He was granted asylum in Russia and faces espionage charges over his actions. Mr Snowden has always maintained that he acted out of a desire to protect privacy and basic liberties.

See Chapter 6.5

3.2.1 Can we still claim the right to be left alone?

What do we mean by 'internet privacy'? What we really mean is personal data privacy which in turn has raised concerns about large-scale computer and data sharing. Privacy can entail either 'Personally Identifying Information' (PII) or non-PII information such as a site visitor's behaviour on a website. Nowadays we leave a cyber footprint the minute we log on to our computers which means we share personal information with complete strangers every single day via the internet.

---

3 *Middleton v Persons Unknown* [2016] EWHC 2354 (QB).

Though the multinational, publicly traded company Google Inc. assures us in its privacy rules that all personal information is stored 'safely', the issue of internet privacy has been in the news since Google changed its rules allowing information to be shared across all its services, such as, 'Google Maps', 'Google Earth', 'YouTube', 'Books', 'Translate', etc. Twitter, Facebook, Yahoo and Microsoft also provide personal information to their affiliates and their privacy policies require the express permission of their users for their information to be released, which subscribers often provide. Who reads dozens of privacy small print pages before signing up? By using social networking websites the onus is placed on the end-user to decide the privacy settings for different elements of information revealed via each site and how many people really use the Google 'incognito' setting?

This means that ISPs are farming out personal data to third parties which in turn raises the question of invasion of people's privacy rights. With many of these providers and services being situated in the United States our personal data transcends all international borders.

Should we then really worry about releasing some of our personal data on the World Wide Web? Most certainly, since we do not know where all our information is going to end up. Is it not extraordinary some people reveal intrinsically personal information and openly share this with their circle of friends on Facebook which can easily become public knowledge?

The media now regularly seize photos and personal details from social networking accounts in times of distress or crisis. Such was the case when British student Meredith Kercher (21) was murdered in Perugia, Italy on 1 November 2007. Initial pictures showed Meredith in unflattering drunk poses or ghoulish Goth attire, taken directly from her own Facebook page.

Wacks argues that the line between a privacy claim and an action for defamation has become somewhat 'fuzzy' – with the overriding obstacle in defamation being 'truth' as a complete defence, thereby providing a valuable safeguard for the media for freedom of expression.[4] But Professor Wacks rightly points out that 'we cannot have it all', that is, the 'right to be left alone' on one hand whilst openly disclosing all our personal likes, dislikes and secrets on social networking sites such as Twitter.[5] There was a time when people's lives were transient; they left no trace. Now via the internet we are all leaving constant 'footprints'. The internet, as Wacks concludes, has become both a nuisance as well as a positive means of communication.

Almost daily the media reveals some scandal and plenty of skeletons are coming out of the cupboard enhanced by blog posts, unregulated web chats and newspaper online coverage. One example is the demise of Lord John Buttifant Sewel, when the *Sun on Sunday* revealed in its headlines of 26 July 2015 that the 69-year-old life peer was displaying some rather improper 'off duty habits'. He had been secretly filmed and photographed in his Dolphin Square flat apparently snorting cocaine up £5 notes in company with 'ladies of the night'. Some clandestine film footage released by the newspaper online showed him dressed in an orange bra. Additional footage of the alleged incident released by *The Sun* appeared to show Lord Sewel bragging of having sex with a BBC presenter as he revealed her name and the programme she worked on.[6] The former junior Labour Minister and Deputy Vice Principal of Aberdeen University, Lord Sewel was forced to resign from the House of Lords, from his post as Deputy Speaker of the House of Lords and that of chairman of the Lords' 'Privileges and Conduct' committee.[7]

The former French finance minister, Dominique Strauss-Kahn (DSK), was also exposed by the French and international media and social networking 'chats' over allegations of sexual assault on a chambermaid in a New York Hotel in 2011. The 'naked Prince Harry in Las Vegas' photos were

---

4   See: Wacks, R. (2013).
5   Ibid. pp. 12–14.
6   Source: 'Lord Sewel quits: Peer "boasts of having sex with BBC presenter and seeing 13 mistresses", by Kashmira Gander, *The Independent*, 28 July 2015 at: www.independent.co.uk/news/uk/politics/lord-sewel-quits-peer-boasts-of-having-sex-with-bbc-presenter-and-seeing-13-mistresses-10420386.html.
7   Source: 'At least he's got some support! Now disgraced Lord Sewel is pictured wearing an orange BRA as secret footage shows him attacking David Cameron and other leading politicians', by Sam Matthew for the *MailOnline*, 27 July 2015 at: www.dailymail.co.uk/news/article-3175569/At-s-got-support-Lord-Sewel-pictured-wearing-orange-bra-latest-revelations-peer-attacking-David-Cameron-leading-politicians.html.

initially published on US websites. *The Sun* then became the first British newspaper to publish the naked photos on 22 August 2012, with the headline 'Harry grabs the Crown Jewels'.

There is no doubt that the internet has considerably widened public interest in what goes on.

 FOR THOUGHT

Do you think the *Sun on Sunday* newspaper (and online edition) made the right decision to publish the clandestine photos and film footage of Lord Sewel? Would you agree with the *Sun* editor that the subject matter of 'naked Prince Harry' was of genuine public interest? Or were these publications simply titillating 'stuff' to increase sales figures of the tabloid? Discuss, using leading authorities.

3.3 Internet libel

How does the law treat ISPs when it comes to the definition of 'publisher'? English and Welsh legislation is partly covered by the Defamation Act 2013 section 5 ('operators of websites')[8] and partly by the Data Protection Act 1998. Various EU regulations and directives can now be applied as well as criminal legislation and Article 8 'privacy' rights of the European Convention.

3.3.1 When is an internet service provider or operator of website a publisher?

The early internet case of *Godfrey* (2001)[9] gave rise to the unwelcome practice of ISPs simply removing material upon complaint without a great deal of scrutiny, causing a chilling effect on freedom of expression and freedom to receive information. As the common law developed over the next decade courts began to send differing and at times confusing messages as to whether an ISP was a publisher or a mere wall on which various people had chosen to inscribe graffiti.

Godfrey hinged on whether the ISP Demon (located in the UK) could be treated as publisher of the defamatory material posted by an unknown person about the university lecturer, Dr Lawrence Godfrey, on a foreign website (soc.culture.thai) in 1997. Dr Godfrey asked Demon to remove the defamatory posting, but Demon failed to remove the message for 12 days; the material was also copied to its servers around the world, containing newsgroup messages.

Morland J – referring to section 1 of the Defamation Act 1996 – held Demon Internet liable for the defamatory statement hosted on its server. He said that the defendants knew of the defamatory posting but chose not to remove it from their Usenet news servers. In his judgement this placed the ISP in an 'insuperable difficulty' which meant there was no available defence provided by section 1 of the 1996 Act. Dr Godfrey was awarded £15,000 plus legal costs, totalling £200,000, by Demon Internet.

The message in *Godfrey* was clear: the ISP Demon was a publisher not a mere 'conduit' of information. As an argument in court, Demon had referred to US case law on electronic commerce in relation to defamation and pointed out that US law clearly states that an ISP is only 'hosting' information on its servers. But the English court rejected this argument.[10]

See Chapter 7.5

Clearly at that time US legislation did not concur with judgments in the UK. In *Prodigy* (1999)[11] the US court in New York ruled that an ISP *cannot* be held liable for any material posted on its server since it is merely a 'host'. In *Prodigy* an unknown imposter had opened a number of accounts with

---

8 Scotland and Northern Ireland did not sign up to the Defamation Act 2013. See Chapter 7.
9 See: *Godfrey v Demon Internet* [2001] QB 201.
10 For further discussion see: Macmillan, K. (2009), pp. 80–82.
11 See: *Lunney (Alexander G.) & c. v Prodigy Services Company et al.* (1999) 99 NY Int 0165.

the ISP, Prodigy Services Company, by assuming and usurping the (real) name of Alexander Lunney, a teenage boy scout claimant in this appeal. The imposter posted two vulgar messages in Lunney's name on a Prodigy bulletin board and sent a threatening, profane email message in Lunney's name to a third person, with the subject line: 'HOW I'M GONNA' KILL U'. Lunney sued Prodigy (through his father), asserting that he had been stigmatized by being falsely cast as the author of these messages. Regarding the defamatory message in question, the court accepted Prodigy's argument that the ISP had not 'participated in preparing the message, exercised any discretion or control over its communication, or in any way assumed responsibility'. Even if Prodigy had been a publisher (which the court held it was not), it was entitled to qualified privilege in the same way that telephone companies are protected from claims for defamation under the US law.

See Chapter
7.2.3

Questions of multiple publications (or re-publications) then arose in relation to past historical postings on the internet. Where did the 'duty to publish' end? Would the author of an original article, the editor, the publishers, etc. all be liable for re-publication of a defamatory statement? The court affirmed the multiple publication rule in *Loutchanski* (2001),[12] a highly controversial judgment.

A decade later, in a groundbreaking judgment, Sharp J, in *Budu v BBC* (2010),[13] ruled that publishers cannot be held liable for libellous material republished out of context on internet search engines. The case concerned a long-running dispute between the BBC and Ghanaian-born Sam Budu. When putting his own name into the Google search engine, he had found three articles about himself which he claimed as libellous.

The first article, which did not refer to the claimant by name, reported that Cambridgeshire police had been compelled to withdraw a job offer from 'an applicant' when it transpired that he was an illegal immigrant. The second and third article, giving Mr Budu's name, reported in June 2004 that Sam Budu, Ipswich and Suffolk Council's racial equality director, was later rejected as diversity manager after security vetting. Although the two later articles put the claimant's side of the story, Mr Budu alleged that they conveyed the defamatory meaning that he had failed a vetting process and posed a security risk.[14]

The High Court deemed that neither a search engine nor an operator of a website (like the BBC) should face libel claims for republished material accessed only via its web archives. Sharp J ruled that the BBC was not liable for the Google 'snippets'.[15] She also held that the case on publication of the first article must be limited to persons who had also seen the later article, because it was only by searching and finding those that it was reasonable for a reader to have found the first article and understood it to refer to the claimant. Any reader who saw the first article would have also read the authoritative rejection of the allegation that the claimant was an illegal immigrant.[16]

The question whether an ISP is a 'publisher' was raised once again in *Tamiz v Google Inc.* (2012).[17] Google Inc. argued successfully in this case that it was not a publisher for the purposes of the English law of defamation. And even if Google were to be regarded as a publisher of the words complained of by Payam Tamiz, the ISP argued that it would be protected against liability by regulation 19 of the Electronic Commerce (EC Directive) Regulations 2002.[18] Google contended in *Tamiz* that the claimant had not pleaded that a 'real and substantial tort' had been committed (referring to *Jameel (Yousef) v Dow Jones & Co. Inc.* (2005)[19]). Eady J referred to the controversial judgment by HHJ Parkes in *Davison v Habeeb* (2011),[20] where it was said that Google *was* a publisher and was liable post-notification.

---

12 See: *Loutchansky v Times Newspapers Ltd* (Nos 2–5) [2001] EWCA Civ 1805.
13 [2010] EWHC 616 (Sharp J) (QB).
14 Ibid., at paras 18, 23 and 25 (Sharp J).
15 Ibid., at para. 70.
16 Ibid., at para. 44.
17 [2012] EWHC 449 (QB).
18 Implemented in UK law by the provisions of Article 14 of Directive 2000/31/EC of the European Parliament and of the Council dated 8 June 2000 relating to electronic commerce.
19 [2005] QB 946.
20 [2011] EWHC 3031 QB (HHJ Parkes QC).

Tamiz (Payam) v Google Inc., Google UK Ltd [2012] EWHC 449 (QB)

Precedent

❖ An ISP is only a 'host' and is granted immunity under regulation 19 of the Electronic Commerce (EC Directive) Regulations 2002.

❖ An ISP (such as 'Google Inc.'[21]) is not a publisher according to common law principles.

Facts

The claimant in this libel action, Mr Payam Tamiz (T), sued both Google Inc. and Google UK Ltd in relation to eight blog posts which were said to be defamatory of him, bearing the name 'London Muslim' at various times between 28 and 30 April 2011. T had been in the news in 2011, following allegations that his resignation as Conservative Party candidate for local elections in Thanet had come about after he had made inappropriate remarks online.[22]

In June 2011 T sent a letter of claim to Google UK, who passed it on to Google Inc. They asked his permission to contact the author of the blog, and the claimant subsequently complained about five further comments. The comments were eventually removed by the blogger himself in August. A claim was issued shortly afterwards, and T was granted permission to serve the claim form on Google Inc. in California on a without notice application on 22 September.

Catrin Evans, acting for the first defendant (Google Inc.), submitted that the claimant (T) had not pleaded that a 'real and substantial tort' had been committed in 'this jurisdiction' (i.e. the UK) because it could not be proved that a substantial number of readers had downloaded or accessed the words complained of (citing: *Jameel (Yousef) v Dow Jones & Co. Inc.* (2005)[23]). Ms Evans also argued that the content of the words complained of did not reach the necessary 'threshold of seriousness required to establish a cause of action in libel'.[24] Even if Google Inc. were to be regarded as a publisher of the words complained of, Ms Evans argued that Google would be protected against liability by regulation 19 of the Electronic Commerce (EC Directive) Regulations 2002.[25]

Decision

Eady J addressed the question whether Google Inc. was a publisher and found that there was – as yet – no common law decision establishing how web publishers fit into the traditional framework of defamation law. Eady J suggested that the position 'may well be fact sensitive', pointing to the differences between the position in law (referring to: *Godfrey v Demon Internet* (2011);[26] *Bunt v Tilley* (2006);[27] *Metropolitan International Schools Ltd (t/a SkillsTrain and/or Train2Game) v Designtechnica Corpn (t/a Digital Trends)* (2009)[28]).

---

21 Interestingly, Google is now an ISP through Google Fiber, which provides internet access in the USA.
22 *Tamiz* [2012] EWHC 449 at para. 6 (Eady J).
23 [2005] QB 946.
24 [2012] EWHC 449 at paras 11–13.
25 These implement in the law of the UK the provisions of Article 14 of Directive 2000/31/EC relating to electronic commerce.
26 [2001] EWHC QB 201.
27 [2006] EWHC 407 (QB).
28 [2009] EWHC 1765 (QB).

On the question of whether Google Inc. could be liable after notification, the judge referred to the Blogger.com platform which contained more than half a trillion words, with 250,000 new words added every minute. He held that accepting the responsibility to notify the offending bloggers did not necessarily change Google's status.[29]

Finally, the judge turned to the statutory 'hosting' defence, found under regulation 19 of the Electronic Commerce (EC Directive) Regulations 2002 (which had succeeded in *Davison*[30]). The provision protects the provider of an 'information society service' – i.e. the ISP.[31] Google was therefore successful and protected by regulation 22 of the e-Commerce Regulation.

Eady J ruled that Google Inc. should not be regarded as a 'publisher' of the offending words and that the ISP was exempted from liability in accordance with Regulation 19 of the Electronic Commerce Regulations 2002[32] (see also: *L'Oréal SA v eBay International AG* (2012)[33]).

Analysis
Eady J's decision in March 2012 in the *Payam Tamiz* case is an important one. He found against the former Conservative council candidate, about whom some outrageously defamatory falsehoods had been posted on Google's blogger.com platform. The court held that the ISP's role was purely passive, that of a host or 'wall' on which any graffiti could be freely posted. Google Inc. was not held to be a 'publisher' and was not capable of having 'authorized' the defamatory publications.

Google Inc. successfully availed itself of the 'hosting' defence provided by regulation 19 of the Electronic Commerce Regulations 2002 in respect of bloggers and similar postings on its server.

The *Tamiz* judgment sent a message of positive inaction taken by the UK courts towards those individuals who were at that time being defamed online. Eady J made the position of ISPs abundantly clear in that they were purely passive hosts.

For the law in the *Lord McAlpine*[34] case discussion see Chapter 7.5.2.

3.3.2 Misuse of private information on the internet
In deciding whether to grant a privacy claim, the courts will look at the circumstances in which the information 'came into the hands of the publisher' (the ISP). Still, looking at the various authorities this appears to be fraught with difficulties when it comes to persuading the ISP or social networking site to reveal the user or registered member of the particular social media community. After all, users of, say, Facebook or Twitter register with the express understanding that their registration

29 *Tamiz* [2012] EWHC 449 at para. 38 (Eady J).
30 *Davison v Habeeb* [2011] EWHC 3031 (QB).
31 *Tamiz* [2012] EWHC 449 at paras 51–54 (Eady J).
32 Ibid., at para. 61.
33 (2012) (Case C-324/09). Judgment of the Court of Justice, Grand Chamber, 12 July 2011 (CJEU).
34 See: *Lord McAlpine of West Green v Sally Bercow* [2013] EWHC 1342 (QB).

enables other members to publish private information about them. This will then limit the standard of 'reasonable expectation' of privacy under Article 8 ECHR and enhance the right to freedom of expression under Article 10.

Bennett notes that due to the instant and widespread nature of publication on Facebook and other such social networking sites, and the effortless means by which any comment can be published, without any vetting process by ISPs, one might have thought that the courts would be concerned that such a decision would open the floodgates for an uncontrollable number of cases of this nature.[35] Increasing legal challenges have emerged, such as the 'right to be forgotten' challenges against Google.

See below 3.6

The so-called *Facebook* case is an important ruling whereby the claim for misuse of private information and 'online libel' was raised (see: *Applause Store v Raphael* below).[36] In this case a false group profile was created on Facebook, attributed to the claimant. In relation to the misuse of private information, damages were awarded 'for the hurt feelings' and distress caused by the 'misuse of their information'.[37]

❖ KEY CASE | The *Facebook* case: *Applause Store Productions Ltd v Raphael* [2008] EWHC 1781 (QB)

Precedent

❖ If a claimant is a member of a social networking site (e.g. Facebook) the court may *not* grant 'reasonable privacy' to the claimant.

❖ If the claimant is not a member of a social network and/or the disclosure of his personal information was by someone else, he can claim a 'reasonable expectation of privacy' under Article 8 ECHR.

Facts

This case concerns an unfortunate dispute between two former Brighton school friends, the claimants being Mathew Firsht (F), a successful businessman, and his company, Applause Store Productions Ltd ('Applause Store' – X), which provided audiences for popular television programmes such as *Big Brother*, *The X Factor* and *Top Gear*. The defendant, freelance lighting cameraman Grant Raphael (R), had since fallen out with his former school friend F.

On 4 July 2007, F, his twin brother Simon and his brother's girlfriend discovered a (false) profile of F and a group page on F and his company X on Facebook. The profile, named Mathew Firsht, included highly personal information on him, such as F's sexual orientation, his relationship status, his birthday, his political and religious views (neither the profile nor the group was set up by F). The Facebook group was entitled 'Has Mathew Firsht lied to you?' F was shocked and extremely upset: he regarded the material as a gross invasion of his privacy, and he was particularly distressed by the fact that his personal details, including false details as to his sexuality, had been 'laid

---

35 See: Bennett, T. D. C. (2010), pp. 145–149.
36 *Applause Store Productions Ltd v Raphael* (the *Facebook* case) [2008] EWHC 1781 (QB); [2008] Info TLR 318 (QBD).
37 Ibid., at 81.

bare for all to see'.[38] He was worried that the defamatory material had the potential to cause serious damage to his professional reputation and that of his company (X).

Counsel for the claimants (F and X) argued that the claim in misuse of private information (by F alone) under Article 8 ECHR arose from the false profile, while the claim in defamation (brought by both F and X) arose from the group page.

It emerged that the profile was set up on R's computer at the premises where R lived. Though there was no dispute that the material was defamatory, R denied responsibility for setting up the profile and the Facebook group and thereby publishing them to those who visited either Facebook address. On 1 August 2007, his solicitors obtained a 'Norwich Pharmacal' order against Facebook Inc. for disclosure of the registration data provided by the user responsible for creating the false material, including email addresses and the IP addresses of all computers used to access Facebook by the owner of those email addresses. Evidence was adduced of an activity log for R's ISP address, showing that R had accessed Facebook during the day the profile was set up. In his defence, R said that that night he had given a party for 12 people, including four strangers who stayed at his flat the following day when he went out. R contended that it must have been someone else who had accessed his computer and set up the profile of F and X on Facebook.

Decision

The court did not accept Grant Raphael's (R) explanation for the Facebook usage and held the evidence as implausible. Richard Parkes QC, sitting as a Deputy Judge of the High Court (QB) on 24 July 2008, called it 'far-fetched' that a complete stranger, visiting R's flat for the first time, would have used R's computer without permission to create a false profile about a man R knew well and had fallen out with. It was also established that R had searched for F's profile via Google, only to discover that F had no profile, and that R had simply made one up by creating a new profile.

In relation to the claim for damages for defamation the judge noted that the profile was only up for 17 days. Whilst the libel was not at the top end of the scale, the words used in the profile suggested that F owed substantial sums of money which he had avoided paying by repeatedly lying, and was not to be trusted in the financial conduct of his business.

Damages for the libel were awarded to F at £15,000 (including aggravated damages); and for X at £5,000. In relation to the claim for misuse of private information, damages were awarded to compensate F for 'hurt feelings and distress caused', at £2,000.

Analysis

The reason why Mr Firsht's privacy claim under Article 8 succeeded was because he was not a member of Facebook, but his profile and that of his company 'Applause Store' was created for him by R, without his knowledge or consent. The entitlement of a company to recover general damages had been affirmed by the House of Lords in the previous year in *Jameel v Wall Street Journal*,[39] where it was held that a company's good name is a thing of value. In *Applause Store* there was no evidence of actual financial loss and it was held that the information was only 'live' on Facebook for a relatively short time (17 days).

---

38 Ibid., at 69.
39 [2007] 1 AC 359.

The case set a precedent that people have a 'reasonable expectation of privacy' online, particularly where claimants have not disclosed their own private information. A company may stand in a slightly different position, for it has no feelings to hurt. It then follows that considerations of aggravated damages may not apply to company claims. The determination of damages will depend on the information revealed, the motive behind disclosure, the effect on the claimant and the frequency with which the claimant uses the social medium himself (if at all). The court ruled that there had been a breach of privacy via a social networking site, which makes this an important decision, particularly in realizing the importance of Article 8 ECHR in relation to online social media contexts. This is also one of the rare cases where Facebook agreed to identify the author of the material in question by way of a court order.[40]

3.4 Social media: bloggers and tweeters

Social media platforms have changed the media landscape forever. Information can easily be transmitted and received via a large number of platforms, such as Facebook, Twitter, WhatsApp, Snapchat and many ever-emerging new platforms. Legal boundaries are arbitrary with servers mostly hosted abroad such as in the USA or Eastern Europe and Russia.

According to *The Economist*, Facebook was the sixth-most valuable public company in the world in 2016, with a market value of around $325 billion. Facebook claims nearly 1.6 billion monthly users for its social network. Around 1 billion people, nearly a third of all those on the planet with access to the internet, log on every day. Facebook takes up 22 per cent of the internet time Americans spend on mobile devices, compared with 11 per cent on Google search and You-Tube combined, according to the market research firm, Nielsen. YouTube (owned by Google) has about 1 billion unique users per month, hosting blogs written in over 120 languages, equating to over 409 million users viewing more than 15.8 billion pages each month. Google users produce approximately 44 million new posts and 59 million new comments on a monthly basis. Most importantly, users can maintain total anonymity in their blogs or tweets. Twitter states that there were about 500 million tweets per day in 2015, equating to an average of nearly 6,000 tweets per second.[41]

See Chapter 6.7

Is there privacy on Facebook? Most probably not. The company, like Google, has large amounts of data about its users, knows as much about their behaviour online and can target them as effectively with advertising. In addition to all the personal and geographical information, interests, social connections and photos users share, the social network is able to see where else they go online. Anywhere with a 'like' symbol feeds back information, as do sites that allow people to log on with their Facebook credentials.

One thing is clear: online communication is no longer constrained by legal boundaries and the use of the internet has increased dramatically over the past five years. Social media transcends all national boundaries. Coe argues that social media is a 'double-edged sword'. On the one hand it enables individuals to circumvent the traditional mass media, converging audience and producer to create millions of 'publishers'. On the other hand this 'power', if used irresponsibly, can lead to 'catastrophic' consequences for the individual.[42]

In January 2011, Liverpool footballer Ryan Babel became the first professional footballer to be censured for comments made on Twitter after the Football Association (FA) fined the Dutch

40 For further discussion see: Mindell, R. (2012) pp. 52–58.
41 Source: 'How to win friends and influence people', *The Economist*, 9 April 2016, pp. 19–22.
42 See: Coe, P. (2015), pp. 75–78.

international £10,000 for posting a mocked-up picture of referee Howard Webb wearing a Manchester United shirt. Babel was fined £10,000 by the FA. Though Babel apologized for his remarks almost immediately, FA Regulatory Commission Chairman Roger Burden said that the punishment fitted the player's irresponsibility in making derogatory comments in a public setting; he said:

> Social network sites, like Twitter, must be regarded as being in the public domain. All participants need to be aware, in the same way as if making a public statement in other forms of media, that any comments would be transmitted to a wider audience. It is their responsibility to ensure only appropriate comments are used.[43]

Though not strictly a legal decision the Babel incident set the standard for further such actions in the football arena. In December 2014 Liverpool's Mario Balotelli was suspended and fined £25,000 for anti-Semitic and racist posts on Instagram.[44]

3.4.1 Anonymity and fake identities on social networking sites

The anonymity of bloggers or those using fake identities on social networking sites can make life intolerable for those individuals who wish to object to what is written about them or seek redress through the courts because naming the abusive individuals in a defamation action is often impossible. Trying to trace a server (or shared server) or reseller of an internet provider (IP) can be time consuming to near impossible. Determining individual users who may have posted defamatory or harassing material on one of the social media platforms can be equally tricky. Generally there is no way to determine *what* is at an IP address, whether the information is sent by a real person or some program running on a machine, or it could be a number of people all using the same IP address. Though the HTTP protocol *does* provide a mechanism for user authentication, where a username and password are required to gain access to a website or individual pages.

In March 2011, Carmarthenshire political blogger Jacqui Thompson sued the Chief Executive of the local council of Llanwrda, Mark James, for libel (see: *Thompson (Jacqueline) v James (Mark) and Carmarthenshire County Council* (2013)[45]). Ms Thompson had posted a series of defamatory internet posts (blogs), falsely accusing Carmarthenshire Council officers of corruption. She had also secretly filmed council hearings in April 2011 and was subsequently arrested. Mr James counter-sued and Ms Thompson lost. In March 2013, after a six-day trial without a jury, the High Court ordered Ms Thompson to pay the Chief Executive £25,000 in damages. Tugendhat J concluded that she had acted irresponsibly and described her blog as an 'unlawful campaign of harassment, defamation and intimidation'. Tugendhat J concluded:

> The strongest point in favour of Mrs Thompson is the fact that the publications on which Mr James has succeeded were to a small number of readers of her blog.[46]

So, who is responsible for defamatory and harassing postings on the internet? The question then remains whether ISPs are classified as 'mere conduits' or access providers rather than 'publishers'. Can ISPs abdicate their responsibility as publisher when defamatory or harassing material is published on its website claiming that ISPs are just intermediaries?

---

43 Source: 'Ryan Babel fined £10,000 over Twitter criticism of Howard Webb', by Rory Smith, *The Daily Telegraph*, 17 January 2011 at: www.telegraph.co.uk/sport/football/teams/liverpool/8264741/Ryan-Babel-fined-10000-over-Twitter-criticism-of-Howard-Webb.html.
44 See: *The Football Association v Mario Balotelli* (unreported) 18 December 2014.
45 [2013] EWHC 515 (QB) 15 March 2013.
46 Ibid., at para. 420 (Tugendhat J).

FOR THOUGHT

Who should be made responsible for libellous or harassing postings on the internet? Compare leading authorities in the UK with US law and discuss any laws necessary to prevent ISPs and operators of websites from restricting content or prioritizing one type of traffic over another.

3.4.2 Internet trolls

What is 'trolling'? It is an online phenomenon which sees users of social media, forums and micro-blogging sites post offensive, upsetting and inflammatory comments where they can be seen publicly. The term can also be applied to those who post opinions and comments, which they may not actually believe, to online discussions in order to throw the debate into disarray. Trolls have become an increasing threat to a person's reputation and can destroy businesses. A 'troll' is a person who sows discord on the internet by starting arguments or upsetting people by posting inflammatory messages. This is usually done under a false identity or pseudonym.

So, is trolling a criminal offence? Yes and no. It is a criminal offence if a profile is created under the name of the victim with fake information uploaded which, if believed, could damage their reputation and humiliate them. It then falls under the definition of 'hate crime' under Crown Prosecution Service (CPS) guidelines, issued in March 2016. Social media trolls who set up fake profiles under their victims' names in order to harass them will face criminal charges.

In October 2014 Brenda Leyland was accused of 'trolling' the parents of Madeleine McCann, Kate and Gerry McCann, after she was identified by Sky News as being one of a number of people posting hate messages aimed at the couple online. Using the Twitter ID @sweepyface, Leyland had tweeted or retweeted 2,210 posts, of which 424 mentioned the McCanns between November 2013 and September 2014.

Sky News crime reporter Martin Brunt had tracked down the 63-year-old to her home in Burton Overy, Leicestershire, and confronted her about her online activities and exposed Mrs Leyland as one of the internet trolls responsible for the hate messages directed at the McCanns. On 4 October 2014, Brenda Leyland was found dead in her Marriott Hotel room in Enderby, Leicester. An inquest found subsequently that she had committed suicide.[47] According to a neighbour who spoke to the *Leicester Mercury*, Mrs Leyland 'fled the village' after the encounter with Mr Brunt. News of the death sparked a storm of angry comments on Twitter many of which attacked Sky News and Martin Brunt for exposing Mrs Leyland. One user called @Oloni wrote: 'Omg so that #sweepyface woman killed herself?! Did Sky News go to [sic] far by ambushing her??' Meanwhile @madmama68 tweeted: 'Having an opinion does NOT make someone a troll and anyone who thinks it does has obvs never come across one !! #mccanns #sweepyface'.[48] Did Brenda Leyland's tweets constitute a criminal offence?

There have been systemic failures of UK police forces to tackle the issue of trolling. A report published by the London Mayor's Office for Policing and Crimes (MOPAC) in 2015 – #ReportHate: Combating Online Hatred – stated that online hate crime was on the rise and draining police force resources. London Assembly Member, Andrew Boff, author of the report, said:

Victims are left feeling isolated by online hate attacks and often feel like there is nobody to turn to.[49]

---

47 Source: 'Brenda Leyland inquest: McCann 'Twitter troll' overdosed on helium after Sky News confrontation', by Yasmin Duffin, *Leicester Mercury*, 20 March 2015.
48 Source: 'McCann "Twitter troll" found dead in hotel', BBC News Online, 6 October 2014.
49 See: Andrew Boff, GLA Conservatives (2015) '#ReportHate: Combating Online Hatred'. Report at: http://glaconservatives.co.uk/wp-content/uploads/2015/06/online-hate-crime.pdf.

Clearly internet users are bound by existing criminal legislation against inciting hatred on the basis of race, religion, transgender or sexual orientation, or disability. But the lack of a coherent, standalone, legislation addressing online hate crime inevitably makes the process of investigating which legislation exactly has been broken harder for the authorities to pursue and prosecute. A prosecution can be avoided if the communication 'was not intended for a wide audience, nor was the obvious consequence of sending the communication' or did not go beyond 'what could conceivably be tolerable or acceptable in an open and diverse society which upholds and respects freedom of expression'.

Improper use of a public electronic communications network has long been an offence contrary to section 127 of the Communications Act 2003. This piece of legislation creates an offence of 'sending', or 'causing to be sent, by means of a public electronic communications network, a message or other matter that is grossly offensive or of an indecent, obscene or menacing character'. In 2011 the CPS brought more than 2,000 prosecutions under section 127.

In September 2012, the then Director of Public Prosecutions (DPP), Keir Starmer QC,[50] clarified the law in respect of the (mis)use of 'public electronic communications networks' (such as Twitter, Facebook, etc.) where communications were said to be 'grossly offensive'. He said that the Communications Act 2003 was sufficient to deal with situations of harassment and trolls via the internet. DPP Starmer noted that the context in which this interactive social media dialogue takes place is quite different to the context in which other communications take place, whereby access to social media is ubiquitous and instantaneous. Starmer noted that banter, jokes and offensive comment were commonplace and often spontaneous. But that such communications intended for a few could potentially reach millions.

Communications which constitute 'credible threats' of violence to the person or damage to property are now regularly prosecuted under section 2A(3) of the Protection from Harassment Act 1997, often falling under the label of 'stalking'. Threats must 'specifically target an individual or individuals'. Section 7(3) of 1997 'stalking' Act makes clear that a 'course of conduct' must involve conduct on at least two occasions. Communications via social networking sites or mobile phones (i.e. text messages) that are considered grossly offensive, indecent or obscene are treated particularly seriously by the prosecution authorities and tend to attract a custodial sentence (under the public interest test). Credible threats to kill are prosecuted under section 16 Offences Against the Person Act 1861.

The CPS social media guidelines were updated to reflect relatively new platforms, such as Snapchat and WhatsApp, including 'revenge porn', aimed at prosecuting those who post explicit images of former partners.[51] The CPS is advising its prosecutors to apply the following charging standards:

- **Category 1**: when online activity results in a credible threat to an individual;
- **Category 2**: when someone is specifically targeted for harassment, stalking, revenge porn or coercive behaviour to former partners or family members;
- **Category 3**: cases resulting in breaches of a court order.

Context and circumstances are highly relevant in these cases and the accused may always raise an Article 10 ECHR defence, relying on the precedent set in *Handyside v UK* (1976),[52] where the court

---

50 Sir Keir Starmer, KCB, QC: Foreword to this edition.
51 See: ss 32–35 Criminal Justice and Courts Act 2015 ('Offences involving intent to cause distress etc.').
52 1 EHRR 737 (ECtHR). A prosecution was brought against the publisher based on the Obscene Publications Act 1959 (as amended by the Obscene Publications Act 1964).

held that 'freedom of expression' also includes the right to say things or express opinions 'that offend, shock or disturb the state or any sector of the population'.

There have been a number of high-profile prosecutions of 'trolls', including single mother from Brighton, Nicola Brookes (45), suffering from Crohn's disease. Brookes had received vicious and depraved abuse on Facebook after she had posted a comment supporting former X Factor contestant Frankie Cocozza when he left the show in 2011. What became known as the RIP (i.e. Rest in Peace) Brookes troll case did not provide adequate justice for Ms Brookes: some 20 months after the abusive trolls had started Sussex Police force was unable to track down Ms Brookes' tormentors. The police had argued that there was no adequate law to protect her. In fact Lee Rimmel (32) of Bourneville, Birmingham, her anonymous tormentor, turned out to be a police constable, serving with West Midlands Constabulary. He had set up a fake Facebook profile in her name using her picture to post explicit comments (i.e. trolls). PC Rimmell learnt in July 2013 that he would not face any criminal charges from the police, having been arrested on suspicion of misuse of a computer following the investigation into online harassment of Nicola Brookes.[53] Ms Brookes subsequently pursued a private action in defamation against her aggressor and the London High Court granted her an injunction in the form of a Norwich Pharmacal order, requesting the US-based Facebook Inc. to reveal the IP address of the troll.

Peter Nunn (33) had sent abusive messages in the form of trolls via Twitter to Labour MP Stella Creasy. He was prosecuted and given an 18 months' prison sentence. His vile messages were sent after Ms Creasy had shown public support for feminist Caroline Criado-Perez for her successful campaign to feature Jane Austen on the new £10 note. Nunn's trolls had retweeted messages threatening to rape the Walthamstow MP and branding her a witch.

In January 2014 Isabella Sorley (23), from Newcastle-upon-Tyne, received a 12-week and her co-defendant John Nimmo (25), from South Shields, Tyne and Wear, an eight-week prison sentence at Westminster Magistrates' Court for trolling Ms Criado-Perez. Sorley's Twitter feeds had read: 'Fuck off and die . . . you should have jumped in front of horses, go die; I will find you and you don't want to know what I will do when I do . . . kill yourself before I do; rape is the last of your worries. I've just got out of prison and would happily do more time to see you berried [sic]; seriously go kill yourself! I will get less time for that; rape?! I'd do a lot worse things than rape you.' Nimmo had used five different Twitter accounts, saying: 'Ya not that gd looking to rape u be fine; I will find you; come to geordieland [Newcastle] bitch; just think it could be somebody that knows you personally; the police will do nothing; rape her nice ass; could I help with that lol; the things I cud do to u; dumb blond bitch.' Sentencing judge Howard Riddle J referred to the trolls as 'life threatening' and 'extreme'.

In July 2013, Reece Elliott (24) was given a two-year prison sentence at Newcastle Crown Court for posting internet threats on Facebook to kill 200 US children. Elliott had left abusive comments on tribute pages set up for two teenagers who died in car accidents in Warren County, Tennessee, in February 2013. A Deputy Sheriff from Tennessee Police Department began investigating, along with the FBI and Homeland Security, asking Facebook to disclose Elliott's identity, tracing him to South Shields, South Tyneside. Elliott admitted one count of making threats to kill and eight Communications Act 2003 offences.

In August 2013, internet troll Oliver Rawlings (20) was made to apologize to academic classicist Professor Mary Beard, after sending hundreds of abusive messages to her. Nottingham University student Rawlings had used his Twitter account to call the Cambridge University professor a 'filthy old slut', making highly offensive sexual comments about her online. But Professor Beard retweeted the remarks to all her followers, saying she would not be 'terrorized' by online abuse. It was by this method that Rawlings was 'outed' and Professor Beard could therefore discover the troll's identity.[54]

53 Source: 'No charges against PC over Facebook trolling of Brighton woman Nicola Brookes', by Anna Roberts, The Brighton Argus, 21 July 2013: www.theargus.co.uk/news/10545030.No_charges_against_PC_over_Facebook_trolling_of_Brighton_woman_Nicola_Brookes.
54 Source: 'Internet troll who abused Mary Beard apologises after threat to tell his mother', by Sam Marsden, Daily Telegraphy, 29 July 2013.

The term 'troll' or 'trolling has now become a catch-all term for everything from minor disagreements through to annoying incivility through to criminal behaviour such as death threats. Brenda Leyland was accused of trolling the McCanns, but questions were subsequently raised over whether her Twitter posts really fell within the 'criminal offence' bracket as they were not sent directly to the McCanns, who were – at that time – not on Twitter.

There is a clear anomaly in the law and the way in which internet abuse is treated and investigated by the police depending on whether the victim is in the public eye or an ordinary member of the public. The Crown Prosecution Service (CPS) guidelines in relation to prosecutions for communications sent by social media now distinguish between different levels of communication, from threats of violence to internet stalking or harassment cases to those which do not fall into any of the above categories but may be grossly offensive or indecent. Even if the identity of the internet troll is being disclosed by a *Norwich Pharmacal* order by, say, Twitter or Facebook, it remains difficult for any 'normal' person to pursue an action in privacy or defamation against the 'persons unknown'.

What are leading internet companies doing about trolls? Both Facebook and Twitter have rules on what can and cannot be posted on their sites and will take down videos that violate them. Facebook, for example, prohibits the use of its network for the commission or celebration of criminal activities. In the Virginia news crew-shooting incident in August 2015, for example, Twitter took down the gunman's account within ten minutes of its being posted. The trouble with most PC or tablet settings is that imbedded video footage plays automatically as soon as people access a news site. The gruesome footage in the Virginia item was that gunman Vester Flanagan (alias 'Bryce Williams') had filmed his shooting of WDBJ reporter Alison Parker and cameraman Adam Ward at close range and had uploaded the video footage on his own Facebook page. All videos about the shooting were removed by YouTube and Facebook.

 FOR THOUGHT

You are the legal adviser for a public broadcasting service. The newsroom has been sent film footage by a news crew based in Africa of a massacre in Kenya. The live footage shows a violent death, bombing and gruesome graphic imagery of many dead bodies in the foreground. The video editor asks your advice whether he should filter and edit out some of these images? The ten o'clock news editor wants to show the full video coverage. What would your advice be before the news goes out that night on national TV?

3.4.3 Revenge porn

There has been an explosion in revenge porn(ography) over the past few years, largely because of the impact of new technology. Thousands of people have had sexually explicit photos and videos of themselves published on the internet without their consent but there were only a few convictions until the law changed in 2015.

In November 2014 Luke King (21), of Aspley, Nottingham, was given a 12-week sentence by Southern Derbyshire magistrates after pleading guilty to 'harassment without violence' under the Protection from Harassment Act 1997. He had published intimate images of a woman on the WhatsApp messaging service in August after making a series of threats to her. King is believed to be the first person in the UK to be imprisoned for posting revenge porn online.

Revenge porn is the sharing of private, sexual materials, either photos or videos, of another person without their consent and with the purpose of causing embarrassment or distress. The images are sometimes accompanied by personal information about the subject, including their full name, address and links to their social media profiles. Revenge porn usually follows the breakdown of an intimate relationship.

Until recently, revenge porn was prosecuted using a range of existing laws – under section 127 Communications Act 2003 or the Malicious Communications Act 1988, where a course of conduct is sexually explicit and shared online without the consent of the pictured individual. Repeat behaviour of this kind (on at least two occasions) could also amount to an offence of harassment under section 2A(3) Protection from Harassment Act 1997.

See above
3.4.1

At the same time the conduct in question has to form a sequence of events and there have to be two incidents (see: Lau v DPP (2000),[55] R v Hills (2001)[56]). Prosecutors would then consider that a course of conduct has to include a range of unwanted behaviours towards the victim ('complainant') and a communication sent via social media has to be one manifestation of this. Where an individual receives unwanted communications from another person via social media in addition to other unwanted behaviour, all the behaviour is then considered together ('in totality') by the prosecutor when determining whether or not a course of conduct was made out.

This complex legislation was amalgamated in one new single offence introduced under the Criminal Justice and Courts Act 2015 providing the police and the CPS with new powers to prosecute. Section 33 created the offence of disclosing private sexual photographs and films with intent to cause distress.[57]

> (1)   It is an offence for a person to disclose a private sexual photograph or film if the disclosure is made –
>
>> (a)   without the consent of an individual who appears in the photograph or film, and
>> (b)   with the intention of causing that individual distress.

Subsection (1) provides that this offence is committed if the disclosure was made without the consent of an individual ('the victim') who appears in the photograph or film, and with the intention of causing that victim distress.

Subsection (1) is subject to subsection (2) which provides that the offence is not committed if the photograph or film was only disclosed to the victim.

Subsections (3), (4) and (5) set out the defences which apply to the offence. Where the defendant provides sufficient evidence to raise an issue in respect to the matters set out in subsections (4) and (5) it will be for the prosecution to disprove those matters beyond all reasonable doubt in order to secure a conviction.

Schedule 8 of the Criminal Justice and Courts Act 2015 ('Disclosing private sexual photographs or films: providers of information society services') addresses the position of 'providers of information society services' (operators of websites and service providers) in respect of the new offence under section 33. Paragraph 1 of Schedule 8 extends liability to a service provider established in England and Wales (E & W) in respect of a photograph or film which is disclosed in a European Economic Area (EEA) state other than the UK. Sub-paragraph (2) of paragraph 1 makes clear that section 33 applies to an E&W service provider who discloses a photograph or film in the course of providing information society services in an EEA state that is not the UK.

Paragraph 3 of the Schedule sets out exceptions for mere 'conduits' and sub-paragraphs (1) to (3) of paragraph 3 set out when an ISP is not capable of being guilty of an offence under section 33. The service provider is not capable of being guilty of an offence if it does not initiate the transmission, select the recipient of the transmission or select or modify the information contained in the

---

55 Lau v DPP [2000] All ER (D) 224 (QBD) 22 February 2000 (Schiemann, Silber JJ) (unreported).
56 R v Hills [2001] 1 FCR 569 (Crim Div) 4 December 2000 (Otton LJ, Hidden J and Sir Richard Tucker).
57 Section 33 of the 2015 Act 'Disclosing private sexual photographs and films with intent to cause distress'.

transmission (i.e. is a mere 'host'). The website operator or service provider is guilty of the offence under section 33 of the 2015 Act if it stores the information for longer than is reasonably necessary for the transmission.[58]

The offence applies both online and offline (including caching) and to images which are shared electronically or in a more traditional way so includes the uploading of images on the internet, sharing by text and email, or showing someone a physical or electronic image.

The new offence criminalizes the sharing of private, sexual photographs or films, where what is shown would not usually be seen in public. Sexual material not only covers images that show the genitals but also anything that a reasonable person would consider to be sexual, so this could be a picture of someone who is engaged in sexual behaviour or posing in a sexually provocative way. This very specific either-way offence attracts a prison sentence of up to two years (on indictment) or on summary conviction, a maximum 6 months' imprisonment or a fine.[59]

3.5 Obscenity, extreme pornography and internet censorship

What are the laws in the UK which cover at least some illegal activity on the internet? In addition to the Obscene Publications Acts 1959, section 63 of the Criminal Justice and Immigration Act 2008 created the offence of possessing extreme pornographic images, aimed mainly at internet users.

Section 63 ('Possession of extreme pornographic images') makes it an offence to possess a limited range of extreme pornographic material. Section 71 of the Act amends the Obscene Publications Act 1959 by increasing the maximum penalty for offences under that Act from three years' imprisonment to five years' imprisonment. Section 63(10) of the Act defines such acts as 'life-threatening acts' or those which would cause serious injury, such as depictions of necrophilia and bestiality.[60]

See Chapter 6.10

Section 63 material goes far beyond what is classified for mainstream cinema by the British Board of Film Classification (BBFC) and beyond the material classified by the BBFC for sale only in licensed sex shops (classified as R18). Section 64(3) of the 2008 Act exempts films that have received a classification from the BBFC, who will have already made a determination that the film is not obscene under the Obscene Publications legislation.[61]

3.5.1 What is 'extreme pornography'?

What is different between the two statutory provisions, namely, section 1 of the Obscene Publications Act 1959 and the new provision under section 63 of the Criminal Justice and Immigration Act 2008? Section 63 of the 2008 Act relates to mere *possession* rather than publication. This means that the offence of possessing extreme pornographic images impacts on private life (Article 8 ECHR) and freedom of expression (Article 10 ECHR).

---

58 Sub-paragraph (4) of para. 3 of Sch. 8. Paragraph 4 of the Schedule sets out exceptions for caching. Sub-paragraph (1) of para. 4 sets out that paragraph 4 applies where an information society service consists of the transmission in a communication network of information provided by a recipient of the service. Sub-paragraphs (2) to (4) of para. 4 set out the circumstances in which a service provider is not capable of being guilty of an offence under s 33 in respect of the automatic, intermediate and temporary storing of information. The circumstances are where: the storage of information is solely for the purpose of making more efficient the onward transmission of information to other recipients of the service at their request; and the service provider does not modify the information, complies with any conditions attached to having access to the information and expeditiously removes the information or disables access to it.

59 Section 33(9) Criminal Justice and Courts Act 2015.

60 Under s 63(10) Criminal Justice and Immigration Act 2008, proceedings must be commenced by the Director of Public Prosecutions (England and Wales). The maximum penalty on conviction on indictment is three years' imprisonment for possession of extreme pornographic images or six months if offences are deemed of a summary nature (s 67 Criminal Justice and Immigration Act 2008).

61 For further discussion see: Munro, V. (2006).

Section 63 defines such material as 'graphic', 'sexually explicit' and *inter alia* 'grossly offensive'. The section is clearly aimed at material on the internet which tends to contain serious violence towards women and men; it generally depicts activities which are illegal in themselves and in which the participants may in some cases have been the victims of criminal offences. The 2008 Act defines an 'extreme' image as one which is grossly offensive, disgusting or otherwise of an obscene character, and portrays the activity in an *explicit and realistic way*.[62]

There are three elements to a section 63(7) offence;[63] an image must come within the terms of *all three elements* before it will fall foul of the offence. Those elements are:

1.   that the image is pornographic;
2.   that the image is grossly offensive, disgusting, or otherwise of an obscene character; and
3.   that the image portrays in an explicit and realistic way, one of the following:

   a.   an act which threatens a person's life; this could include depictions of hanging, suffoca-tion, or sexual assault involving a threat with a weapon;
   b.   an act which results in or is likely to result in serious injury to a person's anus, breast or genitals; this could include the insertion of sharp objects or the mutilation of breasts or genitals;
   c.   an act involving sexual interference with a human corpse; or
   d.   a person performing an act of intercourse or oral sex with an animal, and a reason-able person looking at the image would think that the animals and people portrayed were real.[64]

Section 63 of the Criminal Justice and Immigration Act 2008 does not replace the existing offence contained in the Obscene Publications Act 1959 of *publishing* or having in one's posses-sion for publication an obscene article – although one of its primary purposes is to identify the type of obscene image that might cause the greatest harm and which thus should be subject to prosecution policies. But the principle of moral corruption inherent in the 1959 Act has been retained in section 63 of the 2008 Act. Rowbottom argues that the mainstream entertainment industry, working within current obscenity laws (i.e. the 1959 Act) will not be affected by the section 63 offence.[65]

3.5.2 How is a section 63 offence prosecuted?

What then are the practicalities of prosecuting a section 63 offence? Since the legislation is not articulated clearly and convincingly and contains elements of the Obscene Publications Act 1959, the prosecution needs to evidence a clear link between *possession* and *harm*. The key to accurately assessing what amounts a section 63 offence is to apply all *three elements* (see above) to any example of (online) material under consideration. To focus on just one element in isolation inevitably leads to false conclusions about what is caught. For possession of an 'extreme pornographic' image to be proved, it is necessary to establish some knowledge of its existence (see: *Atkins v DPP; Goodland v DPP* (2000)[66] – see below).

The words 'grossly offensive' and 'disgusting' are not alternatives to 'obscene character' but are examples of it. They are drawn from the ordinary dictionary definition of 'obscene' and reflect different aspects of that concept. They are intended to convey a non-technical definition of that

---

62 Section 63(6) Criminal Justice and Immigration Act 2008.
63 Section 63(2) to (8).
64 See also: Ministry of Justice (2009c).
65 See: Rowbottom, J. (2006), pp. 97–109.
66 [2000] 2 Cr App R 248.

concept. It is a definition which is distinct from the technical definition contained in the Obscene Publications Act 1959, that definition being specifically geared to the concept of publication.

This element of the offence must be read in conjunction with the other two elements. The test as to whether an image comes within the terms of the offence is not simply whether it is grossly offensive, disgusting or otherwise of an obscene character; rather it is a test of whether all elements of the offence are met. It is all three elements working together which should ensure that the only images which are caught are those which would also fall foul of the Obscene Publications Act 1959.

The image then has to be both pornographic and constitute an *extreme* image.[67] An extreme act is one which threatens a person's life, which results or is likely to result in serious injury to a person's anus, breasts or genitals, which involves sexual interference with a human corpse, or which involves a person performing intercourse or oral sex with an animal. But 'life-threatening' is not defined in the 2008 Act.[68]

'Serious injury' is also not defined in the act and this will be a question of fact for the magistrates or jury. The intention is that 'serious injury' should be given its ordinary English meaning. The reference to 'serious injury' was not intended to expressly link into the case law with respect to 'grievous bodily harm' under sections 18 and 20 of the Offences Against the Person Act 1861, which has been interpreted as being capable of including psychological harm. Taking an example which was raised during parliamentary debates on the Criminal Justice and Immigration Bill, the anal sex scene in *Last Tango in Paris*, even if it were to be considered pornographic and of an obscene nature, would not be caught by the offence, because it is not explicit and does not portray an act resulting or likely to result in serious injury to a person's anus.

Only these specific acts will be caught, and only in conjunction with the other two elements of the offence. It will therefore take its ordinary English meaning and will be a question of fact for the magistrates or jury. The image is then of such nature that it must be *reasonably assumed* to have been produced solely or principally for the purpose of sexual arousal. This provision then employs the objective test in the same way as the Obscene Publications Act 1959 – to determine the purpose of the image. This then means that the actual intention of the producer of the image is not really relevant unless that intention points to the presumed intention. A further requirement in respect of an extreme act is that a reasonable person looking at the image would think that the people and animals portrayed were real. The practical effect of that requirement is that only photographs and films, and images which are indistinguishable from photographs and films, will be caught by the offence.

3.5.3 What constitutes 'possession' and 'making' of indecent images of children on the internet?

Increased access to the internet has greatly exacerbated the problem in this area by possessing and making pornographic images of children more easily accessible, and increasing the likelihood of such material being found accidently by others who may subsequently become corrupted by it. This additional risk adds to the culpability of offenders who distribute material of this kind, especially if they post it on publicly accessible areas of the internet. Merely locating an image on the internet will generally be less serious than downloading or 'making' it. Downloading will generally be less serious than taking an original film or photograph of indecent posing or activity involving children.

---

67 Section 63(2) Criminal Justice and Immigration Act 2008.
68 Section 63(3).

The law regarding *possession* of indecent images of children is covered by the following legislation:

●   possession – section 160 Criminal Justice Act 1988 (CJA).

The law regarding 'making' or 'taking' of indecent images of children is covered by:

●   taking, distributing, publishing or possession with a view to distribute or show – section 1 of the Protection of Children Act 1978 (PCA).

The prosecution has to prove 'possession' of an indecent image of a child under section 160 CJA 1988 or of 'extreme pornography' under section 69 Criminal Justice and Immigration Act 2008 which, in turn, extended the remit of the indecent photographs legislation by amending the meaning of 'photograph' within section 7(4)(a) PCA 1978 to include 'derivatives of photographs', such as data (or tracings) stored on a computer disk or by other electronic means, capable of conversion.

Sentencing such offences is a difficult exercise since the public interest in punishing people, who view and download this kind of material, is high. Equally it is important that people who commit such offences are dealt with in a way which is likely to reduce, rather than leave untreated, their need for this kind of imagery.

This complex collection of legislation was put to the test in *Atkins* and *Goodland*.[69] These conjoined cases were significant since the issue was that of 'possession' and 'making' indecent images (of children). The CA held that images stored without the defendant's, Dr Antony Rowan Atkins', knowledge by browser software in a hidden cache, of which he was also unaware, did not amount to knowledge of possession. The situation was akin to a person having a holdall in which, unknown to him, was a gun. Knowledge of the bag was enough, but ignorance of the bag itself made it no crime. Though both cases concerned internet child pornography prosecutions (pseudo-photographs of child images) the ruling can be applied to the section 63 offence of the 2008 Act (see also: *R v Bowden* (1999)[70]). Atkins was convicted at the Bristol Magistrates' Court on 27 May 1999 of ten offences of having in his possession indecent photographs of children contrary to section 160(1) CJA 1988.

Dr Atkins had held a lectureship in the Department of English at Bristol University since October 1997. He had available to him there both a Viglen computer set up in his office and also a departmental computer mostly used by others in the department's main office. On 16 October 1997 another member of the department logged into the departmental computer and was immediately concerned by the menu of internet addresses recently called up. The IT department checked the computer's cache files and found there pictures of naked young girls in crude postures with the PC's history pointing to Dr Atkins. Similar pictures were found in the Viglen cache. The court found that Dr Atkins had deliberately chosen to store the material on the hard drives of the computers, which amounted to 'possession'.

Dr Atkins raised the defence under section 160(2) CJA 1988, namely that he had a legitimate reason for having the photographs in his possession, for the purpose of 'legitimate academic research'. Dr Atkins appealed against his conviction on the ten possession counts; the prosecutor appealed against Dr Atkins's acquittal on 21 of the 'making' counts.

---

69 *Atkins v DPP; Goodlands v DPP* [2000] 2 Cr App R 248 (CA).
70 [1999] EWCA Crim 2270.

In addressing the issue of 'making' contrary to section 1(1)(a) of the Protection of Children Act 1978, Simon Brown LJ found that Dr Atkins had made a directory (named 'J') for the specific purpose of storing the material, thereby agreeing with the prosecution that this would 'call for a conviction'. For possession of an indecent image (of a child) to be proved, it is necessary to establish some knowledge of its existence.

It was by sheer coincidence that both cases of *Atkins* and *Goodland* appeared before the Bristol District Judge. Mr Peter John Goodland was also convicted at Bristol Magistrates' Court (on 21 April 1999) on one count of having in his possession an indecent pseudo-photograph of a ten-year-old girl. The cross-appeal by the Director of Public Prosecutions was allowed, and Mr Goodland was duly convicted. Since the 'sellotaped' copied images of the little girl were so 'pitifully crude' – according to Blofeld J's summing-up in the Court of Appeal – Mr Goodland was sentenced to a two-year conditional discharge with an order to pay £50 costs. He was, however, placed on the Sex Offenders Register (Sex Offenders Act 1997) for a period of five years.

In child pornography cases, the prosecution has to prove that the image was derived (either in whole or in part) from a photograph or pseudo-photograph. Some mobile telephones have effects built into them so that when they take a photograph it produces a tracing rather than a full photograph. If the phone is seized with the image it produced, it can then legitimately be said to be a photograph (because it was taken on a camera) and charged as a section 1 PCA (or section 160 CJA 1988) offence. If the image was sent to someone else or printed out, it would be technically difficult to prove that this was a photograph. In R (on behalf of O'Shea) v Coventry Magistrates' Court (2004),[71] the Divisional Court accepted that it was possible to incite another to distribute indecent images of children even where the 'purchase' of images was a fully automated process.

Pseudo-photographs are generally treated less seriously than real photographs and sentences are generally lower than those involving actual photographs of children under 16. Sentencing for possession of indecent photographs is higher where the subject of the indecent photograph(s) is a child under 13. Registration on the Sex Offenders Register[72] is usually attached to a conviction for this offence dependent upon the age of the subject portrayed in the indecent photograph(s) and the sentence imposed. Courts generally make an ancillary order disqualifying an offender (adult or juvenile) from working with children regardless of the sentence imposed.[73]

In R v McGreen (2010)[74] the defendant pleaded guilty to making indecent photographs of children and possession of extreme pornography. There were videos at levels 1 and 4 and images at level 5. The judge sentenced him to imprisonment accepting his remorse as genuine. R v Rollason (2010)[75] concerned 58 images of children spanning levels 1–4 and an early guilty plea meant a non-custodial sentence, i.e. a two-year community order with supervision. For making images of his stepdaughter as well as possessing a large amount of other images the defendant received a three-year custodial sentence in R v AM (2010).[76]

3.5.4 Defences in relation to possession of indecent images of children and extreme pornography

There are three general defences set out in section 65 of the Criminal Justice and Immigration Act 2008. These are the same as for the possession of indecent images of children under section 160 (2) of the Criminal Justice Act 1988.[77] These are:

71 [2004] EWHC Admin 905.
72 Notification under ss 83 to 96 Sexual Offences Act 2003.
73 Sexual Offences Prevention Order under s 104 Sexual Offences Act 2003.
74 [2010] EWCA Crim 2776 – D 58.
75 [2010] EWCA Crim 2776.
76 [2010] EWCA Crim 1516.
77 Section 160 CJA 1988 covers the offence of possession of an indecent photograph of a child. There are four defences to this offence: three are listed in s 160(2) CJA 1988, Archbold 31–115, and one is listed in s 160A.

- that the person had a legitimate reason for being in possession of the image.

This will cover those who can demonstrate that they have a reason for possessing the image/s. This would include, for example, the police and the prosecuting authorities, those involved in the classification of films (such as the British Board of Film Classification – BBFC[78]), those dealing with complaints from the public about content in the mobile and internet industries and those creating security software to block such images.

- That the person was in possession of an extreme image but had not looked at it and therefore neither knew, nor had reason to suspect that it was an extreme pornographic image.

This will cover those who are in possession of offending images but are unaware of the nature of the images – for example, where a person is sent an electronic copy of an image which he saves without looking at it and which gave rise to no suspicion that it might be extreme pornography.

- That the person had been sent the image without having asked for it, on their own behalf or through someone else, and, having looked at it had not kept it for an unreasonable length of time.[79]

This will cover those who are sent unsolicited material by any means and who act quickly to delete it or otherwise get rid of it.

What constitutes an 'unreasonable amount of time' spent looking at the downloaded images depends on all the circumstances of the case. It is a defence to prove that that the person charged with a section 63 offence had a legitimate reason for being in possession of such an 'extreme' image, had not seen the image concerned and did not know, nor had any cause to suspect, it to be an 'extreme pornographic' image; or that that person was sent the image without any prior request, and did not keep it for an unreasonable time.

What about deleting the images on one's computer? Case law suggests that deleting images held on a computer is sufficient to get rid of them, i.e. this would get rid of the 'possession' element of the offence. An exception would be where a person is shown to have intended to remain in control of an image even though he has deleted it – that will entail him having the capacity (through skill or software) to retrieve the image.

In R v Porter (Ross Warwick) (2006),[80] the CA held that an image (of child pornography) will only be considered to be in *possession* if the defendant had custody or control of the image at that time. If at the time of possession the image is beyond his control, then he will not possess it. Walker had been convicted at Snaresbrook Crown Court in April 2005 (by a majority jury verdict of ten to two) on 15 counts of making an indecent photograph of a child contrary to section 1(1)(a) Protection of Children Act 1978, and two counts (counts 16 and 17) of possessing indecent photographs of children contrary to section 160(1) CJA 1988.

Police forensic experts had recovered 3,575 still images and 40 movie files of child pornography from the hard disk drives of the two computers seized. Of the remaining 3,573 found on the first PC's hard drive, 873 had been deleted in the sense that they had been placed in the 'recycle bin' of the computer, which had then been emptied. The remaining 2,700 still images were saved

---

78 The intention of s 64 Criminal Justice and Immigration Act 2008 is to give certainty to members of the public that they will not be at risk of prosecution if they possess a video recording of a film which has been classified by the BBFC, even if the film contains an image or images, considered by the Board to be justified by the context of the work as a whole, which nevertheless fall foul of the offence in s 63. The fact that the images are held as part of a BBFC classified film takes them outside the scope of the offence.

79 Section 65(2) Criminal Justice and Immigration Act 2008.

80 [2006] EWCA Crim 560 (16 March 2006).

in a database of a program called ACDSee.[81] All of the larger images had, however, been deleted. The effect of deleting the larger images was that the thumbnail could no longer be viewed in the gallery view. But a trace of each thumbnail (the metadata) remained in the database of the program. Of the 40 movie files, seven were recovered from the PC; all of these had been placed in the recycle bin, which had then been emptied. The remaining 33 files were recovered: they had not been saved, but were recovered from the cache (temporary internet files) record of the two hard disk drives.

Mr Porter's appeal rested on the notion of the judge's direction on 'possession'.[82]

The CA held that the judge's summing-up to the jury was flawed in that he directed them that the only issue for them to decide was whether the defendant knew that the images were indecent or likely to be indecent. He did not direct them about the factual state of affairs necessary to constitute possession, and the result was that a vital issue was wrongly removed from the jury. Nor did he direct them about the mental element required to constitute possession. Dyson LJ stated that in principle this would require proof that the defendant did not believe that the image in question was beyond his control. For these reasons, Ross Porter's appeal was allowed and his convictions were quashed.

The *Porter* case has implications for the use of forensic computer examinations if an image has been deleted. 'Possession' will depend on whether the defendant had the know-how and or the software to allow him to retrieve the image. Where, however, the offender admits that he downloaded the image or accessed it on the internet then a charge of 'making' will be laid.[83] Foster argues that the new offence created under section 63 of the Criminal Justice and Immigration Act 2008 ('possession of extreme pornographic images') may well conflict with human rights legislation by restricting free speech under Article 10 ECHR and intruding into adult individuals' private lives under Article 8.[84] He purports that section 63 fails both in regulating truly harmful images that glorify sexual violence and in imposing necessary and proportionate restrictions on free speech and the right to access those images in private.[85]

3.5.5 EU net neutrality law and 'porn filtering'

In October 2015 the European Commission voted in favour of legislation (so-called 'net neutrality laws') to remove all filters that prevent people from viewing online pornography. The European Commission presented its proposal for a telecoms single market ('Connected Continent') in September 2013 and the European Parliament then voted on its first reading of the draft legislation in April 2014. The Council of the European Union then adopted a mandate to negotiate in March 2015 under the Latvian Presidency and these negotiations led to an agreement on 30 June 2015, formally adopted by the Council on 1 October 2015 and by the European Parliament on 27 October 2015. The measure on 'net neutrality' includes a complete overhaul of EU telecoms rules and commenced in January 2016.[86]

This means that all service providers in the EU have to treat online traffic 'without discrimination'. The legislation places the control with the individual browser, giving them the right to 'access and distribute information and content . . . via their internet access'. The UK had introduced adult content filters in July 2013, championed by Conservative Prime Minister David Cameron. Internet users were required to 'opt in' in order to view pornographic material or content showing gratuitous violence, otherwise such sites were automatically blocked. Net neutrality then means 'no

---

81 This programme is designed for viewing graphical images and is used by photographers. When opened in the 'gallery view', the programme creates 'thumbnail' images of the pictures viewed. These would originally have been larger images associated with each thumbnail.
82 [2006] EWCA Crim 560 at para. 8 (Dyson LJ).
83 This is covered by s 1 Protection of Children Act 1978 if this concerns child images.
84 See: Foster, S. (2010), pp. 21–27.
85 For further discussion see: Akdeniz, Y. (2008).
86 Regulation (EU) 2015/2120.

blocking' or 'no throttling' and 'every European must have access to the open internet. All internet traffic will be treated equally.'[87]

In summary, the EU Commission proposed legislative changes to several regulations that realized two key EU Treaty Principles: the freedom to provide and to consume (digital) services within the EU.

Net neutrality

- ends discriminatory blocking and throttling (e.g. of Skype by telecoms companies);
- sets out clear rules for internet traffic management which must be non-discriminatory, proportionate and transparent;
- all net traffic has to be treated equally.

3.6 The right to be forgotten

We are all used to using search engines via Google Chrome, Firefox, Apple's Safari, Bing, Microsoft Internet Explorer and other browsers to trawl the web to find stored data about other people (or even ourselves). The search engine then goes through their databases of information in order to locate the information we are looking for. With each access, pages are then stored as cached data which can be easily accessed in years to come. The processing of data by a browser enables any internet user to access an array of information about a data subject's private life.

Whilst the Google browser 'autocomplete' function undeniably helps us locate data and information more quickly, it can have the negative effect of spreading rumours which, in turn, can lead to false information and seriously harming someone's reputation. The interference with a person's rights (known as the 'data subject') can be very serious. At the same time the economic interest of a browser in processing the data has to be borne in mind (for nothing ever comes free of charge). The main purpose of a search engine is to search for information on the internet. They are software programs that search for websites based on keywords that the user types in.

Unsubstantiated rumours can reach the top of the search list by merely surfacing on some obscure websites on an unregulated server (e.g. in Ukraine).

3.6.1 The *Google Spain* case: the 'right to be forgotten'

In the *Mario Costeja González* case,[88] Google (Spain) was storing historical information data which he wanted removed. The ECJ ruled that that information be confined to 'history' (though the information will still be online – just not indexed by the search engine).

The Court of Justice of the European Union (CJEU) ruled that Google is a 'data controller' and 'processes' personal data for the purposes of the Data Protection Directive (Directive 95/46/EC) (see below). So operators of search engines (like Google) should not retain personal data for longer than necessary for the processing purposes, and this in effect gives data subjects (like Mr Costeja González) a so-called 'right to be forgotten'.

---

87 Regulation 11 (EU) 2015/2120.
88 See: *Google Spain SL v Agencia Espanola de Proteccion de Datos (AEPD)* (C-131/12) [2014] QB 1022 (CJEU).

Article 6 of the Data Protection Directive (95/46/EC)

1. Member States shall provide that personal data must be:

    (a) processed fairly and lawfully
    (b) collected for specified, explicit and legitimate purposes and not further pro-
        cessed in a way incompatible with those purposes. Further processing of data
        for historical, statistical or scientific purposes shall not be considered as
        incompatible provided that Member States provide appropriate safeguards;
    (c) adequate, relevant and not excessive in relation to the purposes for which they
        are collected and/or further processed;
    (d) accurate and, where necessary, kept up to date; every reasonable step must
        be taken to ensure that data which are inaccurate or incomplete, having regard
        to the purposes for which they were collected or for which they are further
        processed, are erased or rectified;
    (e) kept in a form which permits identification of data subjects for no longer than is
        necessary for the purposes for which the data were collected or for which they
        are further processed. Member States shall lay down appropriate safeguards for
        personal data stored for longer periods for historical, statistical or scientific use.

2. It shall be for the controller to ensure that paragraph 1 is complied with.

The request to the Court of Justice arose in the context of proceedings between Google Spain SL and
Google Inc. on the one side and the Agencia Espanola de Proteccion de Datos (AEPD) (the Spanish
National Data Protection Agency) and Mr Mario Costeja González on the other side, concerning
the application of the Data Protection Directive to an internet search engine that Google operated
as service provider.

 KEY CASE

*Google Spain SL v Agencia Española de Protección
de Datos (AEPD)* – European Court of Justice
(Grand Chamber) (ECJ) 13 May 2014[89]

Precedent

❖ Google 'Search' is a 'data controller' within the meaning of Article 2(d) of Directive 95/46 in relation to its provision as a search engine (by providing 'web search
facilities').

❖ The operator of a search engine is obliged (in certain circumstances) to remove
links to web pages that are published by third parties and contain information relating to the data subject from the list of results displayed, following a search made via
the search engine on the basis of that person's name ('de-listing' or 'de-linking').

❖ Courts (or regulators) have to balance the data subject's right to privacy and the
economic interest of the data controller.

---

89 *Google Spain* (C-131/12) [2014] QB 1022 (CJEU).

❖ Activities of search engines and publishers of websites are liable to affect significantly the fundamental rights to privacy and to the protection of personal data.
❖ Article 10 ECHR includes the right of internet users to receive information (via internet search engines).
❖ Individuals playing a role in public life may not benefit from the right to be de-listed ('the right to be forgotten').

Facts

In March 2010 a Spanish national, Mario Costeja González, complained to the Spanish National Data Protection Agency (Agencia Espanola de Proteccion de Datos (AEPD)) that when his name was entered via the Google Spain search engine, the entries which first appeared were pages of the Barcelona newspaper *La Vanguardia* of 19 January and 9 March 1998 with an announcement, mentioning a property of which he was joint owner in connection with attachment proceedings for the recovery of social security debts. He requested, first, that *La Vanguardia* be required either to remove or alter those pages so that the personal data relating to him no longer appeared, and secondly that Google should be required to remove or conceal the personal data relating to him so that they ceased to be included in the search results. He stated that the criminal proceedings against him had been fully resolved and that reference the 'attachment proceedings' was now entirely irrelevant. The AEPD rejected his claim against *La Vanguardia* (the information in the paper had been lawfully published), but upheld the complaint against both Google entities and requested that they 'de-listed' any personal data from their indexes and links on their search engine. Google Spain and Google Inc. brought actions before the Spanish High Court seeking to have the AEPD decision annulled. The national court referred the case for clarification to the CJEU to clarify the territorial scope of application of EU data protection rules, the legal position of internet search engines and the 'right to be forgotten'.

The main issues before the CJEU in Luxembourg were
1. Do the activities Google carries out in compiling its search engine results constitute activities covered by the Data Protection Directive?
2. Is Google a data controller?
3. Is the Data Protection Directive territorially applicable to Google's activities?
4. Do the rights of a data subject (e.g. Mr González) extend to requesting search engines providers to 'de-list' personal data (i.e. 'the right to be forgotten')?

Decision (Preliminary ruling of 13 May 2014 by Judge Skouris, President)
The CJEU noted that:

1. **Data collection**: by searching automatically, constantly and systematically for information published on the internet, the operator of a search engine 'collected' data within the meaning of Article 2(b) Directive 95/46.
2. **Data controller**: the operator (Google), within the framework of its indexing programs, 'retrieved', 'recorded' and 'organized' the data in question, which it then 'stored' on its servers and 'disclosed' and 'made available' to its users in the form of lists of results. Those operations, were to be classified as 'processing', regardless of the fact that the operator of the search engine also carried out the same operations in respect of other types of information and did not distinguish between the latter and the personal data; this made Google a 'data controller' within the meaning of the Article 2(d) of the Directive.

3. **The territorial scope of the Data Protection Directive**: the Court observed that Google Spain was a subsidiary of Google Inc. on Spanish territory and, therefore, an 'establishment' within the meaning of the Directive. Where personal data were processed for the purposes of a search engine operated by an undertaking which, although it had its seat in a non-Member State, had an establishment in a Member State, the processing was carried out 'in the context of the activities' of that establishment (i.e. within the meaning of Article 4(1)(a) Directive 95/46) if the establishment was intended to promote and sell, in the Member State in question, advertising space offered by the search engine in order to make the service offered by the engine profitable.

4. **'The right to be forgotten' (de-listing of personal data)**: the operator was, in certain circumstances, obliged to remove links to web pages that were published by third parties and contained information relating to a person from the list of results displayed following a search made on the basis of that person's name. Such an obligation may also exist in a case where that name or information was not erased beforehand or simultaneously from those web pages, and even, as the case may be, when its publication in itself on those pages was lawful.

Analysis

The *Google Spain* ruling raised a number of issues in relation to the interpretation of Directive 95/46/EC. The CJEU established that URL links found via the Google (Spain) search engine referring to a data subject (here Mr Costeja González) had to be de-listed upon his request. The interference with the person's privacy rights was heightened on account of the important role played by the internet and search engines in a modern society, which render the information contained in such lists of results ubiquitous. However, in as much as the removal of links from the list of results could have effects upon the legitimate interest of internet users, potentially interested in having access to that information, a fair balance should be sought by courts of Member States in particular between that interest (i.e. the right to access information) and the data subject's fundamental rights, in particular the right to privacy and the right to protection of personal data. Following a request by the data subject, that the inclusion of those links in the list was, at this point in time, incompatible with Directive 95/46, the weblinks and information in the list of results via the search engine must be erased. In this regard even initially lawful processing of accurate data may, in the course of time, become incompatible with the Directive where the data appear to be inadequate, irrelevant or no longer relevant, or excessive in relation to the purposes for which they were processed and in the light of the time that had elapsed. To this extent the data subject can exercise his right to have his information 'forgotten'.

The Court observes in this regard that this balance may depend, in specific cases, on the nature of the information in question and its sensitivity for the data subject's private life and on the interest of the public in having that information, an interest which may vary, in particular, according to the role played by the data subject in *public life*. When appraising such a request made by the data subject in order to oppose the processing carried out by the operator of a search engine, it should in particular be examined whether the data subject had a right that the information in question relating to him personally should, at this point in time, no longer be linked to his name by a list of results that was displayed following a search made on the basis of his name. The data subject may address such a request directly to the operator of the search engine ('the data controller') which must then duly examine its merits. Where the controller refuses that request, the data subject may bring the matter before the 'supervisory authority' (i.e. the regulator) or the judicial authority (i.e. the High Court) so that necessary checks can be carried out and the controller be ordered to take specific measures accordingly.

It is worth noting that the *Google Spain* ruling only covers EU-based web browsers, which means that private data can still be accessed via US or non-EU search engines. In any case, the expression 'right to be forgotten' is misleading. Information cannot be deliberately 'forgotten' by an ISP or operator of a website because it cannot be 'consigned to oblivion'. The fact remains that hard (print) copies concerning Mr Costeja González in the Spanish newspaper *La Vanguardia* still exist together with (linked) reports in other Spanish newspapers and Spanish Ministry of Justice court reports. One could even argue that Mr González' case became even more prominent after the ECJ judgment.

Moreover, the Advocate General expressed the view that operators of websites and search engines should not be unduly saddled with the obligation of having to assess an unmanageable number of requests on a case-by-case and day-to-day basis.[90] Operators of websites and search engines will now have to assess de-linking requests against the Directive and the reasons why personal data should (or should not) be withdrawn, depending whether the data subject is a 'public figure' or not.

The *Google Spain* (*González*) ruling is important in relation to the protection of EU data subjects. The ECJ noted that personal data on any subject's private life was easily available and accessible online via aggregation on search engines, meaning that private information was open to the world at large (see also: *Hegglin v Persons Unknown* (2014);[91] also: *Schrems v Data Protection Commissioner* (2015)[92]).

See Chapter 6.5

3.6.2 How is information 'forgotten' and 'erased'?

Google Spain had wide-reaching implications on providers of search engines and operators of websites. Following the 'right to be forgotten' (RTBF), also known as 'right of erasure' ruling by the ECJ in May 2014, Google and others were forced to establish a system to deal with requests for removal of personal (inaccurate or irrelevant) data. By October 2014 some 18,304 requests had been made from UK individuals alone, wanting links to their name removed on google.co.uk. Google Inc. confirmed that it had removed 35 per cent (18,459) of unwanted links to web pages from its UK service by December 2015; UK citizens had made the third highest number of requests behind French and German citizens, with 29,010 and 25,078 respectively.[93] There were nearly 220,000 requests in 2015 in the UK, most of these came from high-profile clients, including criminals, politicians and public figures; fewer than half of the requests were granted.

Following the *Google Spain* ruling, six EU authorities individually initiated enforcement proceedings against Google Inc. One case was that of Dan Shefet, a Danish lawyer working in France. He brought an action against Google.fr via the French data protection authority (CNIL);[94] Google rejected that request by Mr Shefet to be de-listed. The CNIL's Sanctions Committee subsequently issued a monetary penalty of €150,000 to Google Inc. and Google.fr on 3 January 2014, for non-compliance with the provisions of the French Data Protection Act. In its decision, the Sanctions Committee ruled that French law applies to the processing of personal data relating to internet users established in France, contrary to Google's claim.[95] The Committee held the conditions under which Google Inc's 'single policy' was implemented were contrary to several legal requirements under French data protection law; these were:

● The company [Google Inc.] did not sufficiently inform its users of the conditions in which their personal data was processed, nor of the purposes of this processing. Google did not comply

90 See: Advocate General's Opinion in *Google Spain* [2014] QB 1022 at paras 60–68.
91 [2014] EWHC 2808 (QB) 31 July 2014.
92 (Case C-362/14) [2015] All ER 34 (CJEU).
93 The top five countries by October 2015 were: France (14,086), Germany (12,678), the UK (8,497), Spain (6,176) and Italy (5,934).
94 *Commission nationale de l'informatique et des libertés* (CNIL) at: www.cnil.fr/english.
95 See: Deliberation No 2013-420 of the Sanctions Committee of CNIL imposing a financial penalty against Google Inc. Paris, 3 January 2014 at: www.cnil.fr/fileadmin/documents/en/D2013-420_Google_Inc_EN.pdf.

with French-specific data protection legislation, nor the ambit in which data was being collected. Consequently, the company was not able to exercise its rights, in particular their right of access, objection or deletion.

- Google Inc. (France) did not comply with its obligation to obtain user consent prior to the storage of cookies on their terminals.
- The company failed to define retention periods applicable to the data which it had processed.
- Google combined all data collection about its users across all its services (platforms such as Google Search; Docs; Maps; Images; etc.); this was found to be illegal.

The French Sanctions Committee also ordered Google Inc. to publish a communiqué regarding its decision on www.google.fr with immediate effect. The French data protection authorities' ruling was followed by the judgment of the Paris Tribunal de Grande Instance in November 2014 where Google Inc. (France) was ordered to pay daily fines of €1,000, unless links to a defamatory article about Mr Shefet were removed from the company's global network. The financial penalty issued against Google Inc. by the French CNIL's Sanctions Committee was the highest ever issued and was justified by the number and seriousness of the breaches stated in that case.

3.6.3 Implementation of the right to be forgotten and the *Weltimmo* case

The *Google Spain* 'right to be forgotten' ruling (RTBF) vindicates individual data protection and safeguards privacy interests. Arguably the ruling unduly burdens freedom of expression and information retrieval via search engines and weblinks. Many think it depends on the facts.[96] But there is a general feeling amongst privacy lawyers that the implementation of the RTBF ruling should be more transparent for these reasons:

1. the public should be able to find out how social networking sites, operators of websites and search engine providers exercise their power over readily accessible information and the processing of that information; and
2. implementation of the ruling affects global efforts to accommodate privacy rights with other interests in data flows, such as international law enforcement in relation to terrorism-linked offences.

The RTBF ruling was brought into question by the Hungarian *Weltimmo* case (2015).[97] Before declaring the *Safe Harbour* decision invalid (see: *Max Schrems* (2015)[98]), the CJEU released an important, but lesser-known decision in favour of the Hungarian National Authority for Data Protection and Freedom of Information (Nemzeti Adatvédelmi és Információszabadság Hatóság (NAIH)), concerning the interpretation of the applicable law provisions of the EU Data Protection Directive 95/46/EC. The CJEU in *Weltimmo* handed down another landmark judgment on data protection legislation, tackling the issue of jurisdiction when a company is headquartered in one EU country and operates its business in another. The ruling extended the meaning of 'established' as Directive 95/46/EC to include 'real and effective activity' in a Member State through 'stable arrangements'. The decision had significant implications for companies operating across multiple EU countries.

96 See: 'Dear Google': an open letter from 80 academics on the 'right to be forgotten', published in the *Guardian*, 14 May 2015 at: www.theguardian.com/technology/2015/may/14/dear-google-open-letter-from-80-academics-on-right-to-be-forgotten.
97 See: *Weltimmo s.r.o. v Nemzeti Adatvédelmi és Információszabadság Hatóság* (2015) (Case C-230/14) (CJEU –Third Chamber), Luxembourg, 1 October 2015 (*Weltimmo* case).
98 See: *Schrems (Maximilian) v Data Protection Commissioner* (2015) (Case C-362/14) [2015] All ER 34.

The case was brought by the Hungarian Data Protection Authority against Weltimmo which ran property-selling websites, 'ingatlandepo.com' and 'ingatlanbazar.com', concerning Hungarian real estate. However the company was based in Slovakia. The Hungarian regulator fined Weltimmo for infringement of Hungarian Law CXII of 2011 on the 'right to self-determination', regarding information and freedom of information which it had passed on to a debt collection agency.[99] The CJEU found that the Slovakian company pursued real and effective activity in Hungary through stable arrangements. On the question of jurisdiction, the CJEU distinguished between investigative and sanctioning powers. It held that NAIH had the power to investigate the complaint irrespective of the applicable law. However, NAIH only had powers to impose penalties if the applicable law was Hungarian law. To the extent the applicable law is that of a Member State other than Hungary, NAIH would need to request the other Member State's supervisory authority to interfere and impose sanctions. The Court ruling for breach of the EU Directive by Weltimmo meant that the property agency was potentially liable for the 10 million Hungarian forint (£23,650) fine levied by the Hungarian regulator. The CJEU's findings on the applicability of national data protection laws potentially significantly affect the activities of online operators providing services across multiple EU Member States.

Before the *Weltimmo* judgment, companies such as Facebook or Google who choose to head-quarter their European operations in one country and operate in another were thought to be subject to regulation only within that country. These companies could then operate in any EU Member State without having to gain regulatory approval in each country. The *Weltimmo* ruling is pivotal as it allows data protection legislation of a Member State to be applied to a foreign company that has representatives in that country and operates a service in the native language of that country, despite being headquartered in a different country. The implications for the likes of Facebook, Google and others may well dramatically increase compliance costs, particularly where a website is targeted at multiple Member States, making the company subject to multiple data protection authorities.

Until the CJEU ruling in *Weltimmo*, little was known about the kind and quantity of information which was apparently being de-listed from search results, what sources were being de-listed and on what scale? We had no idea what kind of requests failed and in what proportion (i.e. who were the 'public figures' that were being refused) and what were Google's guidelines in striking the right balance between individual privacy and freedom to access information? The practical consequences following the *Weltimmo* decision for online business operators providing cross-border services in Europe can now be challenged. If an online business operator provides services in several languages, has local representatives in different countries and pursues the enforcement of claims in other Member States, such operator might now be compelled to comply with those Member States' data protection laws – including notification, registration and record-keeping requirements – and can also expect audits and sanctions from competent national data protection agencies and regulators.

We then conclude with the question whether – following the Paris and Belgian terrorist attacks in 2015 and 2016 – can one really hide one's identity and personal details on the internet? Can an individual demand the right to remain anonymous when security has become the focus of legislation of all EU governments? As long as there is proper democratic oversight of those handling the data, Europeans will have to give up some anonymity to preserve liberty and security across Europe. But so far, even some of the big companies fail to understand cyber-security. The vast stores of digital information generated by 'free' email systems, communications data, CCTV footage, credit card records etc. are yielding invaluable clues to would be terrorists. Dido Harding, CEO of TalkTalk, was, for instance, unable to say whether her company's database of users' personal and banking information was encrypted (it was not).

See Chapter 6.5

---

99 In the Hungarian original: 'Az információs önrendelkezési jogról és az információszabadságról szóló 2011. évi CXII. Törvény.' The law on information which transposed Directive 95/46 into Hungarian law.

The fact remains, internet users can adopt any name they want when they open an email or social media account, write comments on a web page or set up a website. People living under authoritarian regimes can mask their activities and identities from the authorities. Such freedoms allow people in repressed states to remain private; but they also allow criminals and terrorists to hide. The Edward Snowden revelations disclosed large-scale spying by America's National Security Agency (NSA), but also that data privacy in Western Europe varied markedly between countries. Each government sets different rules for what spies may look at and access. The UK Investigatory Powers Act 2016 ('the Snoopers' Charter') allows bulk collection of metadata and allows eavesdropping on the content of communications of a specific person or group. The General Data Protection Regulation (GDPR) concerns data privacy including biometric data and the use of highly personal information of all EU citizens.[100]

 FOR THOUGHT

The 'right to be forgotten' and the 'right to access information' (via search engines) are proxies for the right to privacy under Article 8 ECHR, Article 12 of the Declaration on Human Rights, and for Article 10 ECHR. Both rights are subject to interpretation and now appear in conflict. How can such a conflict be resolved? Discuss with reference to the *Google Spain* and *Weltimmo* cases.

3.7 Drones and privacy

Since April 2015, figures from the UK Airprox Board suggest, there have been 25 near misses between aircraft and drones at UK airports, with a dozen of these denoted 'Class A' which indicates there was a serious risk of collision.[101] Drones, the common term for 'Remotely Piloted Aircraft Systems' (RPAS) or 'Unmanned Aircraft Systems' (UAS), are no longer the preserve of the military, in that they could be used by private detective agencies and undercover reporters for the purpose of surveillance. News organizations are making routine use of drones to cover stories in remote or disaster areas, and they provide a powerful tool for journalists and paparazzi to invade an individual's privacy. Unmanned drones can, of course, also be used to access difficult, dangerous and remote areas, such as earthquake areas, where they can provide high-definition video, infrared and still images in live situations without the need for dangerous aircraft missions.

In August 2015 Kensington Palace issued a letter to leaders of media industry bodies in the UK providing an overview of the challenges facing the Duke and Duchess of Cambridge seeking to protect Prince George and Princess Charlotte from harassment and surveillance by paparazzi photographers. Communications Secretary, Jason Knauf, pleaded with the media to uphold standards on the protection of children in a rapidly changing media landscape.[102]

---

100 Regulation (EU) 2016/679 (the General Data Protection Regulation). The Data Protection Directive 95/46 EC is repealed.
101 Source: The UK Airprox Board's primary objective is to enhance air safety in the UK, in particular in respect of lessons to be learned and applied from 'Airprox' occurrences reported within UK airspace. An 'Airprox' is a situation in which, in the opinion of a pilot or air traffic services personnel, the distance between aircraft (and now drones) as well as their relative positions and speed have been such that the safety of the aircraft involved may have been compromised. See: www.airproxboard.org.uk/home.
102 Source: A letter from Kensington Palace, by Jason Knauf, Communications Secretary to TRH The Duke and Duchess of Cambridge and HRH Prince Henry of Wales, 14th August 2015 at: www.princeofwales.gov.uk/media/our-view/letter-kensington-palace.

It is clear that long-lens paparazzi photography is being superseded by 'drone journalism' with photo-journalists obtaining Civil Aviation Authority (CAA) licences in the UK to fly RPAS and UAVs with a camera strapped to the device, for commercial purposes. There is as yet no case for 'responsible journalism' or any media regulation apart from data protection regulation and complex CAA rules. Will we be seeing the next picture of a junior royal or a topless princess by obtaining a picture for publication through privacy intrusion?

3.7.1 Trespass, privacy and drones

An early home-made 'drone' was used to take aerial photos over the wall of Manchester Strangeways Prison during the riots in 1990 when a UK broadcast company strapped a camera to a model airplane. Now drones deliver illegal drugs to prison cell windows.

One of the earliest cases concerned aerial kite photography in the mid-1970s was that of *Bernstein*. The case concerned aircraft which fly at a height which in no way affect the use of the land. In this case it was held to be no trespass (see also: *Pickering v Rudd* [1815][103] – it is not trespass to pass over a man's property in a balloon). The case established that a property owner does not have unqualified rights over the airspace above their land. Additionally there is no authority stating that a landowner's right in the airspace over land extends to an unlimited height.

 KEY CASE   *Bernstein of Leigh (Baron) v Skyviews & General Ltd* [1978] 1 QB 479

Precedent
❖   The rights of a landowner in the airspace above his land are restricted to such a height necessary for the ordinary use and enjoyment of his land and the structures upon it.
❖   Above that height the landowner has no greater rights than the general public.
❖   Adjoining landowners have no right to erect structures overhanging their neighbour's land.

Facts
Lord Bernstein (B) complained when he was offered an aerial photograph of his country home, Coppings Farm, in Kent that the photo was taken without his consent and was a gross invasion of his privacy. He demanded that the prints and negative should be handed over to him or destroyed. Defendant, Mr Arthur Ashley, managing director of Skyviews (S), said if he had known of this request he would have undertaken to destroy the photograph and negative and not to take another similar photograph in the future. However, B's letter was answered by an 18-year-old secretary, who offered to sell him the negative for £15.

B started proceedings claiming that S wrongfully entered the airspace above his premises (trespass) in order to take the photograph of his house and also claiming an invasion of his right to privacy. B relied on the old Latin maxim *Cujus est solum ejus est usque ad coelum et ad inferos* (whose is the soil his is also that which is above and below it).[104] B claimed the right to exclude any entry into airspace above his property. S argued in their

---

103   [1815] 171 ER 70.
104   The maxim, first coined in the thirteenth century in Bologna, had been used by English judges in a number cases concerned with structures attached to adjoining land – overhanging buildings, signs, telegraph poles and the like.

defence that the photo was taken while the aircraft was flying over adjoining land. The issue before the court was: does flying over a person's private property constitute trespass of airspace?

Decision

The CA held that S's aircraft did not infringe any rights of B's airspace – thus no trespass. Applying this test to the facts of this case, Griffiths J found that, even though Skyviews' aircraft had flown over Lord Bernstein's property, it did not infringe any of B's rights to airspace, and thus no trespass was committed. B had complained, not that the aircraft had interfered with his use of his land, but that a photograph was taken. His Lordship stated that there was no law against taking a photograph.

Analysis

Lord Bernstein relied on a Latin maxim which meant that an owner of land is the owner of everything up to the heavens above, and everything down to the hell beneath – which the court held inappropriate. S's aircraft flew at such a height which in no way affected the use of the land and could therefore not amount to trespass. There was no law against taking a photograph in public and no authority stating that a landowner's right in the airspace over land extends to an unlimited height. The position is similar in the US, and has been since about 1948 when the US Supreme Court memorably declared that 'The air is a public highway' and that, if it were not, 'every transcontinental flight would subject the operator to countless trespass suits. Common sense revolts at the idea.'

UK rules on flying drones, called the 'Dronecode', have been drawn up by the Civil Aviation Authority (CAA). However, lawyers know only too well, that 'codes' are not the law. The Dronecode states that you should:

- be visible at all times;
- be flown below 400ft (122m);
- not be flown over congested areas.

Additionally:

- unmanned aircraft fitted with a camera should not be flown within 50m of people, vehicles or buildings;
- pilots of drones with cameras must also be mindful of privacy when taking pictures;
- those using a drone for commercial purposes (such as aerial photography) must obtain a CAA licence and complete a training programme.

3.7.2 Drone journalism, paparazzi drones and privacy

How do drone cameras impact on privacy? Some drones fitted with cameras can loiter overhead for long stretches, engaging in 'persistent surveillance'.

Though the CAA has issued guidelines in the form of the Dronecode (see above), persistent aerial surveillance has become the norm and no privacy or transparency measures currently exist in law. The current state of the law in the UK is poorly suited to deal with drone surveillance and paparazzi journalism. This is because privacy law is tailored to questions of whether one is in public – an open field – or in a space where one has a 'reasonable expectation of privacy' (see: *von Hannover* (No 1)). In this era of 'big data', the line between public and private can no longer be delimited by physical boundaries. John Moreland, spokesman for the UAV Systems Association, told the BBC:

> Hundreds of these UAVs are being used commercially these days, typically flying below 400ft (120m) and with a range of about 500m (0.3 miles). Most are engaged in aerial photography and 3D surveying, but applications are expanding all the time.[105]

In April 2014 Robert Knowles from Cumbria was the first person in the UK to be successfully prosecuted by the CAA for the dangerous and illegal flying of a UAV ('the drone'). He was found to have flown the drone in restricted airspace over a nuclear submarine facility. Analysis by the police of video footage taken from a camera fitted to the drone revealed that during its flight it had skimmed over the busy Jubilee Bridge over Walney Channel, well within the legally permitted 50 metres separation distance required. Both offences breached the UK's Air Navigation Order. Knowles was found guilty of 'flying a small unmanned surveillance aircraft' within 50 metres of a structure (contra article 167 of the Air Navigation Order 2009) and flying over a nuclear installation (contra regulation 3(2) of the Air Navigation (Restriction of Flying)(Nuclear Installations) Regulations 2007). Mr Knowles was fined £800 and with costs to the CAA of £3,500 at Furness and District Magistrates' Court. The Robert Knowles case has raised important safety issues concerning recreational flying of unmanned aircraft with cameras attached. Some UK police forces are more 'keen' than others and have issued a number of cautions to photographers for using drones for commercial purposes without permission when trespassing on owners' land without asking for permission.

In December 2014 freelance photo-journalist, Brighton-based Eddie Mitchell,[106] carrying out aerial photography with a drone camera, was arrested by police officers for 'dangerous behaviour'. Mitchell had a CAA licence to fly drones professionally. On 30 December 2014, he was taking aerial photos of a fatal fire at a caravan site in Newchapel, Surrey, where a mother and two children had died. Mitchell flew his 1.2kg drone in order to get a general view picture of the caravan site whilst staying some distance away from the scene of the actual fire. Three Surrey police officers arrested Mitchell, placing him in handcuffs, and used the remote control to attempt to land the drone themselves. Eventually Mitchell had to land it for them still in handcuffs. He was held in a police cell for some five hours for breach of the peace and eventually freed after the intervention of a BBC lawyer. Mitchell claims the 'debacle' came about because police were unaware of the CAA regulations governing drone use.[107]

We already had the discussions about privacy and that it is something worth protecting in Chapter 1. As Louis Brandeis and Samuel Warren defined in 1890, privacy is 'the right to be let alone'.[108] Sadly, their view no longer captures the purpose of privacy in modern society. So persistent surveillance by overhead camera drones or through monitoring internet browsing habits or Facebook's capturing our personal data and 'likes', undermines the formation of liberal individuals in the way that an over-reliance on GPS undermines the formation of a sense of direction. This is because pervasive drone surveillance (by video or aerial photography) tends to shape the actions, thoughts and personalities of those being observed. Such changes happen gradually, even imperceptibly.

See Chapter 1

---

105 Source: 'Sky high thinking: Could we all soon own a drone?', by Matthew Wall, *BBC News online*, 19 February 2013.
106 Mitchell trades under the name 'Aerial News': www.aerialnews.co.uk.
107 Source: 'Licensed drone operator arrested by "dangerous and idiotic" police officers while filming near Gatwick', by Jamie Merrill, *The Independent*, 31 December 2014: www.independent.co.uk/news/uk/home-news/licensed-bbc-drone-operator-arrested-by-dangerous-and-idiotic-police-officers-while-filming-near-gatwick-9951784.html.
108 See: Warren, S. D. and Brandeis, L. D. (1890), 193–220.

3.7.3 Data protection and privacy laws

Presently the use of drones in the UK is partly covered by the Data Protection Act 1998 (DPA) when there is a potential interference with an individual's right to privacy; as well as the General Data Protection Regulation (GDPR) (2016/679 EU). Over the past decade the UK and EU surveillance laws, policies and codes have come under scrutiny as the increasingly expansive and intrusive powers of the state have been revealed and questioned by the media. Small RPAS ('small drones') are the fastest growing sector within the industry and the EU Commission has called for each Member State's data protection agency to create and share guidance for RPAS pilots on this issue.

The European Commission has debated this issue since 2012, i.e. how to regulate the operations of RPAS in EU airspace. A Communication was published in April 2014, setting out this emerging technology and air safety regarding drones.[109] The European Aviation Safety Agency (EASA) released a regulatory framework in March 2015 focusing specifically on 'unmanned aviation' (i.e. drones). Concerns regarding the use of drone journalism and 'paparazzi drones' for surveillance by state authorities was the topic of a debate in the House of Lords in March 2015.[110]

The CJEU ruled in 2014 that EU legislation on mass surveillance contravenes EU data protection law. The case was brought before the ECJ by 'Digital Rights Ireland', together with the Austrian Working Group on Data Retention.[111] In its judgment, the ECJ stated that the European Data Retention Directive (Directive 2006/24/E) did not lay down clear and precise rules governing the extent of the interference with the fundamental rights enshrined in Articles 7 and 8 of the Charter of Fundamental Rights of the European Union. In particular, the Court criticized the untargeted nature of the surveillance measure and it highlighted the absence of any objective criterion by which to determine the limits of the access of the competent national authorities to the data.

The Information Commissioner's Office (ICO) – in charge of enforcing data protection legislation in England and Wales – recommends (perhaps a little unhelpfully) that users of drones with cameras should operate them in a 'responsible' way to respect the privacy of others. The General Data Protection Regulation requires any commercial operation involving the collection and processing of personal data to undertake a Privacy Impact Assessment (PIA). PIAs assess the risk of a project interfering with an individual's informational or physical privacy. The EU General Data Protection Regulation comes into force in all Member States in 2018.

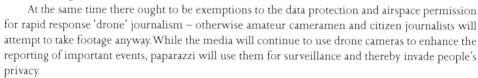

See Chapter
4.4

At the same time there ought to be exemptions to the data protection and airspace permission for rapid response 'drone' journalism – otherwise amateur cameramen and citizen journalists will attempt to take footage anyway. While the media will continue to use drone cameras to enhance the reporting of important events, paparazzi will use them for surveillance and thereby invade people's privacy.

3.8 The Dark Web

Silk Road – the main marketplace of online recreational drug dealing – operates via the Dark Web. One of its main operators, Ross Ulbricht, was found guilty of seven charges in February 2015 by a jury in Manhattan, including running a criminal enterprise, computer hacking and distributing

---

109 COM (2014) 207 'A new era for aviation: Opening the aviation market to the civil use of remotely piloted aircraft systems in a safe and sustainable manner'. 8 April 2014.

110 See: House of Lords (2015) European Union Committee 7th Report of Session 2014–15 Civilian Use of Drones in the EU. 5 March 2015: www.publications.parliament.uk/pa/ld201415/ldselect/ldeucom/122/122.pdf.

111 See: Judgment of the ECJ in 'Digital Rights Ireland data retention challenge', Cases C-293/12 and C-594/12, Luxembourg 8 April 2014.

narcotics over the Dark Web. The drug deals were typically dealt with and paid for in Bitcoin.[112] Ulbricht's cut of the earnings were around £11.8 million in bitcoins. His defence argued that he had been framed by other Silk Road operators, after setting up the site as an 'economic experiment', claiming he was never the 'Dread Pirate Roberts' (the name used by the darknet operator, taken from the name of the hero in the film *The Princess Bride*).[113]

The Dark Web is a term that refers specifically to a collection of websites that are publicly visible, but hide the IP addresses of the servers that run them. The terms Deep Web or Dark Net are used to denote a class of content on the internet that, for various technical reasons, is not indexed by search engines. The Dark Web is a part of the Deep Web that has been intentionally hidden and is inaccessible through standard web browsers.

Internet anonymizer sites such as Pastebin, the Onion Router[114] or Tor[115] – largely sponsored by the US government[116] – are used to exchange contact information and addresses for new hidden services. Tor and other similar networks enable users to traverse the web in near-complete anonymity by encrypting data packets and sending them through several network nodes, called 'Onion Routers' (OR). The Deep Web also includes all user databases, webmail pages, registration-required web forums, and pages behind paywalls. Confusingly, there is also the Dark Internet, a term which defines networks, databases or even websites that cannot be reached over the internet. These contain niche information that few people want or the data exchanged is extremely private.

3.8.1 Who uses the Dark Web?

Since the Edward Snowden revelations we know that the US and UK governments have been 'snooping' on our web use. For this reason some users have migrated to the Dark Web for anonymized communication. If one wants to access the (newly formed) Pirate Bay, for example, one would need to create a virtual private network (VPN). A VPN enables a computer to send and receive data across shared or public networks like the internet as if it were directly connected to a private network. A VPN creates a virtual tunnel between you and the sites and services you need to access, which means the ISP does not know who or indeed where you are, so you will not be blocked off from sites you wish to access.

---

112 Bitcoin is like cash for the internet, also called 'cryptocurrency', first described in 1998 by Wei Dai on the cypherpunks mailing list as a new form of money that uses cryptography to control its creation and transactions rather than a central authority. Bitcoin is a consensus network that enables a new payment system in digital money. It is a decentralized peer-to-peer payment network that is powered by its users with no central authority or middlemen.

113 Source: 'Silk Road Kingpin Ross Ulbricht Found Guilty', *Sky News*, 5 February 2015: http://news.sky.com/story/1421511/silk-road-kingpin-ross-ulbricht-found-guilty.

114 The Onion Routing (OR) program is made up of projects researching, designing, building, and analysing anonymous communications systems. The focus is on practical systems for low-latency internet-based connections that resist traffic analysis, eavesdropping, and other attacks both by outsiders (e.g. internet routers) and insiders (Onion Routing servers themselves). Onion Routing prevents the transport medium from knowing who is communicating with whom; the network knows only that communication is taking place. In addition, the content of the communication is hidden from eavesdroppers up to the point where the traffic leaves the OR network. See: www.onion-router.net.

115 Tor was originally designed, implemented, and deployed as a third-generation onion routing (OR) project of the US Naval Research Laboratory, for the primary purpose of protecting government communications. Today, it is used every day for a wide variety of purposes by the military, journalists, law enforcement officers, activists and many others. See 'The Tor Project' at: www.torproject.org/about/torusers.html.en.

116 Tor received more than $1.8 million in funding from the US government in 2013, even while the NSA was reportedly trying to destroy the network. According to the Tor Projects annual financial statements, the organization received $1,822,907 from the US government in 2013. The bulk of that came in the form of 'pass-through' grants, money which ultimately comes from the US government distributed through some independent third party. Source: The Tor Project, Inc. and Affiliate. Consolidated Financial Statements and Reports Required for Audits in Accordance with Government Auditing Standards and OMB Circular A-133. December 31, 2013 and 2012 at: www.torproject.org/about/findoc/2013-TorProject-FinancialStatements.pdf.

Not all Dark Web sites use Tor. Some use similar encryption services such as I2P (Silk Road Reloaded used this service). But the principle remains the same. The visitor has to use the same encryption tool as the site and – crucially – know where to find the site, in order to type in the URL and visit.

There are some legitimate uses for the Dark Web. For example individuals who live in totalitarian states, such as China, Iran or Syria, use the Dark Web to communicate with the 'outside world'. Since Tor or the Onion Router lets people use the web without revealing who they are or which country they are in this form of internet anonymity has encouraged many people in suppressed states to set up hidden onion sites that offer content but also services and goods (some of which it is illegal to sell openly).

International law enforcement agencies, such as the FBI, Interpol and Europol, are regularly accessing the Dark Web to track down terrorists, paedophiles, gunrunners, drug dealers, sex traffickers and other serious organized criminals. The FBI and Interpol located about 7,000 hidden sites on the Dark Web in 2015 that mark and mask serious crimes by organized crime networks and individuals to avoid detection. Their findings included:

● infiltrating Tor to unmask online users of a child sex abuse site;
● employing undercover police, malware and/or clever technology to take down what was once one of the top markets for illicit drugs and other contraband and services, Silk Road. Silk Road 2.0 was taken down after a successful, six-month attack on Tor;
● Using Deep Web access and cataloguing tools from the Defense Advanced Research Projects Agency (DARPA) to track down sex traffickers for a year before the tools, called Memex, were even revealed.[117]

Chertoff and Simon in their research paper for the think tank Chatham House recommend strongly that these sites need to be kept under constant observation to spot message exchanges containing new Dark Web domains, known as hidden service monitoring. Most hidden services to date tend to be highly volatile and go offline very often, coming back online later under a new domain name. The authors of the report state that it is essential to get a snapshot of every new site as soon as it is spotted, for later analysis or to monitor its online activity.[118]

3.8.2 Global internet governance

In November 2014, the Director of Britain's Government Communications Headquarters (GCHQ), Robert Hannigan, warned that Twitter, Facebook and WhatsApp had become the 'command-and-control' networks of choice for terrorists and criminals.[119] The definition of 'internet governance' was developed at the World Summit on the Information Society (WSIS) in 2005.[120]

---

117 Source: 'FBI again thwarts Tor to unmask visitors to a Dark Web child sex abuse site', by Lisa Vaas, *Naked Security Sophos*, 22 July 2015: https://nakedsecurity.sophos.com/2015/07/22/fbi-again-thwarts-tor-to-unmask-visitors-to-a-dark-web-child-sex-abuse-site/.
118 See: Chertoff, M. and Simon, T. (2015).
119 Source: 'The Web Is a Terrorist's Command-and-Control Network of Choice', by Robert Hannigan, *The Financial Times*, 3 November 2014.
120 Source: Tunis Agenda for the Information Society, 18 November 2005, WSIS-05/TUNIS/DOC6(Rev.1)-E, p. 6 at: www.itu.int/wsis/docs2/tunis/off/6rev1.pdf.

Until September 2015, the internet was 'governed' by the Internet Corporation for Assigned Names and Numbers (ICANN[121]). ICANN – a private sector regulator – made its policy decisions using a multistakeholder model of governance. But increasingly national governments realized that ICANN internet policy decisions intersected with national laws, particularly in areas such as intellectual property, privacy, law enforcement, and cyber security. Some governments – such as the United Kingdom – have advocated increased intergovernmental influence over the way the internet is governed.

In December 2014, Prime Minister David Cameron set up a specialist unit, the National Crime Agency (NCA[122]) which – together with GCHQ – and other law enforcement agencies is responsible for tracking down cyber crime and terrorism threats.[123] The NCA estimated that around 20,000 people from the UK used secret or encrypted networks (such as Tor) each day in 2015.

In November 2015 NCA investigators, assisted by specialist cyber crime officers from Tarian, the Southern Wales Regional Organised Crime Unit, raided the house of a 17-year-old in Cardiff (who cannot be named for legal reasons) and found evidence that he had been involved in distributed denial of service (DDoS) attacks using the 'Lizard Stressor' software (the Dark Web). He had attempted to buy a handgun, a Glock, from an illegal arms dealer in the United States. He was additionally charged with offences under the Computer Misuse Act 1990. The teenager was sentenced to 12 months in a Young Offenders' Institution (YOI) at Cardiff Youth Court on 26 November 2015 and was also ordered to pay more than £1,000 compensation to the victim of the DDoS attack.[124]

In August 2015, Google, Facebook and Twitter joined forces with the UK anti-child abuse organization Internet Watch Foundation (IWF) to remove millions of indecent child images from the web. IWF continuously shares a list of indecent images, identified by unique 'hash' codes on the Dark Net. The IWF's main aim is to take down indecent images of children by allocating to each picture a hash-code (also referred to as a digital fingerprint). By sharing 'hash lists' of indecent pictures of children, Google, Facebook and Twitter are able to stop such images from being uploaded to their sites.[125] The deep web still has great potential to host an increasingly high number of malicious services and activities.[126]

The Internet Assigned Numbers Authority (IANA) was given new functions from 1 October 2016 to allocate domain names and took over from ICANN as temporary stewardship.

3.9 Codifying cyberspace (1)

We know that there are no physical or legal barriers concerning the World Wide Web to prevent access of information from geographically remote places. We also know that in many cases we do not know the physical location of either an ISP or the server or indeed the author of a defamatory or hate message on Twitter or any other social media site.

---

121 ICANN is a not-for-profit public benefit corporation headquartered in Los Angeles, CA, and incorporated under the laws of the state of California. ICANN is organized under the California Non-profit Public Benefit Law for charitable and public purposes, and as such, is subject to legal oversight by the California Attorney General: www.icann.org.

122 The National Crime Agency (NCA) is the UK's law enforcement agency responsible for leading the UK's fight to cut serious and organized crime at: www.nationalcrimeagency.gov.uk.

123 The NCA works closely with the Regional Organised Crime Units (ROCUs), the MPCCU (Metropolitan Police Cyber Crime Unit), partners within industry, government and international law enforcement, and the National Cyber Crime Unit (NCCU).

124 A distributed denial-of-service (DDoS) attack is an attempt to make a machine or network resource unavailable to its intended users. It is analogous to a group of people crowding the entry door or gate to a shop or business, and not letting legitimate parties enter into the shop or business, disrupting normal operations. Criminal perpetrators (or hackers) of DoS (denial-of-service) attacks often target sites or services hosted on high-profile sites, such as banks and credit card payment gateways. Motives are often revenge, blackmail or activism.

125 Source: 'Hash List "could be game-changer" in the global fight against child sexual abuse images online', IWF, 10 August 2015: www.iwf.org.uk/about-iwf/news/post/416-hash-list-could-be-game-changer-in-the-global-fight-against-child-sexual-abuse-images-online.

126 For further information and discussion see: Prestipino, P. (2015).

There is as yet no universally agreed-upon definition of internet governance. Kruger argues that the ongoing debate over internet governance will have a significant impact on how other aspects of the internet may be governed in the future, especially in such areas as intellectual property, privacy, law enforcement, internet free speech, and cyber security. He further contends that the institutional nature of internet governance could have far-reaching implications on important policy decisions that will likely shape the future evolution of the internet.[127]

3.9.1 Internet censorship

See above
3.8.2

The United States has undeniably taken the lead in the regulation of the internet for the last 20 years or so. But as has already been mentioned above, the US government has given up control of the administration of the internet, handing over responsibility for the IP numbering network and Domain Name System (DNS) to the global community. Policing any international legislation across cyber borders is very difficult to impossible and has to be left to individual states. Most protective schemes and attempts to restrict the flow of information on the internet, based on geographical locations, have proved futile so far.

The French courts ruled in 2014 that Yahoo! Inc. must block French users from its sites auctioning Nazi artefacts. Yahoo! argued that it could not possibly limit access to certain geographical regions; alternatively, it could comply with French legislation and block everyone from bidding for the artefacts.

The Kremlin passed a law in 2014 giving Russian prosecutors the right to block, without a court decision, websites with information about protests that have not been sanctioned by the authorities. President Vladimir Putin had described the internet as a project of the CIA, though promised not to put the internet under full government control when he returned to the Kremlin for a third term in 2012. In May 2015 the Russian Federal Service for Supervision in the Sphere of Telecom, Information Technologies and Mass Communications (Roskomnadzor[128]) sent letters to the three US-based internet companies Google, Twitter and Facebook, warning them against violating Russian internet laws. The three US firms were also asked to hand over data on Russian bloggers with more than 3,000 readers per day and take down websites that Roskomnadzor saw as containing calls for 'unsanctioned protests and unrest'. Critics of the Putin regime called this move internet censorship.[129]

The Indian government was accused of internet censorship in July 2015, when the Ministry of Justice's Communication Department ordered ISPs to block access to 857 pornography websites. These had been identified by an anti-porn activist Kamlesh Vaswani (43), a private lawyer from the central Indian state of Madhya Pradesh.[130] Mr Vaswani had previously failed in a private action, when he had asked the Indian Supreme Court to block online pornography. Chief Justice H. L. Dattu had ruled that adults had a fundamental right to watch pornography within the privacy of their own homes. Vaswani had subsequently managed to persuade Prime Minister Narendra Modi to block 857 specific sites, including pornhub.com and indianpornvideos.com.[131] Mr Vaswani began his anti-online-porn campaign as a response to the brutal gang rape of a 23-year-old woman on a New Delhi bus in 2012. He

127 See: Kruger (2015) at: www.fas.org/sgp/crs/misc/R42351.pdf.
128 See: Roskomnadzor at: http://rkn.gov.ru/eng.
129 Source: 'Russia "will block" Google, Twitter and Facebook if they withhold blogger data', *The Guardian*, 22 May 2015 at: www.theguardian.com/world/2015/may/22/russia-will-block-google-twitter-and-facebook-if-they-withhold-blogger-data?CMP=Share_iOSApp_Other.
130 Source: 'India Blocks 857 Pornography Websites, Defying Supreme Court Decision', by David Barstow, *New York Times*, 3 August 2015 at: www.nytimes.com/2015/08/04/world/asia/india-orders-blocking-of-857-pornography-websites-targeted-by-activist.html?_r=0.
131 Source: The Order Notice by the Government of India Ministry of Communication and IT of 31.6.2015. No 813-7/25/2011 – DS (Vol-V).

had analysed internet traffic data of the most popular porn websites in India and subsequently came up with the list of 857 sites for the government communications department to block.

The blocking of the porn websites sparked a furious debate accusing the Indian government of dictating what its citizens could and could not watch online. Within hours of the blocking order there were hundreds of protestors who aired their views on Indian social media platforms, asking why these specific porn-hubs had been blocked and not others? The *Hindustan Times* supported the government writing that the online pornography was 'spreading antisocial activities' in their hyperlinks. Nikhil Pahwa, editor and publisher of MediaNama, which monitors digital policy in India, said he feared that the Modi government was using pornography as 'a ruse' to create a government-controlled web filter for India.[132] Eventually, IT Minister Ravi Shankar Prasad reversed the porn-site ban on 5 August 2015.[133] In a detailed study of India's surveillance policies and laws, Narasimhan, Sharma and Kaushal found that India does not have one unified policy on surveillance.[134]

 FOR THOUGHT

Would you agree with some proponents of internet free speech that any proposed regulations would choke new innovations and freedom of expression? Discuss.

3.9.2 Digital Economy Legislation

The Digital Economy Act 2010 (DEA) was enacted rather hastily during the 'wash-up' period before the dissolution of Parliament in April 2010. It had been championed by Lord Mandelson in the House of Lords in December 2009 and receiving Royal Assent on 8 April 2010. The primary aim of the Act was to regulate digital media and to set out measures to combat online copyright infringement.

Many of the provisions of the DEA have since proved highly controversial, such as 'obligations' on ISPs to send out warning letters to subscribers who have been reported by copyright owners for infringement and providing copyright owners with lists of infringing subscribers. Ofcom was initially tasked with drafting the 'initial obligations' and a code of practice to underpin the duties of ISPs. The DEA also empowered the Secretary of State (for Culture, Media and Sport) to impose certain 'technical measures', such as limiting the internet speed or subscriber access to particular material, to deter further (copyright) infringement. The Digital Economy Bill 2016–17, sponsored by John Whittingdale, makes provision about restricted access to online pornography, data-sharing, functions of OFCOM in relation to the BBC and direct marketing.

See Chapter 5.5

In the *BT and TalkTalk* judicial review case (see below) the applicants claimed the DEA was disproportionate and discriminatory because only the six largest ISPs in the UK would be subject to the 'initial obligations code' provided for in the Act.

132 Source: 'India's porn ban hasn't exactly been lifted: it's conditional & up to ISPs', by Nikhil Pahwa, MediaNama on 4 August 2015: www.medianama.com/2015/08/223-porn-india-ban.
133 Source: 'Govt backs down, asks ISPs to block only child porn', by Pankaj Doval, *The Times of India*, 5 August 2015 at: http://timesofindia.indiatimes.com/tech/tech-news/Govt-backs-down-asks-ISPs-to-block-only-child-porn/articleshow/48352966.cms.
134 For further reading see: Narasimhan, N., Sharma, M. and Kaushal, D. (2012) Accessibility of Government Websites in India: A Report at: http://cis-india.org/accessibility/accessibility-of-govt-websites.pdf.

KEY CASE

R (on the application of (1) BT and (2) TalkTalk) v BPI and others [2012] EWCA Civ 232[135]

Precedent
❖ The DEA is consistent with EU legislation.
❖ There are enough safeguards within the Digital Economy Act 2010 (DEA) to protect the rights of consumers and ISPs.

Facts
On 6 March 2012, the Court of Appeal rejected BT and TalkTalk's appeal in relation to a judicial review of the Digital Economy Act 2010 (DEA). BT and TalkTalk had challenged various provisions of the DEA (sections 3 to 16 regarding internet service providers (ISPs) obligations for online copyright infringement) claiming they were incompatible with various EU directives. In the CA decision the judges dismissed all of the ISPs' grounds of appeal apart from one narrow point on costs. It remains to be seen whether the ISPs will appeal to the Supreme Court as they have indicated they might.

Specifically, BT and TalkTalk claimed the DEA was in breach of, or incompatible with the following:

❖ Technical Standards Directive (98/34/EC) which requires EU Member States to notify any draft technical regulation to the European Commission.
❖ E-Commerce Directive (2000/31/EC) which provides that ISPs who transmit information on behalf of a subscriber, or who provide access to a communications network, are 'not liable for the information transmitted' where they did not initiate the transmission, select the receiver of the transmission or select or modify the information contained in the transmission ('mere conduit' exemption).
❖ Data Protection Directive (95/46/EEC) which prohibits the processing of certain special categories of personal data, such as that revealing racial or ethnic origin, political opinion or religious beliefs unless it 'is necessary for the establishment, exercise or defence of legal claims'.
❖ E-Privacy Directive (2002/58/EC) which provides that the processing of 'traffic data' which is 'data processed for the purpose of the conveyance of a communication on an electronic communications network or for the billing thereof' must comply with certain criteria unless a derogation applies under the E-Privacy Directive.
❖ Authorisation Directive (2002/20/EC) which harmonizes and simplifies the authorization regime for electronic communications networks and services and sets out specific obligations applicable to electronic communications networks and services.

BT and TalkTalk also claimed the DEA was disproportionate and discriminatory because only the six largest ISPs in the UK would be subject to the initial obligations code.

---

135 *R (on the application of (1) British Telecommunications, (2) TalkTalk Telecom Group plc) v Secretary of State for Culture, Olympics, Media and Sport and (1) BPI (British Recorded Music Industry) Ltd, (2) British Video Association Ltd, (3) Broadcasting Entertainment Cinematograph and Theatre Union, (4) Equity, (5) Film Distributors' Association Ltd, (6) Football Association Premier League Ltd, (7) Motion Picture Association Inc., (8) The Musicians' Union, (9) Producers' Alliance for Cinema and Television Ltd, (10) Unite* [2012] EWCA Civ 232; [2011] EWHC 1021 (Admin) 6 March 2012.

Decision

Technical Standards Directive
There was no breach of the Technical Standards Directive.

If a technical regulation is not notified to the European Commission, which the ISPs claimed was the case here, it is unenforceable at national level. The CA ruled there was no need for notification. The true test for deciding what amounted to a 'technical regulation', which required notification, was whether the measure 'by itself' had 'legal effect for individuals'. In this case, the initial obligations under the DEA did not have the prescribed 'legal effect' because the incidence of the initial obligations was made expressly contingent upon the initial obligations code, and the initial obligations were not yet sufficiently particularized so as to be enforceable. It was only the code that would need to be notified in due course as a draft technical regulation.

E-Commerce Directive
The provisions were not incompatible with the E-Commerce Directive.

The ISPs argued that the contested provisions rendered them potentially 'liable for the information transmitted' contrary to Article 12 of the E-Commerce Directive, because of the responsibilities imposed on them in relation to the warning letters and infringing subscriber lists, together with the related financial burden and exposure to liability for costs, compensation and penalties. The CA rejected their arguments saying the provisions did not render ISPs potentially liable for the information transmitted – the initial obligations on ISPs did not impose any liability in respect of underlying copyright infringement.

Data Protection Directive
The provisions were not incompatible with the Data Protection Directive.

The ISPs argued that in a substantial proportion of cases, the procedure prescribed by the DEA was not intended to involve legal claims at all. One of the main aims of the DEA measures was said to be educational and the government had assumed that 70 per cent of infringers would stop infringing if they received a notification from their ISP, who would therefore not need to resort to legal action. The ISPs argued the scheme would operate as extra-judicial and that the processing could not be said to be necessary for the establishment, exercise or defence of legal claims.

It was held that the processing was plainly necessary for the establishment, exercise or defence of legal claims, even if it meant that on receiving a notification, subscribers stopped infringing and no further action was required. Even if the scheme sought to educate users about the legal rights of copyright owners and encouraged them to cease infringing activities without the need for legal action, that did not mean that the copyright owners were not establishing, exercising or defending their legal rights.

E-Privacy Directive
The provisions were not incompatible with the E-Privacy Directive.

The ISPs argued that the data they processed was 'traffic data' and that this processing did not comply with the E-Privacy Directive and that the derogation under Article 15 did not apply. This argument was rejected by the CA which considered that the derogation did apply and that traffic data could be stored to protect IP rights. Member States were entitled to adopt legislative measures to allow for the retention of data for a limited period in order to protect property rights, which would include copyright.

Authorisation Directive

There was a breach of the Authorisation Directive.

The ISPs claimed the DEA imposed onerous costs obligations on ISPs contravening this Directive. The CA held that the provisions of the draft costs order (draft Online Infringement of Copyright (Initial Obligations) (Sharing of Costs) Order 2011) breached the Directive and various fees and charges (qualifying costs, i.e. costs incurred by Ofcom in carrying out its functions under the copyright infringement provisions and case fees, i.e. fees charged by the appeals body in respect of each subscriber appeal received) were administrative costs which could not be imposed on ISPs. This was a partial victory for the ISPs and widened the previous declaration on costs. This means an ISP will only be liable for relevant fees, i.e. those which would be reasonably incurred in carrying out its obligations under the copyright infringement provisions, e.g. costs of sending copyright infringement letters, and ISPs will be able to recover some of those from copyright owners.

Discrimination and proportionality

The proposed exclusion of smaller ISPs and mobile network operators from the scope of the initial obligations was proportionate.

The CA rejected the argument that the proposal in the draft initial obligations code that it would initially cover only fixed-line ISPs with over 400,000 subscribers, i.e. the six largest ISPs, was discriminatory contrary to Article 6 of the Authorisation Directive. The CA agreed with the Court's previous decision that this was reasonable and proportionate and was soundly based on detailed evidence submitted on behalf of the Secretary of State.

Analysis

The government and copyright owners were rather pleased with this decision and by the fact that the court did not refer any questions to the Court of Justice for the European Union, since that would have further delayed the progress of the contested provisions.

The ruling by the Human Rights Court in Delfi v Estonia[136] suggests that operators of websites need to police potential defamatory comments posted online even more carefully. The case concerned the Estonian news website service 'Delfi'. Defamatory comments were posted on the Delfi portal, following a story about a ferry company and one of its ferries which had damaged an ice road in the country, preventing people from using it. The defamatory comments were specifically aimed against L (a major shareholder). Though Delfi accepted the comments were defamatory and removed them as soon as they received L's written complaint, the defamatory postings were left on the website for more than six weeks. L won his action in the Human Rights Court. The ruling in

---

136 *Delfi AS v Estonia* (Application No 64569/09) 10 October 2013 (Grand Chamber) ECtHR.

Delfi created a potentially mammoth workload for busy news websites to monitor comments and 'talking points' on their websites.

What is and is not allowed on the internet is one of biggest challenges facing many national governments. Governments issuing legislation have to balance the interests and freedom of internet users and the protection of personal integrity rights with the requirement for commercial and personal security so that the internet is not being misused. Hurst argues that it is important that UK and other European legislators do not over-regulate the internet in an attempt to deal with privacy, defamation and harassment problems. He states that global internet companies cannot be expected to adopt a legal country-by-country approach but that there ought to be a consistent legislative approach which then can be applied consistently across Europe and beyond. He gives the example of the practical application of section 5 Defamation Act 2013 which provides a statutory defence for website operators. Hurst then argues that the practical procedure for operators of websites remains far too complex thereby making it difficult to deal effectively with anonymous online libel. He concludes, even if EU laws are successfully enacted in the next few years, 'the tech players will be several steps ahead and the law will quickly become outdated'.[137]

See Chapter 7.5

3.9.3 Summary and analysis

Freedom of speech means different things to different societies. Should there be unlimited freedom of expression via the internet? There is precious little that can be banned from the internet today, though there are organizations such as the Internet Watch Foundation (IWF) and the communications regulator Ofcom that have the power to inform and enforce UK domestic law.

See Chapter 5.4

A variety of different interferences fall within the category of 'private life' and interest, including unwanted observation and intrusion into one's home and the workplace as well as the unwanted dissemination of CCTV images (*Peck v UK* (2003)[138]). Recognition of the need to protect against such interferences is unsurprising. The ECtHR has consistently applied its jurisdiction on the subject of Article 8 ECHR when determining what is necessary in a particular state's society where an action is being brought. This is widely acknowledged where the ECtHR has held that it will apply narrower measures with reference to an aspect of a person's private life, such as one's sexuality.[139]

Although English courts have not yet recognized physical intrusion as part of the tort of privacy, there are a number of Strasbourg rulings which could be regarded as persuasive, such as the right to be free from physical assault or bodily searches, surveillance and the dissemination of images (*YF v Turkey* (2004)[140]); or where the ECtHR expressly held that an individual's mental and physical health is part of a person's 'physical or moral integrity' (*Bensaid v UK* (2001)[141]).

This leaves us to conclude that just about anything can be shared and written about via the World Wide Web. The internet has become a worldwide collective of free speech, which some say has spiralled out of control. Others defend it strenuously, arguing that the internet is the one place where the essence of free speech lives unmolested.

---

137 See: Hurst, A. (2015), pp. 187–195.
138 (2003) 36 EHRR 41.
139 *Norris v Ireland* (1989) 13 EHRR 186.
140 (2004) 39 EHRR 34.
141 (2001) 33 EHRR 10.

3.10 Further reading

Bradley, P. (2014) 'Data, data everywhere', *Legal Information Management,* **14(4), 249–252.**
The insightful paper by internet consultant Phil Bradley considers the growth of information on the internet, both in terms of type and amount. His article considers the difficulties that this flood of data brings with it, the challenges facing traditional search engines when faced with access by mobile devices and applications. The role of privacy and the 'internet of things' are also discussed.

Coe, P. (2015) 'Footballers and social media "faux pas": the Football Association's "cash cow"?' *Entertainment Law Review,* **26(3), 75–78.**
Peter Coe discusses the breadth of social media platforms, providing some astounding statistics of internet user data on platforms such as Twitter and Google. He comments that we are now receiving news instantaneously and unfiltered, with opinions expressed which can at times hurt individuals' feelings. Coe concludes that the FA uses these fines as a 'cash cow' that generates significant revenue that it can re-invest into the game.

Easton, S. (2011) 'Criminalising the possession of extreme pornography: sword or shield?', *Journal of Criminal Law,* **75(5), 391–413.**
Susan Easton's article examines the reasons for the introduction of the extreme pornography provisions in section 63 of the Criminal Justice and Immigration Act 2008. She asks whether the provisions can be justified and whether Parliament's goals are practically achievable and whether the provision smacks of repressive paternalism? The impact of the law is assessed with reference to cases and whether banning possession of such extreme material on a personal computer is a legitimate aim and justifiable? In short: was this legislation necessary at all given the relatively few prosecutions.

Hurst, A. (2015) 'Data privacy and intermediary liability: striking a balance between privacy, reputation, innovation and freedom of expression', *Entertainment Law Review,* **26(6), 187–195.**
Ashley Hurst discusses the Data Protection Act 1998 as a 'weapon of choice' for reputation managers. He argues that EU data protection legislation has had a chilling effect on freedom of expression and is stifling innovation. The author (a legal practitioner) points to the plethora of legislation which now exists in relation to the internet and tries to separate the wood from the trees.

Wacks, R. (2013) *Privacy and Media Freedom.* **Oxford: Oxford University Press.**
Raymond Wacks' book is both eminently readable and also extremely detailed in its legal and philosophical discourse on privacy (the book also mentions defamation). American Professor Wacks discusses the notion of privacy in great detail as well as examining rights-based theories of free speech in the US First Amendment. He compares French and German privacy laws and their constitutional 'right to personality' and refers to the individual's right to privacy as a 'mixed blessing'.

Chapter 4

Freedom of information

> ### Key points
>
> This chapter will cover the following questions:
>
> ○ What constitutes freedom of information?
> ○ What type of information can be released under the Freedom of Information Act 2000 (FOIA)?
> ○ Who can request information under FOIA?
> ○ What are the exemptions under FOIA?
> ○ What is the role of the Information Commissioner?
> ○ How can decisions by the Information Commissioner be appealed?
> ○ How have the courts interpreted FOIA legislation?
> ○ Why is the ruling in the *Prince Charles's letters* case (re *Evans*) of constitutional importance?
> ○ What is the difference between data protection and freedom of information laws?
> ○ Has FOIA made a difference to public life?

4.1 Overview

See below
4.5.1

This chapter examines the history of and parliamentary debates leading to the Freedom of Information Act 2000 ('the FOIA'). Some of the exemptions will be scrutinized by way of case law examples, such as section 32 FOIA and *Guardian* journalist Rob Evans's freedom of information quest to have sight of Prince Charles's letters to government ministers. Details of the FOIA will be discussed, looking at the complexity of the legislation and more recent opposition by parliamentarians. Case law focus will be on some legal challenges at the Upper Tribunal, after appeals to the Information Commissioner (IC) were exhausted.[1] The *BBC v Sugar* (2012)[2] case acutely illustrates the complexities and challenges inherent in the FOIA.

The FOIA is generally regarded as a complex though extremely useful piece of legislation. Yet its many complex exemptions[3] and qualifications have led to a controversial area of jurisprudence, resulting in a body of decisions handed down by the courts, from the First Tier Tribunal (FTT) to the Supreme Court.

This chapter looks at the wider remit, including the office of the Information Commissioner (ICO) (and their counterparts in Northern Ireland and Scotland) and the powers the ICO has in law, such as dealing with nuisance telephone calls, unwanted emails and text messages and automated telesales.

We will also look at the differences and similarities of freedom of information (FOIA) and data protection legislation (DPA). Reference will also be made to the Data Protection Act 1998 (DPA) and the Environmental Information Regulations 2004 (EIR), comparing these statutes, how they interact and how they differ when it comes to 'freedom of information' requests.

The question central to this chapter is whether the FOIA has made a difference to public life.

---

1 For further discussion see: Klang and Murray (2004), Chapter 15; see also: Weber (2010).
2 *BBC v Sugar (deceased) (No 2)* [2012] UKSC 4.
3 Under Sch. I, Part VI FOIA.

4.2 Historical overview

The legislative struggle in Britain for freedom of information is inextricably linked to freedom of speech and press freedom. Until it was reformed in 1989, section 2 of the Official Secrets Act 1911 made it an offence for any civil servant or public contractor to reveal any information he had obtained in the course of his work, no matter how insignificant; an offence which successive governments continued to prosecute well into the 1990s, despite recommendations published in 1972 by the Franks Committee calling for reform.[4]

Chapter 1.2

4.2.1 The legislative path to freedom of information in the UK

The Labour Party first pledged itself to a Freedom of Information Bill in its 1974 election manifesto, but the uncertain positions of the Wilson and Callaghan governments made progress impossible. In 1978, Liberal MP, journalist and humorist Clement Freud (1924–2009) introduced an Official Information Bill as a Private Member's Bill. The bill would have repealed the controversial catch-all section 2 of the Official Secrets Act 1911, and would have established the right of freedom of information two decades before the FOIA 2000. Freud secured a second reading of the bill despite entrenched opposition in Whitehall; it was some way through its committee stage when the Callaghan government collapsed in 1979. Two years later, Sheffield Labour MP Frank Hooley introduced another Freedom of Information Bill, which was opposed by the Conservative government and defeated at second reading. Another attempt was introduced by Liberal leader David Steel MP, which was eventually converted into the Data Protection Act passed in 1984. At the same time, Conservative MP Robin Squire promoted the 'Community Rights Project', which led to the Local Government (Access to Information) Act 1985; this Act granted the public wider rights in respect of public authorities, such as public access to council meetings, reports and papers. The Access to Personal Files Act 1987, introduced by Liberal MP Archy Kirkwood (now Lord Kirkwood of Kirkhope), gave citizens the right to see manually held social work and housing records about themselves as well as providing public access to school records.

The Access to Medical Reports Act 1988[5] resulted from another Private Member's Bill by Archy Kirkwood MP. The Act gave people the right to see any report produced by their own doctor for an employer or insurance company. In the same year, the Environment and Safety Information Act 1988 was passed, introduced as a Private Member's Bill by Chris Smith MP, which granted individuals the right to request information from a large number of organizations who had responsibilities for the environment. The Act includes public as well as private authorities, and defines these as bodies that are 'under the control of' a public authority.

In 1991–1992 an amended version of the Freedom of Information Bill was reintroduced by Archy Kirkwood and backed by shadow Home Secretary Roy Hattersley MP, promising a 'Freedom of Information Act' should Labour win the 1992 general election. The bill lasted only 45 minutes in Parliament and did not receive a second reading. At the same time, the Labour front bench published the Right to Information Bill, which was partly based on the Kirkwood Bill, but also included proposals to reform the Official Secrets Act. But the Conservatives won their fourth general election on 9 April that year, defeating Neil Kinnock and his Labour Party.

Though the Conservative government under Prime Minister John Major (1990–1997) did not support any freedom of information legislation, Cabinet Minister William Waldegrave was given responsibility for implementing a policy of more open-style government. John Major introduced the White Paper on 'Open Government' and the 'Right to Know Bill' in July 1993, which proposed

---

4   See: Official Secrets Act debate in Parliament between Prime Minister Edward Heath and opposition leader Harold Wilson, Hansard, HC Deb 12 December 1972 vol. 848 cc 231–234.

5   As amended by the Access to Health Records Act 1990.

two new legal rights to information: public access to manually held personal files and to health and safety information. The bill also proposed to reform the Official Secrets Act 1989.[6] The 'Code of Practice' which was subsequently introduced relating to government openness and access to public official information was established in April 1994, supervised by the Parliamentary Ombudsman (the Parliamentary Commissioner for Administration[7]), who, when publishing his first report in 1996, recommended the introduction of a Freedom of Information Act.

When New Labour won the general election in 1997 under Tony Blair, they were immediately reminded of their earlier party manifesto promise to introduce freedom of information legislation. The White Paper 'Your Right to Know' in 1997 proposed wider public access to information from public bodies such as law enforcement agencies.[8] But first, the new Labour Home Secretary, Jack Straw, prioritized bringing European human rights legislation 'back home',[9] resulting in the Human Rights Act 1998.

The Freedom of Information Bill was introduced by Labour MP Andrew Mackinlay under the ten-minute rule in November 1998 in the House of Commons. It was backed by a slightly amended version in the House of Lords by the Conservative peer Lord Lucas of Crudwell, receiving its second reading in February 1999. The Macpherson Inquiry Report of 1999 into the Stephen Lawrence killing coincided with the second reading of the bill. Apart from the damning declaration that the Metropolitan Police were institutionally racist, Macpherson recommended that the police should be fully and openly accountable to public scrutiny; and the only way this could succeed would be by way of freedom of information legislation.

When the Freedom of Information Act 2000 was ultimately passed, many saw it as a disappointment, with great curtailment of the original proposals in the 'Your Right to Know' White Paper. The range of exemptions and the breadth of grounds on which information could legally be withheld has remained controversial. Tony Blair famously said in his memoirs that he regretted introducing the Freedom of Information Act at all:

> Freedom of Information. Three harmless words. I look at those words as I write them, and feel like shaking my head till it drops off my shoulders. You idiot. You naive, foolish, irresponsible nincompoop. There is really no description of stupidity, no matter how vivid, that is adequate. I quake at the imbecility of it. Once I appreciated the full enormity of the blunder, I used to say – more than a little unfairly – to any civil servant who would listen: Where was Sir Humphrey when I needed him? We had legislated in the first throes of power. How could you, knowing what you know, have allowed us to do such a thing so utterly undermining of sensible government?[10]

See below
4.8.4

The former Labour prime minister claimed that the FOIA was primarily used by the media, calling the Act 'dangerous' because it had deprived government of 'a reasonable level of confidentiality'. FOIA was used to address the invasion of Iraq by UK forces under the Chilcot Inquiry.[11]

---

6   See debates in Parliament, Mr William Waldergrave and Mrs Marjorie (Mo) Mowlam, Labour MP for Redcar, Hansard, HC Deb 15 July 1993 vol. 228 cc 1113–1126.

7   The creation of the post of the Parliamentary Ombudsman was spurred on by the Crichel Down affair in 1954 and by the activism of pressure groups, including the Society for Individual Freedom. The position was created, and his or her powers are documented in, the Parliamentary Commissioner Act 1967. Today the office also covers the NHS in England under the office of the Parliamentary and Health Service Ombudsman (created under the Health Service Commissioners Act 1993). The first Ombudsman was Sir Edmund Compton and Dame Julie Mellor DBE has held the post since January 2012.

8   See: White Paper, 'Your Right to Know' (Cm. 3818). January 1998.

9   Based on the Labour Party Consultation Paper of 1996 headed 'Bringing Rights Home' which set out Labour's plans to incorporate the European Convention if it won the next election.

10 See: Blair (2010).

11 See: The Iraq Inquiry covering the UK's military intervention in Iraq from 2001 to 2009 at: www.iraqinquiry.org.uk.

4.2.2 Lessons from abroad

The public's 'right to know' has existed in Sweden since the eighteenth century, in the USA since 1966, in France since 1978,[12] in Canada, Australia and New Zealand since 1982, and in the Netherlands since 1991.

The Icelandic Parliament in Reykjavik passed 'freedom of information' legislation in 2010 which *inter alia* permitted a high level of protection for journalistic sources and whistleblowers, outlawing 'libel tourism'. The new legislation created a framework which permitted (and indeed encouraged) investigative journalism, access to free information and the promotion of media free speech. It is worth noting that the initial Icelandic parliamentary resolution was drafted by Julian Assange. The renowned Australian internet hacker, and until then rather elusive founder of the electronic whistleblowers' platform WikiLeaks, had surfaced from years of hiding from US intelligence services in order to support the Icelandic freedom of information campaign.

4.3 The Freedom of Information Act 2000 and the big bang approach

The Freedom of Information Act 2000 ('FOIA 2000') came into force on 1 January 2005. The Act provides public access to information held by public authorities; it covers *any* recorded information that is held by a public authority in England, Wales and Northern Ireland, and by UK-wide public authorities based in Scotland.

Information held by Scottish public authorities is covered by Scotland's own Freedom of Information (Scotland) Act 2002. The FOIA does not give people access to their own personal data (information about themselves) such as their health records or credit reference file. If a member of the public wants to see information that a public authority holds about them, they should make a 'Subject Access Request' under the Data Protection Act 1998 (DPA).

At the same time as the FOIA, the Environmental Information Regulations 2004 (EIR[13]) came into force. This dual approach was generally referred to as the 'big bang approach'. The EIR enables public access to all documents containing 'environmental information'.[14]

The FOIA 2000 imposes certain duties on public authorities. Part I of the FOIA 2000 is concerned with 'access to information held by Public Authorities'.[15] Section 1(1) states that:

> Any person making a request for information to a public authority is entitled –
>
> (a)   to be informed in writing by the public authority whether it holds information of the description specified in the request, and
> (b)   if that is the case, to have that information communicated to him.

Whilst FOIA covers all public authorities (e.g. government departments, local authorities, the NHS, state schools and police forces) it does not necessarily cover every organization that receives public money. For example, it does not cover some charities that receive grants and certain private sector authorities that perform public functions. This was tested in the *Kennedy* case.

See below
4.5.3

---

12 Two pieces of French legislation provide the right to access government records: (1) Loi no 78-753 du 17 juillet 1978 de la liberté d'accès au documents administratifs and (2) Loi no 79-587 du juillet 1979 relative à la motivation des actes administratifs et à l'amélioration des relations entre l'administration et le public.

13 S.I. 2004/3391. The EIR 2004 are intended to give effect to the United Kingdom's obligation to implement the 2003 Directive.

14 Regulation 5 EIR 2004.

15 An extensive list is provided in Sch. 1 FOIA of the meaning 'Public Authorities', covering England, Wales, Scotland and Northern Ireland.

4.3.1 Legal purpose of the FOIA

The main principle behind Parliament passing the FOIA was that people now had a right to know about the activities of public authorities, unless there was a good reason for them not to. This is described as a presumption or assumption in favour of disclosure. The FOIA covers more than 100,000 public bodies including local councils, police forces, primary schools and GP surgeries. The Act grants general rights of access in relation to recorded information held by public authorities.

Most public authorities are also covered by the Environmental Information Regulations 2004 (EIR),[16] which make a number of companies subject to the same obligations. These Regulations – based on EU legislation – are more generous and the exemptions much narrower than those contained in the main statute of the FOIA 2000.[17]

The Freedom of Information Act includes some specific requirements regarding datasets. A dataset is a collection of factual, raw data that organizations and public authorities gather as part of providing services and delivering their functions as a public authority which they then hold in electronic form. The EIR do not contain any specific provisions about datasets.

4.3.2 Exemptions under the FOIA: when is information not released?

The exemption sections of the FOIA generally fall within two categories ('class exemptions'):

1.   absolute exemptions;
2.   public interest exemptions.[18]

See below
4.6

All exemptions are time-limited, expiring after 30 years when documents containing previously exempt information become historical records, unless the information is specifically exempted from the 30-year disclosure rule, such as sensitive information relating to correspondence by members of the Royal family; for example the abdication of Edward VIII in 1936 to marry American divorcee Mrs Simpson, which was sealed for 100 years. Worthy of note in relation to the *Rob Evans* case, the FOIA does not apply directly to the Royal Household, as the Royal Household was not included in the Act's definition of a public authority in Schedule 1 of the FOIA.

Exempt information need not be disclosed by the authority. The rights conferred under the FOIA are subject to 'procedural' and 'substantive limitations'. Where access is denied, the public authority has a duty to give reasons.

See below
4.5.1

Section 32 FOIA exemptions remain the most legally challenged. This section covers the following *absolute exemptions* on public information:

- court or tribunal reports of proceedings;
- inquests and post-mortem examinations and records;
- prison custody records.

Section 40 FOIA contains an absolute exemption in relation to 'personal information', subject to the data protection principles set out in the Data Protection Act 1998. Section 41 exempts

16   Replacing the Environmental Information Regulations 1992.

17   The Regulations cover any recorded information held by public authorities in England, Wales and Northern Ireland. Environmental information held by Scottish public authorities is covered by the Environmental Information (Scotland) Regulations 2004.

18   Part II s 21 FOIA 'Exempt Information accessible to applicant by other means'.

information which, if disclosed, 'would constitute an actionable breach of confidence'. Although that is an absolute exemption, public interest in disclosure is normally a defence to a claim for breach of confidence, and it appears to be accepted that it could, in principle, operate as an effective answer to reliance on section 41.

In broad terms the FOIA established that a public authority is not required to publish or disclose information where to do so would put the public authority in contravention of its obligations under the Data Protection Act 1998 (DPA) – in other words, where the disclosure of the information would have a detrimental impact on an individual's expectation of privacy, such as the publication of data about the number of abortions requested from the Department of Health in 2014–2015.

Some *qualified information* that would (not) be in the public interest includes (*inter alia* exemptions under):

- national security (section 23 FOIA)
- defence (section 26 FOIA)
- international relations (section 27 FOIA)
- the economy (section 29 FOIA)
- domestic relationships (section 28)
- law enforcement (section 31 FOIA)
- court records (section 32 FOIA)
- formulation of government policy (section 35 FOIA)
- communications with the monarch or any member of the royal family or household) (section 37 FOIA)
- health and safety (section 38 FOIA)
- legal professional privilege (section 42 FOIA)
- commercial interests (section 43 FOIA).

Here follows a brief summary of *standard class exemptions*[19] of procedural access to 'public interest information':

- **Section 1(3) FOIA** provides that a public authority may refuse to provide information if it is unable to understand what is being asked for. For example, if an inadequately particularized request is made, where the public authority reasonably requires further particulars in order to identify and locate the information requested. The public authority is then not obliged to provide the information until 'further particulars' have been received.
- **Section 9 FOIA** ('fees') allows the public authority to charge a fee before section 1(1) FOIA is complied with; the fees notice must be in writing and, once served, the public authority is not obliged to comply with the request for a period of three months.
- **Section 12 FOIA** allows a public authority not to comply with a request for information if the cost of compliance exceeds the 'appropriate' limit.
- **Section 14 FOIA** provides an exemption if the request for information is vexatious.

---

19 Section 2 FOIA explains the effect of the exemptions in Part II of the Act.

4.3.3 Refusing access to public information on cost grounds

Increasing concern has been expressed by human rights lawyers and freedom of information pressure groups about the charging of fees for access to public information. At the same time FOIA legislation recognizes that freedom of information and environmental requests are not the only demand on the resources of a public authority. They should not be allowed to cause a drain on the public authority's time, energy and finances to the extent that they negatively affect the organization's normal public functions.

Some confusion has arisen between the FOIA and the EIR.[20] Whilst the FOIA states on the one hand that access to public information is free of charge, there are also some sections in both Acts which provide for a public authority to charge a fee, such as for photocopying or the supply of large volumes of published information. Under the EIR, it is only permissible to take into account the costs related to the provision of environmental information.[21]

The cost limit for complying with a request or a *linked series* of requests (FOIA, EIR or DPA) from the same person or group is currently fixed at £600 (for central government, Parliament and armed forces requests), and £450 for all other public authorities' access requests.

A public authority can refuse a request if it estimates that the cost of compliance would exceed this limit.[22] For example a request can be refused if the public body decides that a search of the information required would mean exceeding the cost limit (e.g. when complying with the required search would exceed 60 days).

 FOR THOUGHT – CALCULATING COSTS WHERE A REQUEST SPANS DIFFERENT ACCESS REGIMES

You have been asked to deal with all FOIA requests on behalf of the Ministry of Justice (MOJ). This includes all correspondence between the MOJ and the Department for Environment, Food and Rural Affairs (DEFRA) between certain dates. Because of DEFRA's environmental responsibilities the MOJ thinks it is likely that some, but not all of the information held, will be environmental information. You have been asked by the MOJ to draft a response to an FOIA request by a prisoner to disclose data relating to how many prisons in England and Wales allow prisoners to smoke in their cells. Draft a response to the prisoner giving reasons why the costs of compliance will exceed the appropriate limit.

4.4 The Information Commissioner's Office

The Information Commissioner's Office (ICO) is the UK's independent authority under the FOIA to uphold information rights in the 'public interest' and promote openness by public bodies and data privacy for individuals. The ICO is now handling both data protection and freedom of information requests, and is therefore covered by both data protection and FOIA legislation. What type of information can be obtained is ultimately the decision of the Information Commissioner (IC)[23] who also decides whether the information requested might be exempt because of the risk – for instance – of prejudicing international relations. Following the appointment of (Sir) Christopher

---

20 See: ss 8(4) and (5); 12 (1) FOIA.
21 See: reg. 2(1) EIR.
22 See s 12 FOIA and s 8 EIR.
23 The Data Protection Registrar referred to in the Data Protection Act 1984 became the Data Protection Commissioner by virtue of the Data Protection Act 1998. With the coming into force of certain provisions of the Freedom of Information Act 2000, the Data Protection Commissioner became the Information Commissioner.

Graham as Information Commissioner in 2009,[24] the government extended his remit within the purposes of the FOIA to include four further public organizations, namely academy schools, the Association of Chief Police Officers (ACPO), the Financial Ombudsman Service and the Universities and Colleges Admissions Service (UCAS). In April 2016, the Culture, Media and Sport Select Committee approved Elizabeth Denham[25] as the new Information Commissioner. Ms Denham took up her post in July 2016 and serves a term of five years.

4.4.1 The ICO's law enforcement powers

The ICO has extensive law enforcement powers, including criminal prosecution, non-criminal enforcement and audits. The Commissioner also has the power to serve a 'Monetary Penalty Notice'[26] on a data controller.[27] The Data Protection (Monetary Penalties) (Maximum Penalty and Notices) Regulations 2010 prescribe that the amount of any penalty determined by the Commissioner must not exceed £500,000.[28]

The IC takes a rather restrictive view of commercial interests when it comes to applying the section 43 exemption of the 2000 Act ('commercial interests'). This approach was called into question in the FTT decision in *Student Loans Company (SLC) v Information Commissioner* (2008).[29] The SLC had challenged a decision of the IC that it must disclose a training manual used by staff who dealt with defaulting borrowers. The SLC argued that disclosure of the manual would harm its commercial interests under section 43(2) FOIA, in that it would help borrowers to delay or avoid complying with their obligations. The IC contended that the SLC was not participating competitively in the purchase and sale of goods or services and that a detrimental financial effect of the kind feared by the SLC would not constitute prejudice to the commercial interests of the SLC.

When the matter was appealed before the tribunal, the FTT ruled that the IC's approach to section 43 was too restrictive. The tribunal did not consider it appropriate to tie its meaning directly or indirectly to competitive participation in buying and selling goods or services and to exclude all other possibilities. It held that the word 'commercial' includes debt collection as a commercial activity, even when carried on by a company supported by public funds. The tribunal ruled that a better approach was to ask itself whether a detriment to the SLC, from the delay and reduction of debt collections and increasing the costs of collections, could fairly be described as prejudicing the SLC's commercial interests. For these reasons, the tribunal ordered some parts of the manual to be redacted before disclosure.

A 'breach of privacy' order and fines notice was served on 'Cold Call' under regulation 21 of the Privacy and Electronic Communications Regulations 2003 (PECR).[30] Regulation 21 applies to the making of unsolicited calls for direct marketing purposes.[31]

See Chapter 5.5

---

24 Richard Thomas CBE was the UK's first Information Commissioner in 2002; he was followed by Christopher Graham, who took up his post as IC in June 2009.
25 Ms Denham was previously the Information and Privacy Commissioner in British Columbia, Canada.
26 Under s 55A(1) DPA as adapted by PECR 2011.
27 The ICO publishes a public register of data controllers, its main purpose being that of transparency and openness. The register includes the name and address of data controllers and a description of the kind of processing they do. Notification is a statutory requirement and every organization that processes personal information must notify the ICO, unless they are exempt. Failure to notify is a criminal offence.
28 Under ss 55A to 55E of the Data Protection Act 1998, introduced by the Criminal Justice and Immigration Act 2008, the Information Commissioner may, in certain circumstances, serve a monetary penalty notice on a data controller.
29 IC Application EA/2008/0092.
30 As amended by the Privacy and Electronic Communications (EC Directive) (Amendment) Regulations 2004 and by the Privacy and Electronic Communications (EC Directive) (Amendment) Regulations 2011 (PECR 2011). PECR came into force on 11 December 2003 and revoked the Telecommunications (Data Protection and Privacy) Regulations 1999. PECR adopted Part V entitled, 'Enforcement' and Schs 6 and 9 of the DPA. By virtue of reg. 31(2) of PECR the Commissioner was made responsible for the enforcement functions under PECR.
31 PECR implemented European legislation (Directive 2002/58/EC) aimed at the protection of the individual's fundamental right to privacy in the electronic communications sector. PECR were amended for the purpose of giving effect to Directive 2009/136/EC which amended and strengthened the 2002 provisions. The ICO approaches the PECR so as to give effect to the Directives.

In September 2015, the ICO fined Chichester-based company 'Cold Call Eliminations Ltd'[32] £75,000 for making unsolicited marketing calls to sell cold call-blocking devices. In 2013, 'Cold Call' had been telephoning elderly and vulnerable customers in particular to sell a call-blocking service to stop unsolicited calls, the same type of calls the company itself was making. One complainant reported to the ICO that a sales person from the company had implied they were calling from the statutory Telephone Preference Service (TPS).[33]

4.5 Legal challenges under freedom of information legislation

The FOIA provides a statutory framework within which there are rights to be informed, on request, about the existence of, and to have communicated, information held by any public authority. The right of access to such information is a right that is applicable to everybody, and not merely those who have an interest in the information, such as the media. The duties imposed on public authorities are set out in section 1(1) FOIA and are essentially twofold:

- a duty to communicate that information; and
- a duty to 'confirm or deny' that the requested information exists.[34]

But the FOIA framework is not all-embracing. First, these rights do not apply in cases which are described as *absolute exemptions*[35] and are subject to a large number of other carefully developed qualifications. Secondly, section 78 FOIA specifies that nothing in it 'is to be taken to limit the powers of a public authority to disclose information held by it'.

4.5.1 Appeals before the First Tier Tribunal (FTT): section 32 exemptions

The FTT hears appeals on information rights from appeal notices issued by the Information Commissioner (IC) under the following legislation:

- Data Protection Act 1998;
- Freedom of Information Act 2000;
- Privacy and Electronic Communications Regulations 2003;
- Environmental Information Regulations 2004

(see: Ofcom v The Information Commissioner (2010)[36]).

Section 32 FOIA deals with information held by courts and persons conducting an inquiry or arbitration. The Supreme Court held in *Kennedy* (2014)[37] that its intention was not

---

32 Source: Data Protection Act 1998, Supervisory Powers of the Information Commissioner Monetary Penalty Notice to Cold Call Eliminations Ltd, Suite 1 Metro House, Northgate, Chichester, West Sussex, PO19 1BE. Companies House registration number: 08388416 at: https://ico.org.uk/media/action-weve-taken/mpns/1432532/cold-call-eliminations-ltd-monetary-penalty-notice.pdf.

33 Under reg. 26 Privacy and Electronic Communications Regulations 2003 (PECR), OFCOM is required to maintain a register of numbers allocated to subscribers who have notified the TPS that they do not wish, for the time being, to receive unsolicited calls for direct marketing purposes on those lines. It means that if a company wants to make calls promoting a product or service to an individual who has a telephone number which is registered with the TPS then that individual must have given their consent to that company to receive such calls.

34 Section 1(6) FOIA.

35 Section 2(1)(a) and (b) FOIA.

36 [2010] UKSC 3; on appeal from: [2009] EWCA Civ 90.

37 [2014] UKSC 20.

that such information should *not* be disclosed.[38] Its intention was to take such information outside the FOIA.

With the DPA 1998 the Information Tribunal (IT) came into existence. Its responsibilities were expanded and it began hearing information appeals under FOIA and EIR as well as the Privacy and Electronic Communications Regulations 2003 (PECR). The IT was renamed Information Rights Tribunal (IRT) in January 2010 and appeals are heard by the General Regulatory Chamber. The IRT is part of the First Tier Tribunal (FTT) in the General Regulatory Chamber, part of the Ministry of Justice (MOJ) Tribunal Service.[39]

When a Minister of the Crown issues a certificate on grounds of national security exemption grounds (i.e. a PII notice), the appeal must be transferred to the Administrative Appeals Chamber of the Upper Tribunal (AAC – UT) once the application is received by the FTT (as was the case with the AG's ruling in the '*Rob Evans – Prince Charles letters*' case).

See below 4.6

4.5.2 Reports predominantly for the purpose of journalism: *Sugar v BBC*

Chapter 2.3.2 already discussed the background to the *Sugar* case. The Balen inquiry was commissioned by the BBC's former director of news, Richard Sambrook, following allegations of pro-Palestinian bias. Following the Hutton Report[40] in early 2004, the Balen Inquiry was of an equally sensitive nature and the BBC's Board of Governors set up a panel in late 2004, chaired by Sir Quentin Thomas, to provide an external independent review of reporting of Middle East affairs. The 'Thomas Report' was published in April 2006 and concluded there was 'no deliberate or systematic bias' in the BBC's reporting, but said its approach had at times been 'inconsistent' and was 'not always providing a complete picture', which had meant that it was sometimes 'misleading'. The Balen Report was then presented to the BBC's Journalism Board for consideration in 2004 and Mr Sugar requested to see the report under FOIA.

❖ **KEY CASE**   *Sugar v BBC* (No 2) [2012] UKSC 4[41]

Precedent

❖ The Balen Report was *predominantly* held for purposes of journalism and therefore lay beyond the scope of the FOIA.

❖ Information held by the BBC for the purposes of journalism is exempt from disclosure under the FOIA.

❖ Public broadcasters (like the BBC) must be able to freely gather, edit and publish news and comment on current affairs without the inhibition of an obligation to make public disclosure of or about their work under FOIA.

❖ Article 10 ECHR did not create a general right to freedom of information; the FOIA did not infer such a right when access was refused to documents which were held for journalistic purposes.

---

38 Ibid., at para. 6.
39 See: 'Information rights: appeals against the Information Commissioner'. The General Regulatory Chamber. HM Courts and Tribunal Service at: www.gov.uk/guidance/information-rights-appeal-against-the-commissioners-decision.
40 See: Report of the Inquiry into the Circumstances Surrounding the Death of Dr David Kelly C.M.G. by Lord Hutton, 28 January 2004. HC 247 at: http://fas.org/irp/world/uk/huttonreport.pdf.
41 *Sugar v BBC (deceased)* (No 2) [2012] UKSC 4.

Facts

On 8 January 2005, a commercial lawyer, Steven Sugar, asked to see the Balen Report and made a request to the BBC under the Freedom of Information Act 2000. The BBC governors refused, reasoning that the Balen Report was an internal document aimed at checking its own standards of journalism. This meant that information held by the BBC for the purposes of journalism was effectively exempt from production under the FOIA, even if it was held for other, possibly more important, purposes.[42]

Mr Sugar complained to the Information Commissioner (IC), stating that the BBC – as a public body – was under a duty to disclose the requested information. On 24 October 2005, the IC ruled in favour of the BBC. Mr Sugar subsequently appealed to the Information Tribunal, which ruled in favour of Mr Sugar on 29 August 2006. This meant the BBC had to disclose the report and could not derogate under the FOIA.[43]

The BBC appealed against the tribunal's decision. The grounds of appeal before the High Court were as follows: that the tribunal did not have jurisdiction to hear an appeal from the IC; and, even if it did, the IC's decision had been flawed as a matter of law. On 27 April 2007, High Court judge Davies J backed the IC's decision and held that the Balen Report was 'for the purpose of journalism', i.e. the report was non-disclosable. Additionally, the judge imposed restrictions on potential appeals to the Information Tribunal in the future, stating, *inter alia*, that the tribunal lacked jurisdiction.[44]

Steven Sugar appealed the High Court decision and on 25 January 2008 the Court of Appeal[45] rejected Mr Sugar's appeal, ruling that the Balen Report was to be prohibited and exempt under section 44 FOIA. Importantly, the CA rejected the view that the BBC was a public body, which meant the Corporation did not have to disclose information relating to its journalistic practices.[46] Mr Sugar appealed to the Supreme Court. Regrettably, by the time the case reached the Supreme Court, Mr Sugar had died of cancer in January 2011 aged 60. His wife Fiona Paveley continued the legal battle on his behalf. She argued that his request for disclosure had engaged his *right to receive information* under Article 10(1) ECHR.

Decision

The Supreme Court had to determine, in a situation in which information was held for dual and opposite purposes, whether the information fell within the remit of Schedule1 Part VI FOIA. Mr Sugar's (estate) appeal was dismissed and the Supreme Court held that the BBC could withhold the Balen Report under FOIA exemption since the report was predominantly for the purposes of journalism, meaning that the UK Supreme Court constructed the relevant legislation literally: 'information held for purposes other than those of journalism, art or literature', even if the information was held for other purposes as well. Therefore, the BBC was under no duty to disclose the report.

---

42 'For the purposes of journalism, art or literature' within the meaning of Sch. 1, Part VI FOIA.
43 See: *Sugar v BBC* [2007] EWHC 905.
44 See: [2009] EWHC 2348 (Admin).
45 Lord Buxton J, Lord Lloyd J and Sir Paul Kennedy.
46 For further discussion see: Johnson (2008a).

Analysis

The Supreme Court held that the Court of Appeal in this case had been correct in stating that once it is established that the information sought is held by the BBC for the purposes of journalism, it is effectively exempt from discourse under the FOIA, even if the information is also held by the BBC for other purposes.

Whilst their Lordships found that the purpose of the FOIA was to promote an important public interest in access to information about public bodies, there was however a powerful public interest in public service broadcasters (like the BBC) being free to gather, edit and publish news and comment on current affairs without the inhibition of an obligation to make public disclosure of or about their work.

It is worth noting that the judgments of Lord Walker and Lord Wilson revealed an academic issue, namely whether the definition meant information held solely for purposes other than journalism, art or literature or information held *predominantly* 'for purposes other than journalism, art or literature'.[47] The issue centred on the word and the construction of 'predominantly' and whether this should in effect be inserted into Schedule 1 Part VI before the phrase 'for purposes other than those of journalism, art or literature'. That being the purpose of the immunity, the exemption available under Schedule 1, Part VI would have failed to achieve its purpose if the co-existence of other non-journalistic purposes resulted in the loss of immunity. That was confirmed by the language of Schedule 1, Part VI. The disclosable material was defined in terms which were positive in form but negative in substance.

Their Lordships further commented that Article 10 of the Convention created no general right to freedom of information and where the legislation expressly limited such a right to information held otherwise than for the purposes of journalism, freedom of expression was not interfered with when access was refused to documents which were held for journalistic purposes.[48]

4.5.3 Absolute exemptions under FOIA

Another lengthy case concerning the disclosure of a report under FOIA was that of *Dominic Kennedy*,[49] an experienced *Times* journalist who had long expressed unease in his investigatory reports about the inquiries conducted by the Charity Commission into the 'Mariam Appeal'[50] and its founder, former Glasgow Kelvinside MP, George Galloway. There had been three inquiries by the Charities Commission into the Mariam Appeal. The results of the first two inquiries were published in June 2004 in a 'Statement of Results of the Inquiry' (SORI). At the same time, Mr Galloway had been accused by the *Daily Telegraph* of having received hundreds of thousands of pounds from Saddam Hussein. He successfully sued the *Daily Telegraph* in a libel action (see: *Galloway v Daily Telegraph* (2004).[51]

See Chapter 7

47 [2012] UKSC 4 at para. 61 (as per Lord Walker with Lord Phillips, Lord Brown, Lord Mance agreeing).

48 Ibid., at paras 94 and 98.

49 *Kennedy v Charity Commission* [2014] UKSC 20. On appeal from: *Kennedy (Dominic) v Information Commissioner & Charity Commissioners* [2012] EWCA Civ 317; [2011] EWCA Civ 367; [2011] UKFTT EA/2008/0083; [2010] EWHC 475 (Admin) (QBD) (original IC application EA/2008/0083).

50 The 'Mariam Appeal' was set up to help an Iraqi girl suffering from leukaemia. The fund's known income was nearly £1.5 million until its closure in 2003. The fund's three main backers were Saudi Arabia, the United Arab Emirates and Jordanian businessman Fawaz Zureikat, the Mariam Appeal's chairman.

51 [2004] EWHC 2786 (QB).

In his reports in *The Times*, Kennedy had commented that the Charity Commission's two brief inquiries into the Mariam Appeal left significant questions unanswered. For this reason, he made an FOIA request on 8 June 2007 for disclosure of documentation relating to 'Mariam' from the Charity Commission.[52] His request was refused under the absolute exemption of section 32(2) FOIA ('court records etc' and 'Information held by a public authority'). The Charity Commission further argued that the exemption would last until any document regarding 'Mariam' was destroyed (or to be kept secret for 30 years under section 3 Public Records Act 1958).

When the case reached the Court of Appeal in 2012,[53] Calvert-Smith J held that the Information Tribunal had been *correct* in its ruling that the wording of section 32(2) FOIA had a very wide scope. The CA ruled that there was no absolute right under FOIA to disclosure of documents held by public authorities which had been placed in the custody of or created by a person conducting an inquiry. The judge held that the documents of the Charity Commission fell under the absolute exemptions set out under section 32 FOIA, regardless of their content and the consequences of their disclosure, and notwithstanding the public interest in their disclosure. The case reached the Supreme Court in 2013.

 **KEY CASE**   *Kennedy v The Charity Commission* (UK Supreme Court) [2014] UKSC 20[54]

Precedent

❖ Section 32 FOIA is compatible with Article 10 ECHR ('there is no automatic right to receive information').

❖ Section 62(1) FOIA provides that a record (court; inquiry; inquest; etc.) becomes an 'historical record' at the end of (now) 20 years.[55]

❖ Section 78 FOIA makes it clear that that nothing in the legislation is to limit the powers of a public authority to disclose information held by it.

Facts

The *Dominic Kennedy appeal* reached the Supreme Court more than six years after the *Times* journalist's initial request, after detailed consideration by the Information Commissioner, the Information Tribunal (twice), the High Court and the Court of Appeal (twice).[56] Kennedy had argued that the exemption under section 32(2) FOIA only subsisted for the duration of the inquiry by the Charity Commission; if a natural construction of section 32(2) did not produce that result, Article 10 ECHR required it to be read down to produce that result.

Key issues before the Supreme Court

1. Whether section 32(2) FOIA contained an *absolute exception* which continued *after* the end of the Charity Commissioners' inquiry?

2. If so, whether section 32(2) FOIA ('absolute exception') was compatible with Mr Kennedy's Article 10 rights? (arguing that Article 10 ECHR included the right to *receive* information).

---

52 The Charity Commission's relevant schemes and mechanisms were at that time to be found in the Charities Act 1993, as amended by the Charities Act 2006 (since replaced by the Charities Act 2011).

53 See: *Kennedy (Dominic) v Information Commissioner & Charity Commissioners* [2012] EWCA Civ 317 (as per Calvert-Smith J).

54 [2014] UKSC 20.

55 Amended by s 45(1) Constitutional Reform and Governance Act 2010 (which was 30 years).

56 See: *Kennedy (Dominic) v Information Commissioner & Charity Commissioners* [2012] EWCA Civ 317; [2011] EWCA Civ 367; [2011] UKFTT EA/2008/0083; [2010] EWHC 475 (Admin) (QBD) (original IC application EA/2008/0083).

3. In the event of incompatibility, should section 32 FOIA be read in conjunction with section 3 HRA 1998, as either:

    (i)   ceasing to operate at the end of the inquiry; or
    (ii) being a *qualified exception* that requires a general balancing of the competing public interests?

4. Should the court make a declaration of incompatibility if it was not possible to interpret section 32(2) FOIA in a manner that was compatible with the Convention?

Decision

Their Lordships[57] dismissed the appeal, by a five to two majority (Lords Wilson and Carnwarth dissenting). It was held that:

1. Section 32(2) was intended to provide an absolute exemption which would not cease at the end of inquiry proceedings

The majority of the Supreme Court interpreted the critical phrase 'for the purposes of . . .' in section 32(2) FOIA which qualified the immediately preceding words in that section and referred to the original purpose for which the relevant documents were placed in the custody of, or were created by, a person conducting an inquiry. Their Lordships interpreted section 62(1) in that a record would become an 'historical record' at the end of 20 years.

2. Section 32 FOIA was compatible with Article 10 ECHR

The majority's view was that the effect of section 32 was to take information falling within the absolute exemption outside the scope of the FOIA regime. The FOIA was never intended to determine whether or not such information should be disclosed. Section 78 specified that nothing in the FOIA was to be taken to limit the powers of a public authority to disclose information held by it. Any statutory or common law powers to order disclosure continued to apply alongside the FOIA.

3. In the event of section 32(2) being incompatible with Article 10 ECHR, section 3 HRA did not require the provision to be 'read down'

This point was considered *obiter* due to the majority decision. Lord Mance rejected the applicant's 'radical analysis' that a right to receive information could arise under Article 10, without any domestic right to the information. Lord Toulson agreed and Lords Wilson and Carnwarth dissented on this point; they stated that ECtHR's case law was unsatisfactory (see: *Társaság a Szabadságjogokért v Hungary* (2011)[58]).

---

57 Lord Neuberger, President, Lord Mance, Lord Clarke, Lord Wilson, Lord Sumption, Lord Carnwath and Lord Toulson. Lord Mance and Lord Toulson gave the leading judgments with which a majority of the court agreed. Lord Sumption gave a concurring judgment. Lord Wilson and Lord Carnwath gave dissenting judgments. The appeal was heard on 29 and 31 October 2013. The judgment was given on 26 March 2014.

58 (2011) 53 EHRR 3 (Application No 37374/05) (ECtHR). In *Társaság* the ECtHR had advanced a broader interpretation of the notion of 'freedom to receive information', this was weakly based, clearly aspirational and tentative and not part of the essential reasoning of the Court's decision.

4. No declaration of incompatibility was necessary as section 32 was compatible with the applicant's Article 10 rights

Their Lordships stated that Dominic Kennedy had misunderstood the statutory scheme of the FOIA: he had omitted to take into account the statutory and common law position to which, in the light of ss 32 and 78 FOI, attention should have been given:

> Nothing in this Act is to be taken to limit the powers of a public authority to disclose information held by it.

They concluded that section 32(2) FOIA imposes an *absolute exemption* on disclosure of information and that this continues *after* the end of the relevant inquiry or court hearing. They made it clear that the FOIA was never intended to determine whether or not such information should be disclosed. Instead, any question as to its disclosure would be governed by other rules of statute and common law.

Lord Toulson concluded that Mr Kennedy could have availed himself of the provision of judicial review since the disclosure of the Mariam Appeal Charities' Commission investigations was of genuine public interest and would have had standing (*locus standi*).

Analysis

The *Kennedy* decision is an important ruling by the Supreme Court, particularly for those who seek FOIA disclosure of published documents from public bodies of inquiries or court records. It had been Dominic Kennedy's argument that the FOIA was an exhaustive scheme and that he had a prima facie right to disclosure, also advancing his Article 10 ECHR right to 'receive' information. But the majority of the Supreme Court refused to apply Article 10 and instead focused on the capacity of common law principles. The court referred to recent developments in Strasbourg jurisprudence which the UKSC held was not sufficient to justify a departure from the principle for which Article 10 was intended, namely freedom of expression (see: *Leander v Sweden* (1987),[59] *Gaskin v UK* (1989),[60] *Guerra v Italy* (1998)[61] and *Roche v UK* (2005)[62]).

The effect of the Kennedy judgment by the Supreme Court was not to achieve the openness, transparency and accountability of public bodies in domestic law that we had expected from the FOIA. Varuhas (2015) advances an interesting argument following the Kennedy decision and at the same time the UK Supreme Court's decision in R (on the application of Moseley) v Haringey LBC (2014)[63] – that there are two legal pathways to obtaining information and disclosure. Since the access to freedom of information regarding public authorities failed in Kennedy, there is still the route of judicial review to ensure public power is exercised properly, according to precepts of good administration and the duty to consult.

---

59 (1987) 9 EHRR 433 (A/116) (ECtHR).
60 (1989) 12 EHRR 36 (ECtHR).
61 (1998) 26 EHRR 357 (ECtHR).
62 (2005) 42 EHRR 599 (ECtHR).
63 [2014] UKSC 56; [2014] 1 WLR 3947 (SC).

Varuhas argues that common law in this area of administrative law has developed dynamically in line with contemporary ideas of open and democratic governance under the requirements of natural justice (see: R (on the application of Osborn) v Parole Board (2015)[64]).[65]

4.6 The *Prince Charles 'black spider' letters* case[66]

The long-running *Prince Charles black spider letters* case started in April 2005 with a simple one-line email from the editor of the *Guardian*, Alan Rusbridger, asking whether journalist Rob (Robert) Evans could submit freedom of information requests to ministers to see what letters they had received, and on what subjects, from Prince Charles. Right from the start *Guardian* journalist Rob Evans, who had worked for the newspaper since 1999, knew that asking to have insight into correspondence between the future king and ministers in seven Whitehall departments would be a sensitive issue. Evans had already tracked some of Prince Charles's correspondence back to 1969, the year Charles Windsor was created Prince of Wales at a ceremony at Caernarfon Castle. That memo concerned the overfishing of Atlantic salmon.

4.6.1 FOIA application of 'black spider memos' in April 2012

In April 2005, Rob Evans requested disclosure of communications sent by HRH the Prince of Wales to various government departments between September 2004 and April 2005. The freedom of information request also included the Environmental Information Regulations 2004 (EIR) and concerned some 27 letters and memos which became known as the 'black spider' letters. They were so nicknamed by the media after the prince's distinctive handwriting, with its abundant underlining and exclamation marks.

Evans contended that disclosure of the Prince of Wales's correspondence would be in the public interest, at least to the extent that the correspondence involved 'advocacy correspondence' on the part of Prince Charles. By this the journalist meant correspondence with ministers and government departments in which Prince Charles advocated certain causes which were of particular interest to him, including causes which related to the environment.

In an interview with BBC Radio 4's Joshua Rozenberg (*Law in Action*) Evans explained that his essential reason for insight into the 'black spider' letters was that it would be in the public interest for there to be transparency as to how the future King, Charles III, sought to influence government.[67]

It was well known that the prince had regularly lobbied ministers advocating his environmental policies. Some 'black spider' memos and letters had been leaked to the press in the past, for example in June 2001 when the prince had sent a letter to the then Labour Lord Chancellor, Lord Irvine, on the subject of the Human Rights Act 1998. The prince had complained that the UK was 'sliding inexorably down the slope of ever-increasing petty-minded

---

64 [2015] AC 1115.

65 See: Varuhas, J. N. E. (2015), pp. 215–218.

66 *R (on the application of Evans) v Attorney General* [2015] UKSC 21; [2015] 2 WLR 813, on appeal from [2014] EWCA Civ 254 (sub nom the *Rob Evans* or *Prince Charles black spider letters* case).

67 See: BBC Radio 4, *Law in Action* broadcast with Joshua Rozenberg in an interview with Rob Evans, on 6 November 2014, 'The Prince of Wales Letters', www.bbc.co.uk/programmes/b04n3382 and BBC Radio 4, *The Media Show*, of 5 April 2015, 'The Black Spider Memos', Steve Hewlett in an interview with Rob Evans, following the UK Supreme Court Ruling in *Re Evans* on 26 March 2015, www.bbc.co.uk/programmes/b05nvjhr.

litigiousness' and 'too little is being done to stem the remorseless obsession with rights'.[68] Tony Blair's diaries and the former Labour spin doctor Alastair Campbell's diaries and subsequently published memoirs had commented on Prince Charles's leaked letters to the *Mail on Sunday*, from his objection to the government's 'absurd' Hunting Bill in 2004 to his allegiance with the farming lobby. The former editor of the *Daily Telegraph*, Max Hastings, revealed in the *Spectator* magazine that he had seen a copy of a letter where the prince had lobbied 'for some NHS funds to be diverted from conventional medicine to homeopathy'.[69]

The government departments refused Mr Evans FOIA requests and he subsequently complained to the Information Commissioner (IC), who upheld the departments' refusal. Evans then appealed to the Information Tribunal (IT) and eventually matters were transferred to the Upper Tribunal (UT[70]) (Administrative Appeals Chamber), which determined in September 2012 that the letters should be disclosed.[71] The UT did not order the release of genuinely private correspondence but specifically 27 'advocacy' letters about the prince's lobbying the executive.

The UT's decision was significant and subsequently highlighted by the Supreme Court in its judgment in March 2015. The UT had pointed out that the Prince of Wales had 'strongly held views' on a number of matters, including politically controversial issues and proposed legislation; that his communication of those views to government ministers was well known (not least because he, ministers and others had mentioned this publicly); that he had a 'self-perceived role' which was 'representational' and involved expressing 'views in danger of not being heard'; that some of the letters had been published; and that 'a high degree of publicity' had not stopped his correspondence with ministers.[72] The UT gave some examples, such as letters to the British Bankers' Association and to the trade union UNISON. In some letters the prince had reportedly availed himself of access to ministers in order to 'drive forward charities and promote views'.[73]

But the letters and memos were not released following the UT's ruling for, shortly afterwards, on 16 October 2012 the Attorney General (AG), Dominic Grieve QC, issued a statutory veto certificate under section 53(2) FOIA 2000 and regulation 18(6) EIR 2004, stating that he had, on 'reasonable grounds', formed the opinion that the departments had been entitled to refuse disclosure of the letters. Reasons given for the Attorney General's section 53 order which warranted 'exceptionality' were:

- the fact that the information in question consisted of private and confidential letters between the Prince of Wales and ministers;
- the fact that the request in this case was for recent correspondence;
- kingship;
- the potential damage that disclosure would do to the principle of the Prince of Wales's political neutrality, which could seriously undermine the prince's ability to fulfil his duties when he becomes king;
- the ability of the monarch to engage with the government of the day, whatever its political colour, and maintain political neutrality as a cornerstone of the UK's constitution;
- the fact that the letters in this case formed part of the Prince of Wales's preparation for constitutional framework.

68 Source: 'Too much information: Charles's letters wouldn't tell us anything we didn't already know', by Steve Richards, the i, 18 October 2012.
69 Source: 'Max Hastings's diary: The joys of middle age, and Prince Charles's strange letters', *The Spectator*, 2 April 2015.
70 The UT is of equal status to the High Court.
71 See: *Evans v Information Commissioner* [2012] UKUT 313 (Administrative Appeals Chamber [AAC] (before Walker J, Judge John Angel and Ms Suzanne Cosgrave).
72 *Evans* [2012] UKUT 313 (AAC) at 21.
73 Ibid., at 156–158.

The proposition that a member of the executive – in this case the Attorney General (AG) – can actually overrule a decision of the judiciary because he does not agree with that decision is remarkable, though of course judicially reviewable. The constitutional importance of the principle that a decision of the executive should be reviewable by the judiciary lay behind the majority judgment in *Anisminic*.[74]

Arguably, by overruling the UT's decision the AG had breached FOIA legislation and its main purpose, that of free access to public information. Rob Evans sought judicial review to quash the AG's certificate, arguing that it was invalid on two grounds. First, in domestic law, he contended that section 53 FOIA did not permit a certificate to be issued simply because the accountable person took a different view of the public interest from the Upper Tribunal when it came to the issue of disclosure.[75] Secondly, in EU law, because the advocacy correspondence included environmental information and Evans contended that, once the UT had issued its determination, it was contrary to the provisions of Article 6, supported by the EU Charter, for anyone, especially a member of the executive, to overrule that determination.[76]

The Divisional Court dismissed his claim. However, the Court of Appeal allowed Evans's appeal on both grounds and gave the AG permission to appeal to the Supreme Court.[77] In July 2013, the Administrative Court granted leave for Mr Evans and the *Guardian* for an appeal against the Attorney General's decision to veto any disclosure of the royal letters.[78] The Lord Chief Justice said in his judgment that Prince Charles's correspondence had a 'constitutional function and significance' and that – for this reason – a right to appeal had been allowed. Lord Judge CJ considered the 'extensive public interest'[79] (originally correctly identified by the Information Tribunal), commenting that the Prince of Wales was in no different position from any other lobbyist when making representations to ministers.

The UK Supreme Court (UKSC) in March 2015 dismissed the Attorney General's appeal by a majority of five to two and held that the AG was not entitled to issue a certificate under section 53 FOIA in the manner that he had done; therefore the certificate was invalid. The court held that the AG had impermissibly undertaken his own redetermination of the relevant factual background, including certain constitutional conventions on which the Upper Tribunal (UT) had heard detailed evidence, which he was not entitled to do. The certificate had proceeded on the basis of findings which differed radically from those made by the UT without real or adequate explanation. By a majority of six to one the court held that regulation 18(6) was incompatible with Directive 2003/4 on public access to environmental information and should be treated as invalid.[80]

Lord Neuberger, President of the Supreme Court (with whom Lord Kerr and Lord Reed agreed), concluded that section 53 FOIA did not permit the AG to override a decision of a judicial tribunal (the UT) by issuing a certificate merely because he, a member of the executive, took a different view. The AG's decision had cut across two constitutional principles: firstly, the rule of law, namely that a decision of a court is binding between the parties and could not be set aside; and, secondly, that decisions and actions of the executive were reviewable by the courts, and not vice versa.[81]

---

74 See: *Anisminic Ltd v Foreign Compensation Commission* [1969] 2 AC 147 (HL).
75 Rob Evans argued that reasons given by the AG were not capable of constituting 'reasonable grounds' within the meaning of s 53(2) FOIA.
76 Because the advocacy correspondence was concerned with environmental issues, the certificate was incompatible with Directive 2003/4 on environmental information and/or Article 47 of the EU Charter of Fundamental Rights (the EU Charter).
77 See: *R (on the application of Evans) v Attorney General* [2013] EWHC 1960 (Admin); [2013] 3 WLR 1631 (Lord Judge CJ, Davis LJ and Globe J).
78 See: *R (on the application of Evans) v Attorney General* [2014] EWCA Civ 254; [2014] QB 855 (Lord Dyson MR and Richards and Pitchford LJJ).
79 *Evans* [2013] EWHC 1960 at paras 4–6; 21–22 (as per Lord Judge CJ).
80 *Evans* [2015] UKSC 21 at 100 (per Lord Neuberger and Lord Mance).
81 Ibid., at 52 (per Lord Neuberger).

Lord Wilson, dissenting, accused his fellow justices of rewriting the Freedom of Information Act 2000 (FOIA). He argued that the UKSC majority view undermined parliamentary sovereignty.[82] He said his Supreme Court colleagues should have resisted the temptation to uphold the decision of the Upper Tribunal (UT) against the AG's veto, even though the government had never appealed against the Tribunal's decision. But Lord Neuberger explained that when a court scrutinized the grounds relied upon for a section 53 FOIA certificate, it must do so against the background of the relevant circumstances (in this case in the light of the decision at which the certificate in *Evans* was aimed). Neuberger explained that the UT had adhered to the rule of law in that it heard evidence, called and cross-examined, as well as submissions on both sides, *in public*. In contrast, the AG had not done so. He had consulted *in private*, had taken into account the views of cabinet, former ministers and the IC, and had formed *his own view* without *inter partes* representations.

While the Supreme Court did not find it necessary to make a value judgement as to the desirability of Prince Charles encouraging or warning the government as to what to do, the justices did not think that the departments' fear of disclosing the 27 letters was justified and that the consequences of disclosure would be detrimental. In broad terms the Supreme Court ruling favoured disclosure of the 'advocacy correspondence' in the public interest.

4.6.2 Why is the ruling in the *Rob Evans* case of constitutional importance?

The Supreme Court's ruling in the *Rob Evans* case signified a victory for freedom of information. By coincidence the ruling of the highest court in the UK came in the same year that celebrated Magna Carta's 800th anniversary, heralding freedom of speech. Following the Supreme Court judgment in *Evans*, the *Guardian's* legal team, led by Dinah Rose QC, did not expect the letters to be substantially redacted despite Downing Street's warning of 'preparatory work' before the 'black spider memos' could be released.

On 13 May 2015 Clarence House released Prince Charles's letters and memos (2004–2005) and the public could finally have an insight into the future king's views and concerns. The prince's lobbying topics covered an array of issues, including beef farming and dairy quotas, badger culling and the fate of sea birds, albatrosses and the Patagonian toothfish, the power of supermarkets, Lynx helicopters, derelict hospitals, listed buildings, Scott and Shackleton's Antarctic huts, summer schools, old-fashioned teaching methods and herbal medicines.

The public interest aspect of this case is of undeniable importance in that the release of Prince Charles's letters under FOIA revealed the breadth and depth of the future king's lobbying of the executive, which stretched from Downing Street to Northern Ireland, covering topics such as defence (e.g. the performance of airborne surveillance aircraft in Iraq), the environment, architecture, organic farming, alternative medicine and education. Moreover, as the Supreme Court pointed out, the letters revealed a 'disturbing absence of proportion and self-awareness'. It is presumably for this reason that the former Attorney General, Dominic Grieve QC, fought so hard to stop publication.

The 'black spider' letters may well have engendered a contrary perception of the future monarch which might be difficult to dispel and which therefore might seriously compromise the future role of Charles III. The constitutional implications are about the future king's judgement and the belief that the monarchy ought to be politically neutral. That said, the prince's letters show concern and were considered as fairly 'harmless' by most of the media commentators following publication. What would have been of greater public interest is the ministers' and Whitehall's response to the prince's lobbying memos. That might then have revealed some of the government's policies, openness and transparency in response to the future monarch's private concerns.

---

82 Ibid., at 172 (Lord Wilson dissenting).

4.7 Freedom of information and data protection

What is the difference and interplay between the Data Protection Act 1998 (DPA) and the Freedom of Information Act 2000 (FOIA)? The FOIA provides public access to information held by public authorities but if you wish to obtain information about yourself then you must turn to the Data Protection Act 1998 (DPA).

The DPA grants the right to access (an 'access request') of private personal information such as access to medical records. The DPA sets out rules to make sure that personal information is handled properly by 'data controllers', whereas the FOIA covers the 'right to know' about public authorities. If an organization or business is processing personal data, it usually has to notify the Information Commissioner's Office (ICO) about this activity. Failure to notify is a criminal offence. The ICO is required to keep a register on prescribed data, and the register is available to the public for inspection via the ICO's website.

The IC can override a refusal to publish information in the public interest by issuing an enforcement notice following an appeal by the party whose request was refused. To date, one of the main challenges for the ICO is to tackle the lengthy backlog of cases that her office is struggling with, especially since the ICO also deals with breaches of data protection and law enforcement.

4.7.1 The Data Protection Act 1998

The scope of the DPA is very wide as it applies to just about everything concerned with individuals' personal details; the legislation applies to both manual and electronic systems.[83]

The DPA is based on the following eight principles of good information handling. These give people specific rights in relation to their personal information and place certain obligations on those organizations that are responsible for processing it.

- Principle 1: fair and lawful
- Principle 2: purposes
- Principle 3: adequacy (relevancy)
- Principle 4: accuracy
- Principle 5: retention period
- Principle 6: rights
- Principle 7: security
- Principle 8: international protective conditions for processing

The data protection framework balances the legitimate needs of organizations to collect and use personal data for business and other purposes against the right of individuals to respect for the privacy of their personal details.

The legislation itself is complex, but essentially the 1998 Act gives an individual the right to see personal data held on them by public authorities and other organizations. 'Data' means information which:

(a)   is being processed by means of equipment operating automatically in response to instructions given for that purpose;

---

83 See: Privacy and Electronic Communications (EC Directive) (Amendment) Regulations 2011 inserted ss 55A to 55E DPA 1998 into the Privacy and Electronic Communications (EC Directive) Regulations 2003, enabling the Information Commissioner to serve a monetary penalty notice on a person who breaches the 2003 Regulations.

(b)   is recorded with the intention that it should be processed by means of such equipment;

(c)   is recorded as part (or with the intention that it should form part) of a relevant filing system (i.e. any set of information relating to individuals to the extent that, although not processed as in (a) above, the set is structured either by reference to individuals or by reference to criteria relating to individuals, in such a way that specific information relating to a particular individual is readily accessible); or

(d)   does not fall within paragraph (a), (b) or (c) but forms part of an 'accessible record' (such as an office (manual) filing system of a freelance journalist).[84]

The DPA regulates the 'processing' of personal data. *Processing*, in relation to information or data, means obtaining, recording or holding the information or data or carrying out any operation or set of operations on the information or data, including:

(a)   organization, adaptation or alteration of the information or data;

(b)   retrieval, consultation or use of the information or data;

(c)   disclosure of the information or data by transmission, dissemination or otherwise making available; or

(d)   alignment, combination, blocking, erasure or destruction of the information or data.[85]

A *data subject* is the individual whom particular personal data is about. The Act does not count as a data subject an individual who has died or who cannot be identified or distinguished from others.

It is also worth bearing in mind that the EU General Data Protection Regulation 2016 (GDPR) is due to come into force in May 2018. GDPR affects every business irrespective of Brexit. Individuals have the 'right to be forgotten' and can have their data erased.

4.7.2 What is a data controller?

Under the DPA, anyone has the right to find out what information an organization (or the 'data controller' of an organization) holds about them by making a subject access request. This right allows individuals to find out important information ranging from details recorded on their credit history to data included in their health record. Once received, a *data controller* normally has 40 days to reply to the request.

Legislation frequently mentions the definition of 'data controller'. Understanding the difference between 'data controller' and 'data processor' is crucial to understanding the Data Protection Act 1998 (DPA), particularly in terms of working out where data protection responsibility lies. But the distinction between the two can be misunderstood and we will have a look at the differences here.

Data controller means:

> a person who (either alone or jointly or in common with other persons) determines the purposes for which and the manner in which any personal data are, or are to be, processed.[86]

In other words, a data controller must be a 'person' recognized in law, that is to say:

●   individuals;
●   organizations; and
●   other corporate and unincorporated bodies of persons.

---

84 An 'accessible record' is defined in s 68 DPA and can be summarized here as a health record, educational record (local education authority schools and special schools only), local authority housing record or local authority social services record.

85 Section 1 DPA 'Basic interpretative provisions'.

86 Section 1(1)(e) DPA.

> ### Example: Data controller
>
> A government department sets up a database of information about every child in the country. It does this in partnership with local councils. Each council provides personal data about children in its area, and is responsible for the accuracy of the data it provides. It may also access personal data provided by other councils (and must comply with the data protection principles when using that data). The government department and the councils are data controllers in common in relation to the personal data on the database.

The best example in case law is *Google Spain*,[87] where the Court of Justice of the European Union (CJEU) ruled that an individual can ask a data controller like Google Inc. to delete his data in certain instances. Though a very important 'privacy' case, Señor González' legal complaint against the Spanish Data Protection Authority (AEPD), the Spanish newspaper publisher (La Vanguardia Ediciones SL) and against Google Spain and Google Inc. also established that EU data protection law can catch out a US parent company which has subsidiaries in the EU. As we already concluded in Chapter 3, this is a far-reaching judgment with the potential to impact on other search engine providers such as Safari and Firefox, as well as social networks and digital media companies.

See Chapter 3.6

As with FOIA requests, some types of personal data are exempt from the right of *subject access* and so cannot be obtained by making a subject access request. Exemptions generally include the following areas:

- crime
- taxation
- regulatory activity
- publicly available information
- disclosures required by law
- legal advice and proceedings
- confidential references
- management information
- negotiations
- journalism, literature and art
- domestic purposes.

The definition of *processing* is very wide and it is difficult to think of anything an organization might do with data that will not be processing. A *data processor* in relation to personal data, means any person who processes the data on behalf of the data controller.

> ### Example: Data processor
>
> A utilities company engages a company which operates call centres to provide many of its customer services functions on its behalf. The call centre staff have access to the utilities company's customer records for the purpose of providing those services but may only use the information they contain for specific purposes and in accordance with strict contractual arrangements. The utilities company remains the data controller. The company that operates the call centre is a data processor.

---

87 See: *Google Spain SL v Agencia Espanola de Proteccion de Datos (AEPD)* (C-131/12) [2014] QB 1022 (CJEU – Grand Chamber) 13 May 2014 (*right to be forgotten* case).

The ICO has wide discretion to decide how to undertake a compliance assessment and usually takes the following criteria into account:

- whether the request appears to raise a matter of substance;
- any undue delay in making the request;
- whether the person making the request is entitled to make a subject access request.

There are very often 'grey areas', where data controllers may find it difficult to determine whether or not certain information is subject to the requirements of the DPA 1998 and all subsequent EU regulations. For example, if information about a particular web-user is built up over a period of time – perhaps through the use of tracking technology – with the intention that it may later be linked to a name and address, that information is personal data. Information may be compiled about a particular web-user but without the intention of linking it to a name, address or email address. There might merely be an intention to target that particular user with advertising or to offer discounts when they revisit a particular website without the intention to actually locate that user in the physical world. The IC takes the view that such information is, nevertheless, personal data.

Here follow some common data protection myths and realities which are in the form of 'for thought' boxes with the answers supplied in the footnotes.

 ## FOR THOUGHT NO. 1

The Data Protection Act 1998 stops parents from taking photos at school plays. Is this correct?[88]

 ## FOR THOUGHT NO. 2

A company is never allowed to give a customer's details to a third party. True?[89]

 ## FOR THOUGHT NO. 3

The mother of an 11-year-old girl who sat her flute exam is unable to find out her result. The exam board cited the Data Protection Act 1998 and informs the mother over the telephone that only the person who made the application, the flute teacher, can see the results. Is this correct?[90]

---

88 This is not correct. Photographs taken purely for personal use are exempt from the Data Protection Act 1998. This means that parents, friends and family members can take photographs of their children and friends participating in school activities and can film events at school. The DPA 1998 does apply where photographs are taken for official use by schools and colleges, such as for identity passes, and these images are stored with personal details such as names. It will usually be enough for the photographer to ask for permission to ensure compliance with the 1998 Act.

89 Not true. Where an organization is satisfied that someone asking for information about another person's account is authorized to access it, the DPA 1998 does not prevent this. However, organizations should be cautious about releasing customers' details. There is a market in personal information and unscrupulous individuals try to obtain information about others by deception. Therefore, organizations must have appropriate safeguards in place to ensure that, if staff decide to reveal a customer's personal details, such as bank account information, they are sure that the person they are speaking to is either their customer or someone acting on their behalf; for example, evidence that the account holder has given authority.

90 Not true. The DPA 1998 does not prevent an exam board from giving results to the students or their parents. The decision by this particular exam board is unfair and unnecessary given that the student's mother in this case had to make a subject access request to discover her daughter's exam result – but at least data protection access rights make sure she gets the information to which she was entitled.

4.7.3 Subject access requests: the *Bavarian Lager* case

Which data is an individual entitled to access? This right, commonly referred to as *subject access*, is created by section 7 DPA. This section is increasingly used by individuals who want to see a copy of the information an organization holds about them. However, the right of access goes further than this, and an individual who makes a written request and pays a fee is entitled to be:

● told whether any personal data is being processed;
● given a description of the personal data, the reasons it is being processed, and whether it will be given to any other organizations or people;
● given a copy of the information comprising the data; and given details of the source of the data (where this is available).

An individual can also request information about the reasoning behind any automated decisions, such as a computer-generated decision to grant or deny credit, or an assessment of performance at work (except where this information is a trade secret).

In the *Bavarian Lager* case (see below) a Lancashire beer company was refused access to a draft EU Commission Opinion regarding a possible infringement of European Community (EC) regulations. Advocate General Eleanor Sharpston QC opined in the European Court of Justice (ECJ)[91] on the conflicting Regulations concerning the protection of and freedom of access to personal data and information, namely the 'Access Regulation' 1049/2001 and the 'Data Protection Regulation' 45/2001, which – she commented – contradicted each other.

She recommended that the Commission revise its legislation in this respect to provide individuals (including companies) with clear, legally enforceable rights; furthermore, that the principles of data protection should apply to *any* information concerning an identifiable individual. These rules should then be homogeneously applied in all Member States to safeguard the protection of individuals' fundamental rights and freedoms with regard to the processing of their personal data within the Community.

❖ KEY CASE	The *Bavarian Lager* case [1999] ECR II-3217 (ECJ)[92]

Preliminary Ruling (ECJ)

❖ Under the Access to Documents Regulation,[93] EU institutions can refuse freedom of access to personal information where disclosure may put at risk the protection of the private life of an individual.

❖ Under the Data Protection Regulation,[94] personal data cannot be transferred to recipients other than Community institutions, unless the recipient organization establishes that the data is necessary for the performance of a specific task, carried out in the public interest or subject to the exercise of a public authority.

❖ Where a request based on the Access to Documents Regulation seeks to obtain access to documents including personal data, the provisions of the Data Protection

---

91 Now simply 'The Court of Justice'.
92 *Commission v The Bavarian Lager Co. Ltd* [2009] EUECJ of 15 October 2009 (see also: *Bavarian Lager v Commission* [1999] ECR II-3217(ECJ)).
93 Regulation 1049/2001 of the European Parliament and of the Council of 30 May 2001 regarding public access to European Parliament, Council and Commission documents (OJ 2001 L 145, p. 43).
94 Regulation 45/2001 of the European Parliament and of the Council of 18 December 2000 on the protection of individuals with regard to the processing of personal data by the Community institutions and bodies and on the free movement of such data (OJ 2001 L 8, p. 1).

FREEDOM OF INFORMATION

Regulation become applicable in their entirety, including the provision requiring the recipient of personal data to establish the need for their disclosure (the 'necessity test').

❖ A person requesting access to data information is not required to justify his request and therefore does not have to demonstrate any 'public interest' in having access to the documents requested.

❖ A proper system of personal data protection in each Member State not only requires the establishment of rights for data subjects and obligations for those who process personal data, but also appropriate sanctions for 'offenders' and a proper monitoring by an independent supervisory body (such as the Information Commissioner in the UK).

Facts

During the early 1990s some 2,000 British pubs were 'tied' into Guest Beer Provision (GBP), i.e. exclusive purchasing contracts with breweries; furthermore EU legislation also required that beer was held in casks with specific alcohol content.[95] The *Bavarian Lager Co. Ltd* ('Bavarian Lager'), established in Clitheroe, Lancashire, wanted to import bottled German beer for supply into UK pubs. Because of these 'exclusivity deals' Bavarian Lager could not sell its bottled lager into pubs and for this reason lodged a complaint with the EU Commission in April 1993. The main argument rested on the fact that the measure was incompatible with Article 28 EC Treaty, amounting to the 'equivalent of a quantitative restriction on imports'.

During the administrative procedure before the Commission, a meeting was held on 11 October 1996 between representatives of the Community and UK administrative authorities and the Confédération des Brasseurs du Marché Commun. Bavarian Lager wanted to take part in that meeting, but the Commission refused. On 15 March 1997, the Department of Trade and Industry announced that the GBP provision was to be amended in order for bottled beer to be sold as GBP. The Commission suspended all Treaty infringement proceedings against the UK. By fax of 21 March 1997, Bavarian Lager asked the Director General of the Commission (Internal Market and Financial Services) for a copy of the 'reasoned opinion', and access to the Commission documents concerning the meeting of 11 October 1996. That request was refused. Reasons given included that the related documents were 'data protected' because five individuals wished to remain anonymous.[96]

Bavarian Lager, relying on Article 8(1) and (2) of the Charter, and the Access to Documents Regulation 1049/2001 ('the Access Regulation'), argued for administrative transparency'. The Commission, in turn, relied on Regulation 45/2001 on 'Data Protection' ('DP', the 'Personal Data' Regulation'). The DP requires the person to whom personal data is to be transferred to demonstrate that the transfer is necessary. Bavarian Lager applied to the Court of First Instance[97] for clarification.

---

95 Under Article 7(2)(a) of the Supply of Beer (Tied Estate) Order 1989 (S.I. 1989/2390).
96 See: *Bavarian Lager v Commission* [1999] ECR II-3217(ECJ).
97 Now known as the General Court. As from 1 December 2009, the date on which the Treaty of Lisbon entered into force, the EU has legal personality and has acquired the competences previously conferred on the European Community (EC). Community law has therefore become European Union law. The term 'Community law' will still be used where the earlier case law of the General Court is being cited. The General Court is made up of at least one judge from each Member State.

When the case reached the European Court of Justice, the Commission, supported by the UK, argued that the Court of First Instance had made errors of law in its findings concerning the application of the exemption in Article 4(1)(b) of Regulation No 1049/2001 and thereby rendered certain provisions of Regulation No 45/2001 ineffective.

Decision by the European Court of Justice (ECJ)

In her judgment, the Advocate General ruled that the Access to Documents Regulation[98] established the general rule that the public may have access to documents of public institutions of Member States. But the ECJ equally laid down exemptions by reason of certain public and private interests, particularly in relation to the right of access to a document where the disclosure would undermine the privacy and integrity of an individual or even put that individual at risk. In certain circumstances, however, an individual's personal data may be communicated to the public. Where a request based on the Access to Documents Regulation seeks to obtain access to documents including personal data, the provisions of the Data Protection Regulation[99] become applicable in their entirety, including the provision requiring the recipient of personal data to establish the need for their disclosure (the 'necessity test').

The ECJ set aside the judgment by the Court of First Instance (CFI), meaning that Bavarian Lager lost its appeal; the ECJ reached the following conclusions:

1. The CFI had erred in law because it failed to correctly interpret Article 6 of the Access Regulation 1049/2001, i.e. processing personal data by EU institutions;[100] a person requesting access is not required to justify his request and therefore does not have to demonstrate any interest in having access to the documents requested.
2. The DP Regulation 45/2001 requires consideration of whether the applicant has a legitimate ('necessary') interest in receiving the particular personal data. Accordingly;
3. The Commission had not erred when it decided that Bavarian Lager had not established a legitimate interest in receiving the personal data contained in the documents.
4. The ECJ dismissed the action of Bavarian Lager against the Commission's decision of 18 March 2004, rejecting an application for access to the full minutes of the meeting of 11 October 1996, including all the names, i.e. the data had been lawfully withheld by the Commission. In the absence of the consent of the five participants at the meeting of October 1996, the Commission sufficiently complied with its duty of openness by releasing a version of the document in question with their names blanked out.
5. Since Bavarian Lager was unsuccessful in the appeal, the court ordered Bavarian Lager to pay the full costs relating to the appeal, i.e. all Commission appeal proceedings including the CFI.[101]

Analysis

Though the *Bavarian Lager* case originally concerned the 'free movement of goods' principle, the main issue before the Court of Justice centred on freedom of information and access to personal (or in this case company) data. The ECJ made it clear that a fully fledged

---

98 Regulation 1049/2001, op. cit.
99 Regulation 45/2001, op. cit.
100 See: *Bavarian Lager v Commission* [1999] op. cit.
101 Other cases cited and dealt with at the time by the ECJ were: *Council v Hautala* [2001] ECR I-9565; *Sweden v Commission* [2007] ECR I-11389; *Netherlands v Council* [1996] ECR I-2169 (Case C-58/94). The ECJ ordered the Kingdom of Denmark, the Republic of Finland, the Kingdom of Sweden and the UK to bear their own costs.

system of personal data protection not only requires the establishment of rights for data subjects and obligations for those who process personal data, but also appropriate sanctions for those who breach regulations and monitoring by an independent supervisory body.

The Advocate General's opinion appears to favour freedom of information principles but at the same time she warned that personal data needs to be safeguarded – relying on the fundamental principles of Article 6 EU Treaty and the Charter of Fundamental Rights of the European Union ('the Charter'). The Charter recognizes the primary importance of both the protection of personal data and the right of access to documents. Article 8(1) and (2) of the Charter provide as follows:

1. Everyone has the right to the protection of personal data concerning him or her.
2. Such data must be processed fairly for specified purposes and on the basis of the consent of the person concerned or some other legitimate basis laid down by law. Everyone has the right of access to data which has been collected concerning him or her, and the right to have it rectified.

The AG recommended that measures should be adopted which are binding on Community institutions and bodies. These measures should apply to all processing of personal data by all Community institutions and bodies in so far as such processing is carried out in the exercise of activities all or part of which fall within the scope of Community law, according to Article 6 of the EU Treaty. Access to documents, including conditions for access to documents containing personal data, is governed by the rules in Article 255 EC Treaty.

The *Bavarian Lager* case demonstrates that under the Access to Documents Regulation,[102] EU institutions may refuse freedom of access to information where disclosure would risk undermining the protection of the private life of an individual. The Data Protection Regulation[103] states that personal data cannot be transferred to recipients other than Community institutions, unless the recipient organization establishes that the data is necessary for the performance of a specific task, carried out in the public interest or subject to the exercise of public authority. The General Data Protection Regulation (GDPR) is set to replace the Data Protection Directive 95/46 EC from 25 May 2018. Part 3 of GDPR enhances requirements for obtaining data subject consent.

This means that every EU Member State's public authority ('the controller') must provide access to requested information within reasonable time intervals (usually interpreted as once a year), without charge and 'without excessive delay', meaning usually within three months (see also: *Gillberg v Sweden* (2012)[104]).

4.8 Devolved freedom of information: Scotland and Northern Ireland

The Scottish Information Commissioner (SIC) is a public official appointed by Her Majesty the Queen (or the King) on the nomination of the Scottish Parliament. Much the same as her English counterpart, the Scottish Commissioner promotes and enforces both the public's right to ask for

102 Regulation 1049/2001, op. cit.
103 Regulation 45/2001, op. cit.
104 (2012) (App No 41723/06) of 3 April 2012 (ECtHR).

the information held by Scottish public authorities, and good practice by authorities. The SIC is responsible for enforcing and promoting three pieces of devolved legislation:

- Freedom of Information (Scotland) Act 2002 (FOISA) – very similar to the English/Welsh Act it gives everyone the right to ask for any information held by a Scottish public authority.
- Environmental Information (Scotland) Regulations 2004 (the EIRs) – give everyone the right to ask for environmental information held by a Scottish public authority.
- The INSPIRE (Scotland) Regulations 2009 – create a right to discover and view spatial datasets (e.g. meta data or map data) held by Scottish public authorities.

In July 2012, the Scottish Information Commissioner, Rosemary Agnew,[105] issued a decision requiring Scottish ministers to reveal whether or not they held legal advice in May 2011 on the status of an independent Scotland within the European Union.

A row had broken out when Catherine Stihler MEP[106] had asked for a copy of any legal advice held by Scottish ministers. The ministers took their case to the Court of Session to try to prevent the release of any information. Under Scots FOI law, in limited circumstances a public authority can refuse to reveal whether information is held. A refusal of this type can be issued where:

- the information would be exempt from release under one of a limited number of specified exemptions in the FOI (Scotland) Act if it was held; and
- the authority considers it would be contrary to the public interest to reveal whether the information existed or was held.

Ms Stihler then made an FOI (Scotland) request.

In her consideration of the case, the Scottish Information Commissioner concluded that, if legal advice on this matter was held by ministers, it would, at the time of the request, have been exempt from release under two of the Scottish FOI Act's exemptions. However, she also found that to reveal whether or not the information was held would not have been contrary to the public interest.

In considering the public interest, the Commissioner's decision stated:

> In the Commissioner's view, the role of the [FOI] Act is important not only in ensuring transparency in information held by public authorities, but also in enabling transparency in information about process? In this case, the Commissioner considers that it is in the public interest to know the type of information that the Ministers were taking into account in developing policy in relation to such a significant issue as independence.[107]

The Information Commissioner ordered the disclosure of the information, which eventually took place. As a result of this row First Minister, Alex Salmond, referred himself to the Parliamentary Standards Commissioner to determine whether he had broken the Scottish Ministerial Code. In January 2013 Sir David Bell found that the Scottish First Minister did not breach the Ministerial Code with his stance on legal advice over an independent Scotland's future in Europe.

---

105 Prior to this appointment Ms Agnew was Chief Executive of the Scottish Legal Complaints Commission and prior to that office she was an Assistant Ombudsman at the Local Government Ombudsman's office.
106 Catherine Stihler is a British Labour Party politician and has been a Member of the European Parliament for Scotland since 1999 and is presently the only female MEP representing Scotland.
107 Source: Scottish Information Commissioner. Decision 111/2012. 'Catherine Stihler MEP and the Scottish Ministers. Legal advice: Scotland's membership of the European Union.' Decision: 6 July 2012. The appeal against this decision has since been abandoned.

Between 2013 and 2014, the SIC received 578 appeals with 62 per cent from members of the public. In 67 per cent of cases, the Commissioner found in favour of the applicant requestor.[108] Some decisions taken in 2015 included:

- A request by Mr R (a serving prisoner) who asked the Scottish Prison Service (SPS) for information pertaining to the employment of prisoners in the HMP Edinburgh prison kitchen and about prisoners' wages working in the kitchen.

  ❖ Decision: The SPS provided Mr R with some of the information but informed him that certain information was 'data protected' such as third-party prisoner data and prisoners' earnings.[109]

- A request by Mr McLean about the chime of St Stephen's Church from the City of Edinburgh Council.

  ❖ Decision: The Commissioner ordered the Council to disclose some of the information which the Council had wrongly withheld from Mr McLean, such as the chiming of the historic 1820s clock and why the chime was stopped for some months while work was being carried out in the church between April and August 2014. But that the data should not be released as to the persons who had complained about the noise from the clock's chimes.[110]

- Request by Paul Hutcheon of the Sunday Herald asking Historic Scotland for information regarding the potential refurbishment or relocation of the First Minister's official residence. Historic Scotland withheld information under the exceptions at regulation 10(4)(e) ('internal communications') and 10(5)(a) ('international relations, defence, national security or public safety') of the EIRs.

  ❖ Decision: partly upheld in favour of the applicant. Historic Scotland was entitled to withhold the information under these exemptions. However, the SIC found that Historic Scotland had failed to provide Mr Hutcheon with an adequate level of advice and assistance when responding to his request and as such failed to comply with regulation 9(1) of the EIRs.[111]

4.8.1 Differences and similarities between FOIA in England/Wales and Scotland

The Freedom of Information (Scotland) Act 2002 (FOISA) contains much the same terms as its English and Welsh equivalent – though it is much broader in scope. There are several laws dealing with access to information which apply in Scotland.

Whilst the two Acts (FOIA 2000 and FOISA 2002) are broadly similar in many respects, some of the provisions of the Scottish Act are more rigorous. Some of the main differences between the two regimes are:

- The Scottish Act provides a straightforward right of access to information held, whereas the UK Act provides a right to be told whether or not information is held and to be provided with that information.

---

108 Source: Scottish Information Commissioner. Annual Report 2013–14. 'Taking FOI Forward'.
109 Source: Scottish Information Commissioner Decision 143/2015: 'Mr R and the Scottish Prison Service. Employment of prisoners in prison kitchen'. Reference No: 201500852. Decision: 7 September 2015.
110 Source: Scottish Information Commissioner Decision 128/2015: 'Mr James McLean and the City of Edinburgh Council St Stephen's Church Clock, Edinburgh.' Reference No: 201402393. Decision: 11 August 2015.
111 Source: Scottish Information Commissioner. Decision 033/2015: 'Mr Paul Hutcheon and Historic Scotland Refurbishment or relocation of the First Minister's official residence.' Decision: 16 March 2015.

- The tests for exempt material are different. The Scottish Act requires public authorities claiming an exemption to exercise the public interest test, where applicable, within the 20 working day response period. The UK Act does not give a time limit.
- The harm test in the Scottish Act requires that disclosure would 'substantially prejudice' the effective conduct of public affairs, the commercial interests of an individual, etc. The UK Act stipulates only 'prejudice'.
- Both Acts allow public authorities to recoup a proportion of the costs involved in providing information to individual requests (usually 10 per cent of search costs). In Scotland the first £100 is waived.
- The publication scheme requirements are different. The Scottish Act requires public authorities to take into account the public interest in information relating to: the provision of services, including the cost of provision and the standards of those services; and major decisions made by the public authority, including facts and analyses on which the decisions are based. The UK Act only requires public authorities to have regard for the public interest in allowing public access to the information held by the authority and in the reasons for major decisions made by the authority.
- The UK Act allows information which is due to be published at some future date to be withheld until its publication (where it is reasonable to do so). The Scottish Act limits the withholding of information that is to be published to a maximum of 12 weeks, unless the information relates to a programme of research.
- The UK Act is enforced by the UK Information Commissioner (ICO),[112] the Scottish Act by the Scottish Information Commissioner.

Freedom of Information Act 2000 (FOIA) and Freedom of Information (Scotland) Act 2002 (FOISA)[113]

Comparative Table

	FOI UK (England, Wales & Northern Ireland)	FOI Scotland
Jurisdiction of Commissioner	Commissioner responsible for both FOI (except Scotland) and Data Protection (whole UK). But note responsibility for FOI extends to UK-wide public authorities.	Commissioner responsible for FOI in Scotland. But see overlap with section 38 Data Protection Act 1998.
Duty to inform that the applicant PA[1] has the information requested	UK Act provides for dual rights: • to be informed that PA has information; and if so • to have that information communicated. The UK Act refers to first right as duty to confirm or deny (section 1(6) FOIA). Duty referred to throughout the Act. Arguably goes further than Scottish Act; application can be set aside for virtually every exemption (subject to public interest).	Scottish Act does not structure duty of authority in this way. Provides for one right; to be given the information requested. But does address issue via section 18 FOISA. The duty to confirm whether info exists or not is subject to public interest test. Slightly narrower than UK Act in that it only applies to certain exemptions (sections 28–35, 39(1) or 41).

112 The UK Information Commissioner also polices the Data Protection Act 1998.
113 Source: Scottish Information Commissioner's Office October 2015.

	FOI UK (England, Wales & Northern Ireland)	FOI Scotland
Destruction of information	Destruction of material not specifically addressed in UK Act. Section 77 FOIA makes it an offence to alter, deface, block, erase, destroy or conceal info with intention of preventing disclosure by authority.	Specific section 1(5) FOISA prevents destruction of documents unless not reasonably practicable. Section 65 makes it an offence to destroy material with intention of preventing disclosure.
Harm test	Authorities must show disclosure would prejudice or harm specified interest.	PA must show disclosure would substantially prejudice or harm. Higher standard than UK Act.
Public interest test	Does the public interest in maintaining the exemption outweigh the public interest in disclosing information (section 2(1)(b) FOIA)?	Is the public interest in disclosing the information requested outweighed by the public interest in maintaining exemption (section 2(1)(b) FOISA)?
Information received from UK government 'in confidence'	No reciprocal arrangement in relation to information from Scotland.	Section 3(2)(a)(ii) FOISA provides that information supplied by Minister or Departments of the UK government are held in confidence but not held by Scottish authority; therefore cannot be accessed under FOISA. In such cases UK FOIA will be used.
Disability rights	No specific mention of rights of disabled in relation to applying or receiving information requested.	Specific sections regarding disability rights (section 8; section 11(5) FOISA). Explicit reference to Disability Discrimination Act 1995.
Refusal of request on public interest	Section 17(2) FOIA allows PA more time where authority has not reached decision on the application of section 2(1)(a) or (2)(b) (whether the public interest in relation to duty or confirm or deny or in relation to exempt information applies). PA can issue applicant a notice estimating time within which decision will be reached (PA should aim to reach decision within 40 days).	Section 16 FOISA imposes strict time limits on authority (20 to 30 days) as soon as information is transferred to the 'Keeper of Records' even where public interest needs to be considered.
Information not held by PA	UK Act does not specifically address responsibility of authority when PA does not have info requested.	This issue is specifically addressed in section 17 FOISA. Formal notice must be issued to say that information is not held.

	FOI UK (England, Wales & Northern Ireland)	FOI Scotland
PA review of refusal to disclose	No provision in Act for internal review by authority. Must also refer to right of appeal to Information Commissioner (section 17(7) FOISA). Section 50(2) FOIA states that IC can refuse to entertain application when applicant has not exhausted all remedies.	Scottish authorities have 20 working days (30 days if information held by 'Keeper' and another PA has to carry out review) (section 21) to review their decision if they receive a requirement for review of refusal.
Publication Schemes	The UK Act does not specify the type of information that authorities should consider providing access to via its publication scheme (section 19(3)) but simply refers to need to have regard to public interest.	When adopting publication scheme, an authority must have regard to public interest in allowing access to info relating to costs, standards, facts or analyses (section 23(3)(a)).
National Security Certificates – system of appeal	Section 60 FOIA provides for an appeal by IC or applicant against a certificate issued under section 23 or section 24 (relating to information supplied by security services and national security respectively). Under section 23 (where information is absolutely exempt) tribunal possesses power to quash a certificate where it finds that information is not exempt. Final point of Appeal to UT. Under section 24 (where information is subject to public interest test), the Tribunal can apply principles by court on application for judicial review.	Appeals from national security certificates (issued under section 31) not addressed in Scottish Act. Scottish Information Commissioner cannot challenge on public interest if certificate is conclusive of that fact. Certificate could be challenged via judicial review.
Information intended for future publication	Section 22 FOIA refers to information to be published at some future date.	Section 27 FOISA specifies future date must be not later than 12 weeks from request.
Research	No specific section addressing research.	Detailed provision in relation to programme of research (section 27(2)).
Parliamentary privilege	Information that falls under parliamentary privilege can be exempt. Certificate can be provided to that effect (section 34). The IC cannot challenge the application of this exemption where it is supported by appropriate certificate. However, if no certificate is provided, the claim to this exemption can be challenged by the Commissioner.	The Scottish Act contains no corresponding provision. There is no concept of parliamentary privilege in relation to the Scottish Parliament or its members in the sense understood by Westminster. The Scotland Act 1998 has number of provisions designed to give protection to Parliament so that it can conduct its business.

	FOI UK (England, Wales & Northern Ireland)	FOI Scotland
'Prejudice to public affairs'	Under section 36 FOIA it is left to the reasonable opinion of a qualified person to decide whether disclosure of the information would prejudice the effective conduct of public affairs (subjective test). Exemption becomes absolute in relation to information of both Houses of Parliament.	Opinion of individual is irrelevant in Scottish Act (section 30 FOISA). Applies an objective test.
'Legal professional privilege'	Exemption only applies to lawyer/client relations in England and Wales (s 42). Same section refers to situation in Scotland and uses phrase 'confidentiality of communications'. Wider application when dealing with Scottish public authorities covered by UK Act than other authorities.	Section 36(1) FOISA refers to 'confidentiality of communications' in legal proceedings. This is broader and could include doctor/patient, journalist/sources and possibly priests/penitent.
Commissioner review: time limit	UK Act provides no statutory time limit to review by IC (s 50 FOIA).	Commissioner must report to Parliament annually on number of decisions made outside four-month period (section 46(2) FOISA).
Judicial Review	Equivalent law officers in UK do not have protection accorded to Scottish law officers.	Scottish Commissioner has no power to review refusals to disclose by Lord Advocate and procurators fiscal (s 48) in relation to role as head of criminal investigations.
Appointment of Commissioner	Information Commissioner (IC) appointed by monarch on nomination of government (section 6 Data Protection Act 1998).	Scottish Commissioner appointed by monarch on nomination of Parliament (section 42(1) FOISA).
Information tribunal	FOIA provides for both an Information Commissioner and an Information Tribunal. PA or applicant can appeal to the Tribunal against decision of Commissioner (section 57) whether decision, information or enforcement notice. Section 58 provides two grounds on which Tribunal can allow appeal: (a) notice not in accordance with law (b) if it considers that Commissioner ought to have exercised discretion differently. Tribunal may review any finding of fact on which the notice is based. Further appeal possible to High Court on point of law.	FOISA provides only for an Information Commissioner. Scotland rejected need for Tribunal as introducing unnecessary extra appellate tier. PA/applicant can appeal to Court of Session against decision, information or enforcement notice issued by the Commissioner on point of law.

	FOI UK (England, Wales & Northern Ireland)	FOI Scotland
Commissioner settlement	No provision for settlement by IC contained in FOIA.	FOISA provides for Commissioner to attempt to effect a settlement before reaching decision (section 49(4)).
Potential to override Commissioner	A Minister of the Crown or the Attorney General can issue a certificate in relation to exempt information (see *Rob Evans* case (2015) UKSC). Certificate can only be issued in relation to notice served on government department or PA designated by the order.	Scottish Executive can only issue certificate in relation to certain exemptions: sections 29, 31(1), 32(1)(b), 34, 36(1) and 41(b) (almost all class exemptions). Also information must be of 'exceptional sensitivity' (section 52). Only First Minister can give Commissioner the Certificate and following consultation with other members of the Scottish Executive. Certificate can only be issued in relation to notice served on Scottish Administration (i.e. ministers, junior ministers, non-ministerial office holders and their staff).
Exercise of rights of children	Unlike Scots law, capacity of **children under 16** is largely governed by common law. Guidance from the IC in relation to DPA makes it clear that there is **no minimum age** requirement for applicants. Children can apply for their own records provided they are capable of understanding the nature of the request. A parent or guardian can only apply on the child's behalf if (a) the child has given consent or (b) the child is too young to have the understanding to make an application.	Section 69 FOISA expressly entitles children to exercise their rights under the Act (see similar provision exists in relation to Scotland only in section 66 DPA). See also: Age of Legal Capacity (Scotland) Act 1991; children can consent to certain activities (medical treatment/instructing solicitor) if have sufficient understanding. Presumed to have sufficient understanding if 12 or over.

[1] PA = Public Authority

❖ KEY CASE   *Common Services Agency v Scottish Information Commissioner* (2008) UKHL 47[114]

The background to this case is that for many years concern had been expressed about risks to public health in the area arising from operations at the MOD's Dundrennan firing range, the now decommissioned nuclear reactor at Chapelcross and the nuclear processing facilities at Sellafield. This case raised important questions about the interaction between provisions of the Data Protection Act 1998 (DPA) on the one hand and provisions of the (devolved) Freedom of Information (Scotland) Act 2002 (FOISA) on the other.

114 9 July 2008.

Precedent

❖ Some Scottish and UK-wide FOIA legislation overlaps, specifically section 38(2)(a) FOISA and section 40(3)(a) FOIA.

Facts

On 11 January Mr Collie, acting on behalf of 2005 Chris Ballance MSP, asked the Common Services Agency (CSA) to supply him with details of all incidents of childhood leukaemia for both sexes for the years 1990 to 2003 for all the Dumfries and Galloway ('DG') postal area by census ward. At that time the Agency was a special 'Health Board' whose functions fell partly under the Scottish Parliament but also came under the powers of the National Health Service.[115] There was (and still is) a genuine public interest in the disclosure of this information.

But the CSA refused Mr Collie's request. He was told that the agency did not hold these details for 2002 or 2003 as the data relating to these years was still incomplete. As for the earlier years, there was a significant risk of the indirect identification of living individuals due to the low numbers resulting from the combination of the rare diagnosis, the specified age group and the small geographic area. As a result it was *personal data* within the meaning of section 1(1) DPA and was exempt information for the purposes of FOISA 2002. The agency decided that this 'personal information' was not available under section 38 FOISA (much the same as section 40 FOIA). The agency also maintained that it owed a duty of confidence equivalent to that of the clinicians to whom the information had originally been made available.

Mr Collie applied to the SIC under section 47 FOISA for a decision whether his request for information had been dealt with in accordance with Part I of the Act. The Commissioner published his decision on 15 August 2005 stating that he was minded to release *some* information for each year requested at Health Board level.[116] The Scottish Information Commissioner agreed that the information was personal data, but ruled that the CSA should provide it to Mr Collie after applying a method known as 'barnardization' to disguise personal information.[117] The CSA appealed.

The issues before the HL comprised:

1. Whether the information in barnardized form was information 'held' by the CSA at the time of the request.
2. If so, whether it would constitute 'personal data'.
3. If so, whether its release to Mr Collie would be in accordance with the data protection principles, in particular the conditions for the processing of personal data in Schedule 2 of the DPA 1998.
4. If so, whether the information was also 'sensitive personal data' and whether its release would also meet one of the conditions for processing sensitive personal data in Schedule 3 DPA.

---

115 Functions of the Common Services Agency (Scotland) Order 1974 (S.I. 1974/467) (as amended).

116 On 15 August 2005 the Commissioner issued his decision under s 49(3)(b) FOISA.

117 'Barnardization' is a disclosure control method as employed by the Information Services Division (ISD) of National Health Services in Scotland in July 2005. It sets out a process to be followed when handling statistics where there is a potential risk of disclosure of personal information as a result of small cell counts. ISD uses a modification rule which adds 0, +1, or −1 to all values where the true value lies in the range from 2 to 4 and adding 0 or +1 to cells where the value is 1. 0s are always kept at 0. It does not guarantee against disclosure but aims to disguise those cells that have been identified as unsafe. *See: Draft Guidance on Handling Small Numbers* (2005).

Decision

Their Lordships[118] allowed the appeal and remitted the case back to the Scottish Information Commissioner. The HL decided that information was 'held' by the CSA (a data controller) at the time requested and that barnardizing the information was reasonable in the circumstances. It was only if the result of applying barnardization to the information was that the CSA could no longer identify any living individuals as the subjects of that information that it would not be personal data. Whether barnardization achieved that was a question of fact for the SIC. As barnardization effectively anonymizes the data, condition 6(1) of Schedule 2 ('processing necessary for the purposes of legitimate interests and not unwarranted by prejudice to the data subject') would be met. Whether the data would also be 'sensitive personal data' and whether any of the Schedule 3 conditions were satisfied were questions of fact for the SIC.

Analysis

This case was directly concerned with the interplay between the Data Protection Act 1998 (DPA) and the Freedom of Information (Scotland) Act 2002 (FOIA), but as much of the relevant wording of the latter was (is) also to be found in the Freedom of Information Act 2000 (FOIA), the case is of UK-wide significance. Specifically, there is an overlap of section 38(2)(a) FOISA and section 40(3)(a) FOIA. The HL had therefore been asked for a resolution of these legal 'replicas' which would have a bearing on the interaction between DPA and freedom of information legislation throughout the United Kingdom.

Their Lordships were hindered to an extent by the lack of findings of fact by the SIC, but the case turned on the effectiveness of the barnardization process in rendering the information 'fully anonymous', both to recipients and to the CSA. Lord Hope's speech is particularly notable for his rejection of the submission that whether information was 'sensitive personal data' was to be determined by reference to that information alone and not by other information that was or was likely to come into the data controller's possession.

4.8.2 The Northern Ireland Information Commissioner and NI Law Commission

Legislation in Northern Ireland is much the same as in England and Wales as far as access to freedom of information and data protection are concerned. The Freedom of Information Act 2000 (FOIA) and the Data Protection Act 1998 (DPA) both cover Northern Ireland. The right to request information on public bodies under the 2000 Act is not confined to citizens of the UK; requests can be made by individuals of any nationality from anywhere in the world. The IC for Northern Ireland also influences policy and works closely with the departments of the NI Civil Service and the wider public sector.[119]

The Northern Ireland Law Commission (NILC) is one of the public bodies which is covered by the terms of the FOIA.[120] The NILC was established in 2007 following the recommendations of the Criminal Justice Review Group (2000). The Commission was established under the Justice (Northern Ireland) Act 2002, amended by the Northern Ireland Act 1998 (Devolution of Policing

---

118 Judgment of 9 July 2008: Lord Hoffmann, Lord Hope of Craighead, Lord Rodger of Earlsferry, Baroness Hale of Richmond and Lord Mance.

119 See: Information Commissioner's Office for Northern Ireland: https://ico.org.uk/about-the-ico/who-we-are/northern-ireland-office.

120 Source: 'Freedom of Information anomaly sparks concerns', by John Manley, *The Irish News* 29 July 2015.

and Justice Functions) Order 2010. Legislation requires the NILC to review the law of NI and make recommendations for its systematic development and reform. The Department of Justice must consult with the Attorney General for Northern Ireland before approving any programme of change submitted by the Commission. The Chair of the NILC is drawn from the High Court Bench; four of the Commissioners are drawn from the legal professions and one is appointed from outside the legal professions.

The NILC charges fees where the total cost to provide information exceeds £600,[121] including:

- determining whether NILC holds the information requested;
- locating the information or document containing the information;
- retrieving the information or a document which may contain the information;
- extracting the information from a document containing it.

4.8.3 The Northern Ireland 'Nama' controversy

The National Asset Management Agency (Nama[122]) was a Republic of Ireland government initiative which was aimed at stabilizing and fixing the broken Irish banking system. The agency came under attack by the Irish and UK media following a number of FOIA requests regarding the agency's property development 'interests' between 2003 and 2007. Nama-related properties included those under receivership in Ireland, Northern Ireland and the rest of the UK. Banks such as AIB, Bank of Ireland, Anglo Irish Bank and Irish Nationwide were in turn being paid at discount rates for all their property-related loans over €5 million, good and bad. Properties that had secured the Nama loans – acquired and sold by Nama debtors or the appointed insolvency practitioners – were then placed on the open market. Nama initially tried to evade FOIA requests in Northern Ireland (under FOIA), citing sections 99 and 202 of the Irish National Asset Management Agency Act 2009 which precludes the publication of details relating to debtors or their properties where an enforcement action had not taken place.

The chairman of the NI Stormont Committee, Daithí McKay, had made two separate FOIA access requests from Nama, asking for information about former 'Nama' advisory board member and banker, Frank Cushnahan, in 2015. The FOI requests sought disclosure of all correspondence with Frank Cushnahan and the controversial sales of 'bad banks' of NI debt. All FOIA requests were initially ignored.[123]

The NI Assembly started a public inquiry into Nama in September 2015 at the same time that NI's First Minister, Peter Robinson (Democratic Unionist leader) resigned from his post in the wake of alleged involvement of the IRA in a Belfast killing, that of Kevin McGuigan.[124]

Daithí McKay's FOIA requests were eventually answered by the Department of Finance and Personnel (DFP) and it emerged that Peter Robinson had been among five people who were allegedly going to financially benefit from the sale of a property portfolio worth more than £1 billion, as part of the Nama property sell-offs in NI. Nama was also subject to a criminal investigation by the National Crime Agency (NCA). Mr Robinson denied all allegations.

In December 2015 Peter Robinson received undisclosed libel damages over unfounded allegations in *Private Eye* linking him to a blocked nomination for a peerage. On 9 December Pressdram,

---

121 This equates to a charge of £25 per hour for 24 hours' work (2016).
122 Nama had been introduced as a statutory body by (now deceased) Minister Brian Lenihan (1959–2011) in April 2009, following the enactment of the National Asset Management Agency Act 2009.
123 Source: Northern Ireland Assembly, Committee for Finance and Personnel. Official Report (Hansard) 'Sale of National Asset Management Agency assets in Northern Ireland: Evidence from DFP Officials 23 July 2015' at: http://data.niassembly.gov.uk/HansardXml/committee-14565.pdf.
124 The former Provisional IRA assassin had been struck by at least six bullets fired from two automatic weapons at his house in Comber Court, East Belfast, on 12 August 2015.

the owners of *Private Eye*, published a comprehensive retraction and apology which, together with the payment of a significant sum in damages and costs, vindicated Mr Robinson's position.[125]

4.8.4 The Chilcot Inquiry: the war on Iraq

As soon as the Freedom of Information Act 2000 had come into force in January 2005, there were some 40 requests to various government departments about the process leading up to the Iraq War. The *Daily Telegraph* pursued the Attorney General (AG) at the time, Lord Goldsmith, as to the legality of the Iraq War. Then Labour Prime Minister, Gordon Brown, announced on 15 June 2009 that an 'Iraq Inquiry' would be set up led by Sir John Chilcot, former Permanent Secretary at the Northern Ireland Office in the 1990s. The 'Chilcot Inquiry'[126] was officially launched on 30 July 2009 and completed its final public hearings on 2 February 2011. The 2.6 million-word report took nearly seven years to be published and was finally released on 6 July 2016.[127]

The purpose of the inquiry was to examine the UK's involvement in Iraq, including the way decisions were made and actions taken, and to establish as accurately and reliably as possible what happened and to identify lessons that could be learned. The fundamental question raised under FOIA was whether the war on Iraq was 'legal', questioning the legitimacy of UN Resolution 1441. According to Elizabeth Wilmshurst, Deputy Legal Adviser in the Foreign Office until 2003, the invasion of Iraq lacked legitimacy, and accordingly lacked support from legal advisers in the Foreign Office.[128] She resigned shortly afterwards.

The Chilcot Report's findings are devastating, presenting as fact that the Iraq invasion by British and American troops was not justified in terms of weapons of mass destruction. Chilcot found that then Prime Minister Tony Blair deliberately exaggerated the threat posed by the Iraqi regime of Saddam Hussein as he sought to make the case for military action to MPs and the public in the build up to the invasion in 2002 and 2003. In a six-page memo, Blair had written to US President, George W. Bush, eight months before the Iraq invasion to offer his unqualified backing for war well before UN weapons inspectors had completed their work, saying: 'I will be with you, whatever.'[129]

The Chilcot Report identified some major mistakes by the British intelligence services with 'flawed' information about Saddam's alleged weapons of mass destruction, the basis for going to war. Chilcot rejected Blair's claim that the subsequent chaos and sectarian conflict in the Middle East could not have been predicted and that Tony Blair's hubris ultimately steered Britain into a disastrous course of action. What followed was a destructive and demoralizing war where British soldiers did not have the right equipment, such as the too lightly armoured Snatch Land Rovers, last used in Northern Ireland, which became 'mobile coffins', and a lack of helicopters. The result was too many lives lost unnecessarily.

Regarding the legality of the war, the report is scathing about the indecisiveness of the then Attorney General, Lord Goldsmith, who said there might be a 'reasonable case' under UN Resolution 1441 to invade Iraq.[130] Chilcot concluded that it was neither right nor necessary to invade Iraq in March 2003.

Tony Blair's 6,500-word response following the Chilcot Report finished: 'The aftermath turned out more hostile, protracted and bloody than we ever imagined.'[131]

---

125 Source: 'Peter Robinson wins libel damages and apology from Private Eye magazine over baseless claims he was blocked from peerage', by Alan Erwin, *Belfast Telegraph*, 9 December 2015.

126 See: Iraq Inquiry ('The Chilcot Inquiry into the Iraq War') available at: www.iraqinquiry.org.uk.

127 See: House of Commons (2016) The Chilcot Report, executive summary at: www.iraqinquiry.org.uk/media/246416/the-report-of-the-iraq-inquiry_executive-summary.pdf.

128 Iraq Inquiry at paras 15–19.

129 See: House of Commons (2016) Chilcot Inquiry Report at pp. 69–77 (Executive Summary).

130 Ibid. at pp. 62–68.

131 Source: Video snippets from a two-hour press conference 'Tony Blair unrepentant as Chilcot gives crushing Iraq war verdict', *The Guardian*, 6 July 2016 at: www.theguardian.com/uk-news/2016/jul/06/chilcot-report-crushing-verdict-tony-blair-iraq-war.

 **FOR THOUGHT**

How far has the FOIA played a part in the 'war on Iraq' revelations? Discuss with reference to the Chilcot Report and its inquiry.

4.9 Standards in public life: has the FOIA made a difference?

The revelations about MPs' expenses would not have been available to the *Daily Telegraph* in 2009 had the parliamentary authorities not been preparing a heavily redacted document for FOIA release. Some have criticized the Act as a bureaucratic waste of time and money, with requesters complaining that important information is often redacted or withheld by authorities who are only too aware of the complex rules and exemptions of FOIA legislation.

To date, it has been argued, too much information is being withheld by authorities who try to hide behind the complex exemption clauses. At times, the Information Commissioner has taken years to release information and appeals can take up to four years to process because the ICO is swamped with cases.

4.9.1 Analysis and discussion

It could be argued that freedom of information-type websites, such as WikiLeaks – founded by Julian Assange – have put the complex regime of the FOIA 2000 into question. Critics of the FOIA regime have argued that the Act is too complex with its class exemptions and seemingly long waiting times.

However, the MPs' expenses scandal demonstrates that the FOIA has been a success. With the assistance of the Act, the *Daily Telegraph* was able to access and reveal parliamentary expenses 'abuses' in 2009–2010 which were of genuine public interest. Similarly *Guardian* journalist Rob Evans's access request regarding the disclosure of the Prince Charles letters – though the FOIA requests took nearly a decade for the letters to be released. Though the Prince Charles 'black spider' letters were not earth shattering they still revealed an insight into the future king's views, such as his support for proportional representation in Westminster elections and his opposition to the Human Rights Act. Most would agree that Rob Evans's immense efforts to access some 27 letters and memos written by the Prince of Wales to ministerial departments was a significant and important legal triumph to gain information which the public had a right to know.

There have been many other revelations, such as the naming of paedophile MPs and senior civil servants of the Thatcher government operating in the House of Commons at the time, suggesting a plot to cover up certain MPs' 'penchant for small boys'.

The downside is that appeals to the Information Commissioner's Office (ICO) tend to be lengthy, given that the Commissioner has to balance state, individual, corporate and media interests when making an effective decision as to whether to disclose sensitive information or not under the many exemption clauses of the Act.

4.10 Data protection post-Brexit

On 23 June 2016 the United Kingdom voted to leave the European Union in an advisory referendum (i.e. not strictly legally binding). This coincided with a considerable change in data protection law, namely the implementation across the EU of the General Data Protection Regulation 2016 (GDPR), which comes into force on 25 May 2018.

This might be problematic for the UK, once Article 50 of the Lisbon Treaty is invoked and Britain exits the EU. The UK Information Commissioner's Office (ICO) released a press statement following the Brexit result, noting that the Data Protection Act 1998 (DPA) remains the law, that the GDPR would not directly apply to the UK if the country were no longer part of the EU, but that 'having clear laws with safeguards in place is more important than ever given the growing digital economy, and we will be speaking with government to present our view that reform of the UK law remains necessary'.[132]

Following Prime Minister Theresa May's parliamentary reshuffle and appointments of Boris Johnson as Foreign Secretary and David Davis as Brexit negotiator, we may well see the UK being granted 'adequacy' status by the European Commission, as Canada, Switzerland and several other countries have achieved under the EU Data Protection Directive (95/46/EC). The negotiation period for the UK to leave the EU would then involve Article 45 of the GDPR, as adequate data protection would be assessed as part of Britain's international commitment to commercial companies and trade relationships.

So, how will personal data protection be regulated if the UK leaves the EU before the GDPR comes into force? The Information Commissioner's Office made clear that the UK will not be without data protection legislation and that the Data Protection Act 1998 (DPA) remains the law of the UK. Under the DPA, UK data controllers are permitted to make their own adequacy determination for transferring data outside the UK and EEA. In addition, the UK remains a member of the Council of Europe and a party to the European Convention on Human Rights (e.g. Convention 108 for the Protection of Individuals with regard to Automatic Processing of Personal Data). After all, members to the Convention span some 50 countries, including Turkey, Russia, and Ukraine.

On 12 July 2016, the EU–US 'Privacy Shield' was adopted by the European Commission. The Privacy Shield entered into force immediately in all EU Member States (including the UK at that time). The Privacy Shield replaced the 'Safe Harbour' framework (post the *Max Schrems* ruling[133]) and provides one of the lawful routes for transferring personal data from the EU to those US organizations that have publicly self-certified compliance with the Shield's rules, by providing 'adequate protection' for EU personal data transfer.

See Chapter 6.5

 ## 4.11 Further reading

Brooke, H. (2011) *The Silent State. Secrets, surveillance and the myth of British democracy.* **London: William Heinemann.**
Award-winning investigative journalist Heather Brooke exposed the parliamentary expenses scandal with repeated FOIA requests resulting in the shocking media publications in 2010 of widespread lack of governmental transparency and lack of control of the way parliamentarians spent public money. In this very readable book, Brooke argues that without proper access to the information that citizens pay for, Britain can never be a true democracy.

Grant, H. and Round, N. (2012) 'Recent decisions of the Commissioner and Tribunal', *Freedom of Information,* **9(2), 8–12.**
Hazel Grant and Nicholas Round analyse decisions from the Information Commissioner and First Tier Tribunal in 2012, including *Evans* (2012); *Montford* (2012); *Chagos Refugees Group* (2012); *Magherafelt* (2012). The authors examine sections 38 and 40(2) FOIA concerning personal information exemptions and errors in law.

---

132 Source: Amended statement by the Information Commissioner, Sir Christopher Graham, at the annual report launch on 28 June 2016.
133 See: *Maximillian Schrems v Data Protection Commissioner* (Case C-362/14) (CJEU).

Smartt, U. (2015a) 'Prince Charles's "black spider memos": how a Guardian journalist succeeded in his 10-year quest under the Freedom of Information Act 2000', *European Intellectual Property Review*, **37(8), 529–538.**
This article is an extended case comment on the *Rob Evans* case and the UK Supreme Court's ruling which signifies a victory for freedom of information and the Freedom of Information Act 2001 (FOIA).

Spurrier, M. (2012) *'Gillberg v Sweden*: **towards a right of access to information under Article 10?',** *European Human Rights Law Review*, **5, 551–558.**
Spurrier discusses the ECtHR ruling in *Gillberg v Sweden* (App No 41723/06) of 3 April 2012, where the Human Rights Court recognized and developed a positive right of access to information. The author argues that the Strasbourg Court should take a more principled approach to the development of this right and observes that the changing landscape is provoking much debate in the domestic courts.

Chapter 5

Regulatory authorities 1: the communications industry

Key points

This chapter will cover the following questions:

○ What is the purpose of regulators?
○ What is the difference between statutory and self-regulatory authorities?
○ How is the communications and competition industry regulated?
○ What is the full remit of Ofcom?
○ What are the broadcasting regulations in relation to public service broadcasting?
○ How is the BBC governed?
○ Can the internet be fully regulated?

5.1 Overview

How much does the ordinary member of the public actually know about regulators and government quangos[1]?

This chapter looks at statutory, self- and co-regulators and asks which model of regulation has the most advantages. There are some regulatory authorities which most citizens have never heard of, such as PhonepayPlus – a co-regulator – approved by Ofcom, responsible for premium rate phone services and smartphone applications (apps) in the UK; or ATVOD, the regulator for video-on-demand services.

In some industries, the government might allow self-regulation. Other countries may well have strict government control of the media and the print press. After the 'Law and Justice Party' (PiS) won a clear majority in Poland in the October 2015 elections, President Andrzej Duda enacted controversial laws enabling the new Conservative government to appoint the heads of public TV and radio, as well as civil service directors. The EU Commission expressed concern that Poland was jeopardizing EU values and media freedom.

The regulator for Ukrainian broadcasting – the National Television and Radio Broadcasting Council of Ukraine – signed a Memorandum in May 2015 on protecting minors while providing broadcast services, thereby meeting the requirements of EU legislation.

This and the next chapter discuss the merits and disadvantages of regulatory bodies and whether voluntary regulatory powers are sufficient to deal with wrongdoers or whether court action is still the most effective answer.

5.1.1 Regulatory structure in the UK

The best-known regulators in the UK are OFCOM, the Charity Commission, the Environment Agency, the Law Society and the Civil Aviation Authority. Lesser-known agencies are PhonepayPlus, the Internet Watch Foundation, the Office for Nuclear Regulation or ATVOD,[2] the regulator for video-on-demand services carried over UK TV platforms. There are three regulatory models in the UK. These are:

---

1 Quasi-autonomous non-governmental organization.
2 The Association for Television On-Demand Services at: www.atvod.co.uk.

- statutory regulation control by a statutory body, such as Ofcom, in relation to, for example, complaints about taste and decency, privacy and unfairness in relation to broadcasters;
- industry self-regulation, e.g. the Independent Press Standards Organisation (IPSO) (for print media and online activities) or the Advertising Standards Authority (ASA), the independent regulator of advertising across all media;
- co-regulation, a combination of industry self-regulation with oversight by a statutory body (e.g. PhonepayPlus).

5.2 Regulators: what are their functions?

Scottish moral philosopher and pioneer of political economy, Adam Smith (1723–1790), wrote in his *Wealth of Nations* (1776) that monopolies are inherently harmful and would cause a misallocation of scarce resources, with prices rising well above competitive prices. He recommended regulatory authorities that should closely monitor mergers and competitive behaviour of such monopolies.[3]

From the 1930s onwards most of the public utilities in the UK – gas, water, and electricity – were nationalized to ensure economic survival and efficiency in the face of war and post-war reconstruction. Prime Minister Margaret Thatcher's Conservative policy from 1979 onwards was to privatize these utilities: gas in 1986, electricity in 1990 and water between 1985 and 1989. Her policy led to more than 50 companies being either sold off or privatized. Some of these natural monopolies required regulation and the 'quangos' were formed.

Today the overall regulation of businesses and promotion of competition is undertaken by the Department for Business, Innovation and Skills (BIS), the Competition and Markets Authority (CMA) and the EU Competition Commission. Relevant UK legislation includes:

The Competition Act 1998 (as amended) prohibits:

- formation and operation of cartels;
- price fixing.

The Enterprise Act 2002 (amended the Competition Act 1998):

- detection of and punishing abuse of market dominance and cartels;
- assessment of mergers to be less influenced by politicians;
- regulator can use covert surveillance;
- criminalization of cartels;
- disqualification of directors for breach of the competition rules.

Enterprise and Regulatory Reform Act 2013

- established Competition and Markets Authority (CMA), 1 April 2014 (combined Office of Fair Trading (OFT) and the Competition Commission (CC)).

---

3   See: Smith, A. (1776 – new edition 2008 with explanatory notes by Kathryn Sutherland).

5.3 Models of self-regulation, co-regulation and statutory regulation: converged media services

See Chapter 6

In the UK media self- or co-regulation is primarily achieved by way of codes of practice, drawn up by a variety of professional bodies; such as the Ofcom Broadcasting Code, the CAP Advertising Code (non-broadcast) or the BCAP Code (the UK Code of Broadcast Advertising). Such regulators are largely independent and generally involve public consultation when code changes are proposed. There now exists a mix of regulation and public funding which brings together commercial enterprise and public service broadcasting for consumers.

Media convergence today means an overlap of communications and media activities. Converged devices, such as tablets, iPads or catch-up TV offer media content to a variety of means of access over and above traditional TV and radio services, for example, podcasts, BBC iPlayer, Amazon Prime, Netflix, etc. There are now a large number of video-on-demand (VoD) service providers – all of which need regulating in one form or other.

How much are consumers aware that the content they engage with over the same platform may have a legacy separate from its competitors, leaving it subject to different regulation? How much does the consumer know about content standards and protection in a converged world? How transparent and accountable are suppliers of media content, say, videos imbedded in newspapers online? What impact does convergence have on privacy and data protection? Which regulator should intervene for mixed-media content? Should there be separate regulators for video-on-demand (such as ATVOD – the Authority for Video on Demand service)? The EU Commission is looking at this at present.

Let us have a look at models of regulation in the UK and media regulation in the EU.

5.3.1 Self-regulation

Self-regulatory models are industry designed and led, allowing the industry to define an approach best suited to achieving its desired outcomes. Self-regulatory systems rely on a strong alignment between the incentives of participants and the wider public interest. Membership is voluntary and there is no statutory legal scheme.

The advantages of self-regulators are generally speed and dealing with public complaints out of court; the downside of self-regulation is that these authorities tend not to have legal powers in the form of injunctions, fines or damages (such as does Ofcom).

Traditionally, non-statutory regulatory authorities could not be challenged in the administrative courts by way of judicial review, though Lord Woolf stated in the *Ian Brady* case[4] when the moors murderer challenged an adjudication by the Press Complaints Commission (PCC), that any exercise of jurisdiction over the PCC 'would be reserved for cases where it would clearly be desirable for this court to intervene'. Newsreader Anna Ford also tried to seek judicial review in a PCC decision, but the courts could see no justifiable basis for interfering with a self-regulatory body.[5]

Another negative aspect of self-regulatory regimes is that they are unlikely to prove effective when confronted by circumstances which present a tension between the public interest and the corporate interests of industry players. Critics argue that self-regulation is unlikely to provide sufficient incentive for firms to behave responsibly. If the actions of a voluntary regulator impinge on the rights of the subjects of the decision, particularly their human rights such as freedom of expression or privacy rights, then it is likely that the courts will intervene, which could mean that the

---

4   R v PCC ex parte Stewart-Brady [1997] EMLR 185.
5   R v PCC ex parte Anna Ford [2002] EMLR 5, 31 July 2001 (unreported) (QBD).

strict demarcation between non-statutory (self- or voluntary) and statutory regulators is breaking down. This became the subject of the Leveson Inquiry.

See Chapter 6.3

5.3.2 Statutory regulators

Statutory regulation has the same aims and functions as good quality self-regulation which means the desirable features of statutory regulation are similar to those achieved under self-regulation. The difference is that statutory regulation has the force of the law to ensure that its aims are met; therefore enforcement and monetary fines can be a powerful means of compliance (such as applies to Ofcom). It is usually carried out by an independent body, accountable to the Westminster Parliament and subject to scrutiny by the National Audit Office. It is usually the most effective model where there is a clear divergence between commercial interests and the wider public interest.

There are several ways to achieve statutory regulation. One is for a profession or body to pursue its own Act of Parliament which establishes a statutory regulating body. Regulatory bodies can be set up by order or Royal Charter (e.g. press regulation), subject to affirmative resolution in both Houses of Parliament or the Privy Council.

See Chapter 6.2

The advantages of statutory regulation include that the regulator is then derived from statute which means there is the legal underpinning of a body's disciplinary procedures. For example, a practitioner might be struck off due to misconduct in his or her office (see the 'Sachsgate' affair about the Jonathan Ross and Russell Brand Radio 2 broadcast below at **5.4.4**). Another advantage is that the relevant statutory regulatory body can legally use a particular title (such as Ofcom) and enforce its standards by way of statute. This provision then makes it very easy for the public to determine who is, and who is not, a properly recognized regulator.

5.3.3 Co-regulation

Co-regulatory models typically provide more industry involvement than statutory regulation and can be particularly effective when there is widespread industry support for the objectives of regulation. They require periodic monitoring by a backstop body to ensure effectiveness and can require the backstop body to carry out enforcement activity.

The relevant legislative framework for this regulator is derived from the Audiovisual Media Services Directive 2010/13/EU.[6] One of the aims of the Directive is to provide a fair level of competition between traditional (linear) television broadcasting services and on-demand services that are considered similar enough to compete with them. Section 368BA of the Communications Act 2003 requires that every provider of video on-demand programme services (ODPS)[7] must notify the appropriate regulatory authority of its intention to provide the service.[8] A fee is then levied on that regulator which must be paid to the supervisory 'umbrella' regulator, such as Ofcom.

The Authority for Television On Demand (ATVOD) is such a co-regulator. It co-regulates UK video-on-demand and TV-like services with Ofcom (known as 'on-demand programme services' or ODPS). Examples are catch-up TV such as ITV and Channel 4 'iplayers' (but not the BBC), Amazon Prime (but not Netflix which comes from the USA). ATVOD generally covers 'harm' issues in advertising, sponsorship and children's access to pornography. But it does not cover 'taste and decency',

---

6   Directive 2010/13/EU on the coordination of certain provisions laid down by law, regulation or administrative action in Member States concerning the provision of audiovisual media services (Audiovisual Media Services Directive). The Directive was implemented in UK law by the Audiovisual Media Service Regulations 2010 which came into force on 18 March 2010 and amended the Communications Act 2003 in relation to and regulating video on-demand programme services (ODPS).
7   As defined in s 368A Communications Act 2003.
8   For an ODPS which was already being provided on 18 March 2010, notification should have been made before 30 April 2010. For an ODPS beginning after 18 March 2010, notification should have been made before the service began. Section 368D(3)(ZA) requires that a provider of an ODPS must pay to the appropriate regulatory authority (i.e. Ofcom) such fee as that authority may require under s 368NA of Communications Act 2003.

nor does it regulate fairness or privacy. If a complaint to ATVOD is upheld the regulator will publish a 'determination' on its website citing the breach of its rules.

To demonstrate the complexity of co-regulation in converged media services let us have a look at the Ofcom 'ruling' (known as 'determination') in the *Vice News* case (see below).

Vice News and *BuzzFeed* are relatively new online current affairs brands. The Vice Media, Inc. group is based in New York, though it has bureaus worldwide. *Vice News* was created in December 2013 as a division of Vice Media and primarily consists of documentaries. Vice had some impressive investors, such as Rupert Murdoch's 21st Century Fox, investing some $70 million in Vice Media in 2013 with a 5 per cent stake. A & E Networks, in a joint venture with Hearst Corporation and the Walt Disney Company, acquired a 10 per cent share in Vice in 2014 for $250 million. Vice mainstream news covers events that may not be as well covered by other news sources, distributing written articles and video content on its website and YouTube. Some of its past coverage includes: 'The Battle for Iraq' – covering the post-war insurgency in Iraq, 'Rockets and Revenge' – the Israeli–Palestinian conflict in 2014; 'The Afghan Interpreters' – and their struggle, while working for the US military, in acquiring visas; 'The Islamic State – an inside exclusive'.

BuzzFeed is also an American internet news media company, describing itself on its website as the 'social news and entertainment company . . . redefining online advertising with its social, content-driven publishing technology . . . provides the most shareable breaking news'. Founded in 2006 in New York by Jonah Peretti and John S. Johnson III as a viral lab, the company grew globally by using 'native advertising', a form of online advertising that matches the form and function of the platform on which it appears. For example, an article written by an advertiser to promote their product, but using the same form as an article written by the editorial staff. BuzzFeed receives the majority of its traffic by creating content that is shared on social media websites, such as Twitter and Facebook. The site continues to test and track their custom content with an in-house team of data scientists and external-facing 'social dashboard.' Staff writers are ranked by views on an internal leaderboard.

Vice News and *BuzzFeed* are primarily targeted at a younger demographic audience.

 KEY CASE   *The Vice News Case* (2015)[9]

Facts & background

The regulator 'The Authority for Television On Demand' (ATVOD) determined in 2013 that Vice's UK news office provided 'on-demand programme services' (ODPS) because the video tab constituted 'a service in its own right, the principal purpose of which is the provision of TV-like programmes'. Vice appealed this decision to Ofcom – the 'umbrella' regulator of ATVOD. In July 2015 Ofcom upheld Vice UK's appeal and quashed ATVOD's determination.[10]

Vice's Appeal to OFCOM

Ofcom made its decision on the basis of new information provided by Vice, which submitted that the person with editorial responsibility for its video tab was established in the United States and therefore outside the jurisdiction of the UK for the purposes of the Communications Act 2003. Ofcom agreed with Vice's submission.

---

9 See: Ofcom Determination of 21 July 2015 'Appeal by Vice UK Ltd against a Notice of Determination that the provider of the service 'Vice (Video)' (www.vice.com/en_uk/video) has contravened ss 368BA ('requirement to notify on-demand programme service') and 368D(3)(ZA) ('requirement to pay a fee') of the Communications Act 2003.

10 This decision overturned the previous determination made by ATVOD on 14 August 2013, which judged the video tab made available on the Vice website to be an ODPS.

In determining where Vice's service was established, Ofcom considered Article 2(3) of the Audiovisual Media Services Directive (2010/13/EU), which states:

> For the purposes of this Directive, a media service provider shall be deemed to be established in a member state in the following cases:
>
> (a) ...The media service provider has its head office in that member state and the editorial decisions about the audiovisual media service are taken in that member state;
> (b) If a media service provider has its head office in a member state but decisions on the audiovisual media service are taken in a third country, or vice versa, it shall be deemed to be established in the member state concerned, provided that a significant part of the workforce involved in the pursuit of the audiovisual media service activity operates in that member state.

Decision

Ofcom determined that the entity with editorial responsibility was, for the purposes of Article 2(3)(a) of the Directive, the US-based Vice Media Inc., rather than Vice UK. The decision was based on the following facts:

❖ the UK Vice team had no role in selecting which video content to include;
❖ all US video content had to be included (except if deemed culturally offensive or legally problematic); and
❖ decisions on arranging the content were also made by the team based in the USA.

Ofcom also considered the jurisdiction test at Article 2(3)(c); it found this to be relevant as although Vice's head office was in a third country, some decisions on the audiovisual media service were taken in an EU Member State. Ofcom determined that there was no significant part of the UK workforce involved in the audiovisual media service activity because only an estimated 18 of Vice's 192 staff were based in the UK. In addition, it was determined that the US head office's authority greatly limited the decision-making capacity of the UK-based staff.

Analysis

In *the Vice News case*, Ofcom made some observations for future regulatory reference. The communications regulator said it is necessary to look at what the website offers as a whole: purely written content or audiovisual material or both? Ofcom noted that a video tab could be an *incidental* part of a text- and photo-based magazine-style website. It also said that faced with similar decisions in future, ATVOD may find it helpful to seek evidence to show how consumers in fact access and use the audiovisual material on the site in question.

Ofcom's decision provides a clear indication that where editorial responsibility for an on-demand programme service (ODPS) is established outside the EU, that service will not fall within the definition of an ODPS for the purposes of the UK Communications Act 2003 and so will not be subject to regulation in the UK.[11]

---

11 See: Ofcom Determination of 21 July 2015 'Appeal by Vice UK Ltd', paras 101–102.

Who then is editorially responsible for content on these newly converged media platforms? The answer would seem to be found in the *Vice News* determination: where the majority of content originates from; who selects and arranges the content to be included on the service; and who is responsible for signing off on content?

We have seen that the model of co-regulation can, like self-regulation, struggle where there are pronounced tensions between commercial interests and the wider public interest, but usually less so than self-regulatory models. This is because the existence of the backstop body obliges the participants to find a way of resolving the inherent problems, or else face some kind of sanction from the backstop body.

 FOR THOUGHT

> Does self-regulation by an organization like the Internet Watch Foundation (IWF)[12] pose a threat to civil liberties? Should one not be able to view any material on the internet in the privacy of one's own home?

5.4 Broadcasting regulations: TV and radio

Until the early 1980s, Western European broadcasting was largely state-controlled. For example, advertising 'spots' were either not permitted or strictly controlled by state regulation, and increasingly by EU Treaty provision and EU Regulations.[13] Although this regulatory framework still exists to a certain extent today, it has been frequently challenged by independent broadcasting providers in recent times. The UK was one of the first European countries to dismantle this monopoly by the introduction of commercial broadcasting in September 1955 via 'Independent Television' or ITV. ITV came under the regulatory auspices of the Independent Television Authority (ITA) to provide competition to the public service broadcaster the BBC.[14]

Areas covered by any broadcasting or regulatory standards normally include the following guidelines:

- protection of minors;
- offence to human dignity;
- protection against harm, e.g. flashing lights; on-air hypnosis;
- no encouragement of behaviour which is harmful to health or safety;
- no incitement to crime and disorder;
- no incitement to hatred, contempt, racial hatred or hatred on grounds of national or ethnic origin, colour, religion, sex, sexual orientation, age or mental or physical disability;
- rules on advertising and programming.

The broadcasting and communications sector broadly comprises the following areas of regulation:

- broadcasting equipment, such as cameras and recording transmission equipment;
- data transmission networks and associated cables and ducts; transmission networks, including masts and other large, fixed equipment;

---

12 See: www.iwf.org.uk.
13 See: *Commission v Kingdom of Spain (supported by United Kingdom of Great Britain and Northern Ireland)* (2011) (Case C-281/09) Judgment of the Court (First Chamber) of 24 November 2011. The case concerned 'advertising spots' and transmission times on Spanish national TV and the state's failure to fulfil obligations under Directive 89/552/EEC.
14 For further discussion see: Scherer (2013), Part 3 'Telecommunications laws in EU Member States', pp. 213–285.

- equipment and software that supports fixed and mobile communications, such as telephone lines, video and satellite communications;
- services, such as communications network providers and ISPs, systems integration, communications software, research and development.

A range of factors play a significant role in shaping the communications sector with key drivers in the telecommunications ('telecoms'), radio-communications ('radiocomms') and broadcasting equipment sector, including:

- globalization of the market for the manufacture and design of components, leading to major international players buying smaller, innovative businesses;
- new markets opening up as more countries develop a taste for technology;
- consumers and businesses viewing interaction with telecoms, radiocomms and broadcasting as an everyday experience;
- advances in the mainstream use of technology, such as digital technology, broadband and high definition;
- technology convergence bringing new innovative products to market along with improved performance.

See below
5.5

The UK communications watchdog, Ofcom, has concurrent powers with the relatively new regulator the Competition and Markets Authority (CMA),[15] which investigates breaches of UK and/or EU prohibitions against anti-competitive agreements and abuses of dominant positions, bringing criminal proceedings against individuals who commit the cartels offence under the Enterprise Act 2002 (EA02). The CMA has jurisdiction to carry out all reviews under UK merger control laws and all market investigations. It is the primary enforcer of both civil and criminal competition laws and has co-regulatory powers with the Serious Fraud Office (SFA).[16]

5.4.1 The British Broadcasting Corporation: history and governance

During the first 80 years of the BBC's existence there was comparatively little change in the way in which it was governed. The BBC began its daily radio transmissions in September 1922, and 'listening in' to the 'wireless' quickly became a social and cultural phenomenon in Britain. From 1927 – when the BBC was established by Royal Charter to be the monopoly broadcaster in the UK – until 2006 – when the Royal Charter was last reviewed – the BBC had a Board of Governors which acted as 'trustees' of the public interest.

The BBC governors were constitutionally part of the BBC but were independent of management. They were responsible for:

- appointing the Director-General;
- approving the BBC's strategic direction;
- ensuring that the BBC management implemented its strategy;
- overseeing complaints.

---

15 From April 2014, the CMA took over many of the functions and responsibilities of the Competition Commission and the Office of Fair Trading (OFT) under the Enterprise and Regulatory Reform Act 2013.
16 See CMA and SFO Memorandum of Understanding, 29 April 2014 established under s.188 of the Enterprise Act 2002.

Each of the 12 governors, including the Chairman, was appointed by the Secretary of State. The BBC required the permission of the Secretary of State before it was able to launch a new service. The governors were accountable to Parliament through periodic Charter reviews and by appearing before Parliamentary Select Committees.

The BBC's monopoly lasted until 1955 when Independent Television (ITV) began broadcasting a regional commercial broadcasting service on Channel 3. This heralded the start of an era when a separate regulatory regime was established for commercial television. Whilst in the past governance was often carried out quietly and without much public scrutiny there is now a much greater desire for consistency and transparency when large sums of public monies are being expended. As the BBC spends £3.5 billion of public licence fee money each year it is of no surprise that there have been calls for further clarity over its governance procedures. There is a wealth of literature setting out the variety of options for the future governance of the BBC which were considered in the days leading up to the creation of the Trust at the time of the last renewal of the BBC Royal Charter. The literature regarding the future governance of the BBC includes proposals put forward by the BBC;[17] by a Committee in the House of Lords;[18] and by the HL Select Committee on Communications, chaired by Lord Inglewood.[19]

The BBC Trust was established in 2007, the last time the Charter was renewed. Since then, the Trust has been the sovereign body responsible for the BBC as outlined in the Charter. But in technical legal terms it was not a 'trust' at all but a part of the BBC which was both separate and within the BBC as a whole. The main role of the BBC Trust was to be the guardian of the licence fee and the public interest. The Trust had 12 trustees with the last Chairman being Rona Fairhead. The Trust had a number of sub-committees such as the Editorial Standards Committee and the Remuneration and Appointments Committee.

Since its creation the BBC Trust had been harshly criticized for over-generous payoffs for departing executives. The Corporation had also been condemned for its role in investigating the Jimmy Savile historic child abuse scandal, and the way it dealt with false allegations against Lord McAlpine (see: *Lord McAlpine of West Green v Sally Bercow* (2013)[20]).

See Chapter 7

The issues around the future governance of the BBC, and how it should be regulated, have been much discussed over a considerable period. In his farewell public speech at the London School of Economics before standing down as (the then) Chairman of the BBC Trust at the end of April 2011, Sir Michael Lyons said that changes to the governance structure of the BBC were inevitable following the Hutton Report.[21] Sir Michael described these events as 'the greatest existential threat the BBC has faced in recent times'.[22] As the Royal BBC Charter came to an end in 2016, the Culture Secretary, John Whittingdale, in September 2015 commissioned an independent review, how the future BBC should be governed with recommendations for a new Royal Charter.[23]

Sir David Clementi led the inquiry and in March 2016 published his report (the Clementi Report[24]). The Report asked for a 'fundamental reform' of how the Corporation should be governed

---

17 See: Review of the BBC's Royal Charter: BBC response to a strong BBC, independent of government. May 2005.

18 See: The House of Lords Select Committee on the BBC Charter Review, 1st Report of Session 2005–2006, The Review of the BBC's Royal Charter. HL 50.

19 House of Lords (2011) Select Committee on Communications 2nd Report of Session 2010–12. 'The governance and regulation of the BBC Report'. HL Paper 166. 29 June 2011.

20 [2013] EWHC 1342 (QB).

21 In January 2004 Lord Hutton's report on the death of Dr David Kelly strongly criticized the BBC's management and governors. He said 'the Governors should have recognized more fully than they did that their duty to protect the independence of the BBC was not incompatible with giving proper consideration to whether there was validity in the government's complaints'. See: Report of the Inquiry into the Circumstances Surrounding the Death of Dr David Kelly C. M.G. by Lord Hutton, 28 January 2004, HC 247.

22 Source: 'The BBC Trust – Past Reflections, Continuing Challenges'. Speech by BBC Trust Chairman, Sir Michael Lyons at the London School of Economics, 9 March 2011.

23 See: Department for Culture, Media and Sport (2015). *BBC Charter Review Public Consultation at*: www.gov.uk/government/uploads/system/uploads/attachment_data/file/445704/BBC_Charter_Review_consultation_WEB. pdf.

24 See: Clementi, Sir David (2016) 'A Review of the Governance and Regulation of the BBC'. Presented to Parliament by the Secretary of State for Culture, Media and Sport by Command of Her Majesty. March 2016. Cm 9209 ('The Clementi Report'). Sir David Cecil Clementi was former chairman of Virgin Money and Prudential and previously Deputy Governor of the Bank of England.

in future. Clementi said it would be difficult to achieve a clear separation of BBC Trust and BBC, since the two organizations were 'sitting in one legal entity'. The Report called the BBC Trust model a 'mistake'. Clementi's recommendations included:

- regulatory oversight of the BBC by Ofcom;
- a unitary Board, with a majority of non-executive directors;
- primary responsibility to the licence fee payers should lie with the BBC Board;
- the (Ofcom) Operating Framework should include operating licences;
- the BBC Charter should place on the BBC a duty to consult with the public both as consumers and licence fee payers;
- there should be a 'Broadcaster First' system of complaints; appeal on editorial issues would go to Ofcom.

See below
5.5

5.4.2 Overlapping jurisdictions: the BBC and OFCOM

Until the BBC Charter Review, there existed a degree of uncertainty of overlap of jurisdiction between the BBC Trust and the communications regulator Ofcom. It was unclear whom viewers and listeners could complain to or seek redress from. For example, in cases of 'TV-like' VoD services, complaints about programmes accessed online via BBC iPlayer could be raised with either the BBC or with Ofcom. But, if a BBC iPlayer programme was accessed on another platform (e.g. via Virgin Media or BT Vision), the complaint had to first be raised directly with the BBC. Only once this process had been exhausted could the complainant go directly to the Authority for Video On Demand (ATVOD) since that regulator operates under a 'broadcaster first' system of regulation.[25]

Neither Ofcom nor ATVOD had any jurisdiction over BBC 'non-TV like' online content; so any complaints made about the BBC website had to be made directly to the BBC. Likewise, complaints about BBC radio programmes listened to online via iPlayer Radio had to be made directly to the BBC and could not be appealed to either Ofcom or ATVOD.

Such questions about the complexity of the BBC regulatory system were being asked by John Whittingdale, chairman of the Culture, Media and Sport Select Committee, when chairing the BBC Charter Review in 2015. In May 2016 Culture Secretary John Whittingdale confirmed that the BBC would be regulated by an external organization for the first time in its 90-year history, namely Ofcom. As part of his White Paper the Culture Secretary also announced that the pay of top stars who earn more than £450,000 would be disclosed, which could potentially affect the likes of Graham Norton, Chris Evans and Gary Lineker and that the £145.50 licence fee would increase in line with inflation until 2022, when there would be a new settlement.[26]

5.5 Office of Communications: OFCOM

Ofcom – also known as the 'media watchdog' – is the regulator for the UK communications industries, with responsibilities across television, radio, postal, telecommunications and wireless communications services.

Ofcom was established as a statutory regulator ('a body corporate') by the Office of Communications Act 2002, replacing the Broadcasting Standards Commission (BSC), the Independent

25 Source: Section 2, Memorandum of Understanding between the Office of Communications (Ofcom) and the BBC Trust, March 2007.
26 See: House of Commons (2016).

Television Commission (ITC) and the Radio Authority, the regulators that previously dealt with complaints against broadcasters. Sharon White became the new Chief Executive of Ofcom in July 2015.[27]

The main statute which covers Ofcom's duties is the Communications Act 2003. Section 3(1) states:

> It shall be the principal duty of Ofcom, in carrying out their functions:
>
> (a)   to further the interests of citizens in relation to communications matters; and
> (b)   to further the interests of consumers in relevant markets, where appropriate by promoting competition.

Ofcom operates under a number of statutes, including:

- the Broadcasting Act 1996
- the Broadcasting Act 1990
- the Competition Act 1998
- the Enterprise Act 2002
- the Communications Act 2003
- the Wireless Telegraphy Act 2006
- the Digital Economy Act 2010
- the Enterprise and Regulatory Reform Act 2013
- the Postal Services Act 2011
- EU legislation.

Ofcom's powers will be further enhanced by the Digital Economy Bill 2016–17 which extended its role to enforce copyright infringement. Clauses 74-80 enable the granting by a court of injunctions requiring service providers to block access to websites that are used, or are likely to be used, to infringe copyright. The bill provides for a robust system of appeals, regulation of the BBC, regulation of direct marketing and protection of intellectual property in connection with electronic communications.

Section 355 of the Communications Act 2003 obliges the regulator to carry out periodic reviews and reallocation of (local) radio licences. Part of the remit involves the character of the service, the quality and range of programming and the amount of local content. Ofcom has other responsibilities, such as shaping public policy in the future of broadcasting and new media. Apart from watching over correct allocation of broadband width and ISP compliance, Ofcom also allocates and administers radio frequencies and bandwidths under its periodic 'spectrum trading process', the relevant legislation being the Wireless Telegraphy Act 2006.

Section 264 of the 2003 Act requires Ofcom to report at least every five years on the fulfilment of the public service remit for television by public service broadcasters, namely television services provided by the BBC, Channel 4, Sianel Pedwar Cymru (S4C), Channel 3 services, and Channel 5 and 6. The public service remit involves the provision of a balanced diversity of high-quality content, which meets the needs and interests of different audiences in the UK.[28]

---

27 See: The Culture, Media and Sport Committee holds its first evidence session with the newly-appointed Chief Executive of Ofcom to consider her priorities for the communications regulator: www.parliament.uk/business/committees/committees-a-z/commons-select/culture-media-and-sport-committee/news-parliament-2015/evidence-ofcom-15-16.

28 Paragraphs (b) to (j) of s 264(6) of the 2003 Act provide detailed public service objectives underpinning this remit.

In summary, Ofcom's role has increased considerably since 2010 and now includes the regulation of:

1. **the electro-magnetic spectrum**: the optimal use for wireless telegraphy of the electro-magnetic spectrum;
2. **electronic communications**: that a wide range of electronic communications services is available throughout the UK;
3. **TV and radio services**: that a wide range of TV and radio services of high quality and wide appeal are available throughout the UK;
4. **plurality in TV and radio service**: that sufficient plurality in the providers of different television and radio services is maintained;
5. **protection against offensive or harmful material**: the application of standards that provide adequate protection for members of the public and others against offensive or harmful material in television and radio services;
6. **unfair treatment**: the application of standards that provide adequate protection for members of the public and others against unfair treatment in television and radio programmes and unwarranted infringements of privacy resulting from activities carried on for the purposes of such television and radio services;
7. **provision of a universal postal service**;[29]
8. **regulation of the BBC** (from 3 April 2017).

In July 2015, Ofcom imposed a £1 million fine on EE,[30] Britain's biggest mobile phone operator, for misleading customers who made complaints. The company which had been bought by BT did not tell some of its 27 million customers that their complaint could be decided by an independent adjudicator. EE, whose brands include Orange and T-Mobile, sent letters to customers that did not inform them of their right to take a complaint to alternative dispute resolution (ADR) after eight weeks. Ofcom's investigation into EE's complaints handling between July 2011 and April 2014 found that EE had failed to give certain dissatisfied customers correct or adequate information about their rights. The fine was Ofcom's largest penalty for poor complaints handling in any industry and the regulator's fifth biggest overall.[31]

5.5.1 The OFCOM Broadcasting Code

The Ofcom Broadcasting Code[32] applies to radio and television content (with certain exceptions for the BBC). Broadcasters are required by the terms of their Ofcom licence to observe the Standards Code[33] and the Fairness Code.[34] This includes any local TV and radio broadcast services (including local and community radio services and community digital sound programme services).

The Ofcom Code is divided into ten sections which are primarily drawn from the objectives as set out in section 319(2) Communications Act 2003 and section 107(1) Broadcasting Act 1996, as well as the Representation of the People Act 1983 (as amended).

The Code is set out in terms of principles, meanings and rules and, for sections 7 ('Fairness') and 8 ('Privacy'), also includes a set of 'practices to be followed' by broadcasters. Broadcasters must

---

29 As per s 29(1) Postal Services Act 2011.
30 BT agreed to buy EE from Deutsche Telekom and Orange for £12.5 billion in February 2015.
31 Source: 'EE fined £1m by Ofcom for misleading customers', by Sean Farrell, *The Guardian*, 3 July 2015.
32 The most recent version of the Code is of 9 May 2016.
33 The *Standards* provision is set out in Chapter 4 of the Communications Act 2003 ('Regulatory Provisions').
34 The *Fairness* provision is set out in Part V of the Broadcasting Act 1996. Though the 1996 Act refers to the Broadcasting Standards Commission (BSC) which was replaced by Ofcom and is to be read in that context. The Ofcom Code also deals with unjust and unfair treatment.

ensure that they comply with the rules, as set out in the Code.[35] The main criteria covered by the Code include:

> (a) the degree of harm and offence likely to be caused by the inclusion of any particular sort of material in programmes generally or in programmes of a particular description;
>
> (b) the likely size and composition of the potential audience for programmes included in television and radio services generally or in television and radio services of a particular description;
>
> (c) the likely expectation of the audience as to the nature of a programme's content and the extent to which the nature of a programme's content can be brought to the attention of potential members of the audience;
>
> (d) the likelihood of persons who are unaware of the nature of a programme's content being unintentionally exposed, by their own actions, to that content;
>
> (e) the desirability of securing that the content of services identifies when there is a change affecting the nature of a service that is being watched or listened to and, in particular, a change that is relevant to the application of the standards set under this section;
>
> (f) the desirability of maintaining the independence of editorial control over programme content.

Section 1: Protecting the under 18s[36]

Principle: To ensure that people under 18 are protected.

Rules for scheduling and content information should include 'appropriate scheduling', judged according to:

- the nature of the content;
- the likely number and age range of children in the audience, taking into account school time, weekends and holidays;
- the start time and finish time of the programme;
- the nature of the channel or station and the particular programme; and
- the likely expectations of the audience for a particular channel or station at a particular time and on a particular day;
- television broadcasters must observe the 'watershed' (which is at 21.00);
- material unsuitable for children should not, in general, be shown *before* 21.00 or *after* 05.30 (particularly at a time when young persons are likely to be listening or watching such as breakfast time);
- on premium subscription film services the watershed is at 20.00.

---

35 For further discussion see: Epworth, J. (2005).
36 This section must be read in conjunction with Section Two: Harm and Offence.

Section 2: Harm and offence

Principle: to ensure that generally accepted standards are applied to the content of television and radio services so as to provide adequate protection for members of the public from the inclusion in such services of harmful and/or offensive material. Generally accepted standards include:

- adequate protection for members of the public from the inclusion of harmful and/or offensive material;
- factual programmes must not materially mislead the audience;
- broadcasters must ensure that material which may cause offence is justified by the context (such material may include offensive language, violence, sex, sexual violence, humiliation, distress, violation of human dignity, discriminatory treatment or language, for example on the grounds of age, disability, gender, race, religion, beliefs and sexual orientation);
- broadcast competitions and voting must be conducted fairly.

Section 3: Crime

Principle: to ensure that material likely to encourage or incite the commission of crime or to lead to disorder is not included in television or radio services. These rules include:

- material likely to encourage or incite the commission of crime or to lead to disorder must not be included in television or radio services;
- descriptions or demonstrations of criminal techniques which contain essential details which could enable the commission of crime must not be broadcast unless editorially justified.
- no payment, promise of payment, or payment in kind, may be made to convicted or confessed criminals whether directly or indirectly for a programme contribution by the criminal (or any other person) relating to his/her crime/s. The only exception is where it is in the public interest.
- while criminal proceedings are active, no payment or promise of payment may be made, directly or indirectly, to any witness or any person who may reasonably be expected to be called as a witness. Nor should any payment be suggested or made dependent on the outcome of the trial.
- where criminal proceedings are likely and foreseeable, payments should not be made to people who might reasonably be expected to be witnesses unless there is a clear public interest, such as investigating crime or serious wrongdoing, and the payment is necessary to elicit the information;
- broadcasters must use their best endeavours so as not to broadcast material that could endanger lives or prejudice the success of attempts to deal with a hijack or kidnapping.

Section 4: Religion

Principles:

- to ensure that broadcasters exercise the proper degree of responsibility with respect to the content of programmes which are religious programmes;
- to ensure that religious programmes do not involve any improper exploitation of any susceptibilities of the audience to such a programme;
- to ensure that religious programmes do not involve any abusive treatment of the religious views and beliefs of those belonging to a particular religion or religious denomination.

The rules include that broadcasters must exercise the proper degree of responsibility with respect to the content of programmes which are religious programmes.

Section 5: Due impartiality and due accuracy and undue prominence of views and opinions
Principles:

- to ensure that news, in whatever form, is reported with due accuracy and presented with due impartiality;
- to ensure that the special impartiality requirements of the Act are complied with.

These rules include the meaning of 'due impartiality', which is an important qualification to the concept of impartiality. Impartiality itself means not favouring one side over another; 'due' in this context means adequate or appropriate to the subject and nature of the programme. Broadcasters' approach to due impartiality may vary according to the nature of the subject, the type of programme and channel, the likely expectation of the audience as to content, and the extent to which the content and approach are signalled to the audience. Due impartiality and due accuracy in news should include:

- news, in whatever form, must be reported with due accuracy and presented with due impartiality;
- significant mistakes in news should normally be acknowledged and corrected on air quickly. Corrections should be appropriately scheduled;
- no politician may be used as a newsreader, interviewer or reporter in any news programmes unless, exceptionally, it is editorially justified. In that case, the political allegiance of that person must be made clear to the audience;
- any personal interest of a reporter or presenter, which would call into question the due impartiality of the programme, must be made clear to the audience.

Section 6: Elections and referendums
Principle: to ensure that the special impartiality requirements in the Communications Act 2003 and the Representation of the People Act 1983 (as amended), relating to broadcasting on elections and referendums, are applied at the time of elections and referendums.

The rules include:

- due weight must be given to the coverage of major parties during the election period;
- broadcasters must also consider giving appropriate coverage to other parties and independent candidates with significant views and perspectives;
- discussion and analysis of election and referendum issues must finish when the poll opens.
- broadcasters may not publish the results of any opinion poll on polling day itself until the election or referendum poll closes. (For European parliamentary elections, this applies until all polls throughout the European Union have closed.)

Section 7: Fairness
Principle: to ensure that broadcasters avoid unjust or unfair treatment of individuals or organizations in programmes.

Practices to be followed include:

- broadcasters and programme makers should normally be fair in their dealings with potential contributors to programmes unless, exceptionally, it is justified to be otherwise;

- participants in a programme should be told the nature and purpose of the programme, what the programme is about and be given a clear explanation of why they were asked to contribute and when (if known) and where it is likely to be first broadcast;
- be told what kind of contribution they are expected to make, for example live, pre-recorded, interview, discussion, edited, unedited, etc.;
- be informed about the areas of questioning and, wherever possible, the nature of other likely contributions;
- be told the nature of their contractual rights and obligations and those of the programme maker and broadcaster in relation to their contribution; and
- be given clear information, if offered an opportunity to preview the programme, about whether they will be able to effect any changes to it;
- if a contributor is under 16, consent should normally be obtained from a parent or guardian, or other person of 18 or over *in loco parentis*; persons under 16 should not be asked for views on matters likely to be beyond their capacity to answer properly without such consent.

Section 8: Privacy

Principle: to ensure that broadcasters avoid any unwarranted infringement of privacy in programmes and in connection with obtaining material included in programmes.

This section and the preceding section on fairness are different from other sections of the Code. They apply to how broadcasters treat the individuals or organizations directly affected by programmes, rather than to what the general public sees and/or hears as viewers and listeners. The Broadcasting Act 1996 (as amended) requires Ofcom to consider complaints about unwarranted infringement of privacy in a programme or in connection with the obtaining of material included in a programme. This may call for some difficult on-the-spot judgements about whether privacy is unwarrantably infringed by filming or recording, especially when reporting on emergency situations. A fine editorial balance and judgement in line with the Code has to be made between a strong public interest in reporting on an emergency situation as it occurs and an unwarrantable infringement of a person's privacy. These are factors Ofcom will take into account when adjudicating on complaints. Broadcasters should pay particular attention to the following:

- Any infringement of privacy in the making of a programme should be with the person's and/or organization's consent.
- If the broadcast of a programme would infringe the privacy of a person or organization, consent should be obtained *before* the relevant material is broadcast, unless the infringement of privacy is warranted. (Callers to phone-in shows are deemed to have given consent to the broadcast of their contribution.)
- If an individual or organization's privacy is being infringed, and they ask that the filming, recording or live broadcast be stopped, the broadcaster should do so, unless it is warranted to continue.
- When filming or recording in institutions, organizations or other agencies, permission should be obtained from the relevant authority or management, unless it is warranted to film or record without permission. Individual consent of employees or others whose appearance is incidental or where they are essentially anonymous members of the general public will not normally be required.
- When people are caught up in events which are covered by the news they still have a right to privacy in both the making and the broadcast of a programme, unless it is warranted to infringe it.
- Broadcasters should ensure that words, images or actions filmed or recorded in, or broadcast from, a public place, are not so private that prior consent is required before broadcast from the individual or organization concerned, unless broadcasting without their consent is warranted.

- Doorstepping for factual programmes should not take place unless a request for an interview has been refused or it has not been possible to request an interview, or there is good reason to believe that an investigation will be frustrated if the subject is approached openly, and it is warranted to doorstep. However, normally broadcasters may, without prior warning interview, film or record people in the news when in public places.
- Broadcasters can record telephone calls between the broadcaster and the other party if they have, from the outset of the call, identified themselves, explained the purpose of the call and that the call is being recorded for possible broadcast (unless it is warranted not to do one or more of these practices). If at a later stage it becomes clear that a call that has been recorded will be broadcast (but this was not explained to the other party at the time of the call) then the broadcaster must obtain consent before broadcast from the other party, unless it is warranted not to do so.
- Material gained by surreptitious filming and recording should only be broadcast when it is warranted.
- Broadcasters should pay particular attention to the privacy of people under 16; they do not lose their rights to privacy because, for example, of the fame or notoriety of their parents or because of events in their schools.

Section 9: Commercial references in television programming

This section of the Code covers all commercial references that feature within TV programming (section 10 of the Code concerns radio only).[37]

Principles:

- to ensure that broadcasters maintain editorial independence and control over programming (editorial independence);
- to ensure that there is distinction between editorial content and advertising (distinction);
- to protect audiences from surreptitious advertising;
- to ensure that audiences are protected from the risk of financial harm (consumer protection);
- to ensure that unsuitable sponsorship is prevented.

See Chapter 6.9

The inclusion in a programme of, or of a reference to, a product, service or trade mark (product placement or prop placement) is covered by legislation and EU regulations.

- The BBC is prohibited from accepting most types of commercial revenue in relation to services funded by the public licence fee. However, product placement requirements apply to programmes the BBC acquires or those produced/commissioned by its commercial services or any connected entities.
- Programmes that fall within the permitted genres of product or prop placement must not contain product placement if they are:
  (a) news programmes; or
  (b) children's programmes.
- Product placement of the following products, services or trade marks is prohibited:
  (a) cigarettes or other tobacco products;
  (b) prescription-only medicines;

---

37 Relevant legislation includes, in particular: ss 319(2)(fa), (i) and (j) and 319(4) (a), (c), (e) and (f), s 321(1) and (4) and s 324(3) Communications Act 2003; s 202 Broadcasting Act 1990 (para. 3 in Part 1 of Sch. 2); Articles 9, 10, 11, and Chapter VII (Articles 19 to 26) of the Audiovisual Media Services Directive; reg. 3(4)(d) of the Consumer Protection from Unfair Trading Regulations 2008; s 21(1) Financial Services and Markets Act 2000; para. 3 of the Investment Recommendation (Media) Regulations Act 2005; Article 10 ECHR.

(c) alcoholic drinks;

(d) foods or drinks high in fat, salt or sugar ('HFSS');

(e) gambling;

(f) infant formula (baby milk), including follow-on formula.

● Controlled premium rate services are a subset of premium rate services which are regulated by PhonepayPlus.

Section 10: Commercial communications in radio programming

Principle: to ensure the transparency of commercial communications as a means to secure consumer protection.

The rules cover:

● spot advertisements comprising advertising broadcast in commercial breaks;

● commercial arrangement including sponsorship, competition prize donation and premium rate service provision (commercial arrangements which include payment and/or the provision of some other valuable consideration in return for a commercial reference).

5.5.2 OFCOM's statutory enforcement powers

As a statutory regulator, Ofcom takes enforcement action across a number of industry sectors and is able to use a range of statutory powers granted by the various statutes mentioned above. In practical terms, this means that broadcasting enforcement continues to be the regulator's main aim, namely to secure public protection under the Broadcasting Code – in particular, paying close attention to participation television and the use of premium rate phone services (e.g. for competitions on TV or radio) (see also Digital Economy Bill 2016–17).

Section 392(6) of the Communications Act 2003 gives Ofcom the power to punish breaches of the Code and impose penalties as it sees fit. Before determining how to publish, the regulator must consult the Secretary of State. Ofcom takes over regulation for the BBC from 3 April 2017.

5.5.3 OFCOM adjudications and decisions

Upon the receipt of a complaint, Ofcom will follow a procedure where it investigates cases and applies statutory sanctions to broadcasters where the Code has been breached. When a broadcaster breaches the Code deliberately, seriously or repeatedly, Ofcom may impose statutory sanctions against the broadcaster. Where the Ofcom Broadcasting Code has been breached, the regulator will normally publish a finding and explain why a broadcaster has breached the Code.[38]

Big Brother remains the TV show most complained about according to figures released by the broadcasting watchdog Ofcom. In December 2014, the reality show received 3,784 complaints, mainly about the behaviour of its eventual winner Helen Wood and her treatment of housemates. Celebrity Big Brother was in second place with 1,874 complaints, many of those about Hollywood actor Gary Busey. Soaps Emmerdale, Coronation Street and East Enders also featured in the top ten.

The majority of complaints about Coronation Street related to a 'gay kiss' between characters, Todd Grimshaw (Bruno Langley) and Marcus Dent (Charlie Condou) before the watershed in February 2014. The broadcasting regulator received over 100 complaints about the kiss being too

---

38 These findings are available in Ofcom's Broadcast Bulletins at: www.ofcom.org.uk.

'sexually suggestive'. However, Ofcom decided not to investigate the scene further since it did not breach its Code which does not discriminate between scenes involving opposite sex and same-sex couples.

In November 2014, Ofcom did investigate a controversial rape scene in the long-running soap, *East Enders* after 278 people had complained. Despite the rape being implied rather than explicitly depicted, viewers complained about Queen Vic landlady, Linda Carter (Kellie Bright), being raped by her nephew Dean Wicks (Matt Di Angelo). The episode went out before the watershed on BBC1 at 8pm in October 2014. But the regulator found in January 2015 that the scene did not breach the Ofcom Code; a warning had been issued before the episode, implying a sexual assault.

There have been a number of prominent Ofcom adjudications in recent regulatory broadcasting history. One concerned the 'Shilpa Shetty' incident on Channel 4's fifth *Celebrity Big Brother* series in January 2007. The broadcast created and produced by Brighter Pictures, part of Endemol UK, was broadcast by the Channel Four TV Corporation on its Channel 4 service. Disagreements between the 'housemates' had developed, in particular between Indian film actress and model Shilpa Shetty and the late Jade Goody, famous for being one of the first *Big Brother* contestants, as well as Jo O'Meara, former lead singer of the pop group S Club 7, and Playboy model and former Miss Great Britain, Danielle Lloyd. During the 26-week series, which ran until 28 January 2007, Ofcom received over 44,500 complaints about alleged racist bullying of Ms Shetty.

Following Ofcom's investigation into the 'Shilpa Shetty' affair, the regulator found that there were three events that had breached the Ofcom Broadcasting Code, where Channel 4 had failed to handle the material appropriately and had not adequately protected members of the public from offensive material. These were:

1. remarks about cooking in India by the housemates (transmitted 15 January 2007);
2. Danielle Lloyd's comment: 'I think she should fuck off home' (transmitted 17 January 2007);
3. Jade Goody's comment: 'I couldn't think of her surname. Why would I be talking to someone like that, I don't know what her surname is. What is it? Shilpa Cookamada, Shilpa whatever Rockamada, Shilpa Poppadom?' (transmitted 18 and 19 January 2007).

In particular, Ofcom found that Channel 4 had breached rule 1.3 ('protection of children from offensive and unsuitable material') and rule 2.3 ('offensive material') of the Code. Channel 4 was subsequently fined £1.5 million, which was 5 per cent of the broadcaster's qualifying revenue at that time.[39]

Another Ofcom adjudication concerned the 'prank' played by Russell Brand and Jonathan Ross on their BBC Radio 2 shows on 18 and 25 October 2008 involving a series of messages left on the answerphone of the *Fawlty Towers* TV star, the late Andrew Sachs, who had played 'Manuel' in the 1970s sitcom series. Brand and Ross left lewd answerphone messages on Mr Sachs' phone, telling him that Brand had had sex with his granddaughter. This was broadcast live on radio. There were more than 27,000 public complaints to the BBC and Ofcom. The Ross–Brand show was taken off the air immediately and Russell Brand resigned from the BBC on 29 October 2008 and Jonathan Ross was suspended; BBC Radio 2's controller, Lesley Douglas, also resigned on 25 November.

The Ofcom adjudication in the 'Sachsgate' row in April 2009 found the BBC to be in breach of the Ofcom Broadcasting Code, namely rule 2.1 ('generally accepted standards must be applied in all programmes'); that there had been a lack of clarity about the exact role in the programme of a senior figure at the agency that represented Russell Brand and the executive producer who

---

39 See: Adjudication of Ofcom Content Sanctions Committee – Channel Four Television Corporation in respect of its service Channel 4 of 24 May 2007.

represented the independent production company. Rule 2.3 had also been breached ('offensive material must be justified by the context') in that the radio broadcast had been gratuitously offensive, humiliating and demeaning. Rule 8.1 had also been breached, in that the radio broadcasting standard required 'adequate protection for members of the public from unwarranted infringements of privacy' – in relation to Mr Sachs and the privacy of his family. For the breaches of rules 2.1 and 2.3 Ofcom fined the BBC £70,000 and for rule 8.1 an additional £80,000.[40]

Following the Ofcom finding, Mark Thompson, the then Director-General of the BBC, made a public apology for the serious breach of editorial compliance that had allowed grossly offensive material to be broadcast; he also apologized personally to Andrew Sachs and his family. Clearly, Ofcom's investigation into the 'Sachsgate' affair had identified a general weakness in managerial control and compliance within the BBC.

In August 2015 Ofcom ruled in the *Britain's Got Talent* adjudication that ITV had breached the Broadcasting Code by 'materially misleading' viewers over the use of a stunt-double dog that helped the act 'Jules O'Dwyer and Matisse' win the contest. The act featured a variety of obedience and agility skills, performed by a dog called 'Matisse' under the instruction of his trainer, performed in three shows during the series in May 2015. The act was in fact performed by a 'stunt double' dog called 'Chase'. After the broadcasting regulator had received more than 1,175 complaints, Ofcom launched an investigation and found that Chase had performed the high ropewalk act on the Royal Variety Performance stage, winning his owner O'Dwyer the first prize of £250,000. Four and a half million votes had been cast via the BGT app for free, and by landline or mobile at 50p.

Ofcom adjudicated that ITV broke rule 2.14 of the Broadcasting Code ('broadcasters must ensure that viewers and listeners are not materially misled about any broadcast competition or voting'). However the media regulator did not impose any wider sanction or order ITV to refund voters who felt they had been misled. ITV offered viewers who voted for O'Dwyer to obtain a refund, but did not go as far as looking to hand the title to runner up Jamie Raven.

O'Dwyer and Matisse received 22.6 per cent of the votes cast, narrowly beating magician Raven, who attracted 20.4 per cent. Almost 90 per cent of the votes for O'Dwyer to win were via the free app.[41]

5.5.4 Judicial review and OFCOM

Ofcom's handling of complaints and its adjudications will – at times – be challenged in the courts by way of judicial review applications in the Administrative Court. Allegations of possible breaches of Ofcom's 'Standards' and 'Fairness Codes' as well as its 'Privacy Code' tend to be the most frequent legal challenges – substantially arguing that the programmes complained of were unfair.

The judgment in R (*Traveller Movement*) v Ofcom (2015)[42] contains an important ruling in relation to applications involving regulators and the non-adversarial procedure. In February 2015 Ouseley J dismissed a judicial review application brought against Ofcom by the Traveller Movement (TM), a charity supporting 300,000 gypsies and travellers. The charity had claimed that the Channel 4 broadcasts of *Big Fat Gypsy Wedding* and *Thelma's Gypsy Girls* had depicted children in a sexualized way, that the gypsy communities engaged in and endorsed violent sexual assaults of female children and young women and portrayed men and boys as feckless, violent and criminal as a cultural norm.

TM, the claimant charity, had made a complaint to Ofcom about the programmes in November 2013. The gist of the complaint was that the programmes, particularly *Big Fat Gypsy Wedding*, were unfair and portrayed Irish Traveller, English Traveller, Gypsy and Romany groups in a negative and racially stereotypical way. TM's lawyers argued on grounds of procedural

---

40 Source: 'The Russell Brand Show', Ofcom Broadcast Bulletin Issue 131, 6 April 2009.
41 Source: Ofcom Broadcast Bulletin, Issue 285, 17 August 2015, *Britain's Got Talent* ITV, 31 May 2015, 19:30 in breach.
42 [2015] EWHC 406 (Admin).

unfairness and irrationality and that the regulator had acted unlawfully. TM specifically complained to Ofcom that the 'Standards' and 'Fairness' Codes had been breached. Ofcom found no breach of either Code.

TM's application for judicial review (at standing stage) included procedural impropriety, that Ofcom should have used its powers to seek further information to enable the regulator to reach a properly considered decision; that Ofcom acted irrationally in not accepting the extended assistance of the Equality and Human Rights Commission in considering the complaint; and that the decision not to accept TM's expert evidence as adequate evidence of harm was irrational. The charity also argued on grounds of unfairness that Ofcom's 'draft decision' had only been visible to one party (the broadcaster) but not to the complainant and that this was manifestly unfair.

Ouseley J rejected each of these grounds and held that it was not necessary in the interests of fairness for parties to have sight of a preliminary or provisional view of an adjudicatory body in order for its decision, or the process as a whole, to be fair. He ruled that a 'standards' complaint could be made by anyone, even by someone who had not seen the programme at all. By contrast, the broadcaster (here Channel 4) was directly affected by the outcome of the complaint and decision, and might face sanctions and financial penalties.

In these circumstances, there was nothing unfair or irrational in the 'standards' complaint by the travellers' representatives nor was the procedure unfair for Ofcom to provide its preliminary view to the broadcaster but not to the complainant. Ofcom's counsel, Dinah Rose QC, told the judge that it was fully aware of the sensitivity of potentially racially negative stereotypes and had conducted a 'careful and painstaking' investigation before concluding that the programmes did not breach the broadcasting code.

The judge then agreed Ofcom's decision that Channel 4 had not depicted such stereotypes but that the programmes were, in fact, a balanced portrayal which offered considerable insight into those communities, including the challenges they faced when dealing with prejudice.

The Jon Gaunt case also questioned an Ofcom decision, and therein challenged the Ofcom Broadcasting Code in relation to harmful and offensive broadcasts (here radio).[43] Gaunt also argued that the Code breached his Article 10 ECHR right. The Ken Livingstone case[44] was cited in this case, where the judge said that Mr Livingstone was not to be regarded as expressing a political opinion, attracting a high level of protection, when he indulged in offensive abuse of an Evening Standard journalist outside a City Hall reception.

 **KEY CASE** | ### *R (on the application of Gaunt) v OFCOM* [2011] EWCA Civ 692

Precedent
- An interference with a person's Article 10 rights has to be proportionate to the legitimate aim pursued and must be established convincingly.
- When deciding whether any interference with freedom of expression falls foul of Article 10, the court will have particular regard to the words used, the context in which they were made public and the case as a whole.
- There is a distinction to be drawn between harsh words which constitute a gratuitous personal attack and those which form part of a political debate.

43 Section 319(2) Broadcasting Act 2003.
44 *Livingstone v Adjudication Panel for England* [2006] HRLR 45.

Facts

The case concerned an explosive outburst by radio show host 'Shock Jock' Jon Gaunt on his *talkSPORT* radio programme on 7 November 2008. Around 11am Gaunt interviewed Michael Stark, Cabinet Member for Children's Services for Redbridge London Borough Council, live on radio about the council's controversial proposal to ban smokers from becoming foster parents on the ground that passive smoking has a propensity for harming foster children. Gaunt, himself a foster child, had published a controversial article 'Fags didn't stop my foster mum caring for me', criticizing Redbridge Council as 'health and safety Nazis', referring to a 'master race philosophy' by Redbridge Social Services, whom he called 'the SS', though the High Court did not hold this article to be unduly offensive.[45]

Mr Stark explained the council's stance on the radio show, stating that smoker foster parents would not be used in the future, to which Mr Gaunt responded, 'So you are a Nazi, then?' After Mr Stark protested, Mr Gaunt reiterated, 'No you are, you're a Nazi', with the interview degenerating into an unseemly slanging match. When Mr Stark protested that the insult, as he saw it, was probably actionable, the claimant, Jon Gaunt, replied, 'Take action if you wish', adding, 'You're a health Nazi' and a little later 'you ignorant pig' and 'health fascist' and an 'ignorant idiot'. Gaunt's live broadcast apology an hour later included: 'The councillor wants me to apologize for calling him a Nazi. I'm sorry for calling you a Nazi.' Gaunt was subsequently suspended with his contract terminated immediately.

Ofcom received 53 complaints from listeners and issued its adjudication on 8 June 2009, stating that Mr Gaunt had breached rules 2.1 and 2.3 of the Broadcasting Code.[46]

Jon Gaunt claimed that Ofcom's decision breached his Article 10 right and amounted to an unlawful interference with his freedom of expression. Gaunt was represented by the human rights group Liberty. Mr Millar QC, on behalf of the claimant, submitted there was no pressing social need and that Ofcom's reasons were insufficient to justify the interference with Article 10(2) ECHR[47] (see for this approach: *R v Shayler* (2003);[48] *R (on the application of SB) v Governors of Denbigh High School* (2007);[49] *Belfast City Council v Miss Behavin' Ltd* (2007)[50]).

In July 2010, Mr Gaunt lost his High Court 'freedom of expression' challenge against Ofcom. The High Court ruled that Ofcom's findings did *not* interfere with Mr Gaunt's Article 10 right, but that the 'ignorant pig' comment and the continued bullying and insulting of the Redbridge councillor on live radio amounted to gratuitous and offensive abuse, therefore breaching the Broadcasting Code.

Mr Gaunt's appeal reached the Court of Appeal where he did *not* argue that the Ofcom Code breached his Convention rights. However, Mr Gaunt argued that Ofcom's finding was a breach of his Article 10 rights because it was a *disproportionate* interference and did not meet a pressing social need. The CA dismissed Mr Gaunt's appeal in a judgment given by the Master of the Rolls, Lord Neuberger, endorsing the approach of the Divisional Court (High Court).

---

45 See: *Gaunt and Liberty v Ofcom* [2010] EWHC 1756 (QBD).
46 Rule 2.1 of the Code provides that generally accepted standards must be applied to the contents of television and radio services so as to provide adequate protection for members of the public from the inclusion in such services of harmful and/or offensive materials. Rule 2.3 provides that, in applying generally accepted standards, broadcasters must ensure that material which may cause offence is justified by the context. Such material may include, among other material, offensive language.
47 [2010] EWHC 1756 at para. 17.
48 [2003] 1 AC 247 at para. 23 (Lord Bingham) and para. 61 (Lord Hope).
49 [2007] 1 AC 100.
50 [2007] 1 WLR 1420.

The CA emphasized that the freedom of expression, encompassing the right to say what one wants and how one wants, was the 'lifeblood' of democracy. But freedom of expression also carried with it responsibilities, which necessitated certain restrictions (referring to *Handyside v UK* (1976)[51]). Jon Gaunt applied for judicial review on human rights legislation grounds.

Decision

The CA dismissed Mr Gaunt's claim for judicial review. Reasons included that the public interest aspect (i.e. 'standing') was of limited importance when set in the context of the actual contents of the Michael Stark interview. It concluded that the court's task was to decide whether the amended finding *disproportionately* infringed the claimant's Article 10 right? The court found that there was no 'pressing social need' and that Ofcom's adjudication did not constitute an interference with Mr Gaunt's freedom of expression.

The CA held that the claimant's right to freedom of expression did *not* extend to gratuitous offensive insult or abuse, nor to repeated abusive shouting that served to express no real content.

Analysis

Since it was a live broadcast and Jon Gaunt was considered an experienced interviewer, the interview with the Redbridge Councillor could have been stopped by either Mr Gaunt or the *talkSport* producers, once it had become clear that Jon Gaunt had lost control on live radio. The tone of the interview degenerated from the point where he called Michael Stark a 'Nazi' and the claimant – Mr Gaunt's – conduct of the interview became increasingly abusive, hectoring and out of control. This was followed by the expression 'ignorant pig' which had no contextual justification, said with 'such venom' as to constitute gratuitous offensive abuse.

It was therefore right that the regulator Ofcom found a breach of the Broadcasting Code. The decision of the courts (Divisional Court and CA) acknowledged the adjudication of the statutory regulator was correct. Consequently, there had been no unlawful interference with Mr Gaunt's Article 10 rights. Ofcom was therefore justified in its conclusion, because the offensive and abusive nature of the broadcast was gratuitous, having no factual content or justification, and the 'Amended Finding' constituted no material interference with the claimant's freedom of expression.

 FOR THOUGHT

You act for a broadcaster as legal adviser. Would you say the *Jon Gaunt* case could be relied on as justification for allowing abusive, derogatory and racist language in a new youth TV channel's programme content? Discuss with reference to regulatory and legal authorities.

---

51 (1976) 1 EHRR 737 at para. 59 (ECHR).

5.6 Codifying cyberspace (2)

Is there such thing as 'internet law'? A short answer would be 'no' – since the World Wide Web spans over continents and involves global 'laws'. What we have been looking at so far is the invasion of privacy by those who use social networking sites and by search engines such as Google who look into and pass on personal data of subscribers (most of whom will not have read the lengthy privacy policies of ISPs and social media sites which include the collection of personal information of individuals). And we have established that there are no privacy laws in the UK. There is however the CJEU ruling in *Google Spain*[52] which now provides that a data subject (individual) can ask an ISP to 'de-list' him or her from a specific search engine.

See Chapter 1 and 3.6

5.6.1 Legislation covering online abuse

Let's have a look at UK legislation which can be invoked in instances relating to online harassment and sexual abuse, providing relevant measures to law enforcement agencies:

● Obscene Publications Act 1959 and 1965;
● Protection of Children Act 1978 (England and Wales);
● Civic Government Act 1982 (Scotland);
● Malicious Communications Act 1988;
● Protection from Harassment Act 1997;
● Sexual Offences Act 2003;
● Communications Act 2003 (sections 125–130[53]);
● Police and Justice Act 2006 (sections 35–37[54]);
● Criminal Justice and Immigration Act 2008 (section 63);
● Coroner's and Justice Act 2009 (section 62;[55] section 69[56]);
● Criminal Justice and Licensing (Scotland) Act 2010 (section 42);
● Criminal Justice and Courts Act 2015 (section 33).

In April 2015, the Criminal Justice and Courts Act 2015 created a new criminal offence of revenge pornography, making it a criminal offence to disclose private sexual photographs and films without the consent of an individual who appears in them and with the intent to cause that individual distress.[57] A typical case of revenge pornography might involve an ex-partner uploading an intimate image of the victim to the internet or sending it to their friends and family on Facebook. It is carried out with the intention of causing distress, humiliation and embarrassment to the victim. Previously, these cases were prosecuted under other areas of legislation, such as the Communications Act 2003, Malicious Communications Act 1988 or the Harassment Act 1997. Under the new legislation someone convicted of an offence could face up to two years in prison or receive a fine.

The first defendant believed to have been sentenced, in August 2015 at Reading Magistrates' Court, was Jason Asagba (21). Asagba sent pictures of his ex-girlfriend to the victim's family via text and email. He also hacked into the victim's Facebook account and shared an image on her timeline. He was convicted of posting, texting and emailing intimate photos without the woman's consent with intent to cause her distress under the new 'revenge porn' legislation. He pleaded guilty at the earliest opportunity.

---

52 *Google Spain SL v Agencia Espanola de Proteccion de Datos* (AEPD) (C-131/12) [2014] QB 1022.
53 'Offences relating to networks and services'.
54 'Computer misuse'.
55 'Possession of prohibited images of children'.
56 'Indecent pseudo-photographs of children: marriage etc'.
57 Section 33 Criminal Justice and Courts Act 2015.

Legislation applicable to liability of internet service providers and operators of websites is generally covered by the Directive 2000/31/EC ('Liability of Intermediary Service Providers'), though US legislation will play a major part here since a large number of its operators are located in the USA.

Online copyright infringement is another area where there is no single 'internet law' to cover unlawful file-sharing via peer-to-peer (P2P) networks, therein hampering growth in the creative industries which, in turn, make up a large part of Britain's GDP. The Digital Economy Act 2010 and the Digital Economy Bill 2016–17 create new responsibilities for Ofcom to adopt measures aimed at significantly reducing levels of unlawful file-sharing via P2P networks. The acts also provide powers to the Secretary of State (for Culture, Media and Sport) to require that ISPs implement technical measures against serious repeat infringers (see also: the Enterprise and Regulatory Reform Act 2013 (ERRA)). As part of an effective copyright framework, Ofcom welcomed the recommendation of the Hargreaves Review[58] on copyright of an 'integrated approach' to addressing infringement, which emphasizes the development of legitimate services, alongside education and enforcement. Work by the creative industries to increase the variety of attractive content available legitimately online has been furthered by copyright reform to modernize the licensing process.

See Chapter 9

5.6.2 Self-regulation in the digital age: the Audio Visual Media Services Directive (AVMS)

Since the 'Television without Frontiers' (TVWF)[59] Directive came into force in 1989 – which regulates the audiovisual sector across Europe – new players and platforms have emerged, boosting or requiring more content production for emerging markets. On 25 May 2016, the European Commission published its latest proposals regarding its Digital Single Market (DSM) strategy. The proposals included the updating of the Audio Visual Media Services (AVMS) Directive[60] to include extended provisions for video-on-demand (VoD) and video-sharing services.

In 1989, the AVMS Directive created a new level playing field in Europe for emerging audiovisual media which – *inter alia* – sought to safeguard and preserve cultural diversity, protect children, consumers and media pluralism, and was designed to combat racial and religious hatred.[61]

The key amendments of the AVMS Directive (2016) affecting VoD and video-sharing services include:

1. **Quota of European works** – VoD services must ensure that their catalogues offer at least 20 per cent content share for European works (as defined in the AVMS Directive) and ensure prominence of such works, when they are offering a video-on-demand service in EU Member States (MS).

2. **Financial contributions** – MS can impose financial contributions on VoD services, either by way of direct investments or levies allocated to national film funds.

3. **Hate speech and the protection of minors** – Rules are strengthened that protect minors and prohibit hate speech. These provisions apply to video-sharing platforms (e.g. YouTube), as well as to VoD services. The most harmful content, such as gratuitous violence and pornography, is subject to the strictest measures, such as encryption and effective parental control.

---

58 Hargreaves, I. (2011).
59 EU Directive 89/552 EEC on Transfrontier Television 'Television without Frontiers Directive' (TVWF).
60 EC Directive 2007/65 'Audiovisual Media Services Directive' (AVMS) amended EU Directive 89/552/EEC 'Television without Frontiers Directive' (TVWF) and includes the pursuit of television broadcasting activities including on-demand services since 11 December 2007.
61 See: 2009/C 257/01 Communication from the Commission on the application of state aid rules to public service broadcasting. Official Journal of the European Union, C 257, vol. 52, 27 October 2009.

This now means that VoD services have to review their content in order to see whether they comply with the 20 per cent European content quota. Service providers with a particularly low market presence or turnover may well try and avoid being subject to such requirements. Furthermore, VoD services have to ensure that they have content restriction measures in place with regard to the protection of minors.

Video-sharing services have now been brought in line with the scope of the AVMS Directive. However, the AVMS Directive may not apply to certain VoD services which are located *outside* the EU which then means that some VoD services may be outside the scope of EU legislation.

5.6.3 Does online regulation infringe freedom of expression?

As we have seen in Chapter 2, freedom of expression is fundamental to the functioning of democracy. This applies especially to the communication of opinions and argument about policies which all levels of government pursue, including those made in radio and TV broadcasts (see: R (*Animal Defenders International v Secretary of State for Culture, Media and Sport* (2008)[62]).

Freedom of political expression includes not only the inoffensive, but also the irritating, the contentious, the eccentric, the heretical, the unwelcome and the provocative, provided it does not tend to provoke violence (see: *Redmond-Bate v DPP* (1999)[63]). But in the *Otto-Preminger-Institut v Austria* (1994)[64] case, the ECtHR concluded in relation to the obligations expressed relating to Article 10(2) ECHR, that expressions which are gratuitously offensive to others must be avoided wherever possible. It is then accepted that Strasbourg jurisprudence does not protect gratuitous abuse unrelated to a topic being discussed (on the radio for example), but this is a very limited exception to the broad protection of political expression. For this reason, the regulatory body – Ofcom's – decision in the *Jon Gaunt*[65] case may well be incompatible with Convention Article 10 if tested in the ECtHR; though to date radio broadcaster Jon Gaunt has not pursued his case in the Strasbourg Court.

See above
5.4.4

In the CG case (below), the Belfast court granted a right to privacy to a convicted sex offender, including any publications on social media (here: Facebook).

❖ KEY CASE	*CG v Facebook Ireland Ltd and Joseph McCloskey* [2015] NIQB 11. Queen's Bench Division (Northern Ireland) 20 February 2015

Precedent

❖ Every person has an expectation of privacy online (on the internet) in respect of their personal information – including sex offenders.

❖ Information which can harm the public interest may also create a risk of re-offending.

❖ A social media company (here: Facebook) is a primary publisher and liable for misuse of private information.

❖ An ISP must remove any publication (relevant page/s) from its website which exposes the claimant to vilification and the risk of serious harm.

❖ Regulation 22 of the Electronic Commerce (EC Directive) Regulations 2002 take into account all matters which appear to be relevant with postings on social networking sites.

---

62 [2008] 1 AC 1312 at para. 27 (Lord Bingham).
63 (1999) 163 JP 789.
64 [1994] ECHR 26 at para. 49 (ECHR).
65 See: R (*on the application of Gaunt) v Ofcom* [2011] EWCA Civ 692.

Facts

CG was a convicted sex offender, jailed for five years and released on licence. He lived with his disabled father, and had a disabled son with whom he had regular, supervised contact. He had complied with the terms of his licence, had been assessed as not presenting any significant risk to the public and was under supervision by the authorities. Joseph McCloskey operated a page on Facebook's website named 'Keeping our Kids Safe from Predators 2'. McCloskey had posted a newspaper article with a photograph of CG from the time of his conviction on the Facebook page. In response, between 160 and 180 comments appeared on the page containing abusive and violent language as well as expressions of support for acts of violence against CG. There were also postings of his location, abusive language in relation to his family and allegations of other criminal acts.

CG lived in increased fear of violence, worried about his whereabouts being identified. Direct contact with his son was suspended and relations with other family members were strained. CG told the court that he had been approached and threatened in public as a result of the posts.

Facebook also facilitated a page operated by the father of one of CG's victims, namely RS. The father had posted a photograph of CG and information about his whereabouts which attracted more comments suggesting that CG should be harmed. No proceedings were brought against RS. After receiving letters from CG's lawyers, Facebook refused to investigate the comments until CG provided the URL for each specific comment. Facebook removed the entire series of comments two weeks later.

CG claimed against both defendants that the material posted amounted to a misuse of private information, was in breach of Articles 2, 3 and 8 ECHR and amounted to harassment of him contrary to the Protection from Harassment (Northern Ireland) Order 1997 as actionable negligence. CG further asserted that Facebook was in breach of the Data Protection Act 1998 (DPA). It was further submitted for CG that the case against Facebook was most properly categorized as 'misuse of private information' and against Mr McCloskey as 'misuse of private information and harassment', and it was upon these claims that the judgment was focused.[66]

CG sought damages and injunctions preventing Mr McCloskey from harassing him by publishing any information on Facebook's website, and requiring Facebook to terminate McCloskey's page.

Decision

The case against Joseph McCloskey

The High Court in Northern Ireland found that Mr McCloskey's purpose in setting up the profile and Facebook page was to destroy the family life of sex offenders, to expose them to total humiliation and vilification, to drive them from their homes and expose them to the risk of serious harm. Stephens J found that McCloskey knowingly encouraged harassment of sex offenders by other individuals by the comments he made and by the aim and purpose of his page on Facebook.[67]

---

66 The relevant legislation was the Electronic Commerce (EC Directive) Regulations 2002 and the Protection from Harassment (Northern Ireland) Order 1997 (NI 1997/1180).
67 [2015] NIQB 11 at 74.

The court found that Mr McCloskey had engaged in a course of conduct in relation to harassment of CG so that he 'was extremely concerned and lived in increased fear as he anticipated violence being inflicted on him'.[68]

In relation to misuse of private information and the DPA the court found that CG's privacy, data protection and Article 8 rights had been infringed. The data disclosed via social media had been 'sensitive personal data' under the DPA, including information relating to sexual life, the commission of offences and criminal proceedings. Stephens J said that CG had an expectation of privacy in relation to such information after his conviction had been spent. Accordingly, Mr McCloskey was liable for harassment and misuse of private information of CG.

The case against Facebook

Stephens J ruled that Facebook had misused private information in not deleting the information about CG on the 'Keeping our Kids Safe from Predators 2' profile, the content of which was unlawful being a misuse of private information. The page and postings had incited violence and hatred and had placed CG in serious risk of harm. The judge said that this was indiscriminate and could have led to the development of public order situations. Facebook was the primary publisher and was liable for misuse of private information.

The court ruled that Facebook could not claim lack of knowledge under regulation 22 of the Electronic Commerce (EC Directive) Regulations 2002;[69] and was therefore liable for the whole period of posting.[70] The court reached the same conclusion in relation to the postings on RS's profile page except that liability only arose from the date of receipt of CG's solicitors' letters in relation to each of the two series of postings.

Stephens J pointed out that regulation 22 also provides that the court 'shall take into account all matters which appear to it in the particular circumstances to be relevant'. The judge was highly critical of demands made by Facebook in correspondence for the provision of the URL for every offending posting and comment, together with an explanation in relation to each as to why it transgressed, before it would take any steps to investigate a complaint. Stephens J commented that regulation 22 is 'not an attempt to be prescriptive as to precisely how notice is to be given to a service provider or as to how actual knowledge is required' and must be seen in the context of a requirement to take into account all matters which appear to be relevant.[71]

The court awarded CG damages totalling £20,000. An anti-harassment injunction was made against Mr McCloskey and a mandatory injunction was made against Facebook requiring it to terminate the entirety of the 'Keeping our Kids Safe from Predators 2' profile, including all material referring to other sex offenders.[72]

Analysis

The Northern Ireland High Court's decision in *CG* has a number of notable features. First, a mandatory injunction was made against Facebook requiring it to take down an entire

---

68 Ibid., at 35.
69 Regulation 22 sets out the particular matters that the court shall have regard to in determining whether a service provider has been placed on notice and can therefore be held liable. These include 'details of the location of the information' and 'details of the unlawful nature of the activity or information in question'.
70 [2015] NIQB 11 at 102.
71 Ibid., at 95.
72 Ibid., at 105.

page despite the fact that the offending material had been removed from it immediately following receipt of CG's solicitors' letter. Secondly, the mandatory injunction was made not only to protect the privacy rights of CG but of other sex offenders featured on the web page. Thirdly, the judge used the provisions of the Data Protection Act 1998 for the definitions of sensitive personal data and misuse of private information. Fourthly, Stephens J declared Facebook a primary publisher rejecting its argument that the social media provider had no 'actual knowledge' for the purpose of regulation 22 of the Electronic Commerce (EC Directive) Regulations 2002 for each offending post or comment (unless and until it had provided with the URL) (see also: *AB Ltd v Facebook Ireland Ltd* (2013);[73] *XY v Facebook Ireland Ltd* (2012)[74]).

In December 2008, the European Court of Human Rights handed down its judgment in the *Norwegian Pensioner* case.[75] The ECtHR found that a blanket ban on advertising for political parties violated Article 10 ECHR. The background to the case concerned regional elections in Rogaland province where the Pensioner Party (Pensjonistparti – located in Stavanger) broadcast three political advertising slots on TV ('TV Vest') in the spring of 2003 with elections in September that year. Since political advertising is illegal in Norway and contravenes the broadcasting legislation, the Pensioner Party received a warning from the Norwegian Media Authority. Nevertheless, the commercials were broadcast from 14 August to 13 September and TV Vest was fined NOK 35,000 by the Oslo City Court (Oslo tingrett) for violating the prohibition on political advertising in TV broadcasts.[76]

TV Vest appealed against the decision stating that the prohibitions in the Norwegian Broadcasting Act and Regulations were incompatible with the right to freedom of expression under Article 10 ECHR. The City Court upheld the Media Authority's decision in February 2004, supported by the Norwegian Supreme Court in November of that year. The case progressed to the Strasbourg Human Rights Court where Christos Rozakis, President of the ECtHR (First Section) ruled that there had been a violation of Article 10, because the proportionality aspect had not been addressed; there had not been:

> [a] reasonable relationship of proportionality between the legitimate aim pursued by the prohibition on political advertising and the means deployed to achieve that aim. The restriction which the prohibition and the imposition of the fine entailed on the applicants' exercise of their freedom of expression cannot therefore be regarded as having been necessary in a democratic society, within the meaning of paragraph 2 of Article 10, for the protection of the rights of others, notwithstanding the margin of appreciation available to the national authorities.[77]

The judgment in the *Norwegian Pensioner* case caused great controversy and subsequently had considerable consequences for political advertising in other signature countries to the Convention.

Even where a statement amounts to a value judgement, the proportionality of an interference may depend on whether there exists a sufficient factual basis for the impugned statement, since even a value judgement without any factual basis to support it may be excessive (see: *Dichand v Austria* (2002);[78] also: *Monnat v Switzerland* (2006)[79]).

---

73 [2013] NIQB 14 QBD (NI) 06 February 2013.

74 [2012] NIQB 96 QBD (NI) 30 November 2012.

75 See: *TV Vest AS & Rogaland Pensjonistparti v Norway* (2008) (Application No 21132/05) Judgment of the 11 December 2008 (ECtHR) (the *Norwegian Pensioner* case).

76 Under s 10(3) of the Norwegian Broadcasting Act 1992 and reg. 10(2) of the Norwegian Broadcasting Regulations.

77 *Rogaland Pensjonistparti v Norway* (2008) at para. 78 (Christos Rozakis, President, ECHR).

78 (2002) (Application No 29271/95) of 26 February 2002 (ECHR).

79 (2006) (Application No 73604/01) of 21 September 2006 (ECHR).

5.6.4 Analysis and discussion

The right to freedom of expression includes freedom to seek and receive information. It is a key component of democratic governance as the promotion of a participatory decision-making process in a modern democratic internet society.

While the internet has brought global freedom to communicate and exchange ideas, its growth has introduced difficulties too – for instance, the expression on social networking sites and blogs of personal opinions, with the risk therein of misinformation, defamation, harassment and invasion of privacy. There is also the ability to search the World Wide Web for content of pretty well any extreme nature, ranging from the sexual to the political.

In the light of rather mixed guidance from the Strasbourg Human Rights Court it is then left up to a domestic broadcast or print press regulators to strike a fine balance between the parameters of indecent, obscene and violent material and sensitive issues such as ethics and morals, existing legislation and the effective monitoring of the domestic media services, without being too pro-hibitive. The existence of a discretionary area of judgement means that such decisions can only be made by a domestic court of law, rather than a regulator which may not have full statutory pow-ers, although this may change after the *Max Schrems* ruling in the European Court of Justice (ECJ) in October 2015.[80] In this context, it is submitted that the courts should not regard a regulatory authority as better able than jurisprudence to assess what are 'generally accepted standards', such as the Ofcom Broadcasting Code or IPSO's Editors' Code (see: *R (SB) v Governors of Denbigh High School* (2007);[81] also: *Belfast City Council v Miss Behavin' Ltd* (2007);[82] also: *R (Nasseri) v SSHD* (2010)[83]). It is then up to regulators to introduce safeguards into their codes of practice which express responsibili-ties. As Lord Walker said in the *ProLife case*,[84] in practice the obligation to avoid offensive material is interpreted as limited to what is needlessly or gratuitously shocking or offensive (see also: *Murphy v Ireland* (2000)[85]).

In summary, regulation of the internet as far as online activities are concerned poses ongoing challenges to national governments and for the passing of domestic legislation in line with EU law. The EU Commission's aim for its 2020 agenda is to promote freedoms of opinion and expression as 'online' rights to be exercised by everyone everywhere, based on the principles of equality, non-discrimination and universality. It is the Commission's objective to address and prevent violations of online rights.[86]

Where should the line be drawn between regulating indecency, obscenity and invasion of privacy and freedom of expression and 'freedom to view'? Ultimately should this not be left to the autonomy of and freedom to choose of the end-user? While the international community is fast promoting the transfer of technology and information, there appear to be a number of different policies and laws in place across Europe, the United States[87] and other international jurisdictions, each attempting to regulate, control and curtail the internet and online digital media technology.

---

80 *Schrems (Maximilian) v Data Protection Commissioner* (2015) (Case C-362/14) Luxembourg, 6 October 2015. (CJEU); [2015] All ER (D) 34 (Oct).

81 [2007] 1 AC 100.

82 [2007] 1 WLR 1420.

83 [2010] 1 AC 1 (HL).

84 *R (ProLife Alliance) v BBC* [2004] 1 AC 185 at 121 (Lord Walker).

85 (2000) 38 EHRR 13 (ECtHR).

86 Source: Council of the European Union (2014) 'EU Human Rights Guidelines on Freedom of Expression Online and Offline.' Council meeting Brussels, 12 May 2014.

87 See: The Digital Millennium Copyright Act ('the Copyright Act') (Title 17 of the US Code) to provide in part certain limitations on the liability of online service providers (OSPs) for copyright infringement. Section 512(c) of the Copyright Act provides limitations on service provider liability for storage, at the direction of a user, of copyrighted material residing on a system or network controlled or operated by or for the service provider, if, among other things, the service provider has designated an agent to receive notifications of claimed infringement by providing contact information to the Copyright Office and by posting such information on the service provider's website in a location accessible to the public.

Is it too late to pass any more internet legislation? Is internet governance now dominated by the private sector and self-regulators? The internet is highly robust, dynamic and geographically diverse and can be seen as a positive as well as negative tool. It remains to be seen whether the World Wide Web can really be legally controlled and regulated.

5.7 Further reading

Hurst, A. (2015) 'Data privacy and intermediary liability: striking a balance between privacy, reputation, innovation and freedom of expression', *Entertainment Law Review*, 26(6), 187–195.
Ashley Hurst reviews the problems inherent in the Data Protection Act 1998 (DPA) for ISPs as internet intermediaries since the CJEU ruling in *Google Spain* (2014). The author examines when intermediaries are faced with defamation or privacy claims.

Khan, A. (2012) 'A "right not to be offended" under Article 10(2) ECHR? Concerns in the construction of the "rights of others" ', *European Human Rights Law Review*, 2, 191–204.
This article evaluates the courts' approaches to unpopular political speech and free speech restriction in general. Aatifa Khan considers this development from both a black-letter and jurisprudential point of view, concluding that it is unsupported in law and in principle. The author suggests there should be greater regard to underlying free-speech principles, and a separation between the speech's popularity and the level of legal protection given to it. By looking at *Gaunt v Ofcom*, Khan argues that there is a troubling trend of restricting unpopular speech based on the 'right of others not to be offended'.

Mac Sithigh, D. (2011) '"I'd tell you everything if you'd pick up that telephone": political expression and data protection', *European Human Rights Law Review*, 2, 166–175.
Daithi Mac Sithigh examines EU law, comparing Directive 2002/58 ('Privacy and Electronic Communications Directive') with provisions under Article 10 ECHR ('freedom of expression'). The focus of this article is on 'exemptions' for purposes of journalism. The author argues that EU legislation in this respect has impacted significantly on democratic political activities in Member States. The author concludes that EU data protection law fails to protect communication by parties and candidates, to the detriment of citizen participation in the political process.

Mason, S. (2015) 'The internet and privacy: some considerations', *Computer and Telecommunications Law Review*, 21(3), 68–84.
Stephen Mason discusses the various ways in which online technology can be used to access data about individuals that could be seen as invading their privacy. He analyses the concept of 'privacy' and the harms caused when it is invaded and considers the evidence that privacy is widely acknowledged as a human right. The author then examines how the right to privacy has been interpreted by the UK courts and reviews leading authorities.

Chapter 6

Regulatory authorities 2: press regulation and advertising standards

Key points

This chapter will cover the following questions:

- How is the print press (and their online editions) regulated?
- Has the Leveson Inquiry had an impact on press regulation?
- What is the future of press regulation?
- How should journalistic sources be protected?
- What is the purpose of regulating advertising?
- What are the CAP and BCAP codes in relation to advertising in the UK?
- How can children be protected from unsafe online marketing and advertising content?
- To what extent are films, online videos and games regulated in the UK?
- What is the role of the Competition and Markets Authority (CMA)?

6.1 Overview

This chapter first reflects on the Leveson recommendations, how many have been implemented, the complexities which ensued regarding different press regulators and how many newspapers have actually signed up to the various regulatory bodies. We will look at the new print press regulator IPSO and its rival organization Impress. While IPSO has been backed by the vast majority of the UK press industry – except the *Guardian*, *Independent* and the *Financial Times* – Impress has so far only attracted independent and small publications.

This chapter reflects on the 'phone hacking' scandal at the *News of the World* and looks at ongoing criminal investigations into police forces' hacking into journalists' phones. One such example is the 'Plebgate' affair and how the police misused the provisions of the Regulation of Investigatory Powers Act 2000 (RIPA).

We then move on to the CJEU landmark ruling in the *Max Schrems* (2015) case concerning the Austrian law student who challenged Facebook's international data sharing which led to the collapse of the US–EU 'safe harbour' agreement.[1]

Having looked at the regulation of the print press we examine the self-regulation of the advertising industry via the Advertising Standards Authority (ASA) and EU-wide regulation (such as the CAP Code and the Blue Book). The focus will be – *inter alia* – on the commercial powers of Facebook and YouTube advertising, video-sharing, vlogging and product placement in films and on TV.

Since online advertising strategies have become more aggressive and intrusive we will examine how the regulators and domestic legislation protect children and vulnerable individuals from online abuse.

---

1 Privacy agreement of 2000 ('pact') between the EU and USA regarding online privacy. The pact allows firms to transfer data from the EU to the USA if they provide safeguards equivalent to those required by the EU Data Protection Directive ('safe harbour').

Another self-regulatory body is then the British Board of Film Classification (BBFC), which has been given statutory recognition to classify and regulate not only cinema films, but also music DVDs, videos and games.

The chapter closes with a look at the relatively new UK consumer and competition regulatory authority, the Competition and Markets Authority (CMA), an independent non-ministerial government department (or quango) with responsibility for carrying out investigations into mergers, cartels and price fixing.

6.2 Regulating the print press

The origins of regulation of the British print press can be traced back to the post Second World War period when the Labour government established a Royal Commission in 1947 under the chairmanship of Sir David Ross to review and advise Parliament on the finance, control, management and ownership of the press. When the Commission reported on its findings it recommended the establishment of a self-regulatory press and the Press Council was set up in 1953; a voluntary body that aimed to maintain high ethical standards of journalism and to promote press freedom.

During the 1980s a small number of publications failed in the view of many to observe the basic ethics of journalism. This in turn reinforced a belief among many Members of Parliament that the Press Council, which had lost the confidence of some in the press, was not a sufficiently effective body. Some believed that it would be preferable to enact a law of privacy and right of reply as well as to set up a statutory press council wielding enforceable legal sanctions.[2] Given the serious implications of such a course of action, the Conservative Home Secretary Douglas Hurd appointed a Departmental Committee in 1989 under (later Sir) David Calcutt QC to consider the matter. The Committee's task was to consider what measures were needed to give further protection to individual privacy from the activities of the press and improve recourse against the press for the individual citizen.[3]

6.2.1 Setting up the Press Complaints Commission as self-regulator

The Calcutt Report on 'Privacy and Related Matters' (1990) did not suggest new statutory controls but recommended that a 'Press Complaints Commission' ought to replace the Press Council. The new commission was given just 18 months to demonstrate 'that non-statutory self-regulation can be made to work effectively. This is a stiff test for the press. If it fails, we recommend that a statutory system for handling complaints should be introduced.'[4]

Members of the press responded with vigour to the Calcutt Report, acting with great speed to set up their own self-regulator in the form of the Press Complaints Commission (the PCC) in 1991. Five years later, in July 1995, the Conservative Secretary of State for National Heritage, Virginia Bottomley, reported the findings of the Select Committee on Privacy and Media Intrusion to the House of Commons, that a case had not been made out to enact a privacy law as a form of civil remedy for media intrusion into a person's privacy. The Labour MP for Islington and Finsbury, Chris Smith, asked Mrs Bottomley why a criminal offence had not been introduced specifically designed to prevent physical intrusion from bugging devices planted by the press which seriously invaded a person's private property.[5] The Secretary of State's response was non-committal, stating

2   For further discussion see: Rampal, K. R. (1981).
3   See: House of Commons (1990).
4   Ibid.
5   See: House of Commons (1995) at 1326.

that it was up to the press regulator, the PCC, to keep its journalists in check by way of adherence to their Code of Practice.

In 2003, a House of Commons Parliamentary Select Committee on 'Culture, Media and Sport' considered whether some form of statutory regulation of the print press ought to be introduced since there had been too many calls for the abolition of the PCC. Giving evidence to the Select Committee, Tugendhat J had stated that 'no new laws are necessary because recent changes in the law have already cured the defect in English law. I agree with the PCC that there is no need to introduce new legislation at the present time.'[6] Tugendhat J based his views on the statutory provisions of the Human Rights Act 1998, the Data Protection Act 1998 and the Protection from Harassment Act 1997, as well as common law decisions in *Campbell* (2002),[7] *A v B* (2002)[8] and the Strasbourg Court's ruling in *Peck* (2003)[9] (see below). In other words, no new laws were necessary because recent changes in the law had already cured the defect in English privacy law.

6.2.2 The PCC and its Editors' Code

The Press Complaints Commission (PCC) was established in 1991 as an independent self-regulatory body for the print press (including magazines and, later, online editions). The main role of the PCC was to handle readers' complaints, by administering and upholding the Editors' Code of Practice. By the time the PCC drew to a close in September 2014, the Commission comprised six editorial industry representatives from across a range of newspapers and magazines, and nine lay members – including its chairman, Lord Hunt of Wirral.

The PCC Code was regarded as the cornerstone of (print) press self-regulation, to which the industry and its editors had made a binding commitment. The funding of the PCC was via annual membership of newspaper editors and substantial fees paid to the regulator. Nearly all members of the press who had signed up to the PCC and its Code and had a duty to maintain the highest professional standards. It was then the responsibility of editors and publishers to apply the Code to editorial material in both printed and online versions of publications. *Private Eye*[10] editor Ian Hislop (editor since 1986) never signed up to the PCC. Giving evidence to the Leveson Inquiry, Hislop said he had 'some issues' with the number of tabloid editors sitting on the PCC, particularly the influence of *News of the World* editors.[11]

The PCC included the Editors' Code of Practice Committee ('the Code Committee'), made up of regional editors of newspapers. This Code Committee produced the PCC Code of Practice ('the Code') for the Commission. The Code underwent numerous changes between 1991 and 2013, including *inter alia* an important definition of the 'public interest' and setting the benchmark for ethical press standards. Until 2013, Paul Dacre, editor of the *Daily Mail* and editor in chief of Associated Newspapers, was Code Committee Chairman.

6.2.3 PCC as complaints adjudicator

The PCC said of itself (on its website) that it offered a service which was both 'quick and free' and that 'it costs nothing to complain to the PCC – you do not need a solicitor or anyone else to represent you', thanks to the commitment of the newspaper industry, which self-regulates through tough and effective sanctions without being a burden on the taxpayer. It was true that most disputes

6 Source: House of Commons – Department of Culture, Media and Sport (2003). Supplementary memorandum submitted by Mr Michael Tugendhat QC. Comment on the Supplementary Memorandum submitted by the PCC, 16 June 2003, at para. 501.
7 [2004] 2 AC 457 (HL).
8 [2002] EWCA 337 (QB).
9 *Peck v UK* (2003) 36 EHRR 719 (ECHR).
10 The fortnightly magazine *Private Eye* runs 'Street of Shame', a two-page column devoted to stories about journalistic hypocrisy, misbehaviour and examples of editorial or proprietorial influence in news.
11 Ian Hislop gave evidence to the Leveson Inquiry on 17 January 2012.

were resolved amicably and quickly by the PCC, averaging about 35 working days to do so. The regulator would frequently assist those persons who found themselves at the centre of a media story, usually through no fault of their own, particularly when the individual was particularly vulnerable, for instance as the result of a bereavement. The PCC would then distribute a 'cease and desist' request to newspaper editors, reporters and photographers, to help to ensure that the complainant would receive privacy wherever possible. The outcome of these requests would invariably result in a reduction in physical media intrusion.

Here are some examples of high profile complaints and adjudications of the PCC. In 2008, Professor Sir Roy Meadow[12] complained that a comment piece in The Times, headlined 'A moving response to our family justice campaign', was inaccurate and misleading.[13] His complaint centred on Clause 1 ('Accuracy'). The journalist's point was that the complainant's submission of statistics-based evidence in the Sally Clark[14] case, when he was not a statistician, was an example of his going beyond his remit, and that other women had won their appeals against similar 'cot death' murder convictions also based on the misleading statistical evidence of Sir Roy on 'Sudden Infant Death Syndrome' – simply, that he had misled the jury in the Sally Clark case. As a means of resolving the complaint by Sir Roy, The Times invited the professor to submit a letter for publication outlining his concerns, but the complainant rejected the offer. The PCC did not uphold Professor Meadow's complaint, stating that The Times piece was an opinion piece and that the columnist's interpretation of the 'cot death' cases was accurately based on the appeal judgments, including those in other cases.[15] Above all, they held that the piece had been in the public interest.

Following the untimely death of 33-year-old singer Stephen Gately of pop band Boyzone on 10 October 2009 in Mallorca, the PCC received more than 23,000 complaints from the public about an opinion piece written by the Daily Mail columnist Jan Moir on 13 October. The article was published the day before Gately's funeral in Dublin with the original headline on the Mail's website: 'Why there was nothing "natural" about Stephen Gately's death'. This was later amended in the printed edition and online to: 'A strange, lonely and troubling death'. Moir told her readers that Gately's death after a drunken night out in Mallorca 'strikes another blow to the happy-ever-after myth of civil partnerships'.

The public outcry about Moir's article was fuelled by widespread discussions on social networking sites like Twitter, and resulted in the highest number of complaints the PCC had ever received about a single article. Justifying its public interest responsibility, the Commission got in touch with Gately's family. The Commission also asked the Daily Mail editor, Paul Dacre – a member of the PCC's editorial board – to supply a response. In a new Daily Mail piece on 23 October 2009, Jan Moir expressed regret over her original column, though she stood by her earlier assertion that the circumstances surrounding the pop star's sudden death were 'more than a little sleazy' and that there was 'nothing natural' about Gately's death. The PCC's decision not to uphold the public complaint against the Daily Mail over its publication of Jan Moir's article caused great controversy. The adjudication made the point that one of the primary functions of a self-regulatory system was to defend freedom of speech. The PCC endorsed the newspaper's view that it must allow its journalists freedom of speech, which includes offensive views by its columnists. The PCC's director at the time,

12 Professor Sir Roy Meadow v The Times. PCC adjudication of 17 July 2008.
13 Source: 'A moving response to our family justice campaign', by Camilla Cavendish, The Times, 17 July 2008.
14 Solicitor Mrs Sally Clark was convicted in 1999 of killing her 11-week-old son Christopher in December 1996 and 8-week-old Harry in January 1998 (the 'cot death' case). Her first appeal against the convictions failed in 2000, but the second succeeded and she was acquitted in 2003, when three Appeal Court judges ruled that Mrs Clark's conviction was 'unsafe', based on Professor Sir Roy Meadow's evidence during her trial. Expert witness Professor Meadow (for the prosecution) told the jury that the probability of two natural unexplained cot deaths in a family was 73 million to one. At appeal, the Royal Statistical Society and other medical experts disputed that figure, stating that the odds of a second cot death in a family were around 200 to one. The GMC found Sir Roy guilty of serious professional misconduct in July 2005; he was struck off the medical register. Sally Clark died on 16 March 2007, aged 42.
15 Angela Cannings served 18 months after being wrongly convicted of killing her two sons. Donna Anthony served six years after being wrongly convicted of killing her son and daughter. Trupti Patel was cleared of killing three of her children.

Stephen Abell, said the article contained flaws, but the Commission had decided 'it would not be proportionate to rule against the columnist's right to offer freely expressed views about something that was the focus of public attention'.[16]

The PCC remained under constant criticism for performing inadequately amid claims that the search for an alternative system had become urgent. The Jan Moir decision may not have weighed in the press regulator's favour.

6.2.4 The PCC: a 'toothless poodle'

One question remained: how could the PCC realistically punish its journalistic miscreants when it had no real power to sanction an editor or photographer by imposing a large fine (as does Ofcom)? All the PCC could do was to demand that an offending publication print an apology, publish a relatively small summary of the outcome of its adjudications or present editors with 'cease and desist' notifications which were repeatedly not followed – though *Daily Mail* editor Paul Dacre strongly denied that editors took no notice of the PCC. How effective was the press regulator really in dealing with serious media intrusion into people's private lives?

There was relentless press coverage with extensive media intrusion into the lives of Gerry and Kate McCann following the disappearance of their daughter Madeleine while on holiday in Portugal in May 2007. There was harassment and defamation of a prime suspect, Robert Murat. Neither the McCanns nor Mr Murat were helped by the PCC, so they sought legal redress via the High Court in the tort of defamation, with the result that four national newspaper groups had to apologize to Robert Murat in July 2008 for publishing false allegations about him over claims that he was involved in the abduction of Madeleine McCann. Murat received £600,000 in libel damages from News International, Mirror Group Newspapers, Express Newspapers and Associated Newspapers.[17] The Express Newspapers' titles, including the *Daily Express*, *Daily Star* and *Sunday Express*, were made to apologize to Kate and Gerry McCann for wrongly suggesting that the couple were responsible for Madeleine's death, by printing front-page apologies and paying a settlement of £550,000 damages.[18]

See Chapter 7

When the House of Commons Committee for Culture, Media and Sport launched another inquiry into the possible discontinuation of press self-regulation in 2007, its report concluded that the PCC should continue, since there were now sufficient safeguards in statutory and common law to support private individuals if they could not be granted satisfactory redress by the regulator.

Leading media lawyer Geoffrey Robertson QC disagreed. He had frequently attacked the existence of the PCC, saying that 'the most satisfactory reform of the PCC would be its abolition', and questioning whether its 'lay' members really were 'lay' and truly represent ordinary members of society. In a *Guardian* blog debating the continued existence of the press regulator, Mr Robertson wrote in November 2009:

the PCC tries to function as a poor person's libel court, but why should the vilified poor have to resort to an amateur set of adjudicators who can award them no compensation or damages – not even their bus fare home – and cannot direct newspapers to publish any correction prominently? The PCC's worst feature has been its propagandistic claim that it has raised standards of journalism – which it has not, other than perhaps the reporting of the Royal Family, over whom it is obsessively protective. It goes to extravagant lengths to deter people from asserting their legal rights.[19]

16 Source: Press release by the PCC on 17 February 2010.
17 Source: 'Madeleine McCann: Newspapers pay out £600,000 to Robert Murat', by Oliver Luft and John Pluckett, *Guardian*, 17 July 2008.
18 Source: 'Papers paying damages to McCanns', *BBC News Online*, 19 March 2008.
19 Source: 'What should be done with the PCC?', by Geoffrey Robertson QC, *Guardian*, 23 November 2009.

During a February 2010 debate in the House of Commons on 'Press Standards, Privacy and Libel', the PCC was again criticized for being ineffective and 'toothless' on the issue of use of phone-tapping and clandestine recording devices, particularly by the *News of theWorld*.[20] At the same time, Justice Secretary Jack Straw and Lord Lester proposed that the libel laws and press regulation ought to be reformed at the same time by way of a Defamation Bill. During another parliamentary debate the then Labour opposition leader, Ed Miliband, called the PCC a 'toothless poodle' and asked for an urgent replacement of the press self-regulatory watchdog (House of Commons, 7 July 2011).

See Chapter 7.3

Lord Hunt, who became Chairman of the PCC after predecessor Baroness Peta Buscombe left the post in 2011 amid mounting claims of phone-hacking by the *News of theWorld*, stated he would replace the PCC with a 'robust, independent regulator with teeth'. The PCC ceased to exist on 8 September 2014. The magazine and newspaper industries subsequently created a new, self-regulatory body – the Independent Press Standards Organisation (IPSO) – in accordance with the Leveson principles. IPSO commenced operations in September 2014.

See below 6.4

 FOR THOUGHT

Is self-regulation the best way forward to regulate the print press or should statutory regulation take over, similar to the Irish Press Council?[21] Discuss.

6.3 The Leveson inquiry

Leveson LJ's Inquiry was ordered by the Prime Minister David Cameron in November 2011 as a result of the emerging scandal of 'phone hacking' by the *News of the World* (*NoW*), subsequently closed down by Rupert Murdoch in July 2011 (last edition on 10 July 'Thank You & Good Bye'). The inquiry was ordered, following revelations that someone working for the tabloid had, in 2002, illegally accessed the voicemail messages of the missing schoolgirl, Milly Dowler – who was later found murdered.

The Leveson Inquiry was the culmination of a series of claims and discoveries about the extent of phone-hacking of celebrities and others. Leveson LJ spent nearly 18 months gathering evidence from editors, politicians and victims of press intrusion. The key decision for Lord Leveson was whether to try again with some beefed-up form of pure self-regulation – with the risk that nothing would really change – or argue for formal press regulation enshrined in legislation. Statutory regulation was seen by most sections of the media as tantamount to ending press freedom.

See Chapter 2.2

The Leveson Report ('*Leveson*')[22] made recommendations on how future concerns about press behaviour, media policy, regulation and cross-media ownership should be dealt with and by which authorities; and, in particular, whether statutory intervention was warranted. Leveson made recommendations for a new, more effective policy and regulatory regime designed to encourage the highest ethical and professional standards, without stifling the independence or plurality of the media.

---

20 Source: House of Commons (2010a), at p. 58.
21 See: Press Council of Ireland at: www.presscouncil.ie.
22 The Leveson Inquiry's terms of reference are accessible at: www.levesoninquiry.org.uk/about/terms-of-reference.

6.3.1 The phone-hacking scandal

To understand the background and full impact of *Leveson*, we need to look back to events which led up to the inquiry, namely the phone-hacking scandal and its scale which emerged during the Leveson Inquiry. For many years, there had been complaints that certain parts of the tabloid press were riding roughshod over both individuals and the public at large, without any justifiable public interest. Rumours and jokes about the extent to which phone-hacking was prevalent at the *NoW* were rife, but the press regulator, the PCC, did nothing to investigate in order to expose the unethical conduct tolerated at Rupert Murdoch's News International (publishers of *NoW*). Phone hacking was one of a range of methods of gathering personal information, and was often one of the less directly intrusive. Others included blagging,[23] pinging,[24] paying informants and tailing.[25]

See Chapter
4.4

A report by the Information Commissioner's Office (ICO) – 'What Price Privacy' – was published in 2006. The investigation was led by the then Information Commissioner, Richard Thomas, regarding the unlawful practice of an organized trade in confidential personal data information by newspaper reporters. The ICO report suggested that journalists were increasingly contravening section 55 of the Data Protection Act 1998 by obtaining personal information via illicit means, such as phone-tapping or using private detectives in order to dig up stories at any price.[26]

In 2009 the PCC launched another inquiry into phone-tapping and subterfuge at News International and the *Guardian* subsequently published the results of the Commission's investigation into phone-hacking at *NoW*. Speaking on BBC Radio 4's *Today* programme, the then *Guardian* editor Alan Rusbridger[27] accused the PCC of being 'toothless' for not interviewing a single witness in the 'Goodman' case (see below). Rusbridger told the BBC that the PCC had not inspected any further documents other than those already supplied and inspected by the police in their 2005–2006 investigation.[28]

Clive Goodman, former *NoW*'s Royal Correspondent, had already pleaded guilty a couple of years earlier and was sentenced to four months in prison on 26 January 2007 for intercepting phone messages from Prince William's voicemails. His co-conspirator, private investigator Glenn Mulcaire, had also pleaded guilty to a further five counts of unlawful interception of communications – both were charged under section 1 RIPA. Mulcaire, former striker at AFC Wimbledon, told the court that he had had a year's contract with *NoW* for 'research and information services' worth £104,988 and also received £12,300 in cash from the newspaper. But in reality he was providing the Sunday tabloid with the mobile phone details of celebrities and royals, including the Liberal Democrat MP Simon Hughes, supermodel Elle Macpherson, publicist Max Clifford, football agent Skylet Andrew and Gordon Taylor, Chief Executive of the Professional Footballers' Association. Sentencing judge Gross J described Goodman and Mulcaire's behaviour as 'low conduct, reprehensible in the extreme'; furthermore that this case was not about press freedom; it was about a 'grave, inexcusable invasion of privacy'.[29]

Civil proceedings followed by those whose identity as victims of phone-hacking had been exposed by the prosecution of Goodman and Mulcaire. On 9 July 2009, an article was published in the *Guardian* which alleged a cover-up at *NoW*. Investigative journalist Nick Davies had started to uncover the truth about the extent of phone-hacking at the Sunday tabloid and also found that some incredible settlements with celebrity phone hacking victims had been made with Rupert

---

23 Manage to obtain (something) by using persuasion or guile.
24 'Pinging' can be used to monitor a user's mobile phone and track its location. The technique can pinpoint the location of a mobile phone through a network of cell towers that register its signal every few minutes. Pinging is tightly regulated and is legally restricted to the police, security services and a small selection of other bodies. The practice is often used in situations where there is a threat to life, such as a murder case or suicide risk.
25 To follow someone without being noticed; to 'shadow' someone.
26 See: Information Commissioner's Office (2006a) at paras 5.1–5.4.
27 Alan Rusbridger stepped down as the editor of the *Guardian* on 29 May 2015 after leading the paper for 20 years.
28 Source: Alan Rusbridger, comment on BBC Radio 4's *Today* programme, 9 November 2009.
29 Source: 'Pair jailed over royal phone taps', *BBC News Online*, 26 January 2007.

Murdoch's News Corp., some being paid more than £1 million to settle out of court. By 2015 the phone-hacking scandal at the (by then defunct) *NoW* had risen to £332 million. It had settled 377 compensation claims lodged by celebrities, politicians and public figures including Cherie Blair, Jude Law and former cabinet ministers David Blunkett and Tessa Jowell.[30]

In a complex court action in 2012 – known as *Re Phillips*[31] – the Court of Appeal upheld orders from the High Court requiring the former private investigator, Glenn Mulcaire (known as 'defendant 2' or 'D2'), to provide information regarding his phone-hacking activities. As part of the 50 actions at that time by phone-hacking victims against Rupert Murdoch's 'News Corp.', Nicola Phillips (former PA to PR guru Max Clifford) and actor-comedian Steve Coogan sought disclosure of information from Glenn Mulcaire about his intercepting their voicemails at the time. This, Phillips and Coogan argued, would help their claims against 'News Corp.' for compensation. D2 argued that he should be able to rely on his common law right to privilege from self-incrimination (PSI) in order to negate the obligation to provide information requested from him by the claimants, Phillips and Coogan.

D2 (Mulcaire) objected on the ground that such disclosure may well incriminate him, and he worried that further criminal charges would be brought against him under section 1(1) RIPA ('intercepting phone messages'). Ms Phillips contended that, *inter alia*, section 72 Senior Courts Act 1981 applied to this action, which provides that PSI *cannot* be relied on. The result was that, on 18 July 2012, Glenn Mulcaire was ordered by the court to hand over the information in relation to the hacking of the phones of Nicola Phillips and Steve Coogan. Lawyers acting for 50 further phone-hacking victims argued that this information was vital to their claims. Vos J agreed, citing Article 6 ECHR relating to the individual's right to a fair trial.

From February to August 2013 over 100 arrests were made by the police as part of Scotland Yard's investigation into phone-hacking ('Operation Weeting'). At the same time the 'Yard' was working on 'Operation Elveden' (investigation into alleged corrupt payments to public officials, such as police officers, by journalists) and 'Operation Tuleta' (computer hacking). By mid-2013, the Met had 185 officers and civilian staff working on the investigations: 96 on Weeting, 70 on Elveden and 19 on Tuleta. Among the public officials arrested as part of Elveden were a member of the armed forces, a prison official and several police officers. Police estimated that around 5,500 people had been victims of *NoW* phone hacking.

See below 6.6.1

The 'phone-hacking trial' began on 28 October 2013 at the Old Bailey in London. Former News International Chief Executive Rebekah Brooks (née Wade),[32] her racehorse trainer husband Charlie, Prime Minister David Cameron's former Director of Communications Andy Coulson[33] and seven other defendants faced a number of charges linked to phone-hacking at the by now-defunct *NoW.* The other defendants were Stuart Kuttner, former managing editor of *NoW*, Ian Edmondson, former *NoW* Head of News, Cheryl Carter, Rebekah Brooks's former secretary, and Mark Hanna, Head of Security for News International. All pleaded not guilty to the charges of conspiring to pervert the course of justice.

The trial, which was one of the longest and most expensive in British criminal history, heard allegations of how journalists working at the *NoW* and *The Sun*, under the stewardship of Mrs Brooks and Mr Coulson, routinely broke the law in pursuit of exclusive stories. Jurors were told how reporters at *NoW* hacked mobile phones of hundreds of public and private figures, including celebrities, politicians, even victims of crime: they included Prince William, Prince Harry's ex-girlfriend Chelsy Davy, former Attorney General Lord Goldsmith, former Labour Home Secretary Charles

---

30 Source: 'News Corp hacking scandal costs rise to $512m', by Dominic Ponsford, *Press Gazette*, 8 May 2015.

31 See: *Phillips v News Group Newspapers Ltd* (1) News Group Newspapers Ltd (2) Glenn Mulcaire; Coogan v (1) News Group Newspapers Ltd (2) Glenn Mulcaire [2012] EWCA Civ 48 (also cited as 'Steve Coogan v News Group Newspapers Ltd and Glenn Mulcaire; Nicola Phillips v News Group Newspapers Ltd and Glenn Mulcaire).

32 Rebekah Brooks was also editor of the *Sun* between 14 January 2003 and 1 September 2009.

33 Andy Coulson was the *News of the World*'s deputy editor between 2000 and 2003 and editor between 2003 and 2007.

Clarke, the actor Jude Law, football manager José Mourinho, football pundit Gary Lineker, the parents of Harry Potter actor Daniel Radcliffe, London Mayor Boris Johnson, Angelina Jolie, Simon Cowell, Sir Paul McCartney, former Liberal Democrat leader Charles Kennedy, David Miliband, Elle Macpherson and Heather Mills.

Moore (2015) in his research into the *NoW* phone-hacking scandal found that the majority of the 591 people who settled claims with News International were not celebrities or public figures. 69 per cent were not public figures, compared to 31 per cent who were. These non-public figures were, for the most part, connected to someone that the *NoW* tabloid wanted information about. They might have been the partner or ex-partner of a public figure (33 per cent), or have had a professional connection with one (25 per cent). They might have been a friend or acquaintance (14 per cent) or a parent or step-parent (13 per cent). Almost half the people *NoW* journalists were trying to get information about came from the worlds of entertainment, music or sport. One in five came from politics or journalism. Just under 10 per cent were people who had been involved in personal tragedies. Victims of phone hacking range from teenage boyfriends to 85-year-old fathers, from mothers of murder victims to senior policemen, from friends of a participant in a drug trial to Home Secretaries and royal princes.[34]

On 24 June 2014, former spin doctor for Prime Minister David Cameron at No 10 Downing Street in 2010 and former editor of *NoW*, Andy Coulson,[35] was found guilty and was sentenced to 18 months' imprisonment for plotting to hack phones while he was editor of *NoW* (2003–2007); he had resigned his post on the day of Clive Goodman's conviction in 2007. Saunders J, sentencing Mr Coulson, told the court the evidence heard in the trial revealed that Coulson clearly thought it was necessary to use phone hacking to maintain the *NoW*'s 'competitive edge'. The judge said that Coulson had to take the major share of the blame for the paper's delay in telling police about hacking the voicemail of the missing Surrey schoolgirl Milly Dowler in 2002, the major motivation being to sell the maximum number of newspapers.

Coulson was released after spending fewer than five months in prison and spent the rest of his sentence on home detention curfew. Along with the paper's former chief reporter Neville Thurl-beck, Greg Miskiw, head of news at the tabloid paper, was jailed for six months in July 2014 after pleading guilty to conspiracy to intercept voicemail messages. Miskiw had told the court that he accessed 'routinely, all the time, over and over again' voicemails of former England football captain David Beckham.

Andy Coulson faced further criminal charges, namely perjury, in May 2015 at the Edinburgh High Court. These charges concerned alleged lying under oath at the 2010 trial of ex-MSP Scottish Socialist party leader Tommy Sheridan.[36] In July 2015, Mr Coulson was cleared of the perjury charges after the case against him collapsed. His lawyers had successfully argued that there was no case to answer.

On the same day in June 2014 that Andy Coulson was found guilty at the 'phone hacking' trial at the Old Bailey, the News International Chief Executive and former editor of *NoW*, Rebekah Brooks, was cleared of all charges, including conspiracy to hack phones, conspiracy to corrupt public officials and conspiracy to pervert the course of justice.[37] Mrs Brooks's former personal assistant Cheryl Carter was cleared of conspiracy to pervert the course of justice; also cleared was former

34 See: Moore, M. (2015) at p. 43. The study also includes a comprehensive list of phone-hacked victims in the appendix.

35 Andy Coulson, David Cameron's Communications Director, resigned from his post in January 2011, blaming the continuing row over phone hacking which made his job difficult.

36 *HM Advocate v Sheridan (Thomas) and Sheridan (Gail)* High Court, Glasgow 23 December 2010 (as per Lord Bracadale) (unreported). Thomas (Tommy) Sheridan was sentenced to three years' imprisonment after he was found guilty of perjury i.e. wilfully giving false evidence under oath in judicial proceedings. Gail Sheridan was acquitted.

37 See: *R v Coulson (Andrew) and others* (2014) (unreported). Sentencing remarks of Saunders J Central Criminal Court 4 July 2014 at: www.judiciary.gov.uk/wp-content/uploads/2014/07/sentencing-remarks-mr-j-saunders-r-v-coulson-others.pdf.

managing editor of NoW, Stuart Kuttner. Mrs Brooks's husband Charlie and News International Director of Security Mark Hanna were also cleared of all charges.

A month later, in July 2015, former NoW features editor, Jules Stenson, received a four-month suspended sentence after admitting he oversaw two years of widespread phone hacking at the Sunday tabloid. Stenson pleaded guilty to conspiracy to intercept voicemails, but had to wait for sentencing until the end of the trial of the paper's former deputy editor Neil Wallis, who was acquitted of the same charge.[38] Stenson was also fined £5,000 and given 200 hours of unpaid work in the community ('Community Order'). He was also ordered to pay £18,059.61 in court costs. The Crown Prosecution Service's bill for taking former NoW journalists to court over phone hacking had by this stage reached nearly £2 million.

Numerous criminal trials followed the Leveson Inquiry, where not only journalists were accused of phone-hacking but also police and prisoner officers were accused of bribery, corruption and phone-hacking. In May 2015 a three-week long (civil) trial against the Trinity Mirror Group was heard at the Rolls Building (Royal Courts of Justice) where phone-hacking victims of the Daily Mirror and Sunday Mirror asked for six-figure damages from the Mirror Group in an out-of-court settlement expected to leave the newspaper group with a multi-million pound legal bill. More than 100 high-profile figures, including senior politicians, gave evidence at that trial – some of whom had given evidence at the Leveson Inquiry. At the heart of the High Court trial was the evidence of the former Sunday Mirror journalist Dan Evans. Evans described in detail how he was inducted into phone hacking by two senior Sunday Mirror journalists who showed him how to intercept voicemails.[39]

In June 2015 Mann J awarded substantial sums of damages[40] against Mirror Group Newspapers (MGN) – publishers of the Daily Mirror, The Sunday People and The Sunday Mirror newspapers – ranging from £72,500 to £260,250 to eight celebrity claimants for misuse of private information derived from intercepting voicemail messages left on their telephones (i.e. 'hacking'). MGN appealed and the appeal was dismissed.[41]

Alan Yentob (BBC Executive) was awarded £85,000, Lauren Alcorn (Virgin Airline hostess and former lover of footballer Rio Ferdinand) £72,500, Robert Ashworth (TV producer) £201,250, Lucy Taggart (also known as Lucy Benjamin – East Ender's actress) £157,250, Shobna Gulati (Coronation Street actress) £117,000, Shane Roche (also known as Shane Richie – actor 'Alfie Mon' in East Enders) £155,000, ex-footballer Paul Gascoigne £188,250, actress Sadie Frost £260,250.[42] Mann J said that there had been an invasion of privacy in each case, made up of many different acts over years whilst the individuals' phones were being hacked into. Apart from damages awarded to each victim, the judge also ordered compensation for the distress caused (see also: AAA v Associated Newspapers Ltd (2012);[43] Weller (Paul) v Associated Newspapers Ltd (2014)[44]).

It had become clear that the phone-hacking and bribery scandals were going beyond merely NoW's practices, extending to the Sun, the Daily Mirror and possibly other tabloids. Following her acquittal in June 2014 at the Old Bailey, Rebekah Brooks returned as Chief Executive of Rupert Murdoch's UK newspaper operations in September 2015.[45]

In February 2016 Scotland Yard closed Operation Elveden after nearly five years of investigations into phone-hacking at the NoW. The operation had been prompted by News Corp's

---

38 See: R v Stenson (Jules) (2015) (unreported). Sentencing remarks of Saunders J Central Criminal Court 6 July 2015 at: www. judiciary.gov.uk/wp-content/uploads/2015/07/r-v-stenson-sentencing-remarks1.pdf.

39 Source: 'Phone-hacking victims: lives "torn apart" by decade of mistrust and paranoia', by Josh Halliday, The Guardian, 21 May 2015.

40 For each sum, the court took into account the extent and nature of hacking, private investigators, distress and a small amount for aggravated damages.

41 See: Representative Claimant Respondents v MGN Ltd [2015] EWCA Civ 1291 (Ch) 17 December 2015 (Arden, Rafferty and Kitchin LJJ).

42 Ibid., Schedule to judgment of Arden LJ.

43 [2012] EWHC 2103 (QB).

44 [2014] EMLR 24.

45 Brooks had resigned in 2011 in the wake of the phone-hacking scandal and was given a £16 million payoff by News Corp.

Management and Standards Committee disclosing confidential emails sent between sources and journalists to the police. Eventually 34 people were convicted, including nine police officers and 21 public officials at a cost to the Metropolitan Police of £14.7 million (not including legal fees and not including CPS and prosecution costs).[46]

6.3.2 The Leveson Report 2012[47]

On 13 July 2011 Prime Minister David Cameron announced a two-part inquiry investigating the separate roles of the press and the police in the NoW phone-hacking scandal.

For the sixth time in less than 70 years, a report had been commissioned by the government which was to deal with concerns about the press.[48] Leveson LJ was appointed as Chairman of the inquiry. The inquiry was to be in two parts. Part 1 of the inquiry examined the culture, practices and ethics of the press and, in particular, the relationship of the press with the public, police and politicians.

Part 2 of the inquiry was to look at specific claims about phone-hacking at NoW and what went wrong with the original police investigation. This was (indefinitely) delayed pending the conclusion of criminal prosecutions of police and prison officers.

The Leveson Inquiry commenced its hearings on 14 November 2011 and ended on 24 July 2012. Leveson LJ was assisted by a panel of six independent assessors with expertise in the key issues that were considered. The inquiry was approached in four modules:

● Module 1: The relationship between the press and the public; phone-hacking and other potentially illegal behaviour.
● Module 2: The relationships between the press and police and the extent to which that had operated in the public interest.
● Module 3: The relationship between the press and politicians.
● Module 4: Recommendations for a more effective policy and regulation that supports the integrity and freedom of the press while encouraging the highest ethical standards.

When Leveson LJ opened the hearings on 14 November 2011 he said:

> The press provides an essential check on all aspects of public life. That is why any failure within the media affects all of us. At the heart of this Inquiry, therefore, may be one simple question: who guards the guardians?[49]

From that beginning, the scope of the inquiry was expanded to cover the culture, practices and ethics of the press in its relations with the public, with the police, with politicians; and, as to the police and politicians, the conduct of each. A wide range of witnesses, including newspaper reporters, management, proprietors, police officers and politicians of all parties, all gave evidence to the inquiry under oath and in public. Leveson LJ published his Report on Part 1 of the Inquiry on 29 November 2012.[50]

---

46 Source: 'Operation Elveden closed by Met', by Dominic Ponsford, Press Gazette, 26 February 2016.
47 The Report of An Inquiry into the Culture, Practices and Ethics of the Press was presented to Parliament (HC 780) ('The Leveson Report' or 'Leveson') 29 November 2012.
48 There were Royal Commissions in 1947, 1962 and 1973, the Younger Commission on Privacy and the Calcutt Report.
49 Opening remarks by Lord Justice Leveson at the hearing on 14 November 2011. Lord Justice Leveson published his Report on Part 1 of the Inquiry on 29 November 2012.
50 For further discussion: Wragg, P. (2013a).

The report covers four volumes comprising some 1,987 pages, plus a 46-page executive summary. One of the main recommendations of *Leveson* included changing UK press regulation by reintroducing statutory control of the media after hundreds of years of press freedom.[51]

Leveson: main findings

- **Newspapers recklessly pursued sensational stories** – *Leveson* made no findings on any individual but stated that he was not convinced hacking was confined to one or two people. There had been a recklessness in prioritizing sensational stories by the press, almost irrespective of the harm the stories may cause and the rights of those who would be affected.
- **Covert surveillance** – *Leveson* found that there was a willingness to deploy covert surveillance, blagging and deception in circumstances where stories are difficult to get.
- **Families of actors and footballers also have rights to privacy** – *Leveson* found that some families of famous people had their lives destroyed by the relentless pursuit of the press. Actors, footballers, writers and pop stars were 'fair game' and 'public property' with little entitlement to any private life or respect for dignity.
- **The police** – Senior Met officers were 'too close' to News International. The hospitality police received from the media, including lavish restaurant meals and champagne, did not enhance the Met's reputation, leaving a 'defensive' mindset.

Leveson: key recommendations

Leveson LJ made a range of recommendations to reform the regulatory framework for the press, creating a new framework for press regulation, with the principle of industry self-regulation at its heart. The new framework proposed a system of voluntary self-regulation, overseen by a recognition body established by Royal Charter and strengthened by a series of incentives for members of the press in the application of costs and exemplary damages, encouraging them to join a recognized regulator. Key recommendations included:

- **An independent self-regulatory body** underpinned by statute – 'free of any influence from industry and government'.
- **Powers, remedies and sanctions of the regulator** with fines of 1 per cent of turnover, with a maximum of £1 million. The watchdog should have 'sufficient powers to carry out investigations both into suspected serious or systemic breaches of the code'.
- **A libel resolution unit** – the new regulator should have an arbitration process in relation to civil legal claims against subscribers.
- **Membership** – though this would not be legally obligatory, and editors could *opt out* of the regulatory body.

On 14 June 2016 the House of Commons voted against forcing the government to hold Part 2 of the Leveson Inquiry, with *The Times* reporting that 'the Government had no appetite to launch formally the second part, given the costs involved, and a consensus that this ground had been covered during the criminal trials'. Consultation on the Leveson Inquiry and its implementation closed on 10 January 2017. The Government was seeking views on s.40 Crime and Courts Act 2013 'exemplary damages' and Part 2 Leveson.

See below
6.6.2

---

51 A full copy of the Leveson Report is available from the National Archives and its website. See: The Leveson Inquiry Report No 0780 2012–13.

6.3.3 Statutory versus self-regulation of the print press

Leveson had recommended statutory regulation of the print press – akin to the Irish Press Council model. Fraser Nelson, editor of *The Spectator* magazine, was one of the first of a series of editors who vowed they would not take part in a statutory scheme.[52]

A Royal Charter was subsequently proposed, granted by the Privy Council, to regulate the print media by statute. This would have meant, once incorporated by Royal Charter, the print media 'body' would have surrendered significant aspects of control of its internal affairs to the Privy Council.

Any amendments to Royal Charters can be made only with the agreement of the Sovereign in Council, and amendments to the body's by-laws require the approval of the Council. This would have meant a significant degree of government regulation of the affairs of the print press.

The Coalition government (Conservative and Liberal Democrats) then drafted a Royal Charter[53] on press regulation in February–March 2013, followed by the newspaper industry's counter-proposal of a system of self-regulation (at that time also backed by Royal Charter).

From July 2013, the newspaper and magazine industry pushed ahead with the establishment of a new press regulator. Leading publishers and editors announced that the new regulator – replacing the PCC – would be called the Independent Press Standards Organisation (IPSO). Important policy makers included Rupert Murdoch's News UK (formerly News International), the *Daily Mail* publishers Associated Newspapers, the Telegraph Media Group, the Newspaper Society (representing regional and local papers), the Newspaper Publishers Association (national papers), the Scottish Newspaper Society and PPA (magazine publishers). The 'IPSO Charter' was also supported by the then Mayor of London, Boris Johnson, and the then House of Commons Culture, Media and Sport Committee Chairman John Whittingdale. However, the *Guardian* publisher Guardian News and Media, and the publishers of the *Financial Times, Independent* and *Evening Standard* made clear they would not sign up to the new regulator.

See 6.4 below

A contentious part of the Royal Charter was legislation requiring publishers to pay both sides' costs in a privacy or libel action, even if they won – unless they signed up to IPSO (inherent in section 40 Crime and Courts Act 2013).

Another alternative Royal Charter was proposed by Hacked Off,[54] drafted by Hugh Tomlinson QC and parliamentary counsel Daniel Greenberg. Actor Hugh Grant, a director of the 'Hacked Off campaign', told the BBC's *Andrew Marr Show* that the draft 'Hacked-Off Bill' proposed to set up an appointments commission mainly involving the judiciary which, in turn, would appoint a recognition body that in turn would oversee the body established by the press to regulate itself.[55]

The government's draft Royal Charter Bill went before the Privy Council at the start of the new parliamentary session on 15 May 2013; suffice it to say that very few *Leveson* recommendations were realized in the proposed bill.

In a last-minute attempt to stop the Privy Council introducing a Royal Charter on press regulation, a group of newspaper and magazine publishers sought a High Court injunction. Industry bodies representing the publishers were granted an emergency High Court hearing on 30 October 2013, just hours before the government's Press Regulation Royal Charter – backed by the three main parties and Hacked Off campaigners – was set to go before the Privy Council for sealing by the Queen at 5.30pm that Wednesday afternoon. However, the injunction was *not* granted by Richards LJ and Sales J. The applicant newspaper publishers immediately declared their intention to

---

52   Source: 'Why The Spectator won't sign the Royal Charter', by Fraser Nelson, *The Spectator*, 23 March 2013.
53   See: 'Draft operative provisions for a Royal Charter', 12 February 2013 at: www.gov.uk/government/uploads/system/uploads/attachment_data/file/136347/RC_Draft_Royal_Charter12_February_2013.pdf.
54   Established in 2011, Hacked Off campaigns for a free and accountable press. See: http://hackinginquiry.org.
55   Source: 'Leveson: Hugh Grant slams Cameron's press reform plan', *The Andrew Marr Show*, BBC TV, 17 March 2013 at: www.bbc.co.uk/news/uk-21822040.

take their case to the Court of Appeal. They sought a ruling that any decision to seal the cross-party Charter could be overturned by way of judicial review. Queen Elizabeth II gave her Royal Assent to the Charter on the evening of 30 October 2013.

An arbitration scheme – recommended by *Leveson* – was introduced at the same time by statute. Sections 34 to 42 and Schedule 15 of the Crime and Courts Act 2013 cover 'publishers of news-related material: damages and costs'. These measures set out a new system for 'exemplary damages and costs', as well as defining those who meet the definition of a 'relevant publisher' to whom the new system of exemplary damages applies.[56]

See Chapter 7

Confusingly, by November 2014 there appeared to co-exist two press regulators, the Independent Press Standards Organisation (IPSO) and the Press Recognition Panel (PRP), also set up by (another) Royal Charter. The function of the PRP is to decide whether print press regulator(s) meet the recognition criteria recommended in the Leveson Report. It sees its remit as ensuring that the UK press is independent, properly funded and able to protect the public.[57] Dr David Wolfe became the first Chair of the PRP.

At the same time, a 'third way' of press self-regulation appeared to exist in the form of the 'IMPRESS Project' ('Impress'). Its supporting journalists and philanthropists donors included Sir Harold Evans, Michael Frayn, Terry Gilliam, David Hare, Ian McEwan, J. K. Rowling, William Sieghart and Polly Toynbee. Impress describes itself on its website as: 'We believe in the freedom of the press to tell us what's really going on in our society. But we don't believe in journalism which ruins people's lives just to sell newspapers. That's not press freedom. It's bullying.[58]

6.4 IPSO: Independent Press Standards Organisation

The Independent Press Standards Organisation (IPSO) started on 8 September 2014 after the PCC had been wound up. The new regulator was set up by some of Britain's leading newspaper and magazine publishers. Alongside this, the Royal Charter also remained in force. IPSO's first chairman was Sir Alan Moses. By 2016, IPSO was regulating some 85 publishers, with more than 1,500 printed publications and 1,100 online publications.

Very similar to the PCC's Code there now exists the IPSO Editors' Code of Practice. The Code deals with issues such as accuracy, invasion of privacy, intrusion into grief or shock and harassment – in fact it is strikingly similar to the PCC's Code. IPSO has the power, where necessary, to require the publication of prominent corrections and critical adjudications, and may ultimately fine publications in cases where failings are particularly serious and systemic.

6.4.1 The IPSO Editors' Code

All members of the press who signed up to the new 'press' regulator, IPSO, have a duty to maintain the highest professional standards set out in the Editors' Code. The Code, which includes a definition of the public interest, sets the benchmark for ethical standards, protecting both the rights of the individual and the public's right to know. The Code is regarded as the cornerstone of press self-regulation to which the industry has made a binding commitment. It is of course essential that all newspapers and magazines that have signed up to the IPSO Code agree to follow it to the letter.

---

56 The sanctions under Part 36 of the Civil Procedure Rules (offers to settle) were reformed to encourage early settlement. This was intended to encourage claimants to make, and defendants to accept, reasonable early offers which, in turn, would help reduce the time taken for cases to settle and consequently help to lower overall costs.

57 For further information see: http://pressrecognitionpanel.org.uk.

58 Source: The Impress Project at: http://impressproject.org.

It should not be interpreted so narrowly as to compromise its commitment to respect the rights of the individual, nor so broadly that it constitutes an unnecessary interference with freedom of expression or prevents publication in the public interest.

IPSO revised its Editors' Code in late 2015 and the 2016 Code (see below) includes those changes. The Code's definition of the public interest has been substantially updated in order to comply with the laws of defamation and data protection along with guidance issued by the Crown Prosecution Service.

It is then the responsibility of editors and publishers to apply the Code to editorial material in both printed and online versions of publications. Editors should co-operate swiftly with the regulator IPSO in the resolution of complaints. Any publication judged to have breached the Code must publish the adjudication in full and with due prominence agreed by the regulator, including headline reference to the regulator.

The IPSO Editors' Code (2016 version)[59]

The preamble to the code states that it is 'the duty of editors . . . to resolve complaints swiftly' and to co-operate with the Independent Press Standards Organisation (IPSO). It adds that 'a publication subject to an adverse adjudication must publish it in full and with due prominence, as required by IPSO'.

Clause 1 Accuracy
(i)   The Press must take care not to publish inaccurate, misleading or distorted information, including pictures.
(ii) A significant inaccuracy, misleading statement or distortion once recognized must be corrected, promptly and with due prominence, and – where appropriate – an apology published. In cases involving the regulator, prominence should be agreed with the regulator in advance.
(iii) The Press, whilst free to be partisan, must distinguish clearly between comment, conjecture and fact.
(iv) A publication must report fairly and accurately the outcome of an action for defamation to which it has been a party, unless an agreed settlement states otherwise, or an agreed statement is published.
(v)   Headlines: Newspapers and magazines 'must take care not to publish . . . headlines not supported by the text'.

Clause 2 Opportunity to reply
A fair opportunity for reply to inaccuracies must be given when reasonably called for.

*Clause 3 Privacy
(i)   Everyone is entitled to respect for his or her private and family life, home, health and correspondence, including digital communications.
(ii) Editors will be expected to justify intrusions into any individual's private life without consent. Account will be taken of the complainant's own public disclosures of information.
(iii) It is unacceptable to photograph individuals in private places without their consent. Note – private places are public or private property where there is a reasonable expectation of privacy.

---

59   The most up-to-date version of the IPSO Editors' Code can be found at: www.ipso.co.uk/IPSO/cop.html.

Clause 4 Harassment

(i)   Journalists must not engage in intimidation, harassment or persistent pursuit.

(ii) They must not persist in questioning, telephoning, pursuing or photographing individuals once asked to desist; nor remain on their property when asked to leave and must not follow them. If requested, they must identify themselves and whom they represent.

(iii) Editors must ensure these principles are observed by those working for them and take care not to use non-compliant material from other sources.

Clause 5 Intrusion into grief or shock

(i)   In cases involving personal grief or shock, enquiries and approaches must be made with sympathy and discretion and publication handled sensitively. This should not restrict the right to report legal proceedings, such as inquests.

*(ii) When reporting suicide, care should be taken to avoid excessive detail about the method used.

* *Clause 6 Children*

(i)   Young people should be free to complete their time at school without unnecessary intrusion.

(ii)   A child under 16 must not be interviewed or photographed on issues involving their own or another child's welfare unless a custodial parent or similarly responsible adult consents.

(iii) Pupils must not be approached or photographed at school without the permission of the school authorities.

(iv)   Minors must not be paid for material involving children's welfare, nor parents or guardians for material about their children or wards, unless it is clearly in the child's interest.

(v)   Editors must not use the fame, notoriety or position of a parent or guardian as sole justification for publishing details of a child's private life.

* *Clause 7 Children in sex cases*

1.   The press must not, even if legally free to do so, identify children under 16 who are victims or witnesses in cases involving sex offences.

2.   In any press report of a case involving a sexual offence against a child:

   (i)   The child must not be identified.
   (ii)   The adult may be identified.
   (iii) The word 'incest' must not be used where a child victim might be identified.
   (iv)   Care must be taken that nothing in the report implies the relationship between the accused and the child.

* *Clause 8 Hospitals*

(i)   Journalists must identify themselves and obtain permission from a responsible executive before entering non-public areas of hospitals or similar institutions to pursue enquiries.

(ii) The restrictions on intruding into privacy are particularly relevant to enquiries about individuals in hospitals or similar institutions.

* *Clause 9 Reporting of crime*

(i)   Relatives or friends of persons convicted or accused of crime should not generally be identified without their consent, unless they are genuinely relevant to the story.

(ii) Particular regard should be paid to the potentially vulnerable position of children who witness, or are victims of, crime. This should not restrict the right to report legal proceedings.

Clause 10 Clandestine devices and subterfuge

(i)   The press must not seek to obtain or publish material acquired by using hidden cameras or clandestine listening devices; or by intercepting private or mobile telephone calls, messages or emails; or by the unauthorized removal of documents or photographs; or by accessing digitally held private information without consent.

(ii)   Engaging in misrepresentation or subterfuge, including by agents or intermediaries, can generally be justified only in the public interest and then only when the material cannot be obtained by other means.

Clause 11 Victims of sexual assault

The press must not identify victims of sexual assault or publish material likely to contribute to such identification unless there is adequate justification and they are legally free to do so.

Clause 12 Discrimination

(i)   The press must avoid prejudicial or pejorative reference to an individual's race, colour, religion, gender, sexual orientation or to any physical or mental illness or disability.

(ii)   Details of an individual's race, colour, religion, sexual orientation, physical or mental illness or disability must be avoided unless genuinely relevant to the story.

(iii)   Prejudicial or pejorative reference to an individual's gender identity should be avoided.

Clause 13 Financial journalism

(i)   Even where the law does not prohibit it, journalists must not use for their own profit financial information they receive in advance of its general publication, nor should they pass such information to others.

(ii)   They must not write about shares or securities in whose performance they know that they or their close families have a significant financial interest without disclosing the interest to the editor or financial editor.

(iii)   They must not buy or sell, either directly or through nominees or agents, shares or securities about which they have written recently or about which they intend to write in the near future.

Clause 14 Confidential sources

Journalists have a moral obligation to protect confidential sources of information.

Clause 15 Witness payments in criminal trials

(i)   No payment or offer of payment to a witness − or any person who may reasonably be expected to be called as a witness − should be made in any case once proceedings are active as defined by the Contempt of Court Act 1981.

*(ii)   Where proceedings are not yet active but are likely and foreseeable, editors must not make or offer payment to any person who may reasonably be expected to be called as a witness, unless the information concerned ought demonstrably to be published in the public interest and there is an overriding need to make or promise payment for this to be done; and all reasonable steps have been taken to ensure no financial dealings influence the evidence those witnesses give. In no circumstances should such payment be conditional on the outcome of a trial.

*(iii) Any payment or offer of payment made to a person later cited to give evidence in proceedings must be disclosed to the prosecution and defence. The witness must be advised of this requirement.

* Clause 16 Payment to criminals

(i)   Payment or offers of payment for stories, pictures or information, which seek to exploit a particular crime or to glorify or glamorize crime in general, must not be made directly or via agents to convicted or confessed criminals or to their associates – who may include family, friends and colleagues.

(ii) Editors invoking the public interest to justify payment or offers would need to demonstrate that there was good reason to believe the public interest would be served. If, despite payment, no public interest emerged, then the material should not be published.

The public interest

There may be exceptions to the clauses marked * where they can be demonstrated to be in the public interest.

1.   The public interest includes, but is not confined to:
  ● detecting or exposing crime, or the threat of crime, or serious impropriety;
  ● protecting public health or safety;
  ● protecting the public from being misled by an action or statement of an individual or organization;
  ● disclosing a person or organization's failure or likely failure to comply with any obligation to which they are subject;
  ● disclosing a miscarriage of justice;
  ● raising or contributing to a matter of public debate, including serious cases of impropriety, unethical conduct or incompetence concerning the public;
  ● disclosing concealment, or likely concealment, of any of the above.
2.   There is a public interest in freedom of expression itself.
3.   The regulator will consider the extent to which material is already in the public domain or will become so.
4.   Editors invoking the public interest will need to demonstrate that they reasonably believed publication – or journalistic activity taken with a view to publication – would both serve, and be proportionate to, the public interest and explain how they reached that decision at the time.
5.   An exceptional public interest would need to be demonstrated to override the normally paramount interests of children under 16.

6.4.2 IPSO adjudications

In May 2016 *The Sun* was reprimanded for its headline 'Queen Backs Brexit' published on 9 March 2016 in the run-up to the EU referendum on 23 June 2016.[60] IPSO ruled that the headline was significantly misleading and represented a failure to take care not to publish inaccurate, misleading or distorted information – a clear breach of clause 1 of the Editors' Code of Practice.[61]

In spelling out its ruling, IPSO's Complaints Committee recognized the importance of headlines as a feature of tabloid journalism but believed that there was nothing in the headline, or the

---

60 See: *Buckingham Palace v The Sun*, Decision of the IPSO Complaints Committee 01584–16, 18 May 2016 at: www.ipso.co.uk/IPSO/rulings/IPSOrulings-detail.html?id=367.

61 The newly revised Code (1.1.2016) makes specific reference to headlines not supported by the text as an example of inaccurate, misleading or distorted information.

manner in which it was presented on the newspaper's front page, to suggest that this was the newspaper's conjecture, hyperbole, or not to be read literally. *The Sun*'s headline contained a serious and unsupported allegation that the Queen had fundamentally breached her constitutional obligations in the context of a vitally important national debate. The Committee ordered that the adjudication be published in full on page two of the newspaper. The headline 'IPSO RULES AGAINST SUN QUEEN HEADLINE' was 'splashed' across *The Sun*'s entire front page on 18 May.

In an interview with BBC Radio 4's *Today* programme on the same morning, the editor of *The Sun*, Tony Gallagher, insisted that the Queen 'strongly' believes the UK should leave the EU, despite a ruling by the press watchdog IPSO that his paper's 'Queen backs Brexit' headline was inaccurate. 'Do I accept we made a mistake?' Gallagher told the programme. 'In all conscience I don't.'

In December 2015, *The Daily Mail* was reprimanded by the press regulator for flying a helicopter over the Duke of York's home to take pictures of Princess Eugenie's 'lavish' Disney-themed 25th birthday party. IPSO had received a complaint from the Duke that the use of a helicopter, which made four passes of the grounds at his home at the Royal Lodge in Windsor Park, was an invasion of privacy. The *Daily Mail* published four articles between 20 and 26 June 2015, including information about 'arrangement of tents and a fairground' that had been set up for the party that saw Princess Eugenie dress as Snow White accompanied by seven dwarves. The tabloid had argued that there was a public interest in the plans as Eugenie is eighth in line to the throne and a senior member of the royal family.

IPSO's adjudication included that the Royal Lodge was not publicly accessible or visible to the public and so the Duke of York had a 'reasonable expectation' that the grounds would be respected as a private place, whether he was at home or not. The regulator said aerial photography could be a 'legitimate tool' but in this instance the 'flight over the private space of the grounds of the complainant's home, intended to capture images of the preparations for the event he intended to hold there, was a clear intrusion, regardless of whether the complainant was there'.[62] The Duke of York's complaint was upheld.

At the end of 2015, IPSO regulated more than 2,500 printed and online publications and took forward 463 complaints over its first 12 months since coming into existence on 8 September 2014. Of those complaints, 198 were resolved between the complainant and the publisher. A further 48 of those complaints were mediated to a successful resolution by IPSO and 48 complaints were upheld by IPSO's Complaints Committee. The remaining 169 complaints were not upheld.[63]

According to IPSO's Annual Report (2015) News UK, publisher of *The Sun*, *Times* and *Sunday Times*, was the worst offender. IPSO upheld 11 complaints during 2015.

Once a complaint is upheld, the IPSO Committee considers what remedial action should be required. The Committee has the power to require the publication of a correction and/or adjudication; the nature, extent and placement is determined by IPSO. It may also inform the publication that further remedial action is required to ensure that the requirements of the Editors' Code are met.

In its decision of 6 July 2015, IPSO found against *The Daily Telegraph* on a complaint by First Minister of Scotland, Nicola Sturgeon MSP, about an article published by the newspaper on 4 April 2015. The article reported the contents of a leaked government memorandum which claimed to report details of a private meeting between the Scottish First Minister and the French Ambassador, Sylvie Bermann. The confidential memo of 26 February 2015, claiming that Nicola Sturgeon

---

62 Source: IPSO decision of the Complaints Committee 04839-15 *HRH the Duke of York v Daily Mail*. Date complaint received: 3 August 2015. Date decision issued: 16 November 2015.

63 See: IPSO press release at: www.ipso.co.uk/IPSO/news/press-releases-statements.html.

wanted David Cameron to remain as Prime Minister, had been written in the Scotland Office, but had been circulated elsewhere in government, including the Foreign Office (Sir Jeremy Heywood, Head of the Civil Service, subsequently ordered an inquiry into how it came to be seen by *The Telegraph*). The memo contained details of a private conversation between the First Minister and the French Ambassador.[64]

The complainant, Nicola Sturgeon, told IPSO that the claims contained in the memo and repeated in the article were categorically untrue and regarded the newspaper's decision not to contact Ms Sturgeon for comment as a breach of the Editor's Code clause 1 ('Accuracy'). IPSO's Complaints Committee judged that, while the newspaper was entitled to report on the memorandum, it had published its contents as facts without taking additional steps prior to publication – such as contacting the parties involved for their comment – to verify their accuracy. As a result, the article was held as significantly misleading. The Committee upheld the complaint under clause 1(i) and (ii) and required the newspaper to publish the adjudication on page 2 of the *Daily Telegraph* with a front-page reference, and online (4 April 2015).

❖ **KEY CASE**   *Owens v That's Life* (2015)[65]

That's Life magazine is known for its 'real life' stories. The magazine boasts on its website: 'We're Britain's leading real-life magazine. Every week we pack our pages with the most inspirational, emotional and incredible reads that will leave you stunned and surprised. A multipack of 100% true stories!'[66]

In April 2013, *That's Life* was censored by the then regulator, the PCC, for breaching the Editors' Code. Ms Treena McIntyre had complained to the PCC that *That's Life* magazine had paid a relative of a convicted criminal for an article headlined 'A moment of madness', published on 10 January 2013. The magazine was found in breach of clause 16 ('Payment to criminals') of the then PCC Editors' Code of Practice. In October 2014, IPSO found *That's Life* in breach of its code for inaccuracy (clause 1), for telling a story as if it were 'real life'.[67]

Facts

That's Life magazine had carried an article, published on 16 October 2014, under the by-line of Leanne Owens headlined 'I'd rather die than kill my baby.' Purporting to be a first-person account of the serious illnesses Owens had experienced while pregnant with her fourth child, it reported that she had risked her own life to give birth to a baby girl. By extension, it also suggested she had risked leaving her other children without a mother. But the magazine had got the wrong end of the stick. Owens had not risked her life by continuing with her pregnancy. Instead, she had been told that, with treatment and monitoring, she would survive. It was her unborn baby who might not survive.

Owens complained to IPSO that the magazine had breached clause 1 (Accuracy), clause 2 (Opportunity to reply) and clause 5 (Intrusion into grief or shock) of the Editors' Code of

64 Source: 'Nicola Sturgeon memo claiming she would prefer David Cameron in power was written in Scotland Office', by Simon Johnson and Auslan Cramb, *The Daily Telegraph*, 5 April 2015.
65 Source: IPSO – Decision of the Complaints Committee. Complaint No: 00580-15 'Owens v That's Life'. Date complaint received: 9 February 2015. Date complaint concluded: 26 June 2015.
66 Source: *That's Life* at: www.thatslife.co.uk.
67 Source: IPSO Decision of the Complaints Committee 00580-15 *Owens v That's Life*.

Practice. With regard to clause 5, the complainant said that she had been 'tricked' into including her eldest son in the photographs, when she did not want him to appear in the magazine, and that she had not been advised of the publication date in advance.

In its defence, the magazine's editor believed that the article was an accurate account of the complainant's difficulties during her pregnancy; the editor believed that the copy had been approved by the complainant, Ms Owens. The magazine maintained that it had made every effort to publish a feature with which the complainant was happy: it had removed her surname and address, upon request, and changed the name of her partner. The freelance photographer who had taken the photographs for the feature confirmed that he had not been asked to remove the complainant's eldest son from the images. Though *That's Life* admitted no failure, it still offered to publish a correction on the letters page (last page). But Ms Owens did not think that the magazine's apology was genuine.

Findings of the IPSO Committee

Clause 1: Accuracy
It was of particular importance that the piece had been written in the first person. Therefore such a piece had to accurately reflect the experiences of the subject of the article, under whose name it is published. Since there was no evidence that the complainant had agreed as to the accuracy of the material, the Committee was not able to place any reliance on the read-back. Therefore there was a breach of clause 1.

Clause 2: Opportunity to reply
As the complainant had not requested an opportunity to reply following publication of the article, there was no breach of clause 2.

Clause 5: Intrusion into grief or shock
Given that the photograph of the complainant's children, which included her eldest son, was *posed for*, the Committee was satisfied that it had been reasonable for the magazine to understand that the complainant had *consented* to its publication. The magazine was also not obliged to inform the complainant of the publication date of the feature in advance. There was no breach of clause 5.

Remedial action
The magazine had already offered to publish a correction which stated that the complainant's life had not been put in danger by continuing with her pregnancy. This correction included an apology which, given the nature of the inaccuracy, was required on this occasion. However, given that the inaccuracy was referenced on the front cover of the magazine, the prominence proposed by the magazine was not sufficient under the terms of clause 1(ii). In order to remedy the breach of clause 1, the magazine was required to publish its proposed wording of an apology in full on the first editorial page.

❖ KEY CASE   *Trans Media Watch v The Sun* (2015)[68]

Facts

'Trans Media Watch' complained as a representative group on behalf of Emily Brothers to IPSO that *The Sun* had breached clause 12 (Discrimination) and clause 3 (Privacy) of the Editors' Code in columns published by Rod Liddle on 11 December 2014 and 15 January 2015.

Sun columnist Rod Liddle wrote in the 11 December column:

> Emily Brothers is hoping to become Labour's first blind transgendered MP. She'll be standing at the next election in the constituency of Sutton and Cheam. Thing is though: being blind, how did she know she was the wrong sex?

When Trans Media Watch complained to *The Sun* about the remark, the paper accepted that it was tasteless but denied that it was prejudicial or pejorative. The tabloid did not accept that Liddle had criticized Ms Brothers or suggested anything negative or stereotypical about her blindness or gender identity. Instead, it had been a clumsy attempt at humour. *The Sun* issued an apology from the columnist and offered Brothers a 'response column'. She took up the offer and her article was published on 15 December 2014.

The editor also asked Mr Liddle to apologize in print and the following apology was published in his 15 January 2015 column and online:

> I made a poor joke in bad taste in this column a few weeks back. Well, ok, I suppose I do that every week. But this one was particularly lame . . . a poor joke by any standards even, even if it wasn't meant maliciously. So I apologised to Ms Brothers and said that if I lived in Sutton, where she's standing, I'd vote for her. And I apologise to her again now, in this column. I'd also like to add that having found out more about her I wouldn't vote for her even if she was standing against Nick Clegg, George Galloway and [her former name] Ole Ole Biscuit Barrell from the Silly Party.[69]

Trans Media Watch argued that this 'apology' by Mr Liddle was a deliberate attempt to humiliate Ms Brothers amounting to further discrimination; instead of 'Tarquin' Ole Ole Biscuit Barrell from the Silly Party' (the name of a candidate from a *Monty Python* sketch), Ms Brothers' former name had been used. In its defence, *The Sun* said it had reviewed its editorial processes and introduced a new policy requiring all copy relating to transgender matters to be approved by its managing editor before publication. The newspaper argued that any breach of the Code had been remedied by these measures, and that it would be disproportionate for IPSO to uphold the complaint.

The complainant denied that the apology published was adequate. It had been made on behalf of the columnist, not the newspaper, and did not include acceptance that the Code had been breached, namely clause 3 ('Privacy') and clause 12 ('Discrimination').

---

68 Source: Decision of the Complaints Committee. Complaint No: 00572-15 'Trans Media Watch v The Sun'. Date complaint received: 5 February 2015. Date decision issued: 5 May 2015.

69 A Monty Python reference parodying the coverage of the General Elections in 1970 by including hectic (and downright silly) actions by the media and a range of ridiculous candidates, such as Tarquin Fin-tim-lin-bin-whin-bim-lim-bus-stop-F'tang-F'tang-Olé-Biscuitbarrel from the Silly Party.

Findings of the IPSO Committee

The Committee found initial column discriminatory and although it welcomed the paper's response apology it said its denial that it had breached the Editors' Code gave force to Trans Media Watch's complaint. IPSO's Complaints Committee also did not accept that Rod Liddle's apology was genuine because he had used it as an opportunity for a further attempt at humour at the expense of Ms Brothers. The first column's crude suggestion that Ms Brothers could only have become aware of her gender by seeing its physical manifestations was plainly wrong. It belittled Ms Brothers, her gender identity and her disability, mocking her for no reason other than these perceived 'differences'. The comment did not contain any specific pejorative term, but its meaning was pejorative in relation to characteristics specifically protected by clause 12. Both complaints were upheld, finding breach of clauses 3 and 12.

Remedial action

The IPSO Complaints Committee ordered *The Sun* to publish its adjudication upholding the complaint. The regulator ordered that the adjudication had to be published on the newspaper's front page with immediate effect as well as on the Sun's website, upholding Ms Brother's complaint.

The 'Trans Media Watch' decision was IPSO's first landmark adjudication because the regulator had accepted a complaint from a representative group rather than an individual.

6.5 The surveillance state

The Edward Snowden revelations in 2013 showed the extent of government surveillance, also high-lighting the symbiotic relationship between the US National Security Agency (NSA) and Britain's GCHQ as well as the relationship of giant internet companies (Google, MSN, etc.) with each other and the data sharing across borders.

The archive of whistleblower Edward Snowden revealed that not all encryption technologies live up to what they promise. Encryption – a mathematical process of converting messages, information, or data into a form unreadable by anyone except the intended recipient – protects the confidentiality and integrity of content against third-party access or manipulation. Strong encryption, once the sole province of militaries and intelligence services,[70] is now publicly accessible and often freely available to secure email, voice communication, images, hard drives and website browsers. With 'public key encryption', the dominant form of end-to-end security for data in transit, the sender uses the recipient's public key to encrypt the message and its attachments, and the recipient uses her or his own private key to decrypt them. Encryption is also being used to create digital signatures to ensure that a document and its sender are authentic, to authenticate and verify the identity of a server and to protect the integrity of communications between clients against tampering or manipulation of traffic by third parties. Some online practices have since moved away from the traditional system towards 'forward secrecy' or 'off-the-record' technology such as the Dark Web, in which keys are held ephemerally, particularly for uses such as instant messaging.

See Chapter 3.8

---

70 See: SANS Institute (2001) 'The Weakest Link: The Human Factor Lessons Learned from the German WWII Enigma Cryptosystem', InfoSec Reading Room at: www.sans.org/reading-room/whitepapers/vpns/weakest-link-human-factor-lessons-learned-german-wwii-enigma-cryptosystem-738.

Snowden gave the example of the supposedly completely secure encryption featured in Skype – a program used by some 560 million users to conduct internet video chat. He revealed that sustained Skype data collection by the NSA began in February 2011 when NSA code crackers declared they could access *all* data from Skype. Software giant Microsoft, which acquired Skype in 2011, did not appear to be at all surprised.[71]

The number of requests for user data made by British authorities has more than doubled between 2014 and 2015.

From 1 January to 30 June 2015, UK police and government agencies asked Twitter for information about users 299 times (an increase from 116 in the previous six months and more than the total for the whole of the previous two years). The requests related to a total of 1,041 accounts. The data published by Twitter showed that it provided some or all of the information requested in 51 per cent of cases. This was the highest proportion since the site first published its transparency report in 2012.[72] Twitter's Transparency Report (2015) said the UK remains a top requester, accounting for 7 per cent of the total 4,363 requests around the world. Overall, the number of demands for account information jumped by 52 per cent compared with the second half of 2014.[73] Twitter's report stated this was the largest increase in requests it has observed. The USA remains the most active, making more than half of all requests. That said, should governments not be publishing their own transparency reports, highlighting exactly how many requests are being made, how often they are refused and why?

In his report to the Human Rights Council (2015), Special Rapporteur David Kaye addresses the use of encryption and anonymity in digital communications. Drawing on his research on international and national norms and jurisprudence, his report concludes that encryption and anonymity enable individuals to exercise their rights to freedom of opinion and expression in the digital age and deserve strong protection.[74]

One thing is certain: the intelligence agencies and the information technology companies are in the same business, namely surveillance. Interestingly, both groups provide similar justification for what they do: that their surveillance is both necessary, for national security in the case of governments and for economic viability in the case of the companies (ISPs) – all of which is conducted 'within the law'. For this reason the European Court of Justice's ruling in *Schrems* is of such importance and leads the way to the furtherance of codification and legislation in cyberspace.

6.5.1 The *Maximilian Schrems* case and the 'safe harbour' scheme

The *Schrems*[75] ruling is about the legal basis for the transfer of personal data to businesses that are members of the 'US Safe Harbour' scheme. The Court of Justice of the European Union (CJEU) declared that there must be almost identical degrees of data protection (in the US and the EU) when signing up for any ISPs, browsers, search engines or social networks, such as Google, MSN, Facebook, Twitter, etc. The judgment made clear the important obligation on organizations to protect people's data when it leaves the UK (and other EU Member States).

After the Austrian law student, Maximilian (Max) Schrems, learnt about the Edward Snowden revelations in *der Spiegel* and *The Guardian* in 2013, he wanted to know what was happening to his own

---

71 Source: 'New Snowden revelation shows Skype may be privacy's biggest enemy', by Preston Gralla, *Computerworld*, 12 July 2013.
72 Source: 'Twitter's transparency report is scary, but not always helpful', by Jeff John Roberts, *Fortune Magazine*, 12 August 2015 at: http://fortune.com/2015/08/12/transparency-reports.
73 See: Twitter Transparency Report (2015) at: https://transparency.twitter.com/removal-requests/2015/jul-dec.
74 Human Rights Council (2015) Report of the Special Rapporteur on the promotion and protection of the right to freedom of opinion and expression, David Kaye, 22 May 2015, Document No A/HRC/29/32.
75 *Schrems (Maximilian) v Data Protection Commissioner* (2015) (Case C-362/14) Luxembourg, 6 October 2015 (CJEU); [2015] All ER (D) 34 (Oct).

personal data and records when going online and signing up to Facebook.[76] For example, Schrems was horrified to learn that the US National Security Agency (NSA) was routinely intercepting data from emails, social media, Skype and telephones. This encouraged Mr Schrems to take action. His campaign began in 2010, after studying for a term at the US Santa Clara University in the heart of Silicon Valley.

Following a talk by a Facebook privacy lawyer that allegedly downplayed the importance of Europe's privacy laws in relation to the internet, Schrems (then 24) and some 22 fellow lawyers from Vienna University initially complained to Facebook, asking what happened to their personal data? When the social networking site did not respond, Schrems requested assistance from the Irish regulator, the Data Protection Commissioner, in December 2010; the reason being that Facebook's European headquarters is based in Dublin. With some success. The Irish regulator forced Facebook into a number of concessions, such as greater privacy controls for users and the ability to turn off Facebook's facial recognition feature. But Max Schrems did not stop there.

Schrems then found out that US law did not offer sufficient protection against surveillance by public authorities of any data transferred to the US from, say, Europe – and that this was known as the 'safe harbour' scheme. The scheme included a series of principles concerning the protection of personal data to which US undertakings could subscribe voluntarily.[77] The European Commission decided in July 2000 on 'safe harbour' that US companies complying with the principles were allowed to transfer data from the EU to the US. This decision and the scheme itself were challenged by Max Schrems' action before the CJEU. Schrems used crowd-funding for his legal action (http://europe-v-facebook. org). At €500 per person, some 50,000 people rushed to sign up for Schrems' lawsuit.

Schrems' 'first round' litigation was heard before the High Court in Dublin,[78] where the law student argued that his privacy should have been safeguarded by the Irish regulator against security surveillance. The High Court subsequently made a reference for a preliminary ruling in July 2014 to the Court of Justice of the European Union (CJEU).

The question asked before the CJEU concerned the 'Data Protection Directive' (Directive 95/46/EC),[79] which provides that the transfer of personal data to a third country (here the USA) may, in principle, take place only if that third country ensures an adequate level of protection of the data.

 **KEY CASE**   ***Schrems v Data Protection Commissioner*** (Case C-362/14) Luxembourg, 6 October 2015 (CJEU)[80]

Precedent

 ❖ Where a claim is lodged with the national supervisory authorities (the regulator) they may examine whether the transfer of a person's data to a country complies with the requirements of EU legislation on the protection of that data (here Directive 95/46/EC).

 ❖ Even where the EU Commission has adopted a decision finding that a third country affords an adequate level of protection of personal data, the domestic regulator may still investigate whether the level of data protection is adequate.

---

76 The company was founded by Mark Zuckerberg on 4 February 2014, gained its billionth user in 2012, and on 28 August 2015, Facebook recorded 1 billion users in a single day.
77 The US Department of Commerce website provided a list of organizations that had signed up to 'safe harbour': https://safeharbor.export.gov/list.aspx.
78 *Schrems (Maximillian) v Data Protection Commissioner* (2014) (Case C-362/14) High Court of Ireland 25 July 2014.
79 Directive 95/46/EC of the European Parliament and of the Council of 24 October 1995 on the protection of individuals with regard to the processing of personal data and on the free movement of such data ('the Data Protection Directive') (OJ 1995 L 281, p. 31).
80 *Schrems (Maximilian) v Data Protection Commissioner* (2015) (Case C-362/14) Luxembourg, 6 October 2015 (CJEU); [2015] All ER (D) 34 (Oct).

❖ Alternatively, a person can bring the matter before the national courts, in order that the national courts make a reference for a preliminary ruling for the purpose of examination of the decision's validity.

Facts

Maximilian Schrems lodged a complaint with the Irish regulator and subsequently appealed to the Irish High Court regarding the safe harbour decision,[81] on the ground that there was not an adequate level of protection of his personal data transferred to the US via Facebook (whose headquarters was in the Irish Republic). Schrems lost his claim against the Irish Data Protection Commissioner before Desmond Hogan J. Still, the judge referred the question to the CJEU for a preliminary ruling.

The essential question was whether the Commission's 'Safe Harbour Decision' of 2000 had the effect of preventing a national supervisory authority (i.e. the Irish Data Protection Commissioner) from investigating a complaint, alleging that the third country (i.e. the USA) did not ensure an adequate level of protection and, where appropriate, from suspending the contested transfer of data.

The second question was whether the Irish regulator was absolutely bound by the Community finding (i.e. 'the Safe Harbour Decision') – with the specific provisions of Article 25(6) of Directive 95/46/EC (Data Protection Directive).

Thirdly, whether the 'office holder' could conduct his or her own investigation of the matter given the Safe Harbour Decision?

Decision (CJEU)

The Court stated that no provision of the Data Protection Directive (Directive 95/46/EC) prevents oversight by the national supervisory authorities (the regulator) of transfers of personal data to third countries which have been the subject of a Commission decision. Therefore, even if the Commission had adopted a decision, the national supervisory authorities, when dealing with a claim by a data subject, must be able to examine, with complete independence, whether the transfer of a person's data to a third country complies with the requirements laid down by the Directive.

Consequently, where a national authority or the person who has brought the matter before the national authority considers that a Commission decision is invalid, that authority or person must be able to bring proceedings before the national courts so that they may refer the case to the Court of Justice if they too have doubts as to the validity of the Commission decision. However, only the CJEU has jurisdiction to declare that an EU act is invalid (such as a Commission's 'Safe Harbour' decision).

The CJEU found that national security, public interest and law enforcement requirements of the United States prevailed over the Safe Harbour Scheme. This meant that US undertakings were bound to *disregard* the protective rules laid down by that scheme where they conflicted with such requirements. The US Safe Harbour Scheme thus *enabled*

---

81 Commission Decision 2000/520/EC of 26 July 2000 pursuant to Directive 95/46/EC of the European Parliament and of the Council on the adequacy of the protection provided by the 'safe harbour' privacy principles and related frequently asked questions issued by the US Department of Commerce; having regard to Article 7, Article 8 and Article 47 of the Charter of Fundamental Rights of the European Union (OJ 2000 L 215, p. 7).

interference by United States public authorities, i.e. interference with a person's funda-mental human rights under Article 8 ECHR.

The Court held that the Safe Harbour Scheme was unsafe and fundamentally interfered with an individual's right to respect for private life. The CJEU also found that the 'Safe Harbour Decision' denied the national supervisory authorities (here the Irish Data Pro-tection Commissioner) their powers where a person called into question whether the decision was compatible with the protection of the privacy and of the fundamental rights and freedoms of individuals.

For these reasons, the Court of Justice declared the Safe Harbour Decision invalid.

Analysis

The CJEU's preliminary ruling in *Schrems* is important on many levels. Firstly, it confirms Edward Snowden's courageous whistleblower action as an important service to civil soci-ety. His revelations prompted a wide-ranging reassessment of where our dependence on networking technology has taken us and stimulated some long-overdue thinking about how we might reassert some measure of democratic control over that technology. Snowden has forced all courts – including the CJEU – to rethink the way we share data across borders.

Secondly, it makes a domestic regulator (such as the Irish Data Commissioner or the Information Commissioner in the UK) responsible for ensuring that a data subject receives an adequate level of protection of his or her personal data.

European reaction to the *Max Schrems* case was mixed, generally commending the young lawyer but on the other hand expressing the 'what now after safe harbour' legal conundrum. The reac-tion from the UK Information Commissioner's Office (ICO) mirrored that of its Irish regulatory counterpart, commenting that the *Schrems* ruling is clearly significant and it is important that regula-tors and legislators provide a considered and clear response. Steven Lorber, senior lawyer at Lewis Silkin, commented in the *Data Protection Journal* on the implications of the *Schrems* judgment, namely that the 'Irish data protection authority will need to investigate whether or not transfer of data of Facebook's European subscribers should be suspended on the ground that the US does not afford an adequate level of protection of personal data'.[82]

The *Schrems* decision temporarily put at risk a thriving transatlantic digital economy. The ruling made it harder for the US and the EU to conclude any re-negotiations of the safe harbour pact. The *Max Schrems* ruling revealed that European and American views about personal data protection are radically different. The EU Commission sees protection of personal data as a human right; America considers it mainly in terms of consumer protection ('trade-offs').

Following the Brexit result on 23 June 2016, private data protection in the UK became a com-plex issue. There is the EU General Data Protection Regulation 2016 (GDPR) which comes into force on 25 May 2018 with an EU-wide 'privacy shield'. The existing Data Protection Act 1998 (DPA) per-mitted UK data controllers to assess adequacy and it remained to be seen whether the Information Commissioner's Office would deem certification to the 'Privacy Shield' by US companies adequate

---

82 Source: 'Harbor declared unsafe', by Steven Lorber, *The Data Protection Journal* at: www.lewissilkin.com/Journal/2015/October/ Harbor-declared-unsafe.aspx#.Vh5QuBCrSV5.

even if the UK were outside the EU. Such a stance would not be unprecedented, since other countries, such as Israel, had taken a similar position in relation to the US–EU Safe Harbour Framework before it had been ruled invalid by the CJEU in *Schrems*. If that is the case, then transfers of data to the US on the basis of certification to the Privacy Shield could be deemed per se adequate by the UK.

See Chapter 4.10

Věra Jourová, Commissioner for Justice, Consumers and Gender Equality, announced that the EU–US Privacy Shield 'is a robust new system to protect the personal data of Europeans and ensures legal certainty for businesses' – and that it – 'will restore the trust of consumers when their data is transferred across the Atlantic'.[83]

6.5.2 The Investigatory Powers Tribunal

In October 2015 the Investigatory Powers Tribunal (IPT) ruled that MPs' and peers' private communications are not protected from interception by GCHQ. The IPT was set up under the Regulation of Investigatory Powers Act 2000 (RIPA) and its codes of practice. The tribunal investigates and determines complaints of unlawful use of covert techniques by public authorities infringing our right to privacy. The IPT also investigates claims against intelligence or law enforcement agencies' conduct which breaches a wider range of human rights.[84]

The surprise decision by IPT found that the so-called 'Wilson Doctrine' guarantees no longer applied. The *Wilson Doctrine* was a convention, introduced by Prime Minister Harold Wilson in 1966, banning the tapping of parliamentarians' telephones. This doctrine was extended in 1997 by Prime Minister Tony Blair to cover other forms of electronic surveillance such as email. Subsequently, Mr Blair extended the Wilson Doctrine to 'all forms of warranted interception of communications'.[85]

The original claim was brought by two Green Party parliamentarians, Caroline Lucas, MP for Brighton Pavilion and Baroness Jenny Jones of Moulsecoomb, and former Glasgow and Respect Party MP, George Galloway. The parliamentarians had complained to the IPT that disclosures by whistleblower Edward Snowden had revealed that GCHQ was capturing MPs' communications, which, they argued, breached the Wilson Doctrine.

The tribunal decided that – unlike journalists' and lawyers' communications – there was no leading Strasbourg authority for enhanced privacy protection for parliamentarians. This meant the Wilson Doctrine had no legal effect, and the Security and Intelligence Agencies (SIA) merely had to comply with their own 'Guidance' regulations.[86] This only confirmed that most constitutional conventions do not hold up in law.

6.6 Protecting journalistic sources

The aftermath of the phone hacking affair following the Leveson Inquiry generated a number of enquiries into the relationships between the media, the police and other public services, and the conflict of interests that can arise from them. It emerged that not only journalists had been hacking into celebrities' phones but also that police (particularly the London Metropolitan Police – 'the Met') had been involved in corruption scandals that arose from the Leveson Inquiry.

See below 6.6.3

In separate criminal proceedings and internal police inquiries which ensued it came to light that police officers had frequently obtained telephone records of journalists and newspaper editors without their consent despite legislation which entitles journalists to keep their sources confidential. For example, officers of the Met had obtained call records to *The Sun* newsdesk as well as the

---

83 Source: European Commission Press Release, Brussels, 12 July 2016 at: http://europa.eu/rapid/press-release_IP-16–2461_en.htm?locale=en&cm_mid=5865252&cm_crmid=f34debe6–353a-e611-ad4b-0050569f3e7f&cm_medium=email.
84 See: The Investigatory Powers Tribunal at: www.ipt-uk.com/default.aspx.
85 Source: *Hansard*, The Prime Minister, Interception of Communications, HC Deb 21 January 2002 vol. 378 c589W.
86 See: IPT decision of 4 Oct 2015 – Caroline Lucas MP, Baroness Jones of Moulsecoomb, George Galloway at: www.ipt-uk.com.

See below

6.6.1

editor's phone records in order to identify potential sources of the 'Plebgate' scandal. A conflict of interest had arisen where police officers (and some prison staff) had given preferential treatment to one interest over others, and the behaviour of some Met officers was found to be inappropriate and corrupt.

There have been a number of events in the UK revealing the potential for conflict between a judicial order either prohibiting the publication of details relating to a matter before the courts in the form of superinjunctions, or ordering a journalist to reveal his sources of information.[87] *Wainwright v The Home Office* (2003)[88] confirmed that the UK does not have an established law of privacy (confirming *Kaye v Robertson* (1991)[89]).

January 2016 saw the Court of Appeal ruling in the *David Miranda*[90] case, arguably a *cause célèbre*, hailed as a victory for Miranda because the court noted that the Terrorism Act 2000[91] did not include sufficient protection for journalists carrying sensitive information. However, the CA ruled that Miranda's detention at Heathrow under the Terrorism Act was *lawful*.

David Miranda, a Brazilian citizen, had been part of a professional operation involving the leaking of classified information from the US National Security Agency (NSA) by Edward Snowden, the renegade CIA computer engineer who had been granted asylum in Russia. The Security Service (for which the first defendant Secretary of State is responsible by statute) had undertaken an operation relating to Edward Snowden. They had become aware of David Miranda's movements and had briefed Detective Superintendent Stokley of SO 15, the Counter-Terrorism Command in the Metropolitan Police (the second defendant) on 15 August 2013. The intelligence material – including UK data – found on Miranda included encrypted material derived from data which had been stolen by Snowden and which subsequently formed the basis of articles that appeared in the *Guardian* on 6 and 7 June 2013. Miranda had been questioned at Heathrow airport by police and items in his possession were taken from him. Miranda had been carrying the highly classified material in order to assist his spouse, Glenn Greenwald, in his journalistic activity.

In the judicial review proceedings, Mr Miranda contended that the acts of the police at Heathrow were unlawful because the stop power was exercised for a purpose not permitted by the 2000 terrorism statute; that its use was in breach of his Article 10 right, in particular in relation to journalistic material. The CA held that the publication of material did amount to an act of terrorism if the material endangered life and the person publishing the material intended it to have that effect, provided that it was designed to influence the government or an international governmental organization or to intimidate the public or a section of the public and it was for the purpose of advancing *inter alia* a political or ideological cause.[92]

The court dismissed David Miranda's appeal against the use of the police power, since the power used under the 2000 Act was for a permitted purpose; that is, the police were entitled to consider that material in Miranda's possession might be released in circumstances falling within the definition of terrorism: the 'Schedule 7 stop power in relation to Mr Miranda on 18 August 2013 was lawful.'[93]

The CA rejected Mr Miranda's argument that the use of the stop power against him was an unjustified and disproportionate interference with his right to freedom of expression despite the fact that this was a case involving an interference with press freedom. On the facts of this case, the compelling national security interests outweighed Mr Miranda's Article 10 rights.[94]

---

87 For further discussion see: Geddis, A. (2010).
88 [2003] UKHL 53 (HL).
89 [1991] FSR 62.
90 R (on the application of Miranda [David]) v (1) Secretary of State for the Home Department (2) Commissioner of Police of the Metropolis [2016] EWCA Civ 6 (CA Civ Div) 19 January 2016.
91 Specifically para. 2(1) of Sch. 7 of the Terrorism Act 2000.
92 Miranda [2016] EWCA Civ 6 at paras 38 to 56.
93 Ibid., at paras 25 to 37 and 57 and 58.
94 Ibid., at paras 59 to 93.

That said, the CA held that the stop power, if used in respect of journalistic information or material, is incompatible with Article 10 ECHR because it is not 'prescribed by law' as required by Article 10(2), that is, the power was not subject to sufficient legal safeguards to avoid the risk that it would be exercised arbitrarily. The court therefore granted a certificate of incompatibility and it would be a matter for Parliament to decide how to provide such a safeguard.[95] The most obvious safeguard would be some form of judicial or other independent and impartial scrutiny conducted in such a way as to protect the confidentiality in the material – even though, in this case, there was no breach.

The *David Miranda* case is not about press freedom. It is about the right of the security services to protect secrets vital to their activities and defend national security. Amnesty International however argued that the 'only possible intent' behind Miranda's detention was 'to harass him' for no other reason than his personal relationship to *Guardian* journalist Mr Greenwald.

6.6.1 'Plebgate' and police phone-hacking

The background to 'Plebgate' is that on 19 September 2012 Conservative MP Andrew Mitchell, then the Conservative party's Chief Whip, had a row with armed police officers who would not let him cycle through Downing Street's main gate, alleging that Mitchell called them 'fucking plebs'. On 21 September 2012, the *Sun* newspaper reported that Mr Mitchell had raged against police officers at the entrance to Downing Street in a foul-mouthed rant shouting 'you're f . . . ing plebs'. In the following days, there was considerable media coverage about this incident and on 24 September 2012 the *Daily Telegraph* published an article containing what it claimed was a leaked copy of the police 'log' detailing what Mr Mitchell had allegedly said to the officer on the gate. An investigation was undertaken by the Met's Directorate of Professional Standards – Specialist Investigations (DPS-SI) to find the source of this apparent leak under the operation name 'Operation Alice'. On 19 December 2012 West Mercia Police began a separate investigation into claims that an officer had given false information regarding the alleged abuse by Mr Mitchell.

A year later in October 2013, three Federation police officers, Ken MacKaill, Stuart Hinton and Chris Jones, apologized before the Home Affairs Select Committee for their 'poor judgement' in talking to the media about Mr Mitchell, stating they did not intend to mislead anyone about what occurred. However, they refused to apologize to Mr Mitchell, standing by their 'accurate' account. In January 2014, PC Keith Wallis pleaded guilty to misconduct in a public office at Westminster Magistrates' Court for falsely claiming to have witnessed the 'Plebgate' incident in an email to his MP. He was sentenced to 12 months' imprisonment. Sentencing judge Sweeney J said Mr Wallis had been guilty of 'sustained, and in significant measure, devious misconduct which fell far below the standards expected of a police officer'.

The matter had also been referred to the Independent Police Complaints Commission (IPCC) on 17 December 2012. The IPCC then started its own investigation regarding gross misconduct proceedings against five members of the Met's Diplomatic Protection Group linked to the 'Plebgate' row. Following their investigation, PCs Gillian Weatherley and Susan Johnson were dismissed in April 2014 for gross misconduct in public office over leaks to the press about 'Plebgate'. Subsequently in October 2014, a High Court ruling found that there had been no proper final report prepared by West Mercia Police following the investigation into the three Police Federation officers at the centre of the 'Plebgate' row. The court also quashed the IPCC's decision.

In March 2015 PC Toby Rowland, the police officer who was on duty at Downing Street on 'Plebgate' day, accepted £80,000 damages in a settlement of his libel action against Andrew Mitchell. Mr Rowland had sought initial damages of £200,000 for suggesting he was not telling the truth

---

95 Ibid., at paras 94 to 117.

about the September 2012 altercation by the Downing Street gates. This action was preceded by Mr Mitchell's losing his defamation action against Rupert Murdoch's News Group Newspapers in November 2014 over the story in *The Sun* in 2012 which had claimed he called PC Toby Rowland a 'pleb'. In court Mr Mitchell had admitted that he had used bad language but maintained he had not used 'that' word. The defendant newspaper had pleaded justification and a *Reynolds* public interest defence in its defence.

Giving his ruling, Mitting J said: 'For the reasons given I am satisfied at least on the balance of probabilities that Mr Mitchell did speak the words alleged or something so close to them as to amount to the same including the politically toxic word pleb.' The judge also referred to PC Rowland as, 'not the sort of man who would have had the wit, imagination or inclination to invent on the spur of the moment an account of what a senior politician had said to him in temper'.[96] Mr Mitchell was ordered to pay interim damages of £300,000 with estimated overall costs of £3 million.

In a subsequent separate cost hearing (issued at court before 1 April 2013 when the *Jackson* reforms took effect) – Mr Mitchell appealed against the costs awarded against him. But the court refused to grant relief. Richards MR said that the explanations of Mr Mitchell's solicitors were not unusual and held that there was no evidence of particular prejudice towards the claimant arising from her order.[97] The case was managed in the defamation costs management pilot scheme, which was intended to trial and give effect to the impending civil costs reforms that would later apply to all civil litigation cases. One of the reforms was the requirement for all parties to file and exchange a costs budget within seven days before the case management hearing. Mr Mitchell's solicitors failed to comply in that they did not file their costs in time.[98]

See Chapter 7

In September 2014, the Met's investigation report on 'Operation Alice' was published, concluding that police officers had obtained phone records from *The Sun* journalists involved in the Plebgate affair.[99] The report found that a senior police officer rather than a judge had authorized the 'phone-tapping' of *Sun* journalists. The Met had used police powers under the Regulation of Investigatory Powers Act 2000 (RIPA)[100] which circumvents the Police and Criminal Evidence Act 1984 (PACE); PACE requires police to go to a senior judge to obtain an order for disclosure of journalistic material.

'Operation Alice' had tried to establish the sources of information of the *Sun* newspaper and how police officers had communicated with newspaper reporters ('the whistleblowers') and whether journalists' phone records had been unlawfully obtained by police. The report noted that Tom Newton Dunn, political editor of *The Sun*, had written a series of articles reporting on 'Plebgate', but had refused to give any information to the Met inquiry which might identify his sources. He made it clear however that neither PC Rowland nor PC Weatherley had been the source of his information and that no payment had been made or offered in connection with his 'Plebgate' stories: 'In my opinion this was an example of good faith whistle-blowing about misconduct by a senior politician which was rightfully exposed publicly.'[101]

---

96 Source: 'Plebgate: Andrew Mitchell did call policemen 'plebs,' judge rules', by Martin Evans, 27 November 2014, *Daily Telegraph*.
97 See: *Mitchell MP v News Group Newspapers Ltd* [2013] EWCA Civ 1537 (CA Civ Div) 27 November 2013 (Richards MR and Elias LJJ).
98 At paras 4.1 and 4.2 of CPR PD51D.
99 Source: Metropolitan Police Final Report 'Operation Alice', September 2014 at: www.iocco-uk.info/docs/Met%20Operation%20Alice%20Closing%20Report.pdf.
100 Section 1 RIPA makes it an offence for 'a person intentionally and without lawful authority' to intercept *any* communication in the UK in the course of its transmission either by post or telecommunications networks.
101 Source: Met Police Report 'Operation Alice', September 2014 at paras 5.115–5.118.

The *Sun* subsequently contacted Sir Anthony May,[102] the Interception of Communications Commissioner (ICCO) at the time, to examine how many times the police had sought authorization for journalistic records this way.

See below
6.6.2

6.6.2 The Interception of Communications Commissioner

The office of the Interception of Communications Commissioner (IOCC) was created under section 57(1) of the Regulation of Investigatory Powers Act 2000 (RIPA), the remit being to keep under review the acquisition and disclosure of communications data under Chapter 2 of Part 1 of RIPA.

Following the allegations and serious nature of the concerns about the protection of journalistic sources in the 'Plebgate' affair, the IOCC, Sir Anthony May, launched an inquiry on 6 October 2014[103] into the use of powers by the police under RIPA to acquire communications data relating to the confidential sources of journalists as he shared the concerns raised relating to the protection of journalistic sources.[104] The Met Police's Report on the investigation of the 'Plebgate' affair ('Operation Alice') had been published during September 2014 and a month later Kent Police's 'Operation Solar' was published, relating to the trial of former minister Chris Huhne and his wife for perverting the course of justice. At the same time the *Press Gazette* and the National Union of Journalists (NUJ) launched their 'Save our Sources' campaign, setting out their concerns, and initiated a petition to the Interception of Communication Commissioner's Office (IOCCO), the Rt Hon Sir Paul Kennedy, being interim Commissioner at the time of the investigation (July to December 2014). His report was published in February 2015.

In addition to the IOCC's investigation, the Home Secretary, the Rt Hon Theresa May MP, had also commissioned an inquiry in 2011, led by HM Inspectorate of Constabulary (HMIC), into undue influence, inappropriate contractual arrangements and other abuses of power in police relationships with the media.[105] The report 'Without fear or favour' (2011)[106] scrutinized how the police had handled the phone hacking affairs arising from the Leveson Inquiry and the Plebgate issue – all of which had led to media concerns about police integrity and corruption, and had ultimately undermined public trust in the police service.

6.6.3 The Regulation of Investigatory Powers Act (RIPA)

Invariably when public officials, such as police or the intelligence services, investigate criminal conduct by intercepting phones, internet or social networking sites, acquisition of communications data in such cases is likely to reveal journalistic sources. The main purpose of the RIPA legislation is that it permits communications data to be acquired in relation to *criminality* rather than the identification of a journalist's source.

Police forces are in a privileged position – not least in view of the powers they have to intrude into people's lives and the nature of the information they hold, which will often be of interest to the public. Journalists are conduits of public interest information and generally strive to gather and report this information. There ought to be an overarching principle that police relationships with

---

102 The Rt Hon Sir Anthony May stepped down as Interception of Communications Commissioner on 31 July 2015.
103 See: Interception of Communication Commissioner's Office (IOCCO) Inquiry into the use of Chapter 2 of Part 1 RIPA to identify journalistic sources, 4 February 2015 at: www.iocco-uk.info/docs/IOCCO%20Communications%20Data%20Journalist%20 Inquiry%20Report%204Feb15.pdf.
104 Section 58(1) RIPA imposes a statutory obligation on everyone concerned with Part 1 of the Act to disclose or provide all such documents or information to the Commissioner as he may require for the purpose of enabling him to carry out his functions under s 57.
105 Using her powers under s 11(2) Police Reform Act 2002.
106 HMIC (2011) 'Without fear or favour'. A review of police relationships. December 2011 ISBN 978-1-84987-605-6 at: www. justiceinspectorates.gov.uk/hmic/media/a-review-of-police-relationships-20111213.pdf.

the media should not seek to constrain the media but allow them to accurately report news of which the principal beneficiary is the public.

The protection of journalistic sources and access to records that directly identify journalistic sources are considered by the media as fundamentally important, including the right to freedom of expression (Article 10 ECHR), the public interest and the so-called 'chilling effect' on sources' willingness to provide information.

The HMIC report 'Without fear or favour' (2011) found that these boundaries had become unacceptable particularly in high profile operations such as Plebgate or the phone-hacking fallout of the Leveson Inquiry. Police had been rewarded by the media in cash or kind in exchange for information. The intensity of these relationships were now perceived by the public as 'endemically' corrupt, wishing the police service to act more professionally and in a more businesslike way.

The Interception of Communication Commissioner's Office (IOCCO) Inquiry (2015) into identifying journalists' sources was principally concerned with the acquisition of communications data by police forces under Chapter 2 of Part 1 of RIPA (i.e. 'Lawful acquisition and disclosure of communications data'). Additionally, on 8 April 2014, the Court of Justice of the European Union (CJEU) had published its ruling making invalid the Data Retention Directive 2006/24/EC. The ruling identified, amongst other things, the lack of any exception for communications that was subject to an obligation of professional secrecy.

There are then strict rules governing RIPA as to who can obtain communications data and the circumstances in which the police and security services can access the data retained by Communication Service Providers (CSPs). These are defined in Chapter 2 of Part 1 of the Act. Communications data generally embrace the 'who', 'when' and 'where' of a communication but not the content, what was said or written. In short: traffic data which is data that may be attached to a communication for the purpose of transmitting it and could appear to identify the sender and recipient of the communication, the location from which and the time at which it was sent, and other related material.[107] Additionally, service use information can be accessed, the kind of information that habitually used to appear on CSP's itemized billing documents to customers,[108] and subscriber information, as well as data held or obtained by a CSP in relation to a customer when they sign up to use a service, such as the recorded name and address of the subscriber of a telephone number or the account holder of an email address.[109]

Lawful authority for acquiring and accessing such information can only be undertaken by a 'senior designated person' within the public authority acquiring it. The test for *necessity* is laid out in section 22(2) RIPA comprising:

- in the interests of national security;
- for the purpose of preventing or detecting crime or of preventing disorder;
- in the interests of the economic wellbeing of the United Kingdom;
- in the interests of public safety;
- for the purpose of protecting public health;
- for the purpose, in an emergency, of preventing death or injury; or
- any damage to a person's physical or mental health, or of mitigating such; or for any purpose (not falling within the above which is specified for the purpose of this subsection by an order made by the Secretary of State).[110]

---

107 Section 21(4)(a), (6) and (7) RIPA.
108 Section 21(4)(b) RIPA.
109 Section 21(4)(c) RIPA.
110 Section 81(5) RIPA includes establishing by whom, for what purpose, by what means and generally in what circumstances any crime was committed, the gathering of evidence for use in any legal proceedings and the apprehension of the person (or persons) by whom any crime was committed. In relation to the investigation of crime, the Act does not restrict the acquisition of communications data to serious crime which is defined at s 81(2) and (3) of the Act.

The vast majority of communications data are acquired 'for purpose of preventing or detecting crime or of preventing disorder'. The IOCCO's report found that 76.9 per cent of communications data requests in 2013 were submitted for this purpose.[111]

In addition to the necessity test, there is the 'proportionality' test in obtaining communications data under section 21(1) RIPA. A 'designated person' is forbidden from approving an application for communications data unless s/he believes that obtaining the data in question, by the conduct authorized or required, is *proportionate* to what is sought to be achieved by so obtaining the data.[112] Thus every application to acquire communications data has to address *proportionality* explicitly. This involves balancing the extent of the intrusiveness of the interference against a *specific* benefit to the investigation or operation being undertaken by a relevant public authority in the public interest. The authorizing senior official ('designated person') must also believe that conduct is no more than is *necessary* in the circumstances. Any conduct that is excessive in the circumstances of both the interference and the aim of the investigation or operation, or is in any way arbitrary will not be proportionate. Parliament further reinforced those restrictions with the Data Retention and Investigatory Powers Act 2014 (DRIPA). This Act was challenged and subsequently repealed in December 2016.

See Chapter 8.7

This perhaps rather confusing legislation led to a general misunderstanding amongst journalists regarding the appropriate use of police production orders such as those described at section 9 and Schedule 1 of PACE. Several media reports claimed that the police, when acquiring communications data under RIPA, had circumvented the process of judicial approval for such an order. As the media is normally able to attend any court hearing in order to advance submissions opposing court orders – such as anonymity orders in family courts, grave crimes in youth courts or when police apply for a disclosure order under RIPA – they were not able to do so in the phone hacking and Plebgate incidents.

It was subsequently asserted by the NUJ, the *Guardian* and the *Press Gazette* that the police circumvented judicial approval and denied journalists the opportunity to have a draft order set aside when seeking the disclosure of communications data retained by the CSP in relation to the phone-hacking scandals at the *News of the World* revealed at the Leveson Inquiry and subsequent criminal trials and the Plebgate affair.

Following these allegations and the various reports mentioned above, the Home Office published a draft Code of Practice (2014)[113] on data retention.[114] The relevant section read:

> The degree of interference may be higher where the communications data being sought relates to a person who is a member of a profession that handles privileged or otherwise confidential information (such as a medical doctor, lawyer, journalist, Member of Parliament or minister of religion). It may also be possible to infer an issue of sensitivity from the fact that someone has regular contact with, for example, a lawyer or journalist. Such situations do not preclude an application being made. However applicants, giving special consideration to necessity and proportionality, must draw attention to any such circumstances that might lead to an unusual degree of intrusion or infringement of privacy, and clearly note when an application is made

---

111 See: Interception of Communication Commissioner's Office (IOCCO) Inquiry into the use of Chapter 2 of Part 1 RIPA to identify journalistic sources, 4 February 2015, Figure 7, p. 26, at: www.iocco- uk.info/docs/2013%20Annual%20Report%20of%20 the%20IOCC%20Accessible%20Version.pdf.

112 Section 22(5) RIPA.

113 See: Home Office (2014) Retention of Communications Data Code of Practice Pursuant to regulation 10 of the Data Retention Regulations 2014 and s 71 RIPA 2000 Draft for public consultation 9 December 2014 at: www.gov.uk/government/ uploads/system/uploads/attachment_data/file/383401/Draft_Data_Retention_Code_of_Practice_-_for_publication_2014_ 12_09.pdf.

114 The Code was issued pursuant to s 71 RIPA and relates to the powers and duties conferred or imposed under Part 1 DRIPA and the Data Retention Regulations 2014 (DRR 2014). It provides guidance on the procedures to be followed when communications data is retained under those provisions.

for the communications data of a medical doctor, lawyer, journalist, Member of Parliament, or minister of religion. Particular care must be taken by designated persons when considering such applications.[115]

It became evident that the Codes (past and present) did not provide any clear guidance on how 'designated persons' – such as police officers – should actually apply the principles of necessity, proportionality and collateral intrusion when dealing with data relating to communications with journalists or take account of the added dimension that the requirement may lead to the identification of journalistic sources, whether an intended consequence or not.

The IOCCO's inquiry report was published in February 2015 and the Commissioner, the Rt Hon Sir Paul Kennedy, came to the following conclusions: that neither the RIPA legislation nor the Interception Code of Practice contained any advice on dealing with professions that handle privileged information (e.g. lawyers or journalists). The Commissioner also concluded that Chapter 2 of Part 1 RIPA provided an exclusive scheme to police services whereby communications data could be obtained. This was reinforced by section 21(1), which states that Chapter II RIPA applies to 'any conduct' in relation to obtaining of communications data and to the disclosure to 'any person' of such data, reinforced by section 1(6)(a) DRIPA 2014.

The Commissioner shared an understandable public concern about the necessity and proportionality aspects of the RIPA legislation and therein the potential intrusion caused by access to such information and personal data. He noted the importance of protecting journalistic sources so as to ensure a free press and their Article 10 right regarding freedom of expression.[116] The IOCC made the following two recommendations:

1. Judicial authorization must be obtained in cases where communications data is sought to determine the source of journalistic information.
2. Where communications data is sought that does not relate to an investigation to determine the source of journalistic information (for example where the journalist is a victim of crime or is suspected of committing a crime unrelated to their occupation) Chapter 2 of Part 1 RIPA may be used so long as the designated person gives adequate consideration to the necessity, proportionality, collateral intrusion, including the possible unintended consequence of the conduct. The revised Code contains very little guidance concerning what these considerations should be and that absence needs to be addressed.[117]

The Commissioner concluded that the government be advised to implement these recommendations in the form of legislation in order to provide adequate protection for journalistic sources and enhanced safeguards to prevent unnecessary or disproportionate intrusions.

6.6.4 How can journalists protect their sources?

The cultivation of sources is essential for journalists. It is a basic tool of their trade, the means by which newsworthy and investigative information is brought to the public's attention. Should journalists reveal their sources of information if ordered by a court? The short answer is 'no'.

Still, there are no 'laws' that define whether or not a journalist should reveal his sources, but the various codes of journalism appear to be very clear: journalists should never reveal their sources. Neither the law of confidence nor the Contempt of Court Act 1981 (CCA) explain how 'necessity' and 'in the interests of justice' are to be applied in practice. Section 10 CCA states:

---

115 Home Office draft code on data retention (2014) at paras 3.72 to 3.74.
116 See: IOCCO (2015) Inquiry Report at p. 39.
117 Ibid., at p. 37.

No court may require a person to disclose, nor is any person guilty of contempt of court for refusing to disclose, the source of information contained in a publication for which he is responsible unless it is established to the satisfaction of the court that it is necessary in the interests of justice or national security or for the prevention of disorder or crime.

See Chapter 8.5

The National Union of Journalists (NUJ) drew up its first Code of Ethics in 1936 which later became the bedrock of the language of the Code of Practice for the PCC. Article 7 of the NUJ rule-book states: 'A journalist shall protect confidential sources of information.' But these codes express moral and ethical standards, not legal ones, meaning that not protecting the source is always wrong. While there is no law which covers the fact that journalists must reveal their sources, a court can nevertheless order a journalist to do so.

The law continued to sit uncomfortably with RIPA and new terrorism legislation passed at the start of the new Conservative majority government in May 2015 when the then Home Secretary Theresa May persuaded Parliament to pass new legislation in the form of the Counter-Terrorism and Security Act 2015. Section 21 of the new Terrorism Act concerned the retention of 'relevant internet data' (amending section 2(1) DRIPA – subsequently repealed by the *David Davis and Tom Watson* Judicial Review[118]). The 2015 Terrorism Act went further, allowing any public official to monitor confidential sources, such as between prisoners and MPs, lawyers and their clients, journalists and their confidential sources in an investigative exposé. It is now possible for police and intelligence officers to monitor each person's activity on the internet at any particular place or time.

| ❖ KEY CASE | *Information Commissioner v Colenso-Dunne* [2015] UKUT 471 (AAC)[119] |

Precedent

❖ Businesses are not expected to trawl the internet and other sources to check whether there is any information that, when linked with personal data they hold, would mean the data they hold is in fact sensitive personal data.

❖ Organizations only need to consider 'the immediate context' of data to determine whether it is personal or sensitive personal data under section 2(g) Data Protection Act 1998.

❖ In 'borderline' cases, organizations will have to assess the individual 'circumstances of the case' to determine whether there is too great a risk that disclosing anonymized data would lead to individuals being identified.

Facts

In 2003, the Information Commissioner (IC) had seized information from the home of Mr Steve Whittamore, a private investigator, which included a list of 305 journalists' names who were among his customers as part of 'Operation Motorman'.[120] That investigation by the ICO formed part of the background to the various civil and criminal proceedings generated by the phone-hacking scandal and to the establishment of the Leveson Inquiry. These notebooks along with invoices and remittance notes became

---

118 See: *R (on the application of (1) David Davis MP (2) Tom Watson MP (3) Peter Brice (4) Geoffrey Lewis) v Secretary of State for the Home Department and Open Rights Group; Privacy International; The Law Society of England and Wales* [2015] EWHC 2092 (Admin) High Court of Justice, 17 July 2015 (QB).

119 Upper Tribunal (Administrative Appeals Chamber) 26 August 2015.

120 See: ICO Decision Notice 'Operation Motorman'. Reference: FS50419834. 9 August 2012 at: https://ico.org.uk/media/action-weve-taken/decision-notices/2012/747546/fs_50419834.pdf.

known as the 'Motorman' files. The ICO had found that around 4,000 requests for information had been made by 305 journalists from a wide variety of national newspapers and magazines.

See Chapter 4.4

The ICO refused to release the list of journalists' names in response to Mr Christopher Colenso-Dunne's request citing the exemption under section 40(2) Freedom of Information Act 2000 (FOIA). The reason given was that the journalists' names were 'sensitive personal data' under section 2(g) Data Protection Act 1998 (DPA) as the information related to the alleged commission of criminal offences by at least some of the journalists.

The regulator dismissed Mr Colenso-Dunne's complaint. The First Tier Tribunal (FTT), however, allowed Mr Colenso-Dunne's appeal and the IC, in turn, appealed to the Upper Tribunal (UT) against the FTT's decision. The UT was then asked to consider the public interest in knowing the identities of the journalists who had instructed the private investigator and whether this outweighed the journalists' privacy rights.

Decision
The IC's appeal was dismissed. The Upper Tribunal (UT) upheld the FTT tribunal's decision and allowed the disclosure of the names of certain journalists who had been customers of the private investigator's unlawful trading in confidential personal information. The UT concluded that the journalists' names were not 'sensitive personal data' within the meaning of section 2(g) DPA and were therefore *not* exempt from disclosure under section 40(2) FOIA.

Analysis
Judge Wikeley in the Upper Tribunal noted that the decision of the First Tier Tribunal had been reached properly as to whether the reduced list of journalists' names and contact details constituted sensitive personal data and had rightly concluded that it did not. Certain journalists on Steve Whittamore's contact list had commissioned the private investigator to obtain information. This information did not carry with it any assertion as to the actual or alleged commission of any crime by those journalists in the light of the *News of the World* Leveson phone-hacking inquiry.

The judge also held that any sensitive personal data must essentially speak for itself in its immediate context. Information that on the face of it was ordinary personal data could not suddenly transmute into sensitive personal data because of other information that was out in the public domain. Wikeley J noted the importance when looking at the meaning of the Data Protection Act 1998 (DPA) to distinguish between 'personal data' and the sub-species of 'sensitive' personal data (section 2(g) DPA). When Parliament enacted section 2(g) DPA it had considered that 'the commission or alleged commission' of any offence should attract the heightened level of protection under Schedule 3 to the DPA. So, for instance, a long since spent criminal conviction might be just as much a part of a person's life story and attract enhanced privacy rights as the state of their physical health. Therefore, the fact that some people might misconstrue a journalist's name being in the material seized from the private investigator as an allegation that they had committed an offence did not convert personal data into sensitive personal data.[121]

---

121 See: paras 38–39, 45–46, 48 of the judgment (Judge Wikeley).

It was clear that the UT (and indeed the FTT) had carefully considered the reputations of the journalists and concluded that any damage to their reputational rights was justified in the sense that they would be subject to legitimate criticism for using the private investigator's services. It necessarily followed that in so far as the journalists had a legitimate interest in protecting their reputational rights, that did not carry significant weight: what mattered ultimately were a person's deserved reputational rights. It was also important to note that the tribunal had not actually ordered the disclosure of *all* 305 names that formed the subject matter of the respondent's request. It had explained the process by which it had arrived at the reduced list, and the explanation exemplified the care it had devoted to investigating the evidence. It had sifted out those journalists' names where the enquiry was plainly legitimate or the information was incomplete. Therefore, it had not erred in its approach to balancing the interests of the parties concerned.[122]

6.6.5 Should journalists be forced to reveal their sources?

Some British journalists have chosen to go to prison for 'contempt of court' rather than reveal their sources when ordered by a court to do so. In February 1963 Fleet Street crime reporters Reg Foster of the *Daily Sketch* and Brendan Mulholland of the *Daily Mail* made history by being jailed. They had refused to disclose sources of information on their reporting of the 'Vassall sex and spy scandal' to the Radcliffe Inquiry in 1962. They were sentenced at the High Court for contempt of court; Foster was given three months for refusing to name one source and Mulholland was sentenced to six months' imprisonment for refusing to reveal two.

The journalists had exposed the outrageously inappropriate lifestyle of aristocratic ministers and government mandarins who felt no need to justify themselves to the public. Foster and Mulholland exposed John Vassall, an assistant private secretary to an Admiralty junior minister, as a Soviet spy, who was subsequently sentenced to 18 years' imprisonment. After the trial, held largely in *camera*, the opposition, led by George Brown, succeeded in persuading a reluctant Harold Macmillan to set up the Radcliffe Tribunal of Inquiry, which turned out to be more censorious of the press than of the British security services. Reg Foster, who gave evidence before Lord Radcliffe, chairman of the tribunal inquiring into the activities of John Vassall, about press reports he had written on the case, was asked to say from what type of source he had obtained information about Vassall buying women's clothes in the West End. He refused.

The Vassall affair turned out to be the central link in a chain of events culminating in the Profumo scandal and Prime Minister Harold Macmillan's resignation. Investigative journalism managed to tumble the old order, by exposing the Vassall affair of 1962 and the Profumo and Christine Keeler affair of 1963. Both these rather tasteless affairs became synonymous with a crusade for press freedom and journalistic martyrdom.

In 1971, BBC *Tonight* reporter Bernard Falk served two and a half days in a prison of his own choice, namely Belfast's Crumlin Road Jail, for contempt of court rather than reveal his source, a member of the IRA.[123]

On 22 October 1983, the *Guardian* published an electrifying front-page exclusive which led to a court battle with the government.[124] Documents about cruise missile arrivals at Greenham Common had been anonymously leaked to the newspaper. Peter Preston, then editor of the *Guardian*, was drawn into a legal battle with the government to reveal his source of information and to hand over

---

122 Ibid., at paras 52–55, 66–67.
123 See: Briggs, A. (1995) vol. 5, at pp. 911–912.
124 Source: 'Whitehall sets November 1 Cruise Arrival: Troops stand by for the Greenham Missile Date', by David Fairhall, *Guardian*, 22 October 1983.

all leaked documents – which, in turn, would identify the whistleblower. The *Guardian* lost the battle and Peter Preston was forced to hand over the evidence – one of the great regrets of his time at the *Guardian*. The whistleblower was identified as young civil servant and Foreign Office clerk, Sarah Tisdall, and on 23 March 1984 she was sentenced to six months in prison for leaking government secrets. Peter Preston learnt a hard lesson and was shunned by his fellow journalists for years to come for revealing his sources. Preston defended his action later, strongly believing that section 10 of the Contempt of Court Act 1981 and the various journalistic and PCC codes would provide him with legal protection; he found out, however, that these did not provide any definite guidelines on the obligation not to disclose journalistic sources for sensitive documents and information.[125]

Does present contempt law contravene human rights' freedom of expression? In *Goodwin v UK* (2002),[126] the applicant, Bill Goodwin, a trainee journalist with *The Engineer* magazine, complained of a violation of Article 10 of the Convention. Goodwin had received information regarding the financial status of a company. The information, leaked from a confidential corporate plan, was provided over the telephone from a source who wished to remain anonymous. The company obtained orders preventing Mr Goodwin from disclosing the confidential information under section 10 Contempt of Court Act 1981. The court order then compelled Mr Goodwin to divulge the identity of his source; he unsuccessfully appealed to both the Court of Appeal and the House of Lords. After the journalist continued to refuse to disclose his source he was convicted of contempt and fined £5,000. Bill Goodwin learnt that he had no legal right to protect the source of his story.

When Mr Goodwin sought redress at the ECtHR, the Strasbourg Court commented that it would be difficult to frame the law in this area with absolute clarity and that section 10 CCA 1981 was sufficiently clear (‘*acte clair*’) to satisfy the requirement of foreseeability. The ECtHR ruled that the order for disclosure of the source had not been necessary. This meant that the company's legitimate expectation for disclosure of the source (presumably an employee) and dissemination of the confidential information were outweighed by the interest of a free press (Article 10) in a democratic society.

The *Goodwin* judgment is a significant decision on the protection of journalists' sources. However, the section 10 CCA balancing test still leaves the courts to decide whether or not to make an order requiring a journalist to identify his sources. If journalists are forced to reveal their sources the role of the press as public watchdog could be seriously undermined because of the chilling effect that such disclosure would have on the free flow of information (see also: *Ashworth Hospital v MGN Ltd* (2001)[127]).

In *Financial Times Ltd v UK* (2010)[128] the applicants, four newspapers and an international news agency, had published confidential information relating to a possible takeover bid by Interbrew.[129] The applicants argued that disclosure could lead to identification of a journalistic source (X) and breach Article 10 ECHR. The Court of Appeal had previously upheld a High Court order in 2002 that the applicants were to disclose certain leaked documents to Interbrew.[130] The Strasbourg Human Rights Court held that:

(i)   the disclosure order constituted an interference with the applicants' freedom of expression under Article 10;

---

125 See: ‘A source of great regret’, by Peter Preston, *Guardian*, 5 September 2005.
126 (2002) 35 EHRR 18 (ECtHR).
127 [2001] 1 WLR 515 (CA Civ Div).
128 *Financial Times Ltd v United Kingdom* (821/03) [2010] EMLR 21 (ECHR).
129 Interbrew was a large Belgium-based brewing company which owned many internationally known beers, as well as some smaller local beers. In 2004, Interbrew merged with the Brazilian brewery AmBev to form InBev which at the time became the largest brewer in the world by volume, with a 13 per cent global market share. In 2008, InBev further merged with American brewer Anheuser-Busch to form Anheuser-Busch InBev (‘AB InBev’).
130 See: *Interbrew SA v Financial Times* [2002] EWCA Civ 274.

(ii) the interference authorized by a common law principle[131] and section 10 of the Contempt of Court Act 1981 was prescribed by law and pursued the legitimate aims of protecting the rights of others and preventing the disclosure of information received in confidence;

(iii) X's alleged harmful intent and the doubts surrounding the authenticity of the leaked document were not important factors as neither had been ascertained with the necessary degree of legal certainty in the legal proceedings against the applicants; that ordering disclosure to prevent further leaks would only be justified in exceptional circumstances where no reasonable and less invasive alternative means were available to discover the source; that a chilling effect would arise wherever journalists are seen to assist in the identification of anonymous sources; that Interbrew's interests in eliminating, by proceedings against X, the threat of damage through future dissemination of confidential information and in obtaining damages for past breaches of confidence were insufficient to outweigh the public interest in the protection of journalists' sources.

For decades journalists have depended on members of the public and to a large extent on police and prison staff 'whistleblowers' for the supply of information of public interest. Generally these sources are happy to be quoted in the media. There are times, however, where sources need to be kept secret and protected for their own safety when the information they have provided is of a secret or highly sensitive nature. Anonymity then becomes a precondition for the source's willingness to speak for fear of retaliation if their names are made public. International courts and mechanisms have been mindful that much important information would never reach the public if journalists were unable to guarantee confidentiality to their sources.

Costigan (2007) has suggested it would be helpful if the UK Director of Public Prosecutions (DPP) could produce guidelines setting out when journalists must reveal their sources.[132] This is in addition to the statement issued by the Organization for Security and Co-operation in Europe (OSCE) in its Vienna meeting in 2013 that:

> Journalists . . . are free to seek access to and maintain contacts with, public and private sources of information and that their need for professional confidentiality is respected.[133]

 FOR THOUGHT

Is a court order for journalistic source disclosure necessary in a democratic society for the protection of the rights of an individual or a company? Discuss with reference to legislation and leading authorities.

6.7 Online and social media advertising

Advertisers can reach consumers with laser-like precision. An energy-drink company may target ads at parents of teenage athletes; a retailer can market goods to people from specific neighbourhoods who have visited its website. As a result Facebook claimed 19 per cent and Google 35 per cent of the

131 Norwich Pharmacal Co. v Customs and Excise Commissioners [1974] AC 133 (HL).
132 For further discussion see: Costigan, R. (2007).
133 Source: (OSCE) The Representative on Freedom of the Media (2013) Joint Declarations of the representatives of intergovernmental bodies to protect free media and expression, Vienna, at: www.osce.org/fom/99558?download=true.

$70 billion spent on mobile advertising worldwide in 2015, according to *eMarketer*, a research firm. Twitter and Yahoo had to make do with just 2.5 per cent and 1.5 per cent, respectively.[134]

In 2015 Google banned almost 800 million (780 million) 'bad' adverts from its online ad networks as the web giant continued its crackdown on advertising fraud. This was an increase of almost 50 per cent on 2014 when Google disabled 524 million 'bad ads' and banned 214,000 advertisers.[135] The move comes amid rising scrutiny by advertisers of the actual efficacy of campaigns run across Google's networks, including those that carry malware, promote fake goods or weight-loss scams, or phishing for personal information by financial fraudsters.

Sridhar Ramaswamy, Senior Vice President of Advertising and Commerce at Google, provided some specific figures about Google's 'bad ads' crackdown in 2015. For example, the company stopped showing ads on more than 25,000 mobile apps because of policy violations; it rejected more than 1.4 million applications from website and app developers who wanted to run Google ads but not follow policies. Over 17 million ads were rejected because they either misled or tricked people into clicking on them, such as system warnings. More than 10,000 sites and 18,000 accounts were suspended for trying to sell counterfeit goods. More than 12.5 million ads were blocked for breaking Google's rules on promoting healthcare and medical products. Nearly 7,000 sites were blocked for phishing for web-users' personal information. More than 10,000 sites offering unwanted software were disabled.[136]

Facebook has more data about more users than almost any other company in history. It has used that advantage to become one of the most powerful forces in the advertising business. Its revenues have more than doubled in two years, to $18 billion in 2015. In 2015, Facebook's advertising revenues were eight times greater than Twitter's, largely because it has more users who spend more time generating more data. And this stability allowed Mark Zuckerberg to devote more time and money to working out a suitable format for mobile advertising.[137]

In its *Adults' Media Use and Attitudes Report* (2014) OFCOM provided detailed statistics about the range of online users and the range of devices used, especially by older adults. Over eight out of ten (83 per cent) adults now go online using any type of device in any location. Nearly all 16–24s and 25–34s are now online (98 per cent), and there was a nine percentage point increase in those aged 65+ ever going online (42 per cent in 2013 against 33 per cent in 2012). The number of adults using tablets to go online has almost doubled; from 16 per cent in 2012 to 30 per cent in 2013. While almost all age groups are more likely than previously to use tablets in this way, use by those aged 35–64 has doubled, while use by 65–74s has trebled; from 5 per cent to 17 per cent. Six out of ten UK adults (62 per cent) now use a smartphone, an increase from 54 per cent in 2012. This increase was driven by 25–34s and 45–54s, and those aged 65–74 are almost twice as likely to use a smartphone now compared to 2012 (20 per cent against 12 per cent).[138]

Online vloggers[139] and YouTube 'stars' have emerged as the newest celebrities of the digital age, commanding vast numbers of followers and enjoying ever-broader media profiles. Zoella[140] and Alfie Deyes[141] have enormous audiences, where their fans look to them for recommendations on

---

134 Source: 'How to win friends and influence people', *The Economist*, 9 April 2016, pp. 19–22.

135 Source: Blog post by Vikaram Gupta, Google Director, Ads Engineering, 3 February 2015 at: http://adwords.blogspot.co.uk/2015/02/fighting-bad-advertising-practices-on.html.

136 Source: Blog post 'how we fought bad ads in 2015', by Sridhar Ramaswamy, 21 January 2016 at: https://googleblog.blogspot.co.uk/2016/01/better-ads-report.html.

137 Source: *The Economist*, 9 April 2016, pp. 19–22.

138 Source: Office of Communications (Ofcom) (2014) Adults' Media Use and Attitudes Report April 2014: http://stakeholders.ofcom.org.uk/binaries/research/media-literacy/adults-2014/2014_Adults_report.pdf.

139 Vloggers are people who film themselves talking to camera whilst doing all sorts of stuff, such as make-up, and then put the films up on their YouTube channel. Vlog entries often combine embedded video (or a video link) with supporting text, images, metadata and advertising.

140 Zoe Elizabeth Sugg (aka 'Zoella') is an English fashion and beauty vlogger, YouTuber, and author, including items such as 'I'm definitely a Cadburys & Thorntons girl', and advertising brands such as Selfridges, Estee Lauder, Jo Malone and Lancôme.

141 Alfie Deyes is an English YouTuber and author who runs the YouTube channels PointlessBlog, PointlessBlogVlogs and PointlessBlogGames. Since 2014 he has released three books in his Pointless Book series. Alfie's vlog entries include: 'The disgusting tube challenge'; Halloween costume ideas; the free pizza challenge: www.youtube.com/user/PointlessBlogTv.

what to buy, such as make-up and clothes. These vloggers are invariably sponsored by brands, a surreptitious form of advertising and marketing of specific brands. In the US, YouTubers Shane Dawson, Cameron Dallas, Grace Helbig and Hannah Hart have appeared in films that, when released straight onto iTunes, have outsold some high-profile movies from Hollywood studios. Word-of-mouth has long been an influencer over purchasing decisions and marketing – this has increased substantially with internet recommendations.

Vlogging target audiences tend to be 16–24-year-olds. A study by Global Web Index (GWI) (2015), based on its ongoing survey of more than 170,000 internet users, suggests that fans of vloggers like Zoella, Alfie Deyes and Tyler Oakley look to them more for entertainment and life advice as well as buying new products and brands. According to GWI, 42 per cent of 25–34-year-olds reported using a vlog at least once a month; this rose to 50 per cent for 16–24-year-olds in November 2015.[142]

YouTube star Felix 'PewDiePie' Kjellberg[143] had 40 million fans in 2014; his videos were watched nearly 4.1 billion times and according to documents filed in the Brighton-based Swede's homeland, the 25-year-old earned $7.4 million (£4.8 million). He published *This Book Loves You* with Penguin Random House and was a guest on the high-profile US TV show *The Late Show with Stephen Colbert*.

Vlogging stars have other powerful influences, from Zoella speaking out about panic attacks and anxiety to Tyler Oakley's work with a charity specializing in the prevention of suicide in LGBTQ (lesbian, gay, bisexual, trans and queer) young people. Their cultural influence may well outweigh their commercial influence.

The question pertinent to our chapter on advertising regulation is: who regulates the vloggers and YouTubers whose content contains advertising and brand promotion? It ought to be made clear upfront as part of the vlog that an advertiser has paid for and has editorial control over content produced by a third party, in this case the vlogger's YouTube videos. It is important – particularly for a vulnerable teenage audience – that a brand is being marketed so that the audience can make informed decisions about what they are being told and sold. But many of the YouTube vlogs appear in a format which looks non-promotional. This then amounts to unfair marketing by falsely promoting a product.

One such example can be seen in the Advertising Standards Authority's (ASA) ruling against Mondelez UK Ltd. This involved five YouTube videos, presented by vloggers, who encouraged viewers to participate in a 'Lick Race' challenge in which people competed to lick cream off an Oreo biscuit as quickly as possible. The ASA found that the videos did not clearly indicate that there was a commercial relationship between the advertiser and the vloggers. The ads were on online video channels which were – at that time – regarded as non-promotional. The ASA found that the commercial intent should have been made clear before viewers clicked on the content. The ads breached CAP Code (Edition 12) rules 2.1 and 2.4 (Recognition of marketing communications). The ruling held that the advertisements could no longer appear again in their current format. Mondelez UK Ltd (based in Uxbridge, UK) had to ensure that future ads in the YouTube medium had to make the commercial intent clear prior to consumer engagement.[144]

See below 6.9

It is then perfectly legitimate for vloggers (or bloggers, tweeters, etc.) to enter into a commercial relationship and be paid to promote a product, service or brand, for which they will be earning income. But as soon as a commercial relationship is in place the onus is on the advertiser, and by

142 Source: GWI trends 2015 at: https://app.globalwebindex.net/products/report/gwi-vloggers-trend-report-q1-2015.
143 Felix Arvid Ulf Kjellberg, better known by his online alias PewDiePie, is a Swedish web-based comedian and producer, best known for his 'Let's Play' commentaries and vlogs on YouTube.
144 ASA Ruling on Mondelez UK Ltd, 26 November 2014. Complaint Ref: A14-275018.

extension the vlogger, to be upfront about the commercial relationship and clearly disclose the fact that they are advertising at the start of each video clip or blog.

 FOR THOUGHT

Payday loans,[145] including their advertising, have given rise to much public concern. Should scheduling restrictions on television advertising be introduced? Scheduling restrictions, such as the pre-9pm ban, are some of the best-known restrictions on advertising in the UK. Discuss and consider this proposal in the light of UK regulators such as ASA and Ofcom.

6.8 EU regulatory framework on advertising and marketing

An important element of the European Union's Single Market is advertising and marketing. Self-regulation in advertising exists in most EU Member States and takes widely varying forms in different countries. The underlying ethos however should have a common aim: advertising should be legal, decent, honest and truthful; it should be prepared with a due sense of responsibility to the consumer and society and with respect for the principles of fair competition. For example it is a criminal offence if an advertisement is misleading. Regulation 3(1) of the Business Protection from Misleading Marketing Regulations 2008 states that advertising which is misleading is 'prohibited' and regulation 3(2) defines as misleading advertising which:

(a) in any way, including its presentation, deceives or is likely to deceive the traders to whom it is addressed or whom it reaches; and by reason of its deceptive nature, is likely to affect their economic behaviour; or

(b) for those reasons, injures or is likely to injure a competitor.

A trader is guilty of an offence if he engages in advertising which is misleading under regulation 3.[146]

Although advertising is largely self-regulatory in most EU countries there exists now some legislation and set codes of practice for broadcast and non-broadcast advertising content. In the UK the principal regulator is the Advertising Standards Authority (ASA).

The EU's Single Market provides growth for businesses and creates new jobs and all EU policies and business strategies are geared towards this objective. Whilst marketing and advertising are key elements of any business strategy it is expected that such practices are truthful in their communication, particularly where vulnerable individuals, children or young people are concerned: they need to be protected against misleading advertising or marketing practices. The EU Commission has set out a clear and efficient framework safeguarding fair competition and providing effective means to enforce it. Such provisions have created a necessary regulatory framework in business-to-business marketing where companies enjoy a high degree of contractual freedom.

---

145 High-cost short-term credit (HCSTC), a category of product more commonly referred to as payday loans.
146 Reg 6 Business Protection from Misleading Marketing Regulations 2008.

Since the 'Television Without Frontiers Directive' (TVWF)[147] came into force in 1989, the international audiovisual landscape has changed significantly with the impact of technological developments in the information society. New players and platforms have emerged, boosting or requiring more content production for emerging markets. EU law now covers services delivered over the internet in order to combat internet piracy, copyright infringement and to monitor mass-market advertising on TV and the internet in the 'pay per click' society. Articles 10 and 11 of the Unfair Commercial Practices Directive (2005/29/EC)[148] allow for self-regulation to play an active and complementary role in combating unfair commercial practices and in making sure standards of professional diligence are upheld.

See Chapter 5.6

Since its inception the Audiovisual Media Services Directive (2010/13/EU) (AVMSD) has explicitly encouraged all 28 EU Member States to recognize that self-regulatory systems can complement and operate effectively within the general legal framework. Many of the new Member States were quick to appreciate the benefits of self-regulation in advertising and consumer marketing. The important role of self-regulation is laid down in the *Blue Book*, a detailed analysis of the advertising self-regulatory systems and bodies in place in Europe, produced by the European Advertising Standards Alliance (EASA) (see below).

6.8.1 The European Advertising Standards Alliance

Advertising and marketing campaigns now cross national boundaries. The European Advertising Standards Alliance (EASA), founded in 1992 and based in Brussels, brings together national advertising self-regulatory bodies and organizations representing the advertising industry in Europe. The EASA comprises around 130 representatives from all sectors of the advertising industry under one charter, based on a 'Statement of Common Principles and Operating Standards of Best Practice', and represents some 20 countries. The Alliance operates a cross-border complaints procedure, known as the *Blue Book*.[149]

The EASA ensures best practice in advertising standards across Europe. It has achieved this aim through the application of its Self-Regulation Charter and recommendations which set out a detailed framework model for effective self-regulation. This model was used as the benchmark for the EU Advertising Roundtable discussions on advertising self-regulation in 2015. The EASA Code of Practice encourages best practice and provides a mechanism for dealing with cross-border complaints.[150]

Additionally, the International Council on Ad Self-Regulation (ICAS) publishes an international guide to developing a self-regulatory organization as a tool to provide support in the development of advertising self-regulation at a global level. The EASA and ICAS are globally recognized as a form of best practice regulators with support from the World Federation of Advertisers and the International Advertising Association.[151]

---

147 EU Directive 89/552 EEC on Transfrontier Television 'Television without Frontiers Directive' (TVWF). The 'sans frontières' Directive was replaced by the 'Audio Visual Media Services Directive' (AVMSD) EC Directive 2007/65 'Audiovisual Media Services Directive' (AVMSD) amended EU Directive 89/552/EEC 'Television without Frontiers Directive' (TVWF) and includes the pursuit of television broadcasting activities including on-demand services of 11 December 2007.

148 Directive 2005/29/EC of the European Parliament and the Council of 11 May 2005 concerning unfair business-to-consumer commercial practices in the internal market and amending Council Directive 84/450/EEC, Directives 97/7/EC, 98/27/EC and 2002/65/EC of the European Parliament and of the Council and Regulation (EC) No 2006/2004 of the European Parliament and of the Council ('Unfair Commercial Practices Directive').

149 See: European Advertising Standards Alliance (EASA) *Blue Book*, 6th edn.

150 The EASA website offers further information on the EASA network, advertising standards, self-regulatory (SR) systems, industry members and the Blue Book, available at www.easa-alliance.org.

151 See: International Council on Ad Self-Regulation (ICAS) (2014) International Guide to Developing a Self-Regulatory Organisation. Practical advice on setting up and consolidating an advertising self-regulatory system at: www.easa-alliance.org/binarydata. aspx?type=doc&sessionId=01t3ij45ynsqkb55pqbyot55/EASA_International_Guide_Self-Regulatory_Organisation_2014.pdf.

6.8.2 Codes and sanctions

Each country's advertising regulators will typically receive complaints from members of the general public and the country-specific regulator will then apply the code of practice in order to make a finding, for instance if the advertisement breached unfair competition or indecency rules. The regulator will then investigate the ad by calling on its jury or complaints committee, generally a body responsible for authoritative interpretations of the code. In some systems (particularly in newly created ones) all complaints are usually referred to a jury. If the jury or committee determine a code violation, then the complaint is upheld and the regulator decides on the appropriate action to be taken. Noteworthy is that in the self-regulatory advertising system the burden of proof lies with the advertiser whose advertisement is complained about rather than the complainant. This means that the advertiser has to prove that the claims in the advertisement are true. The advantage of self-regulation and such adjudications complaints is that they are dealt with speedily, generally within two months.

Unlike a statutory regulator (such as OFCOM) advertising self-regulators do not have the power to issue fines. But an adjudication which finds a breach of the code will generally request an immediate amendment of or a withdrawal of the ad. This in itself is costly to the advertising agency and often results in a greater deterrent than a fine. Additionally, jury or regulators' decisions are published and this 'naming and shaming' practice may well result in adverse publicity, which, in turn, can have a negative impact on brand reputation. The consumer is then informed when irresponsible advertising is being practised and this can act as a deterrent to other advertisers and marketing agencies.[152]

6.9 Advertising in the UK

Advertising is generally self-regulated, though at times some ads are close to bribery so that the police have to get involved. In May 2016 the Met Police were investigating a complaint from the 'Vote Leave' campaign in advance of the EU Referendum that a Ryanair advertisement, offering cheap flights to expats who wanted to vote to remain in the EU breached bribery laws. The Ryanair 'Brexit Special' told overseas voters they could 'fly home to vote "remain"' from €19.99 on the day of the referendum, 23 June 2016, or the day before, 22 June. Vote Leave campaign director Dominic Cummings described the offer as 'corrupt' and alleged it broke referendum rules and section 1 of the Bribery Act 2010. Ryanair owner Michael O'Leary, a prominent backer of the 'Remain' campaign, called the complaint 'desperate' and in response extended the airline's offer by a further 24 hours.[153]

In February 2015, *The Daily Telegraph*'s chief political commentator and associate editor of the *Spectator*, Peter Oborne, resigned 'as a matter of conscience'. From the start of 2013 the *Telegraph* investigations team had begun to report on tax evasion schemes and accounts held with HSBC in Jersey. The HSBC bank then suspended its advertising with the *Telegraph* and winning back the HSBC advertising account became an urgent priority for the Barclay brothers, Sir David and Sir Frederick Barclay, the reclusive multi-millionaire owners of London's Ritz Hotel and the *Telegraph* group.

Journalist Peter Oborne told the *Guardian* that from that moment onwards stories critical of HSBC were discouraged by the *Telegraph*. Mr Oborne said interference by management in stories involving the bank was happening 'on an industrial scale' and called the *Telegraph*'s (ceased) coverage of HSBC 'a form of fraud on its readers', claiming the paper deliberately suppressed stories about

---

152 For further discussion on country-specific advertising regulation see: Jordan, P. (2014).
153 Source: 'Ryanair's EU referendum ad investigated by police', by John Plunkett, *The Guardian*, 20 May 2016.

the banking giant. This included revelations that HSBC's Swiss subsidiary helped wealthy customers dodge taxes and conceal millions of dollars in assets, in order to keep its valuable advertising account. Oborne alleged the traditional distinction between the advertising and editorial departments had collapsed and went further in claiming that there was a pattern emerging that could be seen elsewhere in the paper's reporting, including its coverage of student protests in Hong Kong in 2014.[154]

The HSBC story had broken at the beginning of February 2015 after an enormous cache of leaked secret bank account files had been obtained through an international collaboration of news outlets, including the Guardian, the French daily Le Monde, BBC Panorama and the Washington-based International Consortium of Investigative Journalists. A team of journalists from 45 countries had unearthed secret bank accounts maintained for criminals, traffickers, tax 'dodgers', politicians and celebrities. The secret documents indicated that global banking giant HSBC profited from doing business with arms dealers who channelled mortar bombs to child soldiers in Africa, bag men for Third World dictators, traffickers in blood diamonds and other international outlaws.[155] The various news outlets reported that HSBC's Swiss banking arm had helped wealthy customers evade taxes and conceal millions of dollars of assets, handing out bundles of untraceable cash and advising clients on how to circumvent domestic tax authorities.[156]

Following the Telegraph's editorial warning to 'ease off' on HSBC stories in order to regain advertising from the bank, the UK's largest commercial radio group, Global Radio, advised its stations, which include Classic FM, Capital, Heart, Smooth, Xfm, Gold and LBC, to drop the HSBC tax story on the morning of 9 February 2015, the day the story broke, for 'editorial reasons'. Global, which broadcasts to about 23 million listeners a week, advised its stations not to run reports about the banking giant after it was revealed that the bank's Swiss subsidiary helped wealthy customers store assets offshore in an unaccountable way. Coverage of the story was then resumed by the stations 'some days later', according to an inquiry by media regulator Ofcom when this story was first revealed in Private Eye.

During his speech for the departing editor of The Guardian, Alan Rusbridger, Ian Hislop, editor of the Eye, made sure he commented on the HSBC tax scandal, accusing the Telegraph of running reduced coverage of the story out of fear of losing advertising revenue. Hislop pointed out that no such allegations should be levelled at Private Eye:

> I can make this point about advertising, Private Eye has a distinguished history here. When I first joined the paper the advertising staff were very excited because they had a set of full page adverts from Linguaphone, and said 'can we have this facing copy?' and I said I'm not sure you want this, and they said no they'd like it facing copy so Paul Foot wrote a page about what a rip off Linguaphone was. We then topped this, we got a set of adverts from Virgin Atlantic and again they were facing copy. This was during Branson's hot air phase, and we did a picture of a balloon with Branson underneath it with the phrase 'you've got to be careful putting pricks near balloons'.[157]

154 Source: 'Telegraph's Peter Oborne resigns, saying HSBC coverage a "fraud on readers"', by John Plunkett and Ben Quinn, The Guardian, 18 February 2015.

155 Source: 'Banking Giant HSBC Sheltered Murky Cash Linked to Dictators and Arms Dealers', by Gerard Ryle, Will Fitzgibbon, Mar Cabra, Rigoberto Carvajal, Marina Walker Guevara, Martha M. Hamilton and Tom Stites, The International Consortium of Investigative Journalists (ICIJ), 8 February 2015: www.icij.org/project/swiss-leaks/banking-giant-hsbc-sheltered-murky-cash-linked-dictators-and-arms-dealers.

156 Source: 'HSBC files show how Swiss bank helped clients dodge taxes and hide millions', by David Leigh, James Ball, Juliette Garside and David Pegg, The Guardian, 8 February 2015.

157 Source: 'Paul Foot Award 2014: Private Eye wades in on HSBC scandal', by 'Steerpike', The Spectator, 25 February 2015.

FOR THOUGHT

Was it right for the editor and publishers of the *Daily Telegraph* and Global Radio to make the decision to suppress stories about the banking giant HSBC in February 2015 in favour of regaining advertising revenue? What does this say about a journalist's, like Peter Oborne's, Article 10 ECHR right? Discuss.

6.9.1 The Advertising Standards Authority

See Chapter 5.5

The Advertising Standards Authority (ASA) is the UK's independent self-regulator of advertising across all media. The ASA applies the Advertising Codes, which are written by the Committees of Advertising Practice (known as 'the CAP Code'). The regulator's work includes acting on complaints and proactively checking the media to take action against misleading, harmful or offensive advertisements. The ASA is an independent body of 13 directors, chaired by Lord Smith of Finsbury; two-thirds of committee members are drawn from outside the advertising industry. The work of the ASA is held in high regard by government and other regulators, such as Ofcom.

The ASA is funded by advertisers through an arm's length arrangement that guarantees the ASA's independence. Collected by the Advertising Standards Board of Finance (Asbof) and the Broadcast Advertising Standards Board of Finance (Basbof), the 0.1 per cent levy on the cost of buying advertising space and the 0.2 per cent levy on some direct mail ensure the ASA is adequately funded to keep UK advertising standards high. The regulator also receives a small income from charging for some seminars and premium industry advice services. The separate funding mechanism ensures that the ASA does not know which advertisers choose to fund the system or the amount they contribute. The levy is the only part of the system that is voluntary. Advertisers can choose to pay the levy, but they cannot choose to comply with the Advertising Codes or the ASA's rulings.

The ASA responds to approximately 31,000 complaints each year. It reviews the advertisement against the CAP Code and, if it decides to uphold the complaint, takes up the matter with the advertiser. In the majority of cases the advertiser amends or withdraws the ad. If it refuses, the ASA has a range of sanctions it can apply (though these are not statutory). The ASA also proactively conducts compliance surveys in various sectors, particularly those of public concern.

In July 2015 a TV ad for L'Oréal Paris 'Age Perfect' moisturizing cream featuring Helen Mirren attracted a large number of complaints, claiming that the 69-year-old actress's appearance was digitally retouched. The advert showed Mirren being offered a seat at a bus stop and looking unhappy, while her voiceover said 'Ever feel like you go unnoticed? And when you aren't, well, enough.' During the voiceover there were several close-ups of Mirren's face and, towards the end of the ad, she was shown dressed in a leather jacket and bold makeup, and glancing at a younger man. A further press ad featured an image of Mirren's face with a quote from her that stated 'Age is just a number and maths was never my thing!' with added text stating: 'Age spots appear reduced. Skin feels nourished with moisture. Complexion looks more radiant.'

The ASA investigated the ads under the rules regarding misleading advertising, substantiation and exaggeration and invited a response from L'Oréal.[158] They provided four images of Ms Mirren from recent red carpet events and said the images of her in the ads were entirely in line with such public appearances when she had been professionally styled and made up. L'Oréal said the lines around her mouth were consistent in both the ads and the red carpet photos and that no

---

158 The ASA investigated the first advert under BCAP Code rules 3.1 ('misleading advertising'), 3.9 ('substantiation') and 3.12 ('exaggeration'), and the second ad under CAP Code (Edition 12) rules 3.1 ('misleading advertising'), 3.7 ('substantiation') and 3.11 ('exaggeration').

post-production changes had been made to Mirren's face in the TV ad. The ASA concluded that the ads had not altered Helen Mirren's appearance in a way that would exaggerate the likely effect that could be achieved by consumers' use of the product, and concluded that the ads were not misleading. The complaint was not upheld.[159]

6.9.2 Advertising codes and standards

The UK advertising industry is committed to self-regulation for advertising. The requirement for advertising is that it is 'legal, decent, honest and truthful'. Detailed rules setting out what this means in practice have been drawn up by the Committee of Advertising Practice (CAP) and are known as the Advertising Code or CAP Code.[160] The CAP Code – the essential rulebook for the advertising industry – is monitored and enforced by the ASA and its Code Committee.[161]

The Code lays down rules for advertisers and media owners. The Code is primarily concerned with the content of marketing communications and not with terms of business or products themselves. Some rules, however, go beyond content; for example, those that cover the administration of sales promotions, the suitability of promotional items, the delivery of products ordered through an advertisement and the use of personal information in direct marketing. Editorial content is specifically excluded from the Code, though it might be a factor in determining the context in which marketing communications are judged. The main aim of the CAP Code is that advertisements must not mislead or be unfair. There are specific rules that cover advertising to children, and adverts for alcohol, gambling, motoring, health and financial products.

The CAP Code applies to:

a. advertisements in newspapers, magazines, brochures, leaflets, circulars, mailings, emails, text transmissions (including SMS and MMS), fax transmissions, catalogues, follow-up literature and other electronic or printed material;
b. posters and other promotional media in public places, including moving images;
c. cinema, video, DVD and Blu-ray advertisements;
d. advertisements in non-broadcast electronic media, including but not limited to: online advertisements in paid-for space (including banner or pop-up advertisements and online video advertisements); paid-for search listings; preferential listings on price comparison sites; viral advertisements; in-game advertisements; commercial classified advertisements; advertgames that feature in display advertisements; advertisements transmitted by Bluetooth; advertisements distributed through web widgets and online sales promotions and prize promotions;
e. marketing databases containing consumers' personal information;
f. sales promotions in non-broadcast media;
g. advertorials;
h. advertisements and other marketing communications by or from companies, organizations or sole traders on their own websites, or in other non-paid-for space online under their control, that are directly connected with the supply or transfer

159 ASA Ruling on L'Oréal (UK) Ltd, 8 July 2015, Complaint Ref: A15-297452.
160 For a comprehensive list of legislation covering UK advertising see CAP – ASA at: www.cap.org.uk/Advertising-Codes/~/media/Files/CAP/Misc/Legislation%20affecting%20advertising.ashx.
161 See: The CAP Code 'The UK Code of Non-broadcast Advertising, Sales Promotion and Direct Marketing', 12th edition at: www.cap.org.uk/Advertising-Codes/~/media/Files/CAP/Codes%20CAP%20pdf/The%20CAP%20Code.ashx.

of goods, services, opportunities and gifts, or which consist of direct solicitations of donations as part of their own fund-raising activities.

The CAP Code does *not* apply to:

a. broadcast advertisements (the BCAP Code sets out the rules that govern broadcast advertisements on any television channel or radio station licensed by Ofcom) (see below);

b. the contents of premium rate services, which are the responsibility of PhonepayPlus; marketing communications that promote those services are subject to Phonepay-Plus regulation and to the CAP Code;

c. marketing communications in foreign media. Direct marketing communications that originate outside the UK and sales promotions and marketing communications on non-UK websites, if targeted at UK consumers, are subject to the jurisdiction of the relevant authority in the country from which they originate if that authority operates a suitable cross-border complaint system;

d. claims, in marketing communications in media addressed only to medical, dental, veterinary or allied practitioners, that relate to those practitioners' expertise;

e. classified private advertisements, including online;

f. statutory, public, police and other official notices or information, but not marketing communications, produced by public authorities;

g. works of art exhibited in public or private;

h. private correspondence, including correspondence between organizations and their customers about existing relationships or past purchases;

i. live oral communications, including telephone calls and announcements or direct approaches from street marketers;

j. press releases and public relations material;

k. editorial content (e.g. news media or books and regular competitions such as crosswords);

l. flyposting (most of which is illegal);

m. packages, wrappers, labels, tickets, timetables and price lists unless they advertise another product or a sales promotion or are visible in a marketing communication;

n. point-of-sale displays, except those covered by the sales promotion rules or the rolling paper and filter rules;

o. political advertisements;

p. marketing communications for causes and ideas in non-paid-for space, except where they contain a direct solicitation for donations as part of the marketer's own fund-raising activities;

q. website content not covered by d and h, including (but not limited to) editorial content, news or public relations material, corporate reports and natural listings on a search engine or a price comparison site;

r. sponsorship (but marketing communications that refer to sponsorship are covered by the Code);

s. customer charters and codes of practice;

t. investor relations;

u. 'heritage advertising' by or from companies, organizations or sole traders on their own websites, or in other non-paid-for space online under their control, where that advertising is not part of their current promotional strategy and is placed in an appropriate context.

See Chapter 5

The fact that a marketing communication complies with the CAP Code does not guarantee that every publisher will accept it. Media owners can refuse space to marketing communications that break the Code and are not obliged to publish every marketing communication offered to them.

6.9.3 Examples of ASA rulings

Each year, the UK public sees millions of ads, direct marketing and sales promotions about products, services, causes and awareness campaigns. The vast majority of ads comply with the advertising rules. In 2015, the ASA dealt with 31,136 complaints, investigating concerns about ads which allegedly breached the rules of the codes.

As a result, some 4,161 ads were changed or withdrawn.

Sexualized imagery remains one of the most complained about areas in advertising, where the brand owners hope to entice consumers to buy their products, such as Wonderbra with its iconic billboard ad, 'Hello Boys',[162] which built global awareness and drove huge sales on the back of 'nudge-and-wink' imagery. Now, digital channels and social networking communications can be accessed by everyone and the role of the regulator becomes even more crucial.

Sex sells, such as Calvin Klein's ad-campaign featuring racy images overlaid with 'sexting' messages (#mycalvins). New York shots by Mario Sorrenti feature sultry photos overlaid with sexy text messages about threesomes, nude photos and cheating on one's partner. The tagline is: 'Raw texts, real stories', and fine print says the chats are 'inspired by actual events and people'. Tweeters commented on the ads more than 122,000 times worldwide in one day.[163]

The infamous Protein World 'beach body ready' ads caused public outcries but the brand reported £1 million additional revenue over the first four days of the advert going 'viral' (see below). The US brand Groupon seemingly innocently played social media ads containing sexual innuendo around its phallic-looking 'Banana Bunker' product.[164] This resulted in 40,000 YouTube views on the first day increasing revenue for the brand.

Anyone can complain to the ASA free of charge and its self-regulatory value is founded on EC Directives, including those on misleading and comparative advertising.[165] The regulator also watches over product placement in TV productions, sales promotions, direct marketing and online advertisements in the UK. Sanctions include stopping misleading, harmful or offensive advertising, ensuring that sales promotions are run fairly, and reducing unwanted commercial mail (by post, email or SMS) in conjunction with the Information Commissioner's Office. The advertising watchdog also resolves problems with mail-order purchases. The ASA publishes weekly rulings on its website. Decisions are subject to independent review by the Administrative Division of the High Court.

The ASA blacklists traders who continue to make claims on their websites that do not comply with the UK Advertising Code despite repeated requests for changes from the ASA compliance team. Details of each non-conforming trader remain in place until they have appropriately amended their marketing in line with the CAP Code, at which point they are removed.[166]

Ofcom acts as a backstop regulator, which means the ASA can refer cases to Ofcom if advertising continues to appear despite an ASA adjudication against it. Ofcom can then take immediate action on serious breaches of the ASA rules, for instance by using its statutory powers to order the immediate suspension of an advertisement accompanied by a fine. Not all video-on-demand

---

162 Source: '"Hello Boys" Billboard Voted Most Iconic Advert Image Of All Time', by Ruth Doherty, *Huffington Post*, 31 March 2011.
163 Source: 'Calvin Klein Embraces Sexting and Tinder in Racy Campaign About Digital Dating "Conversation through provocation"', by Tim Nudd, *Adweek*, 30 July 2015: www.adweek.com/adfreak/calvin-klein-embraces-sexting-and-tinder-racy-campaign-about-digital-dating-166186.
164 Source: 'How Groupon turned the Banana Bunker into a social media success', by Hazel Sheffield, *The Independent*, 31 March 2015.
165 Directives 2005/29/EC and 2006/114/EC.
166 For a list of non-compliant advertisers online 2015 see: www.asa.org.uk/Rulings/Non-compliant-online-advertisers.aspx.

See Chapters
5.4 and 5.5

(VOD) advertising is subject to the ASA's regulation, however. Only advertisements on services that are subject to statutory regulation will be affected. Services as defined by the Communications Act 2003 are required to notify the Association for Television on Demand (ATVOD) that they are operating.

 **KEY CASE**   *ASA ruling Mulberry Company (Sales) Ltd (23 December 2015)[167]*

The advert

Forty-two complaints were received in the run-up to Christmas 2015, because the video ad showing a nativity scene had replaced baby Jesus with a Mulberry handbag.

The issue

The ad was offensive to Christians who objected that it undermined central messages of their faith; that the important scene was being used for the purpose of consumerism; and that it was blasphemous, breaching CAP Code 4.1 (Edition 12) ('harm and offence').

Response by Mulberry

Mulberry acknowledged that offence was a subjective concept. They believed the Nativity scene was a recognizable and central concept to British society. As such, they believed it was legitimate and would be seen by its customers with the humour, fun and excitement of Christmas time. They believed the video was a light-hearted reference to the Nativity scene, in keeping with the run-up to Christmas time and the gift of a handbag for a loved one. They believed the comment made by the man – 'Guys, it's just a bag' – made it clear that no comparison with the baby Jesus was intended.

Assessment

Not upheld

The ASA acknowledged that the ad might not be to everyone's taste, but considered most viewers would understand it as a light-hearted take on the Nativity story, intended to poke fun at the effect of consumerism on Christmas rather than mocking or denigrating Christian belief. Because of that, the regulator considered the ad was unlikely to cause serious or widespread offence.

ASA Ruling on Protein World Ltd (1 July 2015)[168]

Three hundred and seventy-eight complaints were received regarding the slimming advert, expressing concerns about weight loss claims on a poster seen on the London Underground network. The ad stated: 'ARE YOU BEACH BODY READY?' and featured an image of a toned and athletic woman wearing a bikini.

The issue

The complainants said the ad was grossly offensive and potentially harmful leading to possible eating disorders in young girls, citing *inter alia* breach of rule 1.3 ('responsible advertising') of the CAP Code (Edition 12). The complainants gave reasons to the ASA that the ad implied that a body shape which differed from the 'idealized' one presented was not good enough or in some way inferior and was, therefore, offensive; and the

---

167 ASA ruling Mulberry Company (Sales) Ltd (created by: Adam & Eve DDB), 23 December 2015. Complaint Ref: A15-317950.
168 ASA Ruling on Protein World Ltd (SourProtein World Ltd, Wallington), 1 July 2015, Complaint Ref: A15-300099.

combination of an image of a very slim, toned body coupled with the headline was socially irresponsible in the context of an ad for a slimming product.

Response
Protein World said that the phrase 'beach body' was a common phrase meaning looking at one's best. The question 'Are you beach body ready?' was intended to invite the viewer to consider whether they were in the shape they wanted to be. The ad featured a model who they said used their products and who they felt had a healthy figure. They did not believe that the ad implied everyone should look like the model or that the text and image were irresponsible.

Assessment

Not upheld

The ASA acknowledged that 'beach body' was a well-understood term with connotations of a toned, athletic physique similar to the image of the model in the ad; additionally that feeling sufficiently comfortable and confident with one's physical appearance to wear swimwear in a public environment. They held the phrase 'ARE YOU BEACH BODY READY?' as prompting readers to think about their summer holidays and whether they were fit enough. The ASA concluded that the headline and image were unlikely to cause serious or widespread offence and therefore the ad was not irresponsible. No further action was necessary.

❖ KEY CASE   *ASA Ruling on London Oktoberfest Ltd (4 November 2015)*[169]

Issue
The complainants challenged whether the ad breached CAP Code (Edition 12) rule 18.16 ('Alcohol') because the 'Heidi' model featured appeared to be under 25 years old. The regional press ad for *London Oktoberfest* of 2 September 2015, featured a young woman in traditional Bavarian dress holding a glass of beer in her outstretched arms, headlined: 'Thursdays "special beer girls" – beautiful "heidies"'.

Response
London Oktoberfest Ltd said at the time the photo was taken, the model featured was 25 years old. They also said that the woman was not drinking but only holding a glass of beer.

Assessment

Upheld

The CAP Code requires people shown drinking alcohol in an ad must neither be, nor seem to be, under 25 years of age. The ASA held that the model featured appeared to be younger than 25 years old and, though she was not drinking, played a significant role. The ad breached CAP Code (Edition 12) rule 18.16 (Alcohol).

Action
London Oktoberfest Ltd had to ensure that the ad must not appear again in its current form.

---

169 ASA Ruling on London Oktoberfest Ltd, Blackburn, 4 November 2015, Complaint Ref: A15-312500.

6.9.4 Regulatory framework for broadcast advertising

The Communications Act 2003 sets out provisions for the regulation of broadcasting and television and radio services, including provisions aimed at securing standards for broadcast advertisements. The most relevant sections of the legislation concern the protection of children and young persons:

- section 319(2)(a) that persons under the age of 18 are protected; and
- section 319(2)(h) that the inclusion of advertising which may be misleading, harmful or offensive in television and radio services is prevented.

Furthermore Article 9(g) of the Audiovisual Media Services Directive (AVMS)[170] provides that:

> audiovisual commercial communications shall not cause physical or moral detriment to minors. Therefore they shall not directly exhort minors to buy or hire a product or service by exploiting their inexperience or credulity, directly encourage them to persuade their parents or others to purchase the goods or services being advertised, exploit the special trust minors place in parents, teachers or other persons, or unreasonably show minors in dangerous situations.

The Broadcast Committee of Advertising Practice (BCAP) is contracted by the communications regulator, Ofcom, to write and enforce the UK Code of Broadcast Advertising ('the BCAP Code'). This means the ASA exercises powers 'contracted-out' by Ofcom, when handling complaints about adverts or product placements on licensed TV and radio services. These include traditional spot advertising, teleshopping output and broadcast advertising made available on interactive TV and TV text services.[171]

The CAP and BCAP codes ensure that no ad directly exhorts children to purchase a product or to ask others to purchase it for them. The ASA takes quick and effective action to tackle any ad that falls foul of this important rule.

The ASA also regulates the scheduling of TV and radio advertisements to ensure that audiences are adequately protected from harmful or offensive material. Generally banned products include cigarettes and other tobacco products, medicinal products, alcoholic drinks, salty foods and gambling services. Where relevant to the particular broadcast media, Ofcom remains responsible for the rules governing:

- the insertion of advertising breaks;
- the amount of advertising permitted on TV;
- sponsorship;
- political advertising on TV and radio; and
- participation TV advertising.

6.9.5 Product placement

Product placement is such big business that it has become an industry of its own, with around $14 billion being paid to shoehorn real-world brands into the fictional worlds we see on screen. Product placement in films such as James Bond's *Skyfall* (for which Heineken paid $45 million) was a blink-and-you'll-miss-it moment, but it was still an iconic moment: James Bond sipped from a Heineken bottle rather than a Martini glass. Subsequently Heineken sold out. In total the Skyfall production made around $200 million in product placement from brands such as Sony, Adidas, Heineken and the usual luxury car brands.

---

170 Directive 2010/13/EU ('Provisions applicable to all Audiovisual Media Services').
171 See: Ofcom Broadcasting Code of May 2016 at: www.ofcom.org.uk/__data/assets/pdf_file/0024/49308/Ofcom-broadcast-code-May-2016.pdf.

The entirety of *Mac and Me* movie (ripping off E.T.) is product placement featuring McDonalds and Coca-Cola. *Wayne's World* included Pizza Hut, Doritos, Reebok, Nuprin and Pepsi.

Nowadays, product placement goes further than a film or TV company paying a channel or programme maker to include its products or brands in their storylines. YouTube thrives on it. For example, a fashion company might pay for a presenter or vlogger to wear its clothes during a screening, or a car manufacturer might feature its latest new car in the form of a drama.

Paid-for product placements can then be described as pieces of content that are created specifically for a third party and/or where that third party's brand, message, or product is integrated directly into the content. Product placement in UK television programmes became 'legal' in February 2011 as long as it complied with Ofcom's rules. These rules apply to all programmes broadcast on channels licensed by Ofcom and some channels that broadcast outside the UK (not including the BBC).

Interactive TV is now an advertisers' dream with formats that tie devices together, click-to-act banner ads on screen and inventory management systems that maximize available ad space relevant to the viewers' market at a particular time of day. Forrester's forecast[172] for the next decade is that European marketers' investments in online display and social media advertising will continue to grow at a double-digit rate. Combined, they will grow at 18.7 per cent annually over that period and reach €28.7 billion in 2020, up from €14.4 billion in 2015. Online display and social media advertising already looks much different today: mobile, video, ad blocking, and programmatic buying will impact how both will develop in the coming years.[173]

General rules on product placement include and allow the following genres:

- films (including single dramas and single documentaries);
- series made for television (this includes serials);
- sports programmes;
- light entertainment programmes.

Product placement is *not* allowed in the following genres:

- news;
- children's programmes.

Additional restrictions for programmes produced or commissioned by a UK broadcaster or with a view to their first showing taking place in the UK:

- religious programmes;
- consumer advice programmes;
- current affairs programmes.

Where a magazine show contains product placement but also includes elements of restricted genre content (e.g. news bulletins/items, consumer affairs strands), broadcasters need to ensure that these elements do not contain, or appear to contain, product placement. It may therefore be

---

172 Forrester (Nasdaq: FORR) is one of the most influential research and advisory firms in the world: www.forrester.com/marketing/about/about-us.html.

173 Source: Forrester Advertising and Market Research Report: 'The European Online Display and Social Media Advertising Forecast, 2015 to 2020 Advertisers Increase their Investments in Video and Mobile Ads as Media Consumption Evolves and Targeting Accuracy Improves', by Samantha Merlivat, Luca S. Paderni, Michael O'Grady, Kasia Madej, Laura Glazer, 9 December 2015.

necessary to conduct such restricted items in an area of the studio that does not contain product placement.

Broadcasters must have adequate procedures in place to ensure advertisements carried by them comply with the BCAP Code. Clearcast and the Radio Advertising Clearance Centre (RACC) are privately contracted by many licensees to provide TV and radio advertisement clearance. The RACC clears radio ads with the top 20 commercial radio advertisers including BT, Asda Stores, British Gas, Morrisons, Vodafone, McDonald's, Homebase and TalkTalk.[174] Clearcast, a commercial 'regulator', is funded by the UK's major commercial broadcasters, such as ITV, Channels 4 and 5 and BskyB.[175] They clear about 65,000 ads each year. For instance, adverts for alcohol should not be targeted at people who are under 18. As a result, they must not be shown at times of the day when children are likely to be watching TV, or during programmes aimed at children (so-called 'timing restrictions').

Due to the dramatic changes in technology and media consumption over the past decade high-quality content is more widely available and accessible to audiences including radio and audio content via apps and podcasts. Consumers of radio and audio content in the UK not only have access to 57 BBC radio stations, but also 340 licensed commercial radio stations and 200 community radio stations, plus around 20,000 radio stations from around the world via the *TuneIn Radio* app. In addition to broadcast radio it is now also possible to access music and speech content on demand in a variety of locations and from a range of different sources, using platforms such as *iTunes* or streaming services like *Spotify* (where you pay a fee of around £10 per month not to receive adverts).

6.9.6 Gaming and betting: online gambling

Online gambling is an emotive subject and one that can polarize public opinion. For some it is a sophisticated and glamorous pastime where vast sums of money can be won and lost. For many it is a mainstream leisure activity, seen as a bit of harmless fun, such as bingo or roulette. There are those, however, who suffer from a gambling addiction which can ruin lives. As the amount of ads has increased, so has the number of complaints to the ASA with an increasing trend since 2011, with gambling cases making up 3.5 per cent of all cases dealt with in 2013 by the ASA.[176]

The ASA received 398 complaints about specific gambling ads in 2014, around half referred to potentially misleading content, and in particular concerns about 'free bets' or other promotional offers. The remaining complaints were divided between concerns about potentially harmful or offensive content. 'Harmful' in this context means that ads either 'glamorize' gambling or use bad language or offensive imagery.

The Gambling Act 2005 relaxed legal controls that had previously prohibited gambling advertisers from advertising across media, including TV. The Act recognized gambling as a legitimate leisure activity, but one that needed to be effectively regulated to protect against risks of personal and social harm, for example through excessive or underage play. Since September 2007, betting and gaming companies have been permitted to advertise across all media, but the introduction of strict content rules has ensured that they can do so only in a socially responsible way.[177]

Gaming and betting advertising rules are regulated and controlled by the ASA, placing particular emphasis on protecting children and vulnerable persons (also covered by Part 4 of the Gambling

---

174 Source: Moving annual totals for 2014–2015 calculated from Nielsen Media Research for RACC: www.radiocentre.org/advertising/factsandfigures/top-advertisers-on-radio.
175 See: Clearcast at: www.clearcast.co.uk/about.
176 Source: ASA Gambling Advertising Enforcement Review of the ASA's application of the UK Advertising Codes. October 2014 at p. 3–4 at: www.asa.org.uk/News-resources/Media-Centre/2014/~/media/Files/ASA/Reports/Review%20of%20the%20ASA's%20application%20of%20the%20UK%20Advertising%20Codes%20to%20gambling%20advertising.ashx.
177 Section 4(1)(e) of the Gambling Act 2005 covers 'remote' gambling, including the internet, telephone, radio and 'any other kind of electronic communication'.

Act 2005). The deregulation under the Act has meant that since 2007 there has naturally been an increase in the number of ads appearing. Among the key clauses, the rules state that advertisements for gambling must not:

- portray, condone or encourage gambling behaviour that is socially irresponsible or could lead to financial, social or emotional harm;
- be likely to be of particular appeal to under 18s, especially by reflecting or being associated with youth culture;
- suggest that gambling can be a solution to financial concerns, an alternative to employment or a way to achieve financial security;
- exploit the susceptibilities, aspirations, credulity, inexperience or lack of knowledge of children, young persons or other vulnerable persons;
- link gambling to seduction, sexual success or enhanced attractiveness.

For those advertisers who breach the regulations, they face referral by the ASA to Ofcom or the Gambling Commission for potential additional sanctions.

 FOR THOUGHT

Gambling ads should not be directed to under 18s or vulnerable adults. Consider how you would judge someone as vulnerable? Study the relevant gambling legislation and the CAP Code on the definition of 'vulnerable'. Draft a letter of complaint to the ASA objecting to the following Facebook advertisement. The text reads: 'Addicted to slots?' The Facebook banner ad for a gambling website features a picture of a fruit machine. Further text states: 'Register now on www.666casino & spin. You get a whole year ABSOLUTELY FREE! Get the chance to win every day. No deposit necessary.'

6.10 Film, video and games censorship

Deciding where to draw the line when regulating sexually explicit and violent material relates to the degree of control exercised by a society. Film, video and games regulators in each country have to decide where to place restrictions on access to these images, who can watch them and what is appropriate for adults. They can then decide for themselves what is appropriate. The means of regulating sexually explicit and violent material has been debated for decades. Arguments over what denotes a masterpiece or an obscenity in film, image or literature abound.

The British Board of Film Classification (BBFC – originally the British Board of Film Censors) is an independent, self-financing and not-for-profit media content self-regulator. Its main aim is to protect the public, especially children, from content which might raise the risk of harm.

6.10.1 Early years of film censorship

The British Board of Film Censors (BBFC) was set up in 1912 by the film industry as an independent self-regulatory body to bring a degree of uniformity to the UK's classification of film nationally. From the mid-1920s it became general practice for local authorities to accept the decisions of the board.

When T. P. O'Connor was appointed President of the BBFC in 1916,[178] one of his first tasks was to give evidence to the Cinema Commission of Inquiry, set up by the National Council for Public Morals at the time.[179] He summarized the board's policy by listing 43 grounds for a film's exclusion or rejection. Some of the topics included:

- the irreverent treatment of sacred subjects;
- drunken scenes carried to excess;
- vulgar accessories;
- the modus operandi of criminals;
- nude figures;
- indecorous dancing;
- excessively passionate love scenes;
- realistic horrors of warfare including scenes and incidents calculated to afford information to the enemy;
- subjects dealing with India in which British Officers are seen in an odious light;
- scenes laid in disorderly houses.

Mrs Mary Whitehouse became the first General Secretary of the National Viewers' and Listeners' Association in 1965. The prominent campaigner for public morality made it her life's quest to highlight public decency and the moral decline of television standards – particularly at the BBC. The first chairman of the subsequent BSC (Broadcasting Standards Council), Lord Rees-Mogg, credited Mrs Whitehouse for her influence on the setting-up of the Council in 1988 and for ensuring that the public view was always taken into account. Mrs Whitehouse threatened legal action a number of times, including against programmes such as Monty Python's Flying Circus, The Kenny Everett Television Show – with its skimpily clad dance troupe, Hot Gossip, run by Arlene Phillips – and Doctor Who. Mrs Whitehouse indirectly influenced the BBFC with her quest for public morals and decency.

The American film director Stanley Kubrick had moved to England in 1962 to film Lolita, his motivation being that the UK would prove to have more relaxed censorship laws than the USA. But he fell foul of the Obscene Publications Act 1959 and Mrs Mary Whitehouse. He subsequently made a large number of films including Dr Strangelove (with Peter Sellers), 2001: A Space Odyssey and Eyes Wide Shut.

Kubrick's 1971 film A Clockwork Orange, based on an adaptation of Anthony Burgess's novel of 1962, proved to be another controversial film. It worried the government to such an extent that before the film's general release in January 1972, Home Secretary Reginald Maudling arranged a private viewing of the film. A Clockwork Orange is a dark satirical film depicting Alex (Malcolm McDowell), a charismatic delinquent who engages in 'ultra-violence', including rape, performed to Beethoven's music. The BBFC had passed the film with an 'X' rating, requiring no cuts (the age bar for an 'X'-rated film had just been raised from 16 to 18). With the film's general release, the BBFC had advised the distributors, Warner Brothers, that the film portrayed 'an unrelieved diet of vicious violence and hooliganism'.

Kubrick became a target for hate mail and abusive phone calls in the UK after a number of rapes and murders in the early 1970s were linked to the film, including a sex attack in Lancashire carried out by a gang chanting the Gene Kelly song Singin' in the Rain. This resulted in Kubrick secretly withdrawing the film by arranging with Warners that the film would just be allowed to die off quietly, after further allegations that A Clockwork Orange was inspiring young people to copy its scenes of violence. Stanley Kubrick died on 7 March 1999, aged 70, and the director's widow, German-born

---

178 President from 11 December 1916 to 18 November 1929. Thomas Power O'Connor (1848–1929), known as T. P. O'Connor, was a journalist and Irish nationalist, as well as a Member of Parliament at Westminster for nearly 50 years.
179 Source: National Council for Public Morals (1917).

actress and painter Christiane, retained all consultation rights on the re-released *A Clockwork Orange* in the same year. In the film a large floral oil painting by Christiane can be seen during the famous *Singin' in the Rain* scene.

When the film *The Exorcist* opened in America on 26 December 1973, the response was immediate and extraordinary. It is based on a book by William Peter Blatty, published in 1971, and depicts a demonic possession and subsequent exorcism of a young girl in Washington DC. Despite much press attention in advance of the film's release, the 'Classification and Ratings Administration' of the Motion Picture Academy of America (MPAA) granted *The Exorcist* an uncut 'R' rating ('for strong language and disturbing images'), allowing minors to view the film if accompanied by an adult. MPAA President Jack Valenti pointed out that *The Exorcist* contained 'no overt sex' and 'no excessive violence', a conclusion echoed by the generally cautious Catholic Conference, which rated the film 'A-IV', an adult classification meaning that the film was 'moral, but may offend some [adult] viewers'. Yet Washington police barred persons under the age of 17 from showings of the movie in spite of the MPAA's 'R' rating. Eventually, Marvin Goldman, head of the KB Theatre chain, which owned the Cinema Theatre in DC where the movie was first shown, told the *Washington Post* that he would comply with the (MPAA) ruling, stating that the movie should have been rated X (no one under 17 admitted) in the first place.[180] Walter Cronkite devoted a full ten minutes of his legendary CBS news programme to 'The Exorcist Phenomenon' and the history of demonic possession.

The film struck a unique chord with audiences around the world. In Milan, the crowd at a packed news conference refused to leave a museum where the film's director, William Friedkin, and technical adviser, Father Thomas Bermingham, were answering questions about *The Exorcist*. In Rome, the film made the national news when a sixteenth-century church across the street from a cinema where the film premiered was struck by lightning, causing an ancient cross to plummet from its roof onto the pavement below. At a preview screening in New York, one audience member had to be helped out after becoming dizzy, provoking a wave of press reports of fainting, vomiting and other hysterical reactions. By the time *The Exorcist* came to the UK, rumours of its traumatizing power had grown to such proportions that the St John Ambulance Brigade were standing by for the first showings around London.

But *The Exorcist* was immediately banned by the BBFC, due to Mary Whitehouse's urging them to prohibit it. She called the film 'outright nasty – blasphemous and evil', despite the fact she had never seen a frame of it. She relied purely on adverse media coverage such as Stanley Kaufmann's comment in *New Republic*: 'This is the most scary film I've seen in years – the only scary film I've seen in years ... If you want to be shaken – and I found out, while the picture was going, that that's what I wanted – then *The Exorcist* will scare the hell out of you.'[181] The British film board eventually granted an 'X' certificate to *The Exorcist* in January 1974, which allowed over-18s to view it without cuts or alterations. At the Golden Globe awards of 1974, *The Exorcist* picked up awards for Best Film, Best Director (William Friedkin), Best Screenplay (William Peter Blatty) and Best Supporting Actress (Linda Blair), while the Oscars that year generated ten nominations including Best Picture, Best Screenplay (Blatty) and Best Sound. In box-office terms, the movie became the biggest-grossing hit in Warner Brothers' history, nearly trebling the $34 million gross of the studio's previous record holder, *My Fair Lady*.[182]

Prior to the 1990s it was not an uncommon occurrence that local authorities would ban films in their local cinemas, such as Ken Russell's *The Devils* and Stanley Kubrick's *A Clockwork Orange* in 1971, and Monty Python's *Life of Brian* in 1988. In 1996, Westminster Council banned *Crash* by David Cronenberg, a film first premiered at the 1996 London Film Festival. When Westminster Council demanded cuts to certain parts of this sexually violent film – solely for screenings in Westminster – the

180 Source: 'Exorcist: No one under 17 admitted', by Tom Shales, *Washington Post*, 4 January 1974.
181 Kaufmann's quote in *New Republic*, as quoted in Travers, P. and Reiff, S. (1974), pp. 152–154.
182 Source: 'Entertainment: The Exorcist – hype or horror?', Mark Kermode, BBC Radio 1 Online, 2 November 1998.

distributors declined, and the film was therefore banned from screens in the West End, including Leicester Square. However, cinemagoers could easily see the film in neighbouring Camden, where that council allowed the film to play uncut with its BBFC certificate.

Hally (2012) found that more broadminded councils, such as Manchester, were frequently ahead of BBFC policy and practice during the 1950s and 1960s, first in having an adults-only category before the 'X' certificate, then in relaxing the strictures against screen nudity (the naturist films) and over artistic sex and 'bad language' (e.g. *Ulysses*). Generally Conservative-led councils, such as Sale, continued trying to hold back the tide of 'X' films. Manchester tended to be more liberal-minded than the BBFC on matters of nudity, sex and language but less so on issues of violence and disorder.[183]

The Video Recordings Act 1984 was passed by Parliament to regulate and classify video recordings offered for sale or hire commercially in the UK. The President and Vice Presidents of the BBFC were so designated, and charged with applying the new test of 'suitability for viewing in the home'. At this point the Board's title was changed to the British Board of Film Classification to reflect the fact that classification plays a far larger part in the BBFC's work than censorship.

6.10.2 The British Board of Film Classification

The British Board of Film Classification (BBFC) is an independent regulator and censor of film, video, DVDs and video games. The BBFC is widely regarded as one of the most trusted and highly regarded non-governmental organizations in the UK, funded by the film, DVD and games industries. Generally, the BBFC rejects, bans or passes films (as well as DVDs and some video games). The BBFC remains a not-for-profit self-regulatory organization and its fees are adjusted only to cover its costs. Its income is from the fees it charges for its services, calculated by measuring the running time of films or DVDs submitted for classification. The BBFC consults the Department of Culture, Media and Sport before making any changes to its fees.

The BBFC rates about 10,000 pieces a year, though traditional classified film content has been steadily falling. 2014 saw a shift in the balance of statutory versus non-statutory work with an increase in theatrical submissions (at their highest level since the early 1960s). The regulator licensed 950 films in 2014 and the amount of video work classified under the Video Recordings Act 1984 fell by 7.2 per cent. On the other hand, voluntary classifications for videos saw a dramatic increase of 70 per cent that year whereby content providers and platforms such as Netflix and iTunes self-regulated child protection in their offline content. In 2014 the BBFC also classified more online video content than ever before with a 70 per cent increase.[184]

Trading standards and law enforcement officers have the power to seize illegal video works including, but not limited to, DVDs, Blu-rays and video games. The BBFC is designated by the government (the Department of Culture, Media and Sport) to provide evidence to help secure convictions under the terms of the Video Recordings Act (VRA) 1984 for copyright infringement. The BBFC will issue a Certificate of Evidence under the VRA 1984 or the Criminal Procedure (Scotland) Act 1995. This evidence is admissible in court as 'standalone' evidence and does not require anyone from the BBFC to attend as a witness.

The BBFC has, from time to time, rejected foreign films even though they were openly released in their countries of origin, with sexual topics generally being the norm for rejection, such as *The Best of the New York Erotic Film Festival*, rejected in April 1975, or *Confessions of a Blue Movie Star*, a 1978 West German documentary by Wes Craven and Andrzej Kostenko. The 1969 film *99 Women* (*der Heiße*

183 See: Hally, M. (2012).

184 For more detailed information see: British Board of Film Classification Annual Report and Accounts January 2014–31 December 2014. Presented to Parliament pursuant to s 6(2) of the Video Recordings Act 1984 at: www.bbfc.co.uk/sites/default/files/attachments/BBFC%20Annual%20Report%202014.pdf.

Tod/99 donne/99 mujeres) by Jess Franco, released in Liechtenstein, Spain, Italy and West Germany, was rejected for its 'soft-core' women-in-prison lesbian nature with 'nasty torture sequences'. *The Awakening of Emily* (1976) a soft porn Ann Summers production, featuring Koo Stark,[185] was rejected by the BBFC for its sex scene of two women in a shower in 1983. The regulator has habitually banned prison films that feature women, such as *Deported Women of the SS* (*Le deportate della sezione speciale SS*), a 1976 Italian prison film by Rino Di Silvestro, or *Barbed Wire Dolls* (*Frauengefängnis*), a 1975 Swiss prison drama by Jess Franco, featuring 'caged women'. *Bamboo House Dolls* (*Nu ji zhong ying*), a 1974 Hong Kong film by Chin Hung Kuei, was banned by the BBFC because of its sensitive topic featuring a Japanese women's POW camp.

6.10.3 Legislation covering film and video censorship

The BBFC is governed by several pieces of legislation, the most significant being the Video Recordings Acts (VRA) of 1984 and 2010, which particularly affect classification standards. The 1984 Act requires all 'video works' (films, TV programmes, video games, etc.) which are supplied on a disc, tape or any other device capable of storing data electronically, to be classified by the BBFC, unless they fall within the definition of an exempted work. Section 4A of the 1984 VRA requires 'special regard' to be given to the likelihood of video works being viewed in the home and to any harm that may be caused to potential viewers or, through their behaviour, to society by the manner in which the work deals with criminal behaviour, illegal drugs, violent behaviour or incidents, horrific behaviour or incidents, and human sexual activity, particularly when video works deal with:

(i)   criminal behaviour;
(ii) illegal drugs;
(iii) violent behaviour or incidents;
(iv) horrific behaviour or incidents; or
(v)   human sexual activity.

The Video Recordings Act 2010 repealed and then brought back into force parts of the Video Recordings Act 1984.[186] The reintroduction of the 1984 Act was deemed necessary after Parliament forgot to notify the European Commission in August 2009 of the (original) existence of the 1984 Act.[187] This meant neither the 1984 nor the 2010 VRA were initially in accordance with Directive 98/34/EC.[188] The Digital Economy Act 2010 additionally passed responsibility for games ratings to the Video Standards Council, particularly for those video games that include violence or encourage criminal activity. Video games with specific themes or content – such as the *Grand Theft Auto* series – must also be submitted to the BBFC to receive a legally binding rating in the same way as videos. In considering all these issues, the BBFC needs to be mindful of the possible effect not only on children but also on other vulnerable groups.

The Obscene Publications Acts 1959 and 1964 made it illegal to publish a work in the UK which is regarded as 'obscene' in content (as a whole). The film, DVD, game, etc. must have the tendency to 'deprave and corrupt', unless the 'publication' can be justified as being for the 'public good' on the grounds that it is in the interests of science, art, literature or learning or other objects of general concern.

185 Koo Stark (born 'Kathleen Dee-Anne Stark' on 26 April 1956 in New York City, New York, USA) is a film actress best known for her relationship with Prince Andrew before his marriage. They split up after his return from the Falklands War during the summer of 1982.
186 Section 1 VRA 2010 ('Repeal and revival of provisions of the Video Recordings Act 1984'): ss 1 to 17, 19, 21 and 22 of the VRA 1984 ceased to be in force.
187 See: House of Commons, Parliamentary debate of 6 January 2010, Hansard, cc 181–209.
188 EC Directive 98/34/EC laying down a procedure for the provision of information in the field of technical standards and regulations and of rules on Information Society services of 22 June 1998.

The Public Order Act 1986 makes it illegal to distribute or play to the public a recording of images or sounds which are threatening, abusive or insulting if the intention is to stir up racial hatred or hatred on the grounds of sexual orientation.[189]

There are two Acts which cover animal welfare issues in films. The Cinematograph Films (Animals) Act 1937 renders it illegal to show any scene 'organised or directed' for the purposes of a film that involves the cruel treatment of any animal. The Animal Welfare Act 2006 makes it illegal to show or publish a recording of an animal fight which has taken place in the UK since 6 April 2007. This is to combat illegal dog fighting and the breeding of dangerous dogs for fights, habitually filmed and uploaded by criminals on to YouTube.

6.10.4 Film classification for multi-platform on demand viewing

With increasing online film, video and multi-platform on demand viewing, the BBFC is now working a 'traffic light' censoring system that warns users about the film footage they are about to access online. The regulator has developed the classification system ('Watch & Rate') which allows the public to rate online film content. The BBFC works with the Dutch media regulator NICAM (Netherlands Institute for the Classification of Audiovisual Media) on this system to rate user-generated content that might ordinarily slip through the net and go unclassified. The system involves the viewer uploading the material and providing details about its content. This online film censoring system already exists in Italy, provided by the commercial broadcaster Mediaset. Although the BBFC has no specific powers to rate online material, a number of companies have been keen to seek their classifications on a voluntary basis, including video-on-demand service Netflix, which sought a certificate for online-only series such as *House of Cards*. BBFC examiners log the following details:

- general context: plot, characters, outline of individual scenes;
- timings of classification moments, including camera angles, type of shots, on- and off-screen moments;
- bad language, sex and drug references, etc.

The BBFC then examines the overall tone of a film, DVD or video game and assesses how these may affect the classification of each. A 'U' ('Universal') film should be suitable for audiences aged four years and over, allowing very mild bad language, such as 'damn' and 'hell'; for example, the 1964 Walt Disney film, *Mary Poppins*, featuring Julie Andrews and Dick van Dyke.

A 'PG' (Parental Guidance) film should not disturb a child aged around eight. There may be mild bad language, such as 'shit' or 'son of a bitch', and violence is only acceptable in a historical or fantasy setting. An example would be the 2007 film, *Mr Bean's Holiday*, starring Rowan Atkinson, or Michael Jackson's *This Is It*,[190] released following the legendary pop singer's death in June 2009.

The 12A classification requires an adult to accompany any child under 12 seeing a 12A film at the cinema. Though this ought to be strictly enforced by cinema staff (and a cinema may lose its licence if adult accompaniment is not enforced) – it means that children aged ten could easily get into the cinema to see the latest James Bond film *Spectre*, which was given a 12A certificate, which débued in November 2015.

During post-production of *Spectre*, the distributor sought and was given advice on how to secure the desired classification and reduce the certificate from 15 to 12A. Following the BBFC's advice, certain changes were made prior to submission. Though the BBFC advised that the eye-gouging

---

189 Section 22 Public Order Act 1986.
190 Feature film directed by Kenny Ortega. The cast includes: Michael Jackson, Kenny Ortega and Orianthi. Columbia Pictures Corporation Ltd. Classified 27 October, 2009 as PG.

scene at the start of the film should be taken out, the movie-going families saw the first scene in Mexico City as one bull-necked hitman and Spectre's lead assassin, murders another hitman, starting by pressing his thumbs into the man's eyes and squeezing them out of their sockets. Though this scene was supposedly redacted and the final version of *Spectre* was said to contain only a few scenes of 'moderate action violence', the *Daily Mail* criticized the BBFC for granting the film a 'licence for sadism'.[191]

No one under 15 is legally allowed to see, buy or rent a certificate '15'-rated film, DVD or video game. This classification generally includes strong violence, frequent strong language such as 'fuck', and brief scenes of sexual activity or violence are permitted – so are discriminatory language and drug-taking.

With a few limited exceptions the BBFC does not classify video games. However, the regulator classifies those video games contained on discs which feature primarily linear video content and pornographic video games which include for example:

- images of unsimulated human sexual activity involving genitals or anus;
- sexual fetish material, including bondage or sadomasochistic activity, urination and other bodily functions;
- material likely to encourage an interest in sexually abusive activity;
- the portrayal of sexual activity which involves lack of consent whether real or simulated;
- sexual threats, humiliation or abuse;
- penetration by any object associated with violence or likely to cause physical harm;
- images of sexual activity with animals whether such images or material are of real events or activity or are animated.

Some video games developers are asked by the BBFC to remove certain elements such as those mentioned above. The X-Box game *Castlevania: Lords of Shadow 2* (2014), for instance, was given a '15' rating by the BBFC, after some of the very bloody and extremely violent scenes were redacted.[192] The video game *Call of Duty:World War II* (2015) had difficulties in passing censors in some countries before it could go on sale. The BBFC rating is 18. The German version of game (also 18) removed the gore and reduced the shooting and explosions, the swastikas (against the law in Germany) were replaced with the iron cross and Hitler in the Berlin pictures was replaced with a Luftwaffe officer.

No one under 18 is legally allowed to see a certificate '18'-rated film in the cinema, or to rent or buy the DVD or video game. Films or games rated '18' are essentially adult works, and generally include very strong violence and/or sexual activity with frequently strong language such as 'cunt'. Examples include dystopian crime film *A Clockwork Orange* (1971) directed by Stanley Kubrick, based on Anthony Burgess's 1962 novella.

Fight Club, based on the novel by Chuck Palahniuk, was submitted to the BBFC in 1999. The film caused a sensation at the Venice International Film Festival when some critics reacted strongly to both the film's thesis and its level of personal violence, while others praised its imaginative approach and strong performances from Edward Norton and Brad Pitt. The *London Evening Standard's* famous film critic, Alexander Walker (1930–2003), called the film 'a toxic experience . . . an inadmissible assault on personal decency . . . and on society itself. It resurrects the Führer principle. It promotes pain and suffering as the virtues of the strongest. It tramples every democratic decency underfoot.' The film was given a certificate 18 by the BBFC for its sequences of extreme and bloody male-on-male violence and for encouraging an interest in bare-fist fighting.

---

191 Source: 'Licence to be sadistic: Yes, he loved it. But our critic admits he's a bit queasy about the way new Bond film Spectre glories in cruelty. Is the money-spinning 007 juggernaut so powerful the censors turn a blind eye?', by Film Critic Brian Viner, *The Daily Mail*, 22 October 2015.
192 The game was developed by MercurySteam and published by Konami. It is part of the action-adventure series Castlevania.

As the internet has provided greater choice and freedom to download films and games, the BBFC has recognized that such online content also needs to be classified before a film can be downloaded. The regulator's own research found that the majority of viewers still consider it important to be able to check the suitability of films they download from trusted sources and particularly for parental guidance.[193]

6.10.5 Screen and internet violence

Can screen violence really lead to actual violence? This has been the question that legislators and regulators have asked themselves for years. Dr Guy Cumberbatch, Chartered Psychologist and Director of The Communications Research Group, undertook extensive research in this field. In a report to the Video Standards Council (2004), Cumberbatch established that screen violence does influence children's behaviour, particularly their style of play, which changed in line with the programmes they watched on TV or DVD, or the video games they played. He gave the examples of *Power Rangers, Ninja Turtles* and *Spiderman*.[194]

See Chapter 3.5

Since the arrival of internet-based audiovisual services it has been difficult for a succession of governments to create statutory provisions for movie downloads and interactive internet-based games, particularly those that display an extraordinary amount of screen violence. There is a fine line between privacy – what can be viewed or played in one's own home – and the continuation of freedom of expression.

From 2014 onwards we can observe a shift in the balance of the BBFC's statutory and non-statutory work. Theatrical submissions continued at their highest level since the early 1960s. For the second year running the regulator classified over 950 films, yet video classification declined by 7.2 per cent to 8,860 hours of content. On the other hand, voluntary classifications for videos receiving an online distribution saw a dramatic increase of 70 per cent. Content providers and platforms such as Netflix and iTunes made consumer empowerment and child protection their priority.

Parliament passed two legislative amendments in 2014, improving the protection of children from potentially harmful media content. Firstly, an amendment to the Video Recordings Act 1984, whereby all video content on physical media which is unsuitable for younger children is subject to independent regulation by the BBFC. Previously, certain genres of video, including music, religious and sports videos, had been exempt from classification, even if they contained material unsuitable for younger children. Now content such as strong violence, drug misuse, discriminatory behaviour and language, and dangerous behaviour imitable by impressionable children, is scrutinized separately.

Secondly, an amendment was made to the Communications Act 2003 to better protect children's activities online. This amendment built on the Prime Minister, David Cameron's commitment to align more closely online and offline protections. It requires that any content the BBFC would classify, or has classified, R18 – namely hard core pornography – be placed behind access controls on UK regulated video-on-demand services. It also ensures that any content the BBFC refuses to classify is no longer supplied via these services. This latter content includes abusive pornography and depictions of rape which suggest that women enjoy being raped. Work continues with other regulators, such as ATVOD and Ofcom, to ensure that all three bodies work together in harmony to give effect to the will of Parliament in relation to this change. Although the change only applies to UK-regulated services, it sets an important example to services in other EU Member States.

See Chapters 5.5 and 5.6

193 See: BBFC Classifications (2014) at: www.bbfc.co.uk/sites/default/files/attachments/BBFC%20Classification%20Guidelines%20 2014_2.pdf.
194 See: Cumberbatch, G. (2004).

6.10.6 Classification of music DVDs and online music videos

Many children now have easy access to music videos online and some parents are rightly concerned that some of these contain imagery or lyrics not appropriate for a young audience.

In August 2015 Baroness Shields from the Department of Culture, Media and Sports announced an initiative to protect children from viewing age-inappropriate music videos online and to improve consumer awareness about the content of certain music videos. Vevo and YouTube, working in partnership with the BBFC, initiated a pilot scheme to age-rate all music videos by artists signed to Sony Music UK, Universal Music UK and Warner Music UK that are unsuitable for younger children (under 12s). The government also announced that independent UK music labels would also take part in the pilot scheme.

On Vevo, the BBFC ratings symbol appears in the top left hand corner of the video player for the first few seconds. On YouTube, they appear at the 'Partner Rating' label; or a 12, 15 or 18 in a square box on the smartphone app underneath the video. The record labels now submit to the BBFC any music video by their artists for release online in the UK which they would expect to receive at least a 12 rating. The BBFC then classifies each video, watching it through in its entirety and then assigning an age rating and bespoke content advice (for example, strong language, sex references or sexualized nudity) on the basis of the BBFC's published Classification Guidelines. The sort of issues the BBFC considers in classifying music videos include:

- drug misuse;
- dangerous behaviour presented as safe;
- bad language;
- sexual behaviour and nudity;
- threatening behaviour and violence.

Although the BBFC's online work is not required by UK law, it is upheld on a voluntary basis by digital platforms and distributors. The BBFC's voluntary 'Watch & Rate' digital-only ratings service continues to grow. While submissions of video works under the Video Recordings Act still represent the largest proportion of submissions, the growth in demand for digital-only age ratings reflects the changing UK home entertainment market and an ongoing shift in consumer viewing habits towards video-on-demand (VoD) content.[195]

6.10.7 Public complaints and BBFC rulings

The BBFC receives a relatively small number of complaints about its classification decisions. The film Mr Turner, classified 12A, generated the most public feedback and complaints in 2014. Some 19 members of the public complained about a sex scene in the film.

In the scene in question, Mr Turner's clothed buttocks are seen clenching vigorously, before the scene cuts to a close-up of his face and his thrusting head and shoulders. The scene is relatively brief and does not contain any nudity, but Turner does appear rather distressed. The act ends with shots of Turner sobbing, almost in an exhibition of self-loathing. The BBFC's response to the complaints was that the scene is important in terms of the narrative of the film and that context is central to the question of acceptability of film and video content.

When considering context, the film censors take into account issues such as public expectation in general and the expectations of a work's audience in particular. Given the lack of nudity, the

195 See the full report: British Board of Film Classification Annual Report and Accounts 2014 at: www.bbfc.co.uk/sites/default/files/attachments/BBFC%20Annual%20Report%202014.pdf.

relative brevity of the scene and its importance in terms of narrative, and the audience appeal of the film, the scene is acceptable within the BBFC's Classification Guidelines for sexual content at 12A.

The 15 classification of *12 Years A Slave* generated 12 complaints about the violence, including sexual violence, in the film. The BBFC's justification of a 15-rating was that the film tells its story in a considered and responsible manner, and contains very little in the way of blood or injury detail. The scenes of violence in the film are strong but were held as contextually justified. With very few clear images of the injuries inflicted, the depictions of violence serve to illustrate the very real brutality suffered by many slaves at the hands of their masters. The BBFC censors felt that the rape of a female slave is shocking but is shown in a discreet manner. There is no nudity and the focus of the scene remains on her impassive face.

The 15 classification for *Bad Neighbours* received eight complaints. Correspondents raised the language, drug references and sex scenes in the film as problematic to them at 15. The regulator's response was that there is one use of the word 'cunt' as a man laments the fact that his baby has heard someone swear and worries that soon the baby will begin using this word. The censors noted that the very strong language was neither directed nor aggressively delivered and was, along with the other bad language in the film, within BBFC Guidelines at 15. The scenes of sex are strong but do not challenge the Guidelines at 15. Nudity is limited and most of what occurs is mitigated by the comic context. The associated strong verbal sex references are also permitted at 15.

The Equalizer generated seven complaints from the public for its 15 classification. Correspondents raised the violence in the film as problematic at 15, while others complained that the film had been cut to achieve a 15 classification. The censors commented that the violence in the film was strong in places, particularly during hand-to-hand fight scenes, however that the film did not dwell on the infliction of pain or injury, nor do any of the scenes qualify as the strongest gory images of the type that would require an 18 classification. The BBFC offered advice and when the film was subsequently submitted for a formal classification, edits had been made and the BBFC duly classified the film at 15.

 FOR THOUGHT

How far should games and music DVD censorship go – given the fact that anything can now be viewed in private on the internet? Discuss with reference to BBFC adjudications in addition to statutory measures.

6.11 Competition and appeals

In the UK two sets of competition rules apply in parallel. Anti-competitive behaviour which may affect trade within the UK is specifically prohibited by Chapters I and II of the Competition Act 1998 and the Enterprise Act 2002. Where the effect of anti-competitive behaviour extends beyond the UK to other EU Member States, it is prohibited by Articles 101 and 102 of the Treaty on the Functioning of the European Union (TFEU). Failure to comply with UK or EU competition law can have very serious consequences. Following the merger on 1 April 2014 of the UK Office of Fair Trading (OFT) and the Competition Commission (CC) to form the new Competition and Markets Authority (CMA), businesses operating in the UK are now experiencing tougher enforcement of the competition rules, with high fines and criminal prosecutions in appropriate cases.

6.11.1 The Competition and Markets Authority (CMA)

One part of the government's 'visions and values' business strategies is to look after the welfare of the consumer, for example the protection of consumers' rights, small and enterprising businesses and the impact on the environment. From 2014 a new European Commission clarified and engaged in competition powers for the Financial Conduct Authority and introduced a Payment Systems Regulator. The Competition and Markets Authority (CMA) then brought about these changes in the UK in order to increase the potential for consumers, businesses and the UK economy.[196]

The CMA is a non-ministerial UK government department responsible for strengthening business competition and preventing and reducing anti-competitive activities.[197] Its primary duty is to promote competition, both within and outside the UK for the benefit of consumers. The CMA began operating on 1 April 2014 when it assumed many of the functions of the previously existing Competition Commission and Office of Fair Trading, which were abolished.

The CMA has a wide range of tools available to make markets work well for consumers, businesses and the economy. These include:

(a) **enforcement**, such as prosecution of criminal cartel activity, investigating and taking action against anticompetitive agreements or abuse of a dominant position under the Competition Act 1998, and playing a significant role in the UK consumer protection landscape;

(b) **investigation of markets** where there are concerns that competition is not working well;

(c) **investigation of mergers** to remedy, mitigate or prevent any potential harm to consumers or businesses, including in the form of higher prices, or reduced quality or innovation in a particular market;

(d) **'softer' tools such as targeted compliance** and awareness-raising initiatives, guidance and advocacy and to help firms to comply with the law.

The CMA is also an appeal body for decisions by the sector regulators,[198] including the responsibilities conferred by the Health and Social Care Act 2012, the Civil Aviation Act 2013 and the Financial Services (Banking Reform) Act 2013. Regulatory references and appeals historically comprised up to a quarter of the Competition Commission's workload.

Cartel enforcement was the CMA's priority in 2015–2016 with increased enforcement powers available under the Enterprise and Regulatory Reform Act 2013 (ERRA). A cartel is an agreement between competitors to fix prices, share markets, rig bids or limit output at the expense of the interests of customers.

Apart from a large number of merger investigations such as BT's takeover of EE, the acquisition by Nikkei Inc. of *The Financial Times*, the Ryanair and Aer Lingus merger,[199] the Motor Fuel and Shell merger and the Poundland and 99 pence stores merger (and many others), the CMA launched some criminal investigations into cartels and price fixing as well as 'pyramid selling' schemes.

Pyramid promotional schemes are those where the 'compensation' (that is, money or 'winnings') for participants is derived primarily from introducing others, rather than from the sale of a

---

196 See: Competition and Markets Authority (2015) Annual Plan 2015/16 at: www.gov.uk/government/uploads/system/uploads/attachment_data/file/416433/Annual_Plan_2015–16.pdf.

197 For further details see The Competition and Markets Authority at: www.gov.uk/government/organisations/competition-and-markets-authority.

198 These include decisions of regulators such as Ofcom, Ofgem, Ofwat, Monitor, the Financial Conduct Authority, Payment Systems Regulator, Northern Ireland Utility Regulator, Office of Rail Regulation and the Civil Aviation Authority.

199 The merger was investigated by the Competition Commission (CC) (August 2013, now defunct) and involved the two largest providers of air passenger services between Great Britain and the Republic of Ireland. The CC found that Ryanair's acquisition of a minority shareholding in Aer Lingus had led to a substantial lessening of competition in the markets for air passenger services between Great Britain and the Republic of Ireland. See: Competition Commission Annual Report 2013–14, 31 March 2014. Ordered by the House of Commons. HC 24 at pp. 18–19: www.gov.uk/government/uploads/system/uploads/attachment_data/file/322811/40626_2902424_Web_Accessible_v1.1.pdf.

product or service. Such schemes are automatically unfair commercial practices under the Consumer Protection from Unfair Trading Regulations 2008. They are distinct from promotional arrangements under which compensation payments are derived from the sale of a product or service. Unlawful pyramid promotional schemes may involve products or services, but these will generally be over-priced or have no real resale value, the primary source of the compensation for participants being derived from introducing others to the scheme, such as through large joining fees.

In July 2015, Laura Fox, Carol Chalmers, Jennifer Smith Hayes, Susan Crane, Mary Nash and Hazel Cameron pleaded guilty to pyramid selling schemes at Bristol Crown Court contrary to sections 3 and 4 of the Consumer Protection from Unfair Trading Regulations 2008 ('promoting' and 'operating' a pyramid promotional scheme). His Honour Judge Horton described Laura Fox (chair of the scheme) as the 'driving force behind the scheme'. He sentenced Carol Chalmers (venue organizer for the scheme) and Jennifer Smith Hayes (treasurer of the scheme) to nine months' imprisonment. After pleading guilty, Susan Crane, Mary Nash (charts co-ordinator of the scheme) and Hazel Cameron were sentenced to six months' imprisonment for 'promoting' and 'operating' a pyramid promotional scheme contrary to the Regulations. In the case of Hazel Cameron, her sentence was suspended for two years. Following convictions for their roles in a pyramid selling scheme in July 2015, the CMA secured a total of £535,454 in confiscation orders and prosecution costs from the six organizers. In addition, Laura Fox, Carol Chalmers, Jennifer Smith Hayes, Susan Crane (committee secretary and sub treasurer of the scheme), Mary Nash and Hazel Cameron (games co-ordinator for the scheme) were each ordered to pay a contribution to prosecution costs of £30,362 for a total of £182,172.

The CMA also applied the Proceeds of Crime Act 2002 to the non-committee defendants who pleaded guilty to promoting the scheme. Sally Phillips and Rita Lomas were each found by the court to have obtained a benefit from their criminal conduct, but to have no realizable assets. As a result, the judge ordered the usual nominal sum (of £1) to be confiscated. Jane Smith was found to have benefited to the sum of £51,949 but only to have realizable assets of £20,143.[200]

The Competition and Markets Authority (CMA) – 'Galvanised Steel Tanks' investigation[201]

Facts
Three individuals were charged with an offence under section 188 of the Enterprise Act 2002 ('criminal cartel offence'). Mr Snee, former Managing Director of Franklin Hodge Industries, was arrested in 2012 at the start of an investigation begun by the CMA's predecessor, the Office of Fair Trading.[202] Mr Snee pleaded guilty to dishonestly agreeing with others to fix prices, divide up customers and rig bids between 2005 and 2012 in respect of the supply in the UK of galvanized steel tanks. The tanks were used to store water for sprinkler systems in buildings. Mr Snee co-operated with the investigation and, after pleading guilty to the cartel offence in January 2014, was a witness for the CMA at the subsequent trial of two further individuals. Following a trial at Southwark Crown Court in June 2015 in the same case, two directors, Clive Dean of Kondea Water Supplies Limited and Nicholas Stringer of Galglass Limited, were acquitted of similar cartel offences.

Sentencing remarks by His Honour Judge Goymer
The judge indicated that his starting point in this case was that a prison sentence of two years was appropriate. Taking into account Mr Snee's early guilty plea, his personal

---

200 Source: CMA Press Release 'Pyramid scheme organisers ordered to pay over £500,000', 21 July 2015.
201 CMA case reference: CE/9623/12.
202 The Competition and Markets Authority (CMA) applied the Code for Crown Prosecutors and discharged its duty as a prosecutor by bringing the case in front of a jury.

mitigation and the extent of his voluntary co-operation as a witness, the judge reduced his sentence by the 'higher end' discount of 75 per cent, and concluded that it was appropriate in the circumstances of this case for the resulting six-month sentence to be suspended. The judge remarked that, 'the economic damage done by cartels is such that those involved must expect prison sentences'. On 14 September 2015 Nigel Snee was sentenced to six months' imprisonment, suspended for 12 months, and ordered to do 120 hours of unpaid work within 12 months.

It remains the CMA's statutory duty to promote competition both within and outside the UK which, in turn, helps to create a dynamic economy.

6.11.2 The Competition and Appeals Tribunal

The Enterprise Act 2002 created the Competition Service, a body corporate and executive non-departmental public body whose purpose is to fund and provide support services to the Competition Appeal Tribunal (CAT). The CAT was created by section 12 and Schedule 2 of the Enterprise Act 2002 and came into force on 1 April 2003.

Cases are heard before a tribunal consisting of three members: either the president or a member of the panel of chairmen and two ordinary members.[203] The members of the panel of chairmen are judges of the Chancery Division of the High Court and other senior lawyers. The ordinary members have expertise in law, business, accountancy, economics and other related fields. The tribunal's jurisdiction extends to the whole of the United Kingdom.

The functions of the tribunal are:

● to hear appeals on the merits in respect of decisions made under the Competition Act 1998 by the Competition and Markets Authority (CMA) and the regulators in the telecommunications, electricity, gas, water, railways, air traffic services, payment systems, healthcare services and financial services sectors;
● to hear actions for damages and other monetary claims under the Competition Act 1998;
● to review decisions made by the Secretary of State and the CMA in respect of merger and market references or possible references under the Enterprise Act 2002;
● to hear appeals against certain decisions made by OFCOM and/or the Secretary of State under: Part 2 (networks, services and the radio spectrum) and sections 290 to 294 and Schedule 11 (networking arrangements for Channel 3) of the Communications Act 2003; the Mobile Roaming (European Communities) Regulations 2007.

Who may appeal to the CAT under the Competition Act 1998? Under sections 46 and 47 of the Competition Act an appeal to the tribunal may be made by:

● any party to an agreement in respect of which the CMA (or sectoral regulator) has made a decision;
● any person in respect of whose conduct the CMA (or sectoral regulator) has made a decision;
● any third party (or the representative of third parties) who the tribunal considers has a sufficient interest (or is representative of persons having such an interest) in a decision made by the CMA (or sectoral regulator).

---

203 The Guide to Proceedings 2015 applies to the conduct of proceedings before the tribunal, as at 1 October 2015 in accordance with the Competition Appeal Tribunal Rules 2015.

6.12 Further reading

Chamberlain, P. (2013) 'Where now? The Leveson Report and what to do with it',
Communications Law, **18(1), 21–24.**
Paul Chamberlain looks beyond the scope of the Leveson Report which covered the culture,
practices and ethics of the print press but also the police and politicians. The article focuses
primarily on the Leveson recommendations in relation to the future of press regulation and the
practical consequences.

Costigan, R. (2007) 'Protection of journalists' sources', *Public Law,* **Autumn, 464–487.**
This article critiques the jurisprudence of section 10 of the Contempt of Court Act 1981, which
affords journalists a qualified immunity from compulsory revelation of sources. Ruth Costigan
contends that the courts have failed to appreciate sufficiently the change in the nature of the
decision-making exercise required by section 10 and examines relevant case law. The author
further argues that the HRA 1998 insufficiently protects journalistic sources. Costigan's piece
ends with the argument that the Convention requirement of proportionality is not implemented in
an appropriate and sufficiently demanding manner.

Higgins, A. (2012) 'Legal lessons from the *News of the World* **phone hacking scandal',** *Civil*
Justice Quarterly, **31(3), 274–284.**
Andrew Higgins discusses the phone-hacking scandal at *NoW* between 2010 and 2011. The
author argues that the phone-hacking and corruption scandal provides a salutary reminder of
the limitations of public law enforcement and the value of an effective and accessible civil justice
system in exposing unlawful conduct and providing redress for victims. He further examines the
limitations of the PCC and looks at self-regulation of the print press and the corruption scandals
surrounding the arrests related to phone-hacking, payments to police and attempts to pervert
the course of justice.

Jordan, B. (2011) 'Self-regulation and the British press', *Entertainment Law Review,* **22(8),**
242–243.
Brid Jordan discusses the history of self-regulation of the British media, and looks specifically at
the closure of the PCC following the Leveson Inquiry.

Jordan, P. (ed.) (2014) *International Advertising Law. Practical Global Guide.* **Llandysul: Globe**
Business Publishing.
This 'Club Med' reference guide to advertising laws and regulations comprises some 500 pages
and practices in 31 countries. Editor Paul Jordan – Partner and Head of Advertising at Bristows
LLP (UK) – and 60 other authors – all of whom are practising solicitors and lawyers contributed
to this very useful compendium. This book is essential reading for media and advertising lawyers,
those working in PR as well as marketing and advertising industries. The mighty tome covers
advertising regulations in Austria, Belgium, Denmark, Germany, Greece, France, Czech Republic,
Hungary, Italy, Latvia, Netherlands, Norway, Poland, Spain, Sweden and the United Kingdom.
The text makes reference to state regulation in China, Argentina, Brazil and Mexico. Particularly
attention-grabbing sections are 'ambush marketing', 'online behavioral advertising' and
regulations regarding 'product placement'.

McKean, R. (2015) 'Data transfers to the US: Safe Harbour declared invalid; what are your
options now?', *IT Law Today,* **Oct., 1–2.**
Ross McKean reflects on the Advocate General's decision in *Schrems v Data Protection*
Commissioner (C-362/14) and explains the safe harbour regime. The author considers the
implications of the *Schrems* judgment for EU companies that had relied on safe harbour and
transborder data flows.

Read, G. and Townsend, J. (2015) 'UK Supreme Court upholds CAT's assessment of Ofcom's 08x numbers determinations', *Communications Law,* **20(1), 15–18.**
Graham Read QC and John Townsend review and comment on the highly technical 'competition' case of *BT v 02* (2014),[204] where the UK Supreme Court had the opportunity, for the first time, to consider Ofcom's powers under telecommunications legislation and the EU Common Regulatory Framework (CRF) regarding BT's introducing a 'ladder pricing' system in charging its customers for 08x numbers (such as 080, 0845 and 0870) from 2009. The article carefully talks us through the complex Ofcom dispute resolution (between the four principal mobile network operators (the MNOs), mobile phone operators, such as Telefonica, 02 and EE, etc.) and the involvement thereafter of the Competition Appeal Tribunal (CAT)[205] and the subsequent courts' underlying assessment of the EU framework[206] within which Ofcom and the MNOs operate. The authors explain that Lord Sumption's free market approach in this judgment is an important decision in a field which is becoming an increasingly prominent battleground between BT and other telecommunications operators.

Treacy, B. (2015) 'Expert comment re Schrems v Data Protection Commissioner' (2015) (CJEU), *Privacy & Data Protection,* **15(5), 2.**
Bridget Treacy examines privacy laws in Europe whereby data protection regulators are becoming increasingly proactive in their enforcement activity, despite relatively modest enforcement powers. The author comments on the *Schrems* case in detail and examines similar litigation in the US where such class actions are more frequent against ISPs.

Wragg, P. (2015) 'The legitimacy of press regulation', *Public Law,* **April, 290–307.**
Professor Paul Wragg charts the post-*Leveson* reform of print press regulation and discusses the industry-backed Independent Press Standards Organisation (IPSO) and its refusal to engage with the Royal Charter for the Self-Regulation of the Press. Wragg has been a long-standing commentator in this field.[207] The author examines press freedom and whether it has been curtailed by the Leveson recommendations.[208]

---

204 British *Telecommunications plc v Telefonica 02 UK Ltd & Others* [2014] UKSC 42.
205 Reported at [2011] CAT 24 at para. 215 'As was common ground, BT's ladder pricing for the termination of 080, 0845 and 0870 calls . . . was novel, and so raised novel questions.'
206 Namely Article 8 of Directive 2002/21/EC (Framework Directive).
207 See also: Wragg, P. (2013a) 'Time to end the tyranny: Leveson and the failure of the fourth estate', Communications Law, 18(1), 11–20.
208 See also: Wragg, P. (2013b) 'Mill's dead dogma: the value of truth to free speech jurisprudence', Public Law, April, 363–385.

Chapter 7

Defamation

> Key points
>
> This chapter will cover the following questions:
>
> ○ How do common law and defamation legislation interact?
> ○ What is the meaning of 'reputation' in defamation actions?
> ○ What is the significance of 'malice'?
> ○ What is the difference between the multiple and single publication rules?
> ○ What was the *Reynolds* defence?[1]
> ○ What are defences for operators of websites?
> ○ How are damages assessed?
> ○ Do UK libel laws interfere with 'freedom of expression'?
> ○ Can companies sue in defamation?
> ○ Has the Defamation Act 2013 made a difference to libel tourism?
> ○ Are the Scottish and Northern Irish courts becoming the new libel tourism capitals of the UK?

7.1 Overview

People have been fascinated by high-profile defamation cases for more than 300 years and tabloid journalism has been thriving on libel actions – as well as being regularly sued by the rich and famous. The law of defamation is at times concerned with conflicting issues of great sensitivity, involving both the protection of good reputation and the maintenance of the principle of free speech. In defending a libel action the difference between a statement of verifiable fact and one of honest opinion can be crucial.

This area of law has been profoundly affected by technological change. Whilst Chapter 3 has already touched on internet libel and Chapter 1 on the right to privacy, modern forms of communication have transformed fundamental values in our society and modern law in this respect has to strike a balance between freedom of expression and safeguarding personal rights, such as the protection of one's reputation and the right to privacy.

This chapter looks at recent and historical cases, including social networking libel and internet cases, and the award of damages by courts, said to vindicate injury to reputation and the surrounding publicity of any false statements which have been published. Most cases remain unreported (i.e. in law reports) because they tend to be settled out of court. But there were legal defeats too. In November 2015, former Conservative MP for South Suffolk (1983–2015), Tim Yeo, lost his libel action over a 'cash-for-advocacy' claim against the *Sunday Times* which he said had 'trashed' his reputation.[2] He faced a legal bill of £411,000.

See below
7.4.5

Until recently, defamation claims were heard in the civil courts (county or High Court) by 'libel' juries. This changed with the Defamation Act 2013 which removed the presumption in favour of jury trial.[3] In spite of this area of law being now largely in statute, the Defamation Act 2013 has perhaps not provided a sufficiently clear legal definition for what is meant by 'defamatory'.

---

1   This was repealed by s 4 Defamation Act 2013 ('honest opinion') but the *Reynolds* – 'public interest defence' is still used in Scotland and Northern Ireland and by individual academics.
2   See: *Yeo (Tim) v Times Newspapers Ltd* [2015] EWHC 3375 (QB), 25 November 2015.
3   Section 11 Defamation Act 2013 ('Trial to be without a jury unless the court orders otherwise').

Due to the 'serious harm' test introduced by section 1(1) Defamation Act 2013, libel actions have declined considerably in the English and Welsh courts whilst privacy injunctions have become increasingly fashionable as they can prevent damaging articles from ever seeing the light of day (such as *PJS*[4]). Devolved nations, such as Scotland and Northern Ireland, have not yet incorporated the 2013 Act into their legislation, which will be explored in this chapter.

7.1.1 Definition of defamation

The tort of defamation exists to afford redress for unjustified injury to reputation. By a successful action the injured reputation is vindicated. Though it used to be the case pre-Defamation Act 2013 that individual claimants were not required to prove that they had suffered financial loss, they now have to pass the 'serious harm' test, introduced under section 1(1) of 2013 Act.

Defamation is the generic term for two torts, libel and slander, and occurs when a person communicates material to a third party, in words or any other form, containing an untrue imputation against the reputation of a claimant. Libel is the written or permanent form of defamation, whereas slander is the spoken or transient form. As Lord Atkin defined it:

> Defamation is a publication of an untrue statement about a person that tends to lower his reputation in the opinion of 'right-thinking members of the community'.
>
> *(Sim v Stretch* (1936)[5])

Clement Gatley famously said in his textbook on *Libel and Slander* in the 1930s that 'everyone has a reputation'.[6] In *Brent Walker Group plc v Time Out Ltd*[7] Parker LJ commented on the absurdity of the 'tangled web of the law of defamation'.

Defamation cases tend to 'lift the carpet' on things people want kept out of public view. It is fair to say that the media thrives on gossip stories about celebrities, trying to find any given opportunity to expose their lives. Here are a couple of examples.

In December 2015, boyband heart-throb, Niall Horan, of 'One Direction', won his libel action against the Express Newspaper group after the *Daily Star* had published a number of articles in July 2015 claiming Horan used class 'A' drugs during an evening with fellow musicians Justin Bieber and Cody Simpson.[8] Dingemans J at London's High Court held the article was capable of bearing the defamatory meaning, namely that Horan was 'staring blankly' and there was express reference to 'rumours the singers were using hard drugs'.[9] This was supported by the extensive reference in the tabloid to a 'Breaking Bad-style'[10] drugs pipe.

There was Dr Jose Antonio Serrano Garcia's action against the *Daily Mail*.[11] An article written in April 2012 headlined 'A whole year of hell, thanks to a foreign doctor', by columnist and former *Sun* editor, Kelvin MacKenzie, who had accused the family doctor from Spain, practising in Hastings, of subjecting his patient, bus driver Kevin Jones, to a whole year of hell. The article had falsely claimed that Dr Serrano had misdiagnosed the patient as being alcohol dependent and, without any investigation or tests, had caused him to lose his bus and driving licence so 'robbing' him of

4 *PJS v News Group Newspapers Ltd* [2016] UKSC 26; see also: *PJS v News Group Newspapers Ltd* [2016] EWHC 2770 (QB) (Warby J).
5 [1936] 2 All ER 1237 (Lord Atkin).
6 See: *Gatley on Libel and Slander*, now edited by Milmo, P., Rogers, W. V. H., Parkes, R., Walker, C. and Busuttil, G., in its 12th edition (2013).
7 [1991] 2 QB 33.
8 Source: 'Newspaper loses challenge over Niall Horan "drugs" libel case', *The Herald* (Scotland), 7 December 2015.
9 Source: 'Newspaper loses challenge over Niall Horan "drugs" libel case', *Belfast Telegraph*, 7 December 2015.
10 *Breaking Bad* is a TV series which centres around the manufacture and sale of crystal meth.
11 See: *Serrano Garcia (Jose Antonio) v Associated Newspapers Limited* [2014] EWHC 3137 (QB).

his livelihood for a year. The *Mail* had attempted to justify its pillorying Spanish-born Dr Serrano for being 'a foreign doctor' by claiming Dr Serrano's command of English as a 'non-native-speaker' had played a part in his wrongly referring the patient to the DVLA and the patient losing his driving licences. Dingemans J found the article untrue and defamatory and awarded Dr Serrano £45,000 in damages.[12]

7.2 History of defamation in common law

English libel law was invented by the judges of the Queen's Bench as an alternative to duelling, and conceived for the protection of gentlemen, whose reputations were seen as worthy of the kind of high-class litigation offered by the High Court. No lawyer has been motivated to change defamation laws, least of all claimant lawyers who until recently used conditional fee agreements (CFA) in libel actions.

See below
7.2.7

Until the coming into force of the Defamation Act 2013, the tort of defamation was substantially governed by common law plus some statutory intervention, namely the Defamation Acts of 1952 and 1996. The 'offer of amends' to speed up matters in the courts and to encourage the parties to settle was introduced with the 1996 Act by way of an apology and damages.[13]

7.2.1 The tort of defamation

The tort of defamation developed through the common law tradition over hundreds of years, periodically being supplemented by statute. Nearly 50 years ago Diplock LJ referred to 'the artificial and archaic character of the tort of libel' in *Slim v Daily Telegraph Ltd*.[14]

The basis of the tort of defamation is injury to reputation, so it must be proved that the statement was communicated to someone other than the person defamed – a third party – because it can reasonably be assumed that a third party may well communicate the information independently of the author of it. If the statement is not obviously defamatory, the claimant must show that it would be understood in a defamatory sense, such as by some innuendo[15] or inference.[16] It is not necessary to prove that the defendant intended to refer to the claimant. The test is whether reasonable people would think the statement referred to him. Professor Winfield gave the widely accepted definition of a defamatory statement:

> [one which] tends to lower a person in the estimation of right thinking members of society generally; or which tends to make them shun or avoid that person.[17]

The main tests established by the courts in deciding whether material is defamatory are whether the words used 'tend to lower the claimant in the estimation of right-thinking members of society generally',[18] 'without justification or lawful excuse [are] calculated to injure the reputation of another, by exposing him to hatred, contempt, or ridicule',[19] or tend to make the claimant

---

12 Source: Press Release by Dr Serrano Garcia's lawyer, Daniel Taylor, of Taylor Hampton Solicitors, Chancery Lane, London, *Re Dr Jose Antonio Serrano Garcia v Associated Newspapers Limited* HQ13D00866, 6 October 2014.
13 For further discussion see: Gibbons, T. (1996).
14 [1968] 2 QB 157.
15 An allusive or oblique remark or hint, typically a suggestive or disparaging one.
16 i.e. suggestion or implication.
17 See: Winfield, P. H. (1937), p. 256.
18 *Sim v Stretch* [1936] 2 All ER 1237 (Lord Atkin).
19 *Parmiter v Coupland* (1840) 6 M & W 105 at 108 (Lord Wensleydale; then Parke B).

'be shunned and avoided and that without any moral discredit on [the claimant's] part'.[20] An insult or vulgar abuse is not considered to be defamatory because generally it is not considered likely to lower the reputation of the claimant in the estimation of right-thinking members of society (see: *Skuse v Granada Television Ltd* (1996)[21]).

The standard definition of 'defamation' in common law is:

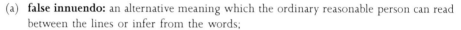
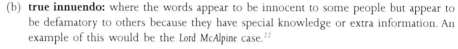

- an imputation which is likely to lower the person in the estimation of right-thinking people;
- an imputation which injures a person's reputation, by exposing them to hatred, contempt or ridicule;
- an imputation which intends to make a person be shunned or avoided.

The law of defamation recognizes two types of meaning:

- **Natural and ordinary meaning of the words:** this is not limited to the literal and obvious meaning but includes any inference which the ordinary, reasonable reader would draw from the words.
- **Innuendo meaning:** there are two types of innuendo meaning:

  (a) **false innuendo:** an alternative meaning which the ordinary reasonable person can read between the lines or infer from the words;
  (b) **true innuendo:** where the words appear to be innocent to some people but appear to be defamatory to others because they have special knowledge or extra information. An example of this would be the *Lord McAlpine* case.[22]

See below
7.5.2

The claimant must show that the defamatory statement referred to him, which is normally not too difficult. If the claimant is not identified by name, then he has to show that the words complained of are understood by some reasonable readers to be referring to him.

Defamation actions also include where the claimant has been the subject of a comical or satirical portrayal which then tended to subject him or her to ridicule or contempt (see: *Dunlop Rubber Co. Ltd v Dunlop* (1921);[23] *Hulton v Jones* (1910)[24]).

A typical example arose in *Gillick v BBC* (1996).[25] Serial litigant Mrs Victoria Gillick, well-known anti-abortionist and mother of ten children, asserted that she would be 'ridiculed, shunned and avoided' during her anti-contraceptive campaign in the 1980s when she claimed being defamed on a live BBC TV chat show (*The Garden Party* on 27 July 1989). It was implied that Gillick was morally responsible for the suicide of pregnant girls, following her campaign to prevent doctors from giving contraceptive advice to under 16-year-old girls without their parents' consent. The words, 'but after you won that battle . . . there were at least two reported cases of suicide by girls who were pregnant', were held by the CA as bearing the defamatory meaning that Mrs Gillick was morally responsible for two girls' deaths.

---

20 *Youssoupoff v MGM Pictures Ltd* (1934) 50 TLR 581 at 587 (Slesser LJ).
21 [1996] EMLR 278 at 286 (Sir Thomas Bingham MR).
22 *Lord McAlpine of West Green v Sally Bercow* [2013] EWHC 1342 (QB); (Lord Alistair McAlpine of West Green 1942–2014).
23 [1921] 1 AC 367 (HL).
24 *Hulton (E) & Co. v Jones* [1910] AC 20 (HL), [1910] AC 20 (HL).
25 [1996] EMLR 267 (CA); see also: *Gillick v Department of Health and Social Security* [1986] AC 112 (HL).

Publication

Words need to be published to a third party. Section 5 Defamation Act 2013 provides a defence to persons who are not authors, editors or commercial publishers of websites if they took reasonable care in the publication and did not know nor had any reason to believe that they had inadvertently contributed to the publication (online) of a defamatory statement. This covers printers, distributors, online device providers, etc.

A defamatory publication is usually in words, but pictures, gestures and other acts, such as a tweet, a blog or a cartoon, can also be defamatory – as the Lord McAlpine[26] case proved.

Juxtaposition

Although a statement may be quite innocent, it can become defamatory in relation to the article if read as a whole or if placed next to a picture, as was the issue in the Petters[27] case, where solicitor Leigh Petters appeared in a Channel 5 Quiz Show called Brainteaser, filmed in Bristol. Mr Petters had beaten the other three contestants to get through to the final round, which he then won together with prize money. On 8 March 2007, Channel 5 disclosed that there had been irregularities in the way in which Brainteaser had been run. In particular, it was revealed that on five occasions, when no member of the public had phoned in, the production company had put up the names of fictional winners and in one case a member of the production team went on air pretending to be the winner. Channel 5 suspended the programme and issued a statement apologizing unreservedly to viewers. In June 2009, Ofcom fined Channel 5 £300,000 for the irregularities on Brainteaser and the show was axed.

The discovery of these irregularities on Brainteaser formed the subject of reports on news bulletins on BBC One News at 6pm and 10pm and BBC News 24 at 6pm, 7pm, 8pm, 9pm, 10pm, 11pm and midnight on 8 March 2007. The story also featured prominently on Newsnight on BBC Two that evening and was again referred to in a subsequent edition of Newsnight on 14 March. These news reports all featured library footage of Brainteaser which showed Mr Petters taking part in the quiz.

Mr Petters claimed that the juxtaposition of these pictures of him with the reports of the quiz irregularities were defamatory of him. He sued the BBC in libel, claiming that viewers would have understood that he was in fact involved in the Brainteaser scam. This allegation was untrue. Mr Petters had taken part in the Brainteaser quiz show in good faith and he had won it fairly. The juxtaposition of pictures coupled with the report were deemed defamatory and Mr Petters won damages of £60,000 from the BBC and Channel 5.

The libel trial between the multi-millionaire financier Nat Rothschild[28] and the Daily Mail offers an intimate glimpse into the lives of the politically powerful and super-rich, such as the billionaire Russian industrialist Oleg Deripaska, Rothschild and the then EU Trade Commissioner Lord Mandelson (pre-2013 Act).

 KEY CASE *Rothschild (the Hon Nathaniel Philip Victor James) v Associated Newspapers Ltd* [2012] EWHC 177 (QB)

Precedent
- ❖ It is a complete defence to a defamatory action that the words complained of are true.
- ❖ The meaning of a defamatory statement must be understood as such by a hypothetical reasonable reader.

26 *Lord McAlpine of West Green v Sally Bercow* [2013] EWHC 1342 (QB).
27 *Petters (Leigh) v BBC*, 22 October 2007 (unreported).
28 [2012] EWHC 177 (QB).

Facts

Mr Rothschild sued the *Daily Mail* publishers, Associated Newspapers Ltd (ANL), for libel for a 'special investigation' article headed: 'EXCLUSIVE: Mandelson, an oligarch and a £500m deal', published on Saturday 22 May 2010. The article extended over pages 2, 8 and 9. The headline on page 9 read: 'Revealed: the astonishing story of the night Lord Mandelson was flown to Moscow by private jet to join a billionaire friend desperate to strike a deal that cost British jobs.' The paper alleged that Lord Mandelson had broken the EU Commissioners' Code of Conduct and that Mr Rothschild's conduct had been 'inappropriate' – thereby alleging corruption of politicians.

Decision

In deciding whether the words complained of bore a defamatory meaning, Tugendhat J stated that the court was not concerned with what the writer or publisher intended, nor with what any actual reasonable reader may have understood. The judge said that there must be a single meaning, 'that is a meaning which the court finds would be understood by the hypothetical reasonable reader' (applying *Slim v Daily Telegraph* (1968)[29]).

The judge cited the test applied by Sir Anthony Clarke MR in *Jeynes v News Magazines Ltd* (2008),[30] as to the meaning of 'defamatory':

1. The governing principle is reasonableness.
2. The hypothetical reasonable reader is not naïve but he is not unduly suspicious. He can read between the lines. He can read in an implication more readily than a lawyer and may indulge in a certain amount of loose thinking but he must be treated as being a man who is not avid for scandal and someone who does not, and should not, select one bad meaning where other non-defamatory meanings are available.
3. Over-elaborate analysis is best avoided.
4. The intention of the publisher is irrelevant.
5. The article must be read as a whole, and any 'bane and antidote' taken together.
6. The hypothetical reader is taken to be representative of those who would read the publication in question.
7. The court should rule out any meaning which 'can only emerge as the produce of some strained, or forced, or utterly unreasonable interpretation'.
8. It follows that it is not enough to say that by some person or another the words might be understood in a defamatory sense.

The court held that ANL had established that the words complained of by Mr Rothschild were substantially true (notwithstanding the admitted inaccuracies); that the allegation – that the purpose of the visit to Moscow was for Lord Mandelson to assist in the closing of the Alcoa deal by discussing tariffs – was so serious that it precluded the finding that the court made, namely that the facts surrounding the trip to Siberia for the joint venture proved that the meaning of the article was substantially true.

Analysis

It is then a complete defence to an action for libel (here against a newspaper) that the words complained of are substantially and materially true – known as 'justification' or

---

29 [1968] 2 QB 157.
30 [2008] EWCA Civ 130 (Sir Anthony Clarke MR).

'fair comment'.[31] Though ANL were able to prove only part of the defamatory allegations made against Mr Rothschild, the law is clear in that a defendant may nevertheless succeed if he can prove, on the balance of probabilities, that what he has alleged is *substantially* true (see: *Sutherland v Stopes* (1925);[32] *Maisel v Financial Times Ltd* (1915)[33]).

It is important to note that a preliminary ruling can be sought from the judge, who has to decide whether the words are legally capable of being defamatory, to avoid the expense of a full trial.[34]

7.2.2 Libel or slander?

We have already established that slander involves the spoken word. The difference between claims for libel and claims for slander is that a claimant must prove some economic loss, such as income, damage to business, or medical expenses, to succeed in a slander action.

In *Westcott v Westcott* (2009)[35] Richard Westcott sought damages for slander and libel as well as an injunction to restrain further publication against his daughter-in-law, the defendant Sarah Westcott, over allegations which she had made about him during an interview with the police. After a heated family argument, Mrs Westcott had telephoned the police and claimed in an oral and written statement that Mr Westcott, her father-in-law, had assaulted her and her baby. But the police decided to take no further action. Mr Westcott then sued Sarah Westcott for defamation. It was held that the police investigation and proceedings were protected by absolute privilege. The Court of Appeal in *Westcott* relied on *Taylor*,[36] establishing that immunity for out-of-court statements was not confined to persons who were subsequently called as witnesses. The policy of 'absolute privilege' was therefore applied and extended to police investigations, enabling people to speak freely, without inhibition and without fear of being sued.

Now section 14 Defamation Act 2013 provides for special damage for slander. Some special damage must be proved to flow from the statement complained of unless the publication falls into certain specific categories. This usually amounts to economic (financial) loss and has to be evidenced in court.

The publication of a statement that conveys the imputation that a person has a contagious or infectious disease no longer gives rise to a cause of action for slander unless the publication causes the person special damage.

7.2.3 The multiple publication rule[37]

One historical relic in defamation law was the long-standing principle that each re-publication of a defamatory statement or broadcast gave rise to a separate cause of action which was subject to its own limitation period. This was known as the 'multiple publication rule', based on a Victorian-era doctrine known as the 'Duke of Brunswick' principle (see: *Brunswick v Harmer* (1849)[38]). This rule still exists in Scotland and Northern Ireland.

---

31 See ss 5 ('Justification') and 6 ('Fair Comment') Defamation Act 1952.
32 [1925] AC 47.
33 (1915) 84 LJKB 2145.
34 See: s 2 Defamation Act 1996 ('offer to make amends').
35 [2009] QB 407; [2009] 2 WLR 838.
36 *Taylor v Director of the Serious Fraud Office* [1999] 2 AC 177 (HL).
37 This was repealed by s 8 Defamation Act 2013 ('single publication rule') but is still used in Scotland and N. Ireland.
38 [1849] 14 QB 185.

The central character in the *Brunswick* case was an exiled German ruler, Karl II.[39] In 1848, the Duke sent a servant to procure a copy of an article which had been published in 1830, containing an alleged defamatory statement about the Duke. The statement had been known to him since its original publication. Clearly, the then six-year limitation period for bringing an action for defamation had expired, but still the Duke sent his servant to procure copies of the offending article and brought defamation proceedings for injury to his reputation. After obtaining a fresh copy of the said article from the London publishers, the Duke promptly sued on the basis that he had the original copy and a fresh copy of the article, thereby suing for re-publication. The Queen's Bench held that the act of procuring the 'fresh' article by the Duke amounted to a new publication of a libel, giving rise to a fresh cause of action in respect of each article; and that was in spite of the fact that there was a statute in place which limited the bringing of such a civil action to six years. The court held that publisher Harmer's back issue of the offending publication in 1848 constituted a separate act of publication and was therefore within the statutory time limit. The new action commenced at the point in time when the publication was received, rather than the date of its original printing and distribution 17 years previously.

The effect of the *Brunswick* doctrine was that each individual access to an allegedly libellous publication could potentially give rise to a separate cause of action, with a separate limitation period attached to it – particularly acute in actions concerning internet archives (though the limitation period was changed under section 4A of the Limitation Act 1980 to *one year* in which an action could be brought (now section 8(6) Defamation Act 2013).

See Chapter 3.3

Kirby J criticized the doctrine in *Dow Jones & Co. Inc. v Gutnick* (2002),[40] where he said that the open-ended liability for publishers made the limitation period pointless in the internet (archive) age. He said that every time the defamatory material was accessed online, the 'stopwatch runs anew from zero'.[41] Each separate publication was then subject to the one-year limitation period.

Jordan (2010a) argued that this open-ended liability amounted to a chilling effect on free speech, which went beyond UK borders.[42] Balin *et al.* (2009) argued that the mere fact that a few English readers accessed via the internet defamatory material published in the USA was enough for a potential defamatory libel action to be brought in the UK courts.[43]

The old *Duke of Brunswick* principle of re-publication was upheld in a range of 'online libel' cases, such as the HL ruling in *Berezovsky v Michaels* (2000).[44]

The controversial judgments in the *Loutchansky*[45] actions (numbers 1–5) highlighted the serious restrictions on press freedom under Article 10 ECHR, implied in the multiple publication rule, and unsuccessfully claimed the necessity of applying the approach taken in the USA where the single publication rule limitation period runs from the first internet posting.[46]

International businessman, Dr Grigori Loutchansky, began libel action against *The Times* publishers in 1999. *The Times* magazine had portrayed Loutchansky as the head of a Russian criminal organization, involved in smuggling nuclear weapons and money laundering. The actions concerned allegations of defamation in the print editions as well as online editions. The defendants claimed qualified privilege under *Reynolds*[47] on the ground that they had a duty to publish and that the public had a right to know the allegations, but were unable to identify sources of their

39 Official title: Herzog zu Braunschweig-Lüneburg-Wolfenbüttel.
40 [2002] CLR 575.
41 Ibid., at para. 92 (Kirby J).
42 Jordan, B. (2010a), pp. 41–47.
43 Balin, R., Handman, L. and Reid, E. (2009), pp. 303–331.
44 [2000] 1 WLR 1004.
45 *Loutchansky v Times Newspapers Ltd (Nos 1–5)* [2001] EWCA Civ 1805.
46 [2002] 1 All ER at p. 312. The first action was brought on 6 December 1999 in respect of two articles published in *The Times* respectively on 8 September 1999 (the first article) and 14 October 1999 (the second article); the second action was brought on 6 December 2000 in respect of the continued internet publication of the same two articles on *The Times* website after 21 February 2000.
47 *Reynolds v Times Newspapers Ltd* [2001] 2 AC 127.

information ('public interest test'). The appellants also invoked Article 10 ECHR before the ECtHR in Strasbourg in 2009.

The High Court ruled in favour of the claimant in April 2001 and *The Times* publishers cross-appealed. The CA dismissed the print and online appeals. In doing so the court considered the 'responsible journalism' test and established *unless* the journalists had acted 'responsibly' he (and the publishers) could not claim qualified privilege.

See below
7.4.3

This involved *inter alia* that the newspaper had a duty to publish the information (whether true or false); whether the publisher would have been open to legitimate criticism had he not published (applying: *Al-Fagih v H.H. Saudi Research and Marketing (UK) Limited* (2001)[48])?

The CA also considered the *Brunswick* re-publication rule. *The Times* claimed that limitation ran from the date when the issue was put on the paper's website, and the claimant that limitation began afresh, each time the site was accessed and transmitted to a reader. The CA dismissed *The Times'* libel defence of 'archive privilege'.

The Master of the Rolls, Simon Brown LJ held:

> The Times' website could not possibly be described as responsible journalism. We do not believe that it can be convincingly argued that the appellants had a *Reynolds* duty to publish those articles in that way without qualification. It follows that we consider that the Judge was right to strike out the qualified privilege defence in the second action although not for the primary reason that he gave for so doing. For these reasons the Internet Single Publication appeal is also dismissed.

7.2.4 On whom lies the burden of proof?

It is common that a claimant in civil law has to prove his case to succeed at trial. Not so in a defamation action: here the claimant alleges that a publication is false and the defendant has to prove the statement at the heart of the case is true. It seems ironic that the defendant's burden of proof was originally established to protect a person's honour and that this ancient common law principle has since been used in favour of libel claimants in the British courts. This has now (slightly) changed in that section 1(1) of the Defamation Act 2013 requires that the claimant must prove 'serious harm' to his or her reputation Otherwise the statement (or 'sting of the libel') is not regarded as defamatory.

See below
7.3.2

It is relatively rare for individuals to defend a libel case successfully against a big corporation as the 'McLibel'[49] case in 2005 demonstrated. Gardener Helen Steel and postman David Morris were found 'guilty' in 1997 of libelling the world's largest hamburger corporation, McDonald's, in a leaflet campaign issued by London Greenpeace.

The 'McLibel Two' spent 314 days in the High Court defending themselves because defamation actions do not warrant legal aid. McDonald's were awarded £60,000 in damages (later reduced to £40,000 on appeal). The ECtHR ruled that Steel and Morris did not have a fair trial under Article 6 ECHR, because of the lack of legal aid available to libel defendants in the UK, and that their freedom of expression had been violated by the 1997 High Court judgment.

In 1997, the *Daily Mail* printed a controversial front page referring to the killing of Stephen Lawrence in 1993 in south-east London. The tabloid subsequently embarked on a campaign to bring five young male racist suspects to justice. On the 14 February 1997, the *Mail* took the unprecedented step of naming them, showing large photographs and the caption 'Murderers' and 'If we are wrong, let them sue us'. The paper named Gary Dobson, David Norris, Neil and Jamie Acourt

---

48   Unreported, 5 November 2001 (Simon Brown LJ's judgment).
49   *Steel and Morris v United Kingdom* [2005] (Application No 68416/01); judgment of 15 February 2005 (ECHR).

and Luke Knight as Stephen's killers and challenged the gang to sue the newspaper in a libel action. They never did.

The paper reprinted the same front page in July 2006 after new evidence emerged in the Stephen Lawrence killing. Gary Dobson and David Norris were eventually convicted of Stephen's racist murder. Gary Dobson was sentenced at the Old Bailey to a minimum of 15 years and two months' and David Norris to 14 years and three months' imprisonment because both had been under 18 at the time of the killing.

Sometimes claimants are disappointed with damages and cost awards by the courts – in spite of their victory. Coronation Street actor Bill (William) Roache won his libel action against The Sun over a claim in November 1990 that he was as boring as his screen character Ken Barlow and hated by his television colleagues.[50] The defendant newspaper, its editor Kelvin Mackenzie and freelance journalist Ken Irwin, pleaded 'fair comment' and, to a limited extent, justification. They paid at first £25,000 and then a further £25,000 into court, but Mr Roache did not accept the amount of damages, arguing that £50,000 would not cover his six-figure court costs. He had expected at least £100,000.

Roache then sued his famous libel lawyer, Peter Carter-Ruck, for negligence over his handling of his libel action against the Sun – which Roache duly lost. He had to declare himself bankrupt in 1999 with debts of around £300,000.

Another litigant who was virtually bankrupted through his libel action was self-professed 'Third Reich' specialist David Irving, who has consistently denied the Holocaust. In Irving v Penguin Books Ltd and Deborah Lipstadt (1996),[51] Irving lost his lengthy libel action against American academic Deborah Lipstadt and her publishers Penguin. Lipstadt said in her 1994 book that Irving had misinterpreted historical evidence to minimize Hitler's culpability in the Holocaust.[52] Gray J – sitting without a jury (because the bulk of evidential material produced by Mr Irving was in German) – ruled that Mr Irving was 'an active Holocaust denier, anti-Semitic and racist' who had 'distorted historical data to suit his own ideological agenda'.[53]

7.2.5 Justification

It is important to note that the defence of justification is now replaced by 'truth' under section 2(1) Defamation Act 2013 (England and Wales). We will however look at the defence historically in common law since it is still used in Northern Ireland and Scotland.

For a plea of 'justification' to succeed, there must be a final finding on the merits by a court on admissible evidence that the defamatory 'sting' of the allegation complained of (the 'sting of the libel') is objectively true as a matter of fact. The defendant does not have to prove that every word he published was true. He has to establish the 'essential' or 'substantial' truth of the sting of the libel. To prove the truth of some lesser defamatory meaning does not provide a complete defence.

Under modern libel practice a defendant must set out in his statement that the defamatory meaning he seeks to prove is essentially or substantially true. This is called the 'Lucas Box meaning'. The Lucas Box principle was formulated by the Court of Appeal in Lucas Box v News Group Newspapers Ltd (1986).[54] It was held that, in a defamation action, a defendant who does not agree with the meaning of the words complained of by the claimant, is entitled to give an alternative meaning and give particulars to justify that meaning ('the Lucas Box meaning').

---

50 See: Roache v Newsgroup Newspapers Ltd [1998] EMLR 161.
51 (1996) judgment of 11 April 2000 (QBD) (unreported).
52 See: Lipstadt, D. E. (1994).
53 See: Lipstadt, D. E. (2006), quoting Gray J at p. 214.
54 See: Lucas Box v News Group Newspapers Ltd; Lucas-Box v Associated Newspapers Group plc and others; Polly Peck (Holdings) plc v Trelford, Viscount de L'Isle v Times Newspapers Ltd [1986] 1 WLR 147 (CA) (as per Ackner LJ).

Whether 'justification' is permitted as a defence depends on the answer to three questions:

1. Is the defence meaning capable of arising from the publication?
2. Does the defence meaning arise from a separate and distinct allegation in the publication, about which the claimant does not complain?
3. Has the defendant provided proper particulars of fact that are capable of supporting the defence?

The *Lucas Box* meaning was applied in the *Elaine Chase* case (2002).[55] Ms Chase, a qualified state registered children's nurse – formerly employed as a paediatric community sister by the South Essex Mental Health and Community Care NHS Trust – alleged that she was being 'fingered' (i.e. exposed) by *The Sun* for a front-page article on 22 June 2002. The headline read: 'NURSE IS PROBED OVER 18 DEATHS: WORLD EXCLUSIVE'. The article did not directly name her but alleged that Ms Chase was suspected of overdosing terminally ill youngsters with painkillers. The tabloid identified the children concerned as nine boys and nine girls, aged between eight weeks and 17 years. Ms Chase argued that a significant number of readers would identify her by way of jigsaw identification. *The Sun* made references to mercy killers, such as Dr Harold Shipman and nurse Beverley Allitt. Ms Chase argued that the implication of such juxtaposition was unmistakable and referred to her. A subsequent edition of *The Sun* published a photograph of the claimant on the front page, although her face was pixelated following an injunction obtained earlier against the newspaper.

The defendant newspaper sought to rely on the fact that allegations were made by largely unidentified third parties in broad terms about the claimant, irrespective of whether those allegations were true or false. This meant a defence of justification based on reasonable grounds for suspicion focusing on some conduct of the individual so as to give rise to the suspicion ('the conduct rule'). The judge rejected the newspaper's defence of justification and entered judgment in favour of Elaine Chase. The newspaper appealed. The court held that the defence of justification, based on 'reasonable grounds for suspicion' must focus on conduct of the claimant that gave rise to the suspicion. It was not permissible to rely on hearsay. The appeal was dismissed.

7.2.6 Unintentional libel and lookalike publications

Some journalists have learned, to the financial detriment of their newspapers, that a sense of humour or, worse still, a joke, finds no favour in the libel courts. The problem arises frequently when a wrong caption to a photo or the wrong TV footage has been added in a newspaper or online edition. Or journalists have got it wrong when their intention was to be either funny or witty in satirical sketches by using innuendo.

The common law rule for 'lookalike' libel dates back to an early twentieth-century case, that of *Artemus Jones* (see: *Hulton v Jones* (1910)[56]). A seemingly simple joke misfired when, in 1910, the *Sunday Chronicle* published a satirical sketch about a certain 'Artemus Jones', said to be a fictional Peckham church warden, who had gone to France with a woman 'who was not his wife'. A Welsh barrister called Thomas Artemus Jones (who was not from Peckham and was not a church warden) complained to the defamation courts and received the then enormous sum of £1,750 in libel damages. He satisfied the House of Lords that reasonable people might conclude that the defamatory words referred to him. The newspaper's assertion that its Artemus Jones was completely imaginary was somewhat undermined by the fact that Thomas Artemus Jones had been a subeditor on the paper seven years earlier. The *Artemus Jones* case remains the precedent for strict liability in defamation law, placing the burden on the publisher, editor and/or author to ensure – as a matter of principle – that

55 *Chase (Elaine) v News Group Newspapers Ltd* [2002] EWCA Civ 1772 (CA).
56 [1910] AC 20 (HL).

no individual has to put up with a damaged reputation as a result of that publication, even if the person concerned suffers damage wholly independently of any fault on the part of the publisher.

The *Artemus Jones* rule was applied in *Dwek v Macmillan Publishers Ltd* (1999),[57] where a book published a photograph – taken some 20 years earlier – showing the claimant Norman Dwek sitting next to a woman who was (correctly) described as a prostitute. The photo in question showed a young woman sitting between two men on a sofa, published in an unauthorized biography of then Harrods owner Mohammed Al Fayed. It was the caption which dramatically transformed the meaning of the image. It read: 'Fantasies: Louise "Michaels" was a prostitute who befriended Dodi (left in photograph).' But the man on the left in the photo was not Dodi Al Fayed,[58] but Norman Dwek, a family dentist from Richmond. The same photograph (with the other man cropped out of the picture) was reprinted in both the *Mail on Sunday* and the *Evening Standard*, with the respective captions: 'Shared: Dodi with high-class prostitute Louise Dyrbusz, who also saw his uncle'.

Mr Dwek successfully sued the book publishers and the newspapers for defamation. The Court of Appeal agreed with Mr Dwek that readers would look at the photograph in the context of the caption and believe that the man in the photo had sex with prostitutes. Mr Dwek rightly argued that many readers would recognize him as being that man, even though it was said to be a photograph of Dodi Al Fayed. The CA held that the photographic juxtaposition was defamatory.

The addition of a caption to a photograph may render it defamatory, so care should be taken when choosing appropriate captions or TV footage, particularly when the subject matter is controversial. The media publisher may seek to defend the libel action on the basis that any reader who identified the person in the photograph would know that the allegation was untrue.

With digital photo-imaging and the ease with which images can now be changed or enhanced, there are additional potential dangers highlighted in the now famous defamation action brought by the *Neighbours* actors Anne Charleston and Ian Smith.[59] The actors, best known as the respectable married couple Harold and Madge Bishop in the soap, sued the publisher and editor of the *News of the World* over photographs showing their faces superimposed on to the bodies of pornographic models. The headlines read: 'Strewth! What's Harold up to with our Madge?' and 'Porn Shocker for Neighbours stars'. The accompanying article made clear that the photographs were from a pornographic computer game and produced by superimposing the actors' faces on the bodies without their knowledge. The argument advanced by Ms Charleston and Mr Smith was that many readers simply scan headlines and 'eye-catching' images without bothering to read the whole of the article. However, the House of Lords decreed that, when determining whether the photograph and text were defamatory, the *whole* of the accompanying article must be taken into account (for example 'bane (poison) and antidote (remedy)' as per *Charleston v News Group Newspapers Ltd* (1995)[60]).

Another case, involving Harrods owner Mohammed Al Fayed, demonstrates how the *Artemus Jones* case[61] is still applied in 'lookalike' situations. On 31 March 2002 Harrods issued a press release headed 'Al Fayed reveals plan to "float" Harrods', inviting the media to contact someone called Loof Lirpa[62] as there was to be an important announcement on the morning of the following day, i.e. 1 April: the launch of a floating shop on a canal boat.[63] The *Wall Street Journal* picked up the story on 5 April under the headline, 'The Enron of Britain?', reporting that 'if Harrods, the British luxury retailer, ever goes public, investors would be wise to question its every disclosure'. Eady J

---

57 *Dwek v Macmillan Publishers Ltd & Others* [1999] EWCA Civ 2002.
58 Emad El-Din Mohamed Abdel Moneim Fayed, better known as Dodi Fayed, was the son of Egyptian billionaire Mohamed Al-Fayed. He was the lover of Diana, Princess of Wales, with whom he died in a car crash in Paris, on 31 August 1997.
59 See: *Charleston v News Group Newspapers Ltd* [1995] 2 AC 65 (HL).
60 [1995] 2 AC 65 (HL).
61 See: *Hulton v Jones* [1910] AC 20 (HL).
62 Note: 'April fool' – spelt backwards!
63 The statement was only available until noon on the chairman's personal website, www.alfayed.com.

determined that the resulting libel action should be heard in the UK, rather than the US, stating that the words could mean that every corporate disclosure of Harrods should be distrusted, and even that 'it is reasonably suspected that if the claimant [Harrods] were to become a public company it would prove itself to be Britain's Enron by deceiving and defrauding its investors on a huge scale'. The case was settled out of court (under the 'offer to make amends') with Harrods demanding an apology and damages to be paid to charity. The journal's defence stated that it was 'meant to be a humorous comment on the bogus press release'.[64] The April fool joke had badly backfired. The history of the 'joke' defence is therefore not a happy one. Words are defamatory and intention is irrelevant.

In *O'Shea v MGN* (2001)[65] Morland J endeavoured to strike a balance between freedom of expression and an individual's right to privacy under Article 8 ECHR when considering strict liability libel. The judge had to decide whether a photograph (of Miss E) would be recognized by those who knew the claimant and would identify her – albeit wrongly – as being the person in the photograph, which would give her the cause of action in libel. Miss E had appeared in an advertisement for a pornographic internet service provider (the second defendant), who in turn had advertised in the *Sunday Mirror*. In this case the claimant bore a striking resemblance to a 'Miss E', though the photograph in question did not name or identify the claimant, other than by virtue of the strong resemblance between her and Miss E. Referring to *Hulton v Jones*, Morland J concluded:

> The test in law is objective. Would the ordinary reader of the advertisement, having regard to the words complained of and the photograph in the context of the advertisement as a whole and clothed with the special knowledge of the publishers, that is that the photograph was the 'spit and image' of the claimant, have reasonably concluded that the woman speaking into the telephone [in the photograph] was the claimant?[66]

Morland J ruled that the strict liability principle should not cover the 'lookalike' situation in this case, and to allow it to do so would be an unjustifiable interference with the vital right of freedom of expression and the democratic principle of a free press. Consequently, Miss O'Shea may well have suffered some embarrassment, but the court held that she was not protected under Article 8 ECHR, nor did she win her libel action.

 FOR THOUGHT

> What happens if a journalist unintentionally refers to a fictitious name which he has made up, and there is such a person 'out there'? Discuss with reference to common law and statutory provision including 'freedom of expression' and any defences the journalist may have.

7.2.7 What are the cost implications of a libel action?

Legal aid is not generally available for defamation cases, so the cost of proceedings will generally have to be paid personally by the defendant – as in the case of *Dr Simon Singh*.[67]

---

64 See also: *Dow Jones & Company, Inc. v Harrods Ltd, and Mohamed Al Fayed* (2003) (Docket No 02-9364). United States Court of Appeals, Second Circuit. Argued: 23 September 2003. Decided: 10 October 2003.
65 [2001] EMLR 40 (QBD).
66 *Hulton v Jones* [1910] AC at 84 (Morland J in *O'Shea v MGN*).
67 *BCA v Singh* [2010] EWCA Civ 350.

Prior to the introduction of conditional fee agreements (or 'CFAs' – commonly known as 'no win no fee'), with recoverable success fees and ATE ('after the event') insurance premiums, claimants could not realistically bring defamation claims, however meritorious, against newspapers because they could not afford the legal fees. Newspapers and media organizations would regularly and deliberately outspend claimants in order to force them into submission. Raphael (1989) cites a lawyer for the *Daily Express*, as he researched the Jeffrey Archer libel action (and others):[68]

> If a newspaper were honest I suspect they would admit to drawing actions out in the hope that a [claimant] runs up large legal bills, loses heart and settles.[69]

Increasingly CFAs were used in defamation cases, such as that of Naomi Campbell in her action against the *Daily Mirror*.[70] Lawyers would typically charge an uplift of up to 100 per cent in 'success fees', which encouraged them to accept cases with a 50/50 chance of success. This meant that newspapers and other media groups were increasingly subject to numerous 'libel' claims from individuals who had until then been unable to enforce their legal rights against them. A CFA agreement then enabled a defamation litigant to engage a lawyer on a total or partial 'no win no fee' basis with an agreement that the lawyer would be paid up to twice their fee if they were successful.

New rules on CFAs, following the Jackson[71] reforms, came into force on 1 April 2013.[72]

7.2.8 Malicious falsehood: the role of malice

As we have seen above in the *McLibel* case for example, claimants will not normally receive any legal aid for pursuing an action in defamation. However, there may be occasions when the claimant is entitled to legal aid if he pursues a 'malicious' or 'injurious falsehood' claim. He must then prove actual economic loss rather than purely non-economic damage to his reputation.

In *Joyce v Sengupta* (1993),[73] the CA allowed an appeal by Linda Joyce, the Princess Royal's maid, when claiming malicious falsehood. The case of Ms Joyce had attracted considerable public and media attention where Linda Joyce had been accused of stealing intimate love letters written to Princess Anne by Commander Timothy Lawrence which, in turn, had sparked rumours about the Princess Royal's troubled 15-year marriage to Captain Mark Phillips. Kim Sengupta, Chief Crime Correspondent of the *Today* newspaper, had published the offending article and allegations on 25 April 1989, headlined 'Royal Maid Stole Letters'. Though the article appeared grossly defamatory, Ms Joyce did not have the money 'up front' to sue in libel and legal aid was clearly not available to her. Ms Joyce argued 'injurious falsehood' (also referred to as 'trade libel') and that the article had caused her financial loss by loss of reputation, loss of employment and by not obtaining references from her former employer, the Royal Household. Ms Joyce's claim of malicious falsehood was successful, in that the article contained serious untruths about her, that it had been published maliciously and the defendants were recklessly indifferent about the falsity of the allegations.

What is important in such a claim is that damages and economic loss have to be quantified as illustrated in the *Stéphane Grappelli*[74] case. Internationally famous jazz violinist Stéphane Grappelli (1908–1997) and guitarist William Charles Disley ('Diz' Disley, 1931–2010) sued their concert

---

68 See: Raphael, A. (1989); the book was written prior to the introduction of CFAs.

69 Ibid., quoting Justin Walford, a lawyer employed at that time by the *Daily Express*.

70 *Campbell v Mirror Group Newspapers Ltd* [2002] EWHC 499 (QB) – initially a defamation action; her privacy action was successful in the House of Lords, see: *Campbell v Mirror Group Newspapers Ltd* [2004] UKHL 22.

71 See: Ministry of Justice (2010b) *Review of Civil Litigation Costs. Final Report* by Rupert Jackson J, December 2009 ('The Jackson Report').

72 These changes were brought about by ss 44 and 46 Legal Aid, Sentencing and Punishment of Offenders Act 2012 (LAPSO) and the Conditional Fee Agreements Order 2013.

73 [1993] 1 WLR 337.

74 *Grappelli v Derek Block (Holdings) Ltd* [1981] 1 WLR 822.

and tour promoters, Derek Block (Holdings) Ltd, in malicious falsehood. Derek Block had arranged 'gigs' for the Grappelli Jazz Trio at Tameside on 26 November 1976 and Milton Keynes on 4 December 1976.

On 21 September 1976 tour promoters cancelled the Tameside and Milton Keynes concerts, with the explanation that Mr Grappelli was 'very seriously ill' in Paris, adding that it would be surprising 'if he [Grappelli] ever toured again'. Lord Denning MR dismissed the original defamation action on the grounds that the statement itself was not defamatory. The claimants filed a new action relying on injurious falsehood and maliciousness, since the announcement was clearly damaging to Mr Grappelli's and the Trio's future success. The claimants were successful in their malicious falsehood action after they had provided the court with evidence of financial losses by way of a statement of quantum of damages.[75]

In *Tse Wai Chun Paul v Albert Cheng* (2001)[76] Lord Nicholls of Birkenhead was concerned with the ingredients of 'malice', which could defeat the defence of 'fair comment', when he said:

> First, the comment must be on a matter of public interest. Public interest is not to be confined within narrow limits today. Second, the comment must be recognisable as comment, as distinct from an imputation of fact. If the imputation is one of fact, a ground of defence must be sought elsewhere, for example, justification or privilege. . . . Third, the comment must be based on facts which are true or protected by privilege . . . the comment must be one which could have been made by an honest person, however prejudiced he might be, and however exaggerated or obstinate his views.[77]

Here follow two example which demonstrate that companies can sue for defamation as well as claim malicious falsehood.

See below
7.7.1

In *Tesco Stores v Guardian* (2008)[78] the supermarket giant sued for 'maliciousness' after the newspaper and its editor, Alan Rusbridger, had claimed the company was avoiding corporation tax through complex offshore property deals. It turned out that Tesco's dealings did aim to avoid tax, but a different one – stamp duty land tax – and for far less than alleged. Before the article was published, Tesco declined to meet the reporters and gave limited written responses. In the circumstances, the newspaper misunderstood the purpose behind the deals, but the story's thrust – regarding tax avoidance – was correct. In May, the *Guardian* nonetheless issued an extensive apology and explanation of its inaccuracies. Tesco, advised by Carter-Ruck, carried on its action in spite of an 'offer of amends' from the *Guardian*.[79] Subsequent investigations by *Private Eye* found that Tesco had offshore schemes to reduce corporation tax too.

At a pre-trial hearing before Eady J, lawyers for Tesco tried to exclude the *Private Eye* evidence and keep the 'offer of amends' on the table, while it pursued the action. The judge ruled against the corporation and struck out the action for 'malicious falsehood'. Two months later, Tesco agreed to a further correction and apology, and a settlement was reached out of court. By then, the costs had become enormous, dwarfing any damages.[80]

After the settlement, Mr Rusbridger argued in his defence that the *Guardian* was guilty of 'erroneous statements honestly made', but was not afforded the same protections as in the United States, quoting the landmark judgment in *New York Times Co. v Sullivan* (1964).[81] The court held that

---

75 Referring *inter alia* to *Wright v Woodgate* (1835) 2 CR M & R 573 at 577.
76 [2001] EMLR 777 (Lord Nicholls of Birkenhead, sitting in the Court of Final Appeal of Hong Kong).
77 Ibid., paras 16–21.
78 See: *Tesco Stores Ltd v Guardian News & Media Ltd and Rusbridger* [2008] EWHC 14 (QB).
79 Source: 'Corrections and clarifications', *The Guardian*, 3 May 2008.
80 *Tesco* [2008] at para. 860.
81 (1964) 376 US 254 (United States Supreme Court). The case established the actual malice test which has to be met before press reports about public officials can be considered to be defamatory and hence allowed free reporting of the civil rights campaigns in the southern United States. It is one of the key decisions supporting the freedom of the press. The actual malice standard

the correct approach to the proposed amendment and apology was to err on the side of generosity, thereby apologize and publish a correction.[82]

'Malicious falsehood' was also advanced in the *Tesla Motors* (2013)[83] case, an action against the BBC's popular programme *Top Gear* in 2008 and its then host, Jeremy Clarkson. Electric sports car maker Tesla Motors Inc., best known for its luxury electric cars, based in Palo Alto, California, claimed that *Top Gear* had faked a scene that appeared to show a Tesla Roadster running out of power, which Tesla claimed led to lower sales. Clarkson had ridiculed the Tesla Roadster running out of battery power after only 55 miles, far short of the 200 miles that Tesla had claimed.

In its ruling in 2013, the CA dismissed the Tesla Motors malicious falsehood claim. Moore-Bick LJ agreed with the first instance judge that the comments made by Clarkson regarding the car's range and reliability whilst testing them on the *Top Gear* test track could not bear the defamatory meaning, specifically that Tesla had intentionally and significantly misled potential customers. With respect to the malicious falsehood claim, the judge held that Tesla had failed sufficiently to particularize any damage the allegedly false statements were calculated to cause. While the court did not go so far as to say Tesla's claim was an abuse of process, it did not consider Tesla's prospect of recovering a substantial sum by way of damages sufficient to justify continuing the proceedings. Moore-Bick LJ found it difficult to believe that Tesla claimed to have suffered loss in revenue in the region of $4 million. The company had not been able to show any 'special damage' right from the outset of its claim in 2008.

In summary, an action in malicious falsehood for a publication or statement in fact must be injurious to the character of another and requires proof of economic loss. It is only then that the law will consider the publication 'malicious', and the courts will interpret the meaning of 'malice' narrowly.

7.3 Defamation Act 2013

See below

7.3.1

It took three years to pass the Defamation Act 2013 in Parliament, following an initial promise by the then Labour Justice Minister and Lord Chancellor, Jack Straw, in 2009, to reform the libel laws after a series of revelations that libel threats had silenced scientists, doctors, biographers, community lawyers, consumer groups and human rights activists. Additionally, the cases of *Singh*[84] and *Flood*[85] had demonstrated the complexities of modern English libel laws with a multifaceted substantive overburdened common law and a costly procedure affordable only to celebrities and rich foreigners.

To reduce the chilling effect on freedom of expression resulting particularly from the *Simon Singh* case, Lord Lester of Herne Hill proposed a private member's Defamation Bill in the House of Lords in July 2010.[86] This was then followed by the government's own bill,[87] championed by Lord McNally, the Liberal Democrat leader in the Lords and Secretary of State for Justice at the time. One of the aims was to reduce foreign defamation actions in the UK which had made London the 'libel capital of the world'.

requires that the claimant has to prove that the publisher of the statement in question knew that the statement was false or acted in reckless disregard of its truth or falsity. Because of the extremely high burden of proof on the claimant, and the difficulty of proving the defendant's knowledge and intentions, such cases – when they involve public figures – rarely prevail.

82 *Tesco* [2008] at para. 868.
83 *Tesla Motors Ltd v British Broadcasting Corporation* [2013] EWCA 152 (CA Civ Div).
84 See: *British Chiropractic Association (BCA) v Singh* [2010] EWCA Civ 350.
85 *Flood v Times Newspapers Ltd* [2011] UKSC 11.
86 [2010–12] First Report: Draft Defamation Bill (HL Paper 203/HC 930).
87 See: Ministry of Justice (2012c).

The legislative fallout from the Leveson Report in 2012,[88] with its proposed Royal Charter, became inextricably linked with the draft Defamation Bill which had been nearing its completion in February 2013. Leveson LJ had recommended that members of the print press who declined to co-operate with a new regulator should be liable for all costs in libel and privacy cases, even when they won, and that politicians and officials should be entitled to curb media reporting, provided 'it is for a legitimate purpose and is necessary in a democratic society'.[89]

See Chapter 6.3

The 'Leveson clause' was introduced by film producer and Labour Peer, Lord Puttnam, in early February 2013, and looked set to sabotage the Defamation Bill, with Prime Minister David Cameron arguing that this was press regulation by the back door. For Labour, which favoured statutory regulation of the press, this was a way to kill two 'media' birds with one legislative stone. In fact, for a while it looked as if the Defamation Bill was totally dead. In a last-minute attempt to quell the revolt in the House of Lords,[90] Lord McNally promised the much-discussed government proposal for a Royal Charter to oversee press regulation in order to save the long-awaited defamation legislation.

The Defamation Act 2013 was enacted on 25 April 2013. The most significant changes included the introduction of a requirement to show 'serious harm' (to reputation of individual(s) or profit loss for profit-making organizations), the reformulation of the defences of truth in the form of 'honest opinion' and publication on matters of public interest (putting *Reynolds* on a statutory footing), and the introduction of greater protection for operators of websites. The 2013 Act was not adopted by either Scotland or Northern Ireland at that time.

7.3.1 Reform of defamation laws in England and Wales

It is important to note that the Defamation Act 2013 reforms aspects of the law of defamation which means that common law continues to co-exist alongside statute (i.e. the Defamation Acts of 1952 and 1996) as well as in common law (particularly in Scotland and Northern Ireland).

The *Flood* ruling in 2011 had marked the end of a six-year legal battle that began with an article by Michael Gillard on 2 June 2006 in *The Times* (and its online edition) headed 'Detective accused of taking bribes from Russian exiles'. The newspaper alleged that DS Flood had accepted bribes from a private security company that was acting for a Russian oligarch. The legal dispute centred on the *Reynolds* defence whereby Tugendhat J had initially ruled in the High Court in 2009 that the newspaper could use *Reynolds* qualified privilege; however, the CA allowed Mr Flood's appeal in 2010 and overturned the High Court ruling.

See below 7.4.3

The Supreme Court (UKSC) ruling in *Flood* (2011)[91] allowed the *Reynolds* defence 'in the public interest'. This ruling was significant in that the media regained their right to freedom of expression. This crucially meant that the truth of the allegations did not have to be proved as long as the matter was of 'serious public concern'. The case also set the precedent for the 'responsible journalism test' (also applied in *Spiller and another v Joseph and others* (2010)[92]).

The Times' reporting serious police corruption in the DS Gary Flood case was seen as being of considerable public interest. What could finally be reported was that Flood had abused his position as a police officer with the Metropolitan Police's Extradition Unit by corruptly accepting £20,000 in bribes from some of Russia's most wanted suspected criminals in return for selling to them highly confidential Home Office and police intelligence about attempts to extradite them to Russia

88 See: Leveson, Lord LJ (2012).
89 Ibid., vol. 4, Part K, 'Regulatory Models for the Future', at para. 15.3, pp. 1703–1704. For a full set of recommendations see: ibid., pp. 1584–1594.
90 The rebellion in the House of Lords included prominent Tories such as Lord Fowler, Lord Hurd and Lord Ashcroft, as well as more than 60 crossbenchers including Baroness O'Neill (the chair of the Equalities and Human Rights Commission) and former Speaker of the House of Commons Baroness Boothroyd.
91 See: *Flood v Times Newspapers Ltd* [2011] UKSC 11.
92 [2010] UKSC 53.

to face criminal charges. DS Flood had 'committed an appalling breach of duty and betrayal of trust' and 'had thereby also committed a very serious criminal offence'.[93]

7.3.2 Defamation Act 2013: key areas

The Defamation Act 2013 comprises 17 sections, with a mixture of codification, revision and general provisions.

Section 1 introduces the 'serious harm' test which now serves as the threshold test to the bringing of a claim. Sections 2 to 7 concern defences. The main common law defences are abolished and replaced. Section 2 restates the 'justification' defence under the label of 'truth', section 3 recasts the honest comment defence as 'honest opinion', and section 4 replaces *Reynolds* privilege with a new defence of 'publication on a matter of public interest'. Section 4(3) restates the reportage variant of the defence, for 'the defendant to believe that publishing the statement was in the public interest'. Section 5 provides a new defence for the operators of websites. Sections 6 and 7 deal with aspects of privilege, including the provision of a qualified privilege for statements made in peer-reviewed scientific or academic journals.

The latter part of the statute concerns publication, jurisdiction, the trial process and remedies. In a revision of particular importance to online publishers, section 8 introduced a 'single publication rule' that limits the period for claims to run from the date of 'first publication', thereby abolishing the *Duke of Brunswick* multiple-publication rule. Section 9 addresses the phenomenon of 'libel tourism', and now compels the court to refuse jurisdiction unless it is satisfied that England and Wales is 'clearly the most appropriate place' for the action to be brought for claimants outside the UK and the EU.

Section 10 provides that an action cannot be brought against persons who are involved in, but not primarily responsible for, publication unless 'it is not reasonably practicable for an action to be brought against the author, editor or publisher'. Section 11 ends the presumption of trial by jury in defamation actions (unless specifically ordered by a judge in exceptional cases). Sections 12 and 13 address the question of remedies. They provide the court with power to order publication of summaries of judgments and to compel the 'take-down' of impugned publications. The final substantive provision, section 14, concerns aspects of the law of slander and special damage.[94]

Summary of contents

Section 1: requirement of serious harm

Section 1(1) Defamation Act 2013 provides the serious harm test: that a statement is not defamatory unless its publication has caused or is likely to cause *serious harm* to the reputation of the claimant.

> 1(1)   A statement is not defamatory unless its publication has caused or is likely to cause serious harm to the reputation of the claimant.

The provision extends to situations where publication is likely to cause serious harm in order to cover situations where the harm has not yet occurred at the time the action for defamation is commenced. This was based on the 1936 HL decision in *Sim v Stretch*[95] cited in the *Sarah Thornton* case

---

93   See: *Flood v Times Newspapers Ltd* [2013] EWHC 4075 (QB) at para. 12 (Nicola Davies J).

94   Section 14(1) repeals the Slander of Women Act 1891.

95   [1936] 2 All ER 1237.

(below),[96] where the threshold for 'seriousness' had been set for what is defamatory. The CA in the *Yousef Jameel v Dow Jones* case (2005)[97] established that there needs to be a 'real and substantial tort'.

The *Sarah Thornton*[98] litigation arose out of a book review by well-known journalist Lynn Barber of Thornton's book *Seven Days in the Art World*. Dr Thornton was successful in her action against the *Telegraph* after a number of cross-appeals. The case made headlines because the defendant's 'offer of amends' was overturned by a finding of 'malice' (on the journalist's behalf) and the court awarded general damages for malicious falsehood. The precedent for the 'serious harm' test in common law was set. Another important precedent set in this case was that 'business libel' was permitted, meaning that a business or organization could sue for defamation in respect of imputations which imply a lack of skill, qualification or efficacy even if they do not imply any moral fault.

 KEY CASE

Thornton (Sarah) v Telegraph Media Group Ltd [2011] EWHC 1884 (QB)

Precedent

❖ There must be a 'threshold of seriousness' in what constitutes a 'defamatory' imputation.

❖ A statement is not defamatory unless its publication has caused or is likely to cause serious harm to the reputation of the claimant.

❖ 'Substantial harm' to the claimant has to be balanced with Article 10 ECHR relating to press freedom.

Facts

The claimant, an author and academic Dr Sarah Thornton, sued for libel and malicious falsehood in respect of a book review published in the *Daily Telegraph*. Part of the words complained of said that Dr Thornton allowed her interview subjects 'copy approval'. Thornton claimed that those words meant that she lacked integrity as a writer. Her primary case was that the article reflected upon her professional reputation ('business libel'), but, from the context of the entire article, it was also a personal libel.[99]

After Ms Thornton's first libel action, the defendants (newspaper and journalist Lynn Barber) made an offer of amends in relation to parts of the review, relying on the defence of 'fair comment'. This was struck out by Sir Charles Gray and the defendant newspaper sought permission to appeal.[100] On 26 July 2011 Tugendhat J handed down a reserved judgment after the trial in *Thornton*, reversing the previous judgment at trial by judge and jury.

Decision

Based on the evidence of journalist Lynn Barber, Tugendhat J found that 'Ms Barber had in fact been interviewed by Dr Thornton' and that Ms Barber had 'lied in the course of giving her oral evidence'.[101] The judge said that this amounted to a 'reckless' and 'malicious'

96 Thornton (Sarah) v Telegraph Media Group Ltd [2011] EWHC 1884 (QB).
97 Jameel (Yousef) v Dow Jones & Co. Inc. [2005] EWCA Civ 75.
98 See: Thornton, S. (2009).
99 Thornton [2011] EWHC 1884 at paras 21–22.
100 Thornton [2009] EWHC 2863 (QB) (Sir Charles Gray).
101 Thornton [2011] EWHC 1884 at para. 82 (Tugendhat J).

action. He additionally allowed the claim for 'business libel' (relying on the principle in *Drummond-Jackson v BMA* (1970)[102]).

On the question of damages, the judge took into account the circulation of the *Telegraph* and the 'serious aggravating factor' of Ms Barber's malice. Taking some mitigation into account, resulting from the newspaper's apology – albeit some ten months after the first publication – the judge held that the least award of damages necessary in this case would be one of £65,000. He attributed £50,000 to the libel and £15,000 to the malicious falsehood.[103]

Analysis

In his ruling, Tugendhat J made clear that the case was not about a bad review or a critic's liberty to loathe a book. *Thornton* was not about opinions, but facts. The judgment sent a 'chill' through book reviewer professions (including academics). It also sent the message to newspaper journalists that if they had made a factual mistake they must publish a correction with immediate effect to put the record straight.

This somewhat controversial judgment introduced the 'serious harm' test which later became part of the Defamation Act 2013. Tugendhat J had balanced the 'substantial harm' test with Article 10 ECHR; that is, if harm is not 'substantial' then it is unlikely that the Article 8 right to reputation will apply in favour of the claimant. He held that the 'threshold of seriousness' had to be consistent with the obligations under Article 10 ECHR, the right to freedom of expression (applying *Jameel v Dow Jones* (2005)[104]).

Section 1(1) of the Defamation Act 2013 was first put to the test in the *Bruno Lachaux* case (2015),[105] where Warby J analysed and clarified the notion of 'serious harm' in relation to damage to reputation: this must be proved and cannot be presumed. The court found serious harm in relation to four of the five articles complained of by the French aerospace engineer in his libel actions against three newspapers and the *Huffington Post*.

❖ **KEY CASE**

Lachaux (Bruno) v Independent Print Ltd; Lachaux v Evening Standard Ltd, Lachaux v AOL (UK) Ltd [2015] EWHC 2242 (QB) of 30 July 2015

Precedent

❖ The 'serious harm' test under section 1(1) Defamation Act 2013 is that a statement is not defamatory of a person *unless* it has caused or will probably cause serious harm to that person's reputation.

❖ Section 1(1) of the 2013 Act requires a claimant to prove on the balance of probabilities that the publication has in fact caused serious harm to the claimant's reputation, or will probably do so in the future.

102 [1970] 1 All ER 1094.
103 Thornton [2011] EWHC 1884 at 189.
104 [2005] QB 946 at paras 60–62, 89(ii), 94.
105 *Lachaux (Bruno) v Independent Print Ltd; Lachaux v Evening Standard Ltd, Lachaux v AOL (UK) Ltd* [2015] EWHC 2242 (QB).

- ❖ The court must consider all the relevant circumstances, including what has actually happened *after* publication.
- ❖ Where the claimant has sued for libel in respect of another publication of the same allegations, that fact is admissible in mitigation of damages (section 12 Defamation Act 1952).
- ❖ Libel is no longer actionable without proof of damage.

Facts

The claimant, Bruno Lachaux, a French national and aerospace engineer, living in the United Arab Emirates (UAE), brought a defamation action against three different news publishers in respect of five articles first published between 20 January and 10 February 2014. Two of the five articles were published online in the *Huffington Post* by AOL (UK) Ltd. Two were published in hard copy in *The Independent* newspaper and its sister paper *i* by Independent Print Ltd (IPL). The *Independent* article was also published online. The fifth article was published in the *Evening Standard* newspaper and online.

Each of the articles complained of by Mr Lachaux contained an account of events in the UAE, including proceedings against the claimant's ex-wife, Afsana Lachaux (a British citizen and ex-civil servant), for 'kidnapping' the couple's son. The articles reported allegations against the claimant – said to have been made by Afsana – who was described in the first *Huffington Post* article as a 'British victim of domestic abuse'. Each article bore similar defamatory allegations about him, such as:

- ❖ Afsana claimed Bruno had 'snatched little Louis from his pushchair after he tracked her down to a shopping centre near her home . . . (and) she has not seen the boy since';
- ❖ she alleged that he 'exploited Dubai's legal system, based in part on Islamic Sharia law, to gain custody of the little boy and have criminal charges brought against her';
- ❖ she claimed that Mr Lachaux divorced her and sued for custody of the boy without her knowledge.

The readership figures for the two *Post* articles online were some 4,800; for the *Independent* around 154,370–231,555 and 523,518–785,277 for the *i*. The *Independent* article had 5,655 unique visitors online. The *Evening Standard* readership was around 1.67–2.5 million for the print edition and 1,955 unique visitors online at the time.

The main issue for the judge's decision was whether the articles had caused or were likely to cause sufficient harm to the claimant's reputation to justify the bringing of these claims and would meet the 'serious harm' test.

The defendant newspapers and online publishers relied on *Cooke v Mirror Group Newspapers Ltd* (2014)[106] – asking for *actual* damage caused to Mr Lachaux's business reputation.

Decision

In four of the five claims Mr Lachaux proved that the publication complained of caused serious harm to his reputation. He did so by inference from the facts that each involved

---

106 *Cooke v Mirror Group Newspapers Ltd* [2014] EWHC 2831 (QB). In Cooke, Bean J accepted that evidence is admissible and may be necessary on the issue of whether serious harm to reputation has been or is likely to be caused, at paras 37–39.

the publication of imputations with a seriously defamatory tendency, in a serious article, in a serious news publication, to a large or at least substantial number of people; from the fact that Mr Lachaux was known by or to a substantial number of people who, it could be inferred, read the publication complained of in one of the relevant places; and from the fact that his reputation amongst those readers in those places to whom he was not yet known was a matter of real significance to him[107] (referring to *Knupffer v London Express* (1944)[108]).

Regarding the serious harm test under section 1(1) of the 2013 Act, Warby J concluded that on the balance of probabilities there were, 'tens of people and possibly more than 100 who knew or knew of the claimant and read one or more of the articles and identified him, and who thought the worse of him as a result'.[109] In addition, there were people to whom the sting of the libel was passed via the 'grapevine', including social media (citing *Jameel*[110]). The court ruled the defamatory meanings as 'serious', especially since the publishers were reputable. All the articles but one had caused serious harm to the claimants' reputation.[111]

Analysis

This seminal judgment in *Lachaux* – nearly two years after the commencement of the Defamation Act 2013 – finally provided a definition of section 1(1) 'serious harm'. We now know that this has to be proved by the claimant on matters of fact. This means the court can have regard to all the relevant circumstances, including evidence of what actually happened *after* the publication. Serious harm may be proved by inference, but the evidence may or may not justify such an inference. Questions of fact as to the meaning of the words spoken or written should be dealt with at first hearing. Warby J ruled that libel is no longer actionable without proof of damage (this was applied in *Ames (Craig) and McGee (Robert) v The Spamhaus Project Ltd and Stephen Linford* (2015)[112]).

Section 2: the defence of 'truth'

Section 2 of the Defamation Act 2013 ('truth') replaces the common law defence of 'justification' with a new statutory defence of truth.[113]

> 2(1)   It is a defence to an action for defamation for the defendant to show that the imputa-
> tion conveyed by the statement complained of is substantially true.

Section 2(1) of the 2013 Act focuses on the imputation conveyed by the defamatory statement and raises two questions:

1.   What imputation is actually conveyed by the statement? And
2.   whether the imputation conveyed is substantially true?

The 'truth' defence was first raised in the case of *Chase v News Group Newspapers Ltd* (2002),[114] where the CA indicated that in order for the defence of 'justification' to be available the defendant

---

107 *Lachaux* [2015] EWHC 2242 at para. 15 (Warby J).
108 [1944] AC 116 at 120.
109 Lachaux [2015] at para. 138 (Warby J).
110 See: *Jameel (Yousef) v Dow Jones & Co. Inc.* [2005] EWCA Civ 75.
111 The second article in the *Huffington Post* published on 6 February 2014 was found not 'serious' enough (at para. 151).
112 *Ames (Craig) and McGee (Robert) v The Spamhaus Project Ltd and Stephen Linford* [2015] EWHC 127 (QB) 21 January 2015 (Warby J).
113 Sections 2(2) and (3) of the 2013 Act replaced and repealed s 5 of the Defamation Act 1952 ('justification').
114 [2002] EWCA Civ 1772.

does not have to prove that every word he published was true. All he has to establish is the 'essential' or 'substantial' truth of the sting of the libel. The new section 2 defence of truth of the 2013 Act applies where the defendant can show that the imputation conveyed by the defamatory statement complained of is substantially true. The defence of 'truth' applies where the imputation is one of fact.

Section 3: the defence of 'honest opinion'

Section 3 of the 2013 Act replaces the common law defence of 'fair comment' with a new defence of 'honest opinion'. This section broadly simplifies and clarifies certain defence elements, but does not include the previous requirement for the opinion to be on a matter of public interest.

> 3(1) It is a defence to an action for defamation for the defendant to show that the following conditions are met.
>
> (2) The first condition is that the statement complained of was a statement of opinion.
>
> (3) The second condition is that the statement complained of indicated, whether in general or specific terms, the basis of the opinion.
>
> (4) The third condition is that an honest person could have held the opinion on the basis of –
>
>> (a) any fact which existed at the time the statement complained of was published;
>>
>> (b) anything asserted to be a fact in a privileged statement published before the statement complained of.

Subsections (1) to (4) provide for the defence to apply where the defendant can show that *three conditions* are met. These are:

- **Condition 1**: that the statement complained of was a statement of opinion;
- **Condition 2**: that the statement complained of indicated, whether in general or specific terms, the basis of the opinion; and
- **Condition 3**: that an honest person could have held the opinion on the basis of any fact which existed at the time the statement complained of was published or anything asserted to be a fact in a privileged statement published before the statement complained of.

Section 4: the defence of publication on a matter of public interest

Section 4(1) of the 2013 Act provides for the defence to be available in circumstances where the defendant can show that the statement complained of was, or formed part of, a statement on a matter of public interest and that he reasonably believed that publishing the statement complained of was in the public interest.

> 4(1) It is a defence to an action for defamation for the defendant to show that –
>
>> (a) the statement complained of was, or formed part of, a statement on a matter of public interest; and
>>
>> (b) the defendant reasonably believed that publishing the statement complained of was in the public interest.

The public interest at the time of publication is an objective test. This section effectively abolishes the *Reynolds* defence[115] (though not in Scotland and Northern Ireland).

Section 5: operators of websites

Section 5 of the 2013 Act creates a new defence for the operators of websites where a defamation action is brought against them in respect of a statement posted on the website.

5(1)   This section applies where an action for defamation is brought against the operator of a website in respect of a statement posted on the website.

(2)   It is a defence for the operator to show that it was not the operator who posted the statement on the website.

(3)   The defence is defeated if the claimant shows that –

(a)   it was not possible for the claimant to identify the person who posted the statement,

(b)   the claimant gave the operator a notice of complaint in relation to the statement, and

(c)   the operator failed to respond to the notice of complaint in accordance with any provision contained in regulations.

Section 6: defence of qualified privilege for peer-reviewed statements in scientific or academic journals

Section 6 of the 2013 Act provides for the defence of 'qualified privilege' relating to peer-reviewed material in scientific or academic journals (whether published in electronic form or otherwise).[116] This was welcome news for the academic community.

6(1)   The publication of a statement in a scientific or academic journal (whether published in electronic form or otherwise) is privileged if the following conditions are met.

(2)   The first condition is that the statement relates to a scientific or academic matter.

(3)   The second condition is that before the statement was published in the journal an independent review of the statement's scientific or academic merit was carried out by –

(a)   the editor of the journal, and

(b)   one or more persons with expertise in the scientific or academic matter concerned.

Sections 6(1) to (3) provide for the defence to apply where *two conditions* are met; firstly, that the statement relates to a scientific or academic matter; and, secondly, that before the statement was published in the journal an independent review of the statement's scientific or academic merit was carried out.

●   **Condition 1**: that the statement relates to a scientific or academic matter; and
●   **Condition 2**: that before the statement was published in the journal an independent review of the statement's scientific or academic merit was carried out by the editor of the journal and one or more persons with expertise in the scientific or academic matter concerned.

---

115 See: *Reynolds v Times Newspapers* [2001] 2 AC 127 (HL).
116 The term 'scientific journal' includes medical and engineering journals.

The requirements in condition 2 are intended to reflect the core aspects of a responsible peer-review process.

Section 6(4) extends the protection offered by the defence to publications in the same journal of any assessment of the scientific or academic merit of a peer-reviewed statement, provided the assessment was written by one or more of the persons who carried out the independent review of the statement, and the assessment was written in the course of that review. This is intended to ensure that the privilege is available not only to the author of the peer-reviewed statement, but also to those who have conducted the independent review who will need to assess, for example, the papers originally submitted by the author and may need to comment.

Section 6(5) provides that the privilege given by the section to peer-reviewed statements and related assessments also extends to the publication of a fair and accurate copy of, extract from or summary of the statement or assessment concerned.

Section 6(6) states that the privilege given by the section is lost if the publication is shown to be made with malice. This reflects the condition attaching to other forms of qualified privilege.

Section 6(7)(b) has been included to ensure that the new section is not read as preventing a person who publishes a statement in a scientific or academic journal from relying on other forms of privilege, such as the privilege conferred under section 7(9) to fair and accurate reports etc. of proceedings at a scientific or academic conference.

Section 6(8) provides that the reference to 'the editor of the journal' is to be read, in the case of a journal with more than one editor, as a reference to the editor or editors who were responsible for deciding to publish the statement concerned. This may be relevant where a board of editors is responsible for decision-making (such as the *Entertainment Law Review* or the *Communications Law Review*).

Section 7: reports etc. protected by privilege

Section 7 of the 2013 extends the defences of 'absolute' and 'qualified privilege' to proceedings in any court of the UK (or territory outside the UK), and any international court or tribunal established by the Security Council of the United Nations or by an international agreement.[117]

Section 8: the single publication rule

Section 8 of the 2013 Act introduces a *single publication rule* to prevent an action being brought in relation to publication of the same material by the same publisher after a one-year limitation period from the date of the first publication of that material to the public or a section of the public. This replaces the 'multiple publication rule' (*Re Brunswick*).

8(1) This section applies if a person –

  (a) publishes a statement to the public ('the first publication'), and
  (b) subsequently publishes (whether or not to the public) that statement or a statement which is substantially the same.

This measure also underpins freedom of expression under Article 10 ECHR by providing far greater protection to publishers. It equally safeguards the right to reputation since the court has discretion to extend the one-year time period whenever it is just to do so. Section 8 only applies to material that is 'substantially the same' as the original publication.

---

117 Section 7(1) of the 2013 Act replaces and repeals s 14(3) of the Defamation Act 1996, which concerns the absolute privilege applying to fair and accurate contemporaneous reports of court proceedings.

Specifically, section 8(1) indicates that the provisions apply where a person publishes a statement to the public (defined in subsection (2) as including publication to a section of the public), and subsequently publishes that statement or a statement which is substantially the same. The definition in subsection (2) is intended to ensure that publications to a limited number of people are covered (for example where a blog has a small group of subscribers or followers).

Section 8(3) has the effect of ensuring that the limitation period in relation to any cause of action brought in respect of a subsequent publication within the scope of this section is treated as having started to run on the date of the first publication. It specifically will not apply to material that is published in a 'materially different manner', taking into account the level of prominence and extent of the subsequent re-publication.

Section 8(4) provides that the single publication rule does not apply where the manner of the subsequent publication of the statement is 'materially different' from the manner of the first publication.

Section 8(5) provides that in deciding this issue the matters to which the court may have regard include the level of prominence given to the statement and the extent of the subsequent publication. A possible example of this could be where a story has first appeared relatively obscurely in a section of a website where several clicks need to be made to access it, but has subsequently been promoted to a position where it can be directly accessed from the home page of the site, thereby increasing considerably the number of hits it receives (see: *Budu v BBC* (2010)[118]).

Section 8(6) confirms that the section does not affect the court's discretion under section 32A Limitation Act 1980 to allow a defamation action to proceed outside the one-year limitation period where it is equitable to do so. It also ensures that the reference in subsection (1)(a) of section 32A to the operation of section 4A of the 1980 Act is interpreted as a reference to the operation of section 4A together with section 8 of the Defamation Act 2013.[119] Section 32A provides a broad discretion which requires the court to have regard to all the circumstances of the case, and it is envisaged that this will provide a safeguard against injustice in relation to the application of any limitation issue arising under this section.

Arguably, the single publication rule under section 8 may have been drafted too narrowly. While it protects the individual who originally published the material once the one-year period has expired, it does not protect anyone else who republishes the same material in a similar manner later. For instance, an online archive that publishes material written by someone else could be sued successfully, even though the original author could no longer be pursued for continuing to make the material available to readers. A publisher who republishes material previously published by a different person will similarly be exposed. It is argued further that the single publication rule should protect anyone who republishes the same material in a similar manner after it has been in the public domain for more than one year. The law is also not clear on merely transferring a paper-based publication onto the internet, or vice versa; does this amount to re-publication which is in a 'materially different' manner? Would this undermine the usefulness of the single publication rule? The answer will lie in the courts' interpretation of section 8 of the 2013 Act.

*Section 9: jurisdiction: action against a person not domiciled in the
UK or a Member State*

Section 9 addresses the issue of 'libel tourism' and focuses the provision on cases where an action is brought against a person who is not domiciled in the UK, an EU Member State or a state which is a party to the Lugano Convention.[120]

---

118 [2010] EWHC 616 of 23 March 2010 (QB).
119 Section 4A concerns the time limit applicable for defamation actions.
120 Convention on jurisdiction and the enforcement of judgments in civil and commercial matters signed in Lugano on 30 October 2007. See: Official Journal on 21 December 2007 (L339/3). Lugano governs issues of jurisdiction and enforcement of judgments between the EU Member States and the European Free Trade Association countries other than Liechtenstein (namely Iceland, Switzerland and Norway).

9   This section applies to an action for defamation against a person who is not domiciled –

      (a)   in the United Kingdom;

      (b)   in another Member State; or

      (c)   in a state which is for the time being a contracting party to the Lugano Convention.

Subsection (2) provides that a court does not have jurisdiction to hear and determine an action to which the section applies unless it is satisfied that, of all the places in which the statement complained of has been published, England and Wales is clearly the most appropriate place in which to bring an action in respect of the statement.

This means that in cases where a statement has been published in a British jurisdiction and also abroad, the court will be required to consider the overall global picture to consider where it would be most appropriate for a claim to be heard. It is intended that this will overcome the problem of courts readily accepting jurisdiction simply because a claimant frames their claim so as to focus on damage which has occurred in the UK jurisdiction only. Section 9 then limits the circumstances in which an action for defamation can be brought against someone who is not the primary publisher of an allegedly defamatory statement. This may well be affected now that Britain has voted to leave the EU.

Section 10: action against a person who was not the author, editor, etc.

Section 10 of the 2013 Act limits the circumstances in which an action for defamation can be brought against someone who is not the primary publisher of an allegedly defamatory statement.

10(1)   A court does not have jurisdiction to hear and determine an action for defamation brought against a person who was not the author, editor or publisher of the statement complained of unless the court is satisfied that it is not reasonably practicable for an action to be brought against the author, editor or publisher.

Section 11: trial without a jury

Section 11 of the 2013 Act removes the presumption in favour of jury trial in defamation cases.[121]

11(1)   In section 69(1) of the Senior Courts Act 1981 (certain actions in the Queen's Bench Division to be tried with a jury unless the trial requires prolonged examination of documents etc.) in paragraph (b) omit 'libel, slander'.

(2)   In section 66 (3) of the County Courts Act 1984 (certain actions in the county court to be tried with a jury unless the trial requires prolonged examination of documents etc.) in paragraph (b) omit 'libel, slander'.[122]

The reality is that defamation cases are now tried without a jury unless a court orders otherwise (except in Northern Ireland and Scotland).

---

121 Provided under s 69 Senior Courts Act 1981 and s 66 County Courts Act 1984 in certain civil proceedings, such as malicious prosecution, false imprisonment, fraud, libel and slander.

122 Subsections (1) and (2) amended the 1981 and 1984 Acts to remove libel and slander from the list of proceedings where a right to jury trial exists.

Section 12: summary of court judgment

Section 12 of the 2013 Act gives the court power to order a summary of its judgment to be published in defamation proceedings more generally.

Subsection (2) provides that the wording of any summary and the time, manner, form and place of its publication are matters for the parties to agree. Where the parties are unable to agree, subsections (3) and (4) respectively provide for the court to settle the wording, and enable it to give such directions in relation to the time, manner, form or place of publication as it considers reasonable and practicable.

That said, section 8 Defamation Act 1996 still grants the power to a court to order an unsuccessful defendant to publish a summary of its judgment where the parties cannot agree the content of any correction or apology.

Section 13: removal of statements

This section is particularly relevant to publications online. Section 13 of the 2013 Act relates to situations where an author may not always be in a position to remove or prevent further dissemination of material which has been found to be defamatory. Section 13 enables the 'author' or operator of a website to remove an alleged defamatory posting during or shortly after the conclusion of proceedings.

Section 14: special damage in actions for slander

Section 14 repeals the Slander of Women Act 1891 and overturns a common law rule relating to special damage. The 1891 Act provided that 'words spoken and published . . . which impute unchastity or adultery to any woman or girl shall not require special damage to render them actionable'.

In relation to slander, some special damage must be proved now to flow from the (oral) statement complained of (unless the publication falls into certain specific categories specified in the Act).

Section 15: general provisions: the meaning of 'publish' and 'statement'

Section 15 of the 2013 Act sets out definitions of the terms 'publish', 'publication' and 'statement'. Broad definitions cover a wide range of publications in any medium, including pictures, visual images and gestures.

Section 16: amendments to existing law

Sections 16(1) to (3) ('Consequential amendments and savings etc.') make consequential amendments to section 8 of the Rehabilitation of Offenders Act 1974 to reflect the new defences of 'truth' and 'honest opinion'. Section 8 of the 1974 Act applies to actions for libel or slander brought by a rehabilitated person based on statements made about offences which were the subject of a spent conviction (e.g. a statement of truth which attracts qualified privilege but where 'malice' may form an important aspect).

Section 17: title and commencement

Section 17 sets out the territorial extent of the provisions and makes provision for commencement. Section 15, the savings-related provisions in subsections (4) to (8) of section 16 and section 17 (short title, commencement and extent) came into force on 25 April 2013.

7.4 Defences

A person who publishes a defamatory statement may be able to rely on the defences of 'absolute' and 'qualified' privilege in a wide variety of circumstances. The defence of absolute privilege, as its name suggests, protects the publisher whatever their motive for publication. The defence of qualified privilege is defeated if the publisher was malicious in the sense that the dominant motive for publication was improper. There are other defences available in statute.

7.4.1 Summary of defences available

This section is particularly relevant to Scotland and Northern Ireland where the Defamation Act 2013 has not yet been enacted. The defences available in a defamation action cut across a number of statutes:

- **justification** that the material is true (section 5 Defamation Act 1952);[123]
- **fair comment (now repealed)**[124] – this in the past protected statements of opinion or comment on matters of public interest (with no malice) (section 6 Defamation Act 1952);
- **absolute privilege** which guarantees immunity from liability in certain situations such as in parliamentary and court proceedings (section 14 Defamation Act 1996);
- **qualified privilege** which grants limited protection on public policy grounds to statements in the media provided that certain requirements are met (section 15(1) Defamation Act 1996 – 'no malice');
- **honest opinion** replaces common law defence of 'fair comment' (see above) (section 3 Defamation Act 2013);
- *Reynolds* **privilege**;
- **publication on matter of public interest** (section 4 Defamation Act 2013);
- **peer-reviewed statement in scientific or academic journal etc.** (section 6 Defamation Act 2013).

The defence of *absolute privilege* gives the author of a 'defamatory' statement utter freedom in the communication of views and information. This privilege of free speech, dating back to Article 9 of the Bill of Rights 1688, is extended to all Members of Parliament and to statements made during judicial or tribunal proceedings. However, absolute privilege does not protect ministers or peers *outside* the Houses of Parliament (such as on College Green) or outside the courthouse (see: *Church of Scientology of California v Johnson-Smith* (1972)[125]).

Examples of absolute privilege include testimony by a witness in court and contemporaneous reports of proceedings in open court (e.g. written statements of witnesses). Although often classified as 'parliamentary privilege', Members of Parliament participating in parliamentary proceedings are similarly protected. This category of privilege reflects a particularly strong public interest in there being no inhibition on being able to speak or write freely even if there is an adverse impact

---

123 Section 2 Defamation Act 2013 ('truth') has replaced the common law defence of justification (England and Wales).
124 Section 3(8) Defamation Act 2013 abolished the common law defence of 'fair comment' and also repealed s 6 Defamation Act 1952.
125 [1972] 1 QB 522.

on the other person's reputation. The defence is central to the proper functioning of an orderly and democratic society.[126]

In addition, section 2 of the Defamation Act 1996 provides a procedure by which a defendant can make an 'offer to make amends' to enable valid claims to be settled without the need for court proceedings. Section 2(2) Defamation Act 1996 reads:

> the offer may be in relation to the statement generally or in relation to a specific defamatory meaning which the person making the offer accepts that the statement conveys
>
> ('a qualified offer').

In the offer to make amends, under section 4 of the 1996 Act: the defendant must:

(a) make a suitable correction of the statement complained of and a sufficient apology to the aggrieved party;

(b) publish the correction and apology in a manner that is' reasonable'; and

(c) pay to the aggrieved party (the claimant) compensation (if any) and costs.

Johnson (2008b) argues that the substantive defences in a defamatory action, such as absolute and qualified privilege, are going 'quite strongly in favour of the publisher of the material' and that the courts and Human Rights Court rulings have been in favour of freedom of expression.[127] But if the basic elements of responsible journalism, such as accuracy and reliable sources, are ignored, the courts will take a dim view of journalists if they put basic economics to sell newspapers or promote their websites before truthful reporting.

While print media may eventually fade in people's memories, online publications and news archives can potentially remain in cyberspace indefinitely. As Tugendhat J remarked in *Clarke* (t/a *Elumina Iberica UK) v Bain & Another* (2008): 'what is to be found on the Internet may become like a tattoo'.[128]

7.4.2 Qualified privilege

The defence of qualified privilege can protect private communications that contain defamatory material where there is a shared duty and interest between the publisher and the recipient. Qualified privilege also applies by statute[129] to a wide range of reports of public proceedings and notices, provided the relevant material is on a matter of public concern and for the public good. This defence arises where media freedom warrants some additional protection from the threat of litigation, particularly relevant to newspaper reports of public meetings or court proceedings.

'Qualified' means it is not 'absolute' and there will be certain conditions put on the author of the statement. A statement made in the performance of a duty may attract the defence of qualified privilege under common law,[130] provided that the person making the statement has a legal, moral or social duty to make the statement and the person receiving it has an interest in doing so in that it allows such person to make a quality decision.

Section 15 Defamation Act 1996 unfortunately does not define 'qualified privilege'; it just states that the publication must not be made with malice. Otherwise 'there is no defence'. There are a number of situations defined in Schedule 1 of the 1996 Act which detail 'qualified privilege' scenarios. The prima facie defence of qualified privilege is lost if the claimant can prove that the

---

126 See: Smartt, U. (2014).
127 See: Johnson, H. (2008b), pp. 126–131.
128 [2008] EWHC 2636 para. 55 (Tugendhat J) (QB).
129 Originally contained in the Defamation Act 1952, now part of the Defamation Act 1996, s 15 and Sch. 1.
130 Common law is recognized by s 15(4) Defamation Act 1996.

defendant was motivated by 'actual' or 'express malice', though there is no sufficient definition in common law as to the meaning of 'malice'. A defendant establishes a prima facie defence of qualified privilege in common law if he can show that the publication was made by him in pursuance of a duty or in protection of an interest to a person who had a duty or interest in having the matter published.[131]

See above
7.2.8

7.4.3 *Reynolds* privilege

The background to the *Reynolds* case itself dates back to 1994. In his libel action against *The Times*, the former Irish Taoiseach, Albert Reynolds,[132] found himself embroiled in a political crisis, when the Irish section of *The Times* alleged that Mr Reynolds had misled the Irish Parliament (Dáil Éireann). The English version of the newspaper had omitted the Taoiseach's 'right of reply'. After a number of cross-appeals, the House of Lords set the precedent for the now famous *Reynolds* qualified privilege defence, which set the tone for future media cases in defamation.

During the series of allegations and cross-appeals it emerged that Reynolds had appointed a new President of the High Court, Harry Whelehan, whom Mr Reynolds had elevated to that post from Attorney General. It emerged that AG Whelehan had delayed the extradition of a couple of Irish priests who were wanted in the Belfast court for alleged child sex abuse, and the newspaper alleged that both Reynolds and Whelehan had deliberately procrastinated in signing the extradition warrants. Mr Reynolds' government fell shortly afterwards, partly as a result of the controversial piece in *The Times*.

During the ensuing defamation action with a jury, Lord Nicholls gave the leading judgment, providing the now legendary ten-point list of factors to take into account when deciding whether the qualified privilege defence ('in the public interest') should be available to journalists. The *ten-point Reynolds test* comprises:

1. **The seriousness of the allegation.** The more serious the charge, the more the public is misinformed and the individual harmed if the allegation is not true.
2. **The nature of the information**, and the extent to which the subject matter is a matter of public concern.
3. **The source of the information.** Some informants have no direct knowledge of the events. Some have their own axes to grind, or are being paid for their stories.
4. **The steps taken to verify the information.**
5. **The status of the information.** The allegation may have already been the subject of an investigation which commands respect.
6. **The urgency of the matter.** News is often a perishable commodity.
7. **Whether comment was sought from the claimant.** He may have information others do not possess or have not disclosed. An approach to the claimant will not always be necessary.
8. **Whether the article contained the gist of the claimant's side of the story.**
9. **The tone of the article.** A newspaper can raise queries or call for an investigation. It need not adopt allegations as statements of fact.
10. **The circumstances of the publication**, including the timing.[134]

---

131 See: *Hebditch v MacIlwaine* [1894] 2 QB 54.
132 Albert Reynolds (1932–2014) was an Irish politician who was Taoiseach (Prime Minister) of Ireland, serving from February 1992 to December 1994. He is credited, along with his British counterpart Conservative Prime Minister John Major, with a crucial role in energizing the long-drawn-out peace process in Northern Ireland.
133 [2001] 2 AC at para. 205 (Lord Nicholls of Birkenhead).

The *Reynolds* defence could be raised where it was clear that a journalist (or 'author' generally), accused of defamation, had a duty to meet the 'ten-point' Lord Nicholls' criteria test in order to claim the defence (as affirmed in *Jameel v Wall Street Journal* (2007[134])).

If and when *Reynolds* was advanced the court was required to interpret and apply this defence in a way that was compatible with Article 10 ECHR and Strasbourg jurisprudence on the importance of free speech and consider at the same time whether Article 8 ECHR was engaged (such was the case in the *Tim Yeo* libel action[135]).

The *Reynolds* ten-point test was (unsuccessfully) applied by the *Daily Telegraph* in the *George Galloway* case,[136] where the former Glasgow MP sued the newspaper and its journalists for publishing libellous articles during April 2003, which claimed that Mr Galloway had 'received money from the Iraqi ruler Saddam Hussein's regime, taking a slice of oil earnings worth £375,000 a year', and that the Scottish MP had asked for 'a greater cut of Iraq's exports' and 'was profiting from food contracts'. A further article had stated that, according to the claimant's Iraqi intelligence profile, the claimant 'had a family history of loyalty to Saddam Hussein's Ba'ath Party', and referred to him as a 'sympathiser with Iraq'.

The High Court (affirmed by the CA) ruled in *Galloway* that the defendant newspaper could not rely on *Reynolds* qualified privilege, because not all of the ten-point criteria had been satisfied. Though the court said that the subject matter was 'undoubtedly of public concern', the sources of information could not be regarded as 'inherently reliable', and the *Telegraph*'s publishers, the editor and journalist had not taken sufficient steps to verify the information. The court, presiding without a jury, ruled in favour of Mr Galloway, who was awarded £150,000 in damages.

What can be concluded from *Galloway* is that a newspaper which obtains critical material from an anonymous or slightly dubious source will not be able to rely on the qualified privilege defence unless the source material passes the *Reynolds* – qualified privilege – test. George Galloway's success against the *Telegraph* effectively meant that by breaching any one of the ten-point *Reynolds* criteria the newspaper's defence had been lost.

Shortly after the Supreme Court ruling in *Flood*,[137] the *David Hunt*[138] libel action made legal headlines. This lengthy and complex action arose from a publication of an article in the *Sunday Times* by investigative journalist, Michael Gillard, about David Hunt in May 2010, headlined 'Underworld Kings Cash in on Taxpayer Land Fund'.[139] It was accompanied by a photograph of the claimant. The article referred to a £20 million fund run by the London Development Authority which sought to acquire land for regeneration. It said that potential beneficiaries of the fund had been implicated in murder, drug-trafficking and fraud, and that these included Hunt, described as a man 'whose criminal network is allegedly so vast that Scotland Yard regards him as "too big" to take on'. The article alleged that the claimant (i) controlled a criminal network involved in murder, drug trafficking and fraud; (ii) in criminal proceedings against him in 1999, assaulted the main prosecution witness; and (iii) in order to obtain a financial benefit from the sale of land to the London Development

---

134 [2007] 1 AC 359.
135 See: *Yeo (Tim) v Times Newspapers Ltd* [2015] EWHC 3375 (QB).
136 See: *Galloway v Telegraph* [2004] EWHC 2786 (QB).
137 See: *Flood* [2011] UKSC 11.
138 *Hunt (David) v Times Newspapers Ltd (No 1)* [2012] EWHC 110 (QB); see also: *Hunt (David) v Evening Standard Limited* [2011] EWHC 272 (QB).
139 The procedural history of the *Hunt* claims are complex. On 2 December 2010, 49 sub-paragraphs of the original plea of justification were struck out following a hearing before Tugendhat J. A separate action had been brought by the Commissioner of Police for the Metropolis and SOCA against the *Sunday Times* and Mr Gillard to restrain them from relying on and disclosing documents said to have been handed to Mr Gillard in breach of confidence (see: *Commissioner of Police of the Metropolis & Anor v Times Newspapers Ltd & Anor* [2011] EWHC 1566 (QB)). Two judgments were handed down which restricted the use the defendant/s could make of leaked documents in this action. The defendants then served an amended defence and Hunt again applied to strike out the pleading, Eady J permitting the defendants to rely on some of the particulars of justification and the *Reynolds* defence (see: *Hunt v Times Newspapers Ltd (No 1)* [2012] EWHC 110 QB). Some of D's reformulated defence was then allowed by Eady J (*Hunt v Times Newspapers Ltd (No 2)* [2012] EWHC 1220 (QB)). On the first day of trial *The Times* was allowed to add new particulars to the plea of justification (*Hunt v Times Newspapers Ltd (No 3)* [2013] EWHC 1090 (QB)).

Agency, attacked and threatened to kill a property developer at a court hearing, and then avoided prosecution by intimidating witnesses.[140]

The defendant newspaper and journalist pleaded defences of 'justification' and *Reynolds* privilege. Mr Hunt argued that the entire justification defence should be struck out, because no particulars survived in the evidential disclosed material to support the most serious defamatory meaning.[141]

In his fifth action (Hunt No 5[142]) in July 2013, Simon J finally dismissed the case, saying that journalist Michael Gillard was highly experienced and gave evidence that was both lucid and entirely credible, allowing the *Reynolds* public interest defence, though noted that a plea of *Reynolds* privilege should not be a longstop for a failed or inadequate plea of justification. The mere fact of existing allegations or rumours could not be found the defence; rather the court had to focus on proportionality and the quality of the research undertaken by *The Times* journalist. Hunt's barrister, Hugh Tomlinson QC, was also Chairman of the 'Hacked Off' campaign and attempted to discredit *The Times* reporter, Michael Gillard during the action. Mr Gillard had been investigating Hunt and his associates for about 11 years and during that time had obtained a significant amount of information which led him honestly to believe that Hunt was a violent and dangerous criminal at the head of a family-based network.[143]

The *Reynolds* qualified privilege defence was newly formulated regarding the 'public interest' test by Lord Phillips in the *Gary Flood* action,[144] when he said:

> [it] protects publication of defamatory matter to the world at large where
>
> (i)   it was in the *public interest* that the information should be published and
> (ii)   the publisher has acted responsibly in publishing the information, a test usually referred to as 'responsible journalism' . . .[145]

See above
7.3.1

Flood also set the precedent for the 'responsible journalism test' (see also: *Hughes v Rusbridger* (2010)[146]).

In summary, the *Reynolds* defence could protect defamatory factual statements which were not or could not be proved to be true.

Some legal critics have commented on *Reynolds* qualified privilege as being divisive and it remains a controversial issue particularly in Scotland and Northern Ireland. Clayton and Tomlinson (2009) argue that *Reynolds* privilege left the law of defamation in a state of uncertainty when it came to investigative journalism and matters of opinion.[147] Whether it could protect comment remains a moot point.

 FOR THOUGHT

Should the reason of the public interest defence not be enough in allowing a high-profile news story to be published without fear that a particular error of fact will restrict the willingness of the press to work in a certain fashion? Discuss.

---

140 Ibid., at para. 2.
141 Ibid., at para. 106.
142 *Hunt (David) v Times Newspapers Ltd (No 5)* [2013] EWHC 1868 (QB).
143 Source: 'Britain's newest "underworld king" unmasked after he loses libel claim against Sunday newspaper that labelled him violent and dangerous', by Simon Tomlinson, *The Daily Mail*, 5 July 2013.
144 See: *Flood v Times Newspapers Ltd* [2012] UKSC 11.
145 Ibid., at para. 2 (Lord Phillips.)
146 [2010] EWHC 491 (QB).
147 Clayton, R. and Tomlinson, H. (2009) at para. 15.249.

See Chapter
7.3

7.4.4 Honest opinion

Section 3 of the 2013 Act broadly reflects and simplifies elements of the common law – replacing the defence of 'fair comment' – but no longer includes the requirement for the opinion to be on a matter of public interest. Subsections (1) to (4) provide for the defence to apply where the defendant can show that three conditions are met.

Condition 1 ('that the statement complained of was a statement of opinion') embraces the requirement established in *Cheng v Tse Wai Chun Paul* (2000)[148] that the statement must be recognizable as comment as distinct from an imputation of fact. It is implicit in Condition 1 that the assessment is on the basis of how the ordinary person would understand it. As an inference of fact is a form of opinion, this would be encompassed by the defence.

Condition 2 ('that the statement complained of indicated, whether in general or specific terms, the basis of the opinion') reflects the test approved by the Supreme Court in *Spiller v Joseph* (2010)[149] that 'the comment must explicitly or implicitly indicate, at least in general terms, the facts on which it is based'.

Condition 3 ('that an honest person could have held the opinion') is based on any fact which existed at the time the statement complained of was published or anything asserted to be a fact in a privileged statement published before the statement complained of. This condition is an *objective* test and consists of two elements. It is enough for one to be satisfied.

The first element of Condition 3 is whether an honest person could have held the opinion on the basis of any fact which existed at the time the statement was published.[150] The second element of Condition 3 is whether an honest person could have formed the opinion on the basis of anything asserted to be a fact in a 'privileged statement' which was published before the statement complained of.[151]

The honest opinion defence is defeated if the claimant shows that the defendant did not hold the opinion 'honestly'.[152] This is a *subjective* test which means the defence of 'honest opinion' will fail if the claimant can show that the statement was actuated by malice.

Section 3(6) makes provision for situations where the defendant is not the author of the statement. For example, where an action is brought against a newspaper editor in respect of a comment piece rather than against the person who wrote it. In these circumstances the defence is defeated if the claimant can show that the defendant knew or ought to have known that the author did not hold the opinion.

Section 3(8) abolishes the common law defence of 'fair comment'. Although this means that the defendant can no longer rely on the common law defence (except in Scotland and Northern Ireland), in cases where uncertainty arises in the interpretation of section 3, case law continues to provide a helpful but not binding guide to interpreting how the new statutory defence should be applied.

What does this mean practically? The defence of honest comment has five requirements: the statement must:

(1) be on a matter of public interest;
(2) be recognizable as comment, as distinct from imputation of fact;
(3) be based on facts which are true or protected by privilege;
(4) explicitly or implicitly indicate those facts, at least in general terms;
(5) be a comment which could have been made by an honest person.[154]

---

148 [2000] 10 BHRC 525.
149 [2010] UKSC 53.
150 Section 3(4)(a) DA 2013.
151 Section 3(4)(b) DA 2013.
152 Section 3(5) DA 2013.
153 As per Lord Nicholls in *Tse Wai Chun v Cheng* [2001] EMLR 777 at paras 16–21 as endorsed by Lord Phillips (with one modification) in *Joseph v Spiller* [2011] 1 AC 852 at para. 105.

Requirement (3) does not demand proof that all the facts indicated as the basis for the comment are true.

Requirement (5) is generously known as 'the objective test' of honest comment. It protects *any* comment which could have been made honestly, even if only by a person who is prejudiced, or holds exaggerated or obstinate views.[154]

A defence of honest comment will fail even though the objective test is satisfied, if the claimant establishes that in fact the defendant was malicious (i.e. did not believe the comment).

7.4.5 The public interest test

Whether an opinion expressed by a journalist or author firstly passes the 'honest opinion' test (as per section 3 DA 2013), and was published in the public interest, thereby passing the 'responsible journalism' test, was first raised in *Jameel v Wall Street*.[155] Lord Hoffmann explained that it requires a two-stage approach:

> The first question is whether the subject matter of the articles [as a whole] was a matter of public interest. In answering that question . . . one should consider the article as a whole and not isolate the defamatory statement . . .
>
> If the article as a whole concerned a matter of public interest, the next question is whether the inclusion of the defamatory statement was justifiable. The . . . allegations . . . must be part of the story. And . . . make a real contribution to the public interest element in the article.[156]

This defence is best illustrated by the *Tim Yeo* case.[157] The articles complained of were written by Jonathan Calvert, *The Sunday Times* 'Insight Editor', and his then deputy, Heidi Blake, in June 2013, resulting from their undercover investigation of the former South Suffolk MP's lobbying practices. Mr Yeo had represented his constituency for more than 30 years until May 2015 and had been chairman of the Energy and Climate Change Select Committee.

The 'sting' by the two *Times* journalists involved one of the them posing as 'Robyn Fox' of a fictitious consultancy firm called 'Coulton & Goldie Global' and during a 'business' lunch discussions had taken place ostensibly with the purpose of providing Mr Yeo with consultancy for a couple of days per month with 'an extremely generous remuneration package'. The work was to relate to a European launch strategy for a leading edge solar technology developer in the Far East. The ensuing articles were headlined: 'Top Tory in new Lobbygate row', and sub-headlined: 'MP coached client before committee grilling', suggesting that Mr Yeo was prepared to, and had offered to, act in a way that was in breach of the House of Commons Code of Conduct by acting as a paid parliamentary advocate who would push for new laws to benefit the business of a client for a daily fee of £7,000 and approach ministers, civil servants and other MPs to promote a client's private agenda in return for cash. The articles also expressed the journalists' opinion, to the effect that Mr Yeo had acted scandalously and shown willingness to abuse his position as an MP.

Mr Yeo then sued the *Sunday Times* for libel over the three 'cash-for-advocacy' stories. Times Newspapers' defence was that its factual allegations were substantially true and made in the public interest. On 9 June 2014, Warby J held that the articles contained a defamatory factual imputation

---

154 See: Turner v Metro-Goldwyn-Mayer Pictures Ltd [1950] 1 All ER 449, 461 (Lord Porter), commenting on an observation in Merivale v Carson (1888) 20 QBD 275, 281 (Lord Esher).
155 *Jameel (Mohammed) v Wall Street Journal Europe Sprl* [2007] 1 AC 359.
156 Ibid., paras 48–51 (Lord Hoffmann).
157 See: *Yeo (Tim) v Times Newspapers Ltd* [2015] EWHC 3375 (QB).

and a defamatory comment.[158] Shortly before that ruling Mr Yeo was cleared by the Parliamentary Commission for Standards of breaking lobbying rules.

The watchdog claimed the newspaper had used 'subterfuge, misrepresentation and selective quotation' in the reporting of the undercover sting.

Times Newspapers Ltd cross-appealed, citing as its defence 'justification', 'honest comment' and '*Reynolds* privilege' in respect of those meanings. At the appeal hearing Warby J dismissed Mr Yeo's claim as 'utterly implausible' and that the former MP did not present his action 'convincingly'. Celebrating the successful 'public interest' and 'responsible journalism' defence, Martin Ivens, editor of *The Sunday Times*, said the decision was 'a victory for investigative journalism'. The *Yeo* case vindicated the role of the press in exposing the clandestine advocacy by some MPs of undisclosed interests.

7.5 Operators of websites

Following conflicting case law – such as *Godfrey* (2011),[159] *Tamiz* (2012)[160] and *Davison v Habeeb* (2011)[161] – the government introduced section 5 of the 2013 Act to clarify the law in relation to operators of websites (which were called 'online intermediaries' in some authorities). The question was whether operators of websites were merely a 'host' or liaison point between the defamed person and the author of the material and against whom the claimant could bring an action. Could he sue the intermediary? US law has always been very clear on this: website operators are merely 'hosts'.

The first landmark judgment in the UK courts was that of *Godfrey v Demon Internet Ltd* (2011)[162] where the court took into account the liability of an internet service provider (ISP) under section 1 Defamation Act 1996. And though *Demon* could have (and should have) removed the defamatory posting about Dr Godfrey from its news server once given notice by the complainant on 17 January 1997, the posting remained on the ISP's server and website for another 15 days. Dr Godfrey was awarded damages in the High Court by Morland J with the routine result that operators of websites would thereafter routinely take down any newsgroup postings and web pages which were allegedly defamatory.

See Chapter 3.3.1

In *Davison v Habeeb* (2011)[163] HHJ Parkes QC noted that it was arguable that Google was liable for publication of the articles at common law, on the basis that it had not merely acted as a passive conduit but could be seen as a publisher, hosting material on its servers and responding to requests for downloads, like the defendant in *Godfrey v Demon Internet Ltd* (2001).[164] Therefore, Google provided an almost infinitely huge electronic 'notice board' which was within its control, so that it became liable once it refused to take the defamatory statements and postings down.[165]

See Chapter 3.3.1

Eady J's decision in *Tamiz v Google Inc.* (2012)[166] somewhat contradicted *Godfrey*, when he ruled that Google (in this case as host of blogger.com) was *not* a publisher at common law, regardless of notification.

---

158 See: *Yeo v Times* [2014] EWHC 2853 (QB) at paras 121–122, 136 and 138 (Warby J); Warby J also held that the online versions of the articles bore the same meanings as the printed versions, at para. 126.
159 See: *Godfrey v Demon Internet Ltd* [2001] QB 201.
160 See: *Tamiz v Google Inc.* [2012] EWHC 449 (QB).
161 [2011] EWHC 3031 (QB).
162 [2001] QB 201.
163 *Davison v Habeeb* [2011] EWHC 3031 (QB) (HHJ Parkes QC).
164 [2001] QB 201.
165 For further discussion see: McEvedy, V. (2013), pp. 108–112.
166 [2012] EWHC 449 (QB) (Eady J).

Website operators now have a complete defence against liability in the UK for defamatory content posted by third parties under section 5 DA 2013, provided that the complainant is able to identify the poster of the defamatory statement.

This section has to be read in conjunction with the Defamation (Operators of Websites) Regulations 2013 ('the Regulations') (see below) which are complex and not altogether helpful. They attempt to define a complete procedure for responding to formal complaints. In a nutshell, the operator must forward the notice to the poster within 48 hours. The poster then has five calendar days to respond.[167]

Section 5 seeks to prevent actions in relation to publications online outside the one-year limitation period for the initial publication, unless the publisher refused or neglected to update the electronic version, on request, with a reasonable letter or statement by the claimant by way of explanation or contradiction. This then reflected the ECtHR ruling in *Times Newspapers v UK* (2009)[168] which recognized the important role played by online archives in preserving and making available news and information as a public service and as an important educational research tool in our information society.

7.5.1 The Defamation (Operators of Websites) Regulations 2013

Though the Ministry of Justice intended for the section 5 procedure to be 'as straightforward as possible', there are at least 20 cross-references linked to the Regulations 2013 which provide further guidance, and it takes a great deal of patience and mental agility to make sense of the section 5 Regulations.

Section 5(2) provides for the defence to apply if the operator of a website can show that they did not post the statement on the website.

Section 5(3) provides for the defence to be defeated if the claimant can show that it was not possible for him to identify the person who posted the statement; that he gave the operator a notice of complaint in relation to the statement; and that the operator failed to respond to that notice in accordance with provisions contained in regulations to be made by the Secretary of State.

Section 5(4) interprets section 5(3)(a) which states:

The defence is defeated if the claimant shows that –

(a)   it was not possible for the claimant to identify the person who posted the statement

and explains that it is possible for a claimant to 'identify' a person for the purposes of that subsection only if the claimant has sufficient information to bring proceedings against the person. This means that the complainant must have sufficient information to be able to bring court proceedings against the poster. By contrast, anonymous (or pseudonymous) content is subject to what amounts to a non-mandatory notice-and-takedown scheme.

Section 5(5) includes provisions for the operators of websites to remove a posting and provisions for time limits for the taking of any action and for conferring a discretion on the court to treat action taken *after* the expiry of a time limit as having been taken before that expiry.

---

167 Source: Paul Norris, Ministry of Justice, Impact Assessment of the Defamation Act and Regulations 2013 of 1 April 2012 at: www. legislation.gov.uk/ukia/2013/146/pdfs/ukia_20130146_en.pdf.
168 *Times Newspapers Ltd (Nos 1 and 2) v United Kingdom* (2009) EMLR 14 (Applications 3002/03 and 23676/03) 10 March 2009 (ECtHR).

Section 5(6) sets out certain specific information which must be included in a notice of complaint. The notice must:

(a)   specify the complainant's name;
(b)   explain why the statement is defamatory of the complainant;
(c)   specify where on the website the statement was posted; and
(d)   contain other information as may be specified in regulations. Regulations may specify what other information must be included in a notice of complaint.

Sections 5(7) to (10) further provide for regulations and secondary legislation (statutory instruments) including notice periods for complaints in different circumstances.

It is important to note: where the poster of a defamatory statement can be identified the website operator may not need to consider section 5. Then section 10 of the 2013 Act comes into play.

Section 10 ('Action against a person who was not the author, editor etc.') provides that:

> A court does not have jurisdiction to hear and determine an action for defamation brought against a person who was not the author, editor or publisher of the statement complained of unless the court is satisfied that it is *not reasonably practicable* for an action to be brought against the author, editor or publisher.

This section then limits the circumstances in which an action for defamation can be brought against someone who is not the primary publisher of an allegedly defamatory statement. Section 10(1) provides that a court does not have jurisdiction to hear and determine an action for defamation brought against a person who was not the author, editor or publisher of the statement complained of unless it is satisfied that it is not reasonably practicable for an action to be brought against the author, editor or publisher. For example, if a claimant wishes to bring an action against a poster based in Canada, it might then not be 'reasonably practicable' to bring an action against that poster. If the poster can be identified, he can easily be served notice by email.

7.5.2 Internet anonymity

The real problem of internet defamation is anonymity. A leading case is that of Lord McAlpine[169] where Sally Bercow's tweet was found seriously defamatory (in its natural and ordinary meaning). Her innuendo that Lord McAlpine was 'trending' on 4 November 2012 alleged that the claimant was a paedophile who was guilty of sexually abusing boys living in care. The tweet – coupled with an emoticon – was found to be defamatory and to have had a serious effect on the Conservative peer. Mrs Bercow did not avail herself of a public interest defence (*Reynolds* privilege or reportage). This unhappy case concluded when the former principal adviser to Mrs Thatcher and successful businessman died shortly after the proceedings. On his death on 17 January 2014 one obituary – written by his long-standing friend, Simon Heffer, in the *Daily Mail* – commented that Sally Bercow's tweet and refusal to apologize to Lord McAlpine had added to 'Alastair's utter distress'.[170]

The background to this case was that a BBC 2 *Newsnight* programme on 2 November 2012 had featured a special investigation into child sexual abuse in North Wales care homes in the 1970s and 1980s. The report claimed that two victims had been abused by 'a leading Conservative politician from the Thatcher years'. The alleged perpetrator was not identified. By the time the *Newsnight* report was broadcast, there had been 12 hours of speculation on social media regarding the identity of the alleged perpetrator.

---

169 See: *Lord McAlpine of West Green v Sally Bercow* [2013] EWHC 1342 (QB).
170 Source: 'I believe this ghastly woman hastened my friend's death: As libel-storm Tory Lord McAlpine dies, an impassioned Simon Heffer pays tribute', by Simon Heffer, *The Daily Mail*, 20 January 2014.

One of the most prominent tweets came from the wife of the Speaker of the House of Commons, Sally Bercow, who, on 4 November 2012 sent the following tweet:

'Why is Lord McAlpine trending?' [followed by the emoticon '*Innocent face*']¹⁷¹

Since Sally Bercow refused to apologize, Lord McAlpine began defamation actions by asking Twitter to disclose the names of 'Twitterers' by way of a High Court order to the US ISP. Mrs Bercow's and other names were disclosed.

The then Director-General of the BBC Executive, George Entwistle, commissioned the 'Mac-Quarrie Report',¹⁷² followed by an unreserved apology to Lord McAlpine on 9 November 2012 for wrongly identifying him as a child sex abuser. Entwistle resigned on 10 November 2012; he had been in the post as DG for just 54 days. At the same time the BBC apologized for the broadcast on *Newsnight* for implicating Lord McAlpine and settled his libel claim for £185,000 plus costs (and the apology) out of court.

Tugendhat J in the libel action against Sally Bercow firstly explained that the emoticon ('innocent face') was to be read as a stage direction and was part of the defamatory sting of the libel. Readers of the tweet were to imagine that they could see an expression of innocence on Sally Bercow's face. Though Mrs Bercow claimed it was a deadpan look. She had, she told the court, simply noticed in all innocence that McAlpine's name was circulating widely on Twitter – 'trending' – and was hoping someone would tell her why. However, the claimant, Lord McAlpine, argued that Mrs Bercow was using irony – that 'innocent face' was meant to be read as the opposite of its literal meaning. Tugendhat J decided the reasonable tweeter would understand Bercow's words as insincere and ironical.

The judge ruled that the tweet was defamatory not only in its 'natural and ordinary meaning' but also through innuendo to Mrs Bercow's 56,000 followers on Twitter at the time. Mrs Bercow settled out of court with an offer to make amends of £150,000, which Lord McAlpine donated to charity.

It was the first time that posters of a defamatory statement via social media could be identified and for this reason action could be taken against the posters on a social networking site. *McAlpine* also demonstrated that Twitter (and other social media sites) are no different from people chatting in the pub. They are a public platform and tweets can seriously harm people's reputation. And if these defamatory tweets are not taken down they will stay on the platform for ever.

At the time the judgment was pronounced in May 2013, other Twitterers were identified. Some, such as *Guardian* columnist George Monbiot, apologized to Lord McAlpine, thereby avoiding further costly legal action against them. Most agreed to an out-of-court settlement and to undertake charitable work in recompense. The comedian Alan Davies had to pay out £15,000 after retweeting an internet post linking Lord McAlpine to the paedophile allegations.¹⁷³

7.5.3 Section 5 notice to website operators

Under the section 5 procedure a complainant is required to send a notice to the website operator containing information prescribed by the 2013 Act and the accompanying Regulations (known as a 'section 5 notice'). Section 5 of the 2013 Act should additionally be read in conjunction with Directive 2000/31/EC ('E-Commerce Directive'),¹⁷⁴ the implementing Regulations of 2013 and the Electronic Commerce Regulations 2002 ('e-Commerce Regs'),¹⁷⁵ which already provide immunities for operators of websites.

---

171 McAlpine [2013] EWHC 1342 at para. 3.
172 See: BBC Trust (2012).
173 Source: 'Lord McAlpine row: George Monbiot reaches "unprecedented" settlement', by Josh Halliday, *Guardian*, 12 March 2013.
174 Directive 2000/31/EC On 'Liability of Intermediary Service Providers' on Electronic Commerce of 8 June 2000 ('E-Commerce Directive').
175 Electronic Commerce (EC) Regulations 2002 (S.I. 2002/2013).

A section 5 notice is only valid if these seven 'boxes' are 'ticked' and the complainant has provided the following:

1. the name and email address of the complainant;
2. the URL or location of the statement complained of;
3. an explanation of what the statement says and why it is defamatory of the complainant;
4. the meaning the complainant attributes to the statement complained of;
5. the aspects of the statement which the complainant believes are factually incorrect or opinions not supported by fact;
6. confirmation that the complainant does not have sufficient information about the author to bring proceedings against them; and
7. confirmation of whether the complainant consents to his name and email address being provided to the poster.

The complainant need not be correct either in law or in fact, for example in identifying words as fact rather than comments or as defamatory as opposed to mere abuse; he simply needs to satisfy the seven 'boxes' (above). If the section 5 notice is missing any of these elements, the website operator can reject it, provided that it does so within 48 hours of receipt and sets out in its response the requirements of a valid notice. The operator need not explain why the notice received was deficient.

Once the notice has been received, the website operator has to communicate the position to the poster (if it has the means to do so), who then has a chance to reply and provide their contact details. Having complied with the process, the website operator can avail itself of the defence under section 5, regardless of the position as between the complainant and the poster. It is then a complete defence for the operator to show that it was not the operator who posted the statement on the website (section 5(2)). This defence can be defeated if the claimant can show that it was not possible for him to identify the person posting the statement, the claimant gave the operator a notice of complaint in relation to that statement and the operator did not respond to the notice of complaint in accordance with these regulations.

Once the website operator has received a section 5 notice, the 'abuse team' has to check whether it complies with the requirements of both section 5(6) of the 2013 Act and regulation 2 of the 2013 Regulations ('Notice of complaint: specified information').

In cases where the poster cannot be identified and the posting is not obviously unlawful or otherwise in breach of the website operator's terms of use, that website operator will have to decide whether to rely on the section 5 procedure, simply take the posting down, or rely on the other defences to defamation, including the important hosting defence provided by regulation 19 of the E-Commerce Regulations 2002 (known as 'the Regulation 19 defence'). If the website operator elects to follow the section 5 procedure, they will need to look carefully at their online complaints procedure, provide training to those responsible for dealing with complaints, and perhaps develop some software to monitor the numerous deadlines included in the procedure.

Section 5(11) provides for the defence to be defeated if the claimant shows that the website operator has acted with malice in relation to the posting of the statement concerned. This might arise where, for example, the website operator had incited the poster to make the posting or had otherwise colluded with the poster of the statement.

Section 5(12) explains that the defence available to a website operator is not defeated by reason only of the fact that the operator moderates the statements posted on it by others. To avoid liability, the operator must remove the allegedly defamatory statement unless the original poster provides a response within that period stating that the poster does not wish for the statement to be removed and including the poster's full name and postal address. However, the poster is entitled to refuse to consent to the disclosure of that information to the complainant.

The Regulations provide for a tight timeline. If the operator has no means of contacting the poster, the allegedly defamatory content must be removed within 48 hours of receiving the complaint. If the operator sends the notice to the poster and receives no reply, the content must be removed within seven days of the operator sending the notice. On its face, there is no provision for the operator to reject a complaint as unfounded and, under regulation 4 ('Defective notices to be treated as notice of complaint') operators are required to respond even to formally defective complaints, albeit only by informing the complainant of the applicable requirements.

In summary, though complex, section 5 DA 2013 provides an extremely useful defence for website operators in circumstances where the poster of the defamatory statement can be identified and served with legal proceedings (as was the case in *Lord McAlpine*). In such circumstances, there is actually no need for the website operator to follow any procedure, or even respond to a notice of complaint at all.

7.6 Defamation in Scotland and Northern Ireland

Defamation law also exists in Scots and Northern Irish law, but there are differences compared with English and Welsh jurisprudence. As we have seen in the previous sections, the Defamation Act 2013 reformed the law of defamation but many of its provisions extend, at present, only to England and Wales. This section will address the key differences between defamation laws in Scotland, Northern Ireland, England and Wales. Since neither Scotland nor Northern Ireland adopted the Defamation Act 2013 into their law, the common law tradition as explained earlier in this chapter prevails for the time being.

See above 7.2

This means, for example, that website operators based in Scotland or Northern Ireland have no general shield from liability for defamation claims over third-party content under the section 5 defence of the 2013 Act. They will have to continue using the 'innocent dissemination' defence. This defence will be defeated where the website operator has actual knowledge of the defamatory content, or even merely has reason to suspect its presence or has been negligent in failing to detect it (as was the case in *Godfrey v Demon*).

7.6.1 Defamation law in Scotland

Scots civil law on defamation has developed largely from the civil Roman law tradition (or Canon law), periodically supplemented by statute – similar to what happened in England and Wales.[176] The main difference between 'English' and Scots defamation law is that in Scottish law we look at the *delict* (or civil wrongdoing) with the award of damages for 'injurious feelings'. The seventeenth-century institutional writer Viscount Stair contributed much information in this area of Scots law.[177]

---

176 For a historical overview, see: Normand, the Right Hon Lord (1938), pp. 327–338.
177 See: Smartt, U. (2006), pp. 231–271.

The main difference between English and Scots defamation law is that an offending state-ment may not necessarily be defamatory and forms part of *delict*. Scots law then refers to 'hurtful words', and is similar to German or French law in this respect i.e. being essentially harmful to the character, honour or reputation of the affected person ('the pursuer') because it is 'deroga-tory' or 'disparaging' or 'demeaning' or 'calumnious' in the eyes of the reasonable person. It is then more akin to 'malicious falsehood' (or 'malice') in English law or a slander of title. Whilst English law makes the distinction between libel and slander, Scots law does not make this distinction, making a 'defamatory communication' a separate delict amounting to 'verbal injury' or *convicium*. Present Scottish law centres on the ('defamatory') statement which must be false and must lower the defamed in the estimation of right thinking members of society (see: Lord Atkin's definition in *Sim v Stretch* (1936)[178]). A Scottish court will ask what that standard is today as it is within this context that the court will look at the allegedly offending statement. It is important to note when accusing someone of 'libel' that that accusation may, in itself, be defamatory.

A pursuer's libel claim bears the nature of *solatium* for hurt feelings and if proved there will be an award of damages for the loss proved or presumed from a reputation unjustly attacked. Since there has been little precedent set to put a precise figure on 'injured reputation' or 'hurt feelings', Scottish judges can at times find it problematic to assess the seriousness of an account for damages in relation to the defender. Allegations of drunkenness made about a minister or of dishonesty made about a solicitor would be treated more seriously than if the same statement were made about an ordinary member of the public.

There is also a separate *delict* of 'invasion of privacy' linked to Article 8 ECHR, in which the making of a statement may give rise to liability for an attack on someone's reputation.[179] Neither of these *delicts* comes under the general heading of 'defamation'.

For a successful defamation action in the Scottish courts, it must be shown that there was a disparaging statement made by one person about another, which is communicated, and for which there is no defence; and 'communication' includes internet posts via blogs or other social media channels such as Facebook or Twitter. But in Scots law a communication need not be to a third party in order to be actionable: communication solely to the victim of a defamatory statement may result in that person suffering relevant insult or affront. Whether material is defamatory (i.e. harm-ful to reputation) is a matter for the courts to determine. The burden of proof in this regard rests with the pursuer. However, the pursuer is not required to show that the material is false; there is a rebuttable presumption that defamatory material is also false material, and it is for the defender to prove otherwise.

Similar to its English counterpart, the development of Scots common law in defamation, cou-pled with 'privacy' challenges, is in a state of flux in that even relatively recent decisions can soon become out of date, best illustrated with reference to cases involving photographs, as was high-lighted in the *Frances Curran* case (below). Scottish courts have frequently referred to the *von Hannover* (No 1)[180] decision in relation to the invasion of someone's privacy when defamatory actions are being considered. When the court considered privacy in the *Ewing*[181] action it referred, *inter alia*, to *Reklos v Greece* (2009).[182]

---

178 [1936] 2 All ER 1237 at para. 1240 (Lord Atkin).

179 Sections 29 and 57 Scotland Act 1998 also provide that the Scottish Parliament and Scottish ministers must not contravene certain Convention Rights, as defined in the Human Rights Act 1998, including Article 10 of the ECHR.

180 *Von Hannover v Germany (No 1)* (2005) 40 EHRR 1 (ECHR).

181 See: *Ewing (Terence Patrick) v Times Newspapers Ltd* [2010] CSIH 67; [2008] CSOH 169 Outer House, Court of Session, Edinburgh.

182 (2009) (Application No 1234/05) ECtHR of 15 January 2009.

9

❖ KEY CASE — *Scottish Daily Record and Sunday Mail Ltd* [2011] CSIH 86 (A952/08). Extra Division, Inner House, Court of Session, 29 December 2011

Facts

The pursuer was Frances Curran;[183] the defenders the publishers of the *Daily Record*. On 7 August 2006 the defenders published a four-page article based on an interview with Tommy Sheridan,[184] in which certain remarks were made about the pursuer and three other MSPs, Colin Fox, Rosie Kane and Carolyn Leckie, accompanied by photographs. The front-page headline read: 'I'll destroy the scabs who tried to ruin me: Tommy vows to win back leadership of Scottish Socialists.' The defenders sought dismissal of the action on the basis that no relevant case of defamation was made out in the pursuer's pleadings and an *esto* position that, were the action to proceed to proof before answer, deletions would be required to be made.

The defenders submitted that criticism by an MSP of another MSP did not amount to defamation because of the permitted latitude in criticizing those who hold public office. Further, it was submitted that the comments made in the article were protected by the *Reynolds* qualified privilege defence. The pursuer would have to prove malice for the defence to fail. This she had not done. The defenders further submitted that the article be looked at as a whole, representing an attack on the public as well as the political activities of the pursuer(s), and that the term 'scab' in the article referred to her being a 'political scab'. Counsel for Ms Curran submitted that the case should be sent to proof and submitted that the tenor of the article was that she was guilty of dishonest conduct with base motives, and that it went beyond fair criticism of a holder of a public office.

Opinion

Temporary Judge Mrs Morag Wise QC dismissed the action. She considered whether the article, taken as a whole, would tend to lower the pursuer in the estimation of right-thinking members of society generally, or be likely to affect her adversely in the estimation of reasonable people generally. She ruled:

> I do not consider that it would have that effect. Right-thinking members of society are well able to read an article of this sort and see it as no more than a robust criticism of the pursuer as a former colleague and ally of Mr Sheridan. The reference to the pursuer as a 'scab' simply has no context without the detail given of the political plot alleged by Mr Sheridan and the references to collaboration with 'the enemy' namely Newsgroup Newspapers Limited.[185] In relation to the photograph this should not be seen in isolation but as part of the whole article, as demonstrated in *Charleston v News Group Newspapers Ltd* (1995),[186] i.e. the defence of 'bane and antidote'.

---

183 Frances Curran (born 21 May 1961, Glasgow) is a former co-chair of the Scottish Socialist Party (SSP) and a former Member of the Scottish Parliament (MSP) for the West of Scotland region during 2003–2007.

184 Tommy Sheridan (born 7 March 1964, Glasgow) then an MSP and leader of the SSP. In a civil jury trial in 2006 Sheridan sought damages for defamation against News Group Newspapers Limited (*News of the World* (*NoW*)). He alleged that articles in *NoW* (e.g. 31 October 2004 an article by Anvar Khan) had falsely accused him of having visited a swingers' club, committed sexual indiscretions, and been unfaithful to his wife. On 4 August 2006 the jury found in his favour and awarded £200,000 in damages. In December 2010 Sheridan was convicted of perjury following the libel trial against *NoW* in 2006. His wife Gail was acquitted after the Crown withdrew charges against her (see: *Her Majesty's Advocate against Thomas Sheridan and Gail Sheridan* [2011] ScotHC HCJ 001).

185 [2010] CSOH 44 at para. 29 (Judge Morag Wise QC).

186 [1995] 2 AC 65 (HL).

Analysis

The Edinburgh court felt that the photo of the Scottish MPs amounted to neither defamation nor an infringement of their privacy under Article 8 ECHR, citing the *Reklos* judgment. Wise J's opinion focused on the 'eye-catching' photograph in particular and stated that the matter was in the public interest, thereby allowing the qualified privilege defence under *Reynolds* (where all the ten-point criteria had been met by the newspaper). She stated that it was of particular public interest – and therein protected by Article 10 ECHR – that the leadership of a political party was explained and the (in this case) inability of some of its members to work with each other. Accordingly, she did not consider that this was an attack on the private character of the main pursuer, Frances Curran, but rather on her political decisions and political loyalties (also applied: *McLeod v News Quest (Sunday Herald) Ltd* (2007)[187]).

See Chapter
6.3

Worth of note is the *Andy Coulson*[188] perjury trial in Scotland which arose from the *Tommy Sheridan* (perjury) trial. Coulson, former editor of the *News of the World* (*NoW*), gave evidence at the *Sheridan* perjury trial on 10 and 11 December 2010 as a defence witness. The Crown alleged that Mr Coulson had perjured himself when giving evidence in the *Sheridan* trial.[189] The perjured evidence was said to have been related to Mr Coulson's knowledge of 'phone hacking' by employees of the paper or people acting for the paper and of payments to them. Lord Burns considered that the false evidence alleged in the indictment against Mr Coulson was not relevant evidence at the original *Sheridan* trial and the charge of perjury in the indictment became irrelevant. For this reason Andy Coulson was cleared of all charges.

The defences available in Scotland are broadly the same as in the English jurisdiction, the most common one being *veritas* (truth or justification); this being equivalent to the English defence of 'truth' (section 2 Defamation Act 2013). The defence of 'fair comment' provides for freedom of expression and protects the inherent public interest in expressing opinions on public figures, political and legal decision makers. An alleged defamer may also offer to make an apology in a reasonable manner as well as offer to pay compensation ('offer to make amends') and this will provide a defence to an action of defamation as long as the defamer did not know, or have reason to believe, that the statement complained of was false and defamatory. If the offer is accepted, the wronged party accepting the offer may not bring, or continue with, defamation proceedings in respect of the defamatory statement. Defences of qualified privilege and absolute privilege apply similarly north and south of the border. Remedies can take the form of *interdict* (injunction) to prevent further publication of the defamatory statement, or damages, which seek to compensate the pursuer for injury to feelings or to reputation. The wider the audience which receives the defamatory statement, the greater damages are likely to be.

7.6.2 Judge-alone trials and damages

Scots defamation law compensates the wronged party who has suffered 'injury to hurt feelings': this generally means a person's reputation (or honour) has been damaged. The greater the circulation of the publication (including online) by the original defamer the greater the sum of damages awarded by the courts. This includes re-publication (for example of a forwarded email or SMS) – since

187 [2007] SCLR 555.
188 *HM Advocate v Andrew Edward Coulson* [2015] HCJ 49.
189 Tommy Sheridan went on trial for perjury committed during his libel action against *NoW* 2006, in which he won substantial damages. Sheridan was subsequently convicted of perjury in December 2010.

the multiple publication rule still exists in Scots defamation law. In cases where publication has been with malice, aggravated damages will be awarded if the case is proved. Even if the statement is truthful but designed to injure the claimant out of malice, an action can be brought when a statement is communicated; but only to the person defamed. This action includes injury to the feelings of the person defamed as well as injury to reputation. The pursuer of such a 'personal injury' claim cannot take advantage of the Court of Session procedure afforded to accident cases, for example.[190]

Although English courts have now abolished 'libel jury' trials, Scottish courts have long abandoned jury trials in defamation actions. In the past libel juries awarded punitive damages in England and Wales (see: *Elton John*[191] and *Esther Rantzen*[192]).

Though the *Tommy Sheridan* libel action in August 2006 was held with a jury, judge-alone trials are more common in Scottish libel actions; the Evidence (Scotland) Act of 1866 (still in force) makes judge-alone trials possible if 'special cause' can be shown.[193] Though 'special cause' is not defined in either common law or statute, it is generally assumed that it means 'special circumstances' depending on each individual case. Once a Scottish court holds the words to be capable of bearing a defamatory meaning, the following are presumed:

1. that the words are false;
2. that the words are spoken with intent to injure; and
3. that the pursuer has suffered some form of material injury which must result in financial compensation being due from the defender.

The Scottish courts regard money damages as the remedy for a wrong done. However, damages are always to compensate, never to punish. In 1908, Lord President Dunedin reviewed the question of punitive or exemplary damages and could find no authority for them in the law of Scotland. In fact, he felt that the heading of 'reparation' under which the matter is treated in the textbooks excluded the very idea of exemplary damages. When the argument was again raised in a defamation case 60 years later, Grant LJC held that the fact that a libel was actuated by malice was not enough to entitle the pursuer to greater damages. The 'offer to make amends' relates to the Defamation Act 1996 (the same as in England and Wales).[194]

In *Baigent v BBC* (1999),[195] temporary Judge Coutts QC awarded exceptionally high damages. The case concerned a TV programme which alleged that the owners of a nursing home were operating 'a callous and uncaring regime'. Mrs Baigent was awarded £60,000, Mr Baigent £50,000 and each of the three Baigent children £20,000 (upheld on appeal). The Baigent case probably marked the turning point when the Scottish courts began to award similarly high damages to the English courts. Coutts J stressed that damages in Scottish libel actions are compensatory rather than punitive. Similarly high awards, each of £60,000, were made in *Clinton v News Group Newspapers Ltd* (1999)[196] and *Wray v Associated Newspapers Ltd* (2000).[197]

Another major difference is the limitation period afforded to a pursuer, which makes litigation in the Scottish courts more attractive to litigants. Section 17 of the Prescription and Limitation Act (Scotland) 1973 grants a litigant three years in which to raise proceedings (compared to the one-year time limit in England and Wales). While Article 6 ECHR permits access to a court, that right is

190 See: rule 43.1 of the Rules of the Court of Session.
191 *John v Mirror Group Newspapers Ltd* [1997] QB 586.
192 *Rantzen v Mirror Group Newspapers (1986) Ltd* [1994] QB 670.
193 See: Chapter 37 Court of Session Rules, r. 37(1) 'Jury Trials'.
194 Its form and application are defined in r. 54 (1) of the Rules of the Court of Session.
195 [1999] SCLR 787.
196 [1999] SC 367.
197 [2000] SLT 869.

not absolute and the granting of an award of caution is a permissible limitation to that right (see: *Monarch Energy Ltd v Powergen Retail Ltd* (2006)[198]).

'Serial litigant' Terence Patrick Ewing (the pursuer and reclaimer) had sued for 'unlimited damages – *solatium* including *actio iniuriarum*' in respect of an article published by the defender and respondent on 11 February 2007 in the *Sunday Times Scotland* edition, and on two related websites. Ewing had a long history of civil litigation, with the High Court of England and Wales declaring him to be a vexatious litigant on 21 December 1989. But Ewing then took advantage of Scottish and later Northern Irish jurisdictions when he sued in both the *delicts* of 'personal injury' and 'injury to privacy'. Pursuer Mr Ewing, co-founder of the Euston Trust, whose members travel around the UK to make objections to planning applications, filed a libel action against the Scottish edition of the *Sunday Times* in respect of an online article of 11 February 2007, entitled 'Heritage Fakers Hold Builders to Ransom', in which investigative journalists Daniel Foggo and Robert Booth had claimed to have exposed Mr Ewing as a fraudster; and also of having considerable debts from statutory demands for non-payment of fines.

On 19 June 2008, the pursuer and reclaimer Mr Ewing applied to the High Court for leave to initiate his action against the defender and respondent in the English courts. This application was refused. Around this time, the Inner House noted the pursuer and reclaimer had travelled to Scotland, where he downloaded the internet version of the article concerned, and also read a hard copy of the article at a public library. The publication in question had been downloaded by Mr Ewing's companion at the Edinburgh City Library.[199]

Mr Ewing sued for defamation, claiming, *inter alia*, breach of data protection, invasion of his privacy and harassment as well as breach of confidence. The court held that there was a 'stateable case' on his pleadings, and confined the pursuer's damages to a claim that would not be 'substantial' because his case did not have 'serious merits' and was an 'artificial litigation',[200] based on Lord Donaldson's ruling in *Henry J Garratt & Co. v Ewing* (1991).[201] One crucial factor for the court's decision was that the pursuer had made 'at least 25 vexatious claims . . . none of this bodes well for the manner in which he is likely to conduct this action in a jurisdiction'[202] (see also: *Rush v Fife Regional Council* (1985)[203]).

From the outset, the defender and respondent newspaper moved the Scottish court to ordain caution in the sum of £50,000 as a condition precedent to continuing the action. This motion was granted by the Lord Ordinary, Lord Brodie, in December 2008. Lord Brodie then took the unprecedented step at the Edinburgh High Court of Sessions in January 2009 and merely granted Mr Ewing a motion for caution in the sum of £15,000, additionally refusing Mr Ewing leave to reclaim any damages at a later hearing. The court granted decree of absolvitor. The pursuer reclaimed against these decisions (see: *Ewing v Times Newspapers Ltd* (2008)[204]).

In considering the pursuer and reclaimer's first submission, the Inner House considered that the Article 6 ECHR right to access to justice was not unqualified, nor absolute. The court noted it was subject to the rights of the other party to be protected against being put to irrevocable expense by an impecunious and irresponsible litigant. The court added that such protection was a legitimate aim, to which a requirement to find caution was properly directed. In relation to the pursuer and reclaimer's second submission, the Inner House noted that the distinction drawn on the timing of the order for caution was of no significance, noting that if the action was unlikely to succeed in any event, it was right that the court should grant caution at an early stage of proceedings; otherwise,

---

198 [2006] SLT 743.
199 Ibid., at paras 3 and 21.
200 Ibid., at para. 25.
201 [1991] 1 WLR 1356 at 1357E (Lord Donaldson MR).
202 [2008] CSOH at para. 29 (Lord Brodie).
203 [1985] SLT 451 (Lord Wheatley).
204 [2008] CSOH 169, Outer House, Court of Session, Edinburgh.

the purpose of the caution itself would be defeated. Finally, the Inner House opined that the proper test to be applied when considering the pursuer's reputation, was whether the Lord Ordinary exercised his discretion as no Lord Ordinary could reasonably have done. Lord Justice-Clerk Gill, in delivering the opinion of the court, noted that Lord Brodie had given a careful account of his reasons for ordering caution, and that he could see no reasons to suggest that his decision was unreasonable. The reclaiming motion was refused and the defender's motion for expenses was granted.[205] Mr Ewing then took his libel actions to the High Court of Justice in Northern Ireland, Queen's Bench Division, Belfast in 2011[206] and subsequently to the courts in Gibraltar.

See below 7.6.5

Henderson (2009) argues that it would be wrong to presume that the finding in the Ewing claim (including privacy) was not stateable, as disclosing any emerging principle of the approach that the Scots courts would take to such actions.[207] First there was an absence of any expectation of privacy on the part of the pursuer and second the context of the libel complaint had to be taken into account in that Mr Ewing had simply supplied a photocopy of the cases cited, where the court held that the pursuer 'did not set out in any comprehensive way in his pleadings the basis upon which he avers that delictual liability has been incurred'.[208]

Despite the differences noted above, it is likely that in many Scottish cases English authorities in defamation will continue to be relied upon, as there are relatively few Scottish decisions reported.

7.6.3 The future of Scottish defamation laws

In the light of the significant changes made by the Defamation Act 2013 in England and Wales, the Scottish Law Commission published a Discussion Paper in March 2016,[209] covering key areas of defamation law, including the defences of public interest, fair comment and truth. The Commission asked whether there should be a mechanism for filtering out claims where little is at stake, and liability for publication of defamatory material online.

The Paper also considered whether the courts should be given power to order that a summary of the court's judgment should be printed by a newspaper or broadcaster which has been found to have defamed someone. It considers if Scottish courts should be given power to order removal of a defamatory statement from a website. The Paper further examined the relationship of the law on verbal injury and defamation law. It also considered whether it should be possible for defamation claims to be brought where the reputation of a person has been unfairly attacked after his or her death. Since reform of defamation law in Scotland remains a 'medium term' objective. It was expected that draft legislation be published by the end of the Ninth Programme of Law Reform in 2017.[210]

The Hon Lord Pentland, Chairman of the Scottish Law Commission, said:

Defamation law potentially affects everyone. It is at the cutting edge of freedom of expression and protection of reputation; two important human rights. The law in this area must be in tune with the values of modern society. We hope that as many people as possible will read our discussion paper and give us their views on the questions we ask. That will allow us to recommend changes to ensure that the law is up to date and in line with current thinking and practice.[211]

205 See: Ewing (Terence Patrick) v Times Newspapers Ltd [2010] CSIH 6.
206 See: Ewing (Terence Patrick) v Times Newspapers Ltd [2011] NIQB 63.
207 See: Henderson, G. (2009), pp. 116–118.
208 [1985] SLT 451 (Lord Wheatley).
209 See: Scottish Law Commission (2016) 'Defamation Law: Time for change?' A Discussion Paper, issued on behalf of the Scottish Law Commission on 17 March 2016.
210 The Scottish Commission had already published comprehensive evidence from various professionals and academics in relation the framework for reform of the defamation law in 2015. See: Scottish Law Commission (2015) at para. 2.18 p. 19.
211 Source: Scottish Law Commission (2016) Discussion Paper p. 1.

In a letter to Professor Hector MacQueen, Chairman of the Scottish Law Commission, Rosalind McInnes, Principal Solicitor for BBC Scotland, expressed her concern regarding the multiple publication rule and the *Reynolds* defence. Ms McInnes said that the restriction on jurisdiction in Scotland, the extension of the defences of qualified and absolute privilege internationally and a shorter time bar period may all combine to encourage 'forum shopping' in favour of Scotland, thereby transferring libel tourism to the High Courts of Justiciary in Edinburgh or Glasgow.[212]

See below
7.6.4

This means that the *Brunswick* multiple publication rule still exists in Scottish libel laws (and indeed in Northern Ireland[213]), making a libellous story in a back-issue of the Sunday *Herald*, for example, a re-publication from its digital or print archive; which means that an original publisher can still be successfully sued if the story was read by someone else. Furthermore, a publisher (or author) in Scotland still has direct responsibility for anonymous online comments made by members of the public.

👁 FOR THOUGHT

Discuss the following scenario in the light of Scottish defamation laws

In private conversations with Ms Grant, Mr McDonald confesses that he owes some money. Shortly afterwards Mr McDonald dies. Ms Grant subsequently publishes statements on Facebook which are clearly defamatory about Mr McDonald, calling him a 'thief'. Mr McDonald's widow, Mrs McDonald, wishes to protect her late husband's memory and to take legal action in relation to the social networking posts by Ms Grant. The postings are clearly defamatory in that they tend to lower the late Mr McDonald in the estimation of right-thinking members of Scottish society. Since she cannot question and cross-examine Mr McDonald in court, how is Ms Grant to prove (as required by standard of Scots defamation law) that her claims are indeed truthful? Advise both Mrs McDonald and Ms Grant. Draft a skeleton argument for the High Court of Justiciary in Glasgow.

7.6.4 Defamation law in Northern Ireland

In a House of Lords debate, Lord Lester (championing the Defamation Bill in Parliament in 2012) had said it would be 'a stain on the reputation of Northern Ireland if it were to replace London as the libel tourist capital by clinging to archaic and uncertain common law – great for the vested interests of wealthy claimants and their lawyers in Belfast but wholly against the public'.

In mid-June 2013, the Northern Ireland Assembly decided *not* to implement the Defamation Act 2013 into Northern Irish legislation. This meant that newspapers (and their online editions) as well as tweeters and bloggers could potentially still face libel tourism claims and threats of legal action by big companies trying to stifle free speech in the High Court in Belfast. It is worth noting though that the Westminster Parliament could have imposed the new defamation legislation on Northern Ireland due to its supremacy, whether Northern Ireland was devolved or not.

On 28 November 2013, the Finance Minister for Northern Ireland, Simon Hamilton MLA, asked the Northern Ireland Law Commission to examine whether the Defamation Act 2013 should be extended to Northern Ireland. Mr Hamilton's department noted that, 'The minister has no preconceived ideas about what [the Northern Ireland Law Commission's] recommendations will be. As with any other Commission Report, the recommendations will have to be thoroughly assessed,

---

212 Source: Letter by Rosalind McInnes to the Scottish Law Commission of 18 July 2014 at: www.scotlawcom.gov.uk/files/8214/3161/0550/Rosalind_M_M_McInnes_Principal_Solicitor_BBC_Scotland.pdf.
213 The Northern Ireland Law Commission launched a consultation on reform of defamation law in October 2014.

with a view to making final policy recommendations.' This reference was formally approved by the Minister of Justice, Mr David Ford MLA, on 7 January 2014. These recommendations were then included in the Commission's Consultation Paper on Defamation Laws (2014),[214] headed by Commissioner Dr Venkat Iyer.

The Department of Justice for Northern Ireland then requested that the Law Commission's Second Programme of Law Reform consider the law relating to defamation in Northern Ireland.[215] The Commission's terms of reference included:

- to review the existing law of defamation within Northern Ireland in light of the recent changes brought about in England and Wales by the introduction of the Defamation Act 2013;
- to assess the strengths and weaknesses of the current system;
- to develop proposals which are tailored to the particular context of Northern Ireland.

7.6.5 Libel claims in Northern Ireland

See above 7.6.2

Current law provides that a libel claim can be summarily dismissed where it discloses no 'real or substantial tort' that has occurred in Northern Ireland. Such an order was affirmed by the Northern Irish Court of Appeal, having been made by the High Court in Ewing v Times (2013).[216]

After a number of unsuccessful defamation claims in the English, Welsh and Scottish courts, serial litigant Mr Ewing tried his luck in in the Belfast High Court. The previous UK jurisdictions had already expressed concern about Mr Ewing's 'forum shopping' as a serial 'libel tourist', calling his claims 'vexatious' and an abuse of process against the Times Newspaper Group.

Gillen J confirmed two mechanisms for dismissing Mr Ewing's claim in the Northern Irish court under the Rules of the Court of Judicature (Northern Ireland) 2009, recognizing the practical hardships that defamation actions could create. Under the Rules the judge set the precedent for a 'new climate' supportive of judges exercising discretion in dismissing such vexatious cases.

Proponents of the status quo in Northern Irish defamation law have argued that the Ewing (Northern Ireland) judgment shows how the common law and procedural rules provide ample means for identifying and dIPSOsing of unmeritorious uses of defamation law before the courts.

However, not deterred by previous rulings across the UK jurisdictions, Mr Ewing then took the matter to the Supreme Court of Gibraltar in relation to copies of the Sunday Times international Madrid edition of 11 February 2007. Puisne Judge, Jack J, pointed out that the claimant had no connection to Gibraltar whatsoever, nor would anyone have known that the offending article in The Times, dating back some seven years, referred to him on the peninsular. Mr Ewing was subsequently remanded in custody for criminal contempt for abuse of process in bringing his vexatious claim again in Gibraltar courts when the courts in England/Wales, Scotland and Northern Ireland had already sufficiently dealt with the matter by way of abuse of process.[217]

Jack J alerted Mr Ewing (as always representing himself) that the maximum punishment for criminal contempt of court in Gibraltar was two years' imprisonment. The judge also said that – to that date – Mr Ewing had never paid any legal costs ordered in the other jurisdictions and that present costs – including Gibraltar – amounted to £30,000. Striking down both claims in defamation and privacy, the judge cited the leading judgment by the Northern Irish High Court by Sir Declan Morgan JC – the only difference being that that claim concerned the Ulster edition of the Sunday Times and this claim the Madrid edition.[218]

---

214 See: Northern Ireland Law Commission (2014).

215 See: Northern Ireland Law Commission (2014).

216 Ewing (Terence Patrick) v Times Newspapers Ltd [2013] NICA (Sir Declan Morgan JC).

217 As per CPR r. 81.16.

218 Ewing (Terence Patrick) v Times Newspapers Ltd (2014) Claim No 2013-E-42 – In the Supreme Court of Gibraltar, Judgment of 17 November 2014 at para. 5 (Adrian Jack J Puisne Judge).

 **FOR THOUGHT**

A defendant Ulster newspaper has archived materials that are or may be defamatory. Would an appropriate notice warning against treating it as the truth remove the sting of the libel from the material or will the Belfast High Court regard this publication as equally important to the dissemination of contemporary material? Discuss.

7.6.6 Defamation law reform in Northern Ireland

Following its consultation period in 2015, the Law Commission for Northern Ireland highlighted the following areas of controversy in relation to the Defamation Act 2013:

- **Section 1 Defamation Act 2013 the 'serious harm' test** – whether this ought to be afforded to commercial bodies that trade for profit (e.g. corporations), and
- the option of adopting a rule barring defamation claims by companies employing more than ten persons (similar to Australian jurisdictions)?
- **Section 3 of the 2013 Act, the 'honest comment' defence** – Northern Irish defamation law reform suggests a two-stage approach, taking the defence even further: (1) whether it should be confirmed that the defence applies to inferences of verifiable fact? This would remove one level of complexity in the deployment of the defence; (2) whether the basis for comment should extend also to include facts that the defendant–publisher 'reasonably believed to be true' at the time of publication. That is, whether the defence should be available when the factual basis for opinion expressed was either true, privileged, or reasonably believed to be true. This extension would be especially useful to those commenting on social media.
- **Section 4 of the 2013 Act, defence of publication on a matter of public interest** – the Commission's recommendation is to retain common law *Reynolds* privilege, plus an extension of the new defence under section 4 to cover opinions as well as statements of fact.
- **The single meaning rule** – the tort of malicious falsehood is to be retained and the 'singular meaning' rule is to be adopted which would simplify the task that must be undertaken by the court when determining defamation claims. This rule would require a court to extract a *singular meaning* from often ambiguous publications on which to base its application of the law. The practical effect of the rule would be to reduce often highly technical, protracted and costly defamation claims to have their interpretations of the publication selected by the court (analogous to the law of trademarks).
- **The prompt correction of falsehoods** – as a means of vindicating reputation. Almost all mainstream Northern Irish (and UK) publishers are committed, in principle, to correcting significant inaccuracies when they are identified.
- **The introduction of a bar on claims** – where timely corrections or retractions have been made; this could mean that defendant–publishers might begin to publish corrections or retractions automatically when complained-of meanings can be seen to be plausible but were unintended. They might also become more willing and able to defend actions in court if they are convinced of the truth of what has been published.
- **Section 6 of the 2013 Act extended qualified privilege to statements published in peer-reviewed articles in scientific or academic journals** – Contributors to academic or scientific discourse can avail themselves of the defences of 'honest comment' or 'honest opinion'. Such primary defences must be readily usable to deter attempts – particularly by large corporations – to bully the academic author of a critical report through the threat of legal action. Otherwise this would have a chilling effect on scientific speech.

- **Section 11 of the 2013 Act presumption that defamation claims will no longer be heard by a jury** – the consultation arguments resulted in favour of retention of the jury in Northern Ireland. Judge-alone trials would weaken the process of determination of meaning and disputes would focus immediately on core errors of factual uncertainty.

Whilst in England and Wales a company can sue for defamation, the present argument in Northern Ireland tends to be against adoption of this rule, one reason being that the concept of 'serious financial loss' does not capture the range of harms that might be caused to corporate reputations; alternatively that harm to corporate reputation may not manifest itself obviously or clearly in specific, identifiable financial losses, and that it might be difficult for a trading company to show loss of profit linked to harm caused by a false publication.

It is therefore highly likely that Northern Irish defamation laws will continue to differ from those of England and Wales. The Northern Irish Law Commissioners argued during the consultation period in 2015 that there is an apparent tendency of some corporations to bring claims to 'bully' opponents.

 FOR THOUGHT

Arguably the Scottish and Northern Irish courts have replaced the London High Court as the forum of choice, as libel tourists seek redress. Discuss.

7.7 Injury to business reputation

Many people tend to think of defamation law in connection with someone's conduct or character in their personal life, the focus being on individual litigants. Corporate reputations are formed and reformed by the near-constant barrage of information available to us every day both in the business sections of newspapers, their online editions and social media. The ability to sue for defamation offers particular advantages in protecting a business reputation. The basic principle remains: the tort of defamation exists to protect against blatantly untrue damaging statements which can potentially ruin a company's business acumen and international standing. As John Disley said when he and Chris Brasher won their libel action in 1995, 'Take away my good name and you take away my life.'[219]

A damaging libel may lower a company's standing in the eyes of the public and even its own staff, and make people less ready to deal with it or less willing and less proud to work for it. If this were not so, corporations would not go to the lengths they do to protect and burnish their corporate images. In his leading judgment in *Jameel*, Lord Bingham found nothing repugnant in the notion that this is a value which the law should protect. He did not accept that a publication, if truly damaging to a corporation's commercial reputation, would result in provable financial loss, since the more prompt and public a company's issue of proceedings, and the more diligent its pursuit of a claim, the less the chance that financial loss would actually accrue.

In the *South Hetton Coal* case (1894),[220] *The Times* publishers argued that a corporation could have no personal character, and that the offending article had not related to the business of the company. Lawyers for the newspaper further argued that defamation laws did not apply to trading

---

219 Source: *The Reunion: The First London Marathon*, BBC Radio 4, 4 April 2010. Brasher and Disley, original founders and organizers of the London Marathon, accepted more than £380,000 in libel damages in an out-of-court settlement on 23 May 1995 over magazine and TV allegations that they used the London Marathon to enrich themselves.

220 *South Hetton Company Limited v North-Eastern News Association Limited* [1894] 1 QB 133.

companies.[221] *The Times* had published an article strongly critical of the way in which the plaintiff, a colliery owner, housed his workers, and the company had not pleaded or proved any actual damage. However, the Court of Appeal unanimously rejected this argument. Lord Esher MR held the law of libel to be one and the same for *all* plaintiffs.[222] While he referred to obvious differences between individuals and companies his conclusion was clear:

> Then, if the case be one of libel – whether on a person, a firm, or a company – the law is that damages are at large. It is not necessary to prove any particular damage; the jury may give such damages as they think fit, having regard to the conduct of the parties respectively, and all the circumstances of the case.[223]

This case established that trading companies that have reputations in the UK could sue for defamation and recover general damages. Since 1993, however, following the case of *Derbyshire County Council v Times Newspaper Ltd* (1993),[224] local authorities, trade unions and unincorporated bodies cannot sue for defamation. Increasingly the UK courts were asked to deal with attacks on international business reputation which – generally – the courts held as defamatory.

The concept that a company can sue for libel was further developed in the *Derbyshire*[225] case. The claimant was a county council constituted as a non-trading corporation. The defendant newspapers questioned the propriety of investments made in the claimant's superannuation funds. The HL clearly established that a trading corporation is entitled to sue in respect of defamatory matters which can be seen as having a tendency to damage it in the way of its business. This became known as the 'Derbyshire Principle'. The *Derbyshire* Principle was applied three years later in *Shevill v Presse Alliance SA* (1996),[226] where a differently constituted committee of the HL decided that a trading company with a trading reputation in the UK may recover general damages without pleading or proving special damage if the publication complained of had a tendency to damage it in the way of its business.

7.7.1 Can a corporation sue for harm to reputation?

There are many defamatory things which can be said about individuals (for example, about their sexual appetite) which cannot be said about corporations. But some statements may well be seriously injurious to the general commercial reputation of trading and charitable corporations; for example, that an arms company has routinely bribed officials of foreign governments to secure contracts; that an oil company has wilfully and unnecessarily damaged the environment; that an international humanitarian agency has wrongfully succumbed to government pressure; that a retailer has knowingly exploited child labour; and so on. Should the corporation be entitled to sue in its own right only if it can prove financial loss? The House of Lords in *Jameel v Wall Street* (No 3) (2007)[227] did not think so.

The contextual circumstances to the *Jameel* case were the 9/11 terrorism atrocities, when, on 11 September 2001, terrorists destroyed the World Trade Center in New York.[228] Shortly afterwards, the *Wall Street Journal* alleged that 15 of the terrorists had been financed by Saudi Arabia. The journal

221 Ibid., paras 134, 137.
222 Ibid., para. 138 (Lord Esher MR).
223 Ibid., paras 138–139.
224 *Derbyshire County Council v Times Newspapers Ltd and Others* [1993] AC 534.
225 Ibid.
226 [1996] AC 959.
227 See: *Jameel and others v Wall Street Journal Europe Sprl* [2006] UKHL 44 (on appeal from [2005] EWCA Civ 74) (HL); see also: *Jameel (Mohammed) v Wall Street Journal Europe Sprl (No 3)* [2007] 1 AC 359.
228 Four passenger airliners (operated by United Airlines and American Airlines) coordinated by Islamic terrorist group Al Qaeda crashed into the North and South Towers of the World Trade Center complex killing 2,996 people and injuring 6,000 others. Within an hour and 42 minutes, both 110-storey towers collapsed.

headlined 'Saudi Officials Monitor Certain Bank Accounts' on 6 February 2002, claiming that the Saudi Arabian Monetary Authority (SAMA[229]) was watching the accounts of certain named Saudi companies at the request of the US Treasury. These included accounts of Mr Jameel, principal director of the holding company named in the article, to trace whether any payments were finding their way to terrorist organizations.[230] The article was written by James Dorsey, the journal's special correspondent in Riyadh and had been checked by financial journalist Glenn R. Simpson for accuracy.

The claimants brought their proceedings in the UK against the publishers of the European edition of the *Wall Street Journal*, where the article had also appeared. Eady J rejected the *Journal*'s claim to *Reynolds* privilege and the jury found that the article was defamatory of both claimants, Mr Jameel and the Jameel Corporation, culminating in awards of £30,000 and £10,000 respectively.[231]

In *Jameel No 3* (2007),[232] the *Journal* argued before the House of Lords that, in accordance with the trend towards enhanced recognition of freedom of expression, the *Derbyshire* Principle should be abolished. Lord Hoffmann – dissenting – agreed.[233] Baroness Hale – also dissenting – quoted the constitutional writer Weir, stating that a 'company has no feelings' which 'might have been hurt and no social relations which might have been impaired'.[234] But by a majority of three to two, the Law Lords (Lord Bingham of Cornhill, Lord Hope of Craighead and Lord Scott of Foscote) agreed that reputation is a thing of value and applies equally to companies as to individuals. This meant that a corporation could sue for defamation on its reputation and could recover damages without proof of special damage (i.e. economic loss). Lord Hope explained:

> this does not mean . . . that it [a company] can only be injured in a way that gives rise to loss which, because it can be calculated, has the character of special damage. What it means is that it must show that it is liable to be damaged in a way that affects its business as a trading company.[235]

Herzfeld (2005) argues that trading corporations should be allowed to sue in defamation only in respect of an attack on their business reputation and not any other reputation (e.g. performing charitable duties). He argued that this would simply be an indirect way to protect the company's business reputation. An example would be a company accused of exaggerating the amount of money it donated to charity. Herzfeld further contended that a company would have to show *actual* loss and be able to prove special damage.[236]

There was a further appeal by the *Wall Street Journal* to the HL[237] which allowed the *Reynolds* privilege defence to the publishers and journalists, reasoning that the story was of international (public) interest, not only because of the identity of the names on the list, but also that there was such a list, evidencing the highly important and significant co-operation between the US and the Saudi authorities in the fight against terrorism. In her leading judgment, Baroness Hale of Richmond said

---

229 On 28 September 2001 the UN Security Council had passed Resolution 1373, which required all states to prevent and suppress the financing of terrorist acts, with the United States making diplomatic efforts to secure the co-operation of the Saudi Arabian Monetary Authority (SAMA).

230 The Abdul Latif Jameel Company Ltd (the second claimant in the law suit) was well known as a substantial Saudi Arabian trading company with interests in a number of businesses, including the distribution of Toyota vehicles, and was part of an international group owned by the Jameel family. The company also included Hartwell plc, a company which distributes vehicles in the UK. Mr Mohammed Abdul Latif Jameel (the first claimant) was General Manager and President at the time.

231 *Jameel (Mohammed)* [2003] EWHC 2322 (Eady J).

232 *Jameel (Mohammed)* (No 3) [2007] 1 AC 359 (HL).

233 Ibid., at para. 91 (Lord Hoffmann dissenting).

234 Ibid., at para. 154 (Baroness Hale dissenting).

235 *Jameel (Mohammed)* [2006] UKHL 44 at para. 95 (Lord Hope).

236 See: Herzfeld, P. (2005), p. 135.

237 *Jameel (Mohammed)* [2006] UKHL 44 (HL).

that the journalists had a professional duty to disclose the vital information amounting to the main criterion of responsible journalism.[238]

Their Lordships then re-qualified the *Reynolds* defence in relation to the meaning of 'responsible journalism':

> 1. Is the publication in the public interest in the context of the work as a whole?
> 2. Will the work or article pass the 'fairness test'?
> 3. How much weight is attached to the professional judgement of the journalist and his reliable sources?

The *Jameel–Reynolds* tests was successfully applied in *Charman v Orion* (2007),[239] where the CA found in favour of BBC reporter Graeme McLagan, whose book *Bent Coppers* was previously judged to have defamed a former Flying Squad officer, Michael Charman.[240] Ward LJ allowed the appeal against the ruling of Gray J in the lower court regarding allegedly defamatory passages in the book.

Since the *Jameel* actions (2006 and 2007) and *Flood* (2001)[241] – we can see a shift towards the (libel) courts' accepting that responsible investigative journalism is embraced by Article 10(1) ECHR as well as being covered by the *Reynolds* qualified privilege defence, particularly where a story is of genuine public interest. *Reynolds* privilege is not exclusively reserved for the media, but it is the media who are most likely to take advantage of it, for it is usually the media that publish to the world at large. The privilege has enlarged the protection enjoyed by the media against liability in defamation (see also: *AB Ltd v Facebook Ireland Ltd* (2013)[242]).

7.7.2 Corporate defamation: summary

The *Jameel* actions formed part of the discussions when the Defamation Bill 'ping-ponged' through Parliament in 2012–2013. Parliament also looked for comparison to the Australian Defamation Act of 2005 which prevents corporations (other than not-for-profit organizations or small businesses of fewer than ten people) from suing for defamation. The law had been passed following concerns that large companies could stifle legitimate public debate by initiating defamation actions. A leading case in the Australian High Court was that of *Radio 2UE Sydney Pty Ltd v Chesterton* (2009),[243] which clarified the law and what could be considered to be defamatory in business reputation cases. This now applies in each of the Australian States and Territories.

Given the reaffirmation by the HL in *Jameel* of the rights of companies to sue in defamation, it was then argued that the law could only be changed by statute if it was desirable to address potential abuses of libel laws by big corporations. Parliament then considered introducing a new category of tort entitled 'corporate defamation' which would require a corporation to prove actual damage to its business before an action could be brought. Alternatively, corporations could be forced to rely on the existing tort of malicious falsehood where damage needed to be shown and malice or recklessness proved.

Eventually Parliament decided not to follow the Australian-style legislation, preventing corporations from suing for defamation. The Defamation Act 2013 made no mention of 'corporations' and case law in this area prevails. The serious financial loss requirement may be difficult for some

238 Ibid., at paras 145–159 (Baroness Hale of Richmond).
239 [2007] EWCA Civ 972 (CA Civ Div).
240 See: McLagan, G. (2004).
241 *Flood v Times Newspapers Ltd* [2011] UKSC 11.
242 [2013] NIQB 14 (QB (Northern Ireland)).
243 [2009] HCA 16 (High Court of Australia) 22 April 2009.

companies to show when suing for defamation, which may well reduce such claims in future; though the HL Joint Committee considering the Defamation Bill recommended that the concept of serious financial loss should be understood 'relative to the nature, size and scope of the claimant business or organisation'.[244]

Section 2(1) DA 2013 ('truth') indirectly seeks to address the area of 'corporate' law in respect of defamation claims. What this means in practice is that a for-profit company must now specify in its defamation claim under 'particulars of claim' that the defamatory statement:

(a) has caused or is likely to cause the body financial loss; and
(b) specify the type of loss; and
(c) that the loss is serious.

7.7.3 Academic criticism and peer-reviewed journals

There have been a number of high-profile libel actions over the past decade involving scientists who have commented on and criticized corporations and conglomerates in academic journals. The US manufacturer NMT Medical Inc., based in Boston, sued British cardiologist Dr Peter Wilmshurst for libel after he criticized its research at a US cardiology conference in 2007. Wilmshurst's remarks concerned a medical trial which he himself designed, called MIST, to find out whether closing small holes in the heart with one of NMT's medical devices could stop migraines. The trial did not succeed. One of Dr Wilmshurst's allegations was that doctors in the medical trials were paid large consultancy fees by NMT and even owned shares in the company.[245] The company argued that the payment of such fees was normal and acceptable, and the shareholdings were below the 'significant' $50,000 (£30,000) level that would have caused concern.

However, NMT did not sue the American specialist online cardiology journal, *Heartwire*, which had published a version of Dr Wilmshurst's remarks; instead, the company sued Dr Wilmshurst personally in the English High Court in 2009. Additionally, NMT claimed that by discussing the details of the case on national radio (BBC Radio 4's *Today* programme in 2011), Dr Wilmshurst defamed the company's reputation further. Wilmshurst paid in excess of £100,000 of his own money to defend himself against NMT in three defamation claims, each time for both libel and slander. In defending the actions he was in danger – similar to Dr Simon Singh[246] – of losing his home. In January 2011, NMT Medical was ordered by the High Court to pay £200,000 into court as security for costs in its case against Dr Wilmshurst. The libel case against the cardiologist appeared to come to an end in April 2011 after NMT Medical went into liquidation.[247] The doctor vowed to take the case to trial in order to defend scientists' rights to free academic debate.

Academic science writer Dr Simon Singh won his long-drawn-out 'libel' action in the Court of Appeal, relying on the defence of 'fair comment' after he had criticized British Chiropractors' claim that they could successfully treat children and babies for conditions such as asthma, colic and ear infections. Dr Singh had suggested there was a lack of evidence in a *Guardian* article in April 2008. The British Chiropractic Association (BCA) sued Simon Singh personally in defamation, rather than bringing an action against the Guardian newspaper group. Dr Singh eventually won an appeal that allowed him to use the 'fair comment' defence, which led to the case against him being dropped.

244 See: Seventh Report: Legislative Scrutiny – Defamation Bill, 2012–2013, HL Paper 84/HC 810 at para. 58.
245 See: Wilmshurst, P. (2011), pp. 1093–1094.
246 See: *British Chiropractic Association v Singh* [2010] EWCA Civ 350.
247 Source: 'NMT Medical, Inc. Assigns All of Its Assets for the Benefit of Creditors', Press Release by NMT Medical, Finance Yahoo online news 19 April 2011 at: http://finance.yahoo.com/news/NMT-Medical-Inc-Assigns-All-iw–3913728736.html.

Many of their fellow scientists have been put off by the *Wilmshurst* and *Singh* actions from voicing their concerns about medical research and reviewing such results in scientific or medical journals. Such fears of the medical, scientific and academic community are well founded, and are also expressed in a report on 'Press standards, privacy and libel' (2010) by the House of Commons Culture, Media and Sport Committee. The report expressed strong concerns about the country's present libel laws in the internet age, in particular the defence of fair comment when challenged in the libel courts over academic and peer-reviewed publications.[248]

7.8 The end of libel tourism?

So-called 'libel tourism' was certainly one of the primary drivers of the libel reform campaign and one of the main reasons the Westminster Parliament changed the defamation laws in 2013 after growing concern that London had become the 'libel capital of the world'.

Most disconcerting had been cases where both the claimant and defendant were from outside the EU (see: *Jameel (Yousef) v Dow Jones* (2005)[249]). There is a wide disparity of views on the facticity of this phenomenon, one of the reasons why Northern Ireland and Scotland did not adopt the Defamation Act 2013 into their devolved jurisdictions at the same time as England and Wales in January 2014. By the end of 2016 it is true to say that very few libel cases had reached the London High Court either due to the high threshold of the 'serious harm' test, or the heightened defence of 'truth' – with the majority of actions being settled out of court.

7.8.1 Foreign libel actions and forum shopping

One of the main reasons why foreign nationals have in the past preferred British courts in their defamation actions is that the law has been perceived as loaded against the defendant (see: *GKR Karate (UK) Ltd v Yorkshire Post Newspapers Ltd* (2000)[250]). British libel laws were regarded as more favourable to pursuing a defamation action than those in the United States, for instance, where libel laws are not only less generous to claimants but there is also the single publication rule, which now no longer exists in English law.[251] It is for these reasons that claimants chose to seek redress in the London courts (see: *Lewis v King* (2004);[252] *Richardson v Schwarzenegger* (2004);[253] *New York Times v Sullivan* (1964)[254]).

Prior to the coming into force of the Defamation Act 2013, there were a number of 'foreign' libel actions in the London High Court. One such action was brought by a Serbian tobacco distributor, Stanko Subotic against Ratko Knezevic,[255] a former Montenegrin trade official, over allegations that had been published in five Serbian or Montenegrin-language publications, suggesting that Subotic was a criminal mastermind linked to murder. Hard copies were not officially circulated in England and Wales. The case was dismissed by Dingemans J in October 2013 as an abuse of process – known now as the '*Jameel*' abuse – because the articles had been read by very few people in the UK,

---

248 See: House of Commons (2010a) at para. 142.
249 [2005] EWCA Civ 75.
250 (No 1) [2000] 1 WLR 2571.
251 For further discussion and comparison with US law, see: Klazmer, E. (2012), pp. 164–168.
252 [2004] EWCA Civ 1329. The case concerned Don King, the US boxing promoter, who was suing Judd Burstein for remarks he made about him on a couple of boxing websites. The High Court and Court of Appeal held that England was an appropriate forum for the case.
253 [2004] EWHC 2422. The claimant was a British TV host who accused actor-turned-politician Arnold Schwarzenegger of touching her breast during the course of his election campaign. Mr Schwarzenegger's publicist alleged that it was Ms Richardson who had behaved provocatively and that Ms Richardson had concocted her story. This allegation was reported in the *Los Angeles Times*. Hard copies of this paper were published in England and the article was also posted on the internet. The High Court refused to set aside the Master's order giving permission to serve the second defendant outside the jurisdiction.
254 376 US 254.
255 See: *Subotic v Knezevic* [2013] EWHC 3011 (QBD).

adding that this had little to do with Mr Subotic's reputation in England and Wales and everything to do with his reputation in the Balkans. *Jameel* abuse is based on a balancing of the extent of publication in England and Wales with the nature and complexity of the proceedings. The judge added that this was a disproportionate and unnecessary interference with freedom of expression.

Another libel action involving non-UK litigants was that of Pavel Karpov, a retired Moscow policeman, against Bill Browder,[256] a British-based businessman, for saying he was complicit in the torture and murder of Sergei Magnitsky, an anti-corruption whistleblower. The disputed claims were made on a Russian website and in Russian TV interviews. Simon J ruled that Mr Karpov could not proceed with his action because he did not have strong links to the UK.

Another example was that of a Russian businessman, Boris Berezovsky (1946–2013), the powerful Russian oligarch who had moved to the UK in 2000. He sued the influential fortnightly US magazine *Forbes*.[257] The magazine devoted considerable resources to the investigation and reporting of the situation in the post-Soviet phase in Russia. In its issue of 30 December 1996 *Forbes* described two men as 'criminals on an outrageous scale'. The first was Nikolai Glouchkov, Managing Director of Aeroflot; the second businessman and politician, Boris Berezovsky,[258] who was described as follows:

> Is he the Godfather of the Kremlin? Power, Politics, Murder. Boris Berezovsky can teach the guys in Sicily a thing or two.

The flavour of the article, which together with a prominent photograph of Mr Berezovsky, was spread over seven pages, was captured in an editorial published by James W. Michaels, the editor of *Forbes*. Both Mr Berezovsky and Mr Glouchkov sued *Forbes* in England for defamation (rather than in Russia or the United States) in February 1997. The allegation was based on his reputation in the UK, applying the *Duke of Brunswick* principle of the multiple publication rule. The High Court had refused leave to try the matter in the London court; this was overruled by the Court of Appeal after new evidence had been admitted by Berezovsky regarding his reputation in England and the effect of the article on his business. *Forbes* then appealed to the House of Lords who dismissed Forbes' appeal, stating that England and Wales was the appropriate forum for trial of the action. Forbes had submitted that the publication of a trans-national libel in England was a separate tort.

Lords Hoffmann and Hope dissented on the ground that the CA should not have interfered with the decision of Popplewell J in the High Court. He had not, they said, misdirected himself in law, and the new evidence presented in the CA would not have affected his decision. Lord Hoffmann described Berezovsky and Grouchkov as 'forum shoppers' and felt that the English courts should not indulge them.

There followed a second action by the Russian oligarch and the whole action took six years before being resolved in the magazine's favour.[259] The ruling in *Berezovsky No 2* (2001) was followed in other common law countries, such as by the High Court of Australia in *Dow Jones v Gutnick* (2002).[260] In response to this, the SPEECH Act was introduced in the United States in 2010, specifically to prevent foreign libel judgments from being enforceable there.[261]

256 See: *Karpov v Browder* [2013] EWHC 3071 (QB).
257 See: *Berezovsky v Forbes Inc.* (No 2) [2001] EWCA 1251; see also: *Berezovsky v Forbes Inc. & Michaels* [2000] UKHL 25.
258 Boris Berezovsky had been Deputy Secretary of the Security Council of the Russian Federation, but in November 1997 President Yeltsin dismissed him. In April 1998 Mr Berezovsky was appointed as Secretary of the Commonwealth of Independent States, with responsibility for co-operation between the various parts of the Russian Federation.
259 See: *Berezovsky v Forbes Inc.* (No 2) [2001] EWCA 1251.
260 [2002] CLR 575.
261 The SPEECH Act (Seeking the Protection of [US] Enduring and Established Constitutional Heritage) was passed in the United States in 2010.

7.8.2 Has the Defamation Act 2013 made a difference? Analysis and discussion

Since 2014, with the coming into force of the Defamation Act 2013 in England and Wales, most claimants have been unable to meet the 'serious harm' threshold under section 1(1) of the 2013 Act, because most defamatory statements (which were disputed) were unlikely to cause serious damage to the claimant's reputation. Here are some reasons:

- The claimant had a bad reputation anyway and there was reasonable doubt that his reputation would be seriously harmed over and above his existing (suspect) reputation.
- The claimant needed to prove an innuendo identification and the people (with the special knowledge) who could have possibly have identified the claimant would not believe the words would seriously harm the claimant's reputation (under the previous law, this would generally not prevent the meaning being defamatory).
- There was only limited publication in the jurisdiction and/or the claimant was not known in that jurisdiction.
- The meaning was borderline vulgar abuse, 'pub talk' or a mere criticism of the claimant (or his goods or services).
- Any damage was transient or short-lived due to a quick retraction, clarification or apology from the publisher.
- There was a *Jameel* abuse-type argument being deployed by the defendant and a 'serious harm' requirement lead to an early strike-out application by the defendants on both grounds.

The 2013 Act has clearly shifted the balance between free speech and the right to reputation, in favour of free speech. In some areas this shift has been significant, particularly where companies who in the past sued for libel now have to prove actual economic harm. What is clear is that the new law prevents a court from hearing an action in defamation in England and Wales *unless* it is satisfied that the UK jurisdiction is the 'most appropriate place for a defamation action to be brought'.

So, has the Defamation Act 2013 made a difference to academics? The short answer is 'yes'. As the law stands at present in England and Wales, a defendant who has to justify a statement of fact, as in the case of *Dr Simon Singh*,[262] has to prove that the defamatory statement is true. This fact has not changed with the Defamation Act 2013. This means that the burden of proof still lies on the defendant, which can involve calling vast amounts of evidence at huge personal cost with no legal aid available.

Hooper *et al.* (2013)[263] argue that the Defamation Act 2013 has not made enough changes, and still favours claimants. The authors examined the passing of the Defamation Bill as it ping-ponged slowly through Parliament looking at the differences the new Act would actually make to publishers and news websites. The authors comment with some consternation how the long-awaited bill was nearly derailed at the last minute before the dissolution of Parliament in the House of Lords by Lord Puttnam who suggested including Leveson LJ's recommendations in the new defamation legislation. The authors predicted, however, that the new 2013 Act would ultimately restrict libel tourism, commenting *inter alia* favourably on the abolition of libel juries and the hurdle of the 'serious harm' threshold.

The unique problems in relation to defamation conducted on the internet have already been explored in detail in Chapter 3 resulting in the discussion and analysis of the concept of self-governance in cyberspace as opposed to governmental territorial legislation.

---

262 *BCA v Singh* [2010] EWCA Civ 350.
263 Hooper, D., Waite, K. and Murphy, O. (2013), pp. 199–206.

Arguably, the existing definition of what is defamatory has not changed with the 2013 Act, and there is still no clear definition of what is meant by defamatory. We still have to resort to leading authority for interpretation of the new statute. However, it has become more challenging to bring an action in defamation, since the bar has been raised before such an action can be brought, this being the threshold from 'substantial harm' to 'serious harm' under section 1 of the 2013 Act.

 FOR THOUGHT

Codifying libel law into statute is very fact-sensitive to account for many different scenarios. Has the Defamation Act 2013 simplified this area of law to account for the finer points such as fact and honest opinion? Discuss.

 7.9 Further reading

Bedat, A. (2015) 'Tim Yeo MP v Times Newspapers Ltd – discretion to order trial by jury under Defamation Act 2013', *Entertainment Law Review,* **26(1), 31–33.**
In her case comment and discussion about the *Tim Yeo*[264] defamation case, Alexia Bedat considers the provisions in the Defamation Act 2013 of 'judge-alone' trial in libel actions – this being the first case under the new provision of juryless libel trials. The essay discusses why it was preferable to have a trial by judge alone in the interests of obtaining a reasoned judgment, for reasons of proportionality and for reasons of case management.

Descheemaeker, E. (2009) 'Protecting reputation: defamation and negligence', *Oxford Journal of Legal Studies,* **29(4), 603–641.**
The article concerns itself with the relationship between defamation and negligence in the protection of the interest in reputation. The author argues that there is no reason why the tort of negligence could not prima facie extend the scope of its protection to reputation.

Klazmer, E. (2012) 'The uncertainties of libel tourism, is diplomacy the answer?', *Entertainment Law Review,* **23(6), 164–168.**
Erica Klazmer compares US libel laws with UK authorities and specifically analyses the approach in the New York court's decision in *Ehrenfeld.*[265] The case concerned a book by Dr Rachel Ehrenfeld, published in 2003 in Chicago entitled, *Funding Evil: How Terrorism Is Financed—and How to Stop It.* In the book, Dr Ehrenfeld stated that Saudi Arabian businessman, Khalid Salim Bin Mahfouz, provided monetary support to Al Qaeda and other terrorist organizations. Mahfouz sued Ehrenfeld in an English court and received a default judgment. Ehrenfeld then retaliated by filing a lawsuit in the US District Court for the Southern District of New York seeking a declaratory judgment that Mahfouz could not prevail on his libel claim. The author also discusses the US Speech Protection Act of 2009 which allows parties to protect assets abroad.

McInnes, R. (2016) *Scots Law for Journalists* **(9th edn). Edinburgh: W Green/Sweet & Maxwell.**
Rosalind McInnes, Principal Solicitor for BBC Scotland, provides a clear and concise guide to Scots law for journalists and editors. The practical and very readable text has been an essential training aid and reference textbook for students studying media law as part of a law, journalism or communications degree.

---

264 *Yeo (Tim) v Times Newspapers Ltd* [2015] EWHC 3375 (QB).
265 *Ehrenfeld v Mahfouz* (2007) 9 N.Y.F 3d 501.

Milmo, P., Rogers, W. V. H., Parkes, R., Walker, C. and Busuttil, G. (eds) (2015) *Gatley on Libel and Slander* **(12th edn). London: Sweet & Maxwell.**
This pivotal work has a high reputation in a number of countries. The mighty tome comprises more than 130 pages of cited cases. Clement Gatley's reference text is primarily concerned with the protection of an individual's reputation and provides relevant legislation and procedural guidance for practitioners in this field.

Whitty, N. R. and Zimmermann, R. (eds) (2009) *Rights of Personality in Scots Law: A comparative perspective*. **Dundee: Dundee University Press.**
This book considers, in a comparative perspective, important trends and issues affecting the law on rights of personality in jurisdictions drawn from the families of common law, civil law and mixed legal systems. The main focus is on the private law of personality rights (including defamation – delict) taking into account the impact of human rights law under the European Convention on constitutional legislation and Scots law conventions.

Chapter 8

Reporting legal proceedings

Key points

This chapter will cover the following questions:

- What can and cannot be reported in a UK court of law?
- How are children protected in the court process in English and Scots law?
- When does a court order reporting restrictions?
- Why are anonymity orders necessary in sexual offence cases?
- How does the public interest test apply in family court proceedings?
- What is common law contempt of court?
- What is statutory contempt?
- What is meant by active and *sub judice* proceedings?
- What is the role of the Attorney General in contempt proceedings?
- What are the general defences for the media when 'contempt' is alleged?
- How are court martial proceedings reported?
- Should court proceedings ever be held in 'secret'?

8.1 Overview

This chapter examines the open justice principle which makes the UK courts quite unique in that all courts (except for youth courts and certain family court proceedings) are open to the public and members of the media. The openness of judicial proceedings is a fundamental principle enshrined in Article 6(1) ECHR ('right to a fair trial').

There are however times when the court orders reporting restrictions or allows complete anonymity orders, or courts are held either in private (*in camera*) or in secret. We will look at occasions when the open justice principle and media access rights are restricted in order to ensure fair trials for and the protection of those who are vulnerable such as children and victims of sexual offences.

In high-profile cases, such as historical child sex offences, media interest can be particularly acute. This chapter focuses on contempt of court legislation, unique to British court reporting. Common law and statutory provision for 'contempt' ensure that *any* court – be it civil or criminal jurisdiction – is free to decide on the matters before it, without undue influence from the media during *sub judice* proceedings.

As more and more members of the British armed forces face court martial charges of desertion or war crime offences we will focus on court martial proceedings and the role of the Judge Advocate General.

The chapter closes with a look at 'secret courts' and 'closed hearings' which tend to involve terrorist suspects, deportation or serious drugs cases. The public interest most regularly engaged in these cases by way of Public Interest Immunity (PII) involves investigations by secret and intelligence services and prosecution of serious crime, often involving police informers and undercover agents and the use of scientific or operational techniques (such as surveillance) which cannot be disclosed without exposing individuals to the risk of personal injury or jeopardizing the success of future operations.

8.2 The open justice principle

The open justice principle, as clearly recognized by Parliament and the courts in *Scott v Scott*,[1] grants the public and media statutory and common law rights to attend all court proceedings in UK courts and tribunals.

There are circumstances when the court may justify hearing a case *in camera*, particularly in cases that threaten national security and acts of terrorism. Witnesses may fear that if their identity is revealed to the defendant, their family or friends may well be at risk of serious harm by way of witness intimidation. The test is one of 'necessity' and an application to proceed *in camera* should be supported by relevant evidence.

8.2.1 Hearings from which the public are excluded

The Lord Chief Justice for England and Wales, the Rt Hon The Lord Thomas of Cwmgiedd, stated in the third edition of *Reporting Restrictions in the Criminal Courts* (2015) that:

> Open justice is a hallmark of the rule of law. It is an essential requisite of the criminal justice system that it should be administered in public and subject to public scrutiny. The media play a vital role in representing the public and reflecting the public interest. However, as is well known, there are some exceptions to these principles. Difficulties and uncertainty can sometimes arise in ensuring they are correctly applied and observed.[2]

In recognition of the open justice principle, the general rule is that justice should be administered in public. This means, unless there are exceptional circumstances laid down by statute or common law, the court must not:

- order or allow the exclusion of the press or public from court for any part of the proceedings;
- permit the withholding of information from the open court proceedings;
- impose permanent or temporary bans on reporting of the proceedings or any part of them including anything that prevents the proper identification, by name and address, of those appearing or mentioned in the course of proceedings.

Like 'without notice' (formerly *ex parte*) hearings, hearings *in camera* raise concerns about fairness, particularly in light of the principle that justice should not only be done but should appear to be done.[3] Before imposing any reporting restriction or restriction on public access to proceedings the court is required to ensure that each party and any other person directly affected is present or has had an opportunity to attend or to make representations.[4]

---

1 *Scott (Morgan) and another v Scott* [1913] AC 417 of 5 May 1913 (as per Lord Atkinson) (HL).
2 See: Judicial College (2015).
3 See: *Hobbs v Tinling and Company Limited* [1929] 2 KB 1 at 33 per Lord Sankey LC; see also: *R v Sussex Justices ex parte McCarthy* [1924].
4 Criminal Procedure Rules 2016, r. 16.

8.2.2 Automatic reporting restrictions: trials held in private

Where a court departs from the open justice principle and Article 6 ECHR, a judge must find exceptional circumstances where a hearing or trial is held in private.[5] Such hearings must be justified by the court in either statute or common law (see: *AG v Leveller Magazine* (1979);[6] *R v Times Newspapers* (2007)[7]). The test is one of necessity. A divorce hearing which might cause the parties embarrassment does not meet the test for necessity as was held in *Scott v Scott* (1913).[8] Neither is it a sufficient basis for a hearing in private that allegations will be aired which will be damaging to the reputation of individuals (e.g. *Global Torch v Apex Global Management Ltd* (2013)[9]). Criminal hearings carry even greater weight to justify public and media presence (see: *R v Wang Yam* (2008)[10]).

Automatic reporting restrictions and, at times, lifelong anonymity orders, apply as follows:

- reporting restrictions for children and young people in criminal proceedings (under 18);[11]
- reporting restrictions for children and young people in non-criminal proceedings (e.g. family court);[12]
- lifetime reporting ban for victims and witnesses under age 18;[13]
- lifetime reporting ban on victims of sexual offences;[14]
- vulnerable adult witnesses;[15]
- withholding information from the public in the interest of the administration of justice;[16]
- reporting restrictions (or postponement) during trial;[17]
- appeals;[18]
- prosecution appeals.[19]

When a party makes an application for anonymity or reporting restrictions (or both), the court must be satisfied that the quality of evidence or level of co-operation by the witness is likely to be diminished by reason of fear or distress in being identified by the public. On appeal, automatic reporting restrictions apply from the moment the prosecution indicates its intention to appeal to prevent the publication of anything other than certain specified factual information.[20]

Because factors known to the media in advance of a court hearing may not be apparent from the case papers in a criminal trial, for instance, neither the prosecution nor the defence may be aware of them or have any particular interest in advancing them. The court will usually invite representations from the media and encourage open debate in advance of a court hearing (see: *R v Teesdale and Wear Valley Justices ex parte M* (2000)[21]).

---

5 CPR 2016, r.16(8) governs procedure 'where a court can order a trial in private'.
6 [1979] AC 440 at 450.
7 [2007] 1 WLR 1015.
8 [1913] AC 417.
9 [2013] 1 WLR 2993 (CA).
10 [2008] EWCA Crim 269.
11 Section 45 Youth Justice and Criminal Evidence Act 1999.
12 Section 39 Children and Young Persons Act 1933.
13 Section 45A Youth Justice and Criminal Evidence Act 1999.
14 Section 1 Sexual Offences (Amendment) Act 1992 (as amended by Sch. 2 of the Youth Justice and Criminal Evidence Act 1999).
15 Section 46 Youth Justice and Criminal Evidence Act 1999.
16 Section 11 Contempt of Court Act 1981.
17 Section 4(2) Contempt of Court Act 1981.
18 Section 35 Criminal Procedure and Investigations Act 1996; s 9(11) Criminal Justice Act 1987.
19 Sections 58 and 82 Criminal Justice Act 2003.
20 Sections 71 and 82 Criminal Justice Act 2003.
21 (2000) of 7 February 2000 (unreported).

8.2.3 Lifetime anonymity in sex offence cases

Whilst the law provides lifetime anonymity for rape victims, such anonymity is not available to rape defendants or those suspected of the offence.

Section 2 of the Sexual Offences (Amendment) Act 1992 applies only to a victim of a sexual offence but not the perpetrator. Once an allegation of a sexual offence has been made, nothing can be published which is likely to lead members of the public to identify the alleged victim. The following cannot be published for the victim's lifetime:

(a) her or his name;
(b) her or his address;
(c) the identity of any school or other educational establishment attended by them;
(d) the identity of any place of work;
(e) any still or moving picture of them.[23]

In March 2016 former editor of The Sun, David Dinsmore, was found guilty of inadvertently identifying a rape victim under section 1 Sexual Offences (Amendment) Act 1992 by Westminster Magistrates. Dinsmore was given a 'compensation order' by the judge, a sentence in its own right, and was ordered to pay £1,000 to the (rape) victim.

The story appeared on 4 March 2016 and concerned a 15-year-old girl who footballer Adam Johnson was accused of having sex with; it showed a heavily pixelated photo of the girl.[23] The story was headlined: 'SOCCER ACE AND GIRL HE BEDDED', with the subheading, 'Johnson in pose with his 15-year-old fan'. The court heard that the girl had been identified by social media users who recognized the photo while the investigation into Johnson's sexual offences was ongoing. Judge Riddle said he was satisfied that Dinsmore and The Sun staff thought they were complying with the law after taking extensive steps to obscure the photo of the girl. But he added that the fact that the original photograph was likely to have been seen by others and that the girl was likely to have been identified found the matter proven.

8.2.4 A question of anonymity for sex offence suspects

Should suspects accused of sex crimes have their identities protected until they are convicted? Under current legislation, people who complain they have been a victim of sexual offences automatically receive anonymity, but suspects do not.

The question of the anonymity of the accused is once again the subject of public debate, for two reasons: the first is the number of well-known people arrested as part of the Met's 'Operation Yewtree' and the second is the advent of social media which has amplified the problem, causing reputational damage by naming a suspect. Operation Yewtree found at least 589 alleged victims linked to the Jimmy Savile abuses post his death on 29 October 2011. The Met also investigated allegations of historical child sexual abuse going back to the Thatcher years. Those linked to historical child sex offences included the late Sir Leon (Lord) Brittan and Cliff Richard in 2015–2016. Allegations were subsequently dropped by the police but those implicated suffered months of incredible stress. In 2014, the BBC Radio 2 DJ, Paul Gambaccini, was arrested on suspicion of sexual abuse. His name was leaked to the tabloid press and once Gambaccini's name was 'out there' by way of 'trial by media', the BBC suspended him without pay, the result of which was lost income and legal fees

---

22 See: Youth Justice and Criminal Evidence Act 1999 Sch. 2 'Reporting Restrictions'.
23 Sunderland footballer, Adam Johnson (28), had pleaded guilty at Bradford Crown Court on 20 February 2016 to one count of sexual activity with a child and one count of grooming.

of around £200,000.[24] He was held on police bail for a year until the CPS determined there was insufficient evidence to prosecute him.

The Sexual Offences (Amendment) Act 1976 initially only offered anonymity to rape victims, but subsequently extended a lifetime reporting ban to other sex offences. The provisions granting anonymity to suspects and accused were repealed in the Criminal Justice Act 1988.

The Heilbron[25] Committee (1975), a Home Office Advisory Committee, had recommended anonymity for rape defendants.[26] The Committee's subsequent report recommended that the identity of rape complainants should be kept secret. They did not recommend anonymity for rape defendants because it felt complainants and defendants were not comparable in principle, and that in cases of other serious crimes where the complainant was often anonymous, defendants were not granted anonymity.

During the passage of the Sexual Offences (Amendment) Act in 1976 in Parliament, apart from lifelong anonymity for rape victims, a concessionary amendment was adopted, providing anonymity for rape defendants as well. The main reason for this was to guard against the possibility of reputation damage for those acquitted of rape and to provide equality between complainants and defendants in rape cases.[27]

With increasing social media and modern technology appearing in court an issue arose in R (Press Association[28]) v Cambridge Crown Court (2012),[29] whereby the Press Association (PA) appealed against a lifelong 'rape' anonymity order on the defendant, imposed by His Honour Judge Hawksworth at Cambridge Crown Court on 16 April 2012, following the defendant's conviction of five counts of rape and four counts of breaching a restraining order in February 2012.[30] The trial had taken place in open court, listed under the defendant's full name. The CA overturned that order and held that the courts do not have power to protect victims of sexual crime by anonymizing defendants who have been named in open court. The judgment highlights the thorny issues that arise whenever anonymity is sought in criminal cases. It also contains an interesting discussion about the role of judicial guidance and journalistic responsibility in relation to media reporting on court proceedings.

In Re B (2006)[31] the CA had to decide whether publication of the defendant's name would create a serious risk of substantial prejudice to the fair trials of his remaining co-defendants? Could the media be trusted with fair and accurate reporting on the defendant's sentencing? This case concerned reporting restrictions post-conviction on Dhiren Barot on 12 October 2006, after he had pleaded guilty to conspiracy to murder. Indian-born Barot admitted in November 2006 at Woolwich Crown Court that he had planned to detonate a radioactive 'dirty bomb' and launch an attack on London's Underground and the Heathrow Express. Reporting restrictions were in place until the conclusion of the trial of his co-defendants. The judge was concerned that reports of Barot's sentencing would cause a risk of substantial prejudice to the trial of the co-defendants, as his reasons for sentence would give rise to a great deal of legitimate public interest and discussion. The CA ruled in favour of media reporting applying the principle in Re Press Association.

The dangers of social media 'reporting' arose in the Ched Evans rape case when a number of people on Twitter identified and named the 19-year-old rape victim of the (then) Sheffield United footballer who had been convicted for rape on 20 April 2012. The former Welsh international

---

24 See: House of Commons (2014), p. 6.
25 Dame Rose Heilbron DBE QC (1914–2005) was the first woman to be appointed King's Counsel and first female judge to sit at the Old Bailey. She chaired the committee on rape laws in 1975.
26 See: Home Office (1975) at pp. 27–31.
27 See: Ministry of Justice (2010c) at p. 2; see also: Criminal Law Revision Committee (1984).
28 The Press Association (PA) provides a global news-collecting and reporting service and delivers continuous feed of news content via a national newswire, including text, images, video and data into newsrooms around the country.
29 Re Press Association [2012] EWCA Crim 2434 (CA).
30 Ibid., at para. 2(ii).
31 R v B [2006] EWCA Crim 2692 (CA).

footballer had been sentenced to five years' imprisonment for rape on 20 April 2012 by a jury at Carnarvon Crown Court. Almost immediately, the hashtag '#ChedEvans' appeared on Twitter, and later, #JusticeForChed. Some tweets questioned why one defendant was found guilty and the other not (Evans's co-accused, Port Vale footballer Clayton McDonald, was found not guilty). Others blamed the victim, particularly focusing on her being drunk.

The Attorney General, Dominic Grieve QC, commenced criminal proceedings against Evans and nine other defendants from the 'Twittermob' for contravening section 5 of the Sexual Offences (Amendment) Act 1992 within the realm of social media networking. They were each fined £624 at Prestatyn Magistrates' Court. Among the accused were Evans's cousin Gemma Thomas from Rhyl, the footballer's friend Craig McDonald, 26, from Prestatyn and 25-year-old biology schoolteacher Holly Price from Prestatyn.[32]

On 21 April 2016, Ched Evans won his appeal against his conviction for raping a 19-year-old woman. Hallett LJ announced that there would be a retrial, and ordered reporting restrictions under section 4(2) of the Contempt of Court Act 1981 applicable to all appeal proceedings until the conclusion of the retrial, to avoid any prejudice to the retrial.[33] On 14 October 2016 Ched Evans was found not guilty at retrial.

The issue of rape defendants' anonymity has arisen frequently in Parliament, and was last debated in Parliament during the passage of the Sexual Offences Bill in the 2002–2003 session. In a hearing before the Home Affairs Committee in March 2015, the Commissioner of the Metropolitan Police, Sir Bernard Hogan-Howe, supported the proposal for granting accused suspects of sexual offences anonymity until charge.[34] In its report to Parliament the Home Affairs Committee recommend that the same right to anonymity should also apply to persons accused of a 'sex' crime, unless and until they are charged with an offence.[35] However, the law has not changed in this respect.

8.3 Reporting on children and young persons

The Children and Young Persons Act 1933 (CYPA) remains the main statute in the UK with the principal aim of protecting the welfare of the child in court proceedings. The Youth Justice and Criminal Evidence Act 1999 (YJCEA) makes further provisions regarding reporting restrictions involving children and young persons under the age of 18.[36] Section 47 CYPA generally bars the public from attending criminal proceedings in the youth court but makes specific exception for representatives of the media.

See below
8.3.2

The freedom of a child to grow up and make mistakes, to act badly and not to have this permanently recorded, is an essential human right recorded in the UN Convention on the Rights of the Child 1989.[37] Article 40 of the UN Convention guarantees the right of a child defendant 'to have his or her privacy fully respected at all stages of the proceedings'. Where the welfare and interest of a child are concerned, the Strasbourg Human Rights Court has sought to protect the privacy of a child under Article 8 ECHR, and any court can now make an order prohibiting the identification of the child. That said, human rights jurisprudence equally states that this power must be used *proportionately*, balancing other interests protected by Articles 6 and 10 of the Convention (see: *McKerry v Teesdale and Wear Valley Justices* (2000)).[38]

---

32 Source: 'Ched Evans: Nine admit naming rape victim on social media', *BBC News Online*, 5 November 2012.
33 See: *Chedwyn Evans v R* (2016) (unreported) Statement in Criminal Court of Appeal by Hallett LJ, 20 April 2012.
34 See: House of Commons (2015b).
35 See: House of Commons (2014), pp. 4–5.
36 See: s 45 YJCEA ('reporting restrictions for children and young people in criminal proceedings').
37 Document A/RES/44/25 of 12 December 1989.
38 [2000] 164 JP 355 (DC).

8.3.1 Reporting on children *not* involved in criminal proceedings: section 39 of the Children and Young Person's Act 1933

Section 39 CYPA permits a court to prohibit *publication* by the media of the name, address, school or any information calculated to lead to the identification of any child or young person concerned in criminal proceedings. Although section 39 CYPA 1933 no longer applies to criminal proceedings, this power to impose a discretionary reporting restriction in relation to a young person aged under 18 continues to be available in family and civil proceedings. Any order made must comply with Article 10 ECHR: it must be:

- necessary;
- proportionate; and
- there must be a pressing social need for it.[40]

New definitions of 'publication' were introduced in 2015, and are included in section 39(3) CYPA.[40] Publication covers print, broadcast and online media (including social media) as well as photographs. That a child's identity is already known to people in the community is not necessarily a good reason for allowing publication of that identity.[41]

The publication of the name, address and other details relating to the child is not in itself prohibited – what a section 39 order seeks to do is to prevent the identification of a child as a witness, victim or defendant in court proceedings.

The court has no power to prohibit the publication of the names of adults involved in the proceedings or other children or young persons not involved in the same proceedings as witnesses, defendants or victims. The CA held in *ex parte Godwin* (1992)[42] that a section 39 order – originally imposed by Judge Laurie at Southwark Crown Court – was only available where the terms of section 39(1) CYPA related to a *relevant* child. In this case the newspapers had previously reported the abusing stepfather's (S) name, referring to the victim as 'an 11-year-old schoolgirl'. There was a serious risk of jigsaw identification in that the composite picture would present the identification of that child.

The appellants, Caroline Godwin, the *Daily Telegraph*, Mirror Group Newspapers and Associated Newspapers Ltd, appealed against the section 39 order[43] arguing that the judge had wrongly interpreted section 39. They further argued that there was no evidence that the naming of the defendant (S) would lead to the identification of the child. The CA subsequently quashed the order in its entirety. After the conclusion of the trial S's child continued to be protected by a lifelong anonymity order provided under section 1 Sexual Offences (Amendment) Act 1992 ('Anonymity of victims in certain offences').

The so-called '*Godwin direction*' means that a section 39 order does not empower a court to prevent the naming of adult defendants in general; section 39 orders, are, by their very nature, specifically related to children and young persons under 18. The court may, however, give guidance to the media if it considers that the naming of an adult defendant would be likely to identify a child ('jigsaw identification'); however, such guidance is not legally binding. The media may, for instance, be able to name a defendant without infringing the order, if the relationship of the victim

---

39 See: *Briffett v CPS* [2002] EMLR 12.
40 Section 39(3) was introduced by s 79(7) of the Criminal Justice and Courts Act 2015.
41 See: *R (Y) v Aylesbury Crown Court* [2012] EWHC 1140 (Admin).
42 *R v Southwark Crown Court ex parte Godwin and Others* [1992] QB 190 (CA (Civ Div)).
43 Under s 159 Criminal Justice Act 1988.

to the defendant is omitted or the nature of the offence is blurred (e.g. 'a sexual offence' rather than incest).

The relationship between Articles 8 and 10 ECHR was put to the test in child proceedings in *Re S (A Child) (Identification: Restrictions on Publication)* (2004).[44] The House of Lords did not consider that there was scope for extending the restrictions on freedom of expression beyond the *Godwin* direction. In *Re S* all the facts were then reported except for the identity of the parties to avoid jigsaw identification of the child. The decision in *Re S* underlines the considerable difficulties confronting a court when carrying out a balancing exercise between a child's right to private life under Article 8 and the right of the press to freely report.

In *Re S (FC) (A Child)* (2005)[45] a child's nine-year-old older brother, DS, had died of acute salt poisoning in the Great Ormond Street Hospital. At a hearing in July 2002, Hedley J found that the salt poisoning had been administered by the child's mother. As a result of this finding, the mother was charged with murder, with a trial set for November 2004. In the pre-trial proceedings, the trial judge was asked in the interests of the child (a five-year-old boy) to ban normal reporting of the trial of his mother for the murder of his nine-year-old brother. Since this terrible situation was going to be known to the boy's school, his neighbours and friends, his guardian applied to the High Court for an injunction to prevent publication of *any* information which might lead to the child's identification under section 39 CYPA, including his name, address, school or any picture of him and his parents. Hedley J declined to do so.

Balancing Articles 8 and 10 of the Convention, Hedley J decided that the order should contain a proviso such that the newspapers were not prevented from publishing the identity of the defendant mother or the deceased child DS or photographs of them in reports of the criminal trial. The appeal to the Court of Appeal was dismissed and the child's guardian appealed to the House of Lords. Both the CA and the HL upheld the trial judge's decision.

The child or young person will be concerned in criminal proceedings if s/he is a victim, defendant or witness in the case, but not merely because he is 'concerned' in the sense of being 'affected' (see: *R v Jolleys; Ex parte Press Association* (2013);[46] or a case brought 'in respect of' a child, which may be sufficient for section 39 as per *R(A) v Lowestoft Magistrates' Court* (2013)[47]). The child must still be alive.[48]

Any journalist who publishes any matter in contravention of any child anonymity order is liable on summary conviction under section 39(2) of the 1933 Act, to a maximum level 5 fine.[49]

Section 57(3) Children and Young Persons Act 1963 extends section 39 CYPA 1933 to Scotland. Unlike in England – where the age of criminal responsibility is ten, in Scotland it is now 12 years old.[50] Young persons under the age of 16 involved in Scottish criminal or Children's Hearing proceedings, or linked with adult offenders, will normally never be named or identified in the Scottish media. The Social Work (Scotland) Act 1968 abolished youth courts following the recommendations of the Kilbrandon Report of 1961. What followed was the Children's Hearing System (CHS), much admired across the world. The Children's Hearings (Scotland) Act 2011 created the post of National Convener of Children's Hearings Scotland (CHS) and established a single national Children's Panel for Scotland which oversees 32 children's hearings panels.[51]

There must be a good reason, apart from age alone, for imposing a section 39 CYPA order. There is a clear distinction between the automatic ban on identification of children in youth court

44 [2004] UKHL 47 (HL).
45 [2005] 1 AC 593.
46 [2013] EWCA Crim 1135, paras 12–13.
47 [2013] EWHC 659 (Admin), paras 8–9.
48 See: *Re S (FC) (A Child)* [2005] 1 AC 593.
49 Upper limits for a level 5 fine (£5000 +) were abolished under s 85 Legal Aid, Sentencing and Punishment of Offenders Act 2012 (LAPSO).
50 See: s 52 Criminal Justice and Licensing (Scotland Act) 2010.
51 See: Children's Hearings Panels Scotland: www.childrenspanelscotland.org.

proceedings and the discretion to impose an order under section 39 of the 1933 Act. Whereas under section 49 CYPA there must be a good reason for lifting the order, under section 39 the onus lies on the party contending for the order to satisfy the court that there is a good reason to impose it. The appellate courts have emphasized that Parliament intended to preserve the distinction between juveniles in youth court proceedings and in the adult courts (see: R v Central Criminal Court ex parte W, B and C (2001)[52]).

In R v Central Independent Television (1994),[53] a wife failed to secure an injunction preventing the broadcasting of a programme identifying her husband as a convicted molester of small boys. She argued that a broadcast would be prejudicial to the welfare of her five-year-old daughter. The identity of the boys was covered by a section 39 order, but the girl was regarded as too remote from the proceedings and the programme had nothing to do with her care or upbringing. More precisely, the little girl was not within the specific categories covered by section 39.

In ex parte Crook (1995),[54] the appellant journalists challenged a section 39 CYPA order which stated that nothing should be published which would lead to the identification of children who were alive and named on the indictment. The indictment included a count of manslaughter of another child of the defendant, whose surviving children were in local authority care. The three young children in this case, for whom the protective order was made, were the alleged victims of cruelty by both parents, charges which were heard together with the allegation of manslaughter in respect of their sibling. The CA, dismissing the appeal, stated that a judge (or magistrate), in making the section 39 order, has complete discretion to allow representatives from the media – who have a legitimate interest – to make representations *before* the order is made. The CA ruled that the original judge had been completely correct in making the section 39 order on receipt of the borough council's report and that any publication would have had an otherwise damaging effect on the surviving children. In making the order, the judge had correctly weighed the children's interest against the freedom of the press to report and had reached the conclusion that the likely harm to the children outweighed the restriction of freedom to publish.

In Re Gazette Media Co. Ltd (2005),[55] the CA considered the scope of a section 39 order where two men, S and L, were being prosecuted (and eventually convicted) for offences contrary to section 1 of the Protection of Children Act 1978 and for conspiracy to rape. S was charged with offences of making or distributing indecent photographs of his daughter and with the offence of conspiracy to rape. L was charged with conspiracy to rape and also with offences of making and distributing indecent photographs of a child. In this case, the Middlesbrough Recorder had made the section 39 order by stating:

> no reporting of any proceedings in respect of R v S and L. No identification of the defendant S by name or otherwise the nature of the case against him, the identification of the alleged victim [S's daughter], her age place of abode or any circumstances that may lead to her identification in connection with these proceedings.[56]

Solicitors acting for Gazette Media wrote to the Recorder complaining about the wording of the section 39 order, citing Godwin: that – as a matter of law – the order did not empower a court to prevent the names of (adult) defendants from being published. Maurice Kay LJ in Re Gazette remarked that it was clear beyond doubt that the order made by the Recorder 'flew in the face of Godwin' in that a section 39 order could not add specifics beyond the words of section 39(1). Therefore, a

52 [2001] 1 Cr App R 7.
53 (1994) 9 February 1994, (CA) (unreported).
54 R v Central Criminal Court ex parte Crook [1995] 1 WLR 139 (CA (Crim Div)).
55 Gazette Media Company Ltd & Ors, R (on the application of) v Teeside Crown Court [2005] EWCA Crim 1983 (CA (Crim Div).
56 Ibid., at 138.

departure from *Godwin* could not be justified. It was not enough to delete the restriction against the reporting of any proceedings in relation to the defendants and the victim; it was also necessary to delete the express restriction on the identification of S and L and the nature of the case against them.

The additional problem in *Re Gazette* was that the restriction provided by section 1 Sexual Offences (Amendment) Act 1992 ('Anonymity of victims in certain offences') was not sufficient to protect the identity of the victim during the proceedings and could be interpreted by the media as 'freedom to report'. While conspiracy to rape was an offence to which section 1 of the 1992 Act applied, other linked offences were not. The order was quashed in its entirety and a new order in conventional *Godwin* terms was substituted. Additionally, it was submitted by the Attorney General that, while a total embargo on the reporting of the proceedings remained unlawful, the prohibition of the naming of a defendant – so as to protect the interests of a child – was now possible within the remit of the human rights provision of Article 8 ECHR and section 3 Human Rights Act 1998, which requires primary legislation to be compatible with Convention rights.

A court may lift a section 39 order, a principle established in *Lee* (1993).[57] This case concerned a 14-year-old boy, convicted of 'grave crimes' (including rape). After conviction and on sentencing, the judge lifted the section 39 order. An interim injunction was made prohibiting identification by another judge, though too late to prevent publication in some newspapers. Lee's lawyers made an application to the sentencing judge to reimpose the section 39 order. The CA upheld the refusal of the judge to ban the media from identifying the 14-year-old, convicted of robbery and rape, because it would involve 'no real harm to the applicant, and [have] a powerful deterrent effect on his contemporaries if the applicant's name and photograph were published'.

This was the first case where the 'naming and shaming' of a young offender was made possible while court proceedings were still active, although Lord Bingham stressed that publicity should not be used as an 'additional punishment' – contrary to the views of successive Home Secretaries (Michael Howard, Conservative, at the time of the case) and ministers of justice (e.g. Jack Straw, Labour; Michael Gove, Conservative).

The *Lee* direction has been used frequently by judges to lift reporting restrictions post-sentence of a young offender. In April 2012, Flaux J lifted the anonymity order on 14-year-old Daniel Bartlam, naming the young killer for murdering his mother Jacqueline Bartlam (47). Nottingham Crown Court heard how Bartlam had been 'obsessed' with *Coronation Street*'s killer character John Stape, who had battered a woman with a hammer before leaving her body in the wreckage of a tram crash to cover up his crime. Bartlam had copied the *modus operandi* and had beaten his mother to death with a claw hammer, then padded her body with paper, doused it in petrol and set fire to it to destroy the evidence. Flaux J sentenced the 14-year-old to life imprisonment,[58] with a minimum tariff of 16 years.

The most notorious case of open court reporting post sentence is that of child killers Jon(athan) Venables and Robert Thompson. The then ten-year-old boys killed 18-month-old James ('Jamie') Bulger on 12 February 1993 after they had snatched the toddler during a shopping trip with his mother at the Strand shopping centre in Bootle. They took Jamie to a disused freight railway line where they brutally tortured him and left him to die. A jury at the (adult) Crown Court in Preston found Venables and Thompson guilty of murder on 24 November. Morland J then lifted the section 39 order 'in the public interest'. A media frenzy ensued, resulting in shocking and distressing facts being openly reported by naming the two (by now) 11-year-olds and their dysfunctional family backgrounds. They were sentenced to be detained for a maximum tariff of eight years in secure youth accommodation.

Following public outrage over the 'short' tariff, the editor of the *Sun* handed a petition bearing nearly 280,000 signatures to the then Conservative Home Secretary, Michael Howard, in a bid

---

57 R v Lee (*Anthony William*) (*a Minor*) [1993] 1 WLR 103 (CA (Crim Div)).
58 Section 53(1) Children and Young Persons Act 1933.

to increase the time spent by both boys in custody where life should mean life. In July 1994 Mr Howard announced that the boys would be kept in custody for a minimum of 15 years; Venables and Thompson challenged this decision under judicial review, arguing the Home Secretary had acted *ultra vires*.[59]

They were successful and, in his judgment, Lord Donaldson criticized the Home Secretary's intervention as *ultra vires*, describing the increased custodial tariff as 'institutionalised vengeance . . . [by] a politician playing to the gallery'. The increased minimum term was overturned by the House of Lords.

The increase of the sentencing term was further criticized by the European Court of Human Rights in *V v UK;T v UK* (1999).[60] The ECtHR stated that the Bulger killers had not received a fair trial and that the UK courts had breached Article 6 ECHR. Not only because proceedings were held in an adult court but also because of the intense media coverage prior to the trial which had put the boys' parents and other siblings' lives at risk. The ECtHR did not rule that youth trials in the UK in the Crown Court were unfair per se.

Following on from the Strasbourg ruling in *V v UK;T v UK*, the Westminster Parliament enacted the Youth Justice and Criminal Evidence Act 1999 (YJCEA). This Act deals with proceedings in the youth court, lifting of reporting restrictions and intimidation, humiliation or distress in court proceedings and the general protection of vulnerable witnesses. Lord Woolf LCJ reinforced the new legislation by a Practice Direction, stating that:

> all possible steps should be taken to assist the young defendant to understand and participate in the proceedings. The ordinary trial process should, so far as necessary, be adapted to meet those ends.[61]

B, aged 14, applied for judicial review of the Winchester trial judge's decision in *R v Winchester Crown Court ex parte B (A Minor)* (1999),[62] to discharge reporting restrictions after sentence in order to identify B; reasons were that reporting restrictions were no longer necessary on the basis that open justice was essential in a civilized society. Judges Simon Brown LJ and Astill J in the Administrative Court dismissed B's application and reiterated that it was well within the Crown Court's powers to discharge a section 39 order in relation to proceedings on indictment after conviction.

A section 39 order automatically lapses when the person reaches the age of 18 and cannot extend to reports of the proceedings after that point (see: *JC & RT v Central Criminal Court* (2014)[63]).

 FOR THOUGHT

> Is it a breach of human rights that children are tried in adult courts in the UK for 'grave' crimes? Discuss in the light of the Strasbourg ruling in *V v UK; T v UK* (1999) (ECtHR).

8.3.2 Reporting on children involved in criminal proceedings: section 45 Youth Justice and Criminal Evidence Act 1999

Section 45 YJCEA permits a criminal court to prevent any information being included in a publication which is likely to lead members of the public to identify the under-18 victim, witness or defendant as a person concerned in the proceedings.

59 See: *Secretary of State for the Home Department ex parte Venables; R v Secretary of State for the Home Department ex parte Thompson* [1998] AC 407.
60 (1999) 30 EHRR 121 (ECtHR).
61 Source: Practice Direction by the Lord Chief Justice of England and Wales (Woolf LCJ): Trial of Children and Young Persons in the Crown Court of 16 February 2000.
62 [1999] 1 WLR 788. B had been sentenced to three years' detention for an offence contrary to s 1 Criminal Attempts Act 1981.
63 [2014] EWHC (1041) (Divisional Court).

Section 45(8) YJCEA identifies particular examples of information that a section 45 reporting restriction may contain, such as:

(a) her or his name;
(b) her or his address;
(c) the identity of any school or other educational establishment attended by her/him;
(d) the identity of any place of work; and
(e) any still or moving picture of her/him.

This list is not exhaustive.

When deciding whether to make an order under section 45 the court must have regard to the welfare of that person. As this restriction is a departure from 'open justice', there must be a good reason for imposing it (see: R v Inner London Crown Court ex parte B (1996)[64]). Furthermore, the court must be satisfied that, on the facts of the case, the welfare of the child outweighs the strong public interest in open justice.

The court, or an appellate court, may dispense with a section 45 reporting restriction if it is satisfied that doing so is in the interests of justice or that the restrictions impose a substantial and unreasonable restriction on the reporting of the proceedings and it is in the public interest to remove or relax the restriction. When considering the 'public interest' the court should have regard, in particular, to the matters identified in section 52 YJCEA:

- the open reporting of crime;
- the open reporting of matters relating to health and safety;
- the prevention and exposure of miscarriages of justice;
- the welfare of the child or young person and the views of the child or young person.

In McKerry v Teesdale and Wear Valley Justices (2000),[65] a 16-year-old boy, with a long record of offending, pleaded guilty at the youth court to a 'TWOCing' offence.[66] Upon request by a local newspaper, the magistrates lifted the reporting restrictions and permitted his identity to be revealed under section 49 of the 1933 Act, giving as reasons that the young offender posed a serious danger to the public and had shown a complete disregard for the law. The Divisional Court held that the magistrates' reasons were completely acceptable because 'no doubt the justices had in mind that members of the public, if they knew the appellant's name, would enjoy a measure of protection if they had cause to encounter him'. The court further added that the power to dispense with anonymity 'must be exercised with very great circumspection' and that the public interest criterion must be met.

In the conjoined cases of R (on the application of T) v St Albans Crown Court; Chief Constable of Surrey v JHG (2002),[67] it was held that antisocial behaviour orders (ASBOs) were very much in the general public interest and that reporting restrictions would not be granted. In the first case, the court had refused to grant anonymity under section 39 Children and Young Persons' Act 1933 to an

64 [1996] COD 17 (DC).
65 [2000] 164 JP 355 (DC).
66 Section 12 Theft Act 1968 ('taking a vehicle without the owner's consent').
67 [2002] EWHC 1129 (Admin) of 20 May 2002 (QBD (Admin).

11-year-old boy (T) in respect of whom an ASBO[68] had been made. T sought a judicial review of that decision. In the second case, the court had granted anonymity to 17-year-old twins (J and D) when making an ASBO, with the Chief Constable of Surrey appealing against that decision. The allegations against T included abuse, minor criminal damage and two assaults, and those against J and D included assault, nuisance, trespass, criminal damage, threatening behaviour and intimidation. T, J and D submitted that, given that ASBOs were civil in character, they were less serious than many of the offences in respect of which section 39 applications were commonly refused in Crown Court proceedings. T submitted that the court had failed to consider relevant matters, including his age and improvement in his behaviour, and in J and D's case the Chief Constable submitted that the court had considered irrelevant matters, including the impact on members of J and D's families.

Applying the *Lee* balancing exercise, that of the public interest test in disclosure of the name versus the welfare of the young person in question, the public interest test weighed in favour of disclosure in T and *JHG*, where it could be reported that the individuals were on an ASBO and the neighbourhood could learn about the orders, assisting the police in making the orders effective to prevent future antisocial behaviour (see also: *R v Winchester ex parte B (A Minor)* (1999).[69]

In summary, the protection of under-18s under a section 45 YJCEA order includes the following:

- A criminal court may make an order preventing the publication of information that identifies a child or young person as being a victim, witness or defendant in the proceedings.
- This restriction applies to traditional print and broadcast media as well as online publications.
- The court must have regard to the welfare of the child or young person.
- The court may remove or relax the section 45 reporting restriction if satisfied that it imposes a substantial and unreasonable restriction on reporting and that it is in the public interest.

Just as with a section 39 order, a section 45 reporting restriction order ceases to apply when the young person reaches the age of 18. In these circumstances, the court has the power to impose lifelong anonymity under section 45A YJCEA if the relevant conditions are met (see below).

8.3.3 Lifelong anonymity orders: section 45A Youth Justice and Criminal Evidence Act 1999

Section 45A YJCEA[70] contains the power for the court to impose a lifelong reporting restriction in the case of an under-18 victim or witness. This provision has long been used for young murderers and means there must be no publication about them during their lifetime.

When Coulson J lifted the reporting restrictions on Ann Maguire's teenage killer, identifying 16-year-old William (Will) Cornick at Leeds Crown Court in November 2014, the media's interest was as intense as in 1993 when Morland J lifted the section 39 anonymity order on Venables and Thompson. After Cornick's guilty plea, Coulson J reasoned that 'there is a public interest in naming

68 Section 1 Crime and Disorder Act 1998.
69 [1999] 1 WLR 788.
70 Inserted by s 78(2) Criminal Justice and Courts Act 2015 'lifetime reporting restrictions in criminal proceedings for witnesses and victims under 18.'

young defendants who are convicted of murder'. He sentenced the young killer to a minimum of 20 years.[71]

The test for making a section 45A order is that the court must be satisfied that fear or distress on the part of the victim or witness in connection with being identified as a person concerned in the proceedings is likely to diminish the quality of that person's evidence or the level of co-operation they give to any party to the proceedings in connection with that party's presentation of its case. When applying the test the court is required to take into account certain particular matters:

- the nature and alleged circumstances of the offence to which the proceedings relate;
- the age of the victim or witness;
- their social and cultural background and ethnic origins;
- their domestic, educational and employment circumstances;
- any religious and political beliefs;
- the views expressed by the victim or witness (victim impact statement).

In summary, under section 45A of YJCEA a criminal court may make a lifetime anonymity order, preventing any publication of information that identifies a child or young person as being a victim or witness in court proceedings. The court must also take Article 10 ECHR into account, the effect that such an order will have on the media's ability to report the proceedings. The court can remove or relax the order and reporting restrictions at any time if reporting is in the public interest.

The issue of a lifelong anonymity order was raised in common law in the 'Mary Bell' case (Re X (1985)[72]), where a lifelong injunction was sought on behalf of the claimant – notorious child killer 'Mary Bell' (not her real name) and her daughter. This is now known as a 'Mary Bell order'. Mary Bell had been convicted of manslaughter by diminished responsibility on 17 December 1968 at Newcastle Assizes for killing two boys aged three and four. Her accomplice, known as 'Norma', aged 13, was acquitted. Cusack J described Mary as 'dangerous' and sentenced her to be detained in secure accommodation at Her Majesty's Pleasure. After conviction, her name was released to the public, resulting in permanent media interest and applications to lift reporting restrictions. After conviction Mary ('X') spent 12 years in secure units, young offender institutions and subsequently prison, during which time her mother repeatedly sold stories about her to the press. Mary Bell was released in 1980 and given a new identity.[73]

There were three major periods when X's identity and whereabouts were either discovered or at risk of discovery by the media. The first was after she formed a settled relationship with a man (the second defendant in Re X), and gave birth to Y on 25 May 1984. Child Y was made a ward of court five days later, granted anonymity until her 18th birthday. In July 1984, the News of the World became aware of the birth and an injunction was granted by Balcombe J in Re X (1985).[74] It is believed that Bell's daughter did not know her mother's identity until it was revealed by reporters (for full background details of the case see: Re X (a woman formerly known as Mary Bell) and others v O'Brien and others (2003)[75]).

71 See: Sentencing remarks by Coulson J in R v William Cornick, Leeds Crown Court, 3 November 2014.
72 X CC v A [1985] 1 All ER 53 (sub nom 'Re X (a minor) (wardship injunction – a woman formerly known as Mary Bell)'.
73 For further insight into the original trial and Mary's development see: Sereny, G. (1998).
74 [1985] All ER 53.
75 Re X [2003] EWHC 1101.

When Y reached 18, X and Y applied for a lifelong anonymity order at the family court. Granting the lifelong anonymity order on 21 May 2003, Dame Elizabeth Butler-Sloss P made an injunctive order preventing the disclosure of their identities, addresses and other information that might identify them for life. Claimants X and Y had argued, *inter alia*, that there was a serious risk that their Article 8 rights would be breached if the *contra mundum* injunctions were not granted.

A 'Mary Bell order' was also made on child killers Jon Venables and Robert Thompson by Dame Elizabeth Butler-Sloss in 2001,[76] granting the 'Bulger killers' lifelong anonymity. When the mother of the murdered James Bulger, Denise Fergus, asked the court in 2010 to lift the lifelong anonymity order on Venables, the then Justice Secretary, Jack Straw, intervened, reiterated the Mary Bell order and the order made by the President of the Family Division in 2001. Appearing via video link at the Old Bailey, 27-year-old Jon Venables pleaded guilty on 23 July 2010, to the offences of downloading and distributing indecent images of children. Bean J partially lifted reporting restrictions to reveal Venables had been living in Cheshire at the time of the offences.[77]

Courts rarely impose lifelong reporting restrictions on adult offenders. Somewhat surprisingly, Eady J granted a *contra mundum* 'Mary Bell' injunction to protect Maxine Carr – then aged 27 – on 24 February 2005.[78] She had provided school caretaker Ian Huntley with a false alibi after he murdered the two ten-year-old schoolgirls, Holly Wells and Jessica Chapman, in 2002 (the 'Soham killings'). After serving 21 months in prison for conspiring to pervert the course of justice, Carr was granted lifelong anonymity, preventing any media organization from identifying her and her whereabouts.

8.3.4 Reporting restrictions on adult witnesses: section 46 Youth Justice and Criminal Evidence Act 1999

Section 46 YJCEA gives the court power to restrict reporting about certain adult witnesses (other than the accused) in criminal proceedings on the application of any party to those proceedings. Again, publication of the name, address, educational establishment, workplace, photo, etc. of the witness, likely to lead to his or her identification as a witness by the public in any criminal proceedings, is not permitted. A section 46 order may also restrict the identification of children where it would lead to the identification of the adult in question.

Such anonymity orders are not granted often by courts since it is a long established principle that the defendant in a criminal trial is entitled to be confronted by his accuser in open court.[79] Media organizations have a right of appeal against section 46 orders,[80] even where the restriction on reporting is confined to photographs or film (see: *ITN News v R* (2013)[81]).

See below
8.5

The court can further exercise its powers to allow a name or *any other matter* to be withheld from the public in criminal proceedings under section 11 of the Contempt of Court Act 1981 (CCA), prohibiting the publication of that name or matter in connection with the proceedings if any evidence in open court would frustrate or render impractical the administration of justice (see: *AG v Leveller Magazine* (1979)[82]). In *Re Trinity Mirror* (2008),[83] the Court of Appeal overturned a Crown Court order under section 11 CCA which, in the interests of the defendant's children, prevented the naming of a defendant who had downloaded paedophile images.

In *A Local Authority and Others v News Group Newspapers Ltd* (2011),[84] Baker J declined to make an order restricting the publication of the names of a surviving child's adult family members, including

---

76 See: *Venables v NGN* [2001] Fam 430.
77 Source: 'Bulger killer Venables jailed over child abuse images', *BBC News Online*, 23 July 2010.
78 See: *Carr (Maxine) v News Group Newspapers Ltd and Others* [2005] EWHC 971 (QB) at para. 5 (Eady J).
79 See: s 88 Coroners and Justice Act 2009.
80 Under s159 Criminal Justice Act 1998.
81 [2013] 2 Cr App R 22 at para. 26.
82 [1979] AC 440.
83 [2008] 2 Cr App R 1 (CA).
84 [2011] EWHC 1764 (Fam) (Baker J).

that of a very vulnerable mother who had been charged with the murder of another child (referring to *Re Evesham Justices* (1988).[85]

 FOR THOUGHT

Do lifelong anonymity orders (*contra mundum* injunctions) contravene the media's right to freedom of expression? Discuss with reference to legislation and leading authorities.

8.4 Anonymity orders and family court restrictions

Thousands of sensitive court decisions affecting vulnerable people in the Court of Protection (COP)[86] and the family courts in the UK were granted greater access to the public in 2016. Such court hearings have, in the past, been held in private and more public hearings were introduced including media reporting.

The *Daily Mail* reported on Wanda Maddocks (50) as being the first person to be sentenced to five months' imprisonment by the COP in April 2013, for trying to remove her father John, suffering from dementia, from a care home where his family thought he was in danger of dying.[87] Cardinal J ruled that Ms Maddocks was in contempt of court for disobeying a number of protection court orders.[88]

When reporting on such proceedings, responsible and ethical journalism must be at the forefront of every media organization when dealing with very difficult issues, such as 'door stepping' bereaved families, taking photographs in hospitals or care homes, or invading the privacy of those who are giving their evidence in family courts.

8.4.1 The Court of Protection

The Court of Protection (COP) makes some momentous decisions about people's lives and for this reason correct and appropriate media reporting of its workings can well improve public understanding. The COP deals with 'capacity' (i.e. mental health) cases and the right to refuse treatment. Non-lawyers (such as relatives) often act as decision makers under the Mental Capacity Act 2005.

In *Re Press Association* (PA) (2014) Peter Jackson J lifted a COP anonymity order on 63-year-old Linda in June 2014. Ms McKenzie, a Jehovah's Witness, had rejected a blood transfusion and any treatment with blood products and had died on 26 February 2014. This followed an earlier hearing where Jackson J ruled it was lawful to refuse treatment.[89] The PA argued that the dead woman could be named since she could no longer be 'injured' by publicity and did not have relatives who might be distressed by reading about her in the press.

---

85 See also: *R v Evesham Justices ex parte McDonagh* [1988] QB 553.
86 The Court of Protection (COP) was set up under the Mental Capacity Act 2005 to deal specifically with decisions involving people who are unable to make them ('lack of mental capacity'), including property, financial affairs, health and welfare.
87 See: *Stoke City Council v Maddocks* (2012) EWHC B31 (COP); (2012) MHLO 111 committal proceedings for contempt of court, issued 3 May 2013 by Lord Judge LCJ and Sir James Munby, President of the Family Division and President of the Court of Protection.
88 Source: 'Jailed in secret – for trying to rescue her father from care home where she believed he would die', by Steve Doughty and Andy Dolan, *The Daily Mail*, 23 April 2013.
89 See: *Press Association v Newcastle upon Tyne Hospitals Foundation Trust* [2014] EWCOP 6 (Jackson J).

Although published judgments may be read by anyone on the internet, the media has a vital role in bringing COP proceedings to wider public awareness, such as *Re V* (2016);[90] or *Re T (Adult: Refusal of Treatment)* (1993)[91].

Re V (with specific reference to an earlier hearing in *Re C*[92]) made tabloid headlines in January 2016. The *Daily Mail* (and other newspapers) had referred to C as a 'woman who had lost her sparkle'. Upon being diagnosed with breast cancer in December 2014 aged 49, C had refused to take medication prescribed for the disease because 'it made her fat'. Kings College NHS hospital trust had argued she did not have the mental capacity to make the decision to die. MacDonald J decided that C *did* have the capacity to make that decision and therefore dismissed the application of the Trust.[93] C was therefore entitled to refuse the treatment and died on 28 November 2015.

MacDonald J had given permission for the judgment to be published and *expressly* pointed out that there were strict anonymity orders in place provided by a schedule available to the media (known as the 'Pilot Order').[94] The media had then 'cherry picked' some sections from the judgment in the 'Pilot Order' which they then sensationalized, such as C's lifestyle, reported as 'impulsive and self-centred', the fact that C had four marriages and a number of affairs and spent her husbands' money on lovers. The *Daily Mail* called her 'reckless', focusing on her 'excessive' consumption of alcohol, her material possessions and 'living the high life'.[95] Lawyers for the dead woman argued for a posthumous anonymity order to protect her daughters and a grandchild and the newspapers appealed. Charles J stated that the order must remain in place until all her children and the grandchild were 18.[96]

8.4.2 Family courts

Family courts make far-reaching decisions, such as whether children should be taken into care or put up for adoption or given contact with parents who are divorcing. They also decide on custody and how finances should be split. Under youth court rules, it is unlawful to publish anything that would identify a minor (under 18) involved in a case, but it is possible to identify adults such as social workers and doctors.

Since the coming into force of the Children, Schools and Families Act 2010, which grants more open access to these courts, proceedings have been under close scrutiny by the media. The 2010 Act is a direct result following pressure groups' argument that family court and wardship proceedings should be part of the open justice principle (see 'fathers for justice' fight for greater court access).[97]

Part 2 of the Children, Schools and Families Act 2010 created a more open and visible justice system in the previously closed family courts by allowing the media access to ensure accountability through professional and public scrutiny of court decisions and thereby increase public confidence in the way the family courts work.[98] This has resulted in more divorce proceedings being reported, involving celebrities, such as the acrimonious divorce of rock star Liam Gallagher and 'All Saints' singer Nicole Appleton. Their undefended petition for a 'quickie divorce', heard at the Principal Registry of the High Court in London in April 2014, only took 68 seconds, according to the

90 *V v Associated Newspapers Ltd, Times Newspapers Ltd, Independent News and Media Ltd, Telegraph Media Group Ltd and Associated Press* [2016] EWCOP 21 (Case No COP1278226) in the matter of proceedings brought by Kings College NHS Foundation Trust concerning C who died on 28 November 2015 COP, 24 April 2016.
91 [1993] Fam 95 at 102 (Lord Donaldson).
92 See: *Kings College Hospital NHS Foundation Trust v C and V* [2015] EWCOP 80.
93 Ibid., at paras 98–100 (MacDonald J).
94 The 'Transparency Pilot Order' provided reporting restrictions in serious medical treatment cases.
95 Source: 'Woman, 50, who lived for "looks, money and men" wins right to refuse life-saving kidney treatment because she doesn't want to be poor, old or ugly', by Keiligh Baker, *The Daily Mail*, 1 December 2015.
96 See: *Re V* [2016] EWCOP 21 at para. 177 (Charles J).
97 See: *R v Central Criminal Court ex parte Crook* [1995] 1 WLR 139 (CA (Crim Div)).
98 See: Part 2, s 13 of the 2010 Act ('Authorised news publication').

Daily Mail.[99] The parties' lawyers had attempted to exclude the media, which failed and the press could report on their substantial assets read out in open court.[100]

At the divorce proceedings of Sir Paul McCartney and Heather Mills, Bennett J ruled against their lawyers' application for *in camera* proceedings (citing *Scott v Scott*). The judgment of 18 March 2008 was made available in full online, reported widely in the media that the former Beatle had to pay a lump sum settlement of £16.5 million to his ex-wife whom he had been married to for seven years.[101] However, the ward proceedings concerning their child Beatrice were held in private (referring to: *Re KD (A Minor) (Ward: Termination of Access)* (1988);[102] *Re W (A Minor) (Wardship: Restrictions on Publication)* (1992);[103] *Re M & N (Minors) (Wardship: Publication of Information)* (1990),[104] *Re Z (A Minor) (Identification: Restrictions on Publication)* (1996)[105]).

The *Clayton* (2006)[106] case raised in acute form the purpose and function of long-term injunctions under section 8 of the Children Act 1989 and the circumstances in which a litigant finds himself when restrained by such an injunction (known as a 'section 8 order').

The background to *Clayton v Clayton* concerns Simon Clayton, a 47-year-old bookseller from Hay-on-Wye in 2003, who abducted his seven-year-old daughter shortly before his divorce hearing, fearing he would lose custody to his wife. He was tracked down to Portugal and brought home under arrest, after which he fought a lengthy custody battle. Mr Clayton found he was legally barred from publishing a book about his case because it would disclose the identity of his daughter.[107] Mr Clayton had become a 'fathers for justice' spokesman and asked for the child anonymity order and reporting restrictions to be lifted.

In a landmark (reversed) ruling, the CA ruled in Mr Clayton's favour in 2006. The President of the Family Division, Sir Mark Potter, set out new guidance on restrictions that could be placed on reporting after the conclusion of proceedings involving a child.[108] He concluded:

> If, for example, the Appellant wishes to put photographs of himself and C on his website, in order to impart the information that they have had a very happy holiday together, this, to my mind, is not different in substance from the activities of many families which operate a 'blog' and exchange information and news about the progress of themselves and their children on a web-site. Against such activities there seems to me to be little point in having a blanket injunction which then exempts social and domestic purposes.[109]

So, have the family court reforms gone far enough with the Children, Schools and Families Act 2010? After the *Clayton* victory it could be argued that the opening up of the family courts has been a positive development; though the Act itself still poses many exemptions and procedural complications, often too complex and time consuming to allow media presence in family courts (see: *Re Child X*

---

99 Source: 'Nicole Appleton granted a "quickie" divorce from Liam Gallagher in just 68 seconds . . . after he admits to adultery', by Fay Strang, *The Daily Mail*, 8 April 2014.
100 See: *Appleton (Nicole) and Gallagher (Liam) v (1) News Group Newspapers Ltd (2) The Press Association* [2015] EWHC 2689 (FAM).
101 Source: 'Sir Paul McCartney and Heather Mills divorce: Judge's full ruling to be made public', by Caroline Gammell and Matthew Moore, *Daily Telegraph*, 18 March 2008.
102 [1988] FCR 657.
103 [1992] 1 WLR 100.
104 [1990] Fam 211, in which a local newspaper intended to publish a story concerning the removal by a local authority of two wards from a long-term foster home without explanation. The CA accepted that there was a clear public interest in knowing more of why the decision to remove had been taken and implemented in this manner. But the welfare of the children dictated that the identity of the children, their previous foster parents, the new foster parents, the parents, the schools and any relevant addresses should not be published.
105 [1996] 2 FCR 164 (CA).
106 [2006] EWCA Civ 878 (CA (Civ Div)).
107 Section 97(2) Children Act 1989 prohibits publication of material likely to identify 'any child as being involved in any proceedings'.
108 *Clayton* [2006] EWCA Civ 878 (CA).
109 Ibid., at para. 137 (Sir Mark Potter P).

(*Residence and Contact – Rights of media attendance*) (2009);[110] *Re A (a child) and B (a child) (Contact) (No 4)* (2015)[111].

 FOR THOUGHT

> Have law reforms increased public confidence by making family courts and court of protection proceedings more 'visible' through the media? Discuss with reference to leading authorities.

8.5 Contempt of court

Contempt of court ('contempt') is the improper interference with the administration of justice. British contempt laws ensure that the court is free to decide on the matters before it, without undue influence from the media. The practical function of the law of contempt has the purpose of preserving the integrity of the legal process in order to provide a fair trial to all parties in court. It is particularly relevant in criminal proceedings, where 'the court is under a duty to ensure the accused a fair trial', covered by Article 6 ECHR.[112]

The courts' jurisdiction to deal with contempt is divided into two broad categories: criminal contempt and civil contempt. In essence, a criminal contempt, such as contempt in the face of the court, is an act which threatens the administration of justice. Courts are empowered to protect the administration of justice by acting on their own initiative, punishing those guilty of such contempt with detention in custody or a fine. Civil contempt involves disobedience of a court order or undertaking by a party who is bound by it. The court's sanction in civil contempt has been seen primarily as coercive or remedial. Civil contempt has largely arisen in respect of an order or undertaking made in civil litigation (see R v M (2008)[113]).

8.5.1 Contempt in the face of the court

This offence covers courtroom behaviour, such as being disrespectful to a bench of magistrates, wearing inappropriate clothing in the public gallery, the use of mobile phones and cameras in the courtroom (see: *DPP v Channel Four Television Co. Ltd* (1993)[114]).

The first published opinion on criminal contempt 'in the face of the court' was that of Wilmot J in *Rex v Almon* (1765)[115] He said:

> it is a necessary incident to every court of justice to fine and imprison for a contempt to the court, acted in the face of it.[116]

---

110 [2009] EWHC 1728 of 14 Jul 2009 (Fam).
111 [2015] EWHC 2839 (Fam) (Case No: FD08P01237) Judgment 14 October 2015 (Cobb J); following on from F1 and F2 (*father 1 and father 2*) v (1) M1 and M2 (*mother 1 and mother 2*); (2) *A (a child) and B (a child) (by their Guardian)* [2013] EWHC 2305 (Fam) 31 July 2013. All judgments were handed down in private and published in a redacted form (removing identifying features of the family).
112 See: *R v Sang* [1980] AC 402.
113 [2008] EWCA Crim 1901.
114 [1993] 2 All ER 517.
115 (1765) Wilm. 243.
116 Ibid., at 254 (Wilmot J).

The issue of taking a mobile phone in a courtroom was first addressed in *R v D (Vincent)* (2004),[117] still prosecuted under the old legislation of section 41 Criminal Justice Act 1925. The Act creates a contempt to take any photograph, make or attempt to make any portrait or sketch of a justice or a witness in, or a party to, any proceedings before a court (either in the courtroom or its precinct, such as the waiting room outside the courtroom or in the immediate circumference of the courthouse).

In this case, the juvenile appellant had taken three mobile phone photos at Liverpool Crown Court: one in the court canteen; one from the public gallery towards the witness box; and the third of his brother in the secure dock, also showing one of the security officers. The trial judge seized the appellant's mobile phone and charged him with the summary offence of criminal contempt. D was convicted and sentenced to 12 months' imprisonment; he appealed against sentence. The CA dismissed his appeal and Lord Aikens noted:

> a person could use photographs of members of the jury or a witness or advocates or even a judge in order to try to intimidate them or to take other reprisals. Witnesses who are only seen on a screen or who are meant to be known only by an initial could possibly be identified. The anonymity of dock officers or policemen who are involved in a case could be compromised if a photograph is taken and is used to identify them.[118]

Section 12 Contempt of Court Act 1981 (CCA) created two further statutory contempts:

- wilfully interrupting the proceedings; and
- otherwise misbehaving in court.

The Crown Court can issue proceedings for contempt 'in the face of the court' in the following circumstances:

- *any* contempt seen by the judge; or
- disobedience of a court order; or
- breach of an undertaking to the court.[119]

The taking of photographs in court can be particularly serious when identification at trial is an evidential issue ('it wasn't me'), as the CA indicated in *R v Bieber* (2006).[120] Once a photo has been published there is greater risk of jury prejudice – especially when the media publish a photo of the accused close to trial proceedings. In such cases a judge may well stay ('halt') 'active' trial proceedings.

In the *Poulson*[121] and *Kray*[122] cases, for example, the respective trial judges said that they could not see how the press could report the evidence without running the risk of being in contempt of other criminal proceedings which had already begun against co-defendants.

---

117 [2004] EWCA Crim 1271.
118 Ibid., at para. 15 (Lord Aikens).
119 See: *DPP v Channel Four Television Co. Ltd* [1993] 2 All ER 517.
120 [2006] EWCA Crim 2776.
121 See: *R v Poulson and Pottinger* [1974] Crim LR 141. The 'Poulson' trials through the 1970s were the most high-profile tax evasion cases brought by the Inland Revenue, resulting in the resignation of the Conservative Home Secretary Reginald Maudling, who had formerly been chairman of two of John Poulson's companies.
122 See: *R v Kray* (1969) 53 Cr App R 412. Ronald Kray (of the Kray twins) had been convicted of murder on 4 March 1969, and on 15 April 1969 he and a number of others were facing a second indictment charging them with murder and other offences. His counsel sought to challenge prospective jurors for cause on the ground that the previous trial had been extensively reported, and that prejudice to Kray resulting from press reporting would be likely to influence the minds of the jurors in the second trial.

In *R v McLeod* (2000),[123] the Court of Appeal held there was no reason why a trial judge could not be considered to be an independent and impartial tribunal for proceedings for contempt of court. The CA further stated that Article 6 ECHR does not add to, or alter, the normal requirement that proceedings should be conducted fairly before an independent and impartial tribunal. Therefore, the trial judge in *McLeod* was entitled to deal with the intimidation of a witness, which had occurred in a corridor outside the courtroom.

8.5.2 Contempt at common law

The concept of contempt was established at common law as 'an act or omission calculated to interfere with the administration of justice'.[124]

One of the leading authorities regarding 'contempt' can be found in Lord Diplock's words in the 'Thalidomide' case, *AG v Times*,[125] when he said:

> [contempt covers] particular conduct in court proceedings which tends to undermine that system or to inhibit citizens from availing themselves of it for the settlement of their disputes.[126]

This case involved decades of civil court actions by 'Thalidomiders' against the manufacturers and distributors of the drug thalidomide, Distillers Co. (Biochemicals) Ltd. The *Sunday Times* and its then editor Harold ('Harry') Evans (now 'Sir') had begun investigatory reporting on thalidomide victims and the 'atrocious' settlements offered to parents of the seriously malformed young children and babies born between 1958 and 1972.[127]

Five Law Lords overruled the CA, and granted a *contra mundum* injunction to the Attorney General against the publishers of *The Times*, thereby restraining the newspaper and all other media organizations from publishing *any* matter which might prejudice present and future court proceedings: *AG v Times* (1974).[128]

After the *Times* publishers and Harry Evans lost their case in the House of Lords, they filed an application with the European Commission of Human Rights in 1978, claiming that the injunction infringed their right to freedom of expression guaranteed by Article 10 of the Convention.[129] The ECtHR held − by 11 votes to nine − that the interference with the applicants' freedom of expression was not justified under Article 10(2) as a 'pressing social need' and could not therefore be regarded as 'necessary'. Following the *Sunday Times* ECtHR ruling, the UK Parliament rushed legislation through Parliament resulting in the Contempt of Court Act 1981.[130]

On 23 December 2009, some 50 years after one of the worst disasters in medical history, the Thalidomiders finally received an apology from the UK government, followed by a £20 million compensation package.[131]

The common law is still the starting point for determining what constitutes 'contempt', and case law has established the powers of courts to deal with contempt. Common law and statutory provision (in the form of the Contempt of Court Act 1981) ensure that *any* court − be it civil or

---

123 [2006] EWCA Crim 2776.
124 See: Fox, J. C. (1927), p. 394.
125 *AG v Times Newspapers* [1974] AC 273 ('Thalidomide').
126 Ibid., at para. 298 (Lord Diplock).
127 The original action concerned 466 victims, born between 1958 and 1961 to mothers who had taken the drug 'Distaval' (first manufactured in Germany under the name 'Contergan' by Chemie Grünenthal GmbH) for morning sickness in the early months of pregnancy. The first cases were settled out of court, but parents found that the *ex gratia* payments were not sufficient and not flexible enough to meet the young people's changing needs.
128 [1974] AC 273.
129 See: *Sunday Times v UK* (1980) 2 EHRR 245 (ECHR) ('Thalidomide').
130 See: Hansard, The Phillimore Report on 'Contempt', HC Deb 25 April 1978 vol. 948 cc 1340−1350.
131 Source: '50 years on, an apology to thalidomide scandal survivors', by Sarah Boseley, *Guardian*, 15 January 2010.

criminal jurisdiction and certain tribunals, such as employment tribunals – is free to decide on the matters before it, without undue influence from the media.

8.5.3 Contempt of Court Act 1981: strict liability contempt

See below
8.5.4

The Contempt of Court Act 1981 (CCA) redefined the strict liability offence of contempt of court, which requires court proceedings to be 'active'.

Section 1 CCA provides for strict liability from the point a case becomes active. This is known as the period of *sub judice*, as set out in section 1 CCA:

> the strict liability rule means the rule of law whereby conduct may be treated as a contempt of court as tending to interfere with the course of justice in particular legal proceedings regardless of intent to do so.

The 'strict liability' rule is defined, whereby conduct may be treated as a 'contempt of court' if it tends to interfere with the course of justice in particular legal proceedings, *regardless of intent* to do so. This means even the most experienced journalist can fall foul of the law of contempt, even if he just wants to write a background piece to a forthcoming trial – it may well be that the publication is deemed to interfere with the course of justice. It is for this reason that every journalist, editor and publisher ought to be familiar with current contempt legislation.

Section 2(1) and (2) CCA ('Limitation of scope of strict liability') limits the scope of the strict liability rule, stating that it only applies to 'publications' including 'speech, writing and other communication in whatever form' which is addressed to the public at large. Only a publication which creates a 'substantial risk' of prejudice will be treated as 'strict liability' contempt. This is governed by case law.

A journalist, editor, broadcaster or publisher is not guilty of strict liability contempt if the publication amounts to fair and accurate reporting of legal proceedings held in public and published 'in good faith'.

Here are some examples of cases which are likely to attract national media interest and where strict liability contempt is particularly acute:

- **The defendant is famous** (e.g. when BBC broadcaster Stuart Hall admitted in May 2013 that he had indecently assaulted 13 girls during the 1960s, 70s and 80s).
- **The complainant is famous** (e.g. when ex-TV 'weathergirl' and TV presenter, Ulrika Jonsson, accused an ex *Blue Peter* presenter of rape in 1988 in her autobiography, serialized in the *Daily Mail*).
- **The case is one of a serial rapist** (e.g. blackcab driver John Worboys, who was convicted as a serial rapist in March 2009 for attacks on 12 women).
- **A high-profile cold case solved because of DNA advances** (e.g. the murder of BBC newsreader and presenter, Jill Dando, by gunshot outside her home in Fulham, West London, on 26 April 1999; Barry George was wrongly convicted of Dando's murder and spent eight years in prison; he lost his legal battle for compensation as a 'victim of a miscarriage of justice' in July 2013. Ms Dando's murder remains an unsolved crime).
- **Criminal appeal cases** (e.g. 'Marine A' case – see: R v Blackman (Alexander Wayne) and Secretary of State for Defence (2014);[132] the Airline Bombers case – see: R v Abdulla Ahmed Ali and Others) (2011).[133]

See below 8.6

---

132 [2014] EWCA Crim 1029 (CA Crim Div).
133 [2011] EWCA Crim 1260 (CA Crim Div).

The trial of Levi Bellfield attracted enormous media attention. He had been found guilty in June 2011 of the murder of 13-year-old schoolgirl Milly Dowler who had gone missing nearly ten years previously, on 21 March 2002. In a separate trial brought by the Attorney General, the *Daily Mail* and the *Daily Mirror* were found guilty of contempt of court over their extensive pre-trial coverage of Bellfield during the *sub judice* period.[134] Sir John Thomas, President of the Queen's Bench Division, fined each newspaper £10,000.

The main areas of the Contempt of Court Act 1981 are summarized below:

- limits liability for contempt under the 'strict liability rule' (sections 1–7);
- deems jury interference as contempt (section 8);
- prohibits the use of tape recorders in court or bringing sound recording equipment into court without leave of the court and deems publication of a sound recording as a contempt (section 9);[136]
- provides limited protection against contempt for a person refusing to disclose the source of information contained in a publication for which he is responsible (section 10);
- empowers magistrates' courts to deal with contempt in the face of the court by imposition of a fine or committal to custody for a maximum of one month or both (section 12);
- restricts the period of committal to prison for contempt where there is no express limitation to two years for a superior court and one month for an inferior court (section 14).

8.5.4 Active proceedings: *sub judice*

The risk of 'contempt' is most prevalent in criminal proceedings. The *sub judice* (or 'active') period starts when a summons has been issued or a defendant has been arrested without warrant (for serious indictable offences). Proceedings cease to be active where they conclude by either an acquittal or sentence, or discontinuance of the charge.[136]

During the *sub judice* period, the media can publish the following:

- the name of the accused;
- his or her address;
- the offence he or she is charged with.

Once appeal proceedings have started a journalist, broadcaster or publisher must adhere to the contempt legislation in the usual way.[137] Civil appellate proceedings are active from the time when arraignments for the hearing are made or from the time the hearing begins, until the proceedings are dIPSOsed of or discontinued or withdrawn.[138]

---

134 *AG v Associated Newspapers Ltd and Mirror Group Newspapers Ltd* [2012] EWHC 2029 (Admin) of 18 July 2012 (*Levi Bellfield contempt* case).
135 Section 31(2) Crime and Courts Act 2013 inserted a new subsection (1A) into s 9 CCA.
136 Schedule 1 paras 5 and 6 CCA; s 1 Powers of Criminal Courts (Sentencing) Act 2000; s 219 or 432 Criminal Procedure (Scotland) Act 1975; Article 14 Treatment of Offenders (Northern Ireland) Order 1976.
137 Schedule 1 para. 12 CCA 1981.
138 Schedule 1 paras 11 and 15 CCA 1981.

When will a judge stay trial proceedings? One answer lay in the trial of Lee Bowyer and Jonathan Woodgate in 2000, at that time still football players for Leeds United.[139] They were standing trial at Hull Crown Court for allegedly seriously wounding 21-year-old student Sarfraz Najeib outside the Majestyk nightclub in Leeds, in January 2000. For fear of 'contempt' during the 'active' trial period, the BBC's *Match of the Day* coverage on 26 November 2000 broadcast a cup match between Leeds United and Arsenal with Woodgate and Bowyer's heads pixelated, running as 'headless' players on the pitch.

During the jury's deliberation in April 2001, the *Sunday Mirror* published an interview with the victim's father, Muhammed Najeib, alleging a racist attack. On application by the defence, Poole J stayed the proceedings, citing contempt of court, and ordered a retrial. He made it clear that the newspaper had seriously prejudiced the jury verdict by its publication, stating that the editor, Colin Myler, should know his 'contempt' legislation better.

At their retrial a year later at Leeds Crown Court in 2002, Woodgate and Bowyer were acquitted of sections 18 and 20 wounding charges (Offences Against the Person Act 1861). Woodgate pleaded guilty to affray and was sentenced to 100 hours' 'community service' and ordered to pay eight weeks' wages as a fine. Bowyer also pleaded guilty to affray and was fined four weeks' wages.

After the conclusion of the second trial, the Attorney General issued contempt proceedings against the Trinity Mirror Group and the *Sunday Mirror*'s editor, Colin Myler. They were found guilty of contempt and subsequently fined a total of £175,000. Colin Myler resigned. Kennedy LJ and Rafferty J contended that the offending article had seriously impeded justice during a lengthy, expensive, high-profile case at a crucially difficult time. (See also: 'the Rosemary West' trial – R v West (Rosemary) (1996).[140])

A murder charge is always serious and an editorial error by a broadcaster or media outlet can seriously impede the course of justice; that includes not granting the accused a fair trial. In the *AG v ITV* case (below) the court upheld the contempt, pointing out that the broadcast had resulted in additional delay and distress to all parties involved in the proceedings.

 KEY CASE — *Attorney General v ITV Central Ltd* [2008] EWHC 1984 (Admin)

Precedent
- ❖ A broadcaster (or other media organization) is guilty of strict liability contempt if he broadcasts or publishes information during 'active' court proceedings or broadcasts any other extraneous information about the case.
- ❖ Where the contemnor has offered an immediate apology and offered to pay third-party costs the court must take this into account in assessing the appropriate amount that the broadcaster should be fined.

Facts
A regional television breakfast news bulletin of 23 seconds by Central TV (ITV) in relation to the trial of five men for murder later that day referred to the fact that one of the men had been convicted of, and was currently serving, a sentence for murder. Defence counsel brought the ITV broadcast to the attention of the trial judge and the trial was stayed. The broadcaster offered an immediate and unreserved apology to the court, agreeing to pay all third-party costs to cover the postponement of the trial. Subsequently, all five defendants were convicted with court costs amounting to £37,014, which ITV paid.

---

139 See: *R v Bowyer (Lee) and Woodgate (Jonathan)* (No 1) (2000) (unreported).
140 [1996] 2 Cr App 374.

After the trial, the Attorney General applied for an order for committal for contempt of court against the broadcaster ITV Central.

Decision
The Divisional Court took the view that the ITV Central news broadcast was a 'serious and basic error' which had caused disturbance to the court, and delays and further distress to third parties. However, in mitigation wasted costs had been voluntarily paid, and allowing for that it would be appropriate to impose a fine of £25,000.

Analysis
The case is a harsh reminder to media editors that there is no scope for honest error in contempt of court offences. The judgment in *AG v ITV* suggests that the courts take the strict liability offence under section 1 CCA 1981 seriously. The AG's application was granted for the reasons that the 'publication' (the broadcast) had amounted to a 'serious and basic error', creating a substantial risk of prejudice that the news bulletin might be seen by members of the jury due to hear the impending trial.

In July 2011, the *Daily Mirror* was fined £50,000 and the *Sun* £18,000 for contempt of court for articles published about a suspect arrested on suspicion of murdering Joanna Yeates.[141] The court ruled that the tabloid newspapers had seriously breached contempt laws with their reporting of the arrest of Christopher Jefferies, Yeates' landlord, who was later released without charge and was entirely innocent of any involvement.

The disappearance and tragic death of Miss Yeates during the Christmas period in 2010 had commanded enormous public interest and concern. Her body was discovered on 25 December and much of the initial criminal investigation had focused on Yeates' landlord Christopher Jefferies. He was arrested on suspicion of her murder on 30 December. The front page of the *Mirror* of 31 December was headlined: 'Jo suspect is peeping Tom: Arrested landlord spied on flat couple', positively asserting that Mr Jefferies was a voyeur.[142] The *Sun* of 1 January 2011 carried the front-page headline 'Obsessed by death', alleging that Mr Jefferies 'scared kids' by a macabre fascination with Victorian murder novels. There were reports that Mr Jefferies might be gay, referring to him as a 'freak'. Further reports described him as 'Hannibal Lecter' and 'a little creepy'.[143] Both papers alleged that Mr Jefferies might be a paedophile. The court held that the material in the two tabloid publications was extreme and prejudicial and that the journalists and editors were guilty of 'strict liability' contempt under section 2(2) CCA.

Had Mr Jefferies been charged with Ms Yeates' murder, these articles would have provided Mr Jefferies with a serious argument that a fair trial would have been impossible. If he had been convicted, he would have argued on appeal that the trial was unfair because of the adverse publicity.[144]

Vincent Tabak, a 33-year-old Dutch engineer, was convicted of murdering his next-door neighbour Joanna Yeates and jailed for a minimum of 20 years in October 2011 at Bristol Crown Court.

We can find parallels with the Joanna Yeates murder coverage where trial by media has taken place, such as in the cases of Peter Sutcliffe (the 'Yorkshire Ripper' trial), Tom Stephens (the 'Suffolk

---

141 See: *AG v Mirror Group Newspapers Ltd and News Group Newspapers Ltd* [2011] EWHC 2074 (Admin) 29 July 2011 (Lord Judge LCJ, Thomas LJ and Owen J).
142 Ibid., paras 5 and 6.
143 Ibid., at para. 8.
144 Though Lord Judge LCJ anticipated that any such appeal would have failed on the 'fade factor'. Ibid., at para. 34.

Ripper' story), Colin Stagg,[145] Robert Murat[146] and Barry George.[147] In each case there were either contempt warnings by the Attorney General (or Solicitor General) to the media, or the newspapers were found guilty of contempt.

In the *Dale Cregan* case,[148] His Honour Judge Gilbart QC imposed strict reporting restrictions under section 4(2) CCA 1981 at Manchester Crown Court on 24 September 2012, on the ground of 'very real risk of prejudice' because the case had attracted high-profile media and public attention. One-eyed Cregan (30) was charged with the murders of police officers Fiona Bone (32) and Nicola Hughes (23) on 18 September 2012 by luring them to their deaths by dialling 999 to report a bogus burglary, then using a Glock handgun and a military grenade to murder the two women in Hattersley, Greater Manchester. This blanket reporting ban meant that there was no further reporting until the jury was sworn in. Any reports of preparatory hearings were limited to basic facts such as the name of the accused and the offences he was charged with.

The *Cregan* case was additionally complex since he was also jointly charged for other offences with his co-defendants Wilkinson and Ward with murdering father and son David and Mark Short on 9 August 2012 by causing an explosion at a property in Luke Road, Droylsden by using a hand-grenade;[149] and additionally with Gorman, Livesey, Hadfield and others for the attempted murders of John Collins, Michael Belcher and Ryan Pridding on 25 May 2012 and Sharon Hark on 10 August 2012[150] and for the possession of illegal firearms with the intent to endanger life.[151]

Dale Cregan admitted the murders of the two policewomen as well as the other offences in May 2013 at Preston Crown Court.[152] He was sentenced to a whole-life tariff by Holroyde J at the end of the four-month trial that laid bare the brutality of Manchester's underworld.

 FOR THOUGHT

In high profile criminal cases such as Dale Cregan (murder of two female police officers and others in Greater Manchester) or Vincent Tabak (murder of Joanna Yeates), where there is intense public and media interest, and the suspect is awaiting trial, is it right that a judge can impose total reporting restrictions under section 4(2) CCA 1981? Or do these restrictions not interfere with the open justice principle and Article 10 ECHR? Is newsworthiness and public interest sufficient reason to impose reporting restrictions? Discuss.

8.5.5 Contempt by publication

Contempt covers media reporting by 'publication' which asserts or assumes, expressly or implicitly, the guilt of the defendant or possible negligence on behalf of the respondent in civil cases. In newspaper reporting terms (and online editions) this can be just a single headline or in broadcasting terms it can be a biased commentary or news item on the radio before or during a

---

145 Colin Stagg was wrongly accused of the killing Rachel Nickell in 1992. Robert Napper, a paranoid schizophrenic, confessed to Rachel Nickell's killing in December 2008.

146 Murat was accused by newspapers of killing or being involved in the disappearance of Madeleine McCann in Praia da Luz, Algarve on 3 May 2007. The Mirror Group Newspapers, Express Newspapers and Associated Newspapers were found guilty of contempt in 2008.

147 Barry George had been found guilty of the murder of TV presenter Jill Dando in 2001. He successfully appealed and was acquitted in November 2007.

148 *R v Cregan (Dale Christopher); Gorman (Damian); Livesey (Luke); Hadfield (Ryan); Ward (Matthew Gary James) and Wilkinson (Anthony)* (2013) (unreported).

149 Section 2 Explosive Substances Act 1883.

150 Section 1(1) Criminal Attempts Act 1981.

151 Section 16 Firearms Act 1968.

152 Source: 'Police killer Dale Cregan pleads guilty to murders of father and son in gun and grenade attacks', by Rob Cooper, *Daily Mail*, 22 May 2013.

trial. It is doubtful that members of the media have short memories and simply do not remember the strict liability rule which is inherent in contempt of court legislation. It is probably fair to say that many of the 'red tops' have taken the risk in order to increase their newspaper sales by printing popular background stories or even the accused's photograph, when the subject matter was *sub judice*, writing off possible legal costs against the benefit of extra sales. 'Publication' then refers to:

- the print media (including photographs);
- broadcasts;
- websites and other online or text-based communication (including Twitter, Facebook, Instagram, etc.).

See below
8.5.7

The element of 'substantial risk' is judged at the time of publication and applies only to legal proceedings that are 'active' at the time of the publication. The longer the gap between publication and the trial the less substantial the risk of serious prejudice is likely to be. This is known as the 'fade factor'.

In the *Geoffrey Knights* case[153] at Harrow Crown Court in October 1995, eight newspapers were referred to the Attorney General, Sir Nicholas Lyell, by trial judge Roger Sanders for 'contempt,' for publishing stories and background about Mr Knights during *sub judice* proceedings.[154] Knights had been charged with wounding with intent on a cab driver and the trial was stayed on the request of Knights' lawyers, stating that their client would not receive a fair trial. The *Daily Mirror* had published stories about Knights' 'stormy' relationship with *EastEnders* actress and later his wife, Gillian Taylforth.[155]

In November 2015, the US publisher of *GQ Magazine*, Condé Nast, was found guilty of contempt over a 'very seriously prejudicial' article about the phone-hacking trial of Rebekah Brooks and Andy Coulson.[156] The article by Michael Wolff – published during the 'phone-hacking trial' in April 2014 – was accompanied by sketches and photos of the court proceedings. The feature also included claims that had not been put before the trial jury, including that Brooks had received a £10.8 million settlement from Rupert Murdoch. Furthermore, the publication contained allegations that Rupert Murdoch, owner of the (now-defunct) *News of the World* (*NoW*) was implicated in phone hacking. The front cover trailed the headline by court reporter, Michael Wolff: 'Hacking exclusive! The Trial of the Century'.[157]

The court heard that at the time of the offending article, GQ had total sales of 90,573, comprising 38,305 newsstand sales, 24,199 subscriber sales, 6,137 digital edition sales and 21,898 multiple copy sales (sales to airline companies, hotels, waiting rooms and the like).[158] What aggravated the 'contempt' by publication was that the article was available to read online during the evidence of some of the defendants: Rebekah Brooks (whose evidence began in February 2014, but who gave evidence until 12 March 2014); Clive Goodman (13 March to 20 March 2014, when

153 *R v Knights (Geoffrey)* (unreported, 1995) Harrow Crown Court 6 October 1995.
154 Source: 'Trial by media: watching for prejudice. After the Geoff Knights fiasco, can we trust the press to allow the accused a fair hearing?', by Grania Langdon-Down, *Independent*, 11 October 1995.
155 Taylforth was married to the late Geoff Knights for 23 years and had two children, Harrison and Jessica, before they separated in 2009. Geoff Knights died in 2013. Source: '"She was broken and devastated": Gillian Taylforth's children recall their mother's split from abusive husband Geoff Knights', by Rebecca Lawrence, *Daily Mail*, 27 March 2016.
156 *Attorney General v The Condé Nast Publications Ltd* [2015] EWHC 3322 (Admin), 18 November 2015 (Lord Thomas of Cwmgiedd LCJ and Nicola Davies J).
157 Ibid., at paras 1–3.
158 Ibid., at paras 10–11.

he became ill); Cheryl Carter (25 March to 27 March 2014); and Charlie Brooks (Mrs Brooks' husband – 28 March to 1 April 2014). The Lord Chief Justice, Lord Thomas, ruled that the article created 'a substantial risk' that the trial of Brooks, Coulson and other employees of NoW 'would be seriously impeded or prejudiced'.[159]

See Chapter 6.3.1

8.5.6 Photographs and contempt

Photographs are a major concern as a source of contempt by publication. This becomes particularly serious in criminal cases where a police suspect has not yet been positively identified by a witness in an ID parade (see the *footballer rape case* – *AG v Express Newspapers* (2004)[160]).

Since publication via social media, the criminal courts have been especially troubled by the dangers to the integrity and fairness of a criminal trial, where juries can obtain easy access to the internet and to other forms of instant communication in order to undertake background 'research' on the accused. Once information is published on the internet, it is difficult if not impossible to remove it completely. However, there will be jurors who disobey the judge's directions regarding the prohibition not to search the internet.

The *Ryan Ward* case[161] demonstrates the need to recognize that instant news requires instant and effective protection for the integrity of a criminal trial. Though the jury in the *Ward* case had been warned not to use the internet, the court could not be completely satisfied that a juror might not have accessed Ward's 'gun' photograph either via the internet or through Twitter. At the start of Ward's trial, *Mail Online* published an article with the caption: 'DRINK-FUELLED ATTACK: Ryan Ward was seen boasting about the incident on CCTV.' The article was accompanied by a photo showing Ward holding a pistol in his right hand with his index finger on the trigger while he indicated firing a handgun with his left hand. The picture remained online for four hours and 54 minutes, until it was removed at 9.58pm.

The *Daily Mail* and the *Sun* were found guilty of contempt in November 2009 for publishing an online photo of the murder trial defendant, posing with a gun on their websites. Ward was about to stand trial for the murder of car mechanic Craig Wass at Sheffield Crown Court when the publication appeared in print and in the respective online editions. Angus McCullough QC, acting for the Attorney General in the contempt proceedings at London's High Court, told the court that the publication of the online photograph (in both *The Sun* and the *Mail*) had created a 'substantial risk' of prejudicing the forthcoming jury trial. Both newspaper publishers (and their online editions) were found guilty under section 1 CCA.

That said, in December 2010, the Lord Chief Justice, Lord Judge, first allowed the use of 'live text-based communication' (e.g. Twitter) in court. A year later, Lord Judge further relaxed the rules, which meant that journalists no longer had to ask for permission to tweet in court, paving the way for more live coverage of court proceedings.[162] Thereafter members of the public could receive instant court reports via Twitter, such as the first extradition proceedings against WikiLeaks founder Julian Assange, at City of Westminster Magistrates' Court, the trial of Vincent Tabak who was found guilty of Jo Yeates' murder in October 2011 and the trial of Gary Dobson and David Norris who were found guilty of murdering teenager Stephen Lawrence in 1993 at the Old Bailey in January 2012.

---

159 Ibid., at paras 39–41.
160 [2004] All ER (D) 394.
161 *Attorney General v Associated Newspapers Ltd and Newsgroup Newspapers Ltd* [2011] EWHC 418 (Admin) (*Ryan Ward* case).
162 Source: Practice Guidance: The use of live text-based forms of communication (including Twitter) from court for the purposes of fair and accurate reporting. Lord Judge The Lord Chief Justice of England and Wales, 14 December 2011 at: www.judiciary.gov.uk/Resources/JCO/Documents/Guidance/ltbcguidance-dec–2011.pdf.

See below
8.5.8

8.5.7 The fade factor: general defences

Once a newspaper or media organization has been charged with 'contempt', the Attorney General will commence proceedings after the original trial has been concluded.

The court will then decide whether the publication has created a 'substantial risk'. Case law tells us that 'substantial risk' does not mean a 'large' or 'great' risk but a risk which is not remote, and the risk must be a practical rather than a theoretical risk.[163] The publication of noticeable prejudicial material during a trial is likely to create a much more substantial risk than the same publication which takes place a year before.

Section 5 CCA 1981 provides a statutory defence concerning 'discussion of public affairs' and further general defences can be found under Schedule 1, section 3 CCA 1981. Section 5 can save a publication that would otherwise fall foul of the 'strict liability' rule (section 1(1) CCA) if it is made a 'discussion of public affairs' and generally passes the public interest test (not defined by statute).

The test of whether the section 5 defence can be successfully applied is left to the Attorney General or the Divisional Court and usually comprises:

1. the size of the risk (of serious prejudice); and
2. the severity of impact of the publication.

Neither a remote risk of serious impediment nor a substantial risk of minor impediment will suffice. Arguably the terms used in section 5 CCA may well form part of the *actus reus* of contempt. But the terms are separately defined in section 2(2) CCA ('limitation of scope of strict liability') in the interests, presumably, of clarity and emphasis. This makes parts of the 1981 Act unclear and confusing: to judge whether an element forms part of the *actus reus* of the strict liability crime or is a defence as strictly defined has of course a bearing on who carries the burden of proof (see: *R v Hunt* (1987);[164] *R v Lambert* (2001)[165]).

This means that the section 5 defence is not altogether satisfactory, particularly where the restraint imposed would interfere with the journalist or publisher's freedom of expression as being 'necessary in a democratic society'.

In *AG v English* (1982),[166] the House of Lords ruled that the section 5 defence was available to the publishers of the *Daily Mail* and columnist Malcolm Muggeridge, because his comment piece had been written in 'good faith' and the piece was held to be 'in the public interest'. The opinion piece had been written by Muggeridge in support of a pro-life candidate running for Parliament. Though no actual mention was made of the 'Dr Arthur Trial'[167] at the time, the journalist made reference in general to medical practices of failing to keep deformed children alive after birth. Lord Diplock opined that section 5 CCA provided the exception to the strict liability rule.[168]

What is the 'fade factor'? The court decides whether the offending publication appeared shortly before an impending trial and whether this may have influenced the decision-making of that trial. If the publication was a long time ago, common law stipulates that this usually amounts to six to nine months prior to the trial; the court will then conclude that the jurors' recollection of adverse publication in the media may well have faded. This will then make the alleged prejudicial reporting no longer contemptuous,

In the (cricketer) Ian Botham case (1987),[169] the court took a robust view of the ability of jurors to decide cases uninfluenced by outside pressures, especially if the trial took place many months after any potentially prejudicial publicity had occurred.

163 See: *AG v Guardian Newspapers (No 3)* [1992] 1 WLR 784 at 881.
164 [1987] AC 352 (HL).
165 [2001] UKHL 37 (HL).
166 [1982] 2 All ER 903 (HL).
167 Sheffield paediatrician, Dr Arthur, was standing trial at the time for murdering a prematurely born, severely disabled baby boy, by not operating on the child or giving life-sustaining treatment. Dr Arthur was later acquitted by the jury.
168 *AG v English* [1982] 2 All ER 903 at paras 918 f–g (Lord Diplock).
169 *Attorney-General v News Group Newspapers* [1987] QB 1 (cricketer Ian Botham case).

❖ KEY CASE *Attorney-General v BBC and Hat Trick Productions Ltd* [1997] EMLR 76 (sub nom *Have I Got News For You* case)

Precedent
❖ A section 5 CCA 1981 defence is not available if the broadcast poses a substantial risk of prejudice to an impending or ongoing trial if the matter is not deemed in the public interest.
❖ The 'fade factor' is not a permissible defence if the trial is imminent (usually amounting to six months).

Facts
News quiz *Have I Got News For You*, chaired by Angus Deayton, on Friday 29 April 1994 on BBC Two, was broadcast between 22.00 and 22.30. The main topic was the forthcoming fraud trial of the Maxwell brothers, Kevin and Ian, sons of the deceased *Mirror* newspaper tycoon Robert Maxwell. The trial was set for 31 October 1994 and the Maxwell brothers were charged with two counts of conspiracy to defraud the trustees and beneficiaries of the Mirror Group Pension Fund.

When team leaders Ian Hislop, editor of *Private Eye*, and actor-comedian Paul Merton played the 'odd one out' round, the fourth photo showed some *Mirror* pensioners. The team members' repeated banter centred on the pensioners being 'allegedly' defrauded by Robert Maxwell, implying the 'guilt' of the Maxwell brothers. The programme was repeated the following night unedited.

At the start of the Maxwell sons' trial, their lawyers applied for proceedings to be stayed, arguing that the BBC news quiz had contravened contempt legislation and that Kevin and Ian Maxwell would not receive a fair trial due to adverse media coverage. Though the trial went ahead, and the Maxwell brothers were acquitted, the AG commenced contempt proceedings against the programme makers Hat Trick Productions and the BBC immediately after the conclusion of the fraud trial.

Decision
The court found both parties guilty of strict liability contempt for the reasons that the programme makers and the BBC should not have broadcast any material in connection with the forthcoming Maxwell trial during the *sub judice* period. The court further held that the public broadcaster had made no attempt to edit out the 'irrelevant' and 'rude' comments, particularly in its repeat programme. Hat Trick and the BBC were each fined £10,000.

Analysis
It was clear in this case that the BBC broadcast alluded to the possible 'guilt' of the Maxwell brothers, amounting to strict liability contempt. It did not matter that the panel members of the satirical TV show did not intend the broadcast to interfere with the impending fraud trial or that the comments were said in jest. The 'fade factor' was not allowed, since the trial was imminent; neither was there a section 5 CCA defence because criminal proceedings were clearly 'active' at the time of the 'publication'.

As we have seen in the *Geoff Knights* case above, serious prejudice can arise if a newspaper publishes the previous criminal convictions of the accused. Whether a publication amounts to a contempt is essentially a value judgement for the court. This was the instance in the *Have I got News for You* case (see above), where the court did not allow either the public interest defence under section 5 CCA nor the 'fade factor'.

Angus Deayton, then chairman of the popular BBC TV news quiz, had made continuous references to Ian and Kevin Maxwell (sons of the deceased Robert Maxwell) who were at that time standing trial for fraud.

At times the Attorney General has shown more leniency in commencing contempt proceedings against the media. Following the atrocities of the 7/7 London bombings in 2005, and the attempted terrorism attacks of 21 July of the same year, the CPS issued new practice guidelines allowing the media to make more extensive use of publishing police intelligence during active proceedings (following pre-trial proceedings), such as photos, CCTV footage and previous convictions of suspects – in this case Hussain Osman (27), Ibrahim Muktar Said (27), Yassin Hussan Omar (26) and Ramzi Mohamed (23). Their trial took two years to come to Woolwich Crown Court. Each accused received a life sentence in July 2007.

 FOR THOUGHT

You are representing a terrorist suspect accused of plotting a pressure-cooker-bomb attack on a famous London nightclub. She is standing trial at the Old Bailey in five months' time. The 'red tops' (and their online editions) continue with their sensational and inflammatory press coverage of your client. Media coverage includes the accused's family and schooling background in Yorkshire, a slur on her faith and reporting on her previous convictions. Produce a skeleton argument for the court to stay the trial under current 'contempt' and human rights legislation and leading authorities.

8.5.8 The role of the Attorney General in contempt proceedings

The Attorney General (AG) is the government's chief legal adviser on domestic and international law and the Solicitor General is his or her deputy. It is the AG's role to commence criminal contempt proceedings against an offending publication or broadcaster, publisher and/or editor, usually after the (original) trial has concluded. Contempt proceedings are public law proceedings and are dealt with in the administrative court.[170]

The AG's office also issues frequent media warnings in high-profile cases that editors should not be complacent and rely on the 'fade factor'.

Attorney General Baroness Scotland stepped in at the last minute to obtain an injunction preventing a book by then Assistant Commissioner of the Metropolitan Police, Andy Hayman, being published, at the time the 'liquid bomb' terrorism trial was 'active' in June 2009. *The Terrorist Hunters* (co-written with Margaret Gilmore) was about to go on sale on 9 July 2009.[171] The book was reissued in March 2010 after the full conclusion of the trial.[172]

---

170 See: Rules of the Supreme Court Ord. 52 (RSC Ord. 52); see also: *R v M* [2008] EWCA Crim 1901.
171 See: *AG v Random House Group* [2009] EWHC 1727 (QB) 15 July 2009.
172 See: Hayman, A. and Gilmore, M. (2009).

The financial penalties for contempt offences can be substantial and unlimited with an additional threat of up to two years' imprisonment for the editor. Fines can be unlimited at the Crown Court.[173] However, the last time an editor was imprisoned was in 1949 (see: *R v Bolam, ex p Haigh*[174]).

Does the Attorney General always prosecute? The rules when 'contempt' actually starts in criminal cases are not quite clear. Some newspapers argue they can still fully report on a suspect before he or she has been charged (i.e. at the point of arrest).[175] This area remains a grey area of the law and the media has habitually ignored contempt legislation in high profile cases.

This occurred in the 'Yorkshire Ripper' case just at the time the Contempt of Court Act 1981 came into force. When Peter Sutcliffe ('the Ripper') was arrested on 2 January 1981 by West Yorkshire police, it marked the *sub judice* period – according to the new legislation. On 5 January 1981, 35-year-old Peter Sutcliffe of 6 Garden Lane, Bradford, was charged at Dewsbury Magistrates' Court with the murder of Jacqueline Hill.[176] Sutcliffe was charged in total with the murder of 13 women, most of them prostitutes, over a five-year period.

The government's Solicitor General, Sir Ian Percival, issued a press warning in line with the new contempt legislation, intimating that the media would be liable to prosecution if their stories impeded a fair trial for Sutcliffe. But long before the 'Ripper Trial', there was extensive newspaper coverage when the 'red tops' alleged that the Ripper's last murder victim, Jacqueline Hill, could have been saved. The papers implied police incompetence during the five-year 'Ripper' investigation.[177]

After a two-week trial at the Old Bailey, Peter Sutcliffe was found guilty of 13 counts of murder and sentenced on Friday 22 May 1981 to 30 years behind bars. Attorney General, Sir Michael Havers QC, did not prosecute any newspaper publishers or indeed any broadcaster for contempt.[178]

However, *Private Eye* was sued in defamation by Peter Sutcliffes' wife, Sonia. The satirical magazine had alleged that she had 'done a deal with the *Daily Mail*' worth £250,000, for telling her story ('My life with the Yorkshire Ripper'). On 24 May 1989, Mrs Sutcliffe won her libel action against the *Eye* and its editor, Ian Hislop.[179] A High Court libel jury awarded Mrs Sutcliffe £600,000 damages, at that time the highest award in the UK. Mr Hislop commented afterwards: 'If this is justice, I'm a banana.' The sum was reduced to £60,000 on appeal.

See Chapter 7

The Byford Report (1981) – released under the Freedom of Information Act 2000 on 1 June 2006 – exposed details of 'systematic failure' by the West Yorkshire Police in the 'Ripper' inquiry and the handling of the press. Sir Lawrence Byford concluded that Peter Sutcliffe never stood a chance of a fair trial.[180]

8.5.9 Contempt proceedings in Scotland

The Contempt of Court Act 1981 covers the whole jurisdiction of the United Kingdom. Scottish contempt proceedings are dealt with by either the Sheriff or the District Court and are known as a 'breach of interdict';[181] there are some leading authorities, such as *Johnson v Grant* (1923);[182] *Johnston*

---

173 See: s 14 CCA 1981. If proceedings are brought by the AG for Northern Ireland under s 18 CCA 1981; s 35 Criminal Justice Act (Northern Ireland) 1945 applies to fines imposed for contempt of court by any superior court other than the Crown Court as it applies to fines imposed by the Crown Court.

174 (1949) 93 *Solicitors Journal* 220.

175 See: *R v Richardson* [2004] EWCA Crim 758.

176 Jacqueline Hill, from Middlesbrough, a 20-year-old student, was found battered to death on 17 November 1980, on waste ground in Leeds. She was Yorkshire-born killer Peter Sutcliffe's final victim.

177 See also: *Hill v Chief Constable of West Yorkshire Police* [1989] AC 53 where the claimant, Mrs Hill, mother of the deceased Jacqueline Hill, the last of the 'Yorkshire Ripper' victims, sued the police in negligence alleging that the police conduct and investigations relating to the earlier 'Ripper' murders in West Yorkshire could have prevented her daughter's killing.

178 Source: Press Council Report, House of Lords Debate; HL Deb 20 July 1983 vol. 443 cc 1159–1170.

179 See: *Sutcliffe v Pressdram Ltd* [1991] 1 QB 153.

180 Source: Home Office (1987), paras 466–482 ('The Byford Report').

181 Section 15 CCA 1981 (incorporated by Criminal Procedure (Scotland) Act 1995).

182 [1923] SC 789.

v Johnston (1996)[183]. Similar to English, Welsh and Northern Irish jurisdictions, Scottish courts are equally strict where the taking of photographs in court, recording proceedings and publications during *sub judice* proceedings are an issue.[184]

Scottish courts have traditionally punished contempt more harshly than English courts. This changed with the case of *Cox and Griffiths*,[185] when Peter Cox, a former *Sun* newspaper executive 'south of the border', became editor of the Glasgow-based *Daily Record* in 1998. In this landmark case, Peter Cox challenged the Scottish courts in contempt proceedings, arguing that the 1981 Contempt of Court Act contravened human rights legislation and press freedom under Article 10 ECHR. Lord Prosser allowed the petition by stating that 'juries are healthy bodies' and that they do not need a 'germ-free' media atmosphere. The finding of contempt was quashed.

The ruling by the Scottish Court of Appeal in *Cox and Griffiths* was seen as rather liberal at the time, demonstrating a more tolerant attitude towards contempt and *sub judice* in the Scottish press. Some Scottish editors have interpreted Lord Prosser's approach in the case as too liberal, worried that *Cox and Griffiths* may be misinterpreted, leading to greater liberties when reporting during a *sub judice* period. Rosalind McInnes undertook a research study in 2009, whereby she examined court reporting and possible contempt situations. She concluded that there was at that time a discrepancy between the Scottish and the English courts' contempt proceedings, arguing that such proceedings 'south of the border' had become 'increasingly rare' compared with Scotland.[186]

The *Aamer Anwar* case[187] demonstrated a change in Scottish proceedings. Solicitor Aamer Anwar had launched a bitter attack on the trial process of his client, Mohammed Atif Siddique, after he had been found guilty of terrorism offences on 17 September 2007. Trial judge Lord Carloway referred Mr Anwar to the High Court for contempt of court.

 **KEY CASE**   *Aamer Anwar (Respondent in contempt proceedings)* [2008] HCJAC (case no 36 IN932/06)

Precedent

❖ Members of the public will not be deterred from performing their public duty as jurors, when called upon to do so, even though they may have heard a potentially contemptuous comment.

❖ Comments and opinions expressed post-trial outside the court do not amount to contempt.

Facts

The background to this (contempt) case was that on 17 September 2007, at the High Court in Glasgow, Mohammed Atif Siddique was found guilty after trial on several charges under the Terrorism Acts 2000 and 2006. He was sentenced to a total of eight years' imprisonment. Mr Siddique's solicitor was Aamer Anwar.

On the day when the jury's verdict was delivered, Mr Anwar read a statement outside the court building in the presence of members of the public and journalists, which was televised. The statement included the observation that Mr Siddique 'was found guilty of

---

183 [1996] SLT 499.
184 See: *Haney v HM Advocate* [2003] Appeal Court, High Court of Justiciary; also: *HM Advocate v McGee* [2005] High Court of Justiciary of 12 October 2005 (Lord Abernethy) (unreported); also: *HM Advocate v Cowan* [2007], 27 February 2007 (Sheriff Sinclair) (unreported).
185 *Cox (Petitioner) and another* [1998] SCCR 561.
186 See: McInnes (2009b).
187 See: *Anwar (Aamer) (Respondent)* [2008] HCJAC (case no 36 IN932/06).

doing what millions of young people do every day, looking for answers on the internet . . .
It is farcical that part of the evidence against Atif was that he grew a beard, had documents in Arabic which he could not even read and downloaded material from a legitimate
Israeli website run by Dr Reuven Paz, ex Mossad . . .'.[188] On 23 October 2007 Mr Anwar
was charged with contempt of court by the Advocate Depute.

Opinion

The opinion was delivered by The Right Honourable Lord Osborne.[189] The court acquitted
Mr Anwar of contempt, stating that Mr Anwar's comments contained 'angry and petulant
criticism of the outcome of the trial process' and 'a range of political comments concerning the position of Muslims in our society' – but this was 'comment' and did not amount
to contempt.[190]

But the court added a postscript criticizing the behaviour of a professional 'officer of the
court'. Lord Osborne said: 'Any solicitor practising in the High Court of Justiciary owes a
duty to the court, a fact recognized in paragraph (I) of the Preamble to the Code of Conduct for Scottish Solicitors of 2002' and 'that a court is entitled to expect better of those
who practice before it'.[191]

Analysis

Though solicitor Mr Anwar was acquitted of contempt of court, it is worth noting the *obiter* opinion of Lord Osborne in relation to Mr Anwar's professional duty and obligations as
a solicitor. Though the court accepted that Mr Anwar's comments outside the courthouse
and on TV did not amount to contempt, their Lordships implied that the Law Society of
Scotland ought to deal with Mr Anwar's behaviour in a professional capacity.

8.5.10 Contemptuous jurors: section 8 Contempt of Court Act 1981

Section 8 CCA relates specifically to proceedings for contempt regarding breaches of confidentiality of jury deliberations in criminal trials. If covering active court proceedings, a court reporter is
allowed to report verbatim and contemporaneously what was said in court.[192]

There have been a number of recent examples where jurors in criminal trials have been tweeting about or researching cases online whilst deliberating. One such example is that of jury foreman,
Michael Seckerson, who published an article in The Times on 29 January 2008, expressing his strong
disagreement with the majority jury verdict of 10:2 in the case of childminder Keran Henderson.
He believed she had been wrongly convicted of manslaughter at Reading Crown Court for shaking
11-month-old Maeve Sheppard from Slough to death.[193]

Following Mr Seckerson's controversial publication, Attorney General, Baroness Scotland QC,
instigated criminal proceedings against The Times and Mr Seckerson, for breaching section 8 CCA
1981. Both The Times publishers and Mr Seckerson argued 'freedom of expression' in their defence,

---

188 Source: 'Press Release – Monday 17 September 2007 – HMA v Mohammed Atif Siddique – Guilty Verdict', statement read on the steps
     of the High Court by Mr Siddique's solicitor – Aamer Anwar.
189 Sitting with Lord Kingarth and Lord Wheatley on 1 July 2008: www.scotcourts.gov.uk/opinions/2008HCJAC36.html.
190 *Aamer Anwar (Respondent in contempt proceedings)* [2008] HCJAC at para. 44 (Lord Osborne).
191 Ibid., at para. 45.
192 See: s 4(1) CCA.
193 Source: 'Juror speaks out' by Mike Seckerson, The Times, 29 January 2008.

but were found guilty on 13 May 2009. *The Times* was fined £15,000 and Michael Seckerson £500 plus costs of £27,426 (paid by the newspaper). Section 8 CCA does not permit the public interest defence. Otherwise Mr Seckerson might have had a strong basis for arguing that alleged child cruelty (in the Keran Henderson case) was in the public interest.

Barsby and Ashworth (2004) argue that the section 5 CCA 1981 defence does not sit comfortably with section 8 of the 1981 Act, because section 5 states that a person is *not* guilty of the strict liability contempt if they can show that publication is part of a discussion in good faith and is a matter of public interest; and that the risk of impediment or prejudice is merely incidental to that discussion.[194] The authors further state that the rules of evidence, developed over hundreds of years of jurisprudence, are there to ensure that the facts that go before a jury have been subjected to scrutiny and can be challenged from both sides. Jurors are not supposed to seek information outside the courtroom. They are required to reach a verdict based only on the facts in the case and they are not supposed to see evidence that has been excluded as prejudicial.

Attorney General Dominic Grieve QC has possibly been the most prolific during his time in office in prosecuting contemptuous jurors. In July 2010, 19-year-old juror Danielle Robinson was found guilty of contempt of court for sending text messages to another woman sitting in a second trial at Hull Crown Court. She had passed on 'gossip' from the jury room, such as: 'Hi, it's Danielle from court. Are you doing the kid's case?' and 'He's been in prison before and is a paedo, and when he broke into the pub he took all the kids underwear xx.' Though both women were subsequently dismissed from sitting on the juries, it was touch and go whether the cases would be allowed to continue. Judge Roger Thorn QC called Robinson's texts a blatant attempt to influence a jury and said that her ignorance was no excuse for such contemptuous behaviour. She received an eight-month suspended sentence.[195]

In June 2011, juror Joanne Fraill,[196] 40, from Blackley, Manchester revealed highly sensitive details about jury room discussions when she swapped online messages with Jamie Sewart, 34, who had been acquitted at the trial. Fraill had used Facebook to contact the defendant in a multi-million-pound drugs trial when the jury was still considering charges against the other defendants. Fraill admitted breaching the Contempt of Court Act 1981 by using Facebook and also conducting an internet search into Sewart's boyfriend, Gary Knox, a co-defendant, while the jury was still deliberating in his case. Fraill's contemptuous actions led to the collapse of that trial, contributing to a £6 million legal bill. The Lord Chief Justice, Lord Judge, and two other senior judges sentenced Ms Fraill to eight months' imprisonment for contempt of court.

Following the Joanne Fraill contempt conviction in 2011, the Lord Chief Justice, Lord Judge, issued a general warning over the need to preserve the integrity of jury trial and the jury system.[197] Lord Judge referred to three separate criminal appeals where appellants were successful because of unsafe jury verdicts in the light of jury irregularities including the dangers of social networking in relation to jury tampering (see: *R v Twomey and Others*;[198] *R v Guthrie & Others*[199]).

Present-day jury directions include a warning by the judge not to consult the internet or any other form of text-based or social networking communication until the full conclusion of the trial.

In the *Paul Chambers* case[200] – also known as the 'Twitter Joke trial' – the administration and finance supervisor, Paul Chambers (26), found himself convicted of tweeting his frustration when being delayed in a snowstorm at Robin Hood Airport in South Yorkshire on 6 January 2010. He had

---

194 See: Barsby, C. and Ashworth, A. J. (2004), pp. 1041–1044.
195 Source: 'Teenager who jeopardised trials with texts to juror escapes jail', by Jo Adetunji, *Guardian*, 14 July 2010.
196 See: *AG v Fraill and another*; see also: *R v Knox* [2011] All ER 103.
197 Source: Press Release by the Judiciary of England and Wales on 9 December 2011: 'The Lord Chief Justice Issues Warning over Jurors Judicial Office news release'.
198 *R v Twomey (John) & Blake (Peter) & Hibberd (Barry) & Cameron (Glen)* [2011] EWCA Crim 8.
199 *R v Guthrie (Riccardo) & Guthrie (Bianca) & Guthrie (Cosimo) & Campbell (Courtney)* [2011] EWCA Crim 1338.
200 *Chambers (Paul) v DPP* [2012] EWHC 2157 (Admin) ('the Twitter Joke trial').

posted a message on Twitter: 'Crap! Robin Hood airport is closed. You've got a week and a bit to get your shit together otherwise I'm blowing the airport sky high!!' Chambers used his own name for this purpose and was registered as '@PaulJChambers', with a personal photograph as his account picture. The message was later found by an off-duty manager at the airport during an unrelated computer search and the matter was duly reported to the local police.

Chambers was arrested by anti-terror police, his house was searched and his mobile phone, laptop and desktop hard drive were confiscated. He was charged with 'sending a public electronic message that was grossly offensive or of an indecent, obscene or menacing character' contrary to section 127(1)(b) of the Communications Act 2003 and section 1 of the Malicious Communications Act 1988. On 10 May, he was found guilty at Doncaster Magistrates' Court and fined £385 and ordered to pay £600 costs. Chambers lost his appeal against his conviction in February 2012. In his second appeal against the DPP, the Lord Chief Justice, Lord Judge, announced a reserved judgment on 22 June 2012. Chambers' conviction was quashed on 27 July 2012. The approved judgment concluded that a 'tweet' does not constitute a criminal office if the message is not of a menacing character (i.e. he did not have the necessary *mens rea* for the Communications Act offence).[201]

In advance of the John Terry trial in February 2012, Newcastle United footballer Joey Barton sent some robust tweets with plain views on Terry and his opinion about the alleged racism charge. Terry had been charged with racially aggravated (verbal) offences against QPR defender Anton Ferdinand (including use of the word 'black') on 23 October 2011. Terry was cleared of the charge in July 2012. In respect of Joey Barton's tweets, the Attorney General, Dominic Grieve QC, decided to take no 'contempt' action, which was good news for Barton. Seemingly, the AG took the view that the tweets did not cause a serious impediment to John Terry's case by influencing any witnesses or the presiding magistrate who heard the case.

Writing in the *Guardian* in February 2012, Dominic Grieve argued that British contempt laws were still fit for the internet age:

> In the UK system, the Contempt of Court Act is part of the apparatus that protects this right, by limiting what can be published about a case while it is live, so that allegations that are not relevant or not tested in court do not form part of a juror's consideration . . . There is no doubt that the characteristics of the internet, and of social media in particular, pose challenges for enforcement. Comment and information – or misinformation – posted from outside the UK jurisdiction can only be addressed with great effort and international co-operation. In the democracy of the internet, what is published by one individual can 'go viral' within hours, with obvious implications. Comments on the web can soon be published far beyond their original, limited audience. And I use the word published advisedly, as publication is, of course, the phrase used within the Contempt of Court Act – an online article that breaches the strict liability rule runs the risk of running foul of the law of contempt.[202]

Do present British contempt laws interfere with freedom of expression? The ECtHR reiterated the right to a fair trial under Article 6(1) ECHR in *Gregory v UK* (1997)[203] (referring to its decision in *Remli v France* (1996)[204]). In *Remli* the trial judge had failed to react to an allegation that an identifiable juror had been overheard to say that he was a racist.

In *Sander v UK* (2000),[205] the Strasbourg Human Rights Court held that there had been a violation of Article 6(1) ECHR on the ground that the trial judge had failed to provide sufficient

201 Ibid., at paras 35–38 (the Lord Chief Justice of England and Wales, Lord Judge).
202 Source: 'Contempt laws are still valid in the internet age', by Dominic Grieve QC, *Guardian*, 8 February 2012.
203 (1997) 25 EHRR 577.
204 (1996) 22 EHRR 253.
205 (2000) 31 EHRR 1003.

guarantees to exclude any objectively justified or legitimate doubts about the impartiality of the court towards an Asian accused. The ECtHR reviewed its decision in *Gregory* regarding the fundamental importance of public confidence in the courts and the rule governing the secrecy of jury deliberations and any outside influences jurors may use.

The same question was addressed by the House of Lords in the two conjoined appeals in *Mirza* and *Connor* (2004):[206] whether evidence about jury deliberations that revealed a lack of impartiality was always inadmissible under the common law secrecy rule. The issue in *Mirza* concerned a juror who had revealed after the verdict that some jury members were associated with a neo-Nazi group, and that, during jury deliberations, they strongly influenced the conviction of the accused because he was a black immigrant. In *Connor*, a juror had revealed after the verdict that a majority of the jury refused to deliberate at all and had made up its mind virtually at the start of the trial; that jury ultimately arrived at a guilty verdict by spinning a coin. Dismissing both appeals, the House of Lords stated that common and statutory provision of contempt of court was well established in the area of jury deliberations under section 8 CCA.

In *Re B* (2006),[207] the BBC and other media organizations appealed against a High Court ruling that had ordered a complete reporting ban under section 4(2) CCA until the conclusion of the trial proceedings. B and D were indicted for 23 offences, including conspiracy to commit murder and acts of terrorism. B had already pleaded guilty to some offences. B and D contended that the extraneous comments made by the media on B's previous sentencing hearing were potentially disastrous to a fair hearing in the present case and D's trial. The defendants argued that the media coverage would seriously prejudice a (yet unselected) jury, arguing, *inter alia*, Article 6 ECHR and their right to a fair trial. Allowing the appeal by the BBC, Sir Igor Judge ruled that media editors ought to be trusted to fulfil their responsibilities and exercise sensible judgment in the publication of such information – reasoning that the media would be familiar with contempt legislation.

During its consultation to review British contempt laws, the Law Commission identified the following areas of difficulty:

● the uncertainty whether a Crown Court and/or the Court of Appeal have the power to detain or bail a person pending determination of an allegation of contempt;
● the restrictive power of the magistrates' courts, which presently do not have the power to deal sufficiently with contempt 'in the face of the court';
● while the Crown Court and Court of Appeal have the power to suspend a committal to custody, it is uncertain whether the magistrates' courts have the same power.[208]

Arguably, British contempt laws have failed to keep pace with the way people access information in the digital age. Current contempt laws as they are enforced come down unduly harshly on UK-based print media and their websites, while leaving live TV relatively untouched, and the internet entirely untamed. It is further submitted that the powers of the criminal courts to deal with contempt committed in the face of the court or by way of breach of court order are unsatisfactory. There is uncertainty as to the scope of the common law powers, gaps in the statutory provisions and unjustifiable inconsistency between them. Additionally, some Attorneys General have not always enforced the strict liability contempt rule, leaving some contemnors unpunished.

---

206 *R v Connor and another; R v Mirza* [2004] (conjoined appeals) UKHL 2 (HL).
207 *R v B* [2006] EWCA Crim 2692 ('Re B').
208 Source: Law Commission (2011) at pp. 6–8 at: http://lawcommission.justice.gov.uk/docs/lc330_eleventh_programme.pdf.

 **FOR THOUGHT**

Should the Contempt of Court Act 1981 be repealed? Are present contempt laws fit for the digital age? Discuss.

8.5.11 Courtroom TV

The argument in favour of courtroom broadcasts is that television has long been the principal source of information for the majority of people. Just as parliamentary broadcasts and UK Supreme Court live streams are freely accessible, it is argued that public broadcasting should now include the full criminal and civil justice system (except youth and family courts).

There have been number of high-profile cases which were broadcast all over the world, for example the trial of former paralympian athlete, Oscar Pistorius, who shot dead his model girlfriend, Reeva Steenkamp, on Valentine's Day in 2013. Parts of the trial and sentencing were broadcast live during 2014 from the South African court and in December 2015 from South Africa's Supreme Court of Appeal after the original verdict of culpable homicide was changed to murder. The O. J. Simpson murder trial, broadcast live for many months from the Los Angeles County Superior Court (November 1994 – October 1995), made courtroom TV history. The former national American football star was acquitted of murdering his ex-wife, Nicole Brown Simpson and waiter Ron Goldman in June 1994.[209]

Filming and recording have been banned in the UK since 1925.[210] British courtroom TV history was made in November 2004 when TV cameras were allowed to film and record a pilot project in the Court of Appeal at the Royal Courts of Justice in the *Speechley* appeal.[211] This concerned the former Lincolnshire County Council leader, Jim Speechley, after he had been convicted at Sheffield Crown Court in April 2003 of 'misconduct in public office' and sentenced to 18 months' imprisonment. During the appeal hearing, robotic cameras were focused on Kennedy LJ (presiding), Bell and Hughes JJ. William Harbage QC and Catarina Sjolin appeared for the appellant; neither the dock nor the witness box was filmed. Both Mr Speechley's conviction and his sentence were upheld, though Kennedy LJ reduced £25,000 court costs to £10,000.

In April 2012, permission was granted by Lord Hamilton, the Lord President and Lord Justice General for Scotland, to record judge Lord Bracadale's sentencing of David Gilroy, 49, at the High Court in Edinburgh for the murder of (missing) bookkeeper Suzanne Pilley. Gilroy, from Edinburgh, was found guilty on 15 March 2012 of murdering 38-year-old Miss Pilley. Broadcaster Scottish Television (STV) focused only on the judge as the sentence of life imprisonment (with a minimum custodial part of 18 years) was read out. Gilroy was not filmed, and neither was anyone else in the courtroom TV footage (except for the macer (mace bearer) and the legal clerk).[212]

The Nat Fraser trial, filmed in the Edinburgh High Court in 2012, was shown on British TV in full in July 2013. The documentary *The Murder Trial* was made by Windfall Films as a Channel 4 production, following the full trial for six weeks as the jury returned a guilty verdict against Fraser on the charge of murdering his wife. The programme provided a rare insight into proceedings in

---

209 See: *People of the State of California v Orenthal James Simpson*, January 24, 1995 (unreported).
210 Under s 41 of the Criminal Justice Act 1925.
211 *R v Speechley* [2004] (unreported) (CA).
212 Source: TV footage: 'David Gilroy jailed for life for the murder of missing bookkeeper Suzanne Pilley', STV, 18 April 2012: http://local.stv.tv/edinburgh/303870-david-gilroy-jailed-for-life-for-the-murder-of-missing-bookkeeper-suzanne-pilley.

Scottish courts. Television viewers heard and saw the same evidence as the jury of the retrial of a man who was found guilty, in 2003, of the murder of his wife Arlene in 1998, but whose conviction had been quashed. They heard the opening statement by prosecutor Alex Prentice QC, and his introductory description of the case as 'tricky', since neither Arlene Fraser's body nor a murder weapon were ever found. Additionally, Fraser had accounted for his movements on the day of the murder. Ultimately, Fraser was found guilty by a majority verdict and the film's biggest shock emerged – a history of domestic abuse that had been inadmissible at the trial.

In March 2016 the Lord Chief Justice, Lord Thomas of Cwmgiedd, announced that Crown Court sentencing remarks could be broadcast from selected 'pilot' courts in England and Wales, these being:

- the Old Bailey (Central Criminal Court, London);
- Southwark, South London;
- Manchester (Crown Square);
- Birmingham;
- Bristol;
- Liverpool;
- Leeds;
- Cardiff.[213]

As the law stands, broadcasting images of the witness box does not comply with victim protection legislation such as the Crime and Disorder Act 1998, the Protection from Harassment Act 1997 or the Vulnerable Witness (Scotland) Act 2004.[214] Arguably, there is a public interest argument in allowing filming of a prosecution or defence opening to a jury and of mitigation and sentence – a powerful teaching tool in law schools and an educational element for the public in general. As the Lord Chief Justice pointed out, judicial discretion should always allow or disallow filming built into contempt of court legislation.[215]

One danger of courtroom TV is that it might be seen as sensationalist and have a potential effect in high-profile trials, as already witnessed in the media circus which surrounded the 'Soham trial' of Ian Huntley in December 2003, or the eight-week historical child sex abuse trial of Rolf Harris in June 2014, when the 84-year-old iconic children's entertainer and veteran TV star was convicted at Southwark Crown Court of indecent assault on four girls aged between seven and 19 over three decades ago.

The argument against courtroom TV rests on the belief that the camera's presence might intimidate witnesses and affect their testimony, thereby creating an O. J. Simpson style media circus. But equally, as the Lockerbie trial and Speechley appeal have shown, there is a strong case for courtroom broadcasting, not just for public interest concerns but also for educational reasons, such as law school training and introducing the open justice principle to schools and colleges.

It remains to be seen whether British courtroom TV will catch on and, if so, whether it will change public opinion towards the justice system by granting greater access to the open court system. However, it may be that courtroom TV could become primarily entertainment like the *Jeremy Kyle Show* or *Judge Rinder*.

---

213 Source: Message from the Lord Chief Justice: 'Broadcasting in the Crown Court', *Judicial News*, 24 March 2016.
214 The Vulnerable Witness (Scotland) Act 2004 is aimed at making it easier for child and adult vulnerable witnesses to give their best evidence by formalizing existing special measures for giving evidence and introducing new measures, such as locations outside the court house known as 'remote sites'.
215 Sections 4(2) and 11 CCA 1981 would still be available to the court should it be felt necessary.

 **FOR THOUGHT**

How does existing contempt law sit with modern social media practices and the introduction of courtroom TV? Do they advance the open justice principle? Discuss.

8.6 Military courts and inquests

This section provides an overview of the constitutional position and function of the British tribunal system such as the court martial, inquests and inquiries.

8.6.1 The court martial

A court martial is a public court with similar powers to a Crown Court. It can impose prison sentences, fines or other forms of justice depending upon the nature of the crime. A court martial hearing is presided over by a Judge Advocate and a board of up to seven military members, individuals with no legal training much like a jury in civilian courts. In line with the government's 'transparency and open data initiative', the Military Court Service now publishes all court martial results in respect of the military court centres.

The Judge Advocate General (JAG) is appointed by the monarch by means of letters patent, on the recommendation of the Lord Chancellor. The JAG is a law officer of the Crown and an independent member of the judiciary and is always a civilian, although he may have served in the armed forces.[216] The JAG is not a general of the army; the word 'general' in this context signifies broad oversight, as in Secretary-General, Attorney-General, etc.

The JAG has a team of full-time judges comprising the Vice-Judge Advocate General[217] and six Assistant Judge Advocates General, and can also call upon the services of Deputy (part-time) Judge Advocates. All the judges are civilians, appointed from the ranks of experienced barristers or solicitors in the same way as other District and Circuit Judges. When conducting a particular trial they are formally titled 'The Judge Advocate', and out of court they are generally referred to and addressed as 'Judge'. In court the judges wear legal costume, comprising a bench wig and black gown, with a tippet (sash) in army red with navy blue and air-force blue edges.

The JAG and many Judge Advocates also sit in the Crown Court. It is also possible for a High Court Judge to be specified to preside in the court martial as a Judge Advocate; this is done for exceptionally serious or unprecedented cases, just as in the Crown Court.

Charges are brought by the Service Prosecuting Authority (SPA),[218] an independent prosecuting authority dealing with all criminal cases and offences contrary to military discipline. The SPA fulfils its functions in support of the operational effectiveness of the British Armed Forces throughout the world. The role of the SPA is to review cases referred to it by the Service Police or Chain of Command and prosecute that case at court martial or Service Civilian Court where appropriate. The

---

216 The current JAG is Jeff Blackett J who is also a circuit judge and who formerly served in the Royal Navy.
217 Judge Michael Hunter (2017).
218 The SPA was formed on 1 January 2009 and at the time of publication its head was Bruce Houlder QC as Director Service Prosecutions (DSP). The SPA was formed with the incorporation of the Navy Prosecution Authority, Army Prosecuting Authority and Royal Air Force Prosecuting Authority and has its headquarters at Royal Air Force Northolt, North West London.

SPA will also act as respondent in the Summary Appeal Court and represent the Crown at the Court Martial Appeal Court.

Serious matters – such as war crimes – including both offences against the civilian criminal law and specifically military disciplinary offences – *may* be tried in the court martial, which is a standing court. A Judge Advocate arraigns each defendant and conducts the trial which is broadly similar to a civilian Crown Court trial in all cases, even when dealing with a minor disciplinary or criminal offence. The jury, known as 'the board', comprises between three and seven commissioned officers or warrant officers depending on the seriousness of the case. Having listened to the Judge Advocate's directions on the law and summary of the evidence, they are responsible for finding defendants guilty or not guilty.

Probably the most high-profile court martial was that of *Marines A–E*. Reporting restrictions and complete anonymity orders on the (initially) five accused were strict, since Judge Advocate General, His Honour Judge Jeff Blackett, had ordered a complete anonymity and reporting ban on 13 October 2012 on all five marines.[219]

This was the first time UK servicemen had been charged with a war crime in modern military history and media interest was heightened, following the *Baha Mousa* atrocity. The death and torture of hotel receptionist Baha Mousa in Basra by British troops in 2003 had cast a dark shadow over the British army's reputation. Mousa had been arrested by British soldiers looking for insurgents, taken into custody for questioning and 36 hours later ended up dead. The shameful circumstances were revealed in Sir William Gage's public inquiry report and only increased the media's interest in reporting on court martial proceedings.[220] Mousa suffered at least 93 injuries prior to his death and seven British soldiers were charged in connection with the case. Six were found not guilty. Corporal Donald Payne pleaded guilty to inhumane treatment of a prisoner and was sentenced to a year in prison and dismissed from the army.[221]

The background to *Marines A–E* was the murder of an injured Taliban fighter in Afghanistan on 15 September 2011, when Royal Marine 3 Commando Brigade was based in Helmand. After the initial arrest of nine Marines by the Service Police in Helmand province video footage was found on a Marine's laptop that showed members of 3 Commando Brigade discussing what to do with a wounded gunman caught inside a compound in Helmand. Four marines were later released without charge. The remaining three Marines could have been tried in a civilian court (as had happened in at least one case arising from the operations of HM Armed Forces in Iraq). However the decision was made by the SPA that the Marines should be prosecuted under the court martial system.

On Friday 8 March 2013, three marines (A, B and C) were arraigned by Blackett J and pleaded not guilty to a joint charge of murder of an Afghan insurgent in September 2011.[222] The trial commenced on 23 October 2013 at Bulford Military Court Centre and the Ministry of Defence (MOD) advanced reasons for the complete anonymity orders on all Marines. One was that the Taliban's killing would be used for their own propaganda purposes. Another concern was the impact on the wider mission: British troops needed to remain in Afghanistan for another two years. The Press Association (PA) appealed against the complete reporting ban.[223] However, the anonymity orders stayed in place on all five defendant Marines.

In the end, Marine A was found guilty of murdering the Afghan insurgent on 5 December 2013, and Blackett J lifted all reporting restrictions so Sergeant Alexander Wayne Blackman (39) could be named. The other two Marines, found not guilty, were also named as Corporal Christopher Watson and Marine Jack Hammond. The Judge Advocate General sentenced Blackman to serve a life sentence of at least ten years in a civilian prison. Blackman was also dismissed with disgrace from Her Majesty's Service.

---

219 The order was made under r. 153 Armed Forces (Court Martial) Rules and s 11 Contempt of Court Act 1981.
220 See: *Baha Mousa Public Inquiry Report* 2011 – all three volumes at: https://www.gov.uk/government/publications/the-baha-mousa-public-inquiry-report.
221 For further discussion see: Williams, A. T. (2012).
222 See: s 42 Armed Forces Act 2006.
223 *R v Marines A–E* (2012) Case Number 2012 CM 00442 (Court Martial – before the Judge Advocate General) 6 November 2012.

The Court Martial found that Blackman's suggestion that he thought the insurgent was dead when he discharged the firearms was made up after he had been charged with murder. Although the insurgent may have died from his wounds sustained in the engagement by the Apache, Blackman gave him no chance of survival. The board found that Sergeant Blackman intended to kill the Afghan soldier and that Blackman's shooting had hastened his death. The video transcript revealed Blackman saying:

Shuffle off this mortal coil, you cunt,

and instructing his fellow marines:

Obviously this doesn't go anywhere, fellas . . . I've just broken the Geneva convention.[224]

Sergeant Blackman's appeal against conviction and sentence was heard before the Lord Chief Justice, Lord Thomas of Cwmgiedd, and the Vice President of the Court of Appeal Criminal Division, Lady Justice Hallett DBE, in the Court Martial Appeal Court (Criminal Division) at the Royal Courts of Justice in London on 22 May 2014. His appeal against conviction for murder was dismissed; the recommendation for parole was reduced to eight years.

Following Sergeant Blackman's conviction, the *Daily Mail* launched an appeal to 'free' the Marine with more than 30,000 supporters donating more than £750,000 by October 2015. Author Frederick Forsyth was spearheading the 'campaign for justice' for Sergeant Blackman.[225]

On 6 December 2016 the Criminal Cases Review Commission referred the murder conviction and sentence of former Royal Marine Alexander Blackman to the Courts Martial Appeal Court. Grounds for the referral include new evidence relating to Mr Blackman's mental state at the time of the offence and the fact that an alternative verdict of unlawful act manslaughter was not available to the Court Martial Board when it considered the case. The Commission concluded that these issues raise a real possibility that the Courts Martial Appeal Court may now quash Mr Blackman's murder conviction. A fresh appeal is now taking place.

8.6.2 The coroners' system

There are some 500,000 deaths in England and Wales every year. Most of these deaths are from natural causes. The Chief Coroner's Report (2015) stated that 223,000 deaths were reported to coroners across England and Wales in 2014–2015. Of these, 25,000 were referred to a coroner's inquest. Of these, only 397 cases were heard by a jury, the majority concerned deaths in prison or police custody.[226]

A coroner's inquest is a formal legal inquiry into the medical cause and circumstances of a sudden or unexplained death. Coroner's courts are held in public and follow the open justice principle.[227] Coroners' inquiries deal with:

- violent or unnatural deaths;
- deaths in prison or police custody;
- unexplained deaths after post-mortem;
- deaths abroad where the body is repatriated to the UK.

A coroner can exclude the public and the media from an inquest where issues of national security are involved. An inquest into a death can be held with or without a jury.

There are 110 separate coroners' jurisdictions in England, Wales and Northern Ireland.[228] Each jurisdiction is locally funded and resourced by local authorities. The Coroners and Justice Act 2009

---

224 Quotation taken from Sergeant Blackman's appeal against sentence in *R v Marines A, B, C, D & E* [2013] EWCA Crim 2367 (CA) at para. 32.
225 Source: 'Fighting fund for jailed Marine tops £750,000: More than 30,000 generous readers help his battle for justice', by Sam Greenhill, *The Daily Mail*, 5 October 2015.
226 Source: Ministry of Justice (2015a) *Report of the Chief Coroner to the Lord Chancellor Second Annual Report: 2014–2015*, paras 23–26.
227 See: Ministry of Justice (2009a).
228 The Coroners Service of Northern Ireland in Belfast is headed by a High Court Judge, Weir J (2016). There were two coroners, Ms Suzanne Anderson and Mr H. Rodgers (2016).

reformed the coroners' inquiry system with new rules on 1 February 2010.[229] The system is now headed by the Chief Coroner,[230] who is head of the coroner system, assuming overall responsibility and providing national leadership for coroners in England and Wales.[231]

In exceptionally high-profile cases, a serving judge is appointed. For example, in 2007 Scott Baker LJ was appointed as Assistant Deputy Coroner for Inner West London for the purposes of hearing the inquests into the deaths in 1997 of Diana, Princess of Wales and Emad El-Din Mohamed Abdel Moneim Fayed (Mr Dodi Al Fayed).

Hallett LJ was appointed Assistant Deputy Coroner for the Inner West London District of Greater London in order to conduct the inquests into the so-called '7/7 London terrorist bombings' in which 56 people were killed on 7 July 2005.

As mentioned, deaths in custody are always heard before a coroner's jury. This was the case with Stephen Chambers, who had taken his own life in his cell at Preston prison.

 **KEY CASE** *Chambers v HM Coroner for Preston and West Lancashire* [2015] EWHC 31 (Admin)[232]

Precedent

❖ In a coroner's inquest, where suicide is at issue, a finding of neglect (here from the HM Prison Service) is only permissible where there has been a *gross failure* to provide (for example) basic medical or psychiatric attention and a clear and direct causal connection between the neglect and the death.

❖ All the facts surrounding every suicide (in prison) must be thoroughly, impartially and carefully investigated.

Facts

On 26 January 2004 Stephen Chambers was found hanging in his cell at HMP Preston. On 14 May 2007 an inquest was held before HM Coroner, Dr James Adeley, and a jury. The jury returned, and the coroner recorded, a verdict that Mr Chambers died from hanging himself in Cell C2-31 which caused his death. The coroner cited as contributing factors his family problems and bullying. The coroner's report evidenced that the prison was aware of this bullying. Stephen Chambers had been in prison on a number of occasions, including from January 2001 to early 2003. During his time in custody in the year 2001 he attempted to hang himself on five occasions.

Since the claimant, Miss Rebecca Chambers, was less than three years old at the time of her father's death, her (divorced) mother, Mrs Deborah Chambers, took judicial review legal action in the administrative court against the coroner's inquest, the prison service and the deceased's mother Mrs Pauline Chambers.

Grounds for review were that (1) the claimant was dissatisfied with the verdict and the 'irregularities of proceedings' of the inquest in 2007 (i.e. failure to notify her or her solicitors that an inquest had taken place) and (2) that there was insufficient inquiry into possible neglect by the prison authorities (re Stephen's self-harm and attempted suicides).

---

229 See: Ministry of Justice (2013).

230 The post holder in 2016 was His Honour Judge Peter Thornton QC, appointed by the Lord Chief Justice on 6 May 2010.

231 Section 35 and Sch. 8 Coroner and Justice Act 2009.

232 *Chambers (Miss Rebecca) (by her mother and litigation friend Mrs Deborah Chambers) v HM Coroner for Preston and West Lancashire and (1) National Offender Management Service for HM Prisons and (2) Mrs Pauline Chambers* [2015] EWHC 31 (Admin).

Deborah Chambers applied to the Attorney General for an order quashing the original inquest verdict of 2007 and to hold a fresh coroner's inquest.[233]

Decision

(1) Allegations of irregularities of proceedings of the coroner's inquest

Deborah Chambers' divorce from Stephen was made absolute 11 days before his death in custody. She was informed by letter of his death which Mrs Chambers acknowledged on 24 May 2004. On 17 January 2006 she was informed of the inquest in early 2007. Since Stephen Chambers' mother, Mrs Pauline Chambers and his brother had instructed a different firm of solicitors, Farleys, from the by now divorced Deborah Chambers, the coroner's office wrote regularly to Farleys since they were the acting family of Mr Stephen Chambers. Counsel instructed by Farleys represented Mr Chambers' mother and brother at the inquest.

The administrative court held that there was no irregularity in the notification period and the proceedings, and therefore this was no ground for quashing the inquest. The family of the deceased had been duly notified and, in Deborah Chamber's case, the claimant (by now divorced from the deceased) did not make sufficient inquiries herself by way of contacting the coroner's office either herself or via her solicitors.

(2) Insufficiency of inquiry (re prison neglect)

The claimant alleged that the coroner's jury ought to have been left with a possibility of returning a finding of neglect; that the coroner failed to hold a sufficiently wide-ranging and appropriately focused investigation into alleged bullying at the prison and domestic problems (see: *R (on the application of Middleton) v West Somerset Coroner* (2004)[234]).

The court noted in Stephen Chambers' suicide case, a finding of neglect is only permissible where there has been a gross failure to provide (for example) basic medical or psychiatric attention and a clear and direct causal connection between the neglect and the death. Where it is found that the deceased has taken his own life that is the appropriate verdict (conclusion), and only in the most extreme circumstances (going well beyond ordinary negligence) can neglect be properly found to have contributed to that cause of death (see: *R v North Humberside Coroner ex parte Jamieson* (1995)[235]).

The court cited Lord Bingham in *R (on the application of Amin) v Home Secretary* (2004):[236]

> The state owes a particular duty to those involuntarily in its custody.[237]

The administrative court cited Lord Hope in *R (on the application of Sacker) v West Yorkshire Coroner* (2004):[238]

> So all the facts surrounding every suicide [in prison] must be thoroughly, impartially and carefully investigated.[239]

---

233 Under s 13 Coroners Act 1988.
234 [2004] 2 AC 182.
235 [1995] QB 1.
236 [2004] 1 AC 653.
237 Ibid., at para. 30 (Lord Bingham).
238 [2004] 1 WLR 796.
239 Ibid., at para. 11 (Lord Hope).

The claimant's application – to quash the original finding of the coroner's inquest and to order a new inquest – was refused.

Analysis

It is the duty of the coroner, acting as an independent judicial officer, to ensure that the process of inquiry during a coroner's inquest (with or without a jury) is rigorous and full. In the *Chambers'* case the court found that the original inquest had been rigorous that there had been no procedural irregularity (alleged by his divorced wife on behalf of their three-year-old child) and no evidence of neglect by HM Prison Service; furthermore that the coroner's court had fully complied with the procedural obligation under Article 2 ECHR which meant the inquest had been 'duly effective'.

The most high-profile inquest in recent history was that of the *Hillsborough Inquests*. These were heard in a purpose-built coroners' courthouse open to the public at Birchwood Park, Warrington, Cheshire, in the north-west of England. The background to this tragic football disaster is that on 15 April 1989 over 50,000 people had travelled to Hillsborough (home of Sheffield Wednesday Football Club) to watch the FA Cup semi-final between Liverpool and Nottingham Forest. Ninety-six people died as a consequence of the crush in the stands and hundreds more were injured and thousands traumatized.

The inquests began on 31 March 2014 with a verdict by the nine members of the jury on 26 April 2016. Over the two years the jury of six men and three women heard evidence from more than 600 witnesses about the design of the Hillsborough football stadium, the disorganized South Yorkshire Police operation and the delayed emergency response.

There had been an inquiry led by Taylor LJ in 1989 following the Hillsborough football disaster resulting in the blaming of the Liverpool fans and a finding of accidental deaths of the victims.[240] There followed 11 years of civil litigations, criminal and disciplinary investigations, and inquests into the deaths of the victims, judicial reviews, a judicial scrutiny of new evidence conducted by Stuart-Smith LJ, and private prosecutions of the two most senior police officers in command on the day. *The Sun*, under the editorship of Kelvin MacKenzie, became famous for its hostile coverage at the time, blaming Liverpool fans. He cleared the front page and, under the banner headline 'THE TRUTH', it read:

> Drunken Liverpool fans viciously attacked rescue workers as they tried to revive victims of the Hillsborough soccer disaster, it was revealed last night.
>
> Police officers, firemen and ambulance crew were punched, kicked and urinated upon by a hooligan element in the crowd.
>
> Some thugs rifled the pockets of injured fans as they were stretched out unconscious on the pitch.[241]

A new inquest was ordered to be held before a jury, following the tireless efforts by the 'Hillsborough Family Support Group'.[242] The original verdict of accidental death was quashed in

---

240 See: The Rt Hon Lord Justice Taylor (1989) *The Hillsborough Stadium Disaster, 15 April 1989, Interim Report*.
241 Source: *The Sun*, 19 April 1989, pp. 1–2.
242 See: *Attorney General v (1) HM Coroner of South Yorkshire (East) (2) HM Coroner of West Yorkshire (West)* [2012] EWHC 3783 (Admin).

December 2012. The Rt Hon Sir John (now Lord) Goldring was appointed as Assistant Coroner for South Yorkshire (East) and West Yorkshire (West) to conduct the new inquests.[243]

The inquest jury's verdict on 26 April 2016 was that the 96 football fans had been unlawfully killed. Reasons given were grave police error, causing the dangerous situation at the turnstiles and failures by commanding police officers to prevent the crush in the stands. Chief Superintendent David Duckenfield was found to be responsible for opening the gates during the Hillsborough disaster and was one of the key figures facing criminal charges. The inquest jury also found that Sheffield Wednesday Football Club failed to approve the plans for dedicated turnstiles for each pen, with inadequate signage at the club and misleading information on match tickets. The CPS was formally considering whether any criminal charges should be brought against any individual or corporate body following the Hillsborough inquests.[244]

Following the jury verdict, *The Sun* (online) headlined:

> *Hillsborough: The real truth.* Cops smeared Liverpool fans to deflect blame, new probe says 41 lives could have been saved. The Sun says: We are profoundly sorry for false reports and families of 96 victims call for prosecutions.[245]

On 1 June 2016, Louise Hunt QC, the Senior Coroner for Birmingham and Solihull, ruled that there would be fresh inquests into the deaths of 21 people killed on 21 November 1974 in the Birmingham pub bombings, widely acknowledged to have been the work of the IRA.

8.6.3 Fatal Accidents Inquiry in Scotland

There is no system of coroners' inquests in Scotland. Accidental, unexpected, unexplained, sudden or suspicious deaths are investigated privately for the local Crown agent by the Procurator Fiscal. Only certain types of death are investigated further at Fatal Accident Inquiries (FAIs).[246]

FAIs were introduced into Scotland by the Fatal Accidents Inquiry (Scotland) Act 1895.[247] That Act was eventually replaced (and repealed) by the 1976 Act supported by secondary legislation, the Fatal Accidents and Sudden Deaths Inquiry Procedure (Scotland) Rules 1977. The 1976 Act made provision for the holding of public inquiries in respect of fatal accidents, deaths of persons in legal custody, sudden, suspicious and unexplained deaths and deaths occurring in circumstances giving rise to serious public concern. It introduced four major changes:

- it dispensed with the need for a jury;
- gave wide powers to the Lord Advocate in relation to such inquiries;
- brought deaths in prisons and of persons in legal custody into the normal FAI system; and
- extended the jurisdiction of sheriffs to cover the offshore oil industry.

Today FAIs take place in local sheriff courts.[248]

---

243 See: House of Commons (2012b) The Report of the Hillsborough Independent Panel Report: http://hillsborough.independent. gov.uk/repository/report/HIP_report.pdf.

244 Source: Press release of statements from the CPS, IPCC and Operation Resolve following Hillsborough inquests verdict, 26 April 2016 at: www.cps.gov.uk/news/latest_news/cps_statement_following_hillsborough_inquest_verdict.

245 Source: *The Sun* (online edition), 26 April 2016 at: www.thesun.co.uk/sol/homepage/news/4535743/23-years-after-Hillsborough-the-real-truth.html.

246 See: Scottish Government (2009) Review of Fatal Accident Inquiry Legislation. The Report by the Rt Hon Lord Cullen of Whitekirk KT: www.gov.scot/resource/doc/290392/0089246.pdf.

247 The 1895 Act was amended by the Fatal Accidents and Sudden Deaths Inquiry (Scotland) Act 1906 to include provisions for inquiries into any case of sudden or suspicious death in Scotland.

248 For an up-to-date record of Fatal Accident Inquiries, see the National Records of Scotland at: www.nrscotland.gov.uk/research/guides/sheriff-court-records.

8.7 Secret courts and the media

Historically, there has always been a certain amount of collaboration between the UK government and the media that has offered a compromise between national security and press freedom. Introduced in advance of World War I, the 'D notice' system became a peculiarly British arrangement between government and the press, in order to ensure that journalists did not endanger national security. It was described as 'a gentleman's agreement', an appropriately quaint term which recalls the most famous news blackout of all – the affair between Edward VIII and the American divorcee – Wallis Simpson, in 1936. A 'DA notice' (Defence Advisory Notice), later called a 'Defence Notice' (D notice), remains an official request to news editors not to publish or broadcast items on specified subjects for reasons of national security.[249] Today, the government D notice system is still intended for stories deemed to affect national security. However, Prince Harry's deployment as a soldier in Afghanistan in 2007–2008 was not considered one of these.

The accountability of MI5 and MI6 and the question of whether they are fully subject to the rule of law lie at the heart of attempts by the media to sweep away the secrecy surrounding terrorism trials since the 9/11 attacks in the USA[250] and 7/7 bombings in London.[251]

It is fair to say, until the revelations by America's National Security Agency (NSA) whistleblower Edward Snowden, most people had no idea of the extensive legislative powers of Britain's digital spy agency, the Government Communications Headquarters (GCHQ), and how close its ties were with NSA. Snowden's exposés further demonstrated that Britain's surveillance laws (on bugging and snooping) were out of date and terrorism legislation confusing and at times conflicting with human rights legislation. Most of these 'terrorism' laws (aimed largely at IRA terrorism in the past) were drafted by Parliament in a pre-internet era, giving sweeping powers to the Home Secretary to authorize the interception and collection of electronic information, and the planting of bugs ('equipment interference'). Snowden had revealed this top-secret information via the *Guardian* and *der Spiegel* in 2013 that both GCHQ and the NSA were spying on all international government executives.

The protection of the UK intelligence and security services in relation to terrorism legislation became clear following the *David Miranda* case (2016).[252] Mr Miranda had been detained by security forces at Heathrow airport in 2013 for carrying files related to information obtained by the US whistleblower Edward Snowden. Miranda was the partner of former *Guardian* journalist Glenn Greenwald who had helped expose Snowden's revelations. The Court of Appeal held Miranda's detention lawful but the clause under which he was held as incompatible with the European Convention on Human Rights (ECHR). Lord Dyson, who made the ruling with Richards and Floyd LJJ, said the powers contained in Schedule 7 of the Terrorism Act 2000 were flawed.

The *Miranda* ruling was seen as an indisputable victory for press freedom. The CA balanced the needs of security and the rights of journalists, that police anti-terror powers to stop and question travellers in and out of the UK were incompatible with Article 10 rights; furthermore, that Mr Miranda should have had the protection of a public interest defence against his detention.

---

249 For a detailed discussion see: Wilkinson, N. (2015).
250 On 11 September 2001, 19 militants associated with the Islamic extremist group Al Qaeda hijacked four airliners and carried out suicide attacks against targets in the United States. Two of the planes were flown into the towers of the World Trade Center in New York City, a third plane hit the Pentagon just outside Washington DC, and the fourth plane crashed in a field in Pennsylvania.
251 On 7 July 2005, four suicide bombers with rucksacks full of explosives attacked central London, killing 52 people and injuring hundreds more. The bombers, Mohammad Sidique Khan (30), Shehzad Tanweer (22) and Hasib Hussain (18), all from West Yorkshire, and Germaine Lindsay (19), detonated four devices. Three of the four bombs went off just before 08:50 BST on Tube trains that had departed King's Cross. The fourth bombing took place at 09:47 BST on the number 30 double-decker bus in Tavistock Square, not far from King's Cross. In total, 52 people were killed and more than 770 injured.
252 See: R (on the application of Miranda [David]) v (1) Secretary of State for the Home Department (2) Commissioner of Police of the Metropolis [2016] EWCA Civ 6 (CA Civ Div) 19 January 2016.

8.7.1 Crown Privilege and Public Interest Immunity

The UK legislation on 'Crown Privilege' – which later became Public Interest Immunity (or PII) – was largely developed in civil cases, dating back to both world wars (see: *Conway v Rimmer* (1968);[253] *Burmah Oil v Bank of England* (1980);[254] *Air Canada v Secretary of State for Trade (No 2)* (1983)[255]).

PII is a common law rule of evidence, meaning that documents may be withheld from parties to legal proceedings when their disclosure would be injurious to the public interest (i.e. national security). PII applications are routinely made and authorized by a Minster of State – such as the Home Secretary or Secretary of State for Justice and Lord Chancellor (a combined position).

In the World War II case of *Duncan v Cammell Laird*,[256] involving the *Thetis* submarine disaster, documents were requested, including blueprints of the submarine. The HL unanimously agreed that a court could never question a claim of 'Crown Privilege' made in the proper form regardless of the nature of the documents to which it referred. It was held that ministers of the Crown were to be the sole arbiters of the public interest. The case attracted considerable criticism in Parliament at the time (see also: *Glasgow Corporation v Central Land Board* (1956)[257] and the Burmah Oil case (1980)[258]).

In highly sensitive cases the prosecution will apply for a PII certificate where the prosecution contends that it is not in the public interest to disclose any sensitive material. The PII application must state why the material should be withheld, i.e. why the public interest in withholding it outweighs the public interest in disclosure.

The courts' current view of PII claims remains complex. Ministers have claimed on a number of occasions that where disclosure is imperative in the interests of justice, claims that documents be withheld on the ground that their disclosure would inhibit candour of communication are unlikely to succeed. Well-supported claims for immunity on class grounds are likely to be respected, but no class of document is automatically immune from disclosure.

The shortcomings of this unsatisfactory regime were vividly exposed by the CA's groundbreaking decision in the *Judith Ward* case.[259] The effect of Ward's miscarriage of justice was to require the prosecution, if it sought to claim PII for documents helpful to the defence, to give notice of the claim to the defence so that, if necessary, the court could be asked to rule on the legitimacy of the prosecution's asserted claim.[260] The procedural implications of the *Ward* judgment were refined by the CA in *R v Davis* (1993)[261] and *R v Keane* (1994).[262]

8.7.2 Secret trials and 'closed material procedures'

Powers to hold secret court hearings were introduced in July 2013 under section 61 of the Justice and Security Act 2013 (JSA) (known commonly as the 'the Secret Courts Act'), so that trials can take place in civil courts without damaging national security.

Part 1 of the Act provides for oversight of the UK security services, the Secret Intelligence Service, the Government Communications Headquarters (GCHQ) and other activities relating to intelligence or security matters, including the parliamentary 'Intelligence and Security Committee'.

---

253 [1968] AC 910.
254 [1980] AC 1090.
255 [1983] 2 AC 394.
256 [1942] AC 624.
257 [1956] SC 1 (HL) – when the HL held that the Scottish courts could go behind a minister's certificate and, after weighing private interests against public ones, decide for themselves whether or not a particular item of evidence should attract immunity on public interest grounds.
258 [1980] AC 1090.
259 *R v Ward* [1993] 1 WLR 619. Ward (25) was convicted to life imprisonment for killing 12 people aboard an army coach which exploded on the M62 motorway in February 1973. Judith Ward spent 18 years in prison before her conviction was quashed in 1992. For a detailed discussion see: Walker, C. and Starmer, K. (1999); see also: Mansfield, M. (2010).
260 See: Ward, J. (1993).
261 [1993] 1 WLR 613.
262 [1994] 1 WLR 746.

Part 2 – the most controversial provision of the 2013 Act – makes provision for the 'closed material procedure' (CMP) involving the (non-) disclosure of sensitive material in trial proceedings.

An application for CMP proceedings is usually made by the Secretary of State in civil proceedings.[263] The High Court (or High Court of Session in Scotland) then makes a declaration – an 'in principle' decision – whether or not a CMP should be available in the case. An application for a declaration is usually supported by some (but not necessarily all) of the relevant sensitive material.[264] A Special Advocate is appointed by the court to represent the interests of the claimant.[265] But the advocate cannot reveal precise details of the evidence held against the claimant; the advocate can only provide the 'gist' of the allegations against the claimant, which means, once the matter comes to criminal proceedings, the claimant may not be aware of all the allegations made against him.

The Ministry of Justice reported in 2015 that the number of secret court hearing applications and CMPs had more than doubled. In the year 2013–2014, there were five secret court hearings; over the same period in 2014, there were 11. Although relatively small in number, the cases include some of the most politically sensitive cases heard in UK courts.[266]

One such application involved 'IRA mole', Martin McGartland[267] (who now has a new identity), who, together with his partner and carer Joanne Asher, was suing MI5 for breach of contract and negligence in his aftercare following a shooting by the IRA which left him unable to work. The Home Secretary, Theresa May, had applied for a declaration under CMP that her lawyers should be allowed to give evidence in secret to defend the damages claim in the High Court.[268] The former undercover agent of the Royal Ulster Constabulary (RUC) Special Branch (1987 and 1991) claimed the MI5 security service failed to provide care for his post-traumatic stress disorder and access to disability benefits.[269]

Three Court of Appeal justices unanimously agreed that secret hearings are lawful, provided they are 'scrutinised with care' and discontinued if they become 'no longer in the interests of the fair and effective administration of justice'.[270] A second application, heard at the same time, was that of *Ahmad Sarkandi*[271] and four other Iranians, subject to asset-freezing orders, who sued Foreign Secretary, Philip Hammond, for damages under the HRA 1998. The *McGartland* ruling enabled government ministers to defend themselves against damages claims (under CMP) while using secret hearings to prevent sensitive material being revealed in evidence in open court. Critics have condemned the ruling as a serious aberration from the tradition of open justice (see also: *Al Rawi v Security Service* (2012)[272]).

IRA and Al Qaeda related terrorism cases are now regularly heard in secret. PII and CMP hearings usually cite the safeguarding of national security as a precautionary approach. In the deportation case, *Secretary of State for the Home Department v Rehman* (2001),[273] Lord Slynn held that such decisions are primarily ones for the discretion of the Secretary of State.[274]

---

263 Section 6 Justice and Security Act 2013 (JSA).
264 Section 12(1) JSA.
265 Section 11 (4) JSA.
266 Source: Ministry of Justice (2015b) Report on use of closed material procedure (from 25 June 2014 to 24 June 2015). October 2015 at: www.gov.uk/government/uploads/system/uploads/attachment_data/file/468375/closed-material-procedure-report-2015.PDF.
267 See: *McGartland (Martin) and Asher (Joanne) v Secretary of State for the Home Department* [2015] EWCA Civ 686, 14 July 2015 (CA).
268 See: *McGartland (Martin) v British Security Service (MI5)* High Court of Justice, London, 19 June 2014 (unreported) (Mitting J).
269 See: McGartland, M. (2009).
270 See: *McGartland* [2015] EWCA Civ 686 at para. 10. Section 7 JSA provides for a s 6 JSA declaration to be kept under review and to be revoked where appropriate (Richards LJ, Lewison LJ and McCombe LJ).
271 See: *R (on the application of Sarkandi and Others) v Secretary of State for Foreign and Commonwealth Affairs* (Case No T3/2014/2545) EWCA Civ 686, 14 July 2015 (CA).
272 [2012] 1 AC 53 (HL).
273 [2001] UKHL 47 (HL).
274 Ibid., at para. 8 (Lord Slynn).

The leading case in common law in advance of security and terrorism legislation, was that of *Chahal* (1996).[275] It involved the deportation of a Sikh separatist, Karamjit Singh Chahal (born 1948), back to India for national security reasons; he had entered the UK illegally in 1971 (the Home Office granted him leave to remain in 1974). Chahal was held in Bedford Prison from 1990 for deportation. He argued violation of his Article 3 ECHR right, that he would face torture at the hands of the Indian authorities. Though there was no question of secret evidence being used against him, the High Court simply could not look at the material that the Home Secretary had used as the basis for his deportation order before the 'three wise men' – Special Immigration Appeals Commission ('SIAC').[276] The Strasbourg Human Rights Court unanimously upheld Mr Chahal's complaint; not only was there a real risk of torture once he was returned to India, but also a breach of procedure under Article 5(4) ECHR because he could not challenge the secret evidence against him[277] (see also: *A and others v Secretary of State for the Home Department* (2004)[278]).

Closed hearings are now widespread. They are both *ex parte* and *in camera*, where the court considers closed or secret evidence laid by the security services. Closed hearings involve the exclusion of one party, as well as members of the public and the press. It is known that defendants in terrorism trials have been convicted on the basis of 'secret evidence'; that is, evidence from anonymous witnesses. Secret evidence can now be used in a wide range of cases, including deportation hearings, parole board cases, asset-freezing applications, pre-charge detention hearings in terrorism cases, employment tribunals and even planning tribunals. The essential test of whether a case involves secret evidence or not is whether both parties have seen and had an equal opportunity to challenge all the evidence that is considered by the court in making its decision.[279] So long as the defendant has disclosure of all the evidence that is used by the court, then no question of the use of secret evidence arises.[280]

In *Re Guardian News and Media Ltd* (2010),[281] the press and other media organizations made an application for open reporting on appeals involving five individuals. Four of them, A, K, M and G, were appellants; the fifth, HAY, was the respondent and cross-appellant in an appeal by the Treasury. The Supreme Court set aside the anonymity order in the case of G, naming him as Mohammed al-Ghabra (his identity was already in the public domain). A, K and M, all brothers, had been informed on 2 August 2007 that they were all subject to an asset-freezing order.[282]

HAY was concerned that his identification would lead to the jigsaw identification of his wife and children, who would suffer adverse consequences from the Egyptian authorities. *The Guardian* argued that articles about him had appeared in the press and Al-Jazeera broadcasts since 1999 (referring to *Youssef v Home Office* (2004),[283] which contained details about him). M's identity was kept anonymized. Lord Rodger, in delivering the Supreme Court judgment, concluded that there was no justification for making an anonymity order in HAY's case and he was duly named as Mr Hani El Sayed Sabaei Youssef (or Hani al-Seba'i).

The approach in *Re Guardian News and Media Ltd* was encouraging: it meant that open reporting in sensitive terrorism trials, including asset-freezing orders, could inform the public regarding

---

275 *Chahal and Others v UK* (1996) 23 EHRR 413 (ECtHR). The second applicant, Darshan Kaur Chahal (born 1956), living in Luton, came to England on 12 September 1975, following her marriage to the first applicant in India. The applicant couple had two children, Kiranpreet Kaur Chahal (born in 1977) and Bikaramjit Singh Chahal (born in 1978), who were the third and fourth applicants. By virtue of their birth in the UK, the two children had British nationality.

276 Under s 15 Immigration Act 1971.

277 *Chahal* (1996) 23 EHRR 413 at paras 130–131.

278 [2004] UKHL 56 (HL).

279 See: s 3(1)(a) Criminal Procedure and Investigations Act 1996 (as amended by s 32 Criminal Justice Act 2003): the prosecution must disclose any material 'which might reasonably be considered capable of undermining the case for the prosecution against the accused or of assisting the case for the accused'.

280 See: *Secretary of State for the Home Department v AHK and others* [2009] EWCA Civ 287 (as per Clarke MR).

281 *Guardian News and Media Ltd and others in Her Majesty's Treasury v Mohammed Jabar Ahmed and others* (FC); also cited as: *HM Treasury v Mohammed al-Ghabra* (FC); *R (on the application of Hani El Sayed Sabaei Youssef) v HM Treasury* [2010] UKSC 1 of 27 January 2010.

282 Under Article 4 Terrorism (United Nations Measures) Order 2006.

283 [2004] EWHC 1884 (QB).

the complexity of terrorism trials. It would also encourage a wider debate about state funding of terrorism. M was eventually named as Michael Marteen (formerly known as Mohammed Tunveer Ahmed) (see also: *A v UK* (2009);[284] *Secretary of State for the Home Department v AF and others* (2009);[285] *Secretary of State for the Home Department v AHK* (2009)[286]).

In 2009 the UK Treasury passed secondary legislation under the Counter-Terrorism Act 2008, namely the Financial Restrictions (Iran) Order 2009. The main purpose of the order was to shut down the UK operations of Bank Mellat[287] and its subsidiaries. Bank Mellat applied to the High Court in London to set the order aside.[288] Some of the evidence in court was heard 'in secret' because the UK government had suspected that the Tehran-based bank had financed firms involved in Iran's nuclear programme since 2009.

In *Bank Mellat*,[289] the appeal before the Supreme Court was primarily concerned with the use of a closed material procedure (CMP) where the Treasury argued that the evidential material was so sensitive that it required the court to sit in a closed hearing. The Supreme Court allowed the bank's appeal, and thereby quashed the Iran bank sanctions. The court criticized the secret hearings. Lord Neuberger commented on the use of closed material procedures:

> A [closed hearing] should be resorted to only where it has been convincingly demonstrated to be genuinely necessary in the interests of justice. If the court strongly suspects that nothing in the closed material is likely to affect the outcome of the appeal, it should not order a closed hearing.[290]

The ruling in *Bank Mellat* was seen as a severe setback for the government's enthusiasm for secret courts.

One of the most secret trials in UK legal history is that of London law student, *Erol Incedal* (2016),[291] a British citizen also holding a Turkish residency permit. Known initially only as 'AB', he and his friend, Mounir Rarmoul-Bouhadjar ('CD'), were charged with planning terrorism offences.[292] Nicol J ruled on 19 May 2014 that the entirety of the criminal trial of both defendants should be in private and the publication of reports of the trial be prohibited.[293] But following a partly successful appeal by *The Guardian* and other media organizations to lift the injunctions and anonymity orders, the CA allowed for limited reporting of proceedings and the identification of both defendants.

Incedal and Rarmoul-Bouhadjar's trial went ahead at the Old Bailey ('Central Criminal Court', London). Only accredited journalists were allowed to hear some of the secret evidence in locked sessions; their notebooks were retained by the court and they could not write about the trial. More than a third of the prosecution case was held in complete secrecy with the jury told they could face

---

284 (2009) Application No 3455/05 [GC], judgment of 19 February 2009 (ECHR).
285 [2009] UKHL 28.
286 [2009] EWCA Civ 287.
287 Bank Mellat (بانک ملت, lit. People's Bank) is a private Iranian bank, established in 1980, with a paid capital of Rials 33.5 billion as a merger of ten pre-revolution private banks, comprising Tehran, Dariush, Pars, Etebarat Taavoni & Tozie, Iran & Arab, Bein-al-melalie-Iran, Omran, Bimeh Iran, Tejarat Khareji Iran and Farhangian. The bank's capital amounted to Rials 13,100 billion (July 2016), one of the largest commercial banks in the Islamic Republic of Iran, ranking among the top 1,000 banks of the world.
288 Under s 63 Counter-Terrorism Act 2008.
289 *Bank Mellat v Her Majesty's Treasury (No 1)* [2013] UKSC 38 (on appeal from: [2011] EWCA Civ 1).
290 Ibid., judgment at paras 119, 126, 133, 173 (Lord Neuberger).
291 See: *Guardian News and Media Ltd and Ors v R and Erol Incedal* [2016] EWCA Crim 11 (CA Crim Div) 9 February 2016 ('Erol Incedal' case) (on appeal from: *Guardian News and Media Ltd; Associated Newspapers Ltd; BBC; BSkyB Ltd; Express Newspapers; Independent Print Ltd; ITN; Mirror Group Newspapers Ltd; News Group Newspapers Ltd; Telegraph Media Group; Times Newspapers Ltd; Press Association v Erol Incedal and Mounir Rarmoul-Bouhadjar* [2014] EWCA Crim 1861 (Case No T2013/7502) 24 September 2014 (formerly known as *R v AB and CD*) (Gross LJ, Simon and Burnett JJ).
292 Charged under s 5 Terrorism Act 2006 ('preparation of terrorist acts') and an offence contrary to s 58 Terrorism Act 2000 ('collection of information').
293 See: *Erol Incedal* [2014] EWCA Crim 1861.

imprisonment under 'contempt' legislation if they ever revealed what they had heard. Part of the evidence alleged that Incedal had planned an attack on Tony or Cherie Blair and that he had been involved in the terrorism attack on the Taj Hotel in Mumbai on 28 November 2008. The jury failed to reach a verdict on Incedal. After a retrial in October 2015, a second jury acquitted him of all charges. Rarmoul-Bouhadjar pleaded guilty to possessing a 'terrorism' manual – identical to that found on Incedal. He was sentenced to three years' imprisonment.

The CA in *Incedal* (2016) set the precedent for a fundamental departure from the principle of open justice, whereby secret courts and CMP were held as 'strictly necessary' in terrorism cases. This meant that any public accountability for matters relating to the prosecution could not be achieved through the media in its function as 'watchdog' of the public interest.

We can then conclude that any issues relating to terrorism offences will in future be tried in secret courts, leaving the evidence by the intelligence and security services unchallenged and unreported.

 FOR THOUGHT

You are representing an Indian citizen with residency in the UK. Your client supports the campaign for an independent Sikh state in the Punjab. The Home Secretary wishes to deport Mr Ravinder Singh to India because she claims that his support for Sikh independence and his past known activities mean that he is a serious threat to national security in the UK, particularly given the current concerns over terrorist activity. Mr Singh tells you that he will be tortured if returned to India. He also fears for his wife and two children who live with him in Southall. On his last return to India some six years ago, he was arrested and detained by the Punjab police for 21 days. During this time your client was kept handcuffed in terrible conditions, beaten until unconscious, electrocuted on various parts of his body and subjected to a mock execution. Later on he was released without charge. Make an application to the High Court opposing your client's deportation.

8.7.3 Increased investigatory powers legislation

The Data Retention and Investigatory Powers Act 2014 (DRIPA) – introduced by then Home Secretary, Theresa May in July 2014 – required internet and phone companies to keep their communications data for a year and regulated how police and intelligence agencies gained access to personal data. DRIPA consolidated interception powers that existed under the Regulation of Investigatory Powers Act 2000 (RIPA) and Wireless Telegraphy Act 2006.[294] The new legislation followed the recommendations in the David Anderson Report of Britain's anti-terrorist legislation.[295]

In July 2015 Tom Watson MP (Labour) and David Davis MP (Conservative) successfully challenged the lawfulness of DRIPA in that it was inconsistent with EU law.[296] They had argued that the legislation was incompatible with Article 8 ECHR ('right to privacy') and Articles 7 and 8 of the EU Charter of Fundamental Rights ('respect for private and family life' and 'protection of personal

---

294 The Act also provided for secondary legislation to replace the Data Retention (EC Directive) Regulations 2009 while providing additional safeguards. This was in response to the ECJ judgment of 8 April 2014 (Grand Chamber) in joined cases *Digital Rights Ireland Ltd v Minister for Communications, Marine and Natural Resources, Minister for Justice, Equality and Law Reform, The Commissioner of the Garda Síochána, Ireland and the Attorney General* (C-293/12) and *Kärntner Landesregierung, Michael Seitlinger, Christof Tschohl and Others* (C-594/12) ('Digital Rights Ireland' case), which declared the Data Retention Directive (2006/24/EC) invalid.
295 See: Independent review of British Terrorism Legislation by David Anderson QC at: https://terrorismlegislationreviewer.independent. gov.uk.
296 See: *R (on the application of (1) David Davis MP (2) Tom Watson MP (3) Peter Brice (4) Geoffrey Lewis) v Secretary of State for the Home Department and Open Rights Group; Privacy International; The Law Society of England and Wales* [2015] EWHC 2092 (Admin) High Court of Justice, 17 July 2015 (QB).

data'). Davis and Watson said that DRIPA had allowed the police and security services to 'snoop' on citizens without sufficient privacy safeguards.

The High Court ruling declared section 1(a) and (b) of DRIPA inconsistent with EU law.[297] The unlawful sections remained in force until the end of March 2016. DRIPA remained in force until December 2016.

Following the *Davis and Watson* ruling Theresa May introduced the Investigatory Powers Bill (known as 'the Snoopers' Charter') (now the Investigatory Powers Act 2016). The Act provides the framework to govern the use and oversight of investigatory powers by law enforcement and the security and intelligence agencies. A controversial measure of the Act is that internet service providers (ISPs) are forced to store personal browsing records for 12 months and allows bulk collection of internet traffic.

There are three main measures in the Investigatory Powers Act 2016:

1. The powers already available to law enforcement, security and intelligence agencies are brought together in the Act to facilitate data collection and personal communications data in bulk form.
2. It introduces a 'double-lock' safeguard for interception warrants: the warrant has to have the Secretary of State's authorization as well as a judge's approval.
3. Provision for the retention of internet connection records for law enforcement to identify the communications service to which a device has connected.

During the passing of the bill, Google, Facebook and Apple had written to the Parliamentary Select Committee to highlight potential conflict of laws (with US legislation) under which Britain might oblige them to hand over data about their clients even when another country expressly prohibited this.[298] Another concern was how GCHQ's intelligence capabilities could be protected from legal challenges in the Court of Justice in Luxembourg and the Human Rights Court in Strasbourg. The biggest objection to the 2016 Act is that it provides GCHQ with unlimited powers to 'investigate' without adequate control mechanisms for the executive. The Investigatory Powers Bill returned to the House of Lords in November 2016.

 CASE STUDY

The use of 'bulk powers'

A group of terrorists are planning a firearms-based attack in the UK. The group has links to known terrorists overseas and as such the threat which they pose is credible. Close monitoring of the group by the police and intelligence agencies is necessary to ensure that their plans can be disrupted. The ability to access communications data in bulk is therefore critical to averting this plot. You act as Government lawyer and have to advise the intelligence and security agencies as well as GCHQ to obtain identifying details for members of the group without the need to resort to intrusive powers and making the terrorists aware that they are being monitored in order to avert the attack. How would you use legislation in your advice?

---

297 *Davis and Watson* [2015] EWHC 2092 (Admin) at para. 114 (Bean LJ and Collins J).
298 See: Joint Committee on the Draft Investigatory Powers Bill at: www.parliament.uk/draft-investigatory-powers.

8.7.4 Summary and conclusion

The imposition of increasing reporting restrictions on court proceedings and secret courts closed to the public and the media amounts to a potential breach of freedom of expression (Article 10 ECHR) and also infringes the open justice principle.

In an age when press freedom and freedom of information are well enshrined in human rights and UK law, there are many who say that any future legislation ought to push for even more openness in the court process. Anything that is done which fetters that freedom should be resisted. The Lord Chief Justice, Lord Thomas of Cwmgiedd, lamented that there is now unprecedented courtroom secrecy due to frequent representations by security agencies to the Director of Public Prosecutions (DPP) for proceedings to be held in private. The Lord Chief Justice said that this interferes with the open justice principle and is a matter of constitutional concern.[299]

8.8 Further reading

Blom-Cooper, L. (2008) 'Press freedom: constitutional right or cultural assumption?',
Public Law, Summer, 260–276.
Louis Blom-Cooper explores the notion of press freedom by stating that the open justice system should prevail and that it is a citizen's right to freely and publicly criticize the executive and legislature. Sir Louis then develops the argument whether it is right that any court proceedings should be kept secret, wondering whether it is not the journalist's careful reporting on such proceedings which opens up the justice system to the public. The author also discusses the Leveson Report.

Jaconelli, J. (2002) *Open Justice: A critique of the public trial*. Oxford: Oxford University Press.
In this topical study, Joseph Jaconelli explores the issues of open justice and the rise of the 'modern media'. He discusses high-profile media reporting of cases which – the author argues – has led to prejudice of potential jurors and witnesses in criminal cases.

Smartt, U. (2015b) "Why I was right to name the teachers' teen killer": naming teenagers in criminal trials and law reform in the internet age', *Communications Law*, 20(1), 5–13.
The author of this book discusses existing (and at times confusing) legislation regarding reporting restrictions on children and young persons in criminal court proceedings. She compares the media coverage on Will Cornick with that of the Jamie Bulger killers, Venables and Thompson, and asks whether the public interest test is now overriding youth anonymity orders?

Walker, C. and Starmer, K. (1999) *Miscarriages of Justice: A review of justice in error*. London: Blackstone Press.
This remains *the* seminal text on miscarriages of justice. The authors discuss in detail the Guildford Four, Birmingham Six, Judith Ward and Tottenham Three cases and how the accused, most of them already serving long prison sentences, were eventually released and the various police services discredited. The authors chart in detail many disturbing features of how the police obtained confessions by unacceptable means, how evidence was fabricated or withheld and how serious failures of disclosure of police evidence led to adverse prosecutions.

Wilkinson, N. (2015) *Secrecy and the Media: The Official History of the United Kingdom's D-Notice System*. Abingdon, Oxon: Routledge.
In his important and very readable book about the official history of the D notice system, retired Rear Admiral Nicholas Wilkinson explains that the Defence-notice system 'emerged amorphously across three decades of increasing concern about army and navy operations being compromised by reports in the British (and sometimes foreign) press' (Preface, xxi). It is rather ironic that Wilkinson book was itself subject to censorship by MI5, MI6 and GCHQ; the

---

299 See: Judicial College (2015), pp. 3–5 (Lord Thomas LCJ).

Foreign, Cabinet, and Home Offices; the Treasury Solicitor and the Attorney General. The book was eventually published in 2009 without five chapters covering the period after Labour's return to power in 1997. Wilkinson provides an historical overview of spying, intelligence, secrecy and government–news media interaction over the course of almost the entirety of the twentieth century, starting with the Boer Wars – the conflicts between Britain and Afrikaaner settlers that determined the fate of Southern Africa.

Chapter 9

Intellectual property and entertainment law

Key points

This chapter will cover the following questions:

- What is intellectual property law?
- What constitutes copyright under the Copyright, Designs and Patents Act 1988 (CDPA)?
- How do durations of copyright differ?
- What are the remedies for copyright infringement?
- What is the purpose and function of the Berne Convention and the WIPO Copyright Treaties in relation to the promotion of creative works across the world?
- How far has EU intellectual property legislation harmonized IP rights within all Member States?
- What amounts to 'passing off'?
- What is music piracy?
- What constitutes 'fair use' in music downloads?
- How far is peer-to-peer (P2P) filesharing 'legal'?
- How have public performance rights changed?
- What do music collecting societies do?

9.1 Overview

Intellectual property (IP) law includes copyright, patents, trademarks and industrial design rights. IP rights are like any other property right; they allow creators, or owners of patents, trademarks or copyrighted works to benefit from their own intellectual work in the form of royalties and earned recognition from what they have invented or created. Some IP rights are automatic; some have to be registered such as patents and trade marks.

IP rights also contain rights to freedom of expression which need to be protected by robust legislation in order for law enforcement agencies to adequately act on copyright theft, piracy and trade mark infringement. Much of what businesses are often seeking to protect is not covered by IP rights, but is instead a concept, idea or know-how. The only way to protect such information is through the law of confidentiality, often by using a non-disclosure agreement (NDA) or contract. But once information is in the public domain (for example once a business has launched and its concept is revealed), an NDA will prove very difficult to enforce.

This chapter examines some of these conflicts in a European legal context. By striking the right balance between the interests of innovators and the wider public interest, the IP system aims to foster an environment in which creativity and innovation can flourish.

However, globalization has enabled counterfeiters to copy luxury goods and fake copies of brands such as Apple's iPhone, Louis Vuitton, Sephora, Christian Dior or Hennessy have become a major headache for these retailers. It is quite common now to buy 'rip offs' on internet shopping platforms such as Alibaba or eBay.

Film piracy is said to have cost the UK economy about £800 million in lost revenues from fake DVD sales and illegal downloads in 2015, though some empirical studies in this area indicate this is not the case and dispute such figures.[1] Since the film industry is a significant contributor to the UK's

---

1   See: Oberholzer-Gee, F. and Strumpf, K. (2005); see also: Fohl, K. (2009).

economy, such a drain on growth is clear copyright theft, making copyright enforcement one of the most challenging areas for law enforcement agencies. According to piracy tracking firm *Excipio*, which monitors illegal activities, the most pirated films in 2015 were also the biggest blockbusters at the box office, such as *Interstellar* (47 million downloads) *Furious 7*, *Avengers: Age of Ultron* and *Jurassic World*. In 2014 it was *The Wolf of Wall Street* with 30 million downloads.[2]

This chapter cannot possibly mention all the IP law suits that are reported daily in UK and international law reports; some make more headlines than others. In January 2015, pop star Rihanna won her trade mark battle against Topshop. The high street store had sold RiRi's 'tank' sleeveless T-shirt without her permission. Kitchin LJ held that the use of her image was damaging to the star's 'goodwill' and represented loss of control over her reputation in the 'fashion sphere'.

New Balance filed a lawsuit against Karl Lagerfeld in 2014 for copyright infringement over claims the designer had 'ripped off' the brand's trademark trainer logo.

This chapter focuses firstly on copyright law with examples from the entertainment industry. Copyright law has two basic functions, a property function and an authenticity function, both seeking to establish who is the author of a work. This means that a person who creates, produces or invests in an original creative work should be the one who receives the rewards in the form of accreditation, payment or royalties; in other words, that this person be recognized as the original rights or copyright owner. Copyright provides that the rights holder determines whether and how copying, distributing, broadcasting and other uses of his work takes place.

The emergence of online music distribution services – such as Amazon's Cloud Player and iTunes, as well as internet radio and free digital services such as Spotify or Pandora – have created challenges for the music industry and the various royalty-collecting and performance rights societies. This chapter looks at a number of copyright challenges in the music industry, such as those of Led Zeppelin and Procol Harum. We will focus on the duration of copyright, including the extended music performance rights from 50 years to 70 years (so-called 'Cliff's law' named after its most ardent campaigner Sir Cliff Richard).

The chapter closes with a look at performing rights' societies and collection agencies that act on behalf of artists and songwriters by collecting their royalties and promoting economic rights of creators in the music and entertainment industries.

9.2 Introduction to intellectual property

See below 9.6

The importance of intellectual property (IP) was first recognized in the Paris Convention for the Protection of Industrial Property (1883) and the Berne Convention for the Protection of Literary and Artistic Works (1886).

IP refers to creations of the mind, such as inventions, literary and artistic works, designs and symbols, names and images used in commerce. The basic idea behind IP is to ensure that a work is not copied or used without permission and to protect the economic rewards ('royalties') of the creators and authors of the works. IP is something unique which is physically created by the 'author', 'creator' or inventor. An idea alone is not IP. For example, an idea for a book does not count, but the words written down do count.

A person will usually not own the IP right for something he has created as part of his work while being employed by someone else (though this tends to be a cause for dispute). IP can have more than one owner or belong to more than one person or business and can be sold ('assigned') or transferred ('licensed').

---

2   Source: 'Top 10 Pirated Movies of 2015' by Andrew Wallenstein, *Variety*, 27 December 2015 at: http://variety.com/t/excipio.

9.2.1 Types of IP protection

See below
9.6.3

The type of protection depends on what has been created. Some IP rights are automatically pro-tected the minute they are created, written down or recorded in physical form; others have to be applied for or registered, such as a trade mark or patent. There is no register of copyright works in the UK (unlike in the USA) – though some authors simply use the copyright symbol (©) to mark their work together with their name and the year of creation. Copyright is also automatically pro-tected in most countries since copyright is territorial in nature.

Automatic protection	
Type of protection	*Examples of intellectual property*
Copyright	Writing and literary works, art, photography, films, TV, music, web content, sound recordings
Design right	Shapes of objects
Protection you have to apply for	
Type of protection	*Examples of intellectual property (time to allow for application)*
Trade marks	Product names, logos, jingles (four months)
Registered designs	Appearance of a product including, shape, packaging, patterns, colours, decoration (one month)
Patents	Inventions and products, e.g. machines and machine parts, tools, medicines (approx. five years)

9.3 Copyright and its historical origins

The 'right to copy' introduced by the Statute of Anne 1710[3] came after nearly three centuries of print technology, during which time monarchs and the Stationers' Company had the right to censor radical literature. The statute introduced the principle of a fixed term of protection.[4] The Statute of Anne provided the conceptual skeleton for copyright law for centuries to come, with economic consequences, affirmed by the House of Lords in *Donaldson v Becket* (1774).[5]

The Scottish case of *Caird v Sime* (1887)[6] established the right of a professor to restrain the publication of lectures orally delivered in his classroom. This case established that the law of property exists in intangible works, such as literature, songs or lectures, irrespective of implied contract or breach of duty.

The HL held in *Walter v Lane* (1900)[7] that copyright subsisted in reports prepared by shorthand writers of *The Times* of public speeches as 'original literary' works. A speech and a report of a speech were therefore held to be two different things. Lord Rosebery was the author of his speeches. The shorthand reporters were the authors of their reports of Rosebery's speeches, because they spent effort, skill and time in writing up their reports of these speeches that they themselves had not written. This is still known as the 'sweat of the brow' doctrine in copyright law, meaning that an author gains rights through simple diligence during the creation of a work.

Walter v Lane is still good law and was confirmed in *Express Newspapers v News* (UK) (1990)[8] and *Sawkins v Hyperion Records Ltd* (2005)[9]

The Copyright Act 1956 introduced no substantive amendments to the 1911 Act, but was significant for the development of the phonogram (record) industry. Most importantly, the 1956 Act extended copyright to sound recordings, cinematographic works (films) and broadcasts. As well as record producers, there were other entrepreneur investors in the phonogram, entertainment and film industry who were now going to be protected under the 1956 Act.

9.3.1 Copyright development in common law

Copyright protects form or expression, but the courts have drawn a limit when it comes to protection of ideas. This was highlighted in the *Rock Follies (Fraser)* case (1983).[10] In this case three female claimants had formed a rock group. Together with their composer and manager, they had developed an idea for a TV series – *Rock Follies*.[11] One of the group, with the consent of the other two, communicated her idea for a TV series in *confidence* to a scriptwriter who then approached the Head of Drama for Thames Television for a possible series. Most importantly, the original rock group members wanted to appear as themselves on TV. Thames Television paid £500 for the rights provided by an option agreement. However *Rock Follies* was produced with other actresses and the real pop group's claimants sued in breach of contract, copyright and confidence.

The CA held in *Fraser* that failure on behalf of Thames TV to offer the rock group claimants parts in the series amounted to breach of contract. There was also a breach of confidence in relation to the idea. On that basis Fraser and the other claimants had brought themselves within

---

3 8 Anne (c. 19), with the full title as 'An Act for the Encouragement of Learning, by vesting the Copies of Printed Books in the Authors or purchasers of such Copies, during the times therein mentioned.'
4 For further discussion see: Baloch, T. A. (2007).
5 (1774) 2 Bro PC 129 (HL).
6 (1887) LR 12 App Cas 326 (HL).
7 [1900] AC 539 (HL).
8 [1990] 1 WLR 1320 (Sir Nicolas Browne-Wilkinson VC).
9 [2005] EWCA Civ 565.
10 See: *Fraser v Thames TV* [1983] 1 QB 44 (the *Rock Follies* case).
11 A 1970s TV cult series, written by Howard Schuman, with music from Andy Mackay, starring Charlotte Cornwell, Julie Covington and Rula Lenska in the title roles.

the requirements of 'breach of confidence' (but not copyright) and were entitled to damages for breach of confidence.

Hirst J's ruling in *Fraser* was applied in *De Maudsley v Palumbo* (1996).[12] This case concerned the idea for a new style all-night nightclub. James (now Lord) Palumbo had offered funding and the idea was subsequently developed by him into what became 'The Ministry of Sound' with a 24-hour licence amid the new wave of dance music. The nightclub opened without the involvement of De Maudsley (the claimant), who saw himself either as shareholder or as part-owner of the company. Since this did not happen, De Maudsley claimed breach of contract and breach of confidence.[13] The CA dismissed the action, applying Hirst J's points made in the *Rock Follies* (*Fraser*) case that there was no significant element of originality and the idea of a 'round the clock' nightclub was not clearly identifiable. The idea was also not sufficiently developed to show some degree of attractiveness to the end-user; additionally, there had been no (written) agreement and no intention to create any legal relations between the parties.

9.4 The Copyright, Designs and Patents Act 1988

The purpose of the Copyright, Designs and Patents Act 1988 (CDPA – also known as the 'UK Copyright Act') (as amended numerous times, e.g. by the Copyright and Related Rights Regulations 2003)[14] is to protect the rights of creators to be paid for, and to control the use of, their works and to address the needs of users who want access to material protected by copyright. The creator's statutory rights are limited by 'exceptions' for the benefit of certain users (e.g. educational establishments, libraries, braille copies or copying for private use).

9.4.1 Categories covered by the Copyright, Designs and Patents Act 1988

The CDPA introduced an immediate copyright which exists automatically in original literary, dramatic, musical or artistic works.

'Literary work' means any work, other than a dramatic or musical work, which is written, spoken or sung, and accordingly includes tables, compilations, computer programmes and databases.[15] 'Dramatic work' includes dance or mime and 'musical work' means a work consisting of music, exclusive of any words or action intended to be sung, spoken or performed with the music.

See below
9.11

Copyright does not subsist in a literary, dramatic or musical work *unless* and until it is recorded, in writing or otherwise,[16] though not necessarily by the author – a recording of an extempore jazz performance at a pub if recorded by a drinker would vest musical copyright in members of the jazz band. 'Recorded' includes the digital medium, storage on a computer hard drive or memory stick, as well as digital music recordings.

Section 4(1)(a) CDPA provides that artistic works, including photographs, are protected as copyright works 'irrespective of artistic quality'.

See below
9.8

A copyright-protected work can have more than one copyright, or another intellectual property right, connected to it. For example, an album of music can have separate copyrights for individual songs, sound recordings, artwork, and so on. While copyright can protect the artwork of the album's logo, it could also be registered as a trade mark.

---

12 [1996] FSR 447.
13 For further discussion see: Carty, H. (2007).
14 The CDPA continues to be amended to implement EC Directives.
15 See: s 3(1) CDPA.
16 See: s 3(2) CDPA.

Immediate copyright subsists in:

- **Literary works**, including novels, instruction manuals, computer programs, song lyrics, newspaper articles.
- **Dramatic works**, including theatrical performances such as plays, pantomimes, musical scores used, scripts, stage directions, set design and ballet. In ballet, for instance, if the choreography of the dance has been recorded in writing or filmed, the dramatic performance of the dance itself can be entitled to copyright.
- **Musical works**, including compositions, opera, musicals. With a song there will usually be more than one copyright associated with it, i.e. the composer of the music is the 'author of the musical work' and has copyright in that music. The lyrics of a song are protected separately by copyright as a literary work. The person who writes the lyrics will own the copyright in the words. If the work is subsequently recorded, the sound recording will also have copyright protection: the producer of the recording will own the copyright in the sound recording. Composers of music may also have moral rights in their work.
- **Artistic works**, including paintings, engravings, photographs, sculptures, cartoons, collages, architecture, technical drawings, diagrams and maps.
- **Typographical arrangements** or **layouts** used to publish a work, such as a book.
- **Recordings** of a work, including sound and film.
- **Broadcasts, TV and films**, including the original screenplay, the music score of a film, and cable, wireless and satellite broadcasts. Films do not have to be original but they will not be new copyright works if they have been copied from existing films. Broadcasts do not have to be original, but there will be no copyright, if, or to the extent that, they infringe copyright[17] in another broadcast.
- **Databases and software**, e.g. computer programs and games; computer languages and codes; databases are usually collections of copyright works, such as a database of poetry.
- **Websites**, copyright applies to the internet in the same way as material in other media; e.g. any photographs posted on the internet are protected in the same way as other artistic works; any original written work will be protected as a 'literary' work.

Moral rights include that an author of a work has the right not to have his work subjected to derogatory treatment,[18] or to have the work falsely attributed to him.[19]

Software for computer games and the PlayStation are protected on the same basis as literary works under UK and EU copyright legislation. Many games developers have tried to establish generic copyrights for their games, some of which have succeeded, such as Wonderstruck, the developers for PS4 and PC gamers in their new creation of *Boundless*.[20] In December 2012, online retailer Amazon.com removed the e-book *Spots the Space Marine* by M. C. A. Hogarth at the request of Games Workshop, who claimed the use of the phrase 'space marine' infringed their trade mark. In February 2013, the argument received some publicity, with authors such as Cory

---

17 See: s 27 CDPA ('Meaning of "infringing copy"').
18 See: s 80(1) CDPA.
19 See: s 84(1) CDPA.
20 *Boundless* is the creation by development studio Wonderstruck (Guildford, UK), which at a glance looks like a hybrid between *Minecraft* and *LEGO* with blocky, over-animated environments that can be scaled and explored using a grapple at: http:// playboundless.com.

Doctorow, Charles Stross and John Scalzi supporting Hogarth; Amazon.com then restored the e-book for sale.[21]

9.4.2 Fundamental principles of the Copyright, Designs and Patents Act 1988

Copyright law is concerned primarily with authorship, ownership and originality. The fundamental principles are summarized in the following sections of the CDPA:

> Section 1(1): Copyright is a property right which subsists in accordance with this Part in the following descriptions of work –
>
> (a) original literary, dramatic, musical or artistic works . . .
>
> Section 2(1): The owner of a copyright in a work of any description has the exclusive right to do the acts specified in Chapter II as the acts restricted by the copyright in a work of that description.
>
> Section 4(1): In this part 'Artistic work' means (a) graphic work, photograph, sculpture or collage, irrespective of artistic quality.
>
> Section 9(1): In this part 'author' in relation to a work means the person who creates it.

When using and working with the CDPA it is important to consult secondary legislation in the form of the Copyright and Related Rights Regulations 2003, which updated the law in line with EU law and measures relating to the prevention of unauthorized use, extraction of contents of databases and the use of works published on the internet.

9.4.3 The protection of literary, dramatic, musical and artistic works and internet ownership

See below
9.6

Can a recording artist or publishing author protect his name, a song or title by copyright? It depends. Copyright may or may not be available for titles, slogans or logos, depending on whether they contain sufficient authorship. In most circumstances copyright does not protect names.

Does an artist or performer need to register his work or sound recording to be protected? Not really, because copyright protection is formality-free in countries party to the Berne Convention, which means that protection does not depend on compliance with any formalities such as registration or deposit of copies.

Under the CDPA 1988, a literary work is defined as 'any work, other than a dramatic or musical work, which is written, spoken or sung'.[22]

'Artistic works' can mean graphic work, a painting, drawing, map, engraving, etching, lithograph, woodcut or similar work, a photograph, sculpture or collage, a work of architecture, such as either a building or a model of a building, or a work of artistic craftsmanship – irrespective of artistic quality.[23] It is not an infringement of the copyright in a work to draw, take a photograph or make a film of, buildings or sculptures or works of artistic craftsmanship which are located in a public place or in premises open to the public. Copyright is not infringed in any material when it is used in legal proceedings.

The landmark case of *Grisbrook v MGN Ltd* (2009)[24] (see below) examined how far licence terms can be implied when technology has moved on beyond what the legislators of the UK Copyright Act initially intended or even imagined.

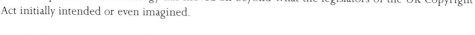

21 Source: "In the Future, All Space Marines Will Be Warhammer 40K Space Marines", The Art and Writing of M. C. A. Hogarth', 5 February 2013 – online at: http://mcahogarth.org/?p=10593.
22 For further discussion, see Gravells, N. P. (2007).
23 See: s 4 CDPA.
24 [2009] EWHC 2520 (Ch D).

Photographer Alan Grisbrook's work was first commissioned in 1981 to provide photographs for the Daily Mirror's 'Diary' page. For the next 16 years he supplied Mirror Group Newspapers (MGN) with hundreds of photographs, such as Ali MacGraw, Alan Bates and Sarah Miles, many of which made the front page. Mr Grisbrook claimed £161,238 in respect of the use of his photographs without his permission between 1982 and October 1997. The newspaper publishers had put his exclusive photos on the paper's website.

❖ KEY CASE   *Grisbrook v Mirror Group Newspapers Ltd* [2009] EWHC 2520 (Ch D)

Precedent

❖ Whether a licence agreement extends to subsequent forms of (new) technology (such as the internet) depends on the form of words used in the contract.

❖ A copyright licence should be limited to what is in the joint contemplation of the parties *at the time* the agreement was made.

Facts

In 1998, Alan Grisbrook commenced proceedings against Mirror Group Newspapers (MGN) to recover unpaid licence fees of £161,238 for photos of his available on various MGN websites for sale (mydailymirror.com, mirrorarchive.co.uk and arcitext.com). By 1998 MGN's website FastFoto held about 350,000 images. As part of the licence fee settlement in 2002, MGN agreed to delete all electronic copies of Mr Grisbrook's photos from the digital photo library. But he discovered in 2008 that MGN were making available back copies of their image library online to paying customers.[25] Alan Grisbrook commenced proceedings for breach of copyright, arguing that the publication of his photographic material on the newspaper's online photo archive amounted to copyright infringement and a breach of undertaking given by MGN. He sought an order for imprisonment of the officers of MGN, and sequestration of MGN's assets. MGN argued that the licence originally granted verbally by Grisbrook permitting publication in the newspaper, also extended to subsequent reproduction of the published material, including archiving on the internet. MGN relied on the defence of public interest under section 171(3) CDPA.

Decision

The CA found that the implied licence did *not* extend to the exploitation of Mr Grisbrook's photos on back-issue websites and databases and therefore amounted to breach of copyright (though perhaps not deliberate on the *Mirror's* part). Patten LJ said that though permission to store pictures for possible future use or for archiving could be an 'implied term' of the oral contract, the same could not be said for the presentation of the archived material to the public for a fee.

The court found that on the facts the licence granted by Mr Grisbrook did *not* allow MGN to publish the images on the websites because this form of commercial exploitation had simply not been in the contemplation of the parties at the time the licence was granted and because

---

25 The MGN archive websites included: mydailymirror.com, launched in June 2006 enabling users to buy *Daily Mirror* front pages in the form of posters, T-shirts or greetings cards; arcitext.com, launched in February 2006 allowing subscribers to access the Mirror's archives as pdf documents which reproduce part of the newspaper as it was printed; and mirrorarchive.co.uk, launched as a test site in April 2007 but intended to be the commercial equivalent of arcitext.com.

this term was not otherwise necessary. MGN had therefore infringed Mr Grisbrook's copyright in the images. Mr Grisbrook was awarded the full amount owed plus costs.

Analysis

Mr Grisbrook and other freelance photographers were obviously aware that MGN, like any other newspaper publisher, would retain an archive of published editions. But this was before the World Wide Web, and photographs were stored in the form of hard copies and microfiche.

The only real issue in this case was whether the verbal licence also extended to making the back numbers database more widely available to members of the public via the internet. The CA held that Mr Grisbrook's photographs on the newspaper's websites were 'a different kind of operation' (at paragraph 65). In effect the exploitation of the photographs of Mr Grisbrook by inclusion in the websites, from which copies could be downloaded and printed at will, was a 'new method of exploitation' which, by reference to the conditions prevailing in the period from 1981 to 1997, was wholly outside anything the parties could have contemplated at the time the photographs were first submitted to MGN.

In the light of the *Grisbrook* judgment, authors of creative works ought to study their licence agreements with media publishers carefully. If they have granted licensed images to a newspaper, which, like MGN, is making back copies of their editions available online to paid subscribers, they may well have a claim in copyright infringement if their licence agreement does not clearly allow such 'extended' use. MGN appealed the High Court ruling but the CA dismissed the appeal.[26]

9.4.4 Copyrights in film

Copyright in the film sector is particularly complex because of the many IP layers involved and the fact that there is no single creator of a film.[27] The following box shows that various copyrights exist in each 'strata' of a film.

Copyrights existing in film

- **artistic** – i.e. the set designs used in the film;
- **dramatic** – if the film is based on a dramatic work, dance or mime material;
- **literary** – within the source material and the original screenplay;
- **musical** – the soundtrack of the film, including both musical score and any lyrics;
- **film** – the images in the 'first fixation' of the film;
- **sound recordings** – the physical recording of the soundtrack;
- **broadcasts** – for sale of the underlying material and film for other exploitation;
- **performance** – any live interpretation of the film;
- **published editions** – within the typographical layout of the page for any published versions of the screenplay.

---

26 See: *Mirror Group Newspapers & Ors v Grisbrook (Alan)* [2010] EWCA Civ 1399 (before the Chancellor of the High Court, Leveson LJ and Etherton LJ) (CA).

27 See: ss 5A and 5B CDPA cover 'film'. Sections 5A and 5B have been substituted by reg. 9(1) (with Pt III) the Performances (Moral Rights, etc.) Regulations 2006 (S.I. 2006/18); s 5B(3)(b)–(d) substituted by s 5B(3)(b) Performances (Moral Rights, etc.) Regulations 2006 (S.I. 2006/18), reg. 2, Sch.

In *Norowzian v Arks Ltd and Others* (1998),[28] film-maker Mehdi Norowzian launched an unsuccessful lawsuit in the High Court Chancery Division in 1998, seeking remuneration for the use of techniques and style from his short film which he made in 1992, called *Joy*. Rattee J had to first decide whether the *Joy* sequence constituted a 'dramatic work' within the meaning of section 1(1) CDPA in order to decide whether an advertising clip for Guinness stout breached Mr Norowzian's copyright. Mr Norowzian further claimed that his film clip of *Joy* fell under section 3 CDPA, as a 'work of dance or mime', which entitled him to be regarded as the maker of it and therefore the 'author' within the meaning of sections 9 and 11 of the 1988 Act.

The background to this case was that drinks giant Diageo had launched a successful Guinness advertising campaign in 1994, promoting the stout with a film clip called *Anticipation*. Mr Norowzian claimed that *Anticipation* was a copy of his *Joy* dance sequence clip and that the makers of the Guinness advert had breached his copyright. *Anticipation* portrayed a man who, having been served by a barman with a pint of Guinness, waits for the frothing liquid in his glass to settle, and, while he waits, carries out a series of dance movements. Was *Anticipation* a copy of *Joy* under section 17(2) CDPA? Rattee J concluded that *Joy* was neither a dramatic work nor a recording of a dramatic work; therefore *Anticipation* did not infringe copyright.

The Court of Appeal in *Norowzian No 2* (1999)[29] clarified the earlier judgment in the first *Norowzian* action (1998) and held that a film might be purely protected as a film (i.e. a dramatic work) and be subject to copyright law, but not the artistic techniques demonstrated in the film, somewhat similar to the French idea of treating the film director as 'the author' (*l'auteur*). While their Lordships did not criticize the original trial judge, they stated that the standards applied by the law in different contexts vary a great deal in precision, and by applying different standards and factors when weighing up what constitutes a 'dramatic' work in a film.[30] In any case section 5(1) CDPA did not specifically define 'film' – it merely stated that it is a 'recording on any medium from which a moving image may by any means be produced'.

Copyright law makes the producer and the principal director of a film joint first owners of copyright,[31] although in practice the director will often assign his interest in the copyright to the production company (or financiers or both jointly). The producer must ensure that all underlying rights in the film, including in the screenplay itself, have been acquired by assignment before they will be able to raise finance for the film. Assignments of rights must be in writing, signed by both parties (although technically they only have to be signed by the assignor) and should include rights to exploit the film (or underlying material) in every imaginable manner, including in ways that have not yet been invented at the time of the assignment.

While an idea for a film cannot be protected by copyright, the title of a film might be protected in limited circumstances. Titles most certainly qualify for trade mark registration and may therefore be protected. It is worth mentioning that not all films are commercial productions; home movies, mobile phone pictures, camcorder images and so on can also constitute 'film', but have a shorter period of protection of 50 years from when they are made.[32] For instance, if a bystander films an important or traumatic event – such as the assassination of US President John F. Kennedy in Dallas in 1963 – and a news agency wants to use that film footage, they may not be able simply to use the whole film without the 'cameraman's' consent.

28 [1998] EWHC 315 (Ch).
29 See: *Norowzian (Mehdi) v Arks Ltd and Guinness Brewing Worldwide Limited (No 2)* [1999] EWCA Civ 3014 (CA).
30 Ibid., (Buxton, Nourse, Brooke LJJ).
31 See: s 9(2)(a) CDPA now substituted by s 9(2)(aa), (bb) in relation to films made on or after 1 July 1994 (S.I. 1996/2967, regs 18(1), 36).
32 See: s 13 CDPA.

Concerns have been raised when dealing with adaptations of plays or books in the making of a film. With either original or adapted works, the film producer needs to ensure that all ancillary rights are acquired, for example to adapt the work for television or to copy the work in the form of a remake, sequel or prequel to the film or to acquire merchandizing rights.[33]

The exploitation of artistic works used in films was addressed in the *Starwars* case, *Lucasfilm Ltd v Ainsworth* (2011).[34] The appeal in the UK Supreme Court was concerned with IP rights in various artefacts made for use in the film, based on artistic drawings and a clay model made in 1976 of a 'military style stormtrooper helmet' by designer Ralph McQuarrie.[35]

Andrew Ainsworth, a then recently qualified industrial designer from Ealing Art School, in West London, produced over 50 stormtrooper helmets for the first Star Wars film in 1976–1977; he applied 'two-dimensional sculpturing techniques' to the original design. Mr Ainsworth later sold replicas of the helmet in both Europe and the USA (mainly via online sales). Lucasfilm claimed, inter alia, that Mr Ainsworth had breached US copyright and trade mark laws, obtaining a default judgment in California with a US$20 million fine against him. Mr Ainsworth counterclaimed to enforce his own copyright in the helmet. The complex case did not only centre on whether the three-dimensional object was a 'sculpture' for the purposes of section 4(2) CPDA, but also on the conflict between the UK, the US and EU law as to the forum conveniens for legal action. Lucasfilm sued for $20 million in 2004, arguing Mr Ainsworth did not hold the intellectual property rights and had no right to sell them – a point upheld by a US court.

Under UK copyright law, it was argued that under section 4(2) CDPA 1988, 'sculpture' includes a cast or model made for purposes of sculpture. The appeal in the Supreme Court raised two distinct legal issues:

(1)   the definition of 'sculpture' in CDPA 1988, and, in particular, the correct approach to three-dimensional objects that have both an artistic purpose and a utilitarian function;

(2)   whether a UK court may exercise jurisdiction (forum conveniens) in a claim against persons domiciled in England for infringement of copyright committed outside the European Union in breach of the copyright law of that country.

Lucasfilm contended that the helmet was 'sculpture' as it had no practical function at all. Its purpose was wholly artistic, to make a visual impression on the filmgoer. That was not, however, how the trial judge and the Court of Appeal had viewed matters. Mann J found the stormtrooper helmet to be a mixture of costume and prop and that its primary function was utilitarian, namely to express an idea as part of character portrayal in the film. He held that this lacked the necessary quality of artistic creation required of a sculpture. The Supreme Court then reviewed the legislative history of the current statutory provisions in UK copyright law as to the meaning of 'sculpture'.

The Supreme Court held that the *Star Wars* film itself was the work of art and that the helmet was utilitarian in the sense that it was an element in the process of production of the film. Importantly, however, the court ruled that the helmet was *not* a sculpture.

The ruling by the UK Supreme Court in July 2011 meant that prop designer Andrew Ainsworth finally won his five-year long copyright battle against movie director George Lucas and his company over his right to sell replicas in the UK and Europe. This meant that US copyright claims

---

33 See: s 21 CDPA ('Infringement by making adaptation or act done in relation to adaptation').
34 [2011] UKSC 39 (the *Star Wars* case).
35 The first *Star Wars* film was released in the United States in 1977. The epic film series, created by George Lucas, won an Oscar for best costume design. It depicts the adventures of various characters 'a long time ago in a galaxy far, far away'.

were justiciable in English proceedings.[36] The Supreme Court hearings were witnessed by dozens of fans dressed in *Star Wars* costumes.

 FOR THOUGHT

> Where should be the *forum conveniens* (the venue where a court has jurisdiction over a case and the parties) when a breach of copyright has occurred in a country *outside* the EU? Why did George Lucas bring the Stormtrooper helmet copyright claim in the forum of the UK courts? Discuss.

9.4.5 Duration of copyright

The original Copyright, Designs and Patents Act 1988 (CDPA) provided for copyright protection of musical, literary, dramatic and artistic works only for 50 years from the death of the author. This was superseded by EU legislation which now states that all have a 70-year duration of copyright after the author's death.[37]

The EC 'Duration of Copyright and Rights in Performances Regulations 1995' harmonized the situation regarding the length of copyright protection for existing works irrespective of when they were created and cover all EU Member States. A summary of duration of copyrights is given below.

Duration of copyrights

i. *Literary, dramatic, musical or artistic works*

70 years from the end of the calendar year in which the last remaining author of the work dies. If the author is unknown, copyright will last for 70 years from the end of the calendar year in which the work was created, although if it is made available to the public during that time (by publication, authorized performance, broadcast, exhibition, etc.), then the duration will be 70 years from the end of the year that the work was first made available.

ii. *Sound recordings*

70 years.[38] The 70-year period runs from the date of first lawful publication or (if none) first lawful communication to the public (if the publication or, as the case may be, communication occurs within 50 years of the date of recording). If neither occurs within 50 years of the date of recording, the term of copyright will expire at that point. The extension will have prospective and retrospective effect. For existing copyrights, the new legislation applies only to sound recordings that are less than 50 years old as at the date falling two years after the date of the amending Directive (2011). In other words, no copyrights will be 'revived' under the new law.

---

36 [2008] EWHC 1878 (Ch) at para. 121 (Mann J, Lord Walker and Lord Collins gave a joint opinion, with which the other members of the court agreed).
37 See: s 12 CDPA, as amended by the Duration of Copyright and Rights in Performances Regulations 1995 (S.I. 1995/3297).
38 See: Extended from 50 to 70 years by Directive 2006/116/EC ('EU Copyright Term Directive').

iii. Films

70 years from the end of the calendar year in which the last principal director, producer, author or composer dies. If the work is of unknown authorship: 70 years from the end of the calendar year of creation or, if made available to the public in that time, 70 years from the end of the year the film was first made available.

iv. Typographical arrangement of published editions

25 years from the end of the calendar year in which the work was first published.[39] Typographical arrangement covers the style, composition, design, layout and general appearance of a page of a published work. In a typical book publication, copyright subsists both in the content of a work and also in the typographical arrangement and design elements of the work. Copyright in the typographical arrangement of a published edition rests with the *publisher* of that published work (in accordance with sections 9(2)(d) and 11 CDPA).

v. Broadcasts and cable programmes

50 years from the end of the calendar year in which the broadcast was made.[40]

vi. Crown copyright

50 years if the work has been published from the end of the year in which the work was published. **125 years** for unpublished works from the end of the year in which the work was made or until 31 December 2039 (which is 50 years from the year in which the CDPA 1988 came into force). Crown Copyright is claimed by government departments and a number of Commonwealth realms (including photographic and film archives). Copyright which has been assigned to the Crown will normally feature one of the copyright lines: © Controller and Queen's Printer or © Queen's Printer for Scotland.

vii. Parliamentary copyright

50 years from the end of the calendar year in which the work was made (e.g. the printing of Acts of Parliament or copies of *Hansard*). It applies to work that is made by or under the direction or control of the House of Commons or the House of Lords.

viii. The creation of artistic works which have been industrially manufactured (repeal of section 52 CPDA[41])

See below
9.4.7

Following the Flos[42] judgment, the UK government announced the repeal of section 52 CDPA.[43] This now means that the period of copyright protection for an *artistic work*, which has been *industrially manufactured*, has been extended from **25 years** to the life of the artist plus **70 years** (the same as all other artistic works).

The repeal of section 52 CDPA is effective from 6 April 2020. This gives the companies that are trading in design copies a period of time to sell off their stock as well as continue dealing in copies.

---

39 See: s 15 CDPA.
40 See: s 14 CDPA.
41 Section 52 reduced the term of copyright protection for artistic works that were industrially exploited. Thus, when more than 50 copies of these artistic works were made the period of protection was limited to 25 years, compared to other artistic works which are protected by copyright for the life of the creator plus 70 years.
42 See: *Flos Spa v Semeraro Casa e Famiglia Spa* (2011) (Case C-168/09) (CJEU).
43 See: s 74 Enterprise and Regulatory Reform Act 2013.

Copyright lifetimes: overview

Literary works	Written works. Includes lyrics, tables, compilations, computer programs, letters, memoranda, email and web pages.	Author's life plus 70 years after death. Anonymous corporation authors: 70 years from year of publication (see above for special rules for unpublished works).
Dramatic works	Plays, works of dance and mime, and also the libretto of an opera.	Author's life plus 70 years after death.
Crown copyright	All works made by Her Majesty or by an officer or servant of the Crown in the course of his or her duties.	Published by HM Stationery Office: 50 years from the end of the year when first published. Unpublished work: 125 years beyond the year it was created.
Parliamentary copyright	All works made by or under the direction or control of the House of Commons or House of Lords.	Mostly 50 years beyond year it was created. Exceptions include bills of Parliament.
Musical compositions and lyrics	Musical composition (music scores) and the lyrics.	This term of protection will (as long as the music and lyrics were specifically created for the relevant work) expire 70 years after the death of the last of the composers of the musical composition and the authors of the lyrics (whether or not those persons are designated as co-authors).
Artistic works	Graphic works (painting, drawing, diagram, map, chart, plan, engraving, etching, lithograph, woodcut), photographs (not part of a moving film), sculpture, collage, works of architecture (buildings and models for buildings) and artistic craftsmanship (e.g. jewellery).	Author's/creator's life plus 70 years after death.
Computer-generated works	Literary, dramatic and musical works.	50 years from first creation or 50 years from creation if unpublished during that time.
Databases	Collections of independent works, data or other materials which (a) are arranged in a systematic or methodical way, or (b) are individually accessible by electronic or other means.	Full term of other relevant copyrights in the material protected. Also, there is a database right for 15 years (this can roll forward).

Performers and sound recordings	Regardless of medium or the device on which they are played.	The copyright term for live performances and sound recordings is 70 years. The 70-year period runs from the date of first lawful recording or live performance or (if none) first lawful communication to the public.
Films	Any medium from which a moving image may be reproduced.	70 years from death of whoever is the last to survive from: principal director, producer, author of dialogue, composer of film music.
Broadcasts	Transmissions via wireless telegraphy through the air (not via cable or wires), includes satellite transmissions.	50 years from when broadcast first made.
Cable programmes	Services via cable.	50 years from when broadcast first made.
Published editions	The typography and layout of a literary, dramatic or musical work.	25 years from first publication.
Orphan works	Copyrighted works for which the owner of the copyright is unknown or cannot be found.	70 years from the year in which the work was created or first made available or until 2039.

9.4.6 Moral and related rights

Linked to UK copyright legislation are 'moral' rights, covered by Chapter IV of the CDPA 1988 ('Right to be identified as author or director'). Moral rights are distinct from any economic rights tied to copyrights. Even if an artist has assigned his or her copyright rights to a work to a third party, he or she still maintains the moral rights to the work. These rights protect non-economic interests, for example the right to claim authorship of a work, to protect the work from harm and distortion and ultimately to protect the creator's reputation.[44] Moral rights may be waived but cannot be assigned or passed on after the author's death.[45]

Moral rights do not extend to computer programs, the design of a typeface or any computer-generated work.[46] Furthermore, the right does not apply to publications in a newspaper, magazine or periodical, or an encyclopedia, dictionary, yearbook or other collective work of reference, or a work in which Crown copyright or parliamentary copyright subsists (such as *Hansard*).[47]

Related rights are a term in copyright law and have developed alongside copyright. They include those of performing artists in their performances, producers of phonograms in their recordings and those of broadcasters in their radio and television programmes. Related rights tend to be of a more limited nature. They are usually of shorter duration and are used in opposition to the term 'author's rights'. Related rights are primarily a result of technological development

---

44 See: s 80 CDPA.
45 See: s 86 CDPA.
46 See: s 79 CDPA.
47 See: s 79(6) and (7) CDPA.

See below
9.11

and generally concern the exploitation of works. The first organized support for the protection of related rights came from the phonogram industry, which sought (and gained, at least in countries following the common law tradition) protection under copyright law against unauthorized copying of phonograms (i.e. records, CDs, etc.) under copyright.

Here follows a summary:

1. **Moral rights** of the author and creator of work include the right of attribution (e.g. name of the author), the right to have a work published anonymously or by pseudonym and the right of integrity of the work. This means that the work is barred from alteration, distortion, or mutilation. Anything else that may detract from the artist's relationship with the work even after it leaves the artist's possession or ownership may bring these moral rights into play.

2. **Related rights** (or 'neighbouring rights' – from the French *droits voisins*) are the rights of a *creative work not* connected with the work's actual copyright (such as fine art, sculpture, paintings, film making, musical composition, literature). The term is used in opposition to the term 'author's rights'. Related rights vary much more widely in scope between different countries than authors' rights. The rights of performers, phonogram producers and broadcasting organizations are covered by the CDPA, the Rome Convention for the Protection of Performers, Producers of Phonograms and Broadcasting Organizations of 1961.

Section 103 CDPA deals with remedies for infringement of moral rights under section 80 CDPA, actionable as a breach of statutory duty owed to the person entitled to the right.

9.4.7 Design rights

Design rights protect aesthetic and visual qualities for shapes and 3D designs (which are not covered by copyright). Design right only applies to the shape and configuration (how different parts of a design are arranged together) of objects.

Design rights are relatively inexpensive to apply for and register. There now exists a unified EU design right which automatically protects your design for ten years after it was first sold or 15 years after it was created – whichever is earliest.[48] However, a registered design right has to be renewed every five years.

The look of a design right includes the

- appearance;
- physical shape;
- configuration (or how different parts of a design are arranged together);
- decoration.

48 See: Council Regulation 6/2002/EC on Community Designs ('the Community Design Right').

> **A registered design right (Community Design Registrations (CDR))**
>
> - protects any aspect of a design, e.g. both the product's shape and decoration;
> - prevents others from using it for up to 25 years;
> - makes taking legal action against infringement and copying more straightforward;
> - once registered the registration number of the design can be displayed on the design.

In the long-running *Trunki* case, Bristol-based company Magmatic, which makes the Trunki case (a ride-on suitcase for children which looks like an animal), argued that 'Kiddee' suitcases, made in Hong Kong by PMS, infringed its registered design rights. Kiddee cases are, like Trunki cases, decorated to look like animals. Robert Law's company, Magmatic, was first granted a judgment in their favour by the High Court in July 2013. However, the ruling was overturned by the CA in March 2014, stating that the Kiddee case looked sufficiently different in design to the Trunki one. Magmatic appealed.

In March 2016, five Supreme Court justices unanimously dismissed Magmatic's appeal, ruling in favour of PMS.[49] Lord Neuberger in his leading judgment centred on the 'Community Design Right'. This provides that a design shall be protected to the extent that it is *new* and has *individual character*. What then mattered in this case was the overall impression created by the design (i.e. a ride-on children's suitcase) and that potential customers would appreciate it on the basis of its *distinctiveness*.[50]

PMS (i.e. 'Kiddee case') claimed that its distinctive design was that of either an insect with antennae or an animal with ears. The Supreme Court justices said that – to the end-user – the overall impression given by the cases' design was that of a horned animal and that a Community Design Registration (CDR) does not merely register a shape, but – in this case – a shape in two contrasting colours. Their Lordships stated that the original judge had been wrong in holding that the design right simply covers a shape.[51] Lord Neuberger expressed sympathy for Magmatic and Mr Law, as the idea of the Trunki case was a clever one; but he stressed that a CDR is intended to protect designs not ideas.[52]

The *Trunki* ruling has far-reaching consequences for the design industry and was seen as disastrous for those who have sought to protect their designs with CDR. The judgment called the legal scope of protection into question.

> **What you can or cannot register**
>
> To register your design, it must:
>
> - be new;
> - not be offensive (e.g. feature graphic images or words);
> - not make use of protected emblems or flags (e.g. the Olympic rings; the European flag; the Royal Crown, etc.);
> - not be an invention or relate to how a product works (this would be a patent);
> - you cannot protect the functionality of a design – e.g. a chair that folds down more quickly than others of the same kind.

---

49 See: *PMS International Group plc v Magmatic Limited* [2016] UKSC 12 (on appeal from: *Magmatic Ltd v PMS International Group plc* [2014] EWCA Civ 181; on appeal from the High Court of Justice Chancery Div (Patents Court) [2013] EWHC 1925 (Pat)) (the Trunki case). The Supreme Court appeal concerned the alleged infringement of CRD No 43427-0001 owned by the appellant, Magmatic Ltd, for the Trunki case.

50 Ibid., at paras 6–10 (Lord Neuberger).

51 Ibid., at paras 51–56.

52 Ibid., at para. 57.

The case which ultimately lead to the repeal of section 52 CDPA is that of Flos.[53] This case concerned the design of the famous 'Arco' lamp,[54] created by the Italian designers Achilles and Pier Giacomo Castiglioni. The Italian lighting manufacturing company Flos held the IP rights in the lamp since the early 1960s. There were a number of cheap copies made in China on the market. Importers Semeraro were marketing the 'Fluida' lamp design in Italy, an imitation copy of the Arco lamp. In 2006 Flos brought an action against Semeraro, claiming that the importer had infringed the IP right in the industrial design for the Arco lamp and that the Fluida lamp 'slavishly imitated all [its] stylistic and aesthetic features'.[55]

The case was eventually decided by the Court of Justice of the European Union (CJEU) in 2011. The court's preliminary ruling concerned the interpretation of Article 17 of the Directive 98/71 in proceedings for breach of copyright between a manufacturer of lamps (Flos) and an importer of lamps (Semeraro).

The CJEU (Second Chamber) ruled that:

1. Article 17 of Directive 98/71/EC ('on the legal protection of designs') must be interpreted as precluding legislation of a Member State which excludes from copyright protection in that Member State designs which were protected by a design right registered in or in respect of a Member State and which entered the public domain before the date of entry into force of that legislation, although they meet all the requirements to be eligible for copyright protection.
2. Article 17 must be interpreted as precluding legislation of a Member State which – either for a substantial period of ten years or completely – excludes from copyright protection designs which, although they meet all the requirements to be eligible for copyright protection, entered the public domain before the date of entry into force of that legislation, that being the case with regard to any third party who has manufactured or marketed products based on such designs in that State – irrespective of the date on which those acts were performed.[56]

The CJEU's judgment in Flos means that a national law cannot refuse copyright protection to industrial designs that are eligible for this protection, even if they have entered into the public domain. The Italian government then amended Article 239 of the Italian Industrial Property Code ('the IPC'[57]) in order to expressly recognize copyright protection to industrial designs which bear 'inherent artistic value'.

Following the Flos decision, the UK Parliament proposed to repeal section 52 CDPA, with transitional arrangements in place. From 2020 onwards it is a criminal offence to sell replica goods unless 70 years have passed from the date the item originally went on sale which means the end of buying cheap designer furniture replicas in the UK, such as the Eames Lounge Chair (designed by Charles and Ray Eames); the Egg chair (by Arne Jacobsen) or the Barcelona Chair (by Mies van der Rohe) – all of which had been sold for less than £500 instead of £5,000.

It is not clear from the CJEU judgment in Flos, whether or not industrial designs which were created before 2001 benefit from full copyright protection. That said, the creative and design industry welcomed the Flos ruling. Legislation now provides extensive copyright protection to industrial designs.

---

53 See: Flos Spa v Semeraro Casa e Famiglia Spa (2011) (Case C-168/09) Judgment of the Court of Justice (Second Chamber) of 27 January 2011 (CJEU).
54 The Arco Lamp was created in 1962 and entered the public domain before 19 April 2001, was eligible for copyright protection as an industrial design under Law No 633/1941, as amended by Legislative Decree No 95/2001.
55 Flos judgment (2011) at paras 20–24 (as per judgment of Advocate General Y. Bot) (CJEU).
56 Ibid., at paras 48–50, 53–56, 61–65.
57 See: Legislative Decree no 30/2005 ('IPC').

9.4.8 The Intellectual Property Act 2014

Following Professor Ian Hargreaves' Report (2011)[58] – an independent review of UK copyright legislation – the Intellectual Property Act 2014 ('IPA' – or 'IP Act')[59] introduced changes to:

> (1) **copyright** regarding home copying, quotation, parody and fair dealing;
> (2) **designs** regarding copying a registered design, first owner, the good faith defence to infringement and unregistered design rights; and
> (3) **patents** regarding the Unified Patent Court, patent notices and patent opinions.

The IPA 2014 modernized intellectual property law to help UK businesses better protect their IP rights. The main changes involved reforms to the designs legislation, which had been described in the Hargreaves Report as messy, complex and confusing. The IP Act introduced a number of new measures, making the law simpler, clearer and more robust.

Key changes in design law include

- a new criminal offence for the copying of registered designs;[60]
- changes to design ownership in relation to commissioned designs;[61]
- private use of unregistered designs;[62]
- scope of an unregistered design right;[63]
- introduction of a design opinions service.[64]

Key changes to patent law include

- marking patented products with a web address;[65]
- expansion of the patent opinions service;[66]
- patents worksharing.[67]

9.5 IP infringement, general defences and remedies

Infringement of IP laws can amount to criminal offences as well as being actionable in civil law. Unfortunately, copyright infringements go undetected most of the time and organized crime, including copying and counterfeiting goods, is on the increase, particularly with auction sales on the internet (e.g. eBay).

---

58 See: Hargreaves, I. (2011) *Digital Opportunity* (The Hargreaves Report).
59 The Intellectual Property Bill 2013–14 was introduced in May 2013 by Lord Younger in the House of Lords; it received Royal Assent on 14 May 2014.
60 See: s 13 IPA 2014 ('Offence of unauthorised copying etc. of design in course of business').
61 See: s 2 IPA 2014 ('Ownership of design').
62 See: ss 2 and 6 IPA 2014; 249A CDPA.
63 See: s 1 IPA 2014.
64 See: s 11 IPA 2014 ('Opinions service'); 28A Registered Designs Act 1949 ('Opinions on designs').
65 See: s 15 IPA 2014 ('Infringement: marking product with internet link').
66 See: s 16 IPA 2014.
67 See: s 18 IPA 2014 ('Sharing information with overseas patent offices').

9.5.1 Primary infringement

Primary infringement of IP rights amounts to a strict liability action. This means the claimant does not have to prove intention, recklessness or carelessness, and purely innocent breaches may be actionable.

> **Examples of IP infringement include when someone:**
>
> - uses, sells or imports your patented product or process;
> - uses all or some of your work under copyright without your permission;
> - makes, offers or sells your registered design for commercial gain;
> - uses a trade mark that is identical or similar to one you have registered.

If the owner of a copyright believes that his work has been copied or pirated, he can enforce these rights in the Patents County Court or the Chancery Division. The courts usually use equitable remedies such as 'specific performance' or injunctions to remedy IP infringement. A decree of specific performance is a court order directed to someone to perform specific obligations, for example, to 'deliver up' the copied manuscript or disclose to the court any royalties already received for a hit single. In addition the High Court can issue a warrant for an inspection of the copiers' premises for evidence of production or possession of the copied or 'pirated' goods (see 'Anton Piller order'). The IP owner can also apply for an interim injunction (or interdict in Scotland) to stop the illegal activities.

In early 2006, authors Michael Baigent and Richard Leigh filed a copyright suit against publishers Random House.[68] The claimants (two of three authors) alleged that significant portions of best seller The Da Vinci Code by Dan Brown had been plagiarized from their text, The Holy Blood and the Holy Grail. Whilst Brown admitted that he had referred to The Holy Blood text in the course of his research, he denied copyright infringement. Lloyd LJ in the CA agreed with the trial judge's decision on the issue of 'substantiality' in that there had been no 'central theme' to copy and accordingly no breach of copyright was found. The claimants were ordered to pay 85 per cent of Random House's legal costs, estimated at £1.3 million.[69]

When assessing breach of copyright that courts will look in detail at how much of the work has been copied. If the court believes that a 'substantial part' of your work has been copied or broadcast, this will still constitute an infringement of the work. A 'substantial part' is assessed qualitatively and could be a very small part of the work if that part was 'distinctive' and 'substantial'.

9.5.2 Secondary infringement of copyright

'Secondary infringement' includes selling, importing, providing premises for primary infringed goods or equipment.[70] In other words, where a person, without a licence agreement from the copyright owner, sells or hires out an article or makes copies of that work, knowing that it is to be used in the course of a business – it amounts to secondary infringement of copyright.[71]

The Privacy and Electronic Communications Regulations 2003[72] introduced the ability for copyright owners (and certain licensees) to take infringement proceedings against anyone who

---

68 See: *Baigent and Leigh v The Random House Group Ltd* [2007] EWCA Civ 247 (CA) (the *Da Vinci Code* case).
69 For further discussion see: Kirk, E. (2006).
70 See: ss 22 to 27 CDPA.
71 See: s 24(2) Copyright and Related Rights Regulations 2003 (EC Regulation 2003/2498) (replacing s 23 CDPA).
72 See: EU Regulation 2003/2426.

circumvents technological measures – such as copy control devices which have been applied to a work – or who removes or alters electronic rights management information associated with a work or imports or sells devices for these acts to be done. This became a challenging issue in the *Karen Murphy (Pub Landlady)*[73] case(s).

The cases related to pubs in the UK which, in order to screen Football Association Premier League (FAPL) football matches, were purchasing foreign decoder cards rather than buying the more expensive authorized BSkyB subscription. The foreign decoder cards enabled the pubs – such as Karen Murphy's 'Red, White and Blue' pub in Portsmouth – to show the Saturday matches, which no UK broadcaster was permitted to show live. Instead of paying for a Sky subscription, landlady Murphy used the Greek TV station Nova to show Premier League matches. She was convicted under section 297(1) CDPA ('Offence of fraudulently receiving programmes').[74]

The CJEU ruled that the FAPL could not stop individuals from seeking better deals for TV sports subscriptions than that offered by BskyB (now 'Sky') at the time. The broadcaster was paying more than £1 billion at the time for broadcast rights for Premier League matches from foreign broadcasters.

The *Karen Murphy* ruling is complex and concerns the applicability of the section 72(1) CDPA (as amended[75]) defence to acts of communication to the public. The defence provides where someone plays or shows a broadcast in public, to an audience which has not paid for admission to their premises, this does *not* infringe any copyright in the broadcast or any film included in the broadcast. The Murphy ruling found that the pubs in question could rely on that defence stating that the transmission in a pub is a 'communication to the public', which means that without the permission of the Premier League Murphy would be in breach of the EU Copyright Directive (Directive 93/83/EEC). But this Directive does not stop individuals from buying foreign decoder cards for domestic use.

The Court of Justice ruled that live match coverage itself was not covered by copyright protection, although the Premier League could claim ownership of FAPL-branded opening video sequences, theme music, on-screen graphics and highlights of previous matches. This means that as long as the FAPL and BSkyB ensure that match coverage includes enough copyright elements pubs will not be allowed to show foreign broadcasts.

9.5.3 The use of hyperlinks

There has been much controversy regarding whether hypertext links between websites, which allow users to surf from one site to another, are infringing copyright under section 20 CDPA.[76]

One of the earliest cases involved two Scottish newspapers and the legal effect of hypertext links. In *Shetland Times v Wills* (1997),[77] both online editors were based in the Shetland Islands. Former student rector of Edinburgh University, Dr Jonathan Wills, former editor of the *Shetland Times*, began to publish the *Shetland News* after falling out with Robert Wishart, owner of the *Shetland Times*. Dr Wills also operated a website for his newspaper, *Shetland News*, using news headlines as the means of access to its stories. From 14 October 1996, *Shetland News* incorporated in its website certain news headlines copied verbatim from the *Shetland Times* site. The *Shetland News* page included *Shetland Times* headlines as hypertext links, and by clicking on these a person would be directed to the relevant stories on the *Shetland Times* website, bypassing the front page of that site altogether.

73 *Karen Murphy v Media Protection Services Ltd* (C-429/08) and *Football Association Premier League Ltd and Others v QC Leisure and Others* (C-403/08) Judgment of the European Court of Justice – Grand Chamber of 4 October 2011.
74 Note: the words in s 297(1) were repealed and substituted by reg. 2(2), Sch. 2 of the Copyright and Related Rights Regulations 2003.
75 Note: the words in s 72 were repealed and substituted by reg. 2(2), Sch. 2, regs 31–40 of the Copyright and Related Rights Regulations 2003.
76 Section 20 has been substituted by the Copyright and Related Rights Regulations 2003 reg. 6(1).
77 [1997] SLT 669.

The *Shetland Times* editor objected primarily because the hyperlinks enabled browsers to bypass the front pages which contained advertising. The *Shetland Times* editor feared that the paper's advertising revenue would accordingly be reduced. The *Shetland Times* alleged copyright infringement in two separate acts:

(1) Their website was a 'cable programme service' in terms of section 7 CDPA, and the use of the *Shetland Times*' headlines in the *Shetland News* site constituted an infringement of copyright under section 20 CDPA.
(2) The headlines attracted copyright protection as original literary works and by storing the headlines by electronic means the *Shetland News* had infringed copyright in them subject to section 17 CDPA.

The Scottish Court of Session accepted that linking to another website does not involve copying material but simply providing a means of access to the other site. The only material which had been copied was the text of the various headlines. The court held that there was an arguable case for the subsistence of both copyrights. Its decision that a website is a 'cable programme service' was to have far-reaching consequences (beyond copyright law) for the regulation and development of the internet. But the court also ruled that the headlines could in fact attract copyright protection despite the *de minimis* rules. On these findings Lord Hamilton granted an interim *interdict* (injunction) – but the case was settled before a full proof could be heard on the facts.

The *Shetland Times* case is now purely of historical value as a result of the introduction of the 'communication right' under section 20 CDPA, which protects works distributed on the World Wide Web.

There are now many 'third-party' websites, whose sole purpose is to link to copyright-infringing content. The leading case is that of *GS Media* – the so-called *Playboy hyperlink* case – involving pornographic photos of Dutch model Britt Dekker. The non-binding opinion,[78] given by the Advocate General of the CJEU, relates to *Playboy Magazine* publishers Sanoma Media and 'hyperlinked porn' posted on a news-gossip website by GS Media. The case itself caused quite a stir (not only in the Netherlands) when Advocate General Wathelet opined that posting a link to a third-party website that contains 'freely accessible' copyright infringing content does *not* itself amount to copyright infringement.

 KEY CASE

GS Media BV v Sanoma Media (2016) (Case C-160/15) Netherlands BV (*Playboy hyperlink* case) (Case C_160/15) (CJEU)[79]

Precedent
❖ Copyright holders in the EU have the exclusive right to control the communication to the public of their works.
❖ Hyperlinking to unauthorized (third party) content does not itself constitute copyright infringement.

Facts
In October 2011, Sanoma Media commissioned a *Playboy* photoshoot of Britt Dekker, a popular figure in the Dutch media. GS Media, which operates the Dutch news-and-scandal

---

78 The preliminary ruling concerns the interpretation of Article 3(1) of Directive 2001/29/EC of the European Parliament and of the Council of 22 May 2001 on the harmonisation of certain aspects of copyright and related rights in the information society ('The InfoSoc Directive').
79 *GS Media BV v Sanoma Media Netherlands BV, Playboy Enterprises International Inc., Britt Geertruida Dekker* (2016) (Case C-160/15) (CJEU). Request for a preliminary ruling by the ECJ from the Hoge Raad der Nederlanden (Supreme Court of the Netherlands). Opinion of Advocated General Wathelet, delivered on 7 April 2016. OJ 2001 L 167, p. 10 (*Playboy hyperlink* case).

website, *GeenStijl*,[80] posted a hyperlink to a third-party website where users could down-load the commissioned pictures. By clicking on a hyperlink on the *GeenStijl* story ('Nude photos . . . Dekker' click: 'HERE'), readers were directed to an Australian data-storage website called Filefactory.com. Readers were then able to open a zip file containing 11 pdf files of Ms Dekker's porn photoshoot.

GS Media repeatedly refused Sanoma's requests to remove the hyperlink from its web-site and even posted links to alternative websites, where the photographs could also be downloaded. As a result of this, the publisher issued a claim in the Amsterdam District Court for copyright infringement against GS Media. The District Court ruled in Sanoma's and Ms Dekker's favour; however, this ruling was overturned by the Dutch CA.

Eventually the case was referred by the Supreme Court of the Netherlands to the CJEU for a preliminary ruling on certain questions regarding the interpretation of Directive 2001/29/EC of the European Parliament and of the Council of 22 May 2001 on the har-monisation of certain aspects of copyright and related rights in the information society (Article 3(1) of the InfoSoc Directive) in respect of hyperlinking to works, which are *freely accessible* on another (third party) website, but which have been posted with-out the copyright owner's consent. The Advocate General was asked to give a prelimi-nary opinion on whether this amounted to copyright infringement under the InfoSoc Directive.

Decision (non-binding legal opinion by the CJEU)

The Advocate General Melchior Wathelet (Belgium) opined that copyright holders (in EU law) have the *exclusive* right to control the communication to the public of their works. An internet user posting a hyperlink to infringing content does not constitute an act of communication to the public within the meaning of the InfoSoc Directive, where the hyperlink is not indispensable to the making available of the infringing works in question, for example where no security measures have been bypassed by using the hyperlink.

In the absence of an 'act of communication to the public', the fact that the person or website posting the link is or ought to be aware that the copyright holder has not authorized the placement of the works in question on that other website, was irrel-evant. Wathelet said that internet users in general do not have the means to verify whether the initial communication to the public of a protected work freely accessible on the internet is with or without the copyright holder's consent. The Advocate Gen-eral felt that this would impede the proper functioning of the internet and limit the development of the information society in Europe, one of the principal objectives of the InfoSoc Directive.[81]

Analysis

Advocate General Wathelet provided the CJEU legal opinion that posting a link to a web-site that contains 'freely accessible' copyright infringing content does not in itself amount to copyright infringement. This meant he did not have to consider whether it was neces-sary for the right holder to have already consented to the work being made available.

---

80 'Geen stijl' roughly translates as 'having no class or style'.
81 Ibid., at paras 32–47 (Advocate General Wathelet).

The AG's opinion may well shut down the argument that a hyperlink infringes copyright if it links to a site on which the copyright work has been posted without the copyright owner's consent. The result could mean serious damage to the creative community's efforts to restrict infringement of their copyrighted content. *GS Media* is good news for ISPs who generate income by (knowingly) hyperlinking to infringing material. But if internet users risked liability for copyright infringement every time they posted a link they would be much more reluctant to do so.

 FOR THOUGHT

Many businesses in the publishing world employ press cuttings agencies to scan international, national and regional newspapers which then provide their clients with cuttings of articles that would be of interest to them. The cuttings supplied by the agency are facsimile copies of parts of the typographical arrangement of the newspapers. Have the agencies copied the whole or a substantial part of the typographical arrangement of the published edition (the newspaper)? Do the new typographical arrangements attract separate copyright within the meaning of the doctrine 'sweat of the brow'? Discuss.

9.5.4 Copyright claims in the music business

Over the past few decades there have been a number of high-profile copyright actions involving musicians and performing artists. Most of these cases involve international artists and laws.

To determine infringement in the music business, courts have relied on the following two-prong test:

1. copying of a prior work; and
2. a substantial similarity to the prior work sufficient to constitute improper appropriation.

The most recent case, in the Californian Federal Court, involved iconic 1970s rock group Led Zeppelin. Led Zeppelin were being sued by the estate of the 1960s psychedelic rock band Spirit's late guitarist, Randy 'California' Wolfe (who died in 1997). A trustee for the late Randy Wolfe, Michael Skidmore, demanded, as part of the lawsuit, that Led Zeppelin would give credit to Wolfe on their 1971 album, *Led Zeppelin IV*, which contains 'Stairway To Heaven'. Randy Wolfe composed the song 'Taurus', which it was alleged, was 'ripped off' by Led Zeppelin. Wolfe's lawyers also claimed substantial backdated royalties. Guitarist Jimmy Page (72) and his co-defendant, singer Robert Plant (67), were relying on the 'Mary Poppins' defence. Led Zeppelin's defence pressed the argument that the descending chromatic scale in 'Taurus', which they were accused of having copied, is exceedingly common in popular music and is not subject to copyright protection. Page explained, by playing 'Stairway to Heaven' on his guitar to the jury, that the song shared its musical DNA with the Mary Poppins song 'Chim Chim Cher-ee', and that the chord sequence in both songs was similar. Page explained that the descending musical motif of the Mary Poppins song was common to both 'Taurus' and 'Stairway to Heaven' and 'had been around forever'.[82]

---

82 Source: 'Led Zeppelin's "Stairway to Heaven" Trial, Day 3: The "Mary Poppins" Connection', by Matt Diehl, *Rolling Stone*, 16 June 2016.

On 23 June 2016, a Los Angeles jury found Robert Plant and Jimmy Page not guilty of stealing the famous passage from the 1971 anthem from the band Spirit. Francis Malofiy, the estate's attorney, said he was sad and disappointed by the jury's decision. 'Stairway to Heaven' remains one of the most played songs on radio and is estimated to have generated more than $500m over the decades. Damages, however, can extend back only three years and into the future.[83]

Led Zeppelin's victory in the USA over allegations the band stole the opening chords of 'Stairway to Heaven' may reverse the surge in copyright infringement lawsuits over pop songs that followed the 'Blurred Lines' verdict in the same court. In that case, Kendrik Lamar was sued by Golden Withers Music and Musidex Music in April 2016 for allegedly replicating the music from the 1975 Bill Withers song 'Don't You Want to Stay' for Lamar's track 'I Do This', without permission. The lawsuit was filed in the same US court where a jury in March 2015 awarded Marvin Gaye's estate some $7.4 million after finding that the Robin Thicke and Pharrell Williams 2013 smash hit 'Blurred Lines' copied parts of Gaye's 1977 song 'Got to Give It Up' (the award was later reduced by the judge to $5.3 million; though subsequently cross-appealed).[84]

To avoid having to expend time, money and resources engaging in a protracted legal dispute, as well as exposure to the possibility of liability for monetary damages and/or injunctive relief as part of an adverse ruling, the most likely conclusion to these kind of disputes is a confidential settlement agreement involving a payment or series of payments to the original artist and composer.

That is precisely how Led Zeppelin resolved prior claims of copyright infringement brought by third-party artists regarding other Led Zeppelin songs including 'Whole Lotta Love', 'Babe I'm Gonna Leave You', 'The Lemon Song' and 'Dazed and Confused'.

In January 2015, three-times Grammy-nominated pop singer, Sam Smith, settled a copyright lawsuit with American singer-songwriter, Tom Petty, over the likeness between Smith's hit 'Stay With Me' and Petty's hit 'I Won't Back Down', co-written with ELO's Jeff Lynne. Smith agreed to a 12.5 per cent writing credit and royalties to Petty and his joint singer-composers Jeff Lynne and Jimmy Napes.[85]

It was even claimed that the world's most popular song, 'Happy Birthday', is under copyright. Music publishers Warner Chappell have earned an estimated $2 million a year from the song by claiming copyright. In 2013, film Director Jennifer Nelson filed a lawsuit claiming the song should not be under copyright. Nelson and 'Good Morning to You Productions' were sued by Warner Chappell's for royalties of $1,500 for the use of the song in a documentary. Nelson claimed she had found a songbook from 1927, containing 'Happy Birthday', with no copyright notice – pre-dating Warner Chappell's copyright claim by eight years.[86]

In 2016, singers Kanye West, Justin Bieber and Ed Sheeran were all facing lawsuits for alleged copyright violations.

9.5.5 Joint authorship of copyright

Where two or more people collaborate in creating a work and their individual contributions are not distinct, they are 'joint authors' of that work (or joint owners of copyright). However, where two or more persons collaborate but it is possible to determine the separate parts attributable to each author, it will not be a work of joint authorship.[87]

---

83 Source: 'Led Zeppelin cleared of stealing riff for Stairway to Heaven', by Rory Carroll, *The Guardian*, 23 June 2016 with a link to a musical comparison: www.theguardian.com/music/2016/jun/23/led-zeppelin-cleared-stairway-to-heaven-lawsuit-spirit?CMP=Share_iOSApp_Other.
84 Source: 'Kendrick Lamar sued for allegedly copying Bill Withers song', *Reuters*, 15 April 2016.
85 Source: 'Sam Smith on Tom Petty Settlement: "Similarities" But "Complete Coincidence"', by Daniel Kreps, *Rolling Stone Magazine*, 26 January 2015.
86 Source: 'World's most popular song is not under copyright, according to lawsuit', by Michael Hann, *The Guardian*, 28 July 2015.
87 See: s 10 CDPA.

In *Ray v Classic* FM (1998),[88] Robin Ray (1934–1998) brought an action against the radio station Classic FM, alleging infringement of his copyright in the playlists which he had created between 1991 and 1997. He had undertaken the mammoth task of drawing up a list of 50,000 pieces of classical music, and rating them for popular appeal, which became the basis for the Classic FM playlist. Classic FM claimed joint authorship of these works on the basis that Mr Ray had simply put into writing ideas initiated by the radio station's representatives at a series of meetings concerning the contents of the catalogue and its categories.

The Chancery Division upheld Mr Ray's claim, not granting joint authorship to Classic FM. The court ruled that, in order to be a joint author for the purposes of section 10 CDPA, a *significant creative contribution* as an author had to be made to the production of the work which was not distinct from that of the other author with whom there was a collaboration. The contribution had to be something which was incorporated into the finished work and protected by copyright. The court observed that Mr Ray was solely responsible for five documents, i.e. the catalogue, playlists and ideas contained in these, and duly awarded Robin Ray the sole copyright in these works.

In the *Spandau Ballet* case,[89] the court ruled that to be a joint owner of copyright the parties must have substantially contributed to the song's creation, not just to its interpretation. As per Park J:

> There is a vital distinction between composition or creation of a musical work on the one hand and performance or interpretation of it on the other.[90]

So, if a drummer just adds a short drum loop, this would not make any material difference to the song, and would not justify the claim that the song was co-written, attracting joint copyright under section 10 CDPA. However, one could argue that the performable arrangement produced by a group would constitute a separate copyright for the new arrangement.

In the landmark case of *Fisher v Brooker* (2009),[91] – one of the last cases heard by the House of Lords – Matthew Fisher managed to assert joint ownership of copyright (retrospectively) in the famous song 'A Whiter Shade of Pale' (1967). The song achieved sales in the millions and is still regarded as one of the greatest songs ever written. Fisher had been the Hammond organist of the pop group Procol Harum. The claimant, Fisher, had composed the familiar organ solo at the beginning of the song and had left the band in 1969. Crucial in this case was that Mr Fisher made his claim some 40 years after the song's release.

❖ KEY CASE — *Fisher v Brooker* [2009] UKHL 41 (HL)

Precedent
- ❖ A claimant cannot be denied the opportunity of exercising his right of intellectual property even after an extensive time period has passed (here nearly 40 years).
- ❖ A claimant of copyright cannot be estopped from asserting his copyright interest on equitable grounds, to declare that the right existed (under the equitable doctrine of proprietary estoppel).

Facts
On 7 March 1967, the original band members of Procol Harum, namely Gary Brooker, Bobby Harrison, Ray Royer and Dave Knight, entered into a recording contract with Essex Music

---

88 [1998] ECC 488 (Ch D).
89 *Hadley v Kemp* [1999] EMLR 589 (the *Spandau Ballet* case).
90 Ibid., at para. 589 (Park J).
91 [2009] UKHL 41 (HL).

Ltd. Shortly after, Matthew Fisher ('the claimant') joined the band as Hammond organist. 'A Whiter Shade of Pale' ('the song') became an instant worldwide hit after the recording was released as a single by the Decca label on 12 May 1967. Around 1993, Essex's recording rights were assigned to Onward Music Ltd, who were registered with PRS–MCPS as owner of the copyright in the song. There were 770 versions of the song performed by other groups and the introductory bars were used commonly as mobile phone ring tones.

During April 2005, the claimant, Mr Fisher (then aged 61 and working as a computer programmer in Croydon) launched his claim against the lead singer of Procol Harum, Gary Brooker, and Essex and Onward Music. The main claim was that Mr Fisher wanted a share of the musical copyright in the song. After his claim was rejected, Mr Fisher began legal proceedings on 31 May 2005. At the High Court, the respondents argued that the claimant was far too late – nearly 40 years – in claiming the copyright for joint authorship in the song. They asked the court for laches and to strike out the claim under the doctrine of estoppel.

The judge held that the claimant was entitled to declarations (i) that he was a joint author of the work, (ii) that he was a joint owner of the copyright to the extent of 40 per cent, and (iii) that the defendants' implied licence had been revoked from the date of issue of proceedings. After a number of cross-appeals, the case reached the House of Lords in 2009.

Decision
The HL declared that Matthew Fisher was joint owner and author of copyright under section 10 CDPA. The reasons being that, 'Mr Fisher's instrumental introduction – the organ solo – is sufficiently different from what Mr Brooker had composed on the piano to qualify in law, and by quite a wide margin, as an original contribution to the work.'[92]

Their Lordships held that it did not matter that the claimant had not asserted his joint authorship for such a long time. His claim was still valid even after 40 years, and they awarded Mr Fisher a 40 per cent share in royalties, backdated to the date of his original claim in 2005. Baroness Hale (one of five Law Lords) commented: 'As one of those people who do remember the Sixties, I am glad that the author of that memorable organ part has at last achieved the recognition he deserves.'

Analysis
It might strike us as extraordinary that Matthew Fisher had waited some 38 years before he brought his joint authorship action, fully in the knowledge, and without reasonable excuse, that the other band members of Procol Harum, in particular Gary Brooker, had exploited the work for so many years.

Fisher v Brooker set the precedent for any future claims of this kind where an artist wishes to assert his (joint authorship) rights in a song or recording during his lifetime; even if the claim is more than 40 years old. The court ruling meant that Matthew Fisher (and his heirs) could receive royalties in 'A Whiter Shade of Pale' for years to come. For the various royalty-collecting societies, such as the PRS and the MCPS, it meant that they had to amend their records and backdate the royalties payable to Mr Fisher to the start of his legal action.

---

92 Ibid., at 42.

See below
9.12

The HL ruling in *Fisher v Brooker* has meant an ongoing music copyright headache for major artists, musicians and their lawyers, who will have all lined up for similar claims for their contributions to successful songs.

9.5.6 Legal measures for copyright infringement

Aside from the CDPA, the TRIPS Agreement[93] describes in some detail how law enforcement measures in IP infringement should be handled, including rules for obtaining evidence, provisional measures, injunctions, damages and other penalties. It states that courts have the right, under certain conditions, to order the dIPSOsal or destruction of pirated or counterfeit goods, covering wilful trade mark counterfeiting or copyright piracy on a commercial level. All governments that have signed up to TRIPS have agreed to ensure that owners' IP rights must receive the assistance of police, trading standards and customs authorities to prevent imports of counterfeit and pirated goods. Increasingly, countries are resorting to criminal law to enforce civil rights. This means that imprisonment is more likely in repeat offence cases. The key issue in a criminal infringement action is that *mens rea* will be required that the defendant knew or ought to have known he was committing an infringing act beyond all reasonable doubt.

The following legislation creates specific IP offences

- **Section 2(1) CDPA** 'Criminal liability for making or dealing with infringing articles etc.' (six months and/or a £50,000 fine, on indictment ten years and/or unlimited fine).[94]
- **Section 2(2) CDPA** 'Criminal liability for making, dealing with or using illicit recordings' (six months and/or a £50,000 fine, on indictment ten years and/or unlimited fine).[95]
- **Section 2(3) CDPA** 'Devices and services designed to circumvent technological measures' (three months and/or a £5,000 fine, on indictment two years and/or unlimited fine).[96]
- **Section 2(4) CDPA** 'Offence of fraudulently receiving programmes', i.e. a broadcasting service provided from a place in the UK with intent to avoid payment of any charge applicable to the reception of the programme (£5,000 fine).[97]
- **Section 2(5) CDPA** 'Unauthorised decoders', i.e. making or exposing for sale, importing, distributing, any unauthorised decoder (six months and/or a £5,000 fine, on indictment ten years and/or unlimited fine).[98]
- **Section 1(1) Trade Mark Act 1994** 'Unauthorised use of a trade mark offence' (six months and/or a £5,000 fine, on indictment ten years and/or unlimited fine).[99]
- **Section 3(1) Registered Designs Act 1949** 'Offence of unauthorised copying etc. of design in course of business', i.e. intentionally copying a registered design exactly in the course of a business, with features that differ only in immaterial details from that design, knowing, or having reason to believe, that the design is a registered design (in England, Wales or Northern Ireland maximum six months' imprisonment

---

93 The Agreement on Trade-Related Aspects of Intellectual Property Rights (TRIPS) is an international agreement administered by the World Trade Organization (WTO) that sets down minimum standards for many forms of intellectual property (IP) regulation as applied to nationals of other WTO Members.
94 See also: s 107(1), (2), (3) CDPA.
95 See also: s 198(1), (2) CDPA.
96 See also: s 296ZB CDPA.
97 See also: s 297 CDPA.
98 See also: s 297A.
99 See also ss 92(1)–(3) Trade Mark Act 1994.

or a fine not exceeding the statutory maximum or to both; in Scotland, to imprisonment for a term not exceeding 12 months or to a fine not exceeding the statutory
maximum or to both).[100]

- **Section 4(1) Video Recordings Act 2010**[101] 'Supplying video recording of unclassified
  work', i.e. a person who supplies or offers to supply a video recording containing a
  video work in respect of which no classification certificate has been issued is guilty
  of an offence (six months and/or a £20,000 fine, on indictment two years and/or
  unlimited fine).[102]
- **Section 4(2) Video Recordings Act 2010** 'Possession of video recording of unclassified work for purposes of supply' (six months and/or a £20,000 fine, on indictment
  two years and/or unlimited fine).[103]
- **Section 4(3) Video Recordings Act 2010** 'Supplying of video recording of classified
  work for purposes of supply' (six months and/or maximum £5,000 fine).[104]
- **Section 4(4) Video Recordings Act 2010** 'Supply of video recording not complying
  with requirements as to labels' (maximum £5,000 fine).[105]
- **Section 5(1) Fraud Act 2006** 'Fraud by false representation' (maximum 12 months
  and/or a £5,000 fine, on indictment ten years and/or a fine)
- **Section 5(2) Fraud Act 2006** 'Possession of any article(s) for use in the course of or
  in connection with any fraud' (maximum 12 months and/or a £5,000 fine, on indictment five years and/or unlimited fine).
- **Section 5(3) Fraud Act 2006** 'Making or supplying articles for use in fraud' (maximum
  12 months and/or a £5,000 fine, on indictment ten years and/or unlimited fine).[106]
- **Section 5(4) Consumer Protection from Unfair Trading Regulations Act 2008**[107] –
  The Regulations introduce a general duty not to trade unfairly and seek to ensure
  that traders act honestly and fairly towards their customers. They apply primarily to
  business to consumer practices (but elements of business to business practices are
  also covered where they affect, or are likely to affect, consumers). When deciding
  which offence(s) are appropriate the date of the offence will be an important factor.

9.5.7 *Anton Piller* orders

An *Anton Piller* order is a search order frequently used in IP infringement.[108] It is a High Court
order obtained *ex parte*, and allows the requesting party to access the premises of the other party
to gather evidence that the court fears may be destroyed if the search is not conducted immediately. *Anton Piller* orders have played an increasingly important role in protecting businesses from
disgruntled or departing employees, who may well take intellectual property with them upon
'clearing their desk'.

---

100 See also: ss 35ZA (1), (3) Registered Designs Act 1949.
101 The 2010 Act repealed and revived provision of the 1984 Act.
102 See also: s 9 Video Recordings Act (VRA) 2010.
103 See also: s 10 VRA 2010.
104 See also: s 11 VRA 2010.
105 See also: s 13 VRA 2010
106 See also: ss 2, 6 and 7 Fraud Act 2006.
107 These regulations implemented the Unfair Commercial Practices Directive (UCPD) in UK law and replaced several pieces of
     consumer protection legislation that were in force prior to 26 May 2008, including the Trade Descriptions Act 1968.
108 See: s 109 CDPA.

The term was established in *Anton Piller KG v Manufacturing Processes Ltd and Others* (1975)[109] which involved an action for copyright infringement and misuse of confidential information. German manufacturers, Anton Piller KG (part of the Piller Group GmbH in Osterode Harz), made electric motors and generators as well as computer parts and frequency converters. They used as their agents in the UK, a company called Manufacturing Processes Ltd (MPL), run by two directors, Mr A. H. S. Baker and Mr B. P. Wallace. In the course of business, Pillers supplied MPL with extensive confidential information about the machines, including manuals and drawings for power machinery such as 'Ferrostaal' and 'Lechmotoren' – all of which were subject to copyright. Pillers claimed that MPL were in secret talks with Canadian and US firms, disclosing the confidential, copyrighted information about Pillers' power units – all of which could be damaging to Piller's business. Pillers applied for an *ex parte* order (interim injunction) to enter MPL's premises to inspect all documents on the site and, if necessary, remove them if they concerned Piller's copyrights. The defendants appealed but Lord Denning MR granted the search and confiscation order with the proviso that such an order must remain 'extremely rare' and should be made only when there was no alternative way of ensuring that justice was done.

Anton Piller orders are not without criticism because therein lies an underlying suggestion that a person (the defendant) cannot be trusted and is likely to destroy evidence if challenged. The order is not simply a search warrant (conducted by the police) – it is an order which is made *without the permission of or notice to* the defendant (*ex parte*). The argument against *Anton Piller* orders (and *Mareva*[110] injunctions[111]) was highlighted by Hoffmann J in *Lock International*[112] where such an order was wrongfully granted, implying dishonesty of the defendant, which, in turn can damage his reputation and business.

9.5.8 General defences
The CDPA allows 'permitted acts' to copy a work without the permission of the copyright owner.[113]

There are two distinct types of permitted acts

- fair dealing;
- exceptions.

9.5.9 Fair dealing
The fair dealing exceptions are fairly limited, such as 'research and private study'[114] and the 'public interest'.[115] The reason is, if copyright laws are too restrictive, it may stifle free speech and news reporting, or result in disproportionate penalties for inconsequential or accidental inclusion.

---

109 [1975] EWCA 12 (Civ Div).
110 See: *Mareva Compania Naviera SA v International Bulkcarriers SA* [1975] 2 Lloyd's Rep. 509 (sub nom 'The Mareva' or 'asset-freezing orders').
111 *Mareva* injunctions (also known as 'freezing orders') are court orders that negate the banker's duty to pay or transfer funds as per the instructions of the customer.
112 *Lock International plc v Beswick* [1989] 1 WLR 1268 (Hoffmann J).
113 See: Chapter III CDPA 'Acts Permitted in relation to Copyright Works', ss 28–76 CDPA.
114 See: s 30 CDPA.
115 See: s 171(3) CDPA.

Fair dealing acts include

- private and research study purposes;
- performance, copies or lending for educational purposes;
- reviews and news reporting (see: *Time Warner v Channel 4* (1994)[116]);
- incidental inclusion;
- copies and lending by librarians;
- acts for the purposes of royal commissions, statutory enquiries, judicial proceedings and parliamentary purposes;
- recording of broadcasts for the purposes of listening to or viewing at a more convenient time ('time-shifting'), including podcasts and the BBC iPlayer;
- producing a backup copy for personal use of a computer program;
- playing a sound recording for a non-profit-making organization, club or society.

One of the exceptions includes the use of photographs (but it does include criticism and reviews). For example, in 2005 the *Daily Mail* cropped and published a now notorious picture of Prince Harry wearing a Nazi uniform at a party, complete with swastika, 'lifted' from *The Sun* which led to a copyright dispute.

In *British Satellite Broadcasting Ltd* (1991),[117] the BBC's copyright action against British Satellite Broadcasting was dismissed by Scott J. The dispute was over the use of highlights from the BBC's exclusive coverage of the 1990 World Cup finals in a sports programme on the satellite channel. Since the BBC had bought exclusive rights, it was found that the use of short clips (all accompanied by a BBC credit line) was protected by the defence of fair dealing.

Scott J referred to Lord Denning's comments in *Hubbard v Vosper* (1972),[118] stating that:

> It is impossible to define what is 'fair dealing' . . . but, short extracts and long comments may be fair . . . after all is said and done, it must be a matter of impression . . . the quality and quantity of BBC copyright material used in each programme seemed . . . consistent with the nature of a news report and to be no more than was reasonably requisite for a television news report.

British Satellite Broadcasting was not ordered to pay damages because they were found to be reporting current news events.

See below
9.5.11

One emerging problem for universities has been the expansion of plagiarism where students make use of copying from websites to write essays and complete their coursework. Such action can be criminally prosecuted under section 84 CDPA ('False attribution of work'); alternatively, the tort of 'passing off' can be used in a civil action against the student when the true identity of the author of a work has not been attributed (see: *Clark v Associated Newspapers Ltd* (1998)[119]).

The courts usually ask these questions: first, is the person really using the work for the stated purpose? For example, if an entire work has been used and it is followed by two lines of vague review, this will not constitute criticism and review. Secondly, has the (alleged) copyright infringer availed himself of the 'fair dealing' exception? And, if so, has he provided a sufficient acknowledgement alongside his work? Has he demonstrated a visible and prominent notice which amounts to

---

116 [1994] EMLR 1 of 22 October 1993 (CA).
117 See: *British Broadcasting Corporation v The British Satellite Broadcasting Ltd* [1991] 3 All ER 833.
118 [1972] 2 QB 84 (Lord Denning). This was a Scientology case where Lord Denning defined the defence of fair dealing under s 6(2) Copyright Act 1956.
119 [1998] All ER 6 of 21 January 1998 (Ch D). [1998] EWHC Patents 345, 21 January, 1998.

a sufficient acknowledgement to the copyright owner? So, it could well be within the scope of 'fair dealing' to make single copies of short extracts of a copyrighted work for non-commercial research or private study, criticism or review, or reporting current events.

In the *Jason Fraser* case (2005),[120] (below) the High Court (Chancery Division) provided further guidance on the application of the fair dealing defence for review and criticism.

❖ **KEY CASE**

Fraser-Woodward Limited v (1) British Broadcasting Corporation (2) Brighter Pictures Ltd [2005] EWHC 472 (Ch) (sub nom *the Jason Fraser case*)

Precedent

❖ Fair dealing for the purpose of criticism or review is an established exclusion in the CDPA – providing only a *reasonable* amount of the work is used.

❖ The section 30 CDPA defence is relied on for day-to-day journalistic practices by all media organizations.[121]

❖ The key requirement for the defence of fair dealing to apply is that the author/s of the allegedly infringing material must demonstrate a genuine intention to criticize or review, rather than a desire to compete with the copyright work or to reproduce the copyright work simply to advance or promote their own product or service.

Facts

The case concerned the use by the BBC and Brighter Pictures of 14 'off-guard' photos of the Beckham family, taken by celebrity photographer Jason Fraser, during the making of a TV programme, *Tabloid Tales*, presented by Piers Morgan. Fraser-Woodward Ltd and its owner Jason Fraser sued for copyright infringement seeking flagrancy damages. The BBC and Brighter Pictures argued that the photos fell within the 'fair dealing' defence of section 30 CDPA 1988. The defendants argued that the programme included criticism of the photos and the tabloid press in general. Mr Fraser argued at first instance that there was no fair dealing and that there was no sufficient acknowledgement. This was rejected and Fraser appealed.

Decision

Mr Fraser's appeal was dismissed. The CA held that all but one of the photographs had been used for the purposes of criticism and review. This meant that the BBC could use his photographs of the Beckhams without his permission and without paying for them because the programme *Tabloid Tales* amounted to a 'review' of the press coverage of the high-profile couple.

Mann J referred to Walker LJ's judgment in the *Pro Sieben* case,[122] that the defence of fair dealing should be interpreted liberally. Mann J also confirmed *Hubbard v Vosper* (1972) that there could be no limitations on the extent of commentary capable of amounting to 'criticism' for the purpose of the defence.

---

120 See: *Fraser-Woodward Limited v (1) British Broadcasting Corporation (2) Brighter Pictures Ltd* [2005] EWHC 472 (Ch).

121 See: s 30 CDPA 'Criticism, review and news reporting'.

122 See: *Pro Sieben Media AG v Carlton UK TV Ltd* [1999] FSR 160 at p. 162 (Walker LJ) (CA).

Analysis

Fair dealing for the purpose of criticism or review is an established exclusion in the CDPA 1988. It is relied on for day-to-day journalistic practices by all media organizations, not just the BBC. The important outcome of the *Jason Fraser* case was that any review or criticism should be considered in its context. The fact that Mr Fraser on occasion licensed his photographs for use in television programmes, and without apparently significantly undermining his ability to license the pictures elsewhere, contradicted his evidence that undue damage to their value was inevitable from their use in the BBC show. Overall, Mann J held that there was not 'excessive use' of the material in question.

Some lawyers have argued that the fair dealing provisions in UK copyright law are too restrictive and that they are asphyxiating the copyright system, calling into question both its credibility and efficacy. The ruling in respect of 'fair dealing' in the *Jason Fraser* case extended the scope of the defence, which now stretches not only to criticism and review of other copyrighted works, but will also cover criticism of works that may not be protected by copyright at all or are unpublished or not identified with any specificity, such as the tabloid press in general. The case also provides guidance as to the meaning of sufficient acknowledgement, in respect of which there is very little case law (see also: *IPC Media Ltd v News Group Newspapers Ltd* (2005);[123] see also: *Ashdown v Telegraph Group Ltd* (2001)[124]).

 FOR THOUGHT

When reporting on the Tottenham riots in August 2011 or on the Oslo attacks by mass killer, Anders Behring Breivik, in August 2012, killing 77 people, the BBC included photographs in its broadcast and online coverage from Twitter, taken by other photographers, whom the BBC did not name. Was the public broadcasting company right in availing itself of the 'fair dealing' defence? Discuss.

9.5.10 Recent exceptions to copyright infringement

Three additional exceptions to copyright infringement entered into force on 1 October 2014:

(i)   private copying (section 28B CDPA);
(ii) quotation (section 30 CDPA);
(iii) caricature, parody and pastiche (section 30A CDPA).

Section 28B CDPA introduced the exception of 'private copying' which permits individuals to make personal copies of *any* copyright works (other than computer programs) for private, non-commercial use, provided the original was acquired lawfully and permanently. This change allows

---

123 [2005] EWHC 317 (Ch).
124 [2001] Ch 685 (Ch).

copying for purposes such as format shifting (e.g. digital storage of music purchased on CDs), backups and storage on a private cloud, provided the copier owns the original.

However, an individual cannot transfer a personal copy to anyone else, except on a private and temporary basis, or give away the original whilst retaining any personal copies. In other EU countries, similar exceptions are supported by levies on copying equipment, but no equivalent system has been introduced in the UK (see the decision in the *BASCA* case (2015)).[125]

Section 30 CDPA allows quotation ('whether for criticism, review or otherwise') provided that:

- it is fair comment or fair use;
- there is sufficient acknowledgement;
- it uses no more than is required; and
- the original work has been made available to the public.

Section 30A CDPA deals with parodies, i.e. an attempt to ridicule an author. In the *Alan Clark's Diaries* case,[126] 'parody' meant an imitation of the style of a particular political sketch writer with deliberate exaggeration for comic effect. The format of the parodies was such that the 'diaries' deceived a substantial number of *Evening Standard* readers into attributing their authorship to the then Conservative MP and established author Alan Clark (1928–1999). Mr Clark was well known for his political diaries, published in 1993.[127]

Mr Clark objected to a couple of articles that had appeared during and after the General Election of 1997 as a weekly column in the *Evening Standard*, written by Peter Bradshaw. The articles were headed 'Alan Clark's Secret Election Diary' and 'Alan Clark's Secret Political Diary', next to a photograph of the claimant. Mr Clark invoked his statutory right under section 84 CDPA 1988 ('false attribution of work'[128]) and his common law right of 'passing off'.

Lightman J asked whether a substantial body of readers of the *Evening Standard* had been or were likely to be misled 'more than momentarily and inconsequentially' into believing that the claimant, Alan Clark, was the author of these articles and whether the claimant, as an author with an established goodwill, had suffered or was likely to suffer damage in consequence? Lightman J found that the claimant had a substantial reputation as a diarist and his identity as author of the articles would plainly be of importance to readers of the *Evening Standard* in deciding whether to read the articles. The consequent identification of the claimant as author was not sufficiently neutralized to prevent a substantial number of readers being deceived.

The *Alan Clark* case set the precedent for the meaning of 'parody': whether rational men and women had been deceived? Lightman J concluded that the defendants, Associated Newspapers, the editor Max Hastings and Peter Bradshaw had been in clear breach of section 84 CDPA and had additionally committed the common law tort of passing off.

How is parody treated in the music business? Until recent changes in the law, parodies amounted to 'copying'. One early example was that of MJ (Morgan Jane) Delaney who – in July 2010 – availed herself of the 'viral marketing' medium when she released her title 'Newport

---

125 See: Jacques, S. (2015), pp. 699–706.
126 See: *Clark v Associated Newspapers Ltd* [1998] All ER 6 (Ch D).
127 See: Clark (1993). Alan Clark's published diaries cover the period 1983 to 1992 after he left the House of Commons, describing the government (and downfall) of Prime Minister Margaret Thatcher.
128 Note: the words in s 84(3)(a), (b) now substituted by regs 31–40 of the Copyright and Related Rights Regulations 2003 reg. 2(1), Sch. 1 para. 10(2) to include 'data bases'.

(Ymerodraeth State of Mind)' on YouTube (Google).[129] EMI records said that her 'spoof' unashamedly breached copyright law (section 84 CDPA) and served YouTube with a take-down notice. MJ claimed that her short video clip, promoting the Welsh city of Newport, was a parody, merely an in-joke of Alicia Keys' and Jay-Z's 'Empire State of Mind,' and that she had never contemplated obtaining a music rights licence.

The 'Newport' music video clip attracted more than 100,000 people within the first 48 hours because it was littered with witty one-liners, among them the city's twinning with Guangxi Province in China ('there's no province finer'). Instead of the Manhattan skyline as a backdrop to their video, scenes from the Welsh town were featured, including Newport rapper Alex Warren and singer Terema Wainwright. The video was later permitted to reappear including viral marketing advertising ('virals').

See Chapter 6.7

Section 30A CDPA now permits the use of copyright material for the purpose of 'caricature, parody or pastiche', and the use has to be 'fair dealing' to benefit from the exception. Once again the CDPA does not further define caricature, parody or pastiche.

> **Essential characteristics of a parody are:**
>
> - to evoke an existing work while being noticeably different from it; and
> - to constitute an expression of humour or mockery.

The Court of Justice (CJEU) provided useful guidance as to the meaning of 'parody' in *Deckmyn v Vandersteen* (2014).[130] This Belgian case involved a parody which conveyed a discriminatory message. In 2011 Mr Deckmyn, a Flemish nationalist and a member of the Vlaams Belang political party (sponsored by Vrijheidsfonds VZW a non-profit association) distributed a calendar in which Mr Deckmyn was named as its editor. The calendar had on its front cover a drawing which resembled a cartoon appearing on the cover of a comic book *Suske en Wiske* (*Spike and Suzy*) entitled 'De Wilde Weldoener' ('The Compulsive Benefactor'). The original drawing of 1961 by Mr Vandersteen had been altered so as to show money being distributed by the Mayor of Ghent, whose image replaced that of the original character, and the persons shown collecting the money had dark-coloured skin and were wearing scarves. No permission had been given to use the original drawing on the cover.

Mr Vandersteen's heirs brought the action against Mr Deckmyn and the Vrijheidsfonds VZW alleging copyright infringement. Mr Deckmyn argued that 'a child could see it [the drawing] was a parody' of the original drawing and that he only intended to make a political point regarding the distribution of taxpayers' money in Ghent. He said that this political cartoon fell within the scope of 'parody' accepted under point (6) of Article 22(1) of the Belgian Law of 30 June 1994 on copyright and related rights.

The CJEU's guidance in the case provides clarity on several points regarding the application of the parody exemption to copyright infringement recently brought into force in the UK under the Copyright and Rights in Performances (Quotation and Parody) Regulations 2014. Under the EU

---

129 Source: 'Jay-Z and Keys spoof is YouTube hit', YouTube, 30 July 2010, available at www.youtube.com/watch?v=maNgAxUnJ8I.
130 See: *Deckmyn (Johan), Vrijheidsfonds VZW v Vandersteen and Others (Helena Vandersteen, Christiane Vandersteen, Liliana Vandersteen, Isabelle Vandersteen, Rita Dupont, Amoras II CVOH, WPG Uitgevers België* (2014) (C-201/13) Judgment of the Court of Justice (Grand Chamber) 3 September 2014 (CJEU).

copyright acquis the Court of Justice held that 'parody' is to be an autonomous concept of EU law and must therefore be uniformly interpreted throughout the EU.[131]

See below
9.6.3

9.5.11 Temporary copying of IP works for the purposes of browsing or caching

Article 5(1) of the Information Society Directive ('InfoSoc')[132] provides for the temporary copying of copyright works in certain circumstances. This defence is mandatory across the EU and was implemented in the UK by introducing section 28A into the CDPA. This section provides that copyright in most types of work (excluding computer programs or databases) is *not* infringed by the making of copies which meet the following criteria:

a. they are temporary;
b. they are transient or incidental;
c. they are an 'integral and essential part of a technological process';
d. their sole purpose is to enable (a) a transmission of the work in a network between third parties by an intermediary or (b) a lawful use of the work; and
e. they have no independent economic significance.

Section 28A CDPA together with the provisions of Article 5(1) InfoSoc Directive means that copies made for the purposes of browsing or caching on the internet are permitted, as confirmed by the Court of Justice in the *Meltwater case* (2014).[133] Section 28A CDPA clarifies situations when a temporary copy created by an ISP would not infringe at all, and accordingly no injunctive relief would be available either (if sought). This may cover, for example, the creation of temporary cached copies of works by an ISP to enable the lawful browsing of the internet by an internet user.

In *Scarlet v SABAM* (2011),[134] the Belgian collecting society SABAM obtained an injunction against the ISP Scarlet. Scarlet's service was being used by internet users for the illegal P2P file-sharing of copyright works administered by SABAM and the injunction required Scarlet to install and implement a system to filter all communications carried over its service in order to identify files containing works in SABAM's catalogue, which would then be blocked.

Scarlet appealed, arguing (successfully) that the injunction was contrary to Article 15 of the E-Commerce Directive and Article 3 of the IP Enforcement Directive.[135] The Court of Justice recognized that national courts must weigh up competing rights and strike a fair balance between users' rights to freedom of expression and privacy rights (e.g. in IP protection). In *Scarlet* the injunction sought failed to strike a fair balance, not least because it could lead to legitimate content being blocked, particularly since copyright exceptions and other provisions for lawful use of copyright material vary from one Member State to another.

---

131 For a detailed discussion see: Arrowsmith, S. (2015), pp. 55–59.
132 Directive 2001/29/EC of the European Parliament and of the Council of 22 May 2001 on the harmonisation of certain aspects of copyright and related rights in the information society ('the InfoSoc Directive'). Official Journal L 167, 22/06/2001 p. 10.
133 See: *Public Relations Consultants Association Ltd v Newspaper Licensing Agency Ltd* [2014] All ER (EC) 959 (C-360/13) (CJEU) (sub nom the Meltwater case).
134 See: *Scarlet Extended SA v Societe Belge des Auteurs, Compositeurs et Editeurs SCRL (SABAM)* (C-70/10) [2011] ECR I-1195
135 Directive 2004/48/EC of the European Parliament and of the Council of 29 April 2004 on the enforcement of intellectual property rights ('the IP Enforcement Directive'). Official Journal L 157, 30/04/2004 p. 45.

Regulations 17, 18 and 19 of the E-Commerce Regulations apply where an ISP is a 'mere conduit' or where it is 'caching' or 'hosting' information. In summary, the defences apply to:

> **Mere conduit:** An ISP is acting as a 'mere conduit' if its services consist of transmitting information or providing network access, which includes the 'automatic, intermediate and transient' storage of information, where the sole purpose of the storage is to carry out the transmission and the information is not stored for longer than reasonably necessary (regulation 17).
>
> **Caching:** Caching is the local storage of information in frequent demand, to enable quicker access to that information by avoiding making repeated requests to the information's source (regulation 18).
>
> **Hosting:** Hosting is the storage of information e.g. the provision of space to internet users; this may be for websites, blogs, discussion boards, etc. (regulation 19).

In *Google France SARL v Louis Vuitton Malletier SA* (2011)[136] the CJEU held that an ISP could rely on the hosting defence only if it,

> has not played an active role of such a kind as to give it knowledge of, or control over, the data stored.

In *L'Oreal v eBay* (2012)[137] the Court of Justice held that eBay would have provided an active role if it provided assistance including:

> optimising the presentation of the offers for sale . . . or promoting those offers.

In this case the internet auction site eBay was not able to rely on the 'hosting' exemption.

See below 9.8

In the *Cartier v BSkyB* case (2014),[138] the London High Court (Chancery Division) granted its first blocking injunction to combat trade mark infringement. Unlike section 97A CDPA, trade mark legislation does not contain a specific power to grant an injunction against an intermediary. But the court granted an injunction under its general power contained in section 37(1) Senior Courts Act 1981.

👁 FOR THOUGHT

The luxury brands of Cartier and Montblanc have asked the big five UK internet service providers (ISPs) – BT, Virgin Media, Sky, TalkTalk and EE – to 'block' (by way of injunction) access to online auction house websites from selling fake versions of their goods, such as jewellery and watches. The operators of websites argue there could be implications for online marketplaces such as eBay and Gumtree, where genuine branded goods are traded alongside some counterfeits. Are injunctions the right way forward? Would it not be simpler to prosecute the company involved in 'counterfeiting'? Discuss.

---

136 (C-236/08) [2011] Bus LR 1 (CJEU).

137 See: *L'Oréal SA and Ors v eBay International AG and Ors* (2012) (Case C-324/09) Judgment of the Court of Justice Grand Chamber, 12 July 2011 (CJEU); [2012] Bus LR 1369.

138 See: *Cartier International and Others v British Sky Broadcasting Ltd and Others* [2014] EWHC 3354 (Ch) 17 October 2014 (sub nom the *Cartier* case).

9.5.12 Remedies

The court will order remedies for infringement of copyright depending on the circumstances, such as how flagrant the infringement was and what benefit the defendant gained from the infringement. Did that person carry out one of the restricted acts without the copyright owner's permission?

Most commonly, damages are awarded for loss of royalties or loss of profit. The calculation is usually based on the licence fee, or alternatively on the equitable remedy of an account for profits which focuses on the illegal gains of the defendant as opposed to the damages suffered by the claimant. Section 97(2) CDPA provides some forms of damages for 'flagrant' copyright infringement depending on the 'benefit' accrued to the defendant rights infringer.

Exemplary (or punitive) damages can be made, though they are rarely awarded in the UK. These are compensation awards in excess of actual damages – a form of punishment awarded in cases of malicious or wilful misconduct or breach of copyright.

9.6 International copyright legislation

Though the Copyright Acts of 1911 and 1956 generally safeguarded the artist's rights in the UK, international law did not grant automatic copyright to the author in another country, such as America. Above all, there were no statutes in the late nineteenth century that governed public performances; and therefore there were no penalties for infringement. This led to widespread copying and passing off of creative works, particularly those originating in English-speaking countries.

The Paris Convention for the Protection of Industrial Property of 20 March 1883 ('the Paris Convention')[139] established basic levels of protection and reciprocal recognition for so-called 'industrial property'. This international agreement was the first major step taken to help inventors ensure that their intellectual works were protected in other countries and at some of the great world exhibitions, such as the Weltausstellung in Wien 1873 (Vienna World Exhibition) and the Exposition Universelle in Paris in 1900.

The Paris Convention applies to industrial property in the widest sense, including patents, trademarks, industrial designs, utility models, service marks, trade names, geographical indications[140] and the repression of unfair competition.

9.6.1 The Berne Convention and the Universal Copyright Convention

The Berne Convention for the Protection of Literary and Artistic Works of 1886[141] ('the Berne Convention') became the first international agreement to unify a system of copyright protection. The Berne Convention creates automatic copyright in works as soon as they are created, asserted and declared (without having to register that right). The Berne Convention is administered by the World Intellectual Property Organization (WIPO). In 2016 WIPO had 188 contracting Member States.[142]

---

139 The Paris Convention has been revised many times: at Brussels on 14 December 1900; at Washington on 2 June 1911; at The Hague on 6 November 1925; at London on 2 June 1934; at Lisbon on 31 October 1958; at Stockholm on 14 July 1967 and 28 September 1979. Summary at: www.wipo.int/treaties/en/ip/paris/summary_paris.html.

140 A geographical indication (GI) is a sign used on products that have a specific geographical origin and possess qualities or a reputation that are due to that origin. In order to function as a GI, a sign must identify a product as originating in a given place, such as: Switzerland's Gruyère cheese, Mexico's Tequila, Roquefort cheese (from the French Roquefort-sur-Soulzon region), etc.

141 The Berne Convention of 9 September 1886, completed at Paris on 4 May 1896; revised at Berlin on 13 November 1908; completed at Berne on 20 March 1914; revised at Rome on 2 June 1928; at Brussels on 26 June 1948; at Stockholm on 14 July 1967; at Paris on 24 July 1971; amended on 28 September 1979. The original signatory countries comprised: Belgium, France, Germany, Italy, United Kingdom, Switzerland and Tunisia, further joined by Luxembourg in 1887, Monaco in 1889, Norway in 1896, Morocco in 1917, Portugal in 1911, the Netherlands in 1912 and Romania in 1927. Summary of the Berne Convention at: www.wipo.int/treaties/en/ip/berne/summary_berne.html.

142 See: WIPO contracting states at: www.wipo.int/members/en.

WIPO's main purpose is to encourage creative activity, with a mandate from its Member States to promote the protection of intellectual property throughout the world.

Though the 'public interest' defence is commonly used in the UK in breaches of copyright challenges, the Berne Convention does not explicitly permit this defence when someone's copyright has been infringed, so it would not necessarily be justifiable if an author's copyright has been infringed to argue that the copying was 'for the greater good of society' (see: *Gartside v Outram* (1856);[143] also: *Beloff v Pressdram Ltd* (1973)[144]). In other words, the Berne Convention does not expressly permit the public interest defence to copyright infringement, whereas UK copyright law will take the public interest defence into account (see: *Ashdown v Telegraph Group Ltd* (2001)[145]).

The Universal Copyright Convention of 1952 (UCC), first created in Geneva, was an alternative to the Berne Convention 1886, because some countries disagreed with certain aspects of the Berne Convention, most notably the United States, who at the time only provided protection on a fixed-term registration basis via the Library of Congress and required that copyright works must always show the copyright symbol ©. The UCC ensures that international protection is available to authors even in countries that would not become parties to the Berne Convention. Berne Convention countries also became signatories of the UCC to ensure that the work of citizens in Berne Convention countries would be protected in non-Berne Convention countries.

9.6.2 Harmonizing international copyright laws

The European Court of Justice's decision in the Danish *Infopaq*[146] case highlighted problems and the need for the harmonization of EU copyright legislation.

Infopaq International A/S (now Infomedia) is an organization, operating in Nordic countries such as Sweden, Denmark and Norway, that uses extracts from daily newspapers, magazines, broadcasting and social networking and produces short text extracts of 11 words. The process of data capture is divided into four parts; the creation of so called TIFF files, the transformation into text files, the data storage and the printing of text files. The purpose of this process is to ease searches and to be able to find relevant articles quickly.

The judgment of the Danish Supreme Court (Højesteret) resulted from an eight-year dispute between Infopaq and Danske Dagblades Forening (DDF)[147] concerning the dismissal of Infopaq's application for a declaration that it was not required to obtain the consent of the copyright owners for acts of reproduction of newspaper articles obtained by collective licensing. The Danish Supreme Court ruled that extracts of newspaper articles comprising no more than 11 words *can* be works protected by copyright.

The ECJ considered (twice – *Infopaq I* and *Infopaq II*) whether short reproductions of extracts from newspaper articles infringed copyright. The two questions referred to the ECJ by the Danish Supreme Court for a preliminary ruling were:

1. Are acts of reproduction of 11 words of articles reproductions that can be protected by the exclusive copyrights of the right holders as set out in Article 2 of the EU Copyright Directive ('Infosoc Directive')?[148]

---

143 (1856) 26 LJ Ch 113.
144 [1973] 1 All ER 24.
145 [2001] Ch 685 (Ch D).
146 See: *Infopaq International A/S v Danske Dagblades Forening* (C-5/08) [2009] ECR I-6569 (ECJ (4th Chamber)).
147 The professional association of Danish daily newspapers; its function is, *inter alia*, to offer advice on copyright issues.
148 Directive 2001/29/EC of the European Parliament and of the Council of 22 May 2001 on the harmonization of certain aspects of copyright and related rights in the information society.

2. Is Infopac's process of data capture an act of temporary and transient reproduction as set out in Article 5 of the Infosoc Directive and as such exempted from the exclusive rights of the right holders according to Article 2?

The ECJ finally ruled in favour of Danske Dagblades Forening, in that the process of data capture was copyright protected and that even 11 printed words were not exempt under Article 5(1) of the Infosoc Directive.[149] Lucas (2010) argues that international copyright litigation nowadays centres on the question of whether the 'reproduction' constitutes an 'expression of the intellectual creation of the author'? This question is now left to the national courts to decide following the *Infopaq* ruling.[150]

 FOR THOUGHT

> Databases enjoy separate protection under the Database Regulations (section 5 Copyright and Rights in Databases Regulations 1997). Generally, the database right is held by the person or organization that has made the arrangements for the database to be created. But what makes a database 'original'? Discuss with reference to relevant copyright legislation and give some practical examples.

9.6.3 EU copyright *acquis*

There has been significant harmonization of the substantive copyright law in Europe to reduce barriers to trade and to adjust the framework to new forms of exploitation. The result has been the so-called EU copyright *acquis*, a French term (*acquis communautaire*) meaning 'the EU as it is'. Accepting the *acquis* on copyright means taking legislation as you find it, that is 'autonomous and uniform' throughout the European Union. This then includes the terms of the copyright directives.

> **Under the EU copyright *acquis* and the WIPO treaties, copyright protection is created automatically when you create**
>
> - original literary, dramatic, musical and artistic work, including illustration and photography;
> - original non-literary written work, e.g. software, web content and databases;
> - sound and music recordings;
> - film and television recordings;
> - broadcasts;
> - the layout of published editions of written, dramatic and musical works.

The judgments by the Court of Justice (CJEU) in this area of harmonized IP laws have set out the terms of international treaties – such as TRIPS – which fall within the scope of EU law (see: *Anheuser-Busch Inc. v Budejovicky Budvar Narodni Podnik* (2004)[151]). However, Handig (2013) argues that the CJEU's interpretations in relation to 'copyright work' are not that straightforward, as there are

149 For further discussion see: Rosati, E. (2011), pp. 746–755.
150 See: Lucas, A. (2010), pp. 277–282.
151 (C-245/02) [2004] ECR I-10989; [2005] ETMR 27 (CJEU).

definitions only for three categories of works – namely computer programs,[152] databases[153] and photographs.[154] He doubts that the term 'copyright work' can (and indeed should) be interpreted uniformly across all copyrighted works in the Member States – as the EU copyright *acquis* suggests. Handig points out that in the recent IP directives there are no more definitions because the Member States could not agree on an 'implantation' to avoid harmonization.[155]

Since the *Karen Murphy* case[156] (see above), a considerable number of changes have been made to protect and harmonize copyright law across Europe. As the numerous footnotes in this chapter indicate, this has had considerable impact on UK copyright law (i.e. the CDPA).[157]

A new licensing scheme on orphan works[158] was introduced in the UK in October 2014 which provided greater access to about 91 million culturally valuable creative works – including diaries, photographs, oral history recordings and documentary films.

Orphan works are works, such as books, newspaper and magazine articles and films that are still protected by copyright but whose authors or other rightholders are not known or cannot be located or contacted to obtain copyright permissions.[159] Under the new scheme, a licence can be granted by the Intellectual Property Office (IPO) so that these works can be reproduced on websites, in books and on TV without breaking the law, while protecting the rights of owners so they can be remunerated if they come forward.

9.7 Passing off

See below 9.8

Passing off is a common law tort and available remedies include injunctive relief, delivery up of the offensive goods and damages to the owner of the rights or an accounting of profits by the offender. There is also 'reverse passing off', where a third party without authorization takes your trade mark or brand name and presents it as theirs.

The most common type of passing off involves the defendant selling goods that purport to be those of the claimant. Most commonly this occurs where a famous trade mark (brand) is copied, where packaging or 'get up' is copied and where websites become 'look-alikes'.

Blythe (2015) argues that the tests for passing off and trade mark infringement have essentially been the same, based on the confusion rationale. This is where the defendant sells goods under a sign that is identical or similar to a registered trade mark, the goods being identical or similar to those for which the mark is registered, and where the average consumer encounters those goods there exists a likelihood of confusion whereby the consumer mistakenly thinks that the defendant's goods are the claimant's goods, or mistakenly believes that there exists an economic link between the two undertakings[160] (see: *Reed Executive plc v Reed Business Information Ltd* (2004)[161]).

To establish this right of action, the claimant must show three elements, sometimes referred to as the 'classic trinity', first established by Lord Oliver of Aylmerton in the House of Lords'

152 Directive 2009/24 on the legal protection of computer programs [2009] OJ L111/16 Article 1(3); originally, Directive 91/250 on the legal protection of computer programs [1991] OJ L122/42.
153 Directive 96/9 on the legal protection of databases [1996] OJ L 77/20 Article 3(1).
154 Directive 2006/116 on the term of protection of copyright and certain related rights (codified version) Article 6, [2006] OJ L372/12 Article 6; originally, Directive 93/98 harmonising the term of protection of copyright and certain related rights, [1993] OJ L 290/9. The directive is sometimes also called the 'Duration Directive'.
155 See: Handig, C. (2013), pp. 334–340.
156 See: *Football Association Premier League Ltd v QC Leisure* (C-403/08) [2012] All ER (EC) 629 (*Karen Murphy* pub landlady case).
157 For detailed discussion see: Cornish, W., Llewelyn, D. and Aplin, T. (2013).
158 Directive 2012/28/EU On certain permitted uses of orphan works sets out common rules on the digitization and online display of so-called orphan works.
159 Section 77 Enterprise and Regulatory Reform Act 2013 (ERRA) ('Orphan Works licensing and extended collective licensing'), added new ss 116A 'Power to provide for licensing of orphan works' and 116B 'Extended collective licensing' to the CDPA 1988.
160 See: Blythe, A. (2015), pp. 484–489.
161 [2004] EWCA Civ 159.

decision of *Reckitt & Colman Products Ltd v Borden Inc.* (1990) (the *Jif Lemon* case).[162] In this case the HL issued a permanent injunction preventing Borden from marketing a lemon-shaped container to sell 'squeezy' lemon juice, which the US firm had done since 1985. Reckitt & Colman had been selling 'squeezy Jif Lemon' juice since 1956. Reckitt sued Borden for passing off their product as Jif Lemon juice. Had the Jif Lemon been a registered trade mark, the case would have been much simpler to prove. For this reason Reckitt & Colman could only resort to a passing off claim in their fight against competition from the US brand 'ReaLemon'. Reckitt succeeded in the House of Lords.

> **The 'classic trinity' test (the *Jif Lemon* principle) for all passing off actions involves**
>
> 1. misrepresentation;
> 2. goodwill;
> 3. damage.

In detail this means:

(1)   The defendant misrepresents his goods or services, either intentionally or unintentionally, so that the public believe or are led to believe that the offered goods or services are those of the claimant.

(2)   Since the claimant supplies his goods or services under a distinctive 'get-up' (e.g. brand or packaging), his goods or services have acquired goodwill and/or reputation in the marketplace that distinguishes the claimant's goods or services from its competitors.

(3)   The claimant suffers damage because of the misrepresentation.[163]

In *Moroccanoil Israel Ltd v Aldi Stores Ltd* (2014),[164] the court applied the *Jif Lemon* principle. Moroccanoil Israel Ltd (MIL) sold its argan oil products worldwide from 2009, the star product being the hair oil, sold in a brown bottle with a blue label. In March 2012, German supermarket giant, Aldi, started selling a new hair oil product called 'Miracle Oil', sold in a similarly shaped bottle with a blue label. MIL alleged customer confusion and in addition to passing off also alleged misrepresentation.[165] MIL enjoyed considerable goodwill in the UK, both in the brand and get-up (i.e. shape, colour, packaging, etc.). The company further argued that the misrepresentation had caused damage to MIL's goodwill. Aldi admitted in court its willingness to 'live dangerously' by marketing products with similar get-up and packaging to their expensive equivalents but argued that this alone did not constitute passing off.

The Intellectual Property Enterprise Court (IPEC) then applied the classic trinity test (*Jif Lemon* principle) in *Moroccanoil*:

(a)   goodwill in MIL's business in the sale of Moroccanoil in the UK, which goodwill is associated with the get-up and name of the product such that they are in combination recognized by the public as distinctive of MIL's product;

---

162   [1990] 1 WLR 491.
163   Ibid., at para. 880 (Lord Oliver).
164   [2014] EWHC 1686 (IPEC).
165   As per s 10 Trade Marks Act 1994, the provision by which Article 5 of Directive 2008/95 was transposed into UK law.

(b)   a misrepresentation on the part of Aldi (whether or not intentional) in relation to the source of Aldi's Miracle Oil product; and

(c)   damage to the goodwill by reason of the misrepresentation.[166]

Additionally His Honour Judge Hacon considered the observations of Morritt LJ in the *Interflora* case[167]. He found that the important point to be taken from this case was that passing off might be established even though most people were not deceived.

The court dismissed MIL's action and concluded that the evidence submitted did not show that members of the public were likely to assume that Aldi's Miracle Oil and Moroccanoil were the same product; that there was no misrepresentation.

See below
9.8

Cases like *Moroccanoil* demonstrate the importance of formally protecting the distinctive elements of a product, particularly in relation to its get-up and packaging. It then makes absolute business sense to register a sign or brand as trade mark in order to seek more effective redress (rather than a passing-off action). While the two actions of passing off and trade mark infringement share many similarities, the fact remains that they are both separate doctrines (see also: *United Biscuits (UK) Ltd v Asda Stores Ltd* (1997)[168] – 'the Penguin and Puffin' case; also: *Specsavers International Healthcare Ltd v Asda Ltd* (2012)[169]).

FOR THOUGHT

What advice would you give a new brand that wants to register its new name 'JamTart'? Discuss relevant legislation and the practicalities.

9.8 Trade marks

A trade mark (or brand) is a badge of origin of goods or services and is usually a name, logo or strap line. Trade marks are signs that distinguish goods or services from one business from those of other businesses. Section 1 of the Trade Marks Act 1994 defines a 'trade mark' as:

(1)   any sign capable of being represented graphically which is capable of distinguishing goods or services of one undertaking from those of other undertakings.

A trade mark may, in particular, consist of words (including personal names), designs, letters, numerals or the shape of goods or their packaging.

Unlike copyright which cannot be registered in the UK, trade marks are registered to ensure that no one else has registered a mark which is the same or similar to the one which is proposed for goods or services. This means you can put the ® symbol next to your brand. Most importantly, the trade mark must be unique.

---

166 *Moroccanoil* [2014] at para. 4 (Hacon HHJ).
167 *Interflora Inc. v Marks and Spencer plc* [2012] EWCA Civ 1501 at para. 30 (Morritt LJ).
168 [1997] RPC 513.
169 [2012] EWCA Civ 24.

Trade marks can include

- words;
- sounds;
- logos;
- colours;
- a combination of any of these.

A trade mark cannot

- be offensive (e.g. contain swear words or pornographic images);
- describe the goods or services it will relate to (e.g. the word 'cotton' cannot be a trade mark for a cotton textile company);
- be misleading (e.g. the word 'organic' for goods that are not organic);
- be a three-dimensional shape associated with a brand (e.g. use the shape of an egg for eggs);
- be too common and non-distinctive (e.g. a simple statement, such as 'we lead the way').

Peppa Pig is a global brand and a registered trade mark.[170] The character is owned by Entertainment One, which makes and distributes TV and films including *Grey's Anatomy, Spotlight* and *The Hunger Games*. The Peppa-brand merchandise brought in more than $1.1 billion in retail sales in 2015–2016, added to which came 500 new or renewed licence deals with TV companies around the world.[171]

In *Interflora Inc. v Marks & Spencer plc* (2015),[172] the claimants, Interflora, brought trade mark infringement proceedings against Marks and Spencer (M & S). Interflora claimed infringement of their UK and Community-registered trade marks for the word 'interflora' and that M & S's activities in the flower delivery market amounted to an infringement of their marks under Article 5(1)(a) and (2) of First Council Directive 89/104 EEC of 21 December 1988 and Article 9(1)(a) and (c) of Council Regulation 40/94 of 20 December 1993 on the Community trade mark.[173] The Court of Justice of the European Union (CFEU) had already granted ISPs a common carrier status similar to the post office, by taking action against platform providers like Google, eBay and Amazon, etc. in relation to claims for trade mark infringement or passing off (see: *Google France SARL v Louis Vuitton Malletier SA* (2011)[174]).

The long-drawn-out *Interflora v M& S* action did not come to a satisfactory conclusion. The CA referred to the complex commercial network of Interflora: as trade mark proprietor it is also composed of a large number of retailers which vary greatly in terms of size and commercial profile. And in such circumstances, it may be particularly difficult for the reasonably well-informed and reasonably observant internet user to determine whose advertisement is displayed in response to a search using that trade mark as a search term.[175] Whilst finding in favour of Interflora, the CA remitted the case back for retrial.

---

170 The trade mark for Peppa Pig was filed by Astley Baker Davies Ltd, London, W1B 5TB on 9 June 20015. The PEPPA PIG trade mark serial number is 78647159.

171 Source: 'Peppa Pig on track to be $2bn brand after making splash in US and Asia', by Mark Sweney, *The Guardian*, 24 May 2016.

172 [2015] EWHC 675 (Ch) 9 March 2015.

173 Now Directive 2008/99/EC of 22 October 2008 and CTM Regulation 207/2009 of 26 February 2009.

174 (C-236/08) [2011] Bus LR 1 (CJEU).

175 *Interflora v M & S* (2015) at paras 51 and 52.

The two key issues that arose in the CA were firstly the issue of the burden of proof and, secondly, the introduction of the controversial initial interest doctrine into the case, i.e. the concept of the 'average consumer' using the internet. Perhaps the *Interflora* case might still be referred to the CJEU for a definitive ruling in the 'initial interest' doctrine.

Swiss company Nestlé failed in its attempt to convince European judges to let it trademark the shape of the four-finger version of a KitKat in the UK.[176] The CJEU ruled in September 2015 that the KitKat's shape was not distinctive enough for consumers to associate it with the chocolate covered wafer.[177] Opposed by the UK's Cadbury, Nestlé had argued before the European Court of Justice in Luxembourg that even without its red and white packaging, the shape of the bar should be regarded as a distinct trade mark. The UK Trade Marks Registry had turned down Nestlé's application to protect the chocolate bar in the UK in 2013, following Cadbury's opposition.[178]

The *Glee Club*[179] ruling in the Court of Appeal in February 2016 ended the long-running legal battle between a small comedy club in the UK and the US giant corporation, Twentieth Century Fox. The case centred on the popular TV show *Glee* – a fictional school singing club and a small UK comedy club concern. Legal action began in 2009 when Comic Enterprises Ltd found that the TV show *Glee* was causing damage to its comedy clubs across the UK, since customers were associating them with the US TV show, which, the comedy club alleged, discouraged customers from attending their clubs. Comic Enterprises registered the name 'The Glee Club' as a trade mark in 2001.

The CA upheld the earlier judgment in the Patents County Court (PCC).[180] Given the similarities between the marks, the Court of Appeal found that the average consumer would consider that the producer of the TV show was also responsible for, or connected with, the UK comedy club. This is known as 'wrong way round' confusion, where a consumer familiar with the accused sign was confused upon seeing the mark, rather than vice versa and therefore it was held a trade mark infringement under section 10(2)(b) Trade Marks Act 1994. In addition, the CA ruled that the broadcast and distribution of a television show are activities that are similar to the provision of venues for live comedy and music shows. The court suggested, for example, that comedy shows could be televised and that a television series could give rise to live tours. The claim for passing off was rejected.

The *Glee* decision demonstrates the importance of registering a brand. The fact that even a Goliath with the financial might of Twentieth Century Fox could be found to infringe a trademark (and was ordered by the court to pay £100,000 on account of damages that could run into millions) shows that trade marks can have a major impact on businesses of any size (see also: *Associated Newspapers Ltd v Bauer Radio Ltd* (2015)[181] – a case concerning the brand *Metro* newspaper and *Metro Radio*).[182]

In 2007 pop legend and frontman of the 1980s pop band Frankie Goes to Hollywood, Holly Johnson, attempted to register the mark 'Frankie Goes to Hollywood' as a Community Trade Mark.

---

176 Article 3(1)(e)(ii) of Directive 2008/95, under which registration may be refused of signs consisting exclusively of the shape of goods which is necessary to obtain a technical result, must be interpreted as referring only to the manner in which the goods at issue function and it does not apply to the manner in which the goods are manufactured.

177 See: *Société des Produits Nestlé SA v Cadbury UK Ltd* (2015) (Case C-215/14) 16 September 2015 (CJEU, First Chamber) (sub nom *KitKat* case).

178 Ibid., at para. 17. On 28 January 2011, Cadbury had filed a notice of opposition to the application for registration putting forward various pleas, in particular a plea alleging that registration should be refused on the basis of the provisions of the Trade Marks Act 1994 which transpose Article 3(1)(b), (e)(i) and (ii) and (3) of Directive 2008/95.

179 See: *Comic Enterprises Ltd v Twentieth Century Fox Film Corp.* [2016] EWCA Civ 41 (CA Civ Div), 8 February 2016 (sub nom the *Glee Club* case).

180 See: *Comic Enterprises Ltd v Twentieth Century Fox Film Corp.* [2012] EWPCC 13 (Patents County Court), 22 March 2012) (the *Glee Club* case).

181 See: *Associated Newspapers Ltd v Bauer Radio* (2015) in the matter of Application No 2233378 by Associated Newspapers Ltd to register the trade marks metro. co.uk and metro.com (*A SERIES*) in classes 9, 16, 35, 36, 38, 39, 41 and 42 Trade Marks Act 1994 and the opposition thereto under No 97043 by Bauer Radio Ltd. (O-241-13) (2015) WL 3750864 (*Metro v Metro Radio*).

182 For further discussion see: Lundie Smith, R. and Kendall-Palmer, C. (2016), pp. 165–168.

The main issue in *Frankie Goes to Hollywood*[183] centred on the law of passing off in relation to a non-registered trade mark. Though Holly Johnson had invented the name, the Office of Harmonization in the Internal Market (OHIM) ruled that the mere act of inventing a name did not, in itself, bring the 'inventor' any rights. It then followed that the use of the non-registered trade mark 'Frankie Goes to Hollywood' was 'of more than mere local significance', in that the original band members could show that the original band name 'Frankie Goes to Hollywood' was very successful both in the UK and in other European countries between 1984 and 1987; moreover, that the band's music continues to be very popular. It was for this reason that the OHIM prevented the registration of a new trade mark in the very same name.[184]

The result then was that Holly Johnson's application was successfully opposed by the four other band members, Peter Gill (in whose name the action was brought), Paul Rutherford, Brian Nash and Mark O'Toole. Relying on Lord Oliver's classic trinity test to establish 'passing off', both the UK Intellectual Property Office (UK-IPO)[185] and OHIM[186] (parallel UK and European actions) decided the rights to the name were owned equally by all five original band members and no one band member had the right to claim exclusivity to that name.

In the *Saxon Trade Mark* case,[187] an agreement over ownership of the 1970s heavy metal band name Saxon was not in place and the court held that a 'partnership at will' arose with the name being an asset of the partnership to be split equally amongst the band members. In 1999 Graham Oliver and Steven Dawson registered 'Saxon' as a trade mark, maintaining they had exclusive rights in the name. They tried to prevent former band member Peter 'Biff' Byford from using the name. Byford then applied to the Trade Mark Registry to have the mark declared invalid, due to 'bad faith' under section 3(6) Trade Marks Act 1994. He brought a passing off action to stop the other two from misrepresenting themselves as Saxon under section 5(4) of the 1994 Act.

The Court of Chancery held that the application had been made in *bad faith* by Oliver and Dawson. The court further established the principle that the name and goodwill of a partnership are owned 'by the partnership' and not the individual partners or band members. This set a new precedent. This means if a band member leaves, and the remaining band members continue in the group, they cannot continue using the band name in the absence of an agreement in contract. The judge concluded that a band would be properly advised to enter into a partnership agreement and register the band name as a trade mark in the event of a band member leaving the group (see also: *Harrods Ltd v Harrodian School* (1996);[188] *Barlow Clowes International Ltd (In Liquidation) v Eurotrust International Ltd* (2005)[189]).

9.8.1 Registered trade marks and EU legislation

Trade mark registration in the UK is by application to the government's Intellectual Property Office (IPO).[190] These marks then provide business exclusivity for a brand, goods or services. However, a mark which simply describes what a business does may not be registered. Section 2 Trade Marks Act 1994 defines a 'registered trade mark' as:

> a property right obtained by the registration of the trade mark under this Act and the proprietor of a registered trade mark has the rights and remedies provided by this Act.

---

183 See: *Gill v Frankie Goes to Hollywood Ltd* [2008] ETMR 4 (Case B 849 069) (OHIM) 27 July 2007.
184 Ibid., at 97–99.
185 UK-IPO 'Frankie Goes to Hollywood', O/140/07 dated 25 May 2007.
186 OHIM Opposition No B849 069 *Gill v Frankie Goes to Hollywood Ltd* [2008] ETMR 4.
187 See: *Byford v Oliver & Dawson* [2003] EWHC 295 (*Saxon Trade Mark* case) (Ch).
188 [1996] RPC 697.
189 [2005] UKPC 37.
190 See: IPO at: www.gov.uk/topic/intellectual-property/trade-marks.

The new EU legislation on Trade Marks and Designs came into force on 23 March 2016 (Regulation (EU) No 2015/2424), making EU-wide registration easier. From that date the European registration office for trade mark regulation (the former Office for Harmonization in the Internal Market (OHIM)) became known as the European Union Intellectual Property Office (EUIPO) located in Alicante, Spain. The Community trade mark is now called 'The European Union Trade Mark' (EUTM). The agency is responsible for registering trade marks and designs valid in all 28 Member States and mediates in trade mark disputes. Trade mark registration costs on average €900 and the EUIPO registers about 100,000 marks each year.[191]

The EU certification allows a certifying institution or organization to use the mark as a sign for goods and services complying with the certification requirements (Article 74b EUTMR). In addition, TRIPS defines what types of signs can be eligible for protection as trade marks and what the minimum rights conferred on their owners must be.

L'Oréal v Bellure (2010)[192] marked two complex landmark rulings, first in 2007 and then in 2010, concerning counterfeit 'smell-alike' perfumes. The CA had to determine whether the Belgian defendants Bellure had contravened Article 5(1)(a) Trademarks Directive ('use of an identical sign for identical goods'[193]) for trading online in 'smell-alike' perfumes ('Stitch', 'Création Lamis' and 'Dorrall'). Each 'creation' smelt like a famous luxury branded perfume with a registered trade mark. All smell-alike products were manufactured in Dubai by Bellure, who, in turn, claimed that the articles were not imitations in the sense of being counterfeits. Bellure argued that the use of trade marks was used only for 'comparative advertising'. L'Oréal had to show that there was detriment to any of the functions of their brands. Lewison J (Chancery Division) found Bellure to have infringed L'Oréal's and other brands' trade marks, and that Bellure had taken unfair advantage of L'Oréal et al.'s reputation in the UK; that is, trying to pass off its own brand as that of L'Oréal (see also: L'Oréal SA v eBay International AG (2009)[194] and the French judgment in L'Oréal SA v eBay France SA (2009)[195]).

The L'Oréal SA v Bellure case[196] reached the Court of Justice (CJEU) for a preliminary ruling on trademark offences. In its decision the court gave guidance on many issues regarding trade mark law, providing a synthesis of several earlier decisions. The decision stresses the wide-reaching protection under Article 5(2) of the Trademarks Directive in that the Directive protects trade marks which have a reputation and protects the brand against the use of unfair advantage and detriment to the brand which is of distinctive character (including its trade mark). The Court of Justice stressed that any comparative advertising which would not meet the requirements of the Directive, while using the trade mark, would constitute a trade mark infringement; for example, if the goods in question are presented as an imitation or replica (which had been the case in L'Oréal v Bellure). The Court of Justice stressed that actual detriment or actual unfair advantage need not be shown, but that it suffices that the use would take unfair advantage of, or would be detrimental to the distinctive character or the trade mark reputation.

Helpfully, the CJEU supplemented the term 'trade mark infringement' with alternative terms, such as 'tarnishment' and 'degradation' to a brand. And the term 'gaining of unfair advantage' was broadly defined with alternative terms such as 'parasitism' and 'free-riding'. These concepts relate not only to the detriment caused to the trade mark but to the unfair advantage taken by the infringer as a result of the use of the identical or similar signs.

---

191 The registration cost for an EU certification mark is the same as for an EU collective mark, i.e. from 850 for one class. See: EUIPO. EUROPA.EU.

192 See: L'Oréal SA; Lancôme Parfums et Beauté & CIE; Laboratoire Garnier & CIE v Bellure NV Malaika Investments Ltd (t/a Honeypot Cosmetic & Perfumery Sales); Starion International Ltd [2010] EWCA Civ 535; See also: L'Oréal SA; Lancôme Parfums et Beauté & CIE; Laboratoire Garnier & CIE v Bellure NV; North West Cosmetics Ltd, HMC Cosmetics Ltd; Malaika Investments Ltd, Sveonmakeup.co.uk; Starion International Ltd [2007] EWCA Civ 968 (Ch).

193 Directive 2008/95/EC to approximate the laws of the Member States relating to trademarks ('the Trademarks Directive').

194 [2009] EWHC 1094 (Ch).

195 (2009) (RG 07/11365) Tribunal de grande instance, Paris, judgment of 13 May 2009 (unreported).

196 L'Oréal SA v Bellure NV (2010) (Case C-487/07) Court of Justice (First Chamber) 10 February 2009 (CJEU); [2010] RPC 1.

Companies which specialize in 'rip-off' (counterfeit) goods have experienced lawyers who advise them on a daily basis on how close to the copyright infringement line they can get without crossing it. However, the *L'Oréal v Bellure* ruling (both in the UK Court of Appeal and the CJEU) is seen by the fashion and cosmetics industries as ground-breaking in deterring future copying and trade mark infringements of genuine brands.

9.8.2 ISP liability in relation to online auction houses

Are online auction 'houses' such as eBay or Gumtree liable for IP infringements committed by their users and dealers? This was the question raised by the Chancery Court with reference to the European Court of Justice (ECJ) in the landmark case of *L'Oréal v eBay* (2012).[197] The claimants were all cosmetics companies bringing claims for trade mark infringement against three defendant companies which facilitated the online auction and sale of goods, as well as seven individual sellers of cosmetic products which, the claimants maintained, infringed a number of Community trade marks and UK trade marks of which they were the proprietors.[198]

The central questions in this case were: did eBay (Europe) itself commit infringements by using trademarks in relation to infringing goods? Or was eBay simply a 'host' and therefore not liable for copyright infringement as a mere auction site?

Furthermore the court raised the important point of sponsored hyperlinks and 'link marks' – a further question referred by the Court of Chancery to the CJEU – this point focusing on the scope of infringement of Article 5(1) of EC Directive 89/104, which approximated the laws of the Member States relating to trade marks. The problem was that this Directive did not specifically define the use of a trade mark by third parties; it only covered the use of a trade mark sign in relation to the proprietor's goods.

In this action the CJEU had to determine whether the sellers had sold goods which infringed the claimants' trade marks in that they were:

(i) counterfeit;
(ii) non-European Economic Area (EEA) goods;
(iii) tester products that were not intended for resale; or
(iv) products which, being unboxed, would have damaged the reputation of claimants' trade marks.

L'Oréal further argued that hyperlinks at the top of the sponsored link led to a page from the eBay Express site showing a search for 'matrix hair' and 'magie noire' which brought up 48 items from international sellers and that all of these were to infringing goods. The basis of this allegation was that the country or region stated was the United States in all cases and the items were priced in sterling. L'Oréal contended that, so far as the auction-style listings were concerned, eBay did in fact conduct an auction. eBay disputed this and L'Oréal accepted at least that eBay's activities differed from those of traditional auctioneers. L'Oréal claimed that each of the fourth to tenth defendants infringed one or more of the trade marks by using signs identical to the trade marks of goods to those for which the trade marks are registered. These claims all concerned the Lancôme marks.[199]

---

197 See: *L'Oréal SA and Ors v eBay International AG and Ors* (2012) (Case C-324/09) Judgment of the Court of Justice Grand Chamber, 12 July 2011 (CJEU) (by reference from the High Court Chancery Division in *L'Oréal SA v eBay International AG* [2009] EWHC 1094 (Ch)).
198 L'Oréal divided the trademarks into two groups for the purposes of their claims. The first group, referred to as 'the Lancôme Marks', consisted of Lancôme, Renergie, Definicils and Amor Amor. The second group, referred to as 'the Link Marks', consisted of Definicils together with the remaining trademarks not included in the first group.
199 The complaint against the fourth defendant concerned advertisements and offers for sale for 'Lancôme Maquicomplet Concealer Light Buff RRP £18.50', sold on 23 November 2006; 'Lancôme Renergie Microlift Active Redefining Treatment', sold on 23 November 2006; and 'Lancôme Definicils Full Size Black Mascara Waterproof', sold on 5 December 2006.

In their defence, eBay argued that they had set up systems and policies which discouraged the sale of infringing products and which enabled trademark owners, by notifying them, to have taken down the webpages on which allegedly infringing products were sold.[200] eBay also argued that they were merely fulfilling the function of an ISP ('hosting site') and were not involved in the sale of infringing goods, relying on Article 14 of Directive 2000/1 (the E-Commerce Directive). eBay submitted that, as a matter of law, eBay Europe was under no duty or obligation to prevent third parties from infringing L'Oréal's (or anyone else's) registered trade marks. The online trading house also argued that it attempted to prevent or at least minimize infringements, in particular through the VeRO programme which filtered infringing goods, such as counterfeit watches by Rolex. Counsel for eBay Europe submitted that in reality L'Oréal's claim of joint tortfeasorship was a thinly disguised attack on eBay's business model.

In this respect, the CJEU did not come to a conclusive decision. It held that EU trademark law had not been completely harmonized in respect of copyright and trade mark infringement via hyperlinks and link marks. Since Article 11 of the EC Enforcement Directive is not clear on third-party obligation with regard to future infringements as a result of online auction site operation, there is, as yet, no liability for past infringements on the ground of joint tortfeasorship. In view of the current uncertainty over this area of law, the CJEU's response to the L'Oréal case does not provide a clear message.

What then was really at the heart of the L'Oréal case? Was it not – as counsel for eBay Europe argued – an attack on eBay's business model? That said, copyright and industrial property rights are at increased risk and it could be argued that the high profits which eBay (and others) make from their sites oblige them to ensure that IP rights are not infringed. The answer lies partly in the Cartier ruling (see below) which followed on from the L'Oréal action, resulting in website-blocking orders.

9.8.3 Website-blocking orders

Section 97A CDPA provides injunctions against service providers which means that the High Court in England and Wales (in Scotland, the Court of Session) now has the power to grant relief in the form of a 'blocking order' against a service provider, where that ISP has actual knowledge of another person using their service to infringe copyright.

In determining whether an ISP has *actual knowledge*, a court will have to take into account all 'matters which appear to it in the particular circumstances to be relevant' (section 97A (2)), such as:

● whether a service provider has received a notice through a means of contact made available in accordance with regulation 6(1)(c) of the Electronic Commerce Regulations 2002; and
● the extent to which any notice includes the full name and address of the sender of the notice; and
● details of the infringement in question.

The leading case is Cartier v BskyB (2014),[201] the first time the High Court in London granted relief ordering five defendant ISPs (namely BskyB [now Sky], BT, EE, Talk Talk and Virgin) who together have a market share of approximately 95 per cent of UK broadband users to block access to a number of counterfeiting websites.

---

200 eBay Europe pleaded defences under ss 10(6) and 11(2) Trademarks Act 1994 (though these were not pursued at trial).
201 See: *Cartier International and Others v BSkyB and Others* [2014] EWHC 3354 (Ch) 17 October 2014 (the *Cartier* case).

KEY CASE   *Cartier International and Others v British Sky Broadcasting Ltd and Others* [2014] EWHC 3354 (Ch)

Precedent

In order to be granted an injunction for website-blocking, the following conditions must be met. The relief must:

* be effective;
* be dissuasive;
* not be unnecessarily complicated or costly;
* avoid barriers to legitimate trade;
* be fair and equitable and strike a 'fair balance' between the applicable fundamental rights;
* be proportionate.

Furthermore:

* the target website must have infringed the trade mark/s, even where they state that the goods are replicas, as this can still lead to customer and post-sale confusion;
* the target websites' operators used the ISPs' services to infringe the trade marks;
* the ISPs had actual knowledge of the infringement.

Facts

The claimants were all companies within the Richemont Group, owners of a portfolio of luxury brands, such as Cartier and Montblanc. Richemont sought injunctions pursuant to section 97A CDPA requiring the ISPs BSkyB *et al.* to block access to six websites that infringed its trade marks by advertising and selling counterfeit goods, target websites such as e.g. www.cartierloveonline.com. Each had targeted UK customers offering for sale replicas of products bearing one of the trade marks.

The key EU provisions which allow rightholders to apply for injunctions against intermediaries are:

* Article 8(3) of the InfoSoc Directive;[202]
* Article 11 of the IP Enforcement Directive.[203]

The main problem was that the UK Parliament implemented Article 8(3) of the InfoSoc Directive (concerning copyright infringement) by inserting section 97A into the CDPA. However, the government did not think it necessary to implement the relevant sentence within Article 11 of the Enforcement Directive, therefore providing no specific statutory provision equivalent to section 97A in relation to trade marks.

---

202 Directive 2001/29/EC of the European Parliament and of the Council of 22 May 2001 on the harmonisation of certain aspects of copyright and related rights in the information society, transposed into UK law by the Copyright and Related Rights Regulations 2003, S.I. 2003/2498 ('the InfoSoc Directive').

203 Directive 2004/48/EC of 29 April 2004 on the enforcement of intellectual property rights, transposed into UK law by the Intellectual Property (Enforcement, etc.) Regulations 2006, S.I. 2006/1028 ('the IP Enforcement Directive').

The question before the High Court was: could the court order such an injunction? Arnold J consulted section 37(1) Senior Courts Act 1981 and interpreted it in light of Article 11 of the IP Enforcement Directive which requires that:

> Member States must ensure that rightholders are in a position to apply for an injunction against intermediaries whose services are used by a third party to infringe an intellectual property right, without prejudice to Article 8 (3) of the [InfoSoc Directive].[204]

Decision

Arnold J granted the orders, finding the likely costs burden on the ISPs was justified and the orders were proportionate. He also acknowledged that ISP costs might be significant in future if applications for such blocking orders grew rapidly in number. On the proportionality aspect in particular, the judge held that the threshold conditions were met.

The Court granted orders substantially in the form sought but with two modifications: (i) a requirement that the notice on the blocked page should identify the party who applied for it to be blocked; and (ii) the orders should contain a 'sunset clause' such that they cease to apply at the expiry of a defined period.

Analysis

The *Cartier* decision marks an important development in the protection of brands online, i.e. as a new option for trade mark holders seeking to limit the online sale of counterfeit goods. The problem had been until then, that there was no specific statutory provision concerning trade marks and blocking websites that sold counterfeit goods.

The 'sunset clause' means that ISPs and operators of websites can now apply to the High Court to discharge or vary such 'blocking' orders following a change in circumstances. The orders will cease to have effect after a defined period (provisionally set at two years) unless either the ISPs consent or the court orders that they should be continued.

Arnold J's additional comments about the effectiveness of alternative measures and the proportionality of imposing the obligation on ISPs may well encourage rights holders to seek site-blocking injunctions.

It remains to be seen whether the ISPs will elect to challenge this decision or if they will continue to oppose future applications under section 97A CDPA, given the additional costs they could face. The public interest in preventing the sale of counterfeit goods was definitely a significant factor in the *Cartier* decision whether to make the blocking order or not. It is fair to say that the case has raised concerns about the impact on online businesses and possible restrictions on freedom of expression on the internet as a market place.

---

204 The Court also considered: Article 5 of Directive 2008/95/EC of October 2008, Articles 5(1)(a) and (3), which were implemented in the UK by s 10(1) and (4) Trade Marks Act 1994; Directive 2000/31/EC of June 2000, which was transposed into UK law by the Electronic Commerce (EC Directive) Regulations 2002 and the Charter of Fundamental Rights of the European Union.

In *Svensson* (2014)[205] the CJEU determined that there would be no infringement where the work is made available on a publicly available website with the authorization of the right holder. *Svensson* was a case brought by the film industry concerning hyperlinks against four websites (viooz.co; megashare.info; www.1.zmovie.tw and watch32.com). Hoy (2015) concludes that the decision in *Svensson* focused specifically on the identification of the 'relevant public', which was, in fact, the same public as that to which the material had originally been lawfully communicated. Where the websites simply collated users' links to torrent files the website operators were communicating to the public and therefore infringing copyright because that public was not the public originally contemplated by the copyright holders, but a 'new' public able to download the uploaded files without authorization and without making any payment.[206]

In summary, where a right holder authorizes his work to appear on a website which is freely available to all via hyperlinks, it will be treated as having authorized all internet users so that linking to the content on the authorized website will not infringe copyright. There will be infringement, however, where the link constitutes availability to a 'new public'. The court in *Svensson* specifically distinguished the situation where a link circumvents measures on the host site which were designed to restrict public access – such as a subscription pay wall, which would then constitute a communication to a new public not contemplated by the right holder.

 FOR THOUGHT

In the light of Arnold J's ruling in the *Cartier* decision (2014),[207] there have been a number of these section 97A CDPA orders granted over recent years. Find out about similar cases where the courts granted 'blocking' injunctions to a number of record companies, for example for breach of copyright in respect of illegal music downloads and music trade mark infringement.

9.9 Patents

A patent protects an invention with a practical application, which is new. Provided it has some practical use, it covers an underlying idea or concept, although it does not mean the holder has a monopoly on a given process, idea or invention.

The right to own a patent derives initially from the inventor or inventors of the invention to be protected by the patent under section 7 Patents Act 1977. However, the inventor may not be entitled to own the patent, for example, because there is a contract or confidentiality agreement which entitles another person to the ownership in preference to the inventor.

A patent application takes a long time and only applies for specific territories. A patent is a title granted by the state to the creator or owner of an invention, which entitles the inventor to prevent others from manufacturing, using, selling and, in some cases, importing the technology without his permission for a specified period of years (TRIPS states 20 years for inventions). Patent protection must be available for both products and processes, in almost all fields of technology.

205 See: *Svensson v Retriever Sverige AB* (C-466/12) [2014] Bus LR 259 (4th Chamber) (CJEU)
206 See: Hoy, R. (2015), pp. 44–47.
207 *Cartier International AG v British Sky Broadcasting Ltd* [2014] EWHC 3354 (Ch).

The HL decision in *Rhone-Poulenc Rorer International Holdings Inc. v Yeda Research & Development Co. Ltd* (2007)[208] restated that the rights to an invention arise from the inventor, and no complexities or uncertainties usually arise in cases where patent rights are claimed under the entitlement provisions. Such proceedings are generally determined simply on the facts of the case.

To stop a patent owner from abusing his rights – for example by failing to supply the product on the market – governments can issue 'compulsory licences', allowing a competitor to produce the product or use the process under license. If a patent is issued for a production process, then the rights must extend to the product directly obtained from the process. Under certain conditions, alleged infringers may be ordered by a court to prove that they have not used the patented process.

UK patent rights can be obtained either through an application made directly to the Intellectual Property Office (IPO) or to the European Patent Office in Munich.[209] The European Patent Register contains all the publicly available procedural information on European patents. Any legal person can apply for a patent application.

However, only the inventors or their successors in title are entitled to the grant of a patent. Before a patent is granted, an indication of how the inventor derived the rights to the invention from the inventor(s) must be filed at the patent office. Employers automatically derive the rights to an invention made by an employee during the course of carrying out the duties of their employment.

Until the creation of the Unified Patent Court (UPC)[210] in 2016–2017, national courts and authorities of the contracting states of the European Patent Convention were competent to decide on the infringement and validity of European patents. However, this gave rise to a number of difficulties when a patent proprietor wished to enforce a European patent – or when a third party sought the revocation of a European patent – in several countries. It meant high costs, risk of diverging decisions and a lack of legal certainty.

Forum shopping became inevitable as parties tried to take advantage of differences in national courts' interpretation of harmonized EU patent law and in procedural laws, as well as differences in speed (between 'slow' and 'quick' courts) and in the level of damages awarded. The 'Agreement on the Unified Patent Court' addresses the above problems by creating a specialized patent court – the Unified Patent Court (UPC) with exclusive jurisdiction for litigation relating to European patents and EU patents with unitary effect (unitary patents).

The UPC began working in Spring 2017. Its divisions and locations are:

- the Court of Appeal in Luxembourg;
- central and local divisions in Germany (Munich); Italy (Milan); Luxembourg; Sweden (Stockholm); and UK (London).

Only EU Member States can be in the UPC. The UPC Committee is composed of all the Signatory States to the Unified Patent Court Agreement (16351/12).[211] The UPC comprises a Court of First Instance, a Court of Appeal and a Registry. By the end of 2016, 25 Member States had ratified the agreement.

---

208 [2007] UKHL 43.
209 See: EPO at: www.epo.org.
210 See: the Unified Patent Court at: www.unified-patent-court.org.
211 See: Regulation (EU) No 1257/2012 of the European Parliament and of the Council of 17 December 2012 implementing enhanced cooperation in the area of the creation of unitary patent protection including any subsequent amendments. OJEU L 361, 31.12.2012, p. 1.

9.10 Music piracy

From 2009 onwards when peer-to-peer (P2P) file-sharing really took off, a number of pop stars declared war on this illegal practice, including Gary Barlow of pop group Take That, music promoter and X Factor creator Simon Cowell and singer-songwriters Lily Allen and Adele. All claimed that P2P file-sharing was the number one enemy of the music industry, condemning millions of people all over the world who were downloading music without paying for it. Other artists disagreed, such as Radiohead, Pink Floyd and Blur. They believed that free releases of their new singles on YouTube would help artists attract a new generation of fans and promote them on a wider platform; and, moreover, that ultimately greater revenue would be generated by live acts and artist-related merchandise.

Several new bands – such as H.U.M.A.N.W.I.N.E[212] – have moved towards a route of publishing songs for free on YouTube, but asking for donations and using 'Kickstarter'[213] to raise funds for recording new material. It is all about being noticed in the first place.

When Apple launched its music streaming service in June 2015 – which allows people to listen to music without buying it for the first three months – American singer-songwriter, Taylor Swift, declared it unacceptable that the corporate giant would not 'be paying writers, producers, or artists for those three months', and threatened to boycott. Apple changed its mind immediately. Apple had indeed planned to give this music away free, and pay no royalties to the artists and record labels for that time. Taylor Swift emerged as a moral saviour for the music industry when she pulled all of her music from Spotify, the market-leading streaming service, in 2014, on the basis that it paid most musicians a pittance. Spotify stated that the payout to rights holders in 2015 per average stream was between $0.006 and $0.0084.[214]

9.10.1 What is piracy?

The commonly used term 'piracy' describes the deliberate infringement of copyright on a commercial scale, including activities that cause economic harm. In relation to the music industry it refers to unauthorized copying. Piracy falls into four categories, namely:

- physical piracy;
- counterfeits;
- bootlegs;
- internet piracy.

Physical music piracy is the making or distribution of copies of sound recordings on physical carriers without the permission of the rights owner whereby the packaging of pirate copies may or may not be different from the original. Pirate copies are often compilations, such as the 'Greatest Hits' or 'Best of' a specific artist or group, or a compilation of a specific genre, such as '400 Best Running Songs' or '40 Best R & B songs'; this extends to music videos, films and games.[215]

---

212 H.U.M.A.N.W.I.N.E. is a band based in Boston, Massachusetts, United States. Their name is an acronym of the phrase 'Humans Underground Making Anagrams Nightly While Imperialistic Not-Mes Enslave'.
213 Kickstarter is an American-based private for-profit company founded in 2009 that provides tools to raise funds for creative projects via crowd funding through its website: www.kickstarter.com.
214 Source: 'How is Spotify contributing to the music business?' at Spotify: www.spotifyartists.com/spotify-explained.
215 For further discussion see: Parsons, K. (2000).

9.10.2 Counterfeiting

See above
9.5 and 9.7

Counterfeits are another form of physical piracy. They are, for example, recordings made without the required permission from the artist or publisher, which are then packaged so that they resemble the original as closely as possible. Original artwork of CD or DVD covers, including trade marks and logos, is reproduced on sophisticated copiers, so that the packaging looks like the real thing and leads to the customer being misled.

Counterfeiting is a global issue and does not only affect the music industry. Counterfeit bottles of whisky, vodka, rum and other spirits are a growing problem for global drinks companies like Diageo, forcing them into cat-and-mouse games with bootleggers as they try to expand sales in Asia and eastern Europe.

9.10.3 Bootlegs

Bootlegs are unauthorized audio or video recordings of live performances, not officially released by the artist. The process of making and distributing such recordings is known as bootlegging. The first bootlegged live recording of a Bob Dylan concert, 'live at the Albert Hall', part of his first UK tour, can be traced back to 1965, with songs including 'The Times They Are a-Changin' and 'Mr Tambourine Man'. 'Dylan Bootlegs' were then duplicated and sold without the artist's permission. A great many such recordings were then simply copied and traded among Dylan fans without any financial reward in the form of royalties to the artist.

By the early 1980s the bootleg industry in Germany and the Netherlands was thriving. Music industry experts claim that there were about 30,000 illegal Dylan bootleg recordings in Italy alone, claiming that the bootleg industry was the most serious form of piracy at that time.[216] Bob Dylan subsequently released his own official edition of a 'bootleg' series in several volumes. Volume 9 (2010), for example, features the legend's studio recordings from 1962 to 1964, also known as the 'Witmark' and 'Leeds' demos in mono format, never previously released on CD; just one way to extend copyright in his recordings and thereby increase royalties (see also: the Bob Dylan case[217]).

It could, however, be argued that in some cases bootlegging serves a useful cultural service. Some of the early recordings of the great opera singer Maria Callas, for example, in her live performances at La Scala Opera House in Milan only exist — and are now sold 'officially' by record companies — because of the illicit activities of members of the audience and technicians. Today, some bootlegged records are sold as rarities for profit, sometimes by adding professional-quality sound engineering and packaging to the raw material.

 FOR THOUGHT

Many people at festivals (e.g. Glastonbury or Isle of Wight) make amateur video recordings of events at the festival, such as impromptu performances of an 'unknown' artist's original songs that do not take place on one of the main stages. If you make bootleg recordings and subsequently compile them for sale on your own website, who has copyright in which aspects of the performance and the recording?

---

216 See: Heylin, C. (1994).
217 *Sony Music Entertainment (Germany) GmbH v Falcon Neue Medien Vertrieb GmbH* (C-240/07) [2009] ECDR 12.

◉ FOR THOUGHT

Is it right to say 'all recordings must be licensed'? If your friends sing 'Happy Birthday' to you in a pub and video-record the 'performance' on their mobile phones, and one of the 'group members' uploads the recording on to Facebook or YouTube, should she obtain a licence? Discuss.

9.10.4 Peer-to-peer file-sharing: 'Napster' and 'The Pirate Bay'

Napster became the first online song-swapping file-share service, based in the USA, attracting more than 60 million users by July 2000. Created by Shawn Fanning, while he was studying at Northeastern University in Boston, the service was named after Fanning's unusual hairstyle. Napster's technology allowed people to share their MP3 music files with other internet users, thereby bypassing the commercial music licensing market and avoiding buying physical CDs. The service operated between June 1999 and July 2000, when Napster was accused of violating US copyright legislation, namely the Digital Millennium Copyright Act of 1998 (DMCA).[218]

A lawsuit was subsequently filed jointly by the Recording Industry Association of America (RIAA), AOL, Time Warner, Bertelsmann, EMI, Vivendi Universal and Sony. Heavy metal band Metallica and rap artist Dr Dre sued in separate legal actions, demanding, *inter alia*, that some 60,000 pages be removed from Napster containing the artists' names. In May 2000, San Francisco Judge Marilyn Hall Patel ruled that Napster was guilty of online copyright infringement and trading copyrighted music without permission. Napster was not entitled to claim protection under the DMCA, because the company did not transmit, route or provide connections for infringing material through its system. Napster was ordered to pay damages and the service was shut down in July 2000.[219]

While appealing against the court's decision, Napster's chief executive, Konrad Hilbers, tried to reach an amicable settlement with the companies concerned, by suggesting various licensing agreements. This resulted in Napster's brand and logo being registered as trade marks in January 2002. Napster then launched a legal file-swapping service as a free beta test version to a selected 20,000 users with more than 100,000 music files on a subscription basis. Shawn Fanning assured the courts that 98 per cent of the code behind the program had been rewritten, adding a music player, chat rooms and instant messaging to the service.[220] There is no doubt that Napster paved the way for decentralized P2P file-sharing and distribution programs.

Music piracy platforms became increasingly difficult to control. Next came the illegal music piracy website, The Pirate Bay (TPB). Founded in Sweden, TPB was offering 'BitTorrent protocol' and 'magnet links' from 2003 onwards to facilitate P2P file-sharing of music, films and TV shows.

On 17 April 2009, the Stockholm district court (Tingsrätt) found the four men behind TPB guilty of internet piracy, i.e. facilitating illegal downloading of copyrighted material.[221] After a 13-day trial, judge Tomas Norström and three namndeman (a jury with extended powers) found Peter Sunde, Gottfrid Svartholm Warg, Fredrik Neij and Carl Lundström guilty of 'assisting in making copyright

---

218 Pub. L. No 105-304, 112 Stat. 2860 (28 October 1998). The DMCA was signed into law by President Clinton on 28 October 1998. The legislation implements two 1996 World Intellectual Property Organization (WIPO) treaties: the WIPO Copyright Treaty and the WIPO Performances and Phonograms Treaty.

219 The movie documentary *Downloaded* (2013) tells the story of Napster.

220 The new service offered standard MP3 music files and 'nap' files, which are MP3s with the addition of a protective layer that prevented them being copied off the host computer or burned onto CDs. There was also a 'buy' button, linking the service to the music retail site CDNow, owned by Bertelsmann.

221 Source: Internationella åklagarkammaren Stockholm, 31 January 2008 (Swedish Criminal Court).

content available', that is, having made 33 copyright-protected files accessible for illegal file-sharing via the TPB website. The Pirate Bay's founders and owners were imprisoned for one year.[222]

Resulting from a parallel civil legal action, the four TPB defendants were fined SEK 30 million (€2.7 million or £3 million) in damages to copyright holders for lost sales, including 17 media and record companies such as Warners, MGM Pictures, Columbia Pictures, Twentieth Century Fox Film, Sony BMG, Universal and EMI. The Pirate Bay website was shut down by a court order. The TPB appellants demanded a retrial on the grounds that the Stockholm Tingsrätt judge had been biased in that he was a member of several copyright protection agencies in Sweden, but their appeal was dismissed by the Swedish Court of Appeal.[223]

By March 2013, The Pirate Bay had regrouped and set up 'shop' in North Korea. To coincide with celebrations of its tenth anniversary, TBP released the 'PirateBrowser', a bundle of Firefox add-ons that helped users 'dodge' ISP filters.[224] Since the Pirate Bay server appears to move constantly (including the use of drones), March 2016 location sightings were from the Republic of Moldova's data centre Trabia.

Google and Apple Music then jumped on the music-streaming bandwagon and launched their own streaming services to compete with Spotify and Deezer as they looked to expand into the fastest growing areas of the music market. Most important for all the music streaming services was the income from premium advertising.

So, are music-streaming services legal? Seemingly so, though songwriter and producer Pete Waterman remarked that streamed music services online were 'scandalous', stating that 'these streaming business models are a disgrace, they devalue our artists, they damage this country economically, culturally and morally'.[225] That said, all the music on Spotify, Pandora or Apple Music has been licensed from and delivered by labels or other rights holders. If an artist asks the server how their music ended up on iTunes or Soundcloud, it often turns out that the artist's music has been licensed and delivered by their label or aggregator without the artist knowing about this.

In autumn 2015 a group of record labels received $90 million from the internet radio site Pandora to settle a dispute over the use of recordings created before 1972. The labels – ABKCO Music & Records, Capitol Records, Sony Music Entertainment, UMG Recordings and Warner Music Group – were represented by the Recording Industry Association of America® (RIAA)[226] and argued that Pandora Music Inc. was violating copyright laws in not paying royalties on music that was more than 43 years old. Songs released after 1972 are protected by US federal copyright laws, but the laws concerning music created prior to that vary from US state to state. The RIAA argued that states including California and New York recognize the copyrights of older recordings and that Pandora was in violation of those copyrights. Pandora settled after the satellite radio provider Sirius XM had lost a similar action, paying out $210 million to record companies to resolve a similar IP dispute between 2013 and 2015.[227] The agreements did not give Pandora and Sirius XM a licence for future use of pre-1972 recordings, but it provided the streaming services legal cover to the end of 2016 to work out deals with the record labels.

9.10.5 Licensing agreements and assignments

The music industry is a complicated business with a number of representative sectors and components interacting to make it work. Despite a shrinking market and slumping sales, there are more pop artists than ever. In 2014, according to the Official Charts Company, 47,751 albums were sold

---

222 Source: 'Artist hoppar av Pirate bay-åtalet', *Svenska Dagbladet*, publicerad Tobias Brandel, 17 April 2009.
223 Source: Reuters 'Swedish court says Pirate Bay judge not biased', 25 June 2009.
224 PirateBrowser also supplies an index of bookmarked torrent sites including Kickass Torrents, Bitsnoop and H33T.
225 Source: 'A bum note for rock 'n' roll', by Justin Stoneman, *Sunday Times*, Culture Supplement, 3 January 2010, p. 27.
226 RIAA® is the trade organization that supports and promotes major music companies. Nearly 85 per cent of all legitimate recorded music produced and sold in the USA is created, manufactured or distributed by RIAA members: www.riaa.com/about-riaa.
227 Source: 'Pandora to pay $90 million to labels over pre-1972 recordings', by Ryan Faughnder, *Los Angeles Times*, 22 October 2015.

for the first time. The comparable figure in 1994 was 11,654. The quantity of recordings has multiplied – and so too have listening figures. Although one million-selling albums are in danger of extinction, the rise of music-streaming services such as Spotify and Apple Music have introduced a whole new order of superlatives. Ed Sheeran, for instance, was Spotify's most-streamed act in 2014 with more than 860 million listens, while his album X was streamed 430 million times.

The UK is the world's fourth-largest music publishing market, providing 10 per cent of world-wide revenues, and is second only to the USA as a source of repertoire. The Music Publishers Association (MPA)[228] has a worldwide catalogue of printed music and links to publishers (digitally and in hard copy). The MPA can act as a link between a performer seeking permission to photocopy printed music or perform it and the copyright owner; that is, the songwriter/s. The Association argues that all recordings should be licensed, even non-commercial recordings. In the UK this is also covered by the MCPS (Mechanical Copyright Protection Society).

See below
9.12

Licensing schemes and assignments of copyright are stated to be within the scope of the UK Copyright Act, namely Chapter V of the CDPA 1988. Assignments tend to be more popular in the United States, whereby artists will assign their copyright to a publishing company. An assignment is an outright transfer of ownership of rights by the copyright owner (e.g. the songwriter) to someone else, which usually covers the life of the copyright: 70 years from the end of the year in which the original author and owner of copyright dies.

The golden rule of music licensing for an artist and producer begins with the knowledge as to which licences exist and how to obtain them. Is the work in the public domain? Is the artist using a composition or a sound recording, or both? Is he creating a cover song? Is he sampling an existing recording? Or is the work out of copyright? Knowing the difference between compositions and sound recordings is key to determining the necessary licence and can be a headache for any budding artist, who may incur high legal costs from copyright violations. The short answer is: unless the artist or producer controls the composition or sound recording, he will need a licence to use it.

The requirements for a valid express assignment are set out in section 90 CDPA;[229] but fortunately for many the law recognizes in addition to express statutory assignments equitable implied assignments based on the circumstances or conduct of the parties; for example, in university research collaboration agreements where the contracted sponsor may wish to own the IP created by the university research assistants or professors. Then the IP needs to be formally transferred, i.e. assigned to the sponsor. The assignment will then give 'full title guarantee' to the sponsor in the 'research collaboration agreement'. If indeed the university agrees to such an assignment, this will have to be formalized in a contract with guarantees and warranties (e.g. promising that it has the right to dIPSOse of the IP); the IP is free from all charges and encumbrances, such as a mortgage, and rights of third parties; licensing back the IP etc. – J. K. Rowling, for instance, assigning rights to her entire *Harry Potter* series at the start of her enterprise in 1993 to Bloomsbury publishing.

It is possible to license a right instead of assigning it. In granting a licence, the copyright owner merely gives another person permission to use that right for the particular purpose as agreed in the licence terms, such as publishing the book from a given manuscript or making a CD from a particular sound recording or live performance. Licensing tends to be more flexible than an assignment as it is possible to license multiple copyrights to many people simultaneously, such as multiple music publishers. This is known as a non-exclusive licence. Usually licences permit sub-licences but generally the 'head licensee' cannot grant more rights to any sub-licensee than were granted to him.

A licence granted by a copyright owner is binding on every successor in title to his interest in the copyright, except a purchaser in good faith for valuable consideration and without notice

228 See: MPA at: www.mpaonline.org.uk.
229 Section 90(1) CDPA states that copyright is transmissible by assignment, by 'testamentary dIPSOsition' or by operation of law, as personal or moveable property.

(actual or constructive) of the licence or a person deriving title from such a purchaser. The licensor can then do anything with the work as he sees fit.[230] This practically means that a music publisher, for example, may do anything with a composer's script, such as issue an abridged or electronic version, subject of course to non-assignable moral rights, though these may be waived by the author. The same is true of book manuscripts. A principle of *de minimis* will be presumed in respect of licensing requirements and that an entitlement would be intended for such an arrangement. The scope of the licence ought to be limited in respect of those opportunities as envisaged by the parties at the time of the agreement. New exploitation and/or unexpected opportunities will not be considered to be included within such scope.

What about implied assignments and licences? Given the often hurly burly world of real commercial practice, parties do not always enter into the appropriate statutory written assignment, which can cause injustice later and frustrate the real intentions of the parties. In certain circumstances English law recognizes an implied assignment or licence. Nowadays, record labels try to persuade recording artists to sign '360°' licence deals so that they can exploit the artists' recordings commercially, including touring and merchandise. Record labels traditionally pay for the recording and mixing of albums and tend to underwrite new acts' touring costs to help raise their profile and sales. In addition, they fund the manufacturing, packaging and distribution of the recordings, plus all the branded merchandise that goes with live performances.

9.11 Sound recordings and performers' rights

Traditionally there are a number of categories of 'performers' involved in the process of music composition and exploitation. Some are direct copyright holders; others indirect.

At the start of the creative process there is the person who is responsible for writing the music: the composer of the music and the lyricist of musical works (remember that there are two separate copyrights here – musical in the notes and literary in the words). Copyright law recognizes them as the 'authors'. Chapter II CDPA deals with rights conferred on performers and persons having recording rights.

> ### Every record track has two rights:
>
> (1) a copyright in the individual musical and lyrical composition; and
> (2) a separate copyright in the total sound recording.

While separate copyright subsists in the recording of the performer, the performance itself is also IP protected. The performance then gives rise to performers' rights which – in turn – are covered by the term 'dramatic performances', which include dance and mime, musical performances, readings and recitations of literary works and variety acts. Circus acts can also be included as well as certain sporting events, such as ice dancing.

The sound recording owner is usually the record company which released the original recording (or 'single') for a public performance and airplay. Live performances are often recorded or transmitted and may be sold for a profit, for example a live recording of a comedy act or classical performance. It is then perfectly acceptable to make your own recording of your own performance

---

230 See: s 90(4) CDPA.

of, say, Mozart's Piano Concerto No 21 (because the composer has been dead for more than 70 years). Provided you performed and recorded the work yourself, then no infringement would have occurred.

In recordings, the phonogram producers ('record producers' or 'record labels') finance the performance and will normally own a sound recording copyright and a recording right in relation to the performers used, in the sense that they may provide finance and recording studio facilities.[231]

Each record label will try to secure an exclusive contract with the artist or group. For example, the Beatles recorded their albums at Abbey Road Studios exclusively with EMI. Tom Jones also used to record with EMI (*What's New Pussycat?* and *Delilah*), and then left for the Island record label (*Praise and Blame*); Deutsche Grammophon have their own classical, jazz and crossover artists like Rolando Vilazón (tenor) and the Three Tenors: José Carreras, Plácido Domingo and Luciano Pavarotti. The Decca label looks after Wynton Marsalis (blues trumpet) and so on.

The record label, by way of licence, will then be able to control the exploitation of the works. Licensing schemes for public performances of sound recordings are firmly grounded in conventional contract law, particularly in relation to 'related rights'. Indirect copyright holders comprise the music publishers, who are not directly involved in the creative process of the works. Their task is to support the authors and ensure that the musical works and scores are exploited by making sure that the repertoires are provided to the public and that the rights holders are granted their copyright; this includes all productions such as musicals or operettas performed by amateur societies.

Does an artist or performer need to register his work or sound recording to be protected? Not really. Copyright protection is formality-free in countries party to the Berne Convention, which means that protection does not depend on compliance with any formalities such as registration or deposit of copies. It exists immediately it is created. The minimum protection guaranteed by the Rome Convention 1961 to performers is to sanction performances without their consent.[232] It is important to remember that the performer of the song has rights as well as the writer of the song (note: a performer's rights ought not to be confused with the performance right in copyright law). This expression was used in order to allow IFPI[233] countries like the UK to continue to protect performers by virtue of penal statutes, determining offences and penal sanctions under public law, such as the Copyright Acts of 1911 and 1956. Under the Rome Convention, record producers ('producers of phonograms') have the right to authorize or prohibit the direct or indirect reproduction of their recordings ('phonograms'). The Convention also provides for the payment of equitable remuneration for broadcasting and communication to the public of phonograms.

The copyright in a sound recording now runs for 70 years from the year of recording, or 70 years from date of release if released in that time.[234]

9.11.1 Extended duration of performers' rights

Royalties in the music industry tend to be a percentage ownership of future production or revenues from a given licence agreement. These include moral rights, that is, the right to be identified as performer.[235] If recordings are made without the consent of the recording company or that of the

---

231 See: ss 185–188 CDPA.
232 Article 10 Rome Convention.
233 The International Federation of the Phonographic Industry (IFPI) represents the interests of the recording industry worldwide. It is a not-for-profit organization registered in Switzerland, with a secretariat in London and regional offices in Brussels, Hong Kong and Miami at: http://ifpi.org.
234 For further discussion see: Yeoh, F. (2015), pp. 119–129.
235 See: ss 205A–F CDPA ('rights in performances' and 'moral rights') plus the Performances (Moral Rights, etc.) Regulations 2006. Rights are also conferred on a performer by Chapter 3 of the Regulations (moral rights) and s 205C CDPA ('right to be identified') and s 205F CDPA ('right to object to derogatory treatment of performance').

performer, this creates an action relating to the use of illicit recordings.[236] Performers' moral rights include the right to object to derogatory treatment of their performance.[237]

In September 2011, the EU Parliament implemented the long-awaited EU Copyright Term Directive 2011.[238] The Copyright and Duration of Rights in Performances Regulations 2013 ('The Regulations') implemented this EU Directive into UK law. The law changed after Sir Paul McCartney and Sir Cliff Richard (and several other famous artistes) had lobbied the EU Commission in April 2006 to extend copyright on sound recordings over several years

Most importantly, the Copyright Term Directive extended the copyright and related performance rights (or 'term of protection') for music performers and sound recordings to 70 years. The implementation of the Europe-wide legislation (which became known as 'Cliff's law') meant that thousands of music performers, from little-known session musicians to Dame Shirley Bassey, would now receive royalties from songs released in the 1960s for an extra 20 years. Many of the most popular songs recorded in the 1960s were due to come out of copyright, including songs recorded by artists such as Tom Jones, the Beatles and the Rolling Stones. Copyright in their hit singles would now not expire until at least 2033.

Recorded performers and musicians, such as session musicians, also benefited from the change in legislation.

9.11.2 Copying for personal and private use

Consent or 'permissions' (by way of licence) are usually by way of a detailed written contract,[239] and allow for the music or composition to be played by other performers ('cover versions') including the right to equitable remuneration for exploitation of sound recordings.[240]

The Copyright and Rights in Performances (Personal Copies for Private Use) Regulations 2014 ('the Regulations') created an exception to copyright based upon personal private use without any mechanism for compensating rightholders. The Regulation introduced section 28B into the CDPA.

However, in the BASCA case[241] (also known as BASCA v BIS) (2015) the court found that the Regulations were unlawful because of a defect in the consultation process. The defendant Business Secretary[242] accepted the ruling by Green J that the Regulations should be quashed.[243]

The claimants, the British Academy of Songwriters, Composers and Authors,[244] sought a declaration that the making of private copies of musical and other copyright works without consent, in the circumstances purportedly authorized by the Regulations, constituted an infringement of copyright (since 1 October 2014).

It had become clear that the law ('the Regulations') had fallen into disrepute. However, the BASCA case involved private litigation between a rightholder and an alleged infringer and the proposed declaration raised potentially complex and far-reaching issues where an alleged copyright infringer might infringe the rights of a specific right holder. For this reason the court declined to make any ruling about whether the 2014 Regulations were retrospectively unlawful. It would be for a defendant in future proceedings to explore and raise that issue. This made the granting of any declaration academic.[245]

---

236 See: s 191(i) and (j) CDPA.

237 See: s 205F CDPA.

238 Directive 2011/77/EU of the European Parliament and of the Council of 27 September 2011 amending Directive 2006/116/EC on the term of protection of copyright and certain related rights ('the EU Copyright Term Directive').

239 See also: s 205A CDPA 'Licensing of performers' property rights'.

240 See: s 182D CDPA.

241 R (on the application of British Academy of Songwriters, Composers and Authors and others) v Secretary of State for Business, Innovation and Skills (The Incorporated Society of Musicians Ltd intervening) (Nos 1 and 2) [2015] EWHC 2041 (Admin) (QBD) 17 July 2015; [2015] Bus LR 1435 (sub nom the BASCA case).

242 The then Rt Hon Sajid Javid MP, Secretary of State for Business, Innovation and Skills.

243 See BASCA judgment (2015) at para. 11 (Green J).

244 Members include Sir Paul McCartney, Dizzee Rascal, Michael Nyman, Gary Barlow, David Arnold, Sir Elton John, Imogen Heap, Howard Goodall, John Powell, Sir Peter Maxwell Davies, Kate Bush, Chris Martin. See BASCA at: http://basca.org.uk.

245 Ibid., at paras 14–21 (Green J).

In summary, since the 2014 Regulations had been hypothetically quashed the essence of the *BASCA* case had disappeared. The Secretary of State had indicated in any case that he wished to have time to consider all options and did not intend to give an indication of when he would seek to reintroduce a copyright exception.

9.11.3 Exclusive rights

A granting of an 'exclusive licence' means the copyright owner grants a person, recording company or (book) publisher permission to exercise a particular right exclusively (even to the exclusion of the copyright owner themselves). An exclusive licence can be limited in the rights given and the time period and firmly falls within the realms of contract law.[246] It is of course possible to grant non-exclusive licences, though these would be economically less valuable to an individual exploiter – but any action for breach of copyright by a non-exclusive licensee might require the copyright owner to be joined as party to the action.[247]

An exclusive licence must be made in writing. For its correct form, this contract must be signed by or on behalf of the copyright owner, who in turn authorizes the licence – to the exclusion of all other persons, including the person granting the licence – to exercise a right which would otherwise be exercisable exclusively by the copyright owner.[248]

The recording right in relation to performers is covered by sections 185 to 188 CDPA. Here the Copyright Act deals with the exclusive recording rights of a performer and the record company, where the label is entitled to the exclusion of all other persons (including the performer) to make recordings of one or more of his performances with a view to their commercial exploitation.[249] This section of the CDPA essentially deals with the problem of 'bootlegging'.[250]

See above
9.10.3

Exclusive recording rights are then 'assigned' to one label ('the qualifying party') by way of an assignment or licence (contract law). This then passes the permanent copyright on to the record label (or music publisher). Both parties then have the benefit of an exclusive recording contract and all recordings and performances will then be subject to exclusive commercial exploitation; this means with a view to the recordings being sold or let for hire, or shown or played in public.[251]

It is worth noting that an exclusive licensee has the same right in title (to sue in their own name) as the copyright owner (such as Warners, Universal or Sony) in this respect. Therefore, the exclusive licence holder – (i.e. a record label) – can take action for copyright infringement without joining the copyright owner to the action – which is what some of the famous labels regularly do against samplers and online file-sharers. An exclusive licence holder has the same rights against a successor in title who is bound by the licence as he has against the person granting the licence.[252]

9.11.4 Sound recordings and derivative works

Sound recordings and film sound tracks are covered by sections 5A and 5B CDPA.[253]

A derivative work is a work that is based on ('derived from') another work; for example a painting based on a photograph, a collage, a musical work based on an existing piece or samples, or a screenplay based on a book. Sound recordings of, for instance, films, are known as 'derivative

---

246 See: s 92(1) CDPA.
247 See: ss 101–101A and 102 CDPA.
248 See: s 92(1) CDPA.
249 See: s 182D(8) CDPA, added by S.I. 2006/18.
250 See: s 5 CDPA.
251 See: s 185 CDPA.
252 See: s 92(2) CDPA.
253 Substituted by reg. 9(1) (with Pt III) The Duration of Copyright and Rights in Performances Regulations 1995.

works', that is they derive from works which themselves are copyrighted (film soundtracks). Legally, only the copyright owner has the right to authorize adaptations and reproductions of their work – this includes the making of a derivative work. The copyright owner is generally the creator of the original work, or it may be someone the creator has given copyright to (e.g. next of kin).

Generally, one needs the permission of the copyright owner before making a derivative work. If copyright has expired (i.e. under present legislation this means the author died over 70 years ago), the work will be in the public domain, and may be used as a basis for a derivative work without permission.

A higher standard is applied by the courts where derivative works are concerned, particularly in the digital age of so-called 'recreative' works. These are works that have been derived from, and which purport to be perfectly accurate copies of, antecedent works that were created at an earlier point in history. They can comprise, for example, ancient religious scholarly works, old compositions or music scores and paintings. The recreative author engages in reproducing the work and it is this process which may or may not be defined as 'copying'. This will depend on what raw materials he has to copy from, what sources of information are available to him to help him accurately identify all the expressive contents of the antecedent work that need to be faithfully reproduced, and what tools and resources are at his dIPSOsal to facilitate the execution of his recreative enterprise. In what form that copying takes place will vary significantly in each case. Recreative derivative works are then identical to the antecedent works from which they were copied. The test for breach of copyright will depend on whether there is a material difference between the original works and the derivative work.[254]

9.11.5 Infringement of a performer's property rights

A copyright owner or performer's rights are infringed by a person who, without his consent:

- makes a copy or recording of the whole or any substantial part of a qualifying work or performance (directly from the live performance);
- broadcasts live the whole or any substantial part of a qualifying performance; or
- makes a copy or recording of the whole or any substantial part of a qualifying work or performance (e.g. directly from a broadcast of the live performance).[255]

The Court of Appeal's judgment in the Dr Sawkins case[256] caused disquiet in the recording industry. The case centred on musical scholar, Dr Lionel Sawkins, the world's leading authority on Lalande's musical works,[257] and Hyperion Records, one of Britain's leading independent classical labels. The copyright battle centred on an acclaimed recording of the French baroque composer Michel-Richard de Lalande for the court of the Sun King, Louis XIV. Dr Sawkins had been commissioned by Hyperion to edit the scores. Dr Sawkins regarded his endeavour as amounting to a new musical work, entitling him to copyright and royalties.

Hyperion Records then produced a compilation CD of early French music, including recordings of performances of Lalande's compositions using the Sawkins' scores. The record label had paid Dr Sawkins a one-off ('killer') fee for providing the performing editions, but refused to pay him

---

254 For further discussion see: Pila, J. (2010).
255 See: ss 183, 184, 187, 188 CDPA.
256 See: *Sawkins v Hyperion Records* [2005] EWCA Civ 565 (CA Civ Div).
257 Michel-Richard de Lalande (1657–1726) was the principal court composer of two French kings during the seventeenth and eighteenth centuries. Few of Lalande's original manuscripts survived.

any subsequent royalties on the basis that an editor was not entitled to copyright in a performing edition of non-copyright music. Dr Sawkins claimed that his performance editions were original musical works with a separate copyright under section 3 CDPA.[258]

The crucial question was whether copyright could subsist in modern performing editions, such as those produced by Dr Sawkins. The second question before the CA was what actually constituted 'music' in copyright terms. Was it the sound or the scores from which music was played? The problem was that the CDPA does not specifically define 'music'. Hyperion's counter-argument was that Sawkins' works were merely transcriptions of Lalande's music, and the company continued to deny Dr Sawkins any royalties because they claimed that he had not created *original* musical works within the meaning of the CDPA.

The CA held that there had been a breach of section 77 CDPA, because the Hyperion CD did not identify Dr Sawkins as the author of the performing editions. The court held that Dr Sawkins had spent hundreds of 'sweat of the brow' hours making the performing editions, which therefore satisfied the requirement of an 'original' work in the copyright sense.[259]

Mummery LJ summarized his reasons why Dr Sawkins's editions were original musical works and therefore entitled to copyright protection in their own right:

(a)   Dr Sawkins originated the performing editions by his own expert and scholarly exertions.
(b)   The editions did not previously exist in that form.
(c)   The contents of his editions affected the combination of sounds produced by the performers.
(d)   The resulting combination of sounds embodied in the CD was music.

The court awarded damages to Dr Sawkins both for infringement of his copyright and for infringement of his 'moral rights' (referring to: *Ladbroke v William Hill* (1964)[260]).

9.11.6 Sampling

The technique of sampling probably dates back to the late 1970s, when a Jamaican-born DJ in the Bronx named Kool DJ Herc began playing the 'break' in a rock, soul, funk or even Latin song over and over by switching between records, while MCs would 'rap' over the beat they created. From rap's inception to the present day, many rap beats contain parts of recognizable songs, such as Run DMC's 1986 hit 'Walk This Way' which borrows a guitar riff, drum beat and chorus from rock band Aerosmith.[261]

In addition to breach of copyright, sampling may also fall foul of the composer's moral rights if it distorts his work in the sample.[262] Sampling is typically done with a 'sampler', which could be a piece of hardware or a computer program. Today sampling artists are at the mercy of large record labels, music publishers and collecting societies – most of whom have legal departments devoted to finding out 'who sampled whom'.[263] Michael Jackson's songs have been sampled on more than 90 songs by other artists. Eminem's single 'Beautiful' used the rock band Queen and singer-songwriter Paul Rodgers' single 'Reachin' Out/Tie Your Mother Down'. Most sampled are James Brown (6519 times) and Public Enemy (2507 times).

That said, sampling is different from 'covering' (or 'covers'), where typically one artist sings the song of another artist (the Beatles got covered 3376 times). If a sampling artist is being confronted by the legitimate copyright holder in a legal challenge, he can possibly use the *de minimis* defence, which means the sample used was small enough so that the rights holder cannot claim that he

---

258 Dr Sawkins completed three modern performance editions of Lalande's original works in 2001. The editions covered *Te Deum Laudamus* (1684), *La Grande Piece Royale* (1695) and *Venite Exultemus* (1701).
259 *Sawkins* [2005] EWCA Civ 565 (CA Civ Div) at 32 (Mummery LJ).
260 [1964] 1 WLR 273.
261 See: Sanjek, D. (1992).
262 See: ss 79–82 CDPA.
263 To check who samples whom see: www.whosampled.com.

See above
9.5.10

'owned' the sampled section. This constitutes 'fair use' of the original. Alternatively, the defendant MC or DJ could claim that the sampling was done in parody, which also amounts to 'fair use' (see: *Twentieth Century Music Corp. v Aiken* (1975)[264]).[265]

After a decades-long battle, the German Bundesverfassungsgericht (Constitutional Court) overturned a ban on a song that used a two-second sample of a recording by the electronic-music band Kraftwerk.[266] In 1997, music producer Moses Pelham had used a clip from the 1977 release 'Metall auf Metall' ('Metal on Metal') in the song 'Nur mir' ('Only Mine'), performed by Sabrina Setlur. Lead singer, keyboardist, and founding member of Kraftwerk, Ralf Hütter, had sued Pelham and won his case for copyright infringement in the German Federal Court of Justice (Bundesgerichtshof). Hütter was awarded damages and was granted an injunction regarding the song 'Nur mir'. In the May 2016 judgment, however, eight federal constitutional judges of the First Senate overturned the judgment of the lower court, stating that it did not sufficiently consider whether the impact of the sample on Kraftwerk might be 'negligible'. Pelham had successfully argued that sampling is common practice in the hip-hop genre and that in some cases,

> . . . artistic freedom overrides the interest of the owner of the copyright.

The Bundesverfassungsgericht agreed that imposing arbitrary royalty fees on composers could stifle creativity and that sampling should be permitted if it did not constitute direct competition to the sampled work, and did not damage the rightholder financially.[267]

Kraftwerk's Ralf Hütter had argued that the process of sampling inherently infringes the copyright in the underlying and original composition and sound recording. Even if a rap artist or DJ wishes to use only a couple of beats, this process should involve either licensing the sample from the copyright holder(s) or asking the artist or right holder for permission (or both).

The ruling by the German Constitutional Court is important for sampling artists and DJs. The court carefully examined how copyright works like a double-edged sword for artists, permitting sampling as a symbol of music creativity – presumably this includes remixes of other songs. The court also explained why licensing is not a solution for artists and the duty to license in lieu of a proper exception can work as a severe impediment to artistic freedom.

Nothing is absolutely legally clear in this area of music licensing law – though the German judgment clarifies the meaning of sampling – but this will be dealt with in different ways in different courts. Using a sample means the use of a pre-recorded track – for example, Van Halen's 'Jump' – in a new recording or rap mix. In this case, the artist, MC or DJ needs to clear the sound recording copyright with Van Halen's record label as well as the mechanical licence from the music publisher in order to legally use the underlying composition.[268]

9.12 Performing rights and music collecting societies

Collective rights management is the practice by which organizations, which were founded by and represent creators and authors, look after the enforcement of the authors' rights (i.e. collect royalties and make sure their music is not copied or sampled).

---

264 [1975] 422 US 151.

265 See: Hampel, S. (1992), p. 559.

266 Source: 'Verfassungsgericht lässt samplen: Zum Rechtsstreit zwischen Moses Pelham und Kraftwerk' ('Constitutional Court allows sampling: about the legal battle between Moses Pelham and Kraftwerk'), Lars Weisbrod, *Die Zeit*, Feuilleton, 2 June 2016, p. 37.

267 Source: From the original judgment and Press Release of the German Constitutional Court (*Bundesverfassungsgericht*): 'Die Verwendung von Samples zur künstlerischen Gestaltung kann einen Eingriff in Urheber- und Leistungsschutzrechte rechtfertigen'. Pressemitteilung Nr. 29/2016 vom 31. Mai 2016. Urteil vom 31. Mai 2016. 1 BvR 1585/13.

268 See: McLeod, K. (2004).

Collecting societies established themselves during the mid-nineteenth century when French composers realized the benefits of operating collectively when licensing public places to use their music – the first collective was the Propriété littéraire et artistique dating back to 1791.[269]

The first official collecting society was then formed in 1926, the International Confederation of Societies of Authors and Composers (Confédération Internationale des Sociétés d'Auteurs et de Compositeurs – or CISAC). Today CISAC's membership extends to nearly 300 authors' collection societies in more than 120 countries.[270]

Collecting societies then act as intermediaries between right holders ('authors') in the music or publishing industries. They license rights, collect royalties, and redistribute revenue to the right holders in circumstances where individually negotiating licences with individual creators would be impractical and entail high transaction costs.[271] Each collecting society has its own unique monitoring systems and detection techniques based on random survey, census, sampling, or digital detection methods.

Collecting societies enjoy considerable market power since their collective practice is largely standardized, such as using the same tariffs, licensing conditions and distribution rights in the repertoire. This system guarantees a certain level of solidarity among rights holders and strengthens the rights of relatively unknown or niche authors and artists, who can expect the same level of protection as popular performers or songwriters. In general, fees are charged to the authors, composers or performers in return for 'collection' services ('collection fee'), and allocating such revenues to the rights holder ('allocation fee').

9.12.1 What do collecting societies do?

Every time a musical work is downloaded via the internet (e.g. via iTunes) – or in the old days a CD, audio cassette or LP is played on the radio for example – the producers require a licence from the owner of the works and they must pay royalties for each song (or copy). The difficulty remains how the various layers of collecting organizations track all of the music samples, covers or remixes, etc. accurately so that royalty monies are correctly paid to songwriters, performing artists, session musicians and publishers, because each of the organizations uses slightly different systems and methods for calculations.

Several countries have different forms of royalty collection. Some record labels and their artists have exclusive rights of reproduction ('private copying') and reprographic reproduction and therefore different rights to remuneration covered by EU legislation.[272] Since there is now a great deal of crossborder representation of artists and performers, collecting societies have created different categories of rights (to existing copyright) under one umbrella, referred to in the industry as the GEMA categories (Gesellschaft für musikalische Aufführungs- und mechanische Vervielfältigungsrechte: Society for musical performing and mechanical reproduction rights). GEMA is the society for musical performing and mechanical reproduction rights which originated in Germany.[273] GEMA, in turn, is a member of the BIEM (Bureau International des Sociétés Gérant les Droits d'Enregistrement et de Reproduction Mécanique: International bureau of societies administering the rights of mechanical recording and reproduction).

That said, there will be those artists who prefer to manage their own conditions and royalties.

---

269 See: Kreile, R. and Becker J. (2001), pp. 85, 89.
270 For further information see: www.cisac.org.
271 See: Koempel, F. (2007), pp. 371–376.
272 See: Directive 92/100/EEC On Rental Rights and Lending Rights and on Certain Rights Related to Copyright in the Field of Intellectual Property which introduced such a right in favour of the authors and performers – the 'unwaivable right to equitable remuneration' in respect of the rental of phonograms and audiovisual works into which their works or, respectively, performances have been incorporated.
273 The reference to the GEMA categories was notably relied on by the EU Commission in its 1971 GEMA Decision. See Decision of 2 June 1971 (IV/26 760–GEMA) [2971] OJ L134/15.

9.12.2 Playing music in public

The two main collecting societies in the UK are the Performing Right Society (PRS) and the Mechanical Copyright Protection Society (MCPS). The PRS and MCPS represent the rights owners and obtain rights clearances. They entered into an operational alliance in 1997 and rebranded in January 2009 as 'PRS-MCPS', which is now the largest UK collecting society. The alliance became one of the founding members of UK Music, an industry-wide body representing all aspects of the music business.[274]

See below
9.12.4

Any person or business wishing to play copyrighted music in public will require a PRS licence from either the copyright owner or the collecting society to do so. If the person does not obtain the required licence, they run the risk of infringing copyright (a criminal offence). Businesses typically applying for music licences from the PRS include fitness clubs, cinemas, shopping centres, funeral parlours, providers of wedding functions and medical premises.

A performance is a 'qualifying performance' relating to a performers' right if it is given by a 'qualifying individual' or takes place in a 'qualifying country' (under the *Berne Convention*).[275]

9.12.3 Mechanical licensing and reproduction rights

'Mechanicals' are publishing rights. Any time an artist or producer produces a recording of a composition which they do not control, they need a mechanical licence. Mechanical rights royalties are different and are paid to the songwriter, composer or publisher when music is reproduced as a physical product (such as sheet music) or for broadcast or online downloads such as iTunes. The mechanical licence royalties are collected by the MCPS.

The distinction between mechanical and performing rights arose at a time when the exploitation of musical works occurred mainly in the public arena – that is in live performances – from the mid-nineteenth century onwards.

A mechanical licence is a broad term that refers to the reproduction for distribution or sale of musical compositions in the form of sound recordings. There are a large number of legal challenges in this area of musical copyright and piracy.

'Mechanical royalties' (to the publisher) are usually based on the amount of 'phonorecords' sold; that is, sales based on sound recordings determined by the record companies through 'Sound Scan' and other reporting systems. While US mechanical royalties are calculated on a 'penny basis' per song, other countries might base mechanical royalties on percentages or 'needle time'.[276]

The PRS-MCPS system grants a mechanical licence for the entire record based on a percentage of the wholesale or retail price, regardless of the number of songs. Public performance monies collected by the organization depend on their survey and consensus of how many times the song is played, when, where and at what time of day, and on what type of medium.

There are few record companies (music publishers) left today. Known as the 'majors'. The 'big three' are Sony BMG, Universal Music Group and Warner Music Group. In 2012 Universal Music took over EMI thus gaining access to major artists such as The Beatles, Pink Floyd, Lady Gaga, Kanye West and many more.

Today, digital music services (such as iTunes or Amazon) involve a combination of mechanical rights (storage of the digital musical work on a hard disk) and performing rights (the musical work is made available to the public on a website). So a performing artist needs to obtain several licences from several entities, each holding either the performing or the mechanical rights. The mechanical licence is usually limited to one configuration, such as a physical CD or album, as opposed to

---

274 UK Music was headed by Feargal Sharkey (co-founder of punk band The Undertones in 1976) until 2011. The CEO is Jo Dipple.
275 See: ss 181–184 CDPA.
276 The term 'needle time' comes from the use of gramophone record players using a gramophone needle.

a digital download, which is different again from a mobile phone ringtone. Almost all publishers require a separate licence for each use.

With music mostly digitized now, the distinction between the two rights (mechanical and performance) has become blurred and performing artists are often not sure whether they need an MCPS or PRS licence.

9.12.4 PPL licences

A 'public performance' occurs whenever sound recordings are played outside the domestic or private circle. There is no statutory definition of 'playing in public' but the UK courts have given guidance on its meaning and ruled that it is any playing of music outside a domestic setting – so, for example, playing recorded music at a workplace, public event or in the course of any business activities is considered to be 'playing in public'.

Public performance rights may be licensed directly from the copyright owner by way of a direct request or from the collection society directly, such as the PRS (or Broadcast Music, Inc. (BMI) in the USA).

Phonographic Performance Ltd (PPL) was formed by EMI and Decca records in May 1934 following its successful action in the *Stephen Carwardine* case.[277] Here, restaurant proprietors were playing music recordings by Auber, played by the LSO, in its tea and coffee rooms. The record label 'The Gramophone Company' (later EMI) argued it was against the law to play the recordings in public without first receiving the permission of the copyright owners. The judge agreed. The case established the principle that owners of sound recordings should be paid for the broadcasting and public performance of their works.[278]

A PPL licence is required when recorded music, including radio and TV, is played in public. In contrast, any recorded music being played as part of domestic home life or when there is an audience entirely comprised of friends and/or family (such as at a private family party) does not require a PPL licence. Each business must register with and pay a fee to PPL, otherwise they risk criminal prosecution under copyright law.

What then is the difference between a PPL licence and a PRS for Music licence? PPL and PRS for Music are two separate independent companies and in most instances a licence is required from both organizations for anyone to legally play recorded music in public. While both organizations licence the use of music and collect royalties for the music industry, each represents different rights holders and has separate licences, terms and conditions. PPL collects and distributes money for the use of recorded music on behalf of record companies and performers; PRS for Music collects and distributes money for the use of the musical composition and lyrics on behalf of authors, songwriters, composers and publishers.

As we have seen, MCPS, PRS and PPL operate many different licences. Even people who work for these collecting societies often do not know how to distinguish between all these different licences and societies. Simply put: a music user who buys a licence can perform or duplicate relevant works under a standard set of limited conditions, set by the collecting societies. Other music applications have separate licences and some music users may need several. The best place to find complete and up-to-date lists of these licences is on the collection societies' individual websites.

So, how many licences does a business need? It can be confusing as to whether one needs a PRS/MCPS or PPL licence in order to play music in public. This issue was addressed in *Re Phonographic Performance Ltd* (Re PPL) (2009),[279] where an action was brought by the British Beer and Pub

---

277 See: *Gramophone Co., Ltd v Stephen Carwardine Co.* [1934] 1 Ch 450 – involving the Copyright Act 1911.
278 See: Jones, R. (2010).
279 See: *Phonographic Performance Ltd v The British Hospitality Association* [2009] EWHC 175 (Ch) ('Re PPL').

Association (BBPA) and the British Hospitality Association (BHA) against PPL for charging additional fees for background music. PPL had demanded from the hotel and catering businesses that they needed two licences, one for public performances (PRS) and another for phonographic playback (background music) from PPL. This had brought in additional subscription fee revenue of about £20 million for PPL.

In *Re PPL*, Kitchin J held that the PPL could not charge a separate licence fee for playing background music of sound recordings because the businesses in question had already paid their PRS fees; a second music licence was therefore not necessary. Based on the Chancery Court's decision, Kitchin J stated that there was nothing in sections 125–128 CDPA to suggest that separate royalties ought to be charged for playing background music, since that was covered by 'public performances'. Kitchin J further ruled that PPL had to pay back all over-charged licence fees to the hoteliers and pub landlords.

The case became a landmark victory for the hospitality industry. The PPL ruling meant that pubs could now play background music with just one music licence.

9.13 Copyright law post-Brexit

Whether Brexit has an impact on some of the IP regimes in the UK is not yet clear in the post-EU world. Since the CDPA is still the main UK copyright legislation (with its numerous amendments) it is assumed that Parliament will not see this area of law as a priority. Other than working out bilateral models of agreements with other trading states, it would seem sensible to work with the World Trade Organization (WTO) rules as a default option. It might be that UK legislators review the recommendations of the Gowers Review of Intellectual Property,[280] the Digital Britain Report[281] and the Hargreaves Review of Intellectual Property and Growth.[282] Since the UK government has been rather restricted in the past by existing EU legislation in the areas of IP law it wished to reform, the Westminster Parliament is now free to implement some of these recommendations.[283] For IP law, the implications of the 'Great Repeal Bill' (2017) remain unclear. However, EU laws have empowered rights holders in trade marks, designs and patents. Until such times that the UK formally exits the EU (possibly in 2019), UK rights holders can continue to protect their IP in the EU.

 **FOR THOUGHT**

> How can copyright be upheld, maintained, claimed and protected in the constantly evolving digital world post-Brexit? Is current UK legislation creaking at the seams and are attempts by legislators to update legislation working or simply confusing matters? Discuss.

---

280 See: HM Treasury (2006).
281 See: HM Department for Culture, Media and Sports (DCMS) and Department for Innovation, Business and Skills (BIS) (2009).
282 See: HM Government (2012).
283 For further discussion see: Vivant, M. (2016), pp. 259–261.

9.14 Further reading

Cornish, W., Llewelyn, D. and Aplin, T. (2013) *Intellectual Property: Patents, Copyrights, Trademarks & Allied Rights* **(8th edn). London: Sweet & Maxwell.**
This is *the* classic textbook by William ('Bill') Cornish and other excellent specialists and reputable authors in the IP field, if you want to read more in depth about intellectual property (IP) law. Since the text is written by practising lawyers, it is up to date, accurate and straight to the point. Additionally, the text provides thoughtful analysis of every area of IP law and guides the reader through complex legislation, particularly recent EU law. There are questions and issues for the reader to develop further. This is a 'flip and find' practitioner reference work, aimed at IP professionals.

Davis, J. and Durant, A. (2011) 'To protect or not to protect? The eligibility of commercially used short verbal texts for copyright and trade mark protection', *Intellectual Property Quarterly,* **4, 345–370.**
Jennifer Davis and Alan Durant's article is concerned with short verbal texts used in a commercial setting, in particular titles and slogans. The authors describe how the protection of these texts against unauthorized third-party use has traditionally been problematic both under the law of trade marks and the law of copyright, and occasionally both. This article examines why this is the case. Davis and Durant argue that one particular difficulty arises from the fact that such texts may give rise to multiple meanings, or kinds of meaning, which are not easily accommodated within the legal reasoning associated with established categories of intellectual property protection. The authors demonstrate that courts have often real practical difficulties to achieve the necessary balance between private and public interest, not least because of the multiple meanings such texts might be thought to convey.

Handig, C. (2013) 'The "sweat of the brow" is not enough! – more than a blueprint of the European copyright term "work"', *European Intellectual Property Review,* **35(6), 334–340.**
Dr Christian Handig examines EU intellectual property legislation and jurisprudence in relation to the term 'copyright work' to receive copyright protection and the importance of EU harmonization in this field. Given that fact and that the European Union established the first copyright provisions more than two decades ago, it comes rather as a surprise that the first substantial decisions on this issue were brought before the Court of Justice of the European Union (CJEU) only fairly recently. The author discusses a small bundle of CJEU decisions that gave the Court of Justice the opportunity to do more than just to lay a foundation in this field (e.g. *Painer v Standard Verlags GmbH* (2012);[284] *Football Association Premier League Ltd v QC Leisure* (2012)[285]).

Harding, T. (2013) 'BitTorrent tracking as a means of detecting illegal file-sharing', *E-Commerce Law & Policy,* **15(2), 8–9.**
The article discusses the legal issues for copyright proprietors who use specialized software to track users of the BitTorrent file-sharing system, detect copyright infringement and apply to the court for disclosure of the names and addresses of the alleged infringers. Harding discusses two cases in this area of copyright infringement and licensing: *Golden Eye v Telefonica* (2012) and *Media CAT Ltd v Adams* (2011). He also considers, *inter alia*, the study by Chothia and Cova, 'The Unbearable Lightness of Monitoring', on the technical aspects of monitoring BitTorrent. An examination of (complex) case law suggests that there are problems with this sort of evidence and its probative value.

Husovec, M. and Peguera, M. (2015) 'Much ado about little – privately litigated internet disconnection injunctions', *International Review of Intellectual Property and Competition Law,* **46(1), 10–37.**
Martin Husovec and Miguel Peguera examine the legal framework of the European Union for injunctions against intermediaries (i.e. private internet injunctions) whose services are used by

---

284 (C-145/10) [2012] ECDR6 (3rd Chamber) (CJEU).
285 (C-403/08) [2012] All ER (EC) 629; *Times,* November 23, 2011 (Grand Chamber) (CJEU) (the *Karen Murphy pub landlady* case).

third parties to infringe an IP right (as per the InfoSoc Directive and the Enforcement Directive[286]) and how the CJEU has construed the conditions. The authors then look at the types of injunctions that right holders may apply for against intermediaries on the basis of Article 8(3) of the InfoSoc Directive, namely those that would consist of enjoining an ISP from providing internet access to one of its users allegedly engaging in copyright infringement. Relevant case law is discussed. The authors then argue that these injunctions raise serious issues regarding their compatibility with the EU Charter of Fundamental Rights[287] and come to the conclusion that these Directives' provisions 'promise much, but if applied correctly, they deliver little'.

Ullrich, H., Hilty, R. M., Lamping, M. and Drexl, J. (eds) (2015) 'TRIPS plus 20. From Trade Rules to Market Principles'. *MPI Studies on Intellectual Property and Competition Law*. Heidelberg: Springer-Verlag.
This book examines the impact and shortcomings of the TRIPS Agreement. The authors argue that the framework conditions of TRIPS have fundamentally changed over the past 20 years. New technologies have emerged, markets have expanded beyond national borders, some developing states have become global players, the terms of international competition have changed, and the intellectual property system faces increasing friction with public policies. The contributors to this text, including the leading academic, Professor William Cornish, inquire whether the TRIPS Agreement should still be seen only as part of an international trade regulation, or whether it needs to be understood – or even reconceptualized – as a framework regulation for the international protection of intellectual property. Various contributors to this text suggest not to define the terms of an outright revision of TRIPS but rather to discuss the framework conditions for an interpretative evolution that could make the agreement better suited to the expectations and needs of today's global economy.

Yeoh, F. (2015) 'Adaptations in music theatre: confronting copyright', *Entertainment Law Review*, 26(4), 119–129.
Francis Yeoh provides an extensive overview of music copyright in the UK dating back to the Statute of Anne 1710 and examples of musical and dramatic works and compositions dating back to the nineteenth century, such as the works by Gilbert and Sullivan. For example, *HMS Pinafore* (1878) was widely pirated and copied particularly in the United States. G & S's predicament was due to the fact that copyright established in the United Kingdom was not recognized in the United States at the time. The author then raises awareness as to music adaptations and the acquiring of copyright. He discusses the concept of copyright as 'property' and the 'economic' approach to copyright. Yeoh's criticism of current copyright law is the proposition that the increases in authorial rights have been exploited to destroy the delicate balance between authorial rights and the public interest. He compares international copyright legislation (e.g. Berne Convention) with UK provisions and investigates how these have encroached on the freedom of expression. Yeoh argues the shortcomings of harmonized copyright law in the context of the adaptor/author's rights as owner and user in the context of UK and US copyright legislation.

---

286 Directive 2001/29 on the harmonization of certain aspects of copyright and related rights in the information society [2001] OJ L167/10; Article 8 Directive 2004/48 on the enforcement of intellectual property rights [2004] OJ L157/45.
287 See: Article 11 Charter of Fundamental Rights of the European Union [2000] OJ C364/1.

Bibliography

Advertising Standards Authority (ASA) and Committee of Advertising Practice (CAP) (2012) *Annual Report 2012: Keeping Ads Honest: A fair deal for consumers and competitors*. London: ASA/CAP.

Ainger, M. (2002) *Gilbert and Sullivan: A dual biography*. Oxford: Oxford University Press.

Akdeniz, Y. (2008) *Internet Child Pornography and the Law: National and international responses*. Aldershot: Ashgate.

Allen, T. and Seaton, J. (1999) *The Media of Conflict: War reporting and representations of ethnic violence*. London: Zed Books Ltd.

Anderson, J. Q. and Rainie, L. (2006) *The Future of the Internet*. Washington DC: Pew Internet & American Life Project ('The Pew Report').

Andrew, C. (2009) *The Defence of the Realm: The authorized history of MI5*. London: Allen Lane.

Angelopoulos, C. (2012) 'The myth of European term harmonisation — 27 public domains for 27 Member States', *International Review of Intellectual Property and Competition Law*, 43(5), 567–594.

Archbold, *Criminal Pleading, Evidence and Practice*, see Richardson (2014).

Arrowsmith, S. (2015) 'What is a parody? Deckmyn v Vanderstee'. Case Comment, *European Intellectual Property Review*, 37(1), 55–59.

Atkin, W. R. (2001) 'Defamation law in New Zealand "refined" and "amplified"', *Common Law World Review*, 30, 237.

Aubrey, W. H. S. (orig. 1895 — reprint 2007) *The Rise and Growth of the English Nation, with Special Reference to Epochs and Crises: A history of, and for, the people*. Whitefish, MT: Kessinger Publishing.

Bainham, A. and Cretney, S. (1993) 'Children', *The Modern Law*, 409–413.

Balin, R., Handman, L. and Reid, E. (2009) 'Libel tourism and the Duke's manservant: an American perspective', *European Human Rights Law Review*, 3, 303–331.

Baloch, T. A. (2007) 'Law booksellers and printers as agents of unchange', *Cambridge Law Journal*, 66(2), 389–421.

Bar Council, The (2011) 'Jackson: The Next Chapter'. Peter Lodder QC Chairman's Report. May 2011.

Barber, N. W. (2003) 'A right to privacy?', *Public Law*, Winter, 602–610.

Barendt, E. (1989) 'Spycatcher and freedom of speech', *Public Law*, PO 204.

Barendt, E. (1990) 'Broadcasting censorship', *Law Quarterly Review*, 106 (July), 354–361.

Barendt, E. (2007) *Freedom of Speech* (2nd edn). Oxford: Oxford University Press.

Barendt, E. (2009) *Media Freedom and Contempt of Court: Library of essays in media law*. London: Ashgate.

Barendt, E., Lustgarten, L, Norrie, K. and Stephenson, H. (1997) *Libel and the Media: The chilling effect*. Oxford: Clarendon Press, p. 1032 (referred to in *Reynolds* [2001] 2 AC 127).

Barnum, D. G. (2006) 'Indirect incitement and freedom of speech in Anglo-American law', *European Human Rights Law Review*, 3, 258–280.

Barron, A. (2012) 'Kant, copyright and communicative freedom', *Law & Philosophy*, 31(1), 1–48.

Barsby, C. and Ashworth, A. J. (2004) 'Juries: Contempt of Court Act 1981, s. 8. Case comment', *Criminal Law Review*, Dec., 1041–1044.

BBC Trust (2012) *Findings of the Editorial Standards Committee of the BBC Trust* (The 'MacQuarrie Report'), 14 December 2012, at: http://downloads.bbc.co.uk/bbctrust/assets/files/pdf/appeals/esc_bulletins/2012/newsnight_2nov.pdf.

Beaujon, A. (1999) 'It's not the beat, it's the Mocean', *CMJ New Music Monthly*, April, 25.

Bedat, A. (2015) 'Tim Yeo MP v Times Newspapers Ltd — discretion to order trial by jury under Defamation Act 2013', *Entertainment Law Review*, 26(1), 31–33.

Bennett, T. D. C. (2010) 'Horizontality's new horizons – re-examining horizontal effect: privacy defamation and the Human Rights Act (Part 2)', *Entertainment Law Review*, 21(4), 145–149.

Bentham, J. (1843a) 'Draft of the Organization of Judicial Establishments', *The Works of Jeremy Bentham, Published under the Supervision of His Executor, John Bowring*, 11 volumes, 1838–1843. Edinburgh: W. Tait.

Bentham, J. (1843b, reprinted 2001) 'The anarchical fallacies', *The Works of Jeremy Bentham, Published under the Supervision of His Executor, John Bowring*, 11 volumes, 1838–1843. Boston, MA: Adamant Media Corporation.

Bernard, N. (1996) 'Discrimination and free movement in EC law', *International and Comparative Law Quarterly*, 45, 82–108.

Bilton, M. (2003) *Wicked Beyond Belief: The hunt for the Yorkshire Ripper*. London: HarperCollins.

Bindman, G. (1989) 'Spycatcher: judging the judges', *New Law Journal*, 139, 94.

Bingham, T. (1996) 'Should there be a law to protect rights of personal privacy?', *European Human Rights Law Review*, 5, 455–462.

Blackett, HHJ, J. (2009) *Rant on the Court Martial and Service Law*. Oxford: Oxford University Press.

Blackstone, Sir W. (1765) *Commentaries on the Laws of England* (16th edn – revised in 1825). London: University of Cambridge.

Blair, A. (2010) *A Journey*. London: Hutchinson/Random House.

Blom-Cooper, L. (2008) 'Press freedom: constitutional right or cultural assumption?', *Public Law*, Summer, 260–276.

Blythe, A. (2015) 'Misrepresentation, confusion and the average consumer: to what extent are the tests for passing off and likelihood of confusion within trade mark law identical?', *European Intellectual Property Review*, 37(8), 484–489.

Bonnington, A. J. and McInnes, R. (2010) *Scots Law for Journalists* (8th edn). Edinburgh: W. Green/ Sweet & Maxwell Ltd.

Bower, T. (2006) *Conrad and Lady Black: Dancing on the edge*. London: Harper Collins.

Bradley, P. (2014) 'Data, data everywhere', *Legal Information Management*, 14(4), 249–252.

Brems, E. (1996) 'The margin of appreciation in the case law of the European Court of Human Rights', *Zeitschrift für ausländisches öffentliches Recht und Völkerrecht* (Heidelberg Journal of International Law), 56, 240–314.

Briggs, A. (ed.) (1995) *The History of Broadcasting* (5 vols). Oxford: Oxford University Press.

Brimsted, K. (2003) 'Commission reports uneven playing field for data protection', *Privacy Laws & Business International Newsletter*, 68 (May/June), 22–23.

Brisby, P. (2006) 'The regulation of telecommunications networks and services in the United Kingdom', *Computer and Telecommunications Law Review*, 12(4), 114–139.

British Board of Film Classification (BBFC) (2011) *On-line Media Regulation Research Findings* by Bernice Hardie at: www.bbfc.co.uk/sites/default/files/attachments/Media%20Regulation%20 Research_0.pdf.

Britton, D. (1989) *Lord Horror*. London: Savoy Books.

Broadway, J. (2008) 'Aberrant accounts: William Dugdale's handling of two Tudor murders in the antiquities of Warwickshire', *Midland History*, 33(1) (Spring), 2–20.

Brooke, H. (2011) *The Silent State. Secrets, surveillance and the myth of British democracy*. London: William Heinemann.

Brooks, T. (2004) 'A defence of jury nullification', *Res Publica*, 10(4), 401–423.

Burchill, R., White, N. D. and Morris, J. (eds) (2005) *International Conflict and Security Law: Essays in memory of Hilaire McCoubrey*. Cambridge: Cambridge University Press.

Burke, E. (1790) *Reflections on the Revolution in France and on the Proceedings in Certain Societies in London Relevant to the Event in a Letter Intended to Have Been Sent to a Gentleman in Paris* (10th edn). London: Printed for J. Dodsley in Pall Mall.

Burns Coleman, E. and White, K. (2006) *Negotiating the Sacred in Multicultural Societies: Blasphemy and sacrilege in a multicultural society*. Canberra: University of Australia National University Press.

Busch, D. and MacGregor, L. (2009) *The Unauthorised Agent: Perspectives from European and Comparative Law*. Cambridge: Cambridge University Press.

Calender Smith, R. (2015) *Celebrity and Royalty Privacy, the Media and the Law*. London: Sweet & Maxwell.

Callery, C. (2010) 'John Terry: reflections on public image, sponsorship, and employment', *International Sports Law Review*, 2, 48–52.

Campbell, A. (2012) *The Burden of Power: Countdown to Iraq – The Alastair Campbell Diaries*. London: Hutchinson/Random House.

Campbell, W. J. (2001) *Yellow Journalism: Puncturing the myths, defining the legacies*. Opa-Locka, FL: Praeger.

The CAP Code (2010) 'The UK Code of Non-broadcast Advertising, Sales Promotion and Direct Marketing', 12th edn: www.cap.org.uk/Advertising-Codes/~/media/Files/CAP/Codes%20 CAP%20pdf/The%20CAP%20Code.ashx.

Capp, B. (2004) 'The Potter Almanacs', *Electronic British Library Journal*, 1–2: www.bl.uk/eblj/ 2004articles/pdf/article4.pdf.

Carter-Ruck, P. F. (1990) *Memoirs of a Libel Lawyer*. London: Weidenfeld & Nicolson.

Carter-Silk, A. and Cartwright-Hignett, C. (2009) 'A child's right to privacy: "Out of a parent's hands"', *Entertainment Law Review*, 20(6), 212–217.

Carty, H. (2007) 'The common law and the quest for the IP effect', *Intellectual Property Quarterly*, 3, 237–266.

Carty, H. (2008) 'An analysis of the modern action for breach of commercial confidence: when is protection merited?', *Intellectual Property Quarterly*, 4, 416–455.

Chamberlain, P. (2013) 'Where now? The Leveson Report and what to do with it', *Communications Law*, 18(1), 21–24.

Chertoff, M. and Simon, T. (2015) *The Impact of the Dark Web on Internet Governance and Cyber Security*. Chatham House Series. No 6. February 2015: https://ourinternet-files.s3.amazonaws.com/pub-lications/GCIG_Paper_No6.pdf.

Christie, A. and Gare, S. (2008) *Blackstone's Statutes on Intellectual Property* (9th edn). Oxford: Oxford University Press.

Clark, A. (1993) *Diaries*. London: Weidenfeld & Nicolson.

Clark, B. (2009) 'Princess Caroline: German Federal Supreme Court again considers the lawfulness of the publication of a celebrity photograph', *Entertainment Law Review*, 20(3), 107–111.

Clayton, R. and Tomlinson, H. (2009) *The Law of Human Rights* (2nd edn). Oxford: Oxford University Press.

Clementi, Sir David (2016) 'A Review of the Governance and Regulation of the BBC'. Presented to Parliament by the Secretary of State for Culture, Media and Sport by Command of Her Majesty. March 2016. Cm 9209 ('The Clementi Report').

Clutterbuck, R. (1981) *The Media and Political Violence*. London: Macmillan.

Coad, J. (2005) 'The Press Complaints Commission: Are we safe in its hands?', *Entertainment Law Review*, 16(7), 167–173.

Cobbett, W. (1806) *Cobbett's Parliamentary History of England*, vol. 6, col. 1063. London: House of Commons. Oxford University Digital Library.

Coe, P. (2015) 'Footballers and social media "faux pas": the Football Association's "cash cow"?', *Entertainment Law Review*, 26(3), 75–78.

Colligan, C. (2003) 'Race of born pederasts: Homosexuality, and the Arabs', *Nineteenth Century Contexts*, 25(1) (March), 1–20.

Colston, C. and Galloway, J. (2010) *Modern Intellectual Property Law* (3rd edn). London: Routledge.

Competition and Markets Authority (2015) *Annual Plan 2015/16*. Presented to Parliament pursuant to paragraph 13(2) of Schedule 4 to the Enterprise and Regulatory Reform Act 2013 March 2015. ID 12031503 03/15 at: www.gov.uk/government/uploads/system/uploads/attachment_ data/file/416433/Annual_Plan_2015–16.pdf.

Competition Commission Annual Report 2013–14, 31 March 2014. Ordered by the House of Commons. HC 24 at pp. 18–19: https://www.gov.uk/government/uploads/system/uploads/ attachment_data/file/322811/40626_2902424_Web_Accessible_v1.1.pdf.

Cook, T. (2010) *EU Intellectual Property Law*. Oxford: Oxford University Press.

Cornish, W. (2009) 'Conserving culture and copyright: A partial history', *Edinburgh Law Review*, 13(1), 8–26.

Cornish, W., Llewelyn, D. and Aplin, T. (2013) *Intellectual Property: Patents, Copyrights, Trademarks & Allied Rights* (8th edn). London: Sweet & Maxwell.

Costigan, R. (2007) 'Protection of journalists' sources', *Public Law*, Autumn, 464–487.

Council of Europe (1996) 'The European Convention on Human Rights in the New Architecture of Europe'. General Report presented by Lord Lester of Herne Hill, QC, in Proceedings of the 8th International Colloquy on the European Convention on Human Rights, pp. 227–240.

Council of Europe (2009) *International Justice for Children*. Brussels: Council of Europe Publication.

Council of Europe (2010) 'Blasphemy, insult and hatred: Finding answers in a democratic society', *Science and Technique of Democracy 47*. Brussels: Council of Europe Publication.

Coutts, J. A. (1999) 'Contempt by scandalising the court', *Journal of Criminal Law*, 63, 472.

Craig, R. (2009) 'Non-jury courts in Northern Ireland', *Criminal Law and Justice Weekly*, 5 June: www.criminallawandjustice.co.uk/features/Non-Jury-Courts-Northern-Ireland.

Criminal Law Revision Committee (1984) *Fifteenth Report of the Criminal Law Revision Committee, Sexual Offences*. Cmnd 9213, April 1984.

Crossan, S. J. and Wylie, A. B. (2010) *Introduction to Scots Law: Theory and practice* (2nd edn). London: Hodder Gibson.

Crossman, R. H. S. (1976a) *The Diaries of a Cabinet Minister, 1964–1966*. Volume I. New York: Holt, Rinehart & Winston.

Crossman, R. H. S. (1976b) *The Diaries of a Cabinet Minister: Lord President of the Council, 1966–68*. Volume II. London: Hamish Hamilton.

Crossman, R. H. S. (1977) *The Diaries of a Cabinet Minister: Secretary of State for Social Services, 1968–70*. Volume III. London: Penguin.

Crown Prosecution Service (2012) 'Interim guidelines on prosecuting cases involving communications sent via social media', issued by the Director of Public Prosecutions on 19 December 2012.

Cumberbatch, G. (2004) 'Villain or victim? A review of the research evidence concerning media violence and its effects in the real world with additional reference to video games', A report prepared for The Video Standards Council.

Currie, E. (2002) *Diaries, 1987–1992*. London: Times Warner Books UK.

Daly, M. (2013) 'Is there an entitlement to anonymity? A European and international analysis', *European Intellectual Property Review*, 35(4), 198–211.

Darnton, R. (1990) *What Was Revolutionary about the French Revolution?* Waco, TX: Baylor University Press.

Davies, M. (2010) 'The demise of professional selfregulation? Evidence from the "ideal type" professions of medicine and law', *Professional Negligence*, 26(1), 3–38.

Davis, J. and Durant, A. (2011) 'To protect or not to protect? The eligibility of commercially used short verbal texts for copyright and trade mark protection', *Intellectual Property Quarterly*, 4, 345–370.

De Waele, H. (2012) 'Implications of replacing the Data Protection Directive with a Regulation – a legal perspective', *Privacy & Data Protection*, 12(4), 3–5.

Dehin, V. (2010) 'The future of legal online music services in the European Union: A review of the EU Commission's recent initiatives in cross-border copyright management', *European Intellectual Property Review*, 32(5), 220–237.

Denning, Lord (1949) 'Freedom under the Law'. The Hamlyn Lectures, First Series. London.

Department for Culture, Media and Sport (2015). *BBC Charter Review Public Consultation* at: www.gov.uk/government/uploads/system/uploads/attachment_data/file/445704/BBC_Charter_Review_consultation_WEB. pdf.

Descheemaeker, E. (2009) 'Protecting reputation: defamation and negligence', *Oxford Journal of Legal Studies*, 29(4), 603–641.

Devlin, Sir Patrick (1956, reprinted 1966) *Trial by Jury*. London: Methuen.

Doley, C., Starte, H., Addy, C., Helme, I., Griffiths, J., Scott, A. and Mullis, A. (eds) (2009) *Carter-Ruck on Libel and Slander*. London: Butterworths.

Duncan, A. G. M., Gordon, W. M., Gamble, A. J. and Reid, K. G. C. (1996) *The Law of Property in Scotland*. Edinburgh: Butterworths.

Dunlop, R. (2006) 'Article 10, the Reynolds test and the rule in the Duke of Brunswick's case – the decision in *Times Newspapers Ltd v United Kingdom*', *European Human Rights Law Review*, 3, 327–339.

Dupré, C. (2000) 'The protection of private life against freedom of expression in French law', *European Human Rights Law Review*, 6, 627–649.

Easton, S. (2011) 'Criminalising the possession of extreme pornography: sword or shield?', *Journal of Criminal Law*, 75(5), 391–413.

Edwards, S. M. (1997) 'A safe haven for hardest core', *Entertainment Law Review*, 8(4), 137–142.

Edwards, S. M. (1998) 'On the contemporary application of the Obscene Publications Act 1959', *Criminal Law Review*, December, 843–853.

Edwards, S. M. (2000) 'The failure of British obscenity law in the regulation of pornography', *Journal of Sexual Aggression: An international, interdisciplinary forum for research, theory and practice*, 6(1), 111–127.

Elder, W., Jadot, R., Hanbury, T. , Bebe Epale, A. and Burton, A. (2014) 'Preparing for the swarm: ensuring our airwaves and airspace can accommodate transformational commercial drone technology', *Computer and Telecommunications Law Review*, 20(5), 123–126.

Elliott, D. W. (1993) 'Blasphemy and other expressions of offensive opinion', *Ecclesiastical Law Journal*, 3(13), 70–85.

Epworth, J. (2005) 'Protecting your private life: The future of OFCOM privacy complaints', *Communications Law*, 10(6), 191–196.

Ericson, E. E. and Mahoney, D. J. (eds) (2009) *The Solzhenitsyn Reader: New and essential writings, 1947–2005.* Wilmington, NC: ISI Books (Intercollegiate Studies Institute).

European Advertising Standards Alliance (EASA) *Blue Book* (6th edn). Brussels: EASA.

European Commission (2007) *Green Paper on Copyright in the Knowledge Economy.* COM (2007) 724 final, Brussels, 20 November.

European Commission (2010) *A Digital Agenda for Europe.* COM (2010) 245 final, Brussels, 19 May.

European Commission (2011) *A Single Market for Intellectual Property Rights. Boosting creativity and innovation to provide economic growth, high quality jobs and first class products and services in Europe.* COM (2011) 287. Brussels, 24 May.

European Commission (2012) *Proposal for a Directive of the European Parliament and the Council on collective management of copyright and related rights and multiterritorial licensing of rights in musical works for online uses in the internal market.* COM (2012) 372 final 2012/0180 (COD), Brussels, 11 July.

European Commission (2013a) *Proposal for a Regulation of the European Parliament and of the Council amending Regulation (EU) No 1215/2012 on jurisdiction and the recognition and enforcement of judgments in civil and commercial matters.* COM (2013) 554. 2013/0268 (COD), Brussels, 26 July.

European Commission (2013b) *Proposal for a Regulation of the European Parliament and for the Council laying down measures concerning the European single market for electronic communications and to achieve a Connected Continent, and amending Directives 2002/20/EC, 2002/21/EC and 2002/22/EC and Regulations (EC) No 1211/2009 and (EU) No 531/2012. Brussels, 11.9.2013 COM(2013) 627. 2013/0309 (COD).*

Evans, H. (1983) *Good Times, Bad Times.* London: Weidenfeld & Nicolson.

Farrand, B. (2012) 'Too much is never enough? The 2011 Copyright in Sound Recordings Extension Directive', *European Intellectual Property Review*, 34(5), 297–304.

Fenwick, H. and Phillipson, G. (2006) *Media Freedom under the Human Rights Act.* Oxford: Oxford University Press.

Fohl, K. (2009) 'Which factors leading to decreasing sales in the music industry can be influenced by online marketing tools?' Budapest Business School. Faculty of International management and Business: http://elib.kkf.hu/edip/D_15267.pdf.

Foster, S. (2010) 'Possession of extreme pornographic images, public protection and human rights', *Coventry Law Journal*, 15(1), 21–27.

Foster, S. (2015) 'Reclaiming the public interest defence in the conflict between privacy rights and free speech', *Coventry Law Journal*, 19(2), 1–23.

Fox, Sir John C. (1927) *The History of Contempt of Court. The form of trial and the mode of punishment.* Oxford: The Clarendon Press.

Foxon, D. (1965) *Libertine Literature in England 1660–1745.* New York: New Hyde Park Publishing, pp. 19–30.

Freud, S. (1976) *The Interpretation of Dreams.* London: Penguin Books. (1900, 1st edn, *Über den Traum.* Wiesbaden: Verlag J. F. Bergmann).

Fritscher, J. (2002) 'What happened when? Censorship, gay history and Robert Mapplethorpe', in D. Jones (ed.) *Censorship: A world encyclopaedia.* New York: Fitzroy Dearborn Publishers, pp. 67–98.

Frost, C. (2015) *Journalism, Ethics and Regulation* (4th edn). Harlow: Longman.

Gaber, I. (2009) 'Three cheers for subjectivity: Or the crumbling of the seven pillars of traditional journalistic wisdom', *Communications Law*, 14(5), 150–156.

Garzaniti, L. (2009) *Telecommunications, Broadcasting and the Internet: EU competition law and regulation* (3rd edn). London: Sweet & Maxwell.

Gatley, J. C. C. (2013) *Gatley on Libel and Slander* (12th edn) (eds Milmo, P., Rogers, W. V. H., Parkes, R., Walker, C. and Busuttil, G.). London: Sweet & Maxwell.

Geddis, A. (2010) 'What we cannot talk about we must pass over in silence: judicial orders and reporting Parliamentary speech', *Public Law*, July, 443–451.

Gibbons, T. (1996) 'Defamation reconsidered', *Oxford Journal of Legal Studies*, 16(4), 587–615.

Giles, P. (2000) 'Virtual Eden: *Lolita*, pornography, and the perversions of American studies', *Cambridge Journal of American Studies*, 34(1), 41–66.

Gillieron, P. (2006) 'Performing Rights Societies in the Digital Environment', unpublished thesis, Stanford Law School: www.law.stanford.edu/sites/default/files/biblio/108/143082/doc/slspublic/GillieronPhilippe-tft2006.pdf.

Gilvarry, E. (1990) 'Mapplethorpe retrospective sparks pornography debate', *Law Society Gazette*, 87(33), 10–11.

Goldberg, D. (2009) 'Freedom of information in the 21st century: bringing clarity to transparency', *Communications*, 14(2), 50–56.

Goldsmith, J. and Wu, T. (2008) *Who Controls the Internet?: Illusions of a borderless world*. London/ New York: Oxford University Press.

Gordon, S. (2008) *The Future of the Music Business. How to succeed with the new digital technologies. A guide for artists and entrepreneurs* (2nd edn). San Francisco, CA: Backbeat Books (Hal Leonard Corporation).

Grant, H. and Round, N. (2012) 'Recent decisions of the Commissioner and tribunal'. *Freedom of Information*, 9(2), 8–12.

Gravells, N. P. (2007) 'Authorship and originality: The persistent influence of *Walter v Lane*', *Intellectual Property Quarterly*, 3, 267–293.

Grest, L. (2015) 'The drone revolution: can privacy and data protection legislation keep up with the technology?', *Computer and Telecommunications Law Review*, 21(5), 120–122.

Griffiths, J. (2010) 'Rhetoric and the "Three-Step Test": Copyright reform in the United Kingdom', *European Intellectual Property Review*, 32(7), 309–312.

Groll, L. (1980) *Freedom and Self Discipline of the Swedish Press*. Stockholm: The Swedish Institute.

GSMA (2014) Fourth Implementation Review of the European Framework for Safer Mobile Use by Younger Teenagers and Children. April 2014 at: www.gsma.com/gsmaeurope/wpcontent/uploads/2012/04/Fourth_Implementation_Review_of_the_European-Framework_for_Safer-Mobile-Use-by-Younger-Teenagers-and-Children.pdf.

Habermas, J. (1962, translation 1989) *The Structural Transformation of the Public Sphere: An inquiry into a category of bourgeois society* (original in German *Strukturwandel der Öffentlichkeit. Untersuchungen zu einer Kategorie der bürgerlichen Gesellschaft*). Cambridge: Polity Press.

Habermas, J. (1992, translation 1996) *Between Facts and Norms: Contributions to a discourse theory of law and democracy* (original in German *Faktizität und Geltung*). Cambridge: Polity Press.

Habermas, J. (1994) 'Three normative models of democracy', *Constellations: An International Journal of Critical and Democratic Theory*, 1(1) (December), 10.

Haig, S. (2013) 'The Defamation Act 2013 and what it means for the internet', *E-Commerce Law & Policy*, 15(6), 14–15.

Hain, P. (2012) *Outside In*. London: Biteback Publishing.

Hally, M. (2012) 'Local authorities and film censorship: a historical account of the "Naughty Pictures Committees" in Sale and Manchester', *Entertainment and Sports Law Journal*, 11 (ISSN 1748-944X): www2.warwick.ac.uk/fac/soc/law/elj/eslj/issues/volume11/hally/hally.pdf.

Handig, C. (2013) 'The "sweat of the brow" is not enough! – more than a blueprint of the European copyright term "work"', *European Intellectual Property Review*, 35(6), 334–340.

Hanison, D. (2013) 'Performers, session musicians and record producers set to have their rights extended from November 2013', *Entertainment Law Review*, 24(3), 73–77.

Hampel, S. (1992) 'Note: Are Samplers Getting a Bum Rap? Copyright infringement of technological creativity?', *University of Illinois Law Review*, 559.

Harding, T. (2013) 'BitTorrent tracking as a means of detecting illegal file-sharing', *E-Commerce Law & Policy*, 15(2), 8–9.

Hargreaves, I. (2011) *Digital Opportunity. A Review of Intellectual Property and Growth* ('The Hargreaves Review'). Newport: Intellectual Property Office: www.ipo.gov.uk/ipreview-finalreport.pdf.

Harris, D., O'Boyle, M., Warbrick, C., Bates, E. and Buckley, C. (2009) *Law of the European Convention on Human Rights* (2nd edn). Oxford: Oxford University Press.

Harrison, A. (2011) *Music: The Business. The essential guide to the law and the deals* (5th edn). Chatham: Virgin Books/Random House.

Hauch, J. M. (1994) 'Protecting private facts in France: The Warren and Brandeis tort is alive and well and flourishing in Paris', *Tulane Law Review*, 68, 1219.

Hayman, A. and Gilmore, M. (2009) *The Terrorist Hunters: The ultimate inside story of Britain's fight against terror.* London: Bantam Press.

Hedley, S. and Aplin, T. (2008) *Blackstone's Statutes on IT and e-Commerce* (4th edn). Oxford: Oxford University Press.

Henderson, G. (2009) 'A new form of libel tourist? *Ewing v Times Newspapers Ltd.* Case Comment', *Scots Law Times*, 20, 116–118.

Herring, J. (2015) *Family Law* (7th edn). Harlow: Longman.

Herzfeld, P. (2005) 'Corporations, defamation and general damages: back to first principles', *Media and Arts Law Review*, 10, 135.

Hewitt, S. (2010) *Snitch! A history of the modern intelligence informer.* London: Continuum.

Heylin, C. (1994) *The Great White Wonders: A history of rock bootlegs.* London: Viking.

Higgins, A. (2012) 'Legal lessons from the *News of the World* phone hacking scandal', *Civil Justice Quarterly*, 31(3), 274–284.

Hildebrand, L. (2009) *Inherent Vice: Bootleg histories of videotape and copyright.* Durham, NC: Duke University Press.

Hirst, M. (2002) 'Cyberobscenity and the ambit of English criminal law', *Computers and Law*, 13, 25.

Hixson, R. (1987) *Privacy in a Public Society: Human rights in conflict.* Oxford: Oxford University Press.

HM Department for Culture, Media and Sports (DCMS) and Department for Innovation, Business and Skills (BIS) (2009) *Digital Britain.* Presented to Parliament by The Secretary of State for Culture, Media and Sport and the Minister for Communications, Technology and Broadcasting. June 2009. London: The Stationery Office, Cm 7650.

HM Government (2012) *Consultation on Copyright. Summary of Responses.* June 2012 ('The Hargreaves Review') at: www.ipo.gov.uk/copyright-summaryofresponses-pdf.

HM Treasury (2006) *Gowers Review of Intellectual Property.* London: HMSO.

HM Treasury (2009) *Taking Forward the Gowers Review of Intellectual Property: Proposed Changes to Copyright Exceptions.* Second stage consultation on copyright. London: HMSO.

HMIC (2011) *Without fear or favour. A review of police relationships.* December 2011 ISBN 978-1-84987-605-6 at: www.justiceinspectorates.gov.uk/hmic/media/a-review-of-police-relationships-20111213.pdf.

Hoffmann, Lord (2009) 'The universality of human rights', *Law Quarterly Review*, 125 (July), 416–432.

Holdsworth, W., Sir (1920) 'Press control and copyright in the 16th and 17th centuries', *Yale Law Journal*, 29, 841.

Holdsworth, W., Sir (1942) *A History of English Law* (5th edn). London: Methuen & Co.

Hollingsworth, M. and Fielding, N. (1999) *Defending the Realm: MI5 and the David Shayler affair.* London: Andre Deutsch Ltd.

Home Office (1965) *Report of the Departmental Committee on Jury Service* ('The Morris Report'), Cmnd 2627. London: HMSO.

Home Office (1975) *Report of the Advisory Group on the Law of Rape* ('the Heilbron Report'), Cmnd 6352, December. London: HMSO.

Home Office (1987) *The Byford Report.* Home Office papers 1981–86. London: HMSO.

Home Office (1997) *No More Excuses: A new approach to tackling youth crime in England and Wales.* A White Paper presented to Parliament by the Secretary of State for the Home Department, Mr Jack Straw MP. November. Cm 3809. London: HMSO.

Home Office (2002) *The Criminal Justice Bill: Justice for All.* Cm 5563, July. London: Stationery Office.

Home Office and The Scottish Executive (2005) *Consultation: On the Possession of Extreme Pornographic Material.* August. London and Edinburgh.

Home Office (2014) Retention of Communications Data Code of Practice Pursuant to regulation 10 of the Data Retention Regulations 2014 and section 71 of the Regulation of Investigatory Powers Act 2000 Draft for public consultation 9 December 2014 at: www.gov.uk/government/uploads/system/uploads/attachment_data/file/383401/Draft_Data_Retention_Code_of_Practice_-_for_publication_2014_12_09.pdf.

Hooper, D., Waite, K. and Murphy, O. (2013) 'Defamation Act 2013 – what difference will it really make?', *Entertainment Law Review*, 24(6), 199–206.

House of Commons (1973) 'Privacy: Younger Committee's report', HC Debate 6 June 1973. Hansard, vol. 343: cc 104–178.

House of Commons (1974) *Report of the Committee on Contempt of Court*. Cmnd 5794. London: HMSO.

House of Commons (1980) *Contempt of Court. A discussion paper*. Cmnd 7145. London: HMSO.

House of Commons (1981) *Report of the Committee on Contempt of Court*. Cmnd 5794. London: HMSO.

House of Commons (1990) 'The Calcutt Report'. HC Debate 21 June 1990. Hansard, vol. 174: cc 1125–1134.

House of Commons (1994) *First Report of the Committee on Standards in Public Life: The Nolan Report*. Volume 1: Report, Cm 2850-I; Volume 2: Transcripts of Oral Evidence, Cm 2850–II. London: HMSO.

House of Commons (1995) 'Privacy and media intrusion'. HC Debate 17 July 1995, Hansard, vol. 263: cc 132–139.

House of Commons – Department of Culture, Media and Sport (2003) *Privacy and Media Intrusion. Select Committee Report*. Session 2002–03. 16 June. HC 458-I. London: The Stationery Office.

House of Commons (2004) *Report of the Inquiry into the Circumstances Surrounding the Death of Dr David Kelly C.M.G. by Lord Hutton* ('The Hutton Report'). HC 247. London: The Stationery Office.

House of Commons – Department of Culture, Media and Sport (2007) *Report by the Select Committee on 'Self-Regulation of the Press'*, 7th Report, 3 July. Session 2006–07, HC 375. London: The Stationery Office.

House of Commons (2009) *Intelligence and Security Committee Report: 'Could 7/7 have been prevented? Review of the intelligence on the London terrorist attacks on 7 July 2005'*. Cm 7617. London: The Stationery Office.

House of Commons – Department of Culture, Media and Sport Select Committee (2010a) *Second Report on 'Press standards, privacy and libel'*, 9 February. London: The Stationery Office: www.publications. parliament.uk/pa/cm200910/cmselect/cmcumeds/362/36202.htm.

House of Commons (2010b) *The Government's Response to the Culture, Media and Sport Select Committee on Press Standards, Privacy and Libel*. April. Cm 7851: London: The Stationery Office: www.official-documents. gov.uk/document/cm78/7851/7851.pdf.

House of Commons – Department of Culture, Media and Sport Select Committee (2010c) *Press Standards, Privacy and Libel*, Session 2009–10, HC 362. London: The Stationery Office.

House of Commons – Department of Culture, Media and Sport Committee (2012a) *News International and Phonehacking*. Eleventh Report of Session 2010–12 Volume I: Report, together with formal minutes; Volume II: Oral and written evidence. 1 May 2012 HC 903-I. London: The Stationery Office: www.publications.parliament.uk/pa/cm201012/cmselect/cmcumeds/903/903i.pdf.

House of Commons (2012b) *The Report of the Hillsborough Independent Panel*. September. HC 581 London: The Stationery Office: http://hillsborough.independent.gov.uk/repository/report/HIP_report.pdf.

House of Commons (2014) Home Affairs Committee. 'Police, the media, and high-profile criminal investigations: Government Response to the Committee's Fifth Report of Session 2014–15'. Sixth Special Report of Session 2014–15. 3 December 2014. HC 867.

House of Commons (2015) Home Affairs Committee Oral evidence: Policing in London, HC 929 Tuesday 10 March 2015 at: http://data.parliament.uk/writtenevidence/committeeevidence. svc/evidencedocument/home-affairs-committee/policing-in-london/oral/18518.pdf.

House of Commons (2016) BBC Charter renewal. Briefing Paper Number 3416, 13 May 2016 (by Philip Ward).

House of Commons (2016) Chilcot Inquiry Report. Number CBP 6215, 1 July 2016.

House of Lords and House of Commons (2010) *Human Rights Joint Committee. Counter-Terrorism Policy and Human Rights*. 16th Report. Annual Renewal of Control Orders Legislation 2010. Internet publication: www.publications.parliament.uk/pa/jt200910/jtselect/jtrights/64/6402.htm.

House of Lords (2011) Select Committee on Communications 2nd Report of Session 2010–12. 'The governance and regulation of the BBC Report'. HL Paper 166. 29 June 2011.

House of Lords (2015) European Union Committee 7th Report of Session 2014–15 Civilian Use of Drones in the EU. 5 March 2015: www.publications.parliament.uk/pa/ld201415/ldselect/ ldeucom/122/122.pdf.

Hoy, R. (2015) 'Internet blocking injunctions are alive and well in the post Svensson world', *Entertainment Law Review*, 26(2), 44–47.

Human Rights Council (2015) Report of the Special Rapporteur on the promotion and protection of the right to freedom of opinion and expression, David Kaye, 22 May 2015, Document No A/HRC/29/32.

Hurst, A. (2015) 'Data privacy and intermediary liability: striking a balance between privacy, reputation, innovation and freedom of expression', *Entertainment Law Review*, 26(6), 187–195.

Husovec, M. and Peguera, M. (2015) 'Much ado about little – privately litigated internet disconnection injunctions', *International Review of Intellectual Property and Competition Law*, 46(1), 10–37.

Independent Police Complaints Commission (IPCC) (2013) *Commissioner's report IPCC independent investigation into Surrey Police's knowledge of the alleged illegal accessing of Amanda (Milly) Dowler's mobile phone in 2002* by Deborah Glass, IPCC Deputy Chair, April 2013.

Information Commissioner's Office (ICO) (2006a) *What Price Privacy? The unlawful trade in confidential personal information*, presented by the Information Commissioner to Parliament pursuant to section 52(2) of the Data Protection Act 1998. 10 May 2006. HC 1056. London: The Stationery Office.

Information Commissioner's Office (ICO) (2006b) *A Report on the Surveillance Society, for the Information Commissioner by the Surveillance Studies Network.* September 2006. Online report: www.ico.org.uk/~/media/documents/library/Data_Protection/Practical_application/SURVEILLANCE_SOCIETY_FULL_REPORT_2006.ashx.

Information Commissioner's Office (2013) *Implications of the European Commission's proposal for a general data protection regulation for business. Final report to the Information Commissioner's Office.* May 2013 at: www.ico.org.uk/about_us/research/~/media/documents/library/Data_Protection/Research_and_reports/implications-european-commissions-proposal-general-data-protection-regulation-for-business.ashx.

Intellectual Property Office (IPO) (2013a) *Intellectual Property Rights in India.* Newport: Intellectual Property Office, April: www.ipo.gov.uk/ipindia.pdf.

Intellectual Property Office (IPO) (2013b) *Copyright in Europe. Call for views.* Consultation Paper. Newport: Intellectual Property Office: www.ipo.gov.uk/consult-2013-copyrighteurope.pdf.

Intellectual Property Office (IPO) (2013c) *Consultation on the Implementation of Directive 2011/77/EU Amending Directive 2006/116/EC on the Term of Protection of Copyright and Certain Related rights* at: http://webarchive.nationalarchives.gov.uk/20140603093549/http://www.ipo.gov.uk/consult-2013-copyterm.pdf.

Interception of Communication Commissioner's Office (IOCCO) (2015) Inquiry into the use of Chapter 2 of Part 1 of the Regulation of Investigatory Powers Act (RIPA) to identify journalistic sources, 4 February 2015 at: www.iocco-uk.info/docs/IOCCO%20Communications%20Data%20Journalist%20Inquiry%20Report%204Feb15.pdf.

International Council on Ad Self-Regulation (ICAS) (2014) International Guide to Developing a Self-Regulatory Organisation. Practical advice on setting up and consolidating an advertising self-regulatory system at: www.easa-alliance.org/binarydata.aspx?type=doc&sessionId=01t3ij45ynsqkb55pqbyot55/EASA_International_Guide_Self-Regulatory_Organisation_2014.pdf.

Internet Watch Foundation (2011) *Annual and Charity Report.* Cambridge: Internet Watch Foundation: www.iwf.org.uk/assets/media/annual-reports/annual%20med%20res.pdf.

IPSOS-MORI (2014) OFCOM and ICO – Research into the Effectiveness of the Telephone Preference Service (TPS). A Randomised Control Trial. July 2014 at: http://stakeholders.ofcom.org.uk/binaries/research/telecoms-research/tps/tps-effectiveness.pdf.

Isocrates (1980) *Isocrates: with an English Translation in three volumes*, by George Norlin, PhD, LLD. Cambridge, MA: Harvard University Press; London: William Heinemann Ltd.

Iyer, V. (2009) 'The media and scandalising: time for a fresh look', *Northern Ireland Legal Quarterly*, 60, 245.

Jackson, R. M. (1903) *Jackson's Machinery of Justice*: see Spencer, J. R. (1989).

Jackson, R. M. (1937) 'Common law misdemeanours', *Cambridge Law Journal*, 6, 193–201.

Jaconelli, J. (2002) *Open Justice: A critique of the public trial.* Oxford: Oxford University Press.

Jaconelli, J. (2007) 'Defences to speech crimes', *European Human Rights Law Review*, 1, 27–46.

Jacques, S. (2015) 'Are the new "fair dealing" provisions an improvement on the previous UK law, and why?', *Journal of Intellectual Property Law & Practice*, 10(9), 699–706.

James, J. and Ghandi, S. (1998) 'The English law of blasphemy and the European Convention on Human Rights', *European Human Rights Law Review*, 4, 430–451.

Jerrold, C. (1913) *The Married Life of Queen Victoria.* London: G. Bell & Sons Ltd.

Johnson, H. (2006) 'Family justice: open justice'. *Communications Law*, 11(5), 171–174.

Johnson, H. (2008a) 'Freedom of information – confidence and journalism exemptions from Disclosure', *Communications Law*, 13(5), 174–176.

Johnson, H. (2008b) 'Defamation: the media on the defensive?', *Communications Law*, 13(4), 126–131.

Johnson, H. (2013a) 'Leveson and feelings of anti-climax', *Communications Law*, 18(1), 1–2.

Johnson, H. (2013b) 'Loss of sensitive health data – challenging a monetary penalty: *Central London Community Healthcare Trust v Information Commissioner* (EA/2012/00111). Case Comment'. *Communications Law*, 18(1), 25–28.

Jones, R. (2010) 'Intellectual property reform for the internet generation: an accident waiting to happen', *European Journal of Law and Technology*, 1(2).

Jordan, B. (2010a) 'Existing defamation law needs to be updated so that it is fit for the modern age. The government's consultation on the multiple publication rule', *Entertainment Law Review*, 21(2), 41–47.

Jordan, B. (2010b) 'Reputation and Article 8: *Karako v Hungary*. Case Comment', *Entertainment Law Review*, 21(3), 109–111.

Jordan, B. (2011) 'Self-regulation and the British press', *Entertainment Law Review*, 22(8), 242–243.

Jordan, B. and Hurst, I. (2012) 'Privacy and the Princess – a review of the Grand Chamber's decisions in *Von Hannover* and *Axel Springer*', *Entertainment Law Review*, 23(4), 108–113.

Jordan, P. (ed.) (2014) *International Advertising Law. Practical Global Guide*. Llandysul: Globe Business Publishing.

Judge, Lord LCJ (2008) 'Time of change: The criminal justice system in England and Wales'. Speech to the University of Hertfordshire, 4 November: www.judiciary.gov.uk/Resources/JCO/Documents/Speeches/lcj-speech-uni-hertfordshire–041108.pdf.

Judge, Lord, LCJ (2011) 13th Annual Justice Lecture: Press Regulation, 19 October 2011.

Judicial College (2015) Reporting Restrictions in the Criminal Courts, 3rd edn: file:///D:/Media%20Law%203rd%20ed/reporting-restrictions-guide-2015-final%20(1).pdf.

Kearns, P. (2000) 'Obscene and blasphemous libel: Misunderstanding art', *Criminal Law Review*, Aug., 652–660.

Keeling, D. T., Llewelyn, D. and Mellor, J. (2011) *Kerly's Law of Trade Marks and Trade Names* (15th edn). London: Sweet & Maxwell.

Kendrick, W. (1997) *The Secret Museum: Pornography in modern culture*. Ewing, NJ: University of California Press.

Kennedy, J. (2010) *Music How, When, Where You Want It – but not without addressing piracy*. London: International Federation of the Phonographic Industry (IFPI).

Kerly, Sir D. M., Keeling, D. T., Llewelyn, D. and Mellor, J. (eds) (2014) *Kerly's Law of Trade Marks and Trade Names* (15th edn). London: Sweet & Maxwell.

Khan, A. (2012) 'A "right not to be offended" under Article 10(2) ECHR? Concerns in the construction of the "rights of others"', *European Human Rights Law Review*, 2, 191–204.

Kilbrandon, Lord (1964) *Report of the Committee on Children and Young Persons, Scotland* ('The Kilbrandon Report'). Cmnd 2306, London: HMSO.

Kilbrandon, Lord (1971) 'The Law of Privacy in Scotland', 2 *Cambrian Law Review*, 35, 128.

Kirk, E. (2006) 'The *Da Vinci Code* case – *Baigent & Leigh v Random House*: ideas v expression revisited', *Intellectual Property & Information Law*, 11(3), 4–6.

Klang, M. and Murray, A. (2004) *Human Rights in the Digital Age*. Oxford: Routledge-Cavendish.

Klazmer, E. (2012) 'The uncertainties of libel tourism, is diplomacy the answer?', *Entertainment Law Review*, 23(6), 164–168.

Kleinwachter, W. (2012) 'Internet governance outlook 2012: cold war or constructive dialogue?', *Communications Law*, 17(1), 14–18.

Koempel, F. (2005) 'Data protection and intellectual property', *Computer and Telecommunications Law Review*, 11(6), 185–187.

Koempel, F. (2007) 'If the kids are united', *Journal of Intellectual Property Law & Practice*, 2(6), 371–376.

Kreile, R. and Becker, J. (2001) 'Rechtedurchsetzung und Rechteverwaltung durch Verwertungsgesellschaften in der Informationsgesellschaft' ('Rights enforcement and management by collecting societies in the information society'), *GEMA Yearbook 2000/2001*, pp. 85, 89. Berlin: GEMA.

Kruger, L. G. (2015) Internet Governance and the Domain Name System: Issues for Congress. Specialist in Science and Technology Policy June 24, 2015. Congressional Research Service Publications. Washington DC at: www.fas.org/sgp/crs/misc/R42351.pdf.

Ky Chan, G. (2013) 'Corporate defamation: reputation, rights and remedies', *Legal Studies*, 33(2) (June), 264–288.

Laddie, H., Prescott, P. and Vitoria, M. (2011) (Vitoria, M., Speck, A., Lane, L., Alexander, D., Tappin, M., Clark, F., Onslow, R., May, C., Berkeley, I. and Whyte, J. eds) *The Modern Law of Copyright and Designs* (4th edn). London: Butterworths.

Larusson, H. K. (2009) 'Uncertainty in the scope of copyright: the case of illegal file-sharing in the UK', *European Intellectual Property Review*, 31(3), 124–134.

Law Commission (1982) *Criminal Libel*. Working Paper No 84. London: HMSO.

Law Commission (2002) *Defamation and the Internet: A preliminary investigation*, Scoping Study No 2, December 2002. London: HMSO.

Law Commission (2011) *Eleventh Programme of Law Reform*. Presented to Parliament pursuant to section 3(2) of the Law Commissions Act 1965. (Law Com No 330) HC 1407. 19 July 2011. London: The Stationery Office.

Law Commission (2012a) *Contempt of Court: Scandalising the Court*. Consultation Paper No 207. London: The Stationery Office. ID P002506634 08/12 22941 19585: http://lawcommission.justice. gov.uk/docs/cp207_Scandalising_the_Court_for_web.pdf.

Law Commission (2012b) *Contempt of Court*. Consultation Paper No 209. November 2012. London: The Stationery Office: http://lawcommission.justice.gov.uk/docs/cp209_contempt_of_ court.pdf.

Law Commission of New Zealand (2011) *The News Media meets 'New media': Rights, responsibilities and Regulation in the Digital Age*, December 2011: www.lawcom.govt.nz/project/review-regulatory-gaps-and-new-media.

Lawrence, D. H. (1928; first UK publication 1960) *Lady Chatterley's Lover*. London: Penguin Classics.

Lee, S. (1987) 'Spycatcher', *The Law Quarterly Review* 103, 506.

Leigh, I. (1992) 'Spycatcher in Strasbourg', *Public Law*, 200.

Lennon, C. (2005) *John*. London: Hodder & Stoughton.

Lester, Lord, of Herne Hill (1993) 'Freedom of expression', in Macdonald, R. J., Matscher, F. and Petzold, H. (eds) *The European System for the Protection of Human Rights*. Dordrecht: Martinus Nijhoff, pp. 465–481.

Lester, Lord, of Herne Hill, Panick, Lord David and Herberg, Javan (eds) (2009) *Human Rights Law and Practice* (3rd rev. edn). London: LexisNexis.

Leveson, Lord, LJ (2012) *An Inquiry into the Culture, Practices and Ethics of the Press. Report by The Right Honourable Lord Justice Leveson in 4 Volumes*. Volume I 'The Inquiry', Volume II 'The Culture, Practices and Ethics of the Press', Volume III 'The Press and Data Protection', Volume IV 'Aspects of regulation: the law and the Press Complaints Commission'. November 2012. London: The Stationery Office. ID P002525215 11/12 22930 19585. (Also cited as: The Report of An Inquiry into the Culture, Practices and Ethics of the Press as presented to Parliament (HC 780) ('The Leveson Report' or 'Leveson')). 29 November: www.officialdocuments.gov.uk/document/hc1213/ hc07/0780/0780.asp.

Lewis, T. (2002) 'Human Earrings, Human Rights and Public Decency', *Entertainment Law*, 1(2), Summer, 50–71.

Lindon, M. (1998) *Le Procès de Jean-Marie Le Pen*. Paris: POL.

Lipstadt, D. E. (1994) *Denying the Holocaust: The growing assault on truth and memory*. London: Penguin.

Lipstadt, D. E. (2006) *History on Trial: My day in court with David Irving*. New York: Harper Collins.

Litvinenko Report, The (2016) The Litvinenko Inquiry Report into the death of Alexander Litvinenko. Chairman: Sir Robert Owen, January 2016. The Litvinenko Inquiry. Presented to Parliament pursuant to Section 26 of the Inquiries Act 2005 Ordered by the House of Commons to be printed on 21 January 2016. HC 695: www.litvinenkoinquiry.org/files/Litvinenko-Inquiry-Report-web-version.pdf.

Lloyd-Bostock, S. (2007) 'The Jubilee Line jurors: Does their experience strengthen the argument for judge-only trial in long and complex fraud cases?', *Criminal Law Review*, April, 255–273.

Lovelace, L. (Linda Susan Boreman) (1976) *Inside Linda Lovelace*. London: Pinnacle Books.

Loveland, I. (2000) *Political Libels: A comparative study*. Oxford: Hart Publishing.

Lucas, A. (2010) 'For a reasonable interpretation of the three-step test', *European Intellectual Property Review*, 32(6), 277–282.

Lundie Smith, R. and Kendall-Palmer, C. (2016) 'No Glee in the United Kingdom with reverse confusion: Comic Enterprises Ltd v Twentieth Century Fox Film Corp.', Entertainment Law Review, 25(4), 165–168.

Mac Sithigh, D. (2011) '"I'd tell you everything if you'd pick up that telephone": political expression and data protection', European Human Rights Law Review, 2, 166–175.

Macmillan, K. (2009) 'Internet publication rule survives', Communications Law, 14(3), 80–82.

MacQueen, H. (2012) Studying Scots Law (4th edn). Edinburgh: Bloomsbury Professional.

Mahoney, P. (1997) 'Universality versus subsidiarity in the Strasbourg case law on free speech: Explaining some recent judgments', European Human Rights Law Review, 4, 364–379.

Manchester, C. (1988) 'Lord Campbell's Act: England's first obscenity statute', Journal of Legal History, 9(2), 223–241.

Mansfield, M. (2010) Memoirs of a Radical Lawyer. London. Bloomsbury Publishing.

Markesinis, B. S. (1990) The German Law of Torts: A comparative introduction (2nd edn). Oxford: Clarendon Press.

Markesinis, B. S. and Unberath, H. (2002) The German Law of Torts: A comparative treatise. London: Hart.

Marsh, K. (2012) Stumbling over Truth. London: Biteback Publishing.

Mason, S. (2015) 'The internet and privacy: some considerations', Computer and Telecommunications Law Review, 21(3), 68–84.

Master of the Rolls (2011) Report of the Committee on Super-Injunctions: Super-Injunctions, Anonymised Injunctions and Open Justice ('the Neuberger Report'): www.judiciary.gov.uk/Resources/JCO/Documents/Reports/super-injunction-report-20052011.pdf.

Matthews, R., Hancock, L. and Briggs, D. (2004) Jurors' Perceptions, Understanding, Confidence and Satisfaction in the Jury System: A study in six courts. Research Development and Statistics Directorate. Home Office Report No 05/04: http://library.npia.police.uk/docs/hordsolr/rdsolr0504.pdf.

McEvedy, V. (2013) 'Defamation and intermediaries: ISP defences', Computer and Telecommunications Law Review, 19(4), 108–112.

McGartland, M. (2009) Fifty Dead Men Walking. London: John Blake Publishing Ltd.

McGlynn, C. and Rackley, E. (2007) 'Striking a balance: arguments for the criminal regulation of extreme pornography', Criminal Law Review, Sep., 677–690.

McGlynn, C. and Rackley, E. (2009) 'Criminalising extreme pornography: a lost opportunity', Criminal Law Review, 4, 245–260.

McGonagle, M. and Barrett, N. (2007) 'Reforming media law in Ireland: Broadcasting', Communications Law, 12(1), 11–17.

McInnes, R. (2009a) 'Footballers' faces: Photographs, identification and publication contempt', Scots Law Times, 21, 123–126.

McInnes, R. (2009b) 'The ones which got away? Reporting of criminal trials', Scots Law Times, 25, 149–152.

McInnes, R. (2016) Scots Law for Journalists (9th edn). Edinburgh: W Green/Sweet & Maxwell.

McKean, R. (2015) 'Data transfers to the US: Safe Harbour declared invalid; what are your options now?', IT Law Today, Oct., 1–2.

McKittrick, D. and McVea, D. (2001) Making Sense of the Troubles. London: Penguin.

McLagan, G (2004) Bent Coppers: The inside story of Scotland Yard's battle against police corruption. London: Orion.

McLeod, K. (2004) 'How copyright law changed hip hop', Stay Free magazine, 20, 23 June: www.stayfreemagazine.org/archives/20/public_enemy.html.

McLuhan, M. (1962) The Gutenberg Galaxy. Toronto: University of Toronto Press.

McLuhan, M. (1964; reprint 2013) Understanding Media: The extensions of man. Berkeley, CA: Gingko Press.

McLuhan, M. (1967) The Medium is the Message. London: Penguin.

Mill, J. S. (1859) On Liberty (4th edn). London: Longmans, Green, Reader and Dyer.

Miller, F. P., Vandome, A. F and McBrewster, J. (eds) (2009) Intellectual Property: Government-granted monopoly, exclusive right, copyright, trademark, patent, industrial design right, trade secret, history of patent law, history of copyright law. Beau Bassin, Mauritius: Alphascript Publishing/VDM Publishing House Ltd.

Milmo, P., Rogers, W. V. H., Parkes, R., Walker, C. and Busuttil, G. (eds) (2015) Gatley on Libel and Slander (12th edn). London: Sweet & Maxwell.

Milo, D. (2008) *Defamation and Freedom of Speech*. Oxford: Oxford University Press.

Milton, J. (1644) *Areopagitica: A Speech for the Liberty of Unlicensed Printing to the Parliament of England*. London: printed in the Year 1644. (Reprinted edn 1915. London: Macmillan and Co. Limited).

Mindell, R. (2012) 'Rewriting privacy: the impact of online social networks', *Entertainment Law Review*, 23(3), 52–58.

Ministry of Justice (2001) *A Review of the Criminal Courts of England and Wales by The Right Honourable Lord Justice Auld* ('The Auld Review'). London: HMSO.

Ministry of Justice (2007) *Diversity and Fairness in the Jury System*, Research Analysis by Thomas, C. and Balmer, N., Ministry of Justice Research Series 2/07 June 2007. London: HMSO.

Ministry of Justice (2009a) *Sensitive Reporting in Coroners' Courts – Response to Comments 2006–2008*, Coroners and Burials Division, January 2009. London: Ministry of Justice.

Ministry of Justice (2009b) *Defamation and the Internet: The Multiple Publication Rule*, Consultation Paper, CP20/09, 16 September 2009. London: Ministry of Justice.

Ministry of Justice (2009c) *Defamation and the Internet: The Multiple Publication Rule*, Response to Consultation, CP(R) 20/09, 23 March 2010. London: Ministry of Justice.

Ministry of Justice (2009d) 'Possession of Extreme Pornographic Images and increase in the maximum sentence for offences under the Obscene Publications Act 1959: Implementation of Sections 63–67 and Section 71 of the Criminal Justice and Immigration Act 2008'. Circular No 2009/01, 19 January 2009. London: Ministry of Justice.

Ministry of Justice (2010a) *Are Juries Fair?* Research conducted by Professor Cheryl Thomas of the Centre for Empirical Legal Studies, University College London. Ministry of Justice Bulletin Number 39, March 2010.

Ministry of Justice (2010b) *Review of Civil Litigation Costs*. Final Report by Rupert Jackson J, December 2009. P002341871 c7 01/10 860 19585 ('The Jackson Report') London: HMSO: www.judiciary.gov.uk/NR/rdonlyres/8EB9F3F3-9C4A-4139-8A93-56F09672EB6A/0/jacksonfinalreport140110.pdf.

Ministry of Justice (2010c) *Providing Anonymity to those Accused of Rape: An assessment of evidence*. Ministry of Justice Research Series 20/10, November 2010.

Ministry of Justice (2011a) *Draft Defamation Bill: Consultation Paper* CP3/11, March 2011. Cm 8020. London: HMSO.

Ministry of Justice (2011b) *Family Justice Review*. Final Report. November 2011: www.justice.gov.uk/downloads/publications/moj/2011/family-justice-reviewfinal-report.pdf.

Ministry of Justice (2012a) *Swift and Sure Justice: The Government's Plans for Reform of the Criminal Justice System*. White Paper. July 2012. Cm 8388: www.justice.gov.uk/downloads/publications/policy/moj/swift-and-sure-justice.pdf.

Ministry of Justice (2012b) *Putting Victims First: More effective responses to anti-social behaviour*. White Paper, 22 May 2012: www.official-documents.gov.uk/document/cm83/8367/8367.pdf.

Ministry of Justice (2012c) *The Government's Response to the Report of the Joint Committee on the Draft Defamation Bill*. Cm 8295. London: Stationery Office.

Ministry of Justice (2013) *Implementing the Coroner Reforms in Part 1 of the Coroners and Justice Act 2009. Consultation on Rules, Regulations, Coroner Areas and Statutory Guidance*. Consultation Paper CP2/2013, 12 April 2013.

Ministry of Justice (2015a) *Report of the Chief Coroner to the Lord Chancellor Second Annual Report: 2014–2015*. Presented to Parliament Pursuant to Section 36(6) of the Coroners and Justice Act 2009 by the Chief Coroner, His Honour Judge Peter Thornton QC, at: www.gov.uk/government/uploads/system/uploads/attachment_data/file/443090/chief-coroner-report-2015.pdf.

Ministry of Justice (2015b) Report on use of closed material procedure (from 25 June 2014 to 24 June 2015). October 2015 at: www.gov.uk/government/uploads/system/uploads/attachment_data/file/468375/closed-material-procedure-report-2015.PDF.

Mitchell, P. (2005) *The Making of the Modern Law of Defamation*. Oxford: Hart Publishing.

Mommsen, T. (1954) *The History of Rome*, Volumes I–V. (orig. *Römische Geschichte* 1854–1856). New York: Appleton & Co.

Moore, B. (1984) *Privacy: Studies in social and cultural history*. Armonk, NY: M. E. Sharpe Publishing.

Moore, M. (2015) *Who was hacked? An investigation into phone hacking and its victims*, Parts I and II. The Media Standards Trust. March 2015.

Moreham, N. A. (2008) 'The right to respect for private life in the European Convention on Human Rights: A re-examination', *European Human Rights Law Review*, 1, 44–79.

Morgan P. (2005) *The Insider: The private diaries of a scandalous decade*. London: Ebury Press.

Mullis, A. and Scott, A. (2012) 'The swing of the pendulum: reputation, expression and the re-centring of English libel law', *Northern Ireland Legal Quarterly*, 63(1), 27–58.

Munro, V. (2006) 'Sex, laws and videotape: the R18 category', *Criminal Law Review*, Nov., 957–968.

Munro, V. (2007) 'Dev'l-in Disguise? Harm, Privacy and the Sexual Offences Act 2003' in Munro, V. and Stychin. C. (eds) *Sexuality and the Law – feminist engagements*. Abingdon: Routledge.

Music Managers Forum (2003) *The Music Management Bible* (2nd edn). London: Sanctuary Publishing Ltd.

Nabokov, V. V. (1958) *Lolita*. New York: Berkley Publishing Group (first published 1955 in French, Paris: Olympia Press; first British edition 1959, published by Weidenfeld and Nicolson, London).

Nagle, E. (2009) 'Keeping its own counsel: The Irish Press Council, self-regulation and media freedom', *Entertainment Law Review*, 20(3), 93–99.

Narasimhan, N., Sharma, M. and Kaushal, D. (2012) Accessibility of Government Websites in India: A Report at: http://cis-india.org/accessibility/accessibility-of-govt-websites.pdf.

National Audit Office (2009) *The Procurement of Criminal Legal Aid in England and Wales by the Legal Services Commission*. Report by the Comptroller and Auditor General. Session 2009–10. HC 29. London: HMSO.

National Council for Public Morals (1917) *The Cinema: Its present position and future possibilities*, Report of Chief Evidence. London: Williams and Norgate.

Neethling, J., Potgieter, J. M. and Scott, T. J. (1995) *Casebook on the Law of Delict/Vonnisbundel oor die Deliktereg* (2nd edn). Cape Town: Juta Legal and Academic Publishers.

Neethling, J., Potgieter, J. M. and Visser, P. J. (1996) *Neethling's Law of Personality*. Cape Town: Juta Legal and Academic Publishers.

New York Times (2001) *Political Censorship*. 20th Century Review. Chicago, IL: Fitzroy Dearbourn Publishers.

Nokes, G. D. (1928) *A History of the Crime of Blasphemy*. London: Sweet & Maxwell.

Normand, the Right Hon Lord (1938) 'The Law of Defamation in Scotland', *The Cambridge Law Journal*, 6, 327–338.

Northern Ireland Law Commission (2014) *Consultation Paper: Defamation Law in Northern Ireland*. NILC 19 (2014), November 2014. ISBN 978-1-908820-49-5.

Oats, L. and Sadler, P. (2002) '"This great crisis in the republic of letters" – the introduction in 1712 of stamp duties on newspapers and pamphlets', *British Tax Review*, 4, 353–366.

Oberholzer-Gee, F. and Strumpf, K. (2005) 'The effect of file sharing on record sales. An empirical analysis.' Harvard Business School UNC Chapel Hill: www.unc.edu/~cigar/papers/FileSharing_June2005_final.pdf.

Office of Communications (Ofcom) (2012a) *Annual Report and Accounts*. For the period 1 April 2011 to 31 March 2012. HC 237. London: The Stationery Office.

Office of Communications (Ofcom) (2012b) *Communications Market Report 2012*. Research Document of 18 July 2012: http://stakeholders.ofcom.org.uk/binaries/research/cmr/cmr12/CMR_UK_2012.pdf.

Office of Communications (Ofcom) (2012c) *Online Infringement of Copyright: Implementation of the Online Infringement of Copyright (Initial Obligations) (Sharing of Costs) Order 2012*. Consultation document. June 2012: http://stakeholders.ofcom.org.uk/binaries/consultations/onlinecopyright/summary/condoc.pdf.

Office of Communications (Ofcom) (2012d) *Review of Postal Users' Needs. A consultation document on the reasonable needs of users in relation to the market for the provision of postal services in the United Kingdom*. December 2012: http://stakeholders.ofcom.org.uk/binaries/consultations/review-of-user-needs/summary/condoc.pdf.

Office of Communications (Ofcom) (2014) *Adults' Media Use and Attitudes Report*. April 2014: http://stakeholders.ofcom.org.uk/binaries/research/media-literacy/adults-2014/2014_Adults_report.pdf.

Ormerod, D. (1995) 'Publicity and children cases', *Family Law*, 25, 686.

Ormerod, D. and Williams, D. H. (2007) *Smith's Law of Theft* (9th edn). Oxford: Oxford University Press.

Orwell, G. (1941) 'The Art of Donald McGill', in *Critical Essays*. London: Horizon (also in *Critical Essays* (1946). London: Secker and Warburg).

Oswald, J. F. (2010) *Contempt of Court, Committal, and Attachment and Arrest upon Civil Process*. London: Lightning Source UK Ltd.

Owen, L. (ed.) (2007) *Clark's Publishing Agreements: A book of precedents* (7th edn). Haywards Heath: Tottel Publishing.

Oxford Economics (2009) 'Respect for Film: Economic impact of legislative reform to reduce audio-visual piracy'. March 2009, Final Report. Oxford: Oxford Economics.

Page, W. (2007) 'Economics: It's time to face the music', *The Report*, 178 (18 October), 7–8.

Pagefair (2015) 'The cost of ad-blocking. Third Annual Report' at: http://downloads.pagefair.com/reports/2015_report-the_cost_of_ad_blocking.pdf.

Palmer, H. (1997) 'Queen Victoria's not so "Victorian" writings: About pregnancy, children, marriage and men', *Victoriana Magazine*. Online publication: www.victoriana.com/doors/queenvictoria.htm.

Palmer, T. (1971) *Trials of Oz*. London: Blond & Briggs.

Parsons, K. (2000) 'Pirates' web', *European Lawyer*, 1(1), 38–39, 41–42.

Passman, D. S. (2011) *All You Need to Know about the Music Business* (8th edn). London/New York: Viking.

Pedley, P. (2008) *Copyright Compliance: Practical steps to stay within the law*. London: Facet Publishing.

Pfeifer, K.-N. (2008) 'The return of the commons: Copyright history as a helpful source?', *International Review of Intellectual Property and Competition Law*, 39(6), 679–688.

Phillips, J. (2009) *Copyright in the UK and the European Community*. London: Butterworths.

Phillipson, G. (2003) 'Breach of confidence, celebrities, freedom of expression, legal reasoning, newspapers, privacy, public interest, right to respect for private and family life', *European Human Rights Law Review* (Special Issue 'Privacy'), 54–72.

Pike, L. O. (1894) *A Constitutional History of the House of Lords*. London: Macmillan.

Pila, J. (2010) 'Copyright and its categories of original works', *Oxford Journal of Legal Studies*, 30(2), 229–254.

Pillans, B. (2012) 'Private lives in St Moritz: von Hannover v Germany (no 2). Case Comment', *Communications Law*, 17(2), 63–67.

Pimlot, N. (2007) 'ICSTIS – 20 years on', *Entertainment Law Review*, 18(4), 135–137.

Politkovskaya, A. (2001) *A Dirty War: A Russian reporter in Chechnya*. London. Harvill Press.

Poole, T. and Shah, S. (2009) 'The impact of the Human Rights Act on the House of Lords', *Public Law*, April, 347–371.

Press Complaints Commission (2009) *The Editor's Code Book* (2nd edn). London: Press Complaints Commission.

Press Council (1983) 'Fair trial and the presumption of innocence', Report on Media Events Surrounding the Peter Sutcliffe Trial. London: The Press Council (as reported in House of Lords Debates, Hansard – see House of Lords (1983) above).

Prestipino, P. (2015) *Domains 360. The Fundamentals of Buying and Selling Domain Names*. Amazon Media EU. Kindle edn only.

Price, D., Cain, N. and Duodu, K. (2009) *Defamation: Law, procedure and practice*. London: Sweet & Maxwell.

Price, M. E., Verhulst, S. G. and Morgan, L. (eds) (2013) *Routledge Handbook of Media Law*. Abingdon and New York: Routledge.

Rachels, J. (1975) 'Why privacy is important', *Philosophy and Public Affairs*, 4, 323.

Rampal, K. R. (1981) 'The concept of the Press Council', *International Communication Gazette*, 28, 91–103.

Rana, I. S. (1990) *Law of Obscenity in India, USA and UK*. London: Mittal Publications.

Raphael, A. (1989) *My Learned Friends: An insider's view of the Jeffrey Archer Case and other notorious libel actions*. London: W. H. Allen/Virgin Books.

Rawls, J. (1971; 1999 reprinted edn) *A Theory of Justice*. Oxford: Oxford University Press.

Raymond, J. (1998) 'The newspaper, public opinion, and the public sphere in the seventeenth century', *Prose Studies*, 21(2) (August), 109–136.

Read, G. and Townsend, J. (2015) 'UK Supreme upholds CAT's assessment of Ofcom's 08x numbers determinations', *Communications Law*, 20(1), 15–18.

Reid, E. (2010) *Personality, Confidentiality and Privacy in Scots Law*. Edinburgh: W. Green.

Reid, K. G. C. (1993) *The Laws of Scotland*, Stair Memorial Encyclopaedia, vol. 18. Edinburgh: Butterworths.

Reid, K. G. C. and Zimmermann, R. (2000) *A History of Private Law in Scotland*. Oxford: Oxford University Press.

Richardson, J. (ed.) (2014) *Archbold: Criminal Pleading, Evidence and Practice 2014*. London: Sweet & Maxwell.

Richardson, M. and Thomas, J. (2012) *Fashioning Intellectual Property: Exhibition, advertising and the press 1789–1918*. Cambridge: Cambridge University Press.

Rimington, S. (2002) *Open Secret: The autobiography of the former Director-General of MI5*. London: Arrow Books Ltd.

Roberts, A. and Guelff, R. (2000) *Documents on the Laws of War* (3rd edn). Oxford: Oxford University Press.

Rogers, W. V. H. and Parkes, R. (eds) (2010) *Gatley on Libel and Slander* (11th edn). London: Sweet & Maxwell.

Rogerson, P. (2010) 'Conflict of laws – foreign copyright jurisdiction', *Cambridge Law Journal*, 69(2), 245–247.

Rosati, E. (2011) 'Originality in a work, or a work of originality: the effects of the Infopaq decision', *European Intellectual Property Review*, 33(12), 746–755.

Rösler, H. (2008) 'Dignitarian posthumous personality rights – An analysis of U.S. and German constitutional and tort law', *Berkeley Journal of International Law*, 26 (9 December), 153–205.

Ross, A. (2015) 'Orphan works – the law's in place; now here's the process', *Entertainment Law Review*, 26(2), 40–43.

Routledge, G. (1989) 'Blasphemy –The Report of the Archbishop of Canterbury's Working Paper on Offences against Religion and Public Worship', *Ecclesiastical Law Review*, 4, 27–31.

Rowbottom, J. (2006) 'Obscenity laws and the internet: targeting the supply and demand', *Criminal Law Review*, February, 97–109.

Rowbottom, J. (2012) 'To rant, vent and converse: protecting low level digital speech', *Cambridge Law Review*, 71(2), 355–383.

Royal Commission (1993) *Report of the Royal Commission on Criminal Justice* ('The Runciman Commission'). London: Stationery Office Books.

Rushdie, S. (1989; new edition 1998) *The Satanic Verses*. Minneapolis, MI and London: Consortium Press.

Rushdie, S. (2012) *Joseph Anton*. London: Jonathan Cape/Random House.

Samuels, A. (2009) 'Obscenity and pornography', *Criminal Law and Justice Weekly*, 173(12), 187–189.

Samuels, E. (2001) *The Illustrated Story of Copyright*. New York: Palgrave Macmillan.

Sanders, K (2003) *Ethics and Journalism*. London: Sage.

Sanjek, D. (1992) '"Don't have to DJ no more": Sampling and the "autonomous" creator', *Cardozo Arts and Entertainment Law Journal*, 10(2), 612–615.

SANS Institute (2001) 'The Weakest Link: The Human Factor Lessons Learned from the German WWII Enigma Cryptosystem', InfoSec Reading Room at: www.sans.org/reading-room/whitepapers/vpns/weakest-link-human-factor-lessons-learned-german-wwii-enigma-cryptosystem-738.

Scherer, J. (ed.) (2013) *Telecommunication Laws in Europe: Law and regulation of electronic communications in Europe* (6th edn). Haywards Heath: Bloomsbury Professional.

Schudson, M. (2003) 'The sociology of news media', in Alexander, G.C. (ed.), *Contemporary Societies*. New York: W. W. Norton & Co.

Schwabach, A. (2011) *Fan Fiction and Copyright: Outsider work and intellectual property protection*. Farnham: Ashgate.

Scottish Children's Reporter Administration (2012) *Reforming Scots Criminal Law and Practice: The Carloway Report*. 5 October 2012: www.scra.gov.uk/cms_resources/Reforming%20Scots%20Criminal%20Law%20and%20Practice%20The%20Carloway%20Report%20response.pdf.

Scottish Executive; Northern Ireland Office; Home Office (2006) *Making Sure that Crime Doesn't Pay: Proposals for a new measure to prevent convicted criminals profiting from published accounts of their crimes*. November: www.scotland.gov.uk/Resource/Doc/154027/0041420.pdf.

Scottish Government (2009) Review of Fatal Accident Inquiry Legislation. The Report by the Rt Hon Lord Cullen of Whitekirk KT: www.gov.scot/resource/doc/290392/0089246.pdf.

Scottish Government (2011) *Death of a Good Name: Defamation and the Deceased. A Consultation Paper*. Produced for the Scottish government by APS Group Scotland. DPPAS11019 (01/11). Edinburgh: Scottish Government.

Scottish Government (2015) 'Consultation on further extension of coverage of the Freedom of Information (Scotland) Act 2002 to more organisations'. Friday, June 12, 2015.

Scottish Law Commission (2015) Ninth Programme of Law Reform. SCOT LAW COM No 242 SG/2015/17, February 2015 at: www.scotlawcom.gov.uk/files/6414/2321/6887/Ninth_Programme_of_Law_Reform_Scot_Law_Com_No_242.pdf.

Scottish Law Commission (2016) 'Defamation Law: Time for change?' A Discussion Paper, issued on behalf of the Scottish Law Commission on 17 March 2016.

Sellars, S. (2011) 'Online privacy: do we have it and do we want it? A review of the risks and UK case law', *European Intellectual Property Review*, 33(1), 9–17.

Senftleben, M. (2004) *Copyright, Limitations and the Three-Step Test: An analysis of the three-step test in international and EC Copyright Law*. The Hague: Kluwer Law International.

Sentencing Guidelines Council (2009) *Overarching Principles: Sentencing youths*. London: Sentencing Guidelines Council (November).

Sereny, G. (1998) *Cries Unheard: The story of Mary Bell*. London: Macmillan.

Shannon, R. (2001) *A Press Free and Responsible: Self regulation and the press complaints commission, 1991–2001*. London: John Murray Publications.

Simon, I. (2006a) 'The introduction of performers' moral rights: Part 1', *European Intellectual Property Review*, 28, 552–561.

Simon, I. (2006b) 'The introduction of performers' moral rights: Part 2', *European Intellectual Property Review*, 28(12), 600–610.

Simpson, A. W. B. (2004) *Human Rights and the End of Empire. Britain and the genesis of the European Convention*. Oxford: Oxford University Press.

Singh, S. and Ernst, E. (2009) *Trick or Treatment: Alternative medicine on trial*. London: Transworld Publishing.

Smartt, U. (1999) 'Constitutionalism in the British Overseas Territories', *European Journal of Crime, Criminal Law and Criminal Justice*, 3 (June), 300–314.

Smartt, U. (2004) 'Stay out of jail: Performance, multimedia and copyright laws', in L. Hill and H. Paris, *Guerrilla Performance and Multimedia* (2nd edn). London/New York: Continuum Press.

Smartt, U. (2006) *Media Law for Journalists*. London: Sage Publications.

Smartt, U. (2007) 'Who still observes the law of contempt?', *Justice of the Peace Journal*, 171 (3 February), 76–83.

Smartt, U. (2008) 'Crime and punishment in the Turks and Caicos Islands', *Justice of the Peace Journal*, 172 (April), 200–203.

Smartt, U. (2010a) 'Criminal actions – copyright in the digital age', *Criminal Law & Justice Weekly*, 174(42), 645–647.

Smartt, U. (2010b) 'Crime and punishment in the Turks and Caicos Islands', in J. P. Stamatel and H.-E. Sung (vol. eds); G. R. Newman (ed.) *Crime and Punishment Around the World. The Americas*, vol. 2, pp. 322–328. Santa Barbara, CA, Denver, CO and Oxford, UK: ABC-CLIO, LLC-Greenwood Press.

Smartt, U. (2011) 'Twitter undermines superinjunctions', *Communications Law*, 16(4), 135–140.

Smartt, U. (2012) 'Safety first: the Ryan Giggs superinjunction Part 2 of March 2012', *Communications Law*, 17(2), 50–52.

Smartt, U. (2014) 'Internet libel: will the new Defamation Act 2013 make a real difference?' In: Criminal Law and Justice Weekly, *CLJW* 174(42), 645–647.

Smartt, U. (2015a) 'Prince Charles's "black spider memos": how a Guardian journalist succeeded in his 10-year quest under the Freedom of Information Act 2000', *European Intellectual Property Review*, 37(8), 529–538.

Smartt, U. (2015b) 'Why I was right to name the teachers' teen killer: naming teenagers in criminal trials and law reform in the internet age', *Communications Law*, 20(1), 5–13.

Smith, A. (1776 – ed. Kathryn Sutherland, new edition 2008) *An Inquiry into the Nature and Causes of the Wealth of Nations*. Oxford: Oxford Classics.

Smith, J. C. *The Law of Theft*; see Ormerod and Williams (2007).

Smith, T. B. (1964) 'Civil jury trial: A Scottish assessment', *Virginia Law Review*, 1.

Solzhenitsyn, A. (1962) *One Day in the Life of Ivan Denisovich*. London: Penguin (reprinted in 1996. London: Bantam Press).

Spencer, J. R. (1977) 'Criminal libel: A skeleton in the cupboard', *Criminal Law Review*, 383.

Spencer, J. R. (1989) *Jackson's Machinery of Justice* (8th edn of the original publication by Professor R. M. Jackson in 1903). Cambridge: Cambridge University Press.

Spencer, J. R. (2006) 'Can juvenile offenders be "named and shamed" when they are adults?', *Justice of the Peace & Local Government Law*, 170(34), 644–647.

Spurrier, M. (2012) '*Gillberg v Sweden*: towards a right of access to information under Article 10?', *European Human Rights Law Review*, 5, 551–558.

Stahl, J. M. (1997) 'CDA is DOA: Zoning the information superhighway to exclude adult motels and community service organisations', *Entertainment Law Review*, 8(5), 166–175.

Stair, Viscount (The Stair Society, 1981) *The Tercentenary of the First Publication of Viscount Stair's Institutions of the Laws of Scotland*. Papers delivered at a Conference held in the University of Glasgow. The Stair Society. Edinburgh: W. Green & Son.

Stein, E. (2000) *Thoughts from a Bridge. A retrospective of writings on new Europe and American federalism*. Michigan, MI: University of Michigan Press.

Stephen, J. F. (1883) *A History of the Criminal Law of England*. London: Macmillan and Co.

Stephens, K., Fuller, Z. and Atherton, H. (2013) 'Copyright: Norwich Pharmacal orders against ISPs', *Chartered Institute of Patent Agents Journal*, 42(1), 45.

Sterling, A. L. (2008) *World Copyright Law* (3rd edn). London: Sweet & Maxwell.

Stobbs, J., Weller, G. and Zhou, J. (2015) 'Review of United Kingdom trade mark and design decisions', *International Review of Intellectual Property and Competition Law*, 46(2), 238–245.

Strachan, J. F., Lord (1959) *Civil Jury Trial in Scotland*, The Scotland Committee on Civil Jury Trial. Edinburgh: HMSO.

Swami, V., Chamorro-Premuzic, T. and Furnham, A. (2009) 'Faking it: Personality and individual difference predictors of willingness to buy counterfeit goods', *The Journal of Socio-Economics*, 38(5), 820–825.

Synodinou, T. E. (2013) 'E-books, a new page in the history of copyright law?', *European Intellectual Property Review*, 35(4), 220–227.

Taylor, The Rt Hon Lord Justice (1989) *The Hillsborough Stadium Disaster, 15 April 1989, Interim Report*. Cm 765, London: Her Majesty's Stationery Office.

Tehranipoor, M., Ujjwal Guin, M. and Domenic Forte, D. (2015) *Counterfeit Integrated Circuits: Detection and Avoidance*. Heidelberg, New York, Dordrecht: Springer-Verlag.

Thomas, N. M. (2012) 'An education: the three-step test for development', *European Intellectual Property Review*, 34(4), 244–260.

Thompson, B. (ed.) (2012) *Ban This Filth! Letters from the Mary Whitehouse Archive*. London: Faber & Faber (Kindle edition).

Thornton, S. (2009) *Seven Days in the Art World*. London: Granta Books.

Tomkinson, M. and Gillard, M. (1980) *Nothing to Declare: Political corruptions of John Poulson*. Richmond, Surrey: Calder Publications.

Traub, F. (2009) 'Bob Dylan's albums protected in Germany', *Entertainment Law Review*, 20(4), 144–146.

Travers, P. and Reiff, S. (1974) *The Story Behind 'The Exorcist'*. New York: Signet Books.

Treacy, B. (2015) 'Expert comment re Schrems v Data Protection Commissioner (2015) (CJEU)', *Privacy & Data Protection*, 15(5), 2.

Trend Micro (2015) 'Forward-Looking Threat. Below the Surface: Exploring the Dark Web'. Research team publication by Dr Vincenzo Ciancaglini, Dr Marco Balduzzi, Robert McArdle, and Martin Rösler. A TrendLabs Research Paper at: www.trendmicro.co.uk/media/wp/exploring-the-deep-web-whitepaper-en.pdf.

Tugendhat and Christie (2016) *The Law of Privacy and The Media* (Warby, M., Mareham, N. and Christie. I., eds) (3rd edn). Oxford: Oxford University Press.

Ullrich, H., Hilty, R. M., Lamping, M. and Drexl, J. (eds) (2015) 'TRIPS plus 20. From Trade Rules to Market Principles'. MPI Studies on Intellectual Property and Competition Law. Heidelberg: Springer-Verlag.

Van Vechten., V. (1903) 'The History and Theory of the Law of Defamation I', *Columbia Law Review*, 3, 546.

Van Vechten, V. (1904) 'The History and Theory of the Law of Defamation II', *Columbia Law Review*, 4, 33.

Varuhas, J. N. E. (2015) 'Judicial review at the crossroads', *Cambridge Law Journal*, 74(2), 215–218.

Vivant, M. (2016) 'Building a common culture of IP?', *International Review of Intellectual Property and Competition Law*, 47(3), 259–261.

Wacks, R. (2013) *Privacy and Media Freedom*. Oxford: Oxford University Press.

Walker, C. and Starmer, K. (1999) *Miscarriages of Justice: A review of justice in error*. London: Blackstone Press.

Wall, L. J. (1995) 'Publicity in children cases – a personal view', *Family Law*, 25, 136.

Wallis, R., Baden-Fuller, C., Kretschmer, M. and Klimis, G. M. (1999) 'Contested collective administration of intellectual property rights in music: The challenge to the principles of reciprocity and solidarity', *European Journal of Communication*, 14(1), 5–35.

Ward, J. (1993) *Ambushed*. London: Vermillion.

Warren, S. D. and Brandeis, L. D. (1890) 'The right to privacy', *Harvard Law Review*, 4(5) (15 December 1890), 193–220.

Weber, R. H. (in collaboration with M. Grosz and R. Weber) (2010) *Shaping Internet Governance: Regulatory challenges*. Zürich: Springer.

Whitty, N. R. (2005) 'Rights of personality, property rights and the human body in Scots law', *Edinburgh Law Review*, 9(2), 194–237.

Whitty, N. R. and Zimmermann, R. (eds) (2009) *Rights of Personality in Scots Law: A Comparative Perspective*. Dundee: Dundee University Press.

Wilkinson, N. (2015) *Secrecy and the Media: the Official History of the United Kingdom's D-Notice System*. Abingdon, Oxon: Routledge

Williams, A. T. (2012) *A Very British Killing: The death of Baha Mousa*. London: Jonathan Cape.

Wilmshurst, P. (2011) 'The regulation of medical devices', *British Medical Journal*, 342, 1093–1094.

Wilmshurst, P. (2012) 'CLOSURE 1 seen through the MIST', *British Medical Journal*, 344, 51.

Winfield, P. H. (1937) *A Textbook of the Law of Tort*. London: Sweet & Maxwell.

WIPO (World Intellectual Property Organization) (2003) *WIPO Study on Limitations and Exceptions of Copyright and Related Rights in the Digital Environment*. Study by the Standing Committee on Copyright and Related Rights. 9th Session, Geneva, June 23 to 27, 2003: www.wipo.int/edocs/mdocs/copyright/en/sccr_9/sccr_9_7.pdf.

Witzleb, N. (2009) 'Justifying gain-based remedies for invasions of privacy', *Oxford Journal of Legal Studies*, 29, 325.

Wragg, P. (2013a) 'Time to end the tyranny: Leveson and the failure of the fourth estate', *Communications Law*, 18(1), 11–20.

Wragg, P. (2013b) 'Mill's dead dogma: the value of truth to free speech jurisprudence', *Public Law*, April, 363–385.

Wragg, P. (2015) 'The legitimacy of press regulation', *Public Law*, April, 290–307.

Wright, P. (1987) *Spycatcher: The candid autobiography of a secret intelligence officer*. Australia: William Heinemann and Viking Press.

Wulff, B. and Maibaum, N. (2012) *Jenseits des Protokolls*. München: Riva Verlag.

Yeoh, F. (2015) 'Adaptations in music theatre: confronting copyright', *Entertainment Law Review*, 26(4), 119–129.

Zuckerman, A. (2010) 'Super injunctions – curiosity-suppressant orders undermine the rule of law', *Civil Justice Quarterly*, 29, 131.

Internet sources and useful websites

Advertising Standards Authority (ASA): www.asa.org.uk
Associated Press (AP) (Global News Network): www.ap.org
Association for Television on Demand (ATVOD): http://atvod.co.uk
Association of American Publishers: www.publishers.org
Attorney General's Office (England & Wales): www.attorneygeneral.gov.uk
Authors' Licensing and Collecting Society (ALCS): www.alcs.co.uk
BBC News Online: www.bbc.co.uk/news
BBC Northern Ireland Service online: www.bbc.co.uk/northernireland
BMI – Broadcast Music, Inc.: www.bmi.com
British Board of Film Classification (BBFC): www.bbfc.co.uk
British Phonographic Industry (BPI): www.bpi.co.uk
Cabinet Office (UK): www.gov.uk/government/organisations/cabinet-office
CISAC (Confédération Internationale des Sociétés d'Auteurs et Compositeurs – the
    International Confederation of Societies of Authors and Composers): www.cisac.org
Competition and Markets Authority: www.gov.uk/government/organisations/competition-
    and-markets-authority
Court martial (the military court service): www.gov.uk/the-military-court-service
Court of Justice of the European Union (CJEU): www.curia.eu
Department for Culture, Media and Sport: www.culture.gov.uk
English PEN: www.englishpen.org
European Advertising Standards Alliance (EASA): www.easa-alliance.org
European Commission: http://ec.europa.eu
European Court of Human Rights: www.echr.coe.int
European Parliament: www.europarl.eu
European Patent Office (Munich): www.epo.org
Featured Artists Coalition (FAC): www.featuredartistscoalition.com
Federation Against Copyright Theft (FACT): www.fact-uk.org.uk
Freedom of Information Advocates: www.freedominfo.org
GEMA (Gesellschaft für musikalische Aufführungs- und mechanische Vervielfältigungsrechte –
    Musical copyright association): www.gema.de
Hansard: https://hansard.parliament.uk
HUDOC (database for case law of the European Court of Human Rights): http://hudoc.echr.
    coe.int/eng
IMPRESS (independent press regulator): http://impress.press
Independent Press Standards Organisation (IPSO): www.ipso.co.uk
Information Commissioner for Northern Ireland: https://ico.org.uk/about-the-ico/who-we-
    are/northern-ireland-office
Information Commissioner's Office (ICO): www.ico.gov.uk
Intellectual Property Office UK: www.ipo.gov.uk
Interception of Information Commissioner: www.iocco-uk.info
International Confederation of Societies of Authors and Composers (Confédération
    Internationale des Sociétés d'Auteurs et Compositeurs): www.cisac.org
International Council on Advertising Self-Regulation (ICAS): www.easa-alliance.org
International Federation of Journalists: www.ifj.org/en
International Federation of the Phonographic Industry (IFPI): www.ifpi.org

International Press Institute (IPI): www.freemedia.at
Internet Corporation for Assigned Names and Numbers (ICANN): www.icann.org
Internet Watch Foundation (IWF): www.iwf.org.uk
Irish Department of Justice and Law Reform: www.justice.ie
Irish Parliament for the Dáil – Houses of the Oireachtas: www.oireachtas.ie
Judiciary (England & Wales – courts & tribunals): www.judiciary.gov.uk
Mechanical Copyright Protection Society (MCPS) – see: PRS
Music Managers Forum (MMF): www.musicmanagersforum.co.uk
Music Publishers Association (for sheet/printed music): www.mpaonline.org.uk
Musicians' Union (MU): www.musiciansunion.org.uk
National Archives: www.nationalarchives.gov.uk
National Union of Journalists (NUJ): www.nuj.org.uk
Northern Ireland Assembly: www.niassembly.gov.uk
Northern Ireland Courts and Tribunal Service: www.courtsni.gov.uk
Northern Ireland Law Commission: www.nilawcommission.gov.uk
Ofcom (Office of Communications): www.ofcom.org.uk
Office for Harmonization in the Internal Market (OHIM) (EU Trademark Office): http://
    oami.europa.eu
Office of National Statistics (UK): www.statistics.gov.uk
Office of Public Sector Information: www.opsi.gov.uk/psi
Parliament, UK: www.parliament.uk
Performing Right Society (PRS): www.prsformusic.com
PhonepayPlus (regulates phone-paid services in the UK): www.phonepayplus.org.uk
Phonographic Performance Ltd (PPL): www.ppluk.com
Press Association: www.pressassociation.com
Press Council of Ireland: www.presscouncil.ie
Scots Law Online: www.scottishlaw.org.uk
Scottish Court Service: www.scotcourts.gov.uk
Scottish Information Commissioner: www.itspublicknowledge.info/home/
    ScottishInformationCommissioner.asp
Scottish Law Commission: www.scotlawcom.gov.uk
Scottish Parliament: www.scottish.parliament.uk
Society of Authors: www.societyofauthors.net
Society of Editors: www.societyofeditors.co.uk
Trading Standards Institute (TSI): www.tradingstandards.gov.uk
UK Copyright Service: www.copyrightservice.co.uk
Unified Patent Court (EU): www.unified-patent-court.org
US Patent Office (Patents & Trademarks): www.uspto.gov
Video Standards Council (VSC): www.videostandards.org.uk
Welsh Assembly: www.assembly.wales
Welsh Music Foundation: www.welshmusicfoundation.com
WIPO Phonogram Treaties: www.wipo.int/treaties/en/ip/phonograms
World Intellectual Property Organization (WIPO): www.wipo.int
World Summit on the Information Society (WSIS): www.itu.int/wsis
World Trade Organization (WTO): www.wto.org
Youth Justice Board (England/ Wales): www.gov.uk/government/organisations/youth-justice-
    board-for-england-and-wales

Index